PERSONNEL
MANAGEMENT OF
HUMAN RESOURCES

Michael R. Carrell
University of Louisville

Frank E. Kuzmits
University of Louisville

Charles E. Merrill Publishing Company
A Bell & Howell Company
Columbus   Toronto   London   Sydney

Published by
Charles E. Merrill Publishing Company
A Bell & Howell Company
Columbus, Ohio 43216

This book was set in Optima and Perpetua.
Photo Acquisitions Editor: Cindy Donaldson
Design Consultant: Ann Mirels
Production Editor: Clare Wulker
Cover Design Coordinator: Will Chenoweth
Cover Photo: Larry Hamill

Photo Credits:
Chapters 1, 13, 16, 17: The Archives of Labor and Urban Affairs, Wayne State
University
Chapters 3 and 8: Ben Chandler
Chapter 4: Western Electric
Chapter 5: Strix Pix
Chapter 7: United Nations/Y. Nagota
Chapters 9 and 11: Tennessee Valley Authority
Chapters 10 and 19: Larry Hamill
Chapter 12: Bell and Howell Company
Chapter 14: ACTION/Foster Grandparent Program
Chapter 15: Annan Photo Features

International Standard Book Number: 0-675-09927-7

Library of Congress Catalog Card Number: 81-82314

1 2 3 4 5 6 7 8 9 10—87 86 85 84 83 82

Printed in the United States of America.

To Mary and Shari

To My Parents
Frank M. and Helen Kuzmits

PREFACE

Today, the personnel function has an important bearing on the success of the organization because it directly affects the "bottom line" by enhancing profits and/or reducing operating and labor costs. The philosophy that underscores this premise is often called *human resource management*—an approach that values the employee group as an *investment* which can improve organization effectiveness through satisfaction of personal needs and goals.

Our book focuses on the policies, programs, methods, and techniques that modern professional personnel managers create and implement to achieve a human resource philosophy. We stress, however, that all managers are managers of personnel; therefore, we have written our book for all business students, not simply those who intend to pursue a career in the personnel field. Much of the material we present—employee selection, job design, performance appraisal, training and development, career management, safety and health, labor relations, and personnel problem solving—is as important to the operating manager as it is to the personnel manager. For this reason, we have emphasized not only what effective human resource programs *are*, but how they are *applied and managed*. Throughout the text, we have included many practical illustrations and examples to help students understand the personnel manager's roles, responsibilities, and relationship with other managers and administrators.

Acknowledgements

Many people have directly or indirectly contributed to this project. First, we sincerely wish to thank those who have influenced our careers: Marc J. Wallace, Jr., John Ivancevich, James L. Gibson, and Lynn Spruill of the University of Kentucky; Robert Myers, Jerald Smith, Joe Grant, and John Paul Nelson of the University of Louisville; John E. Dittrich of the University of Colorado; Andrew Hailey of the University of North Carolina-Greensboro; and Warren S. Blumenfeld of Georgia State University. We also wish to thank the office staff who helped prepare our manuscript, especially Kathy Ostermiller, as well as Janice Pollard, Jewell Howard, Gay Alexander, and Diane Heitzman. Special thanks go to Jane Goldstein for seeing that our manuscript deadlines were somehow always met. Particular thanks should also go to William H. Peters, Dean of the School of Business, University of Louisville, whose cooperation and positive reinforcement were critical to this project. Several reviewers made very helpful suggestions for improving the manuscript: Laurence M. Vukelich of Portland Community College, Anthony F. Campagna of The Ohio State University, John Dittrich of the University of Colorado, and Michael Farley of Del Mar College. John Mead of the University of Louisville also provided many helpful comments on the labor relations chapters. Steven G. Smith, developmental editor of the Charles E. Merrill Publishing Company, was a continual source of assistance and encouragement throughout the project. Finally, we would like to acknowledge Bremer Ehrler, a "textbook" administrator whose enthusiasm has always been motivating, as well as Archie V. and Myrtle Carrell and Frank M. and Helen Kuzmits, whose confidence in their sons enabled them to complete this project as well as many others in their careers.

CONTENTS

1   Introduction to Personnel Management   1
Rap Session at O'Malley's   2
Personnel: Past and Present Perspectives   4
Current Problems and Issues   8
Personnel Functions   16
Career Opportunities   19
The Pet Store   24
Reading: A Decade of Rapid Change: The Outlook for Human
             Resources Management in the '80s   25

2   Management and the Personnel Function   33
Akron Steel Products Company   34
Management Functions   35
Organizations   38
Personnel Department Functions   43
Management/Personnel Interaction   47
Personnel Department Organization   52
Armadillo Auto Parts Company   59
Reading: What the Chief Executive Expects of the Personnel
             Function   61

3   Job Analysis   71
Cateon Company   72
Program Implementation   75
Job Analysis Problems   86
Job Descriptions   88
The Outside Consultant   96
Reading: When the Traditional Job Description is Not
             Enough   97

4   Job Design and Alternate Work Schedules   105
Well Paid or Challenged?   106
Designing Jobs   107
Alternate Work Schedules   118
Design or Scheduling Problem?   132

5   Federal Employment Guidelines and Laws   137
Wirtz, Secretary of Labor v. Basic, Inc.   138

Federal Legislation   138
Federal Guidelines   144
EEOC v. Local 638   161
Reading: Should Courts Write Your Job Descriptions?   162

6   **Personnel Recruitment   167**
College Recruiting   168
Labor Market Information   171
Cost/Benefit Analysis of Recruitment   174
Recruitment Sources   176
Methods of Recruitment   178
Overtime and Temporary Help   184
Successful Recruitment   187
Ostermiller, The Accountant
Reading: The State Employment Service: An Aid to Affirmative
                    Action Implementation   195

7   **Personnel Selection   201**
Minority Candidates   202
The Best-Guess Process   203
The Selection Process   204
The Selection Decision   222
The New Personnel Director   226
Reading: Personal Privacy and the Personnel Record   228

8   **Appraisal of Human Resources   235**
Annual Performance Evaluation   236
Performance Appraisal   238
Appraisal Process   239
Appraisal Interview   258
Centralized Performance Appraisal   268
Reading: The "Refined" Performance Evaluation Monitoring
                    System: Best of Both Worlds   270

9   **Employee Training   275**
Georgia Trust Bank   276
Training Process   282
Effective Training   296
Training Responsibilities   299
Mayflower Manufacturing Corporation   306
Reading: Changing Demands on the Training
                    Professional   309

10 Management Development 315
Management Development at Cabinet Craft 316
Managerial Skills 319
Management Development Process 319
Female Managers 333
Management Development Problems 336
Successful Programs 336
Cincinnati Trust Bank 344

11 Organizational Development 349
Southwester Plastics 350
Organizational Problems 353
Organizational Development 354
Chicago Mercantile Company 377
Reading: Merging Personnel and OD: A Not-So-Odd
                 Couple 382

12 Internal Staffing and Career Management 389
Citizens Savings and Loan 390
Internal Staffing 392
Internal Staffing Policies 403
Career Management 406
Assessment Center at Piedmont Insurance 418

13 Compensation 423
Perceived Pay Inequity 424
Compensation Objectives 426
Job Evaluation 435
Designing the Pay System 450
Job Evaluation 461
Reading: Five Years with a Scanlon Plan 463

14 Employees' Benefits 471
Funeral Leave Policy 472
Benefit Increases 473
Types of Benefits 475
Employee Services 490
Total Benefit Planning 492
Publicizing Benefits 497
Cafeteria Planning 500
Reading: Some Practical Implications of the Pregnancy
                 Discrimination Act 501

15 Employees' Health and Safety   509
Unsafe Office Conditions   510
Occupational Safety and Health Administration   512
Health Maintenance Organizations   520
Health and Safety Program   524
Family Health Insurance   533

16 Labor Unions   537
Riverside Packing Company   538
Impact on Management   540
Union History   541
Union Goals   548
Labor Management Legislation   552
Union Structure and Management   554
A Union Time Study on Company Premises?   567

17 Collective Bargaining and Grievance Handling   575
Grievances at Midwest Steel   576
Bargaining Structures   577
Collective Bargaining   579
Public Sector Collective Bargaining   588
Grievance Handling   589
Making Coffee on Company Premises   599
Reading: Critical Issues and Problems in Collective Bargaining:
          A Management Perspective   602

18 Personnel Research and Problem Solving   607
Absenteeism at Digitronics, Inc.   608
Personnel Research   610
Research Techniques   613
Personnel Information Decision System   618
Researching Personnel Problems   620
Better Bread Baking Company   638
Reading: Personnel Research for Problem Solving   647

19 Discipline and Counseling   653
Midwestern Chemicals   654
Causes of Poor Performance   656
Objectives of Discipline   658
Strand-O'Mally Publishing Company   678
Reading: Guidelines to Corrective Discipline   682

Assembly line workers lowering an engine into an automobile frame at a Ford factory in 1934.

1

INTRODUCTION TO PERSONNEL MANAGEMENT

*Personnel: Past and Present
Perspectives*

Current Problems and Issues

Personnel Functions

Career Opportunities

The Problem: Rap Session at O'Malley's

O'Malley's Bar and Grill is a popular watering hole near one of Detroit's largest automobile plants. Assembly workers, supervisors, middle managers, administrators, and top-level executives are counted among the regulars. Why is O'Malley's so popular? Proprietor Tim O'Malley feels "People can come in here and unwind after a grueling day on the line or in the office. And in here everybody is the same—you can see big-shot vice-presidents sitting next to greasy assembly line workers enjoying good conversation. And the fact that you can still get a glass of beer for thirty-five cents here doesn't hurt business, either!"

This particular day found three engine-assembly supervisors tucked in a corner booth hotly discussing a common supervisory topic: employee motivation. Part of the conversation went like this:

Rafe Arnold: I tell you, man, sometimes I could just wring their necks. Out of thirty-four employees, I had twenty-two show up on time today! My section of the line was held up for an hour. And who catches hell because of it? Me! All the yelling and screaming I do must go in one ear and out the other. Well, when I see somebody slough off from now on, I'm really going to crack down hard on them. I'll show no mercy! That'll shape them up!

Paul Ashbury: Rafe, old buddy, you've got it all wrong. Haven't you heard the old saw "you catch more flys with sugar than vinegar"? You've got to be nice to people. Treat them like human beings, not mindless robots. Say good morning to them. Send them a little card on their birthdays. Sit down and talk to them one-on-one every now and then. That's what employees really want—someone they can look up to and be real friends with. You've got to get out of the dark ages, Rafe. This is the twentieth century! Am I right, Leo?

Leo Avery: Well, I don't know. But I heard something interesting the other day from our personnel manager. In Sweden, they make Volvos with small teams of workers instead of using assembly lines. The workers also make several decisions about their work, such as how the work should be planned and scheduled. And they take breaks whenever they want to. They're given a weekly quota and pretty much left alone to decide how to get the job done. Apparently, most workers are really satisfied with this arrangement. Absenteeism is low and quality is really high. I guess with this kind of work design, the employees take a lot more pride in their work than our workers do. Maybe we ought to look at the team work concept over here. We sure need something to help us compete with the imports.

Rafe: Ha Ha! Leo, you must have sniffed too much cleaning solvent today. You gotta be kidding. Are you going to let a twenty year old kid with a high school diploma decide how to build an $8,000 car? Come on! These guys

and gals just want to come to work, do a
simple job, get their pay checks and split at
the end of the shift. I know, I've been
around!

The name of the game in business today is personnel . . . you can't hope to show a good financial or operating report unless your personnel relations are in order, and I don't care what kind of a company you're running. A chief executive is nothing without his people. You've got to have the right ones in the right jobs for them, and you've got to be sure employees at every level are being paid fairly and being given opportunities for promotion. You can't fool them, and any chief executive who tries is going to hurt himself and his company. . . .[1]

The preceding statement was not made by a professor in an attempt to foster student interest in a personnel management course. It was voiced by Tom Beebe, chief executive officer of one of the nation's largest air carriers, Delta Airlines. And, the facts indicate that Beebe's philosophy about managing people pays off. In a time when skyrocketing fuel costs and fewer passengers have squeezed the profits of most major airlines, Delta continues to enjoy healthy profit margins and steady organizational growth. To many industry observers, Delta's success is no accident or stroke of luck. Rather, it stems from management's commitment to the growth and development of its human resources at all levels of the organization.

These statements illustrate why increas-

ing attention is being given to the personnel management in organizations today. Admittedly, not all top managers agree that personnel management is a key organizational function. But the consensus among decision makers is that the effectiveness of an organization's personnel and human resource program will have a direct bearing on its ability to grow and prosper in a highly competitive environment.

What is a personnel management program? What does it include? Who is responsible for the management of personnel? Is personnel management "situational?" What specifically are "good" personnel management practices and how are they implemented? Questions such as these are the focus of this book.

Personnel management may be defined as a set of programs, functions, and activities designed to maximize both personal and organizational goals. The terms personnel management, personnel administration, and human resource management may all be used synonymously.

PERSONNEL: PAST AND PRESENT PERSPECTIVES

Personnel management today is, of course, radically different from personnel

---

1. Herbert E. Meyer, "Personnel Directors are the New Corporate Heroes," *Fortune*, February 1976, p. 88.

management many decades ago. Since the turn of the century, the managerial philosophy that has defined the personnel function has undergone significant changes. In the last eighty years, the *scientific management* and *human relations* movements have appeared and declined; today what has popularly become known as the *human resources* approach has emerged. We will briefly discuss each of these philosophies and describe how the personnel function has been affected by each.

Scientific Management

The father of scientific management, Frederick Taylor, believed that "One of the very first requirements for a man who is fit to handle pig iron as a regular occupation is that he shall be so stupid and so phlegmatic that he more nearly resembles in his mental makeup the ox than any other type."[2] While Taylor's often–quoted comment overshadows the many benefits that were derived from the scientific management movement, it underscores a widespread managerial attitude during the early twentieth century: that along with raw materials, capital, and machinery, the employee was simply another *factor of production*. As such, the scientific management approach resulted in work methods and techniques which showed great concern for employees' output but little concern for employees' satisfaction. Time and motion studies replaced "rule of thumb" work methods with the "one best way" to perform a task. Typically, the "one best way" to do the job was highly specialized and routine, involving little

mental effort and few opportunities to make decisions or use judgment. Proponents of the scientific management philosophy are quick to point out—as it perhaps should be—that the "average" turn of the century worker with little formal education had few skills and abilities that could be applied to organizational problems.

The "economic man" concept was also embraced by many managers and administrators during this period. This concept suggested that the worker is motivated primarily by economic gain and that workers' output can be maximized only through additional financial incentives. Following this assumption, Taylor created the differential piece rate system whereby workers would receive a higher piece rate after the daily output standard had been achieved. With the differential piece rate system, in addition to the other scientific management techniques, workers were expected to produce at the maximum level and, in turn, to satisfy their only work-related need: money.

In addition to the traditional responsibilities of recruiting, selection, training, and health and safety, the personnel function in large manufacturing companies during the early years of this century centered around the creation and implementation of scientific management techniques. For example, the personnel staff conducted time and motion and fatigue studies, performed job analyses, prepared job specifications, and created wage incentive programs.[3] During this period, many personnel departments also

---

2. Frederick W. Taylor, *Scientific Management* (New York: Harper & Brothers, 1947) pp. 45–46.

3. For a description of personnel functions and activities undertaken by large companies during the scientific management era, see Ordway Tead and Henry C. Metcalf, *Personnel Administration* (New York: McGraw-Hill Book Company, 1920).

actively supported *welfare movement* programs to enhance the well-being of their workers. Designed to strengthen the physical, social, and educational conditions of the worker these programs included vacations, personal hygiene, training, instruction in English and naturalization (a great many factory workers were immigrants), lunchrooms, company housing, employee loans, insurance plans, and recreational programs. Unfortunately, many welfare programs were initially implemented to minimize employment resentment against long hours, low wages, harsh working conditions and exploitive supervision. Furthermore, welfare programs generally reflected paternalistic attitudes prevalent during this time: "We know what is best for you. Do as we say, and everything will be all right." However, paternalistic practices often failed to bring about the passive acceptance of unquestioned authority that management expected. Primarily for these reasons, the popularity of employee welfare programs declined somewhat during the 1920s and 1930s.

Human Relations

During the 1930s and 1940s, with impetus provided by the classic Hawthorne Studies, management's attention shifted from human engineering to *human relations*. The Hawthorne Studies demonstrated that employee productivity was affected not only by the way the job was designed and the manner in which employees were rewarded economically, but by certain social and psychological factors as well.[4]

4. For a detailed description of the Hawthorne Studies, see F. J. Roethlisberger and W. J. Dickson, *Management and the Worker* (Cambridge, MA: Harvard University Press, 1939).

Hawthorne researchers Elton Mayo and F. J. Roethlisberger discovered that employees' feelings, emotions, and sentiments were strongly affected by certain work conditions such as group relationships, leadership styles, and support from management. According to the researchers, employees' feelings could, in turn, have a significant impact on their productivity. Thus, the presumption that treating employees as human beings would enhance not only employees' satisfaction but enable achievement of organizational goals for higher productivity as well. The Mayo-Roethlisberger research led to the wide scale implementation of behavioral science techniques in industry which included supervisory training programs emphasizing support and concern for workers, programs to strengthen lines of communication between labor and management, and counseling programs whereby employees were encouraged to discuss both work and personal problems with trained counselors. The personnel staff was primarily responsible for designing and implementing these programs.

The human relations movement was also influenced by the growing strength of unions during the late 1930s and 1940s. The rise of unionism during this period was largely due to the passage of the Wagner Act which gave workers the legal right to bargain collectively with employers over matters concerning wages, job security, benefits, and many other conditions of work. While the Wagner Act did not legislate "good human relations," the act compelled many employers to improve their personnel programs and employee relations in an effort to keep unions out. Further, with the existence of a formal grievance procedure, unionization also provided employees with a measure of protection against arbitrary and hostile supervision. While unionization has led to an erosion of labor-management relations in some firms, in many other companies it resulted in greater acceptance of human relations principles.

While the human relations movement was no doubt instrumental in improving the working environment of a great many workers, it achieved only minimal success in bringing about large scale increases in worker output and job satisfaction. The lackluster performance of the movement is attributable to:

- The human relations philosophy which presented a highly oversimplified concept of human behavior in an organizational setting. The notion that "a happy worker is a hard worker" generally presented to management as an untested hypothesis is now recognized to be valid for only part of the workforce.

- This philosophy failed to consider the concept of individual differences: Each worker is a unique and highly complex individual with different wants, needs, and values. What motivates one worker may not motivate another, and "being happy" or "feeling good" may have little or no impact on the productivity of certain employees.

- The philosophy failed to recognize the need for job structure and controls on employee behavior. The approach largely neglected the importance of sound policies, procedures, standards, and work rules in guiding employees' behavior toward organizational goals.

- The philosophy failed to recognize that good human relations are but one of many conditions necessary to sustain high levels of employee motivation. The movement largely overlooked potential improvements in productivity that could result from sound performance appraisal systems, career development programs, job enrichment, and selection and placement systems that successfully match the employee with the job.

Largely for the reasons cited above, the human relations approach fell from favor with management during the 1950s and 1960s and is considered passé today. While good human relations is still an important organizational objective, human relations no longer is the predominant philosophy guiding human behavior within organizations. Good human relations are necessary, but certainly not sufficient to ensure peak levels of employee satisfaction and productivity.

Human Resources

The emerging trend in personnel management is clearly toward the adoption of the human resource philosophy. With the effective utilization of this approach, organizations benefit from two significant payoffs: increased organizational effectiveness and the bona fide satisfaction of individual employee's needs. Rather than viewing the achievement of organizational and employee needs as separate and exclusive events, supporters of the human resource philosophy contend that organizational needs and human needs are mutual and compatible. One need not be gained at the expense of the other.

Human resources is a relatively new concept in the jargon of management and organization. The term became popular during the early 1970s as behavioral science research showed that managing people as resources rather than factors of production or simply as human beings with feelings and emotions could result in real benefits to both the organization and the employee. Unfortunately, the term *human resources*—much like many terms in management literature—is hard to define with a great deal of clarity and specificity. Nonetheless, a number of principles provide the base for a human resources approach. Figure 1-1 highlights the main tenents of the human resource philosophy by comparing it with the human relations philosophy.

FIGURE 1-1: *Human Resources Philosophy*

1. Employees are viewed as *investments* that will, if effectively managed and developed, provide long-term rewards to the organization in the form of greater productivity.

2. Managers create policies, programs, and practices which satisfy both the economic and emotional needs of employees.

3. Managers create a working environment in which employees are encouraged to develop and utilize their skills and abilities to the maximum extent.

4. Personnel programs and practices are created with the goal of balancing the needs and requirements of the organization and the employee.

CURRENT PROBLEMS AND ISSUES

To a large extent, the personnel department's new found yet well-deserved status and prestige are due to the enormous responsibilities undertaken by personnel managers and administrators today. Of course, many traditional problems and issues are still largely "personnel": the recruitment, selection, orientation, and training of high quality personnel; job analysis and job evaluation; the maintenance of sound labor relations; and the design and administration of employee appraisal systems, to name a few. In recent years unique problems have created a new area of professionalism in personnel management. Some of these problems and issues are:

Productivity Crisis

How productive is America [in comparison] with the rest of the world? Person for person, the U.S. still leads the world in total output. But the American lead is shrinking; many of this country's closest competitors are catching up fast in output per person. Japan's performance jumped from only 31 percent of U.S. per capita output in 1960 to 68 percent in 1977. In 1979, particularly, productivity in the U.S.—output per hour of work—actually dropped, compared with increases in many places abroad.[5]

The above data give ample reason why we do not refer to the productivity problem, but the productivity *crisis*. Undesirable by-products of the productivity crisis include the double-edged dilemma of unemployment and inflation, a weakening position in the international economic environment, and for many a serious decline in a standard of living that they have taken for granted. All sectors of our industrial society—government, labor, and business—are searching for ways to

5. "U.S. Output—How It Stacks Up Against Other Nations," *U.S. News and World Report*, April 28, 1980, p. 29.

improve our nation's productivity and strengthen our economy.

To be sure, the productivity crisis stems from not one but a broad spectrum of economic ills: poor labor-management relations, an often hostile business-government relationship, outmoded plants and equipment, and lack of capital for plant modernization. Today the management of people is recognized to have an important bearing on employees' productivity. Many companies report that the implementation of modern personnel management practices has led to greater output and improved quality. Because research has shown that a sound personnel management program can make a difference in a firm's rate of productivity, personnel's role in productivity improvement should increase in the years ahead.

Quality of Working Life

Sociologists have spoken of the quality of life concept for years. Recently, behavioral scientists have added a similar term to the human resource jargon: *quality of working life (QWL)*. Quality of working life refers to the extent to which employees' personal needs and values are met through their work. Quality of work life improves as more and more personal needs—such as security, responsibility, and self-esteem—are met. Personnel policymakers have a two-fold concern about the QWL issue. First, many organizations consider QWL as a social responsibility to employees as well as a moral and ethical responsibility. Second, there are strong indications that improvements in QWL correlate with organizational performance measures. For example, job redesign projects at assembly plants involving

the replacement of traditional mechanically-paced assembly lines with work teams to assemble cars and trucks has led to lower turnover, less absenteeism, and improvements in product quality.[6]

Safety and Health

Creating a work environment which minimizes the likelihood of an accident or injury has long been a goal of both personnel specialists and operating managers. In addition, a number of second generation safety and health issues are taxing the skills of personnel decision makers in not only manufacturing organizations but service-oriented concerns as well. First, there is mounting evidence that some work environments are responsible for cancer, infertility, lung disease, and other diseases. Unlike an accident or injury, occupational diseases are difficult to detect—often they remain undetected until it is too late to remedy them. More and more, the work place is being labeled as hazardous to one's long-term health.

A second health-related issue deals with job stress. Unlike accidents and injuries which are most problematic in construction, manufacturing, mining, and transportation industries, job stress can be a problem in any kind of firm in any job—blue-collar, clerical, managerial, or professional. Extreme stress can lead to ulcers, heart failure, nervous conditions, and other physiological and psychological impairments. The potential impact of stress on job performance is obvious. Managers are now beginning to recognize potential personal and organizational job

6. "Job Redesign on the Assembly Line: Farewell to Blue-Collar Blues?" *Organizational Dynamics*, 2, no. 2 (1973): 51–67.

stress dangers and to seek ways to recognize and reduce the problem.

A third issue concerning employee health focuses upon the alcoholic employee. About *one in every ten employees* suffers from a drinking problem that may negatively affect performance. In the past, the alcoholic employee was either ignored or fired. Recognizing that these alternatives do not rehabilitate individuals, a growing number of firms are creating and implementing employee assistance programs (EAP) whereby troubled employees (mostly alcoholic employees) are recognized, counseled, rehabilitated, and placed back on the job. Not every alcoholic employee can be rehabilitated, but EAP's are said to enjoy up to a 70 percent success rate.[7] Most EAP's are administered within the personnel department.

Equal Employment Opportunity

The Civil Rights Act of 1964 provided the legal framework for equal opportunity in all conditions of employment without regard to race, color, religion, sex, or national origin. With the passage of the act, civil rights leaders envisioned a business environment devoid of discrimination and foresaw a day when minorities would enjoy the same economic status as the majority. But in the years since the passage of the act, the dreams of many minorities have gone unanswered. While gains have been scored by minorities in the past decade, discriminatory practices still constitute an immoral and illegal part of personnel programs in many organizations today.

7. "Summary of Third Report on Alcohol and Health," National Institute on Alcohol Abuse and Alcoholism, November 30, 1978, p. 6.

Creating an environment in which equal employment opportunity is reality rather than a popular slogan is no doubt one of the personnel manager's toughest jobs. Much like the plant foreman who is often referred to as the "man in the middle" of labor and upper management, the personnel manager has the federal government pushing for compliance on one side, while the operating manager presses for greater autonomy in personnel decisions on the other. The problem is greatly compounded by the fact that the national labor pool of qualified minorities is not yet large enough to satisfy the equal employment goals administrators strive to achieve. While equal opportunity legislation has scored successes for countless minorities, it also poses challenges that many personnel managers are finding difficult to meet.

A major equal employment opportunity problem involves the development and promotion of women into management. Generally women still face formidable barriers to management jobs—particularly for jobs above the first-line supervisory level. Among the many barriers is the stereotype that women can't handle "men's" work and that women lack the unemotional, rational temperament that decision makers must possess. Because of this reasoning, women are often excluded from training and development programs that would enable them to acquire management skills and abilities.

By designing programs and activities to strengthen opportunities for female employees, the personnel department can remove the barriers that keep many women from upper-level management jobs. These programs include the scientific testing and assessment of managerial potential, the elimination of bias in performance appraisal programs, the implementation of training programs designed specifically for women, and the development of career path programs illustrating the potential routes that women may take to achieve management positions. Women are demanding their rights in the workplace, and these demands will continue until equality is fully achieved.

Professionalism in Personnel

Years ago, an important requirement for the personnel manager was that he or she "like people." Theoretically personnel activities were conducted to keep people happy and satisfied; personnel staff members were selected largely because they possessed an appropriate human relations orientation. Even today, many students opt for a career in personnel management because they "like people and want to help people."

To be sure, showing concern for the welfare of the employee group is an important trait for the personnel staff, and for that matter, for all managers and administrators. But "liking people" does little to describe the skills and abilities of the effective personnel executive today and even less to describe the effective personnel manager or administrator of tomorrow. As the personnel function continues to grow in importance and complexity, the capabilities of the personnel staff must also expand. During the next decade, personnel practitioners must become true *professionals* who can effectively contribute to organizational goals through high quality human resource programs.

The rising demand for professionalism in personnel has led to the creation of several educational programs designed specifically to prepare personnel decision makers for the challenges they will face. Several colleges and universities, such as Indiana University and the University of Louisville, have created an undergraduate major in Personnel Administration/Industrial Relations (PAIR). The PAIR degree enables the student to concentrate coursework in areas related to the personnel function. In addition, the American Society for Personnel Administration (ASPA) has developed programs for practitioners including the Accredited Executive in Personnel (AEP) and the Accredited Personnel Manager (APM); both programs are designed for personnel generalists. Programs for personnel specialists include the Accredited Personnel Diplomate (APD) and the Accredited Personnel Specialist (APS). The APD and APS may be granted to practitioners, as well as educators and consultants.

In addition to ASPA, other associations and societies that promote professionalism in the personnel field include the Academy of Management, the American Society of Training Directors (ASTD), the International Personnel Management Association (IPMA), the American Management Associations, and the Society for the Advancement of Management.

These organizations meet regularly to discuss important topics and new developments in the field of personnel. Many personnel organizations also conduct educational seminars and publish journals; examples are the American Management Associations' *Personnel* and ASPA's *Personnel Administration*. Journals such as these contain new developments in personnel in addition to methods and techniques for improving traditional personnel functions.

External Influences

Our preceding discussion has provided ample proof that the personnel function today is shaped and molded by forces and influences outside the organization, as Figure 1-2 illustrates. Because the personnel manager exerts little control over many—or perhaps most—of these forces, the external environment constrains and challenges the personnel staff. Personnel administrators must understand the nature and importance of the external environment and recognize its impact upon current and future personnel activities.

LEGAL

The Equal Pay Act of 1963. The Civil Rights Act of 1964. The Age Discrimination Act of 1967. The Occupational Health and Safety Act of 1970. The Vocational Rehabilitation Act of 1973. The Employee Retirement Income Security Act of 1974. The Federal Privacy Act of 1974. The Pregnancy Discrimination Act of 1978.

The legal environment which engulfs business organizations today is a far cry from the laissez-faire philosophy which Adam Smith espoused over two hundred years ago in his classic work, *Wealth of Nations*. The laws cited above are but a portion of the legislation passed within the last twenty years that affect the management of personnel. Today, personnel programs must satisfy the needs of the organization, the needs of the employee, and the needs of government: they must be legal. Increasingly, legislative requirements are helping to shape personnel programs today. This has forced personnel administrators to study the laws, and to know how they are to be interpreted and how they affect the firm.

LABOR UNIONS

In 1980 members of unions or employees' associations made up about 22 percent of the labor force. The vast majority of these employees' rewards, rights, and work conditions were determined through collective bargaining between management and the workers' representative—the union. In a unionized organization, the union constitutes, perhaps, the single most powerful force upon the way in which people are managed and how personnel programs and activities are designed.

Obviously, the union can have a pronounced impact upon an organization's effectiveness; this impact may be viewed as positive or negative. A recent *Wall Street Journal*/George Gallup study found a wide divergence in attitudes toward unions among 782 top corporate executives. While management spoke of unions in positive terms, most corporate leaders felt the union was a detriment to organizational effectiveness. On the plus side, unions were recognized as aiding labor-management communication, cooperating in attempts to increase productivity, helping to reduce labor costs, and working jointly in Washington against tariff reductions. Negative comments sug-

FIGURE 1-2 *External Influences Upon the Personnel Function*

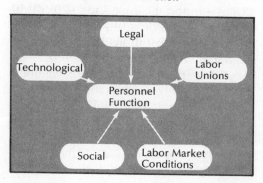

gested that unions hurt productivity, create inflexible work rules, make excessive wage demands, and cause inflation.[8] Regardless of the attitudes managers hold toward the union, most agree that the influence of the union is felt in practically every personnel policy, program, and activity designed for the union employee.

LABOR MARKET CONDITIONS

A recurring problem for personnel managers is the recruitment and selection of qualified, motivated people at reasonable wages or salaries. Thus, labor market conditions—which are heavily influenced by the supply and demand for labor—determine if an organization can satisfy its staffing and compensation objectives. Like the legal environment, the labor market cannot be influenced or controlled by any single organization. This problem is intensified by the fact that labor market conditions are highly dynamic and sometimes unpredictable. For this reason, the labor market often adds an element of frustration and uncertainty to a variety of personnel activities.

The federal government regularly publishes labor market information to assist the personnel specialist in the collection and analysis of labor market data. The U.S. Department of Labor's Bureau of Labor Statistics (BLS) is the primary collector and publisher of labor market information. In addition, federal, state, and local government agencies; employers' associations; and private groups also collect and publish data on labor market conditions. Some of their findings include:

- About 100 million workers were in the labor force in 1980. Slightly more than two-fifths of all workers were women.

- About 50 percent of all females and about 78 percent of all males work. Slightly over half of all black workers were women. Over one-fourth of all female workers held part-time jobs.

- The median education for workers is 12.6 years of school.

- White-collar jobs—technical, clerical, administrative, and managerial—are expanding at a much faster rate than blue-collar jobs. By 1985 the jobs in service industries are expected to expand by 26 percent over 1976 figures; during the same time period, jobs in goods producing firms are expected to rise by only 17 percent.

- Through the mid-eighties opportunities are expected to be favorable in health care, government, banking, insurance, and construction. Stable employment is expected in mining, manufacturing, transportation, and wholesale and retail trade. Significant employment declines are predicted in the agriculture sector.

SOCIAL

To a great extent, societal values, attitudes, and beliefs influence what workers want from their jobs. In stark contrast to workers of generations past, today's workers are demanding more than a "fair day's wage" and a safe and healthy place to work. Many seek a greater involvement in their jobs and increased attention by management to their particular work problems and needs. Such demands are likely to intensify in the coming years as workers' aspirations rise concurrently, with increases in their educational levels.

---

8. "Bosses Say Unions Do More Bad Than Good," *Wall Street Journal,* December 11, 1980, p. 28.

Specific worker demands that personnel managers and administrators will address most likely will include:

More intrinsically satisfying work. Most behavioral scientists agree that organizations today do a satisfactory job of fulfilling the lower level needs of employees. The American worker is among the highest paid in the world, and able to enjoy a fairly comfortable standard of living. But more and more, workers are demanding satisfaction from their work. Growing up in an age which constantly preaches self-fulfillment and self-actualization, they now insist that their work help them achieve more satisfying and rewarding lives. The rebellion against boring, repetitious, and demeaning work is demonstrated in low employee morale, lagging productivity, high levels of absenteeism, and other manifestations of the "blue-collar blues."[9]

In the coming years, organizations must increase efforts to satisfy human needs for self-esteem by designing highly productive work systems which improve the quality of workers' lives. Personnel managers must study the feasibility of using work teams in place of individualized assembly line work. Through teamwork, jobs gain a more humanizing and rewarding potential, thus improving employees' satisfaction at work. *Job enrichment*, a technique which allows employees more control over their work, is another work redesign strategy that may fulfill human needs. Although the virtues of job enrichment have consumed countless pages in many hundreds of journals and books, they are infrequently used in factories and offices today. Personnel decision makers must look much more closely at this technique and determine its potential in their own organizations.

Finally, in studying and evaluating strategies to improve the quality of work life, administrators must recognize and respect the most basic of all psychological tenents: people differ. In matching employees' needs to organizational needs, employees' needs should be effectively diagnosed before making sweeping changes in the way the work is performed or in the way managers and supervisors behave. Many failures in work redesign are caused by a mismatch between organizational problems and their solutions. A sound personnel research function will accurately pinpoint which employee needs are being met and those remaining unfulfilled.

Careers versus Jobs. Today, a greater number of individuals are seeking more than jobs that offer paychecks and security from the unemployment line. Instead, they are searching for organizations that will develop their skills and abilities, offering them meaningful careers with greater job challenges, increasingly responsible work, and enhanced economic rewards. Turnover research indicates that job-hopping is due in large part to the lack of career advancement and promotional opportunities. Recent college graduates, for example, find that developmental efforts and promotions are very slow to come. In addition, more and more operative level employees—blue-collar and clerical workers—are frustrated with the organization's lack of concern over their career development. They, too, are voicing demands for programs that enable them to develop and progress into management and professional positions.

9. See *Work in America: Report of a Special Task Force to the Secretary of Health, Education and Welfare*, (Cambridge, MA: MIT Press, 1973).

In this decade, personnel professionals will be challenged to implement career development programs that are truly effective. Many existing programs look good on paper but, in reality, pay little more than lip service to the concept of career development. Managers and administrators must enlarge and strengthen programs that affect career development: training and development, performance appraisal, career counseling, and career paths. In addition, these programs must not operate in a vacuum; they must be coordinated and managed in a systems fashion to ensure that human resources are being utilized to the greatest extent possible.

Alternate Work Schedules. Increasingly, workers are seeking a greater balance between their work lives and their personal lives, more leisure time and greater flexibility in scheduling time away from work. Feeling severely restricted with the typical Monday-through-Friday, nine-to-five routine they find it difficult—if not impossible—to schedule doctors appointments, accommodate children's school schedules, and satisfy other personal needs away from work. Employees are demanding that management look more closely at work schedules which accommodate their needs in addition to the needs of the organization.

These demands are expected to increase in the future. Thus, the use of alternative work schedules such as the four-day workweek is expected to rise in the coming years. Personnel managers will be called upon to study various forms of work schedules and assist in the design and implementation of arrangements that will fit the unique needs of the organization and its human resource group.

TECHNOLOGICAL

An organization's technology—the methods and techniques that are used to produce goods and services—profoundly impacts upon the skills and abilities that its employees must possess. A prime example is the computer. As computers became permanent fixtures in organizations during the 1960s, bookkeeping and clerical skills were no longer marketable; keypunching, programming, and systems analysis were in demand. Similar effects are expected to result from an increasing trend toward *robotics*—the operation of robots to perform routine assembly operations. What happens when robots enter the plant? The personnel department will be affected by:

1. Possible union resistance at unionized plants. This may mean a guarantee by management that no workers will be laid off because of the installation of robots.

2. Displaced workers must be retrained to perform new jobs.

3. New jobs may be created for persons repairing and maintaining the robots. Each new job must be studied to determine skill requirements and appropriate pay levels.

4. Management must be prepared to face the discontent which is likely to erupt as the organization's social system is damaged. Robotics will force many changes in informal group membership and informal communication patterns.

Is the trend toward robotics likely to continue? According to James Grier, president of Milacron, a leading manufacturer of industrial robots, annual sales are expected to grow from $100 million in 1980 to $700 million by 1990.[10] Should this forecast prove valid, many personnel managers will become very familiar with the problems and promises of robotics. The robot may not gripe, grumble, get bored, call in sick, or complain about the pay, but many other less obtrusive personnel dilemmas will result as assembly lines are invaded by squadrons of robots.

PERSONNEL FUNCTIONS

The personnel management program of each organization is unique. Even though personnel activities will vary somewhat from firm to firm, trends clearly indicate that the scope of personnel responsibilities is increasing in organizations of all sizes. Personnel functions described in this book include:

- Designing and Analyzing Jobs
- Acquiring Human Resources
- Developing Human Resources
- Determining Compensation and Health
- Maintaining Labor Relations
- Solving Personnel Problems

Designing and Analyzing Jobs

Under the scientific management philosophy, jobs were created to be simple and routine so that relatively unskilled workers could be easily and quickly trained to do each job. A primary assumption of the

10. Barnaby J. Feder, "Milacron's Aim: No. 1 in Robots," *The New York Times*, February 10, 1981, p. 1 (Business).

scientific management approach to job design was that the average worker had neither the skill nor the inclination to participate in work decisions or the need to gain satisfaction from work. No doubt, many assumptions about the turn-of-the-century needs and motivations of workers were valid. But while employee needs and motives have experienced many changes since the formative years of industrialization, job design in many organizations today still smacks of scientific management. Organizational research shows that in addition to demanding more satisfying and rewarding work, employees are demonstrating that their involvement in decision making can enhance, rather than impair, organizational effectiveness. In Chapter 4, we will explore alternative ways to design jobs and work schedules and discuss their relative advantages and disadvantages.

In order to perform at a satisfactory level, an employee's skills, abilities, and motives to perform the job must match the job requirements. Clearly, a mismatch may lead to poor performance, absenteeism, turnover, and other organizational problems. Through a process termed job analysis, the skills, knowledge, and abilities to perform a specific job are determined. In Chapter 3, we will present various job analysis techniques and discuss the problems that may accompany the job analysis function.

Acquiring Human Resources

To a great degree, organizational effectiveness depends on personnel effectiveness. Without a quality labor force, an organization is destined to mediocre performance—if it survives at all. For this reason, the acquisition of human resources is a critical personnel function today. Acquiring a qualified labor force involves a variety of personnel activities: labor market analysis, human resources planning, recruiting, interviewing, and testing to name a few. Chapter 6 and 7 are the focus of these topics.

One of the most important factors shaping recruiting and selection functions during the past several years, perhaps, has been the legal environment. Federal legislation—notably the Civil Rights Act of 1964—has modified the way employers search for and select a workforce. Because of the significance of legislation on the acquisition of people today, Chapter 5 has been devoted to this subject.

Developing Human Resources

Organizational growth is closely related to the growth of its human resources. Whenever employees fail to grow, a stagnant organization most likely will result. A strong employee development program does not guarantee organizational success, but generally is part of the personnel programs of successful, growing organizations.

A professional development program will help achieve personal as well as organizational goals. Many employees seek jobs in which growth and advancement are an integral part of the job. Once their goals are recognized, employees will perform effectively and be satisfied with their jobs. If these goals are not met, there is a good chance employees will seek organizations with employee development programs. For these reasons, the developmental function has increased in importance and value in many types of organizations today.

One important developmental function is the appraisal of employees' performance. During the performance appraisal process, employees are told of any performance deficiencies and what they must do to improve performance and perhaps become promotable. Various methods and techniques of performance appraisal, with their advantages and disadvantages will be described in Chapter 8.

For many organizations, the heart of the development process is on- and off-the-job activities that teach employees new skills and abilities. Because managers now recognize the benefits derived from the developmental process, expenditures for employee education are at an all-time high. This rise in employee education has been accompanied by growing professionalism in the training field and a demand for competent, qualified trainers.

Training and development is a complex function, offering many rewards but also posing many potential problems for training personnel: Who should be trained and why? What training techniques should be used? Is training cost effective? The activities and issues that center around the training and development of managerial and nonmanagerial personnel are the focus of Chapters 9 and 10.

Chapter 11 includes a discussion of a unique form of human resource development—organizational development. The purpose of organizational development is to reduce organizational conflict and resistance to change, improve decision making, and create a working environment that fosters a high commitment to the achievement of both personal and organizational goals. Drawing heavily on the behavioral sciences of psychology and sociology, most developmental techniques are geared toward work groups and project teams rather than individual employees.

A final chapter in this section deals with a relative newcomer to the personnel field: career management. In recent years, increasing attention has been given to processes and activities that enhance career advancement and solve problems that employees encounter along their career paths. While career management is difficult to implement, advances in recent years have brought about improvements in the decision making processes that affect employees' careers.

Determining Compensation and Health

The issue of compensation has long posed problems for the personnel manager. How should jobs be evaluated to determine their worth? Are wage and salary levels competitive? Are they fair? Is it possible to create an incentive compensation system tied to performance? Techniques for evaluating the financial worth of jobs and other issues pertaining to the design of pay systems are included in Chapter 13.

Included in indirect compensation are employee benefits. Because the costs of benefits for many organizations are now averaging—and occasionally exceeding—40 percent of total payroll costs, employers are trying to control benefit costs without seriously affecting the overall compensation program. The kinds of benefits that employers may offer and the considerations that should be given to planning a total benefits package are discussed in Chapter 14.

The final chapter in this section centers around an increasingly important concern to the employee today: health and safety.

Each year accidents and injuries cost billions of dollars in medical expenses, medical insurance, equipment damage, and production problems. While much is being done to improve the workplace today, there is still considerable room for improvement. In Chapter 15 we will explore important health and safety legislation and describe various strategies for strengthening an organization's health and safety program.

Maintaining Labor Relations

Labor unions exert a powerful force upon employers and influence personnel policies and programs for union employees. Because union participation in personnel decision making may have a pronounced impact on the economic condition of the firm, managers should understand the union's philosophies and goals, and explore ways in which a cooperative rather than adversarial relationship may be achieved. In the two chapters devoted to labor relations we will examine union goals, union organizational structure, the union organizing drive, the collective bargaining process, and techniques for handling employees' grievances.

Solving Personnel Problems

The final two chapters of this text are devoted to recognizing and solving common personnel problems. Absenteeism, turnover, job dissatisfaction, and unfair employee treatment are costly to the organization and aggravate labor-management relations. Today's personnel administrators are challenged to scientifically create strategies to resolve these problems. They must possess a complete understanding of the research process:

the role of personnel research, research strategies, how to analyze research data, and how to apply research to strengthen the personnel program. Chapter 18 explores these issues and describes ways in which common personnel problems may be researched and solved.

The final chapter focuses upon a problem that has no doubt plagued managers for centuries: the unsatisfactory employee. The employee who fails to perform up to management's expectations not only poses a potentially large economic cost to the employer but may also suffer stress, frustration, and tension. For these reasons, managers must recognize the factors that cause unsatisfactory performance and be able to bring about a permanent improvement in job behavior. In this chapter, specific emphasis will be placed upon discipline and counseling philosophies and techniques.

CAREER OPPORTUNITIES

The future holds numerous opportunities for students who will seek careers in personnel and human resource management. The U.S. Department of Labor projects 450,000 jobs in personnel fields by 1985. Only 335,000 such jobs existed in 1970. The *Occupational Outlook Handbook* states that:

> The number of personnel and labor relations workers is expected to grow faster than the average for all occupations through 1985, as employers, increasingly aware of the benefits to be derived from good labor-management relations, continue to support sound, capably staffed employee relations programs. In addition to new jobs created by growth of the occupation, many openings will become available each year because of

the need to replace workers who die, retire, or leave their jobs for other reasons.

Legislation setting standards for employment practices in the areas of occupational safety and health, equal employment opportunity, and pensions has stimulated demand for personnel and labor relations workers. Continued growth is foreseen, as employers throughout the country review existing programs in each of these areas and, in many cases, establish entirely new ones. This has created job opportunities for people with appropriate expertise. The effort to end discriminatory employment practices, for example, has led to scrutiny of the testing, selection, placement, and promotion procedures in many companies and government agencies. The findings are causing a number of employers to modify these procedures and to take steps to raise the level of professionalism in their personnel departments.[11]

Career Patterns of Personnel Professionals

A personnel career may be pursued in three basic ways: One way is to be promoted from a clerical/support position in the personnel department. This alternative normally exists only for superior performers who show a great deal of promise as personnel specialists. A second, more common method is to assume a staff specialist's job upon receiving a bachelor's or master's degree in business or a related field such as industrial psychology or social psychology. Recent graduates usually receive on- and off-the-job training in order to acquire skills and abilities in a functional specialty such as recruiting or employee development. A third, less common method is to be transferred from

11. U.S. Department of Labor, *Occupational Outlook Handbook* 1978–79 Edition (Washington, DC: U.S. Government Printing Office, 1979), pp. 150–53.

FIGURE 1–3: *Career Patterns for Personnel Professionals*

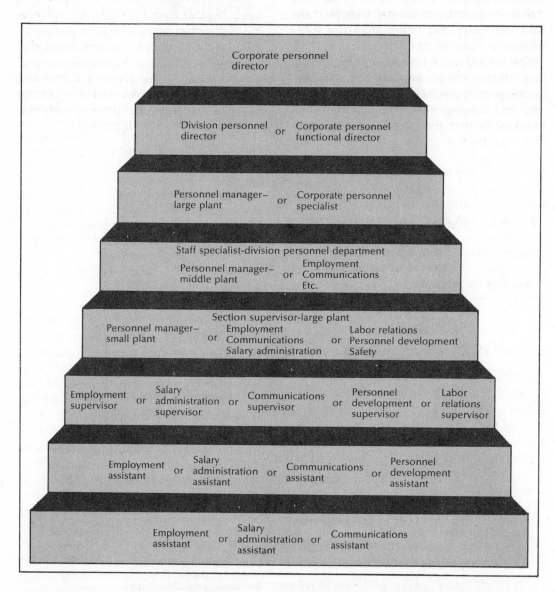

SOURCE: H. H. Mitchell, "Selecting and Developing Personnel Professionals." Reprinted with permission, *Personnel Journal,* Costa Mesa, CA, copyright July 1970.

a line job (e.g. manufacturing supervisor) or another staff job (e.g. purchasing or accounting) to a personnel staff position. This technique is not widely practiced because interdepartmental transfers are still the exception rather than the rule. However, line to staff and staff to line transfers are more common today than a few decades ago and will, no doubt, increase in the future. One advantage of the line management-to-personnel staff transfer is that the employee is experi-enced in the operating sector of the organization and brings greater breadth and knowledge to the personnel function.

The personnel chain of command in a large organization provides the achievement-oriented employee with numerous goals and challenges. The personnel staff member may pursue a number of functional areas or work toward a career as a personnel manager. An example of career patterns that personnel professionals may follow are shown in Figure 1–3.

The Solution

Perhaps since the dawn of organized activity, there has been considerable disagreement about how employees should be motivated and managed to satisfy the needs of both the individual and the organization. This fact is illustrated by Rafe's conversation with Paul and Leo. Rafe, with his attitude that people want simple jobs and that they work only to earn a paycheck, maintains attitudes that were popular during the scientific managment era. Paul, on the other hand, with his emphasis on friendship and paternalism, may be matched with the human relations approach. Leo's discussion about the job enrichment program at Volvo is a classic example of an organization's desire to implement a human resources philosophy whereby personnel programs are designed to meet the economic and psychological needs of employees in addition to the goals of the organization.

Not all managers subscribe to the human resource philosophy, and it is important to note that scientific management and human relations methods, principles, and techniques are still very much an important part of the *personnel practices of many organizations today. Managers would do well to borrow methods and techniques from each of these approaches which best fit the particular needs of the organization and their employees.*

KEY TERMS AND CONCEPTS

Personnel Management	Human Resources
Human Resource Management	Quality of Working Life (QWL)
Scientific Management	External Environment
Human Relations	Robotics

FOR REVIEW

1. How do the scientific management, human relations, and human resources approaches to managing people differ? Why is the human resource philosophy considered by many to be a favored approach over the traditional ways of managing people?

2. What are the critical problems and issues facing personnel decision makers today?

3. What changes in society and within organizations have been instrumental in reshaping the personnel role?

4. Describe the elements that make up personnel's external environment.

5. What is the career outlook for individuals who wish to enter the field of personnel/industrial relations?

DISCUSSION

1. One often hears that the scientific management philosophy of managing employees is still widely used in blue-collar work involving manufacturing and other forms of unskilled/semi-skilled work. Why might this be so? Will scientific management principles still be used in the year 2000? Explain.

2. Why did the human relations movement decline in popularity? How important are "good human relations" today? What else

must a good manager do in addition to practicing good human relations?

3. In the years ahead, the use of automated manufacturing processes is expected to increase. Some behavioral scientists also predict that job enrichment techniques in manufacturing environments will also increase. Is job enrichment compatible with automated work processes? Discuss.

4. The question of government interference in private enterprise has long been a "hot" topic for business practitioners. Have equal employment opportunity laws been, overall, good or bad for business? Good or bad for minorities? Do you feel more EEO legislation will be enacted in the coming years?

5. The outlook for professionals in the field of personnel/industrial relations is expected to remain strong through the mid 1980s. Between 1985 and 2000, do you expect the demand for personnel professionals to continue to increase, stabilize, or decrease? Discuss.

SUPPLEMENTARY READINGS

Dressnack, Carl H. "Financial Impact of Effective Human Resources Management." *Personnel Administrator*, December 1979, p. 62–66.

Dunnette, Marvin. *Work and Nonwork in the Year 2001*. Monterey, California: Brooks/Cole Publishing Co., 1973.

English, Jack W. "The Road Ahead for the Human Resources Function." *Personnel*, March-April 1980, pp. 35–39.

Foulkes, Fred K. "The Expanding Role of the Personnel Functions." *Harvard Business Review*, March-April 1975, p. 71–84.

Odiorne, George S. "Personnel Management for the 80's." *The Personnel Administrator*, August 1977, pp. 20–24.

Scheavoni, Michael J. "Employee Relations: Where Will It Be in 1985?" *The Personnel Administrator*, March 1978, pp. 25–29.

Walker, James. "Human Resource Planning: An Odyssey to 2001 and Beyond." *Pittsburg Business Review*, March 1978, pp. 2–8.

For Analysis: The Pet Store

Mike Roberts opened his first pet store ten years ago, a life long dream. Today with his wife and three daughters he manages six stores in three cities. The stores employ eighteen full-time employees and twenty-four part-time employees. Until last summer there were only two stores, both located in the same city.

Last month Roberts' store was inspected by a safety inspector from the state Occupational Safety and Health Office. The inspector was following up a complaint received from an employee. One of the new stores is located in an old building where the wiring is outdated causing overuse of extension cords and overloading of electrical circuits. One employee was severely injured as a result of an extension cord shorting out on a wet floor.

Recently some employees inquired about Roberts helping them set up Individual Retirement Accounts (IRA) so that they could utilize the tax-free provisions. Roberts confessed that he did not know anything about IRA's but would look into the matter. This inquiry led Roberts to question whether he needed a personnel officer for the stores. He has always assumed that his bookkeeper and attorney would keep him out of any real legal trouble, but now he is not so sure.

Questions:

1. How should Roberts proceed in making this decision?

2. Which personnel activities might be included in the duties of the personnel officer?

3. Are there alternatives to hiring a personnel officer?

SELECTED PROFESSIONAL READING

A Decade of Rapid Change: The Outlook for Human Resources Management in the '80s

JAMES C. TOEDTMAN

The start of a new decade and the opening of a new chapter for personnel just happen to come at the same time this month. Put them together and you have good reason to predict a wave of substantial and progressive change in human resources management in the years just ahead. But this change will be engendered by a wide range—social, political and technological—of sensitive problems: work force retrenchment, inflation, energy crises, mergers and consolidations, government regulations—each one a force to be reckoned with. We must counter these short-term problems with long-range planning. In fact, planning is one of the three key words that kept showing up in the more than 100 interviews, meetings and surveys about human resources management that we conducted or covered in the past several months. The other two keys are resilience and change.

PLANNING, RESILIENCE AND CHANGE

The official news these days is gloom and discouragement. And truly, there are no quick and easy answers to the complexities of high interest rates, energy crises, inflation . . . Moreover, Washington has an ever-tightening grip on practically everything we do.

But a revealing demonstration of the creativity of Americans, and particularly of American business, came at a recent meeting of ASPA/ International in Cambridge, Massachusetts, during a discussion of unemployment in Europe and the United States. The effects of minidata-processing technology on both continents have resulted in two completely opposite views. The United States speakers were looking at the development of the minicomputer systems as an exciting new opportunity and a commitment to expand industry, which will *create* jobs, while European speakers were extremely negative, predicting that as many as 30 percent of existing service jobs will be eliminated by computerization.

It's not that the American attitude is one of indifference to the problem of unemployment due to technology, but that there is a resolve to create opportunities out of seeming problems. The computer capacity in the United States has doubled every two and a half years, and there is no reason to doubt its continued growth. Dr. Anthony J. Weiner, coauthor with Herman Kahn of *The Year 2,000—A Framework for Speculation,* says the consequence of this growth is a "two–edged sword." He explained his views at a recent MSA, Inc. conference by applauding the advances in technology that have created vast economic opportunities and have freed people from hours of wasteful busy work, but at the same time expressed concern that "more must be done to encourage the development of new jobs or leisure activities to replace the skills which have become obsolete. No other area of technology will change people's lives as quickly or spread more rapidly than data processing and communications."

Weiner feels that one solution to this problem lies in the natural growth of the computer industry itself. This growth should create great economic and informational opportunities. "When there is economic growth, people usually find work. And the new information made possible through advances in software should spur more social and professional communications.

"The current and prospective growth of information technology is the most important development society has experienced since the automobile, the cotton gin, and the steam engine—the industrial revolution itself.

"One outgrowth of this computerized society is an intellectual elite whose jobs do not depend upon electronics and possibly a vast work force with nothing to do," said Weiner. "While the increasing use of information technology will mean greater productivity for less work, some people will not be able to cope with the increased options for work or enforced leisure.

"While I believe in Parkinson's Law that work expands to meet the labor force available," he continued, "the problem will not be solved unless people recognize its existence and start doing something about it."

We all remember the warnings of twenty years ago about the computer—that automation would be putting millions out of work. The next twenty years may be different, but the quickening, innovative pace of change, as well as new opportunities for our social concerns, environmental interests and alternate-energy demands, also means many new job developments. A tremendous surge of interest in just improving our lot is apparent all around us. Industry, for example, is accelerating its efforts to improve the way we do business. Its research and development budgets increased 16 percent in 1977, went up another 10 percent in 1978, reaching $21.8 billion, and are expected to go up yet again in 1980, to result in a continuing wealth of innovation in every business. We have the proper tools to plan and cope with such innovation; we now need to mobilize our attitude and our desire to do so, rather than just express them. So the first key to the future is planning.

The second key to the future is resilience. If there is one American quality that is showing up again, it is our ability to bounce back. After political scandal. After a crippling strike. After a demoralizing setback at the stadium. "Wait until next year!" is what we hear after a disappointing showing by our favorite team.

The third key word that is being discussed everywhere is change. And that seems to be at the heart of much work place unrest. We resist change when it affects us personally—at our jobs, in our departments. It would be redundant to dwell on all the discussions to which we've listened lately about the changes coming up in the '80s in human resources management, but there is a recurring concept. This was brought up some years ago by one of the leaders in personnel–preparedness thinking, Clyde Benedict, vice president of Integon Corporation, and is currently espoused by Terrance S. Hitchcock, vice president—human resources for Leaseway Corporation. Benedict talked about the personnel director as a change agent; Hitchcock asks for innovative personnel leadership.

Let's continue our survey of recent conferences, seminars, reports and general observations. We talked to the personnel people themselves about what the future holds for human resources management. We confirmed our own interviews with surveys made during the past few months. We asked management professionals how they felt about their own personnel departments. These views, interestingly enough, all held together quite well.

Next we turned to the marketplace to see how the people and companies who sell personnel products and services view the new decade. Their comments, by the way, were wonderfully encouraging.

A MANAGER'S VIEW OF QWL

Eaton Corporation's chairman, E.M. DeWindt, had this to say about an important corporate concern for the '80s, the quality of working life: "About ten years ago, Eaton launched a massive expansion program, a long-range project involving the building of nearly a score of new plants around the nation. We knew that each plant design would incorporate the most modern methods and machinery for productivity. And, realizing that productivity is really a function of people, we decided that our employee relations practices and policies should get as much streamlining as the plants and equipment. When we looked at our traditional practices, it was obvious that they weren't designed for rushing into the 21st century. These practices were born of mistrust, agitation and negotiation. This was apparent in the paraphernalia and terminology that went along with them. We had the tyrannical time clocks and mindless bells and buzzers. We had probationary periods, posted work rules, disciplinary proceedings and restrictive holiday-eligibility rules for production workers that stamped them as second-class members of the total team.

"The building of so many new plants gave us a unique opportunity to start from scratch, and our employee relations people were challenged to break away from tradition and develop a program built on mutual trust.

"They responded with vigor and enthusiasm, and today nearly twenty Eaton plants operate under the new philosophy. There are no time clocks in these plants, no bells or buzzers or whistles to remind people that Big Daddy is watching them. All employees of these plants—management, office and production—are salaried, and all participate in major decisions concerning the operation. There are no paycheck penalties for casual absences or tardiness, no segregated parking lots.

"The results have been dramatic and productive. Absenteeism averages 2 percent in these plants and turnover is almost zero. Productivity ranges from 30 to 40 percent higher than in traditional plants. There is a genuine feeling of involvement and belonging throughout the plants. The program has passed the tests of good and bad times, and many of its elements are working their way into older, organized plants.

"While it is true that such sweeping changes could only be made in new and unorganized plants, this is not a program to combat the unions, but rather to combat the climate of mistrust that so often and so easily pervades a manufacturing operation. It has helped bring about productive negotiations in unionized plants, and we are convinced that both management and labor will pursue the course of mutual trust at a greater degree than ever before," DeWindt concludes.

PERSONNEL SPEAKS UP, TOO

The personnel professionals have a similar positive attitude toward their work. Members of the American Society of Personnel Administration, in a survey of personnel issues, paint a clear picture of how personnel managers see the 1980s affecting their role. They see, for example, that their role must broaden beyond the traditional interviewing, hiring, compensation and labor relations, into such areas as:

- Design and control of the oganizational structure (77 percent).
- Support of line managers through communications (75 percent).
- Computer systems for personnel forecasting and planning (84 percent).
- Support of line managers in planning long-range personnel needs for their business units (93 percent).

They also see the importance of moving into a more proactive role in public affairs, political action and economic education (92 percent), the better to cope with social responsibility issues, government regulations and consumer pressures.

These personnel managers especially agree (97 percent) that the personnel function must be upgraded in the '80s to fulfill all of these needs. They feel the challenge will result in experienced line managers from other functions being attracted to the personnel profession.

PERSONNEL ISN'T JUST TALKING TO ITSELF

Separating the wheat from the chaff in the widespread talks about personnel professionalism, leadership stance and personnel as a change agent isn't always easy. The quest for professional stature is a longstanding one, regardless of position, and the personnel director is now falling in line with the physicists, the chemists, the technicians, the physicians and a host of other professionals.

Everyone wants to be recognized and respected, and rightly so. But here is a case of professional stature that is not only desirable, but comes at the right time as well. In a recent Coopers and Lybrand study, "The Management of Human Assets," the economists at this international firm of public accountants say, "Companies now recognize that effective personnel management is no longer simply a desirable goal; it is mandatory if an organization is to achieve optimum productivity and is to attract and retain talented people."

To continue this objective outside analysis, Coopers and Lybrand affirm, "For a manager to maximize the return on the assets changed to his care, a company should establish a systematic program in human resources management that parallels the effective planning process utilized for capital projects."

AREAS OF OPPORTUNITY

We have heard of all of the following areas suggested as ground on which personnel can prove itself in the '80s:

- Planning.
- Forecasting required human resource skills.
- Organizing processes to identify skills.
- Searching and recruiting to put qualified talent in the right positions.
- Designing total compensation systems.
- Upgrading work life.
- Proving cost/benefit results.

In the recent Information Science Incorporated survey of corporate personnel executives, the CPEs were asked how they could best contribute to their companies profits. Their responses indicate that the profession takes its new leadership role seriously. Here are the most popular suggestions:

- Improving cost-control measures, such as reductions in turnover, absenteeism and time lost through accidents.
- Developing productivity programs.
- Negotiating low-cost insurance coverage.
- Working to keep employee morale high.
- Designing benefit plans within established cost parameters.
- Designing new reward systems.
- Controlling compensation levels.
- Implementing human resource planning and development programs.
- Putting the lid on employment levels.
- Developing safety programs.
- Employing cost-effective measurements.

When asked what kind of research program they would institute on the job, the clear favorite was a combination of comprehensive human resource planning and development and productivity studies.

AREAS OF CHANGE

Here are what our study shows will be the principal changes in the personnel department in the decade ahead.

Information: The computer has arrived in personnel management, somewhat belatedly, but encouragingly. MSA, Inc.; Information Science Incorporated; Comshare, Inc.; Wang Laboratories, Inc.; IBM and other software firms specializing in human resource management systems predict rapidly expanding service. Planning and decision making require an integrated approach, involving information resource management, data processing, and telecommunication services. These are the elements of the new informatics, to use a term that coordinates the collection, integration and application of information. It's a government term, but expect to hear it a lot in the '80s. Of course, it also means new jobs and concept changes.

This evolution won't always be easy, warns the Technology Research Group, based in Pasadena, California. Office workers may be classed EDP or non-EDP staff, technological enclaves may emerge, and it will be easy to become too wrapped up in the intricacies of sophisticated equipment. A new function will be information resource management, which will keep organizations up to date as to the most effective use of EDP applications.

Remember yet again: informatics will be the lifeblood of your organization in the '80s. The company with the superior information flow is the one that makes better decisions, is managed more efficiently, achieves higher productivity and alleviates employee frustration more successfully. Emphasis continues to be on reduced paperwork, not on designing a beautiful system. By 1985, according to *Information System News,* virtually every personnel director will be buying software products, of which there are currently 5,500 being marketed by more than 2,000 vendors. (If you're not sure about the meaning of "software," John P. Imlay, president of MSA, Inc., displayed a player piano at a recent conference. "The piano roll is the software," he summarized.)

Finally, human resource planning will be a particularly important concern in the automated personnel office. These computerized personnel information systems can also have substantial cost-saving benefits, a Comshare study shows.

Education: Personnel as a career will attain new status in the '80s. (A trend to graduate degrees in the field has accelerated in the last few years.) M.B.A. programs are putting more emphasis on personnel, and sabbaticals for graduate study and civic and social work (such as those granted by Xerox, IBM and others) will be evident. Expect a trend toward printed services, video tape and closed-circuit instruction to expand; seminars may lag in growth rate in favor of personalized and in-house study. The energy crunch may also regionalize more meetings and conferences.

Affirmative Action: There is no turning back, and we are now adjusting to regulatory procedures after almost 16 years of civil rights in employment. Eleanor Holmes Norton, head of the Equal Employment Opportunity Commission, talks of "status change" for women and blacks, and much progress can be reported for these groups in managerial positions. But government programs for the unskilled and untrained have been held up substantially by red tape, and employers will have to take a much more prominent role in tackling the "hard-core jobless" problem.

Men still hold 78 percent of managerial jobs, by the way. About the same percentage of women are in clerical, service, sales or factory jobs. We're getting used to women moving into nontraditional jobs now, so expect more of it in the '80s, but women can also look for more competition for advancement as the novelty wears off.

Labor Relations: European trends to social policies like codetermination and work councils can be expected to accelerate in the United States, especially now that Chrysler Corp. has appointed a union member to its board. Look for computer assistance in contract negotiations. The Empire Division of Applied Data Research, Inc., in fact, takes data processing right to the bargaining table to quickly verify discussions in regard to regulatory requirements, inflation, benefit costs and projections. Unions will also push for membership in diversified employment areas, but there will be little change in union–management attitudes. Professional unions are growing in strength, particularly in government and education, though labor and craft unions will continue to have membership problems.

Temporary Help: Expect this resource to expand from 2.5 to 10 percent of our total labor force by 1990, according to a Kelly Services study. The quality of temporary workers will improve, too. Manpower Temporary Services, for example, has a new interviewing and testing system that improves selection and determines not only the best qualified workers, but also the most adaptable.

Temporary engineers and technicians will be more available in the '80s. Manpower Temporary Services and others now have medical divisions with health care temporaries, while

Accountemps emphasizes skilled accounting and data processing help for overloads. Industrial workers can also be found through the temporary services. The major growth, however, will continue to be in traditional office staffing—expanding to include government and service sectors, especially since there is currently an estimated shortage of 3 million skilled office people. (Note that some firms, such as Staff Builders, do recruiting and training as well.) Look for more decentralized temporary services to place workers in jobs near their homes—both because they like the convenience, and because it cuts down on energy use.

Retirement: Second careers, reeducation, consulting and part-time work will be common activities for our older population. Retirement advisers say vast changes in the type of retirees are already showing since the recent amendments to the Age Discrimination in Employment Act, and these people are better adjusted to their new life-styles. Company retirement-preparation programs are steadily improving, while incentives for retirement and the indexing of benefits grow in importance. Second-career training is also in the picture. In fact, Canteen Corporation is launching its Univance Career Centers on the West Coast to counsel older people about their careers.

Older workers are also more visible in the temporary–help field. Mature Temps, a division of Colonial Penn Life Insurance Company, specializes in placing people 59 or older in clerical and secretarial jobs, as they tend to be both reliable and productive. Finally, about 20 percent of the adult population is now 45 to 64 years old, and their number will increase to 38 percent by the year 2000.

Relocation: This rapidly expanding service has grown into a huge industry, but it hasn't yet really stabilized, due to changing life-styles and the present economy. However, Equitable Relocation's growth rate of 20 percent a year is expected to continue, and this seems to represent an industry trend. Improved "relocation training" for transferred employees is coming in the '80s also. ABC is introducing a comprehensive overseas relocation videocassette film service, "Touch of Home," to ease foreign transfers. Spouse relocation will be a growing problem, due to job-shifting difficulties.

A recent Merrill-Lynch Relocation survey shows that a significant number of firms expect to upgrade and more clearly define their policies for relocation, and most companies reaffirmed that they do not penalize employees for refusing to move, another continuing trend. There was also an increase noted in reimbursements for additional tax liability in the new location. About one–third of the companies surveyed offer assistance in helping to find jobs for transferees' spouses. What's more, relocation must now include consideration of energy conservation. Where commuting is a problem, some large firms are allowing lateral or functional job changes in order to cut traveling time and expense. (Company buspools will be an everyday personnel concern in the future, while carpooling is already a special activity. Avis is doing an excellent public service in this area.) Coming, too, is more flexibility in vacating dates and lease contracts, a higher-cost policy on hard-to-sell older homes, additional house-hunting time, increased temporary living expenses, and improved relocation counseling.

Health Care: This will be an increasing concern for personnel executives as the cost/benefit factor continues to reach alarming levels. People want more comprehensive health plans, but they also want their employers to pay for them. A growing service will be group clinics and specialized ambulatory care centers, all of which will cut hospital stays. Mobile testing services for chest x-rays, blood and urine analysis, visual screening, toxicology and cytology will fill an increasing demand for effective and preventive employee health care. Personnel must take a more active role in this area in order to develop group action for cost control.

Work Schedules: Get used to more flexibility, more personally arranged work programs. Part-time work and flexitime are increasing, particularly for women. Entrance-level training is also on the increase, since vocational training has been curtailed due to school budget cuts in many areas.

Here is a prediction from the American Management Associations' Center for Management Development: To make the most of high office rents and the higher cost of equipment, look for great changes in the traditional office schedules. Look to conducting business from air terminals, home or automobiles. Three-shift offices will change life-styles and call for added incentives for night work, possible 25 percent salary premiums and other perks.

Office Equipment: An information–processing industry consortium headquartered in Washington DC has opened. Companies cooperating in the innovative center have donated over $600,000 worth of equipment for a work place test of the latest systems and technology. An administrative laboratory developed by the consulting firm of Micronet, Inc., the experiment tells us that you must expect to spend much more than the $2,000 per employee for equipment that was typical in the '70s. In addition to the demonstrations of equipment and office systems, this "paperless office" laboratory offers seminars and workshops to help train executives in the use of the automated office.

Outplacement Counseling: We will be seeing more of it, with more specialists/consultants and more formal programs. Executive assistance in counseling and job development is expected to grow ten times over in the new decade.

Recruitment: About 20 million people change jobs every year. Turnover is particularly high among EDP employees—34 percent. Executive search has quadrupled in the past ten years, and the trend is still with us. However, human resource inventory and organizational audit systems are being developed that will help career pathing and thereby reduce turnover. Job posting may be on the increase, and recruitment advertising definitely is, for personnel department ad budgets are expected to double by 1983.

Employee Incentives: These were separated as a major area of incentives only three years ago, but they have increased by about 7 percent each year since, and this yearly rate will probably increase to 10 percent very soon. Incentives for employee performance is a $7 billion business, so don't be surprised to see companies developing new incentive systems or packages.

ATTITUDE = PROGRESS AND SURVIVAL

That's a lot of changes, and they are obviously complex ones as well, affecting just about every facet of the personnel professional's field. As we pointed out earlier, such changes can only be met with long–range planning—and planning is a matter of awareness, communication and hard work. But whether you wish to think of yourself as a change agent or simply an innovative personnel manager, remember: your attitude toward change in the new decade is a clue not only to how much progress your organization will make, but also to your professional survival in this increasingly competitive corporate era.

One of a personnel specialist's duties is reviewing the company's personnel manual with new employees.

2

MANAGEMENT AND THE PERSONNEL FUNCTION

Management Functions

Personnel Department Functions

Management/Personnel Interaction

Large, Medium, and Small Personnel Departments

The Problem: Akron Steel Products Company

Mary Brice, personnel manager for the Akron Steel Products Company, was not looking forward to her meeting with Carl Mead, the vice-president of production. Mead was known to have great distain for the personnel department. Brice was going to explain the details of Akron Steel's new affirmative action program to Mead as well as the program's impact on recruiting, hiring, promoting, and transferring employees within the production department. The program was recently approved by Akron Steel's president and board of directors and the Equal Employment Opportunity Commission.

A medium-sized manufacturer of steel products located in Ohio, Akron Steel employs about 2,200 employees, most of whom work in production. The firm has had a long history of labor problems involving charges of discrimination against black persons and women. A recent legal suit resulted in promotions and back pay for many minority employees. The presiding judge also ordered Akron Steel to create and implement an affirmative action program to insure that more blacks and women were recruited, hired, trained, placed and then promoted into skilled, administrative, and managerial jobs.

Brice met with Mead in the production department conference room and began to explain the details of the program. Face reddening, Mead sharply broke in after about ten minutes:

"Mary, it's the same old story. You're trying to tell me how to run my business. Now you're telling me who I can and can't hire and promote. Well, how would you like the responsibility for meeting production goals every week? You

*want to interfere with my job and the running of my
department but you don't want to assume any responsibility
for our personnel problems. Well, I'm sorry, Mary, but I think
this affirmative action program is a bunch of garbage and I'll
fight it tooth and nail."*

*Brice tried to explain to Mead that the company had no
choice—the program was ordered by the court.*

*"I don't care," said Mead. "I'll drag my feet like you've
never seen before. "Besides, what will you do—fire me?"*

The personnel job is every manager's responsibility. Because managers accomplish their goals through other people, each manager by definition, is a "manager of personnel." The accomplishment of organizational objectives depends upon the selection, development, and retention of human resources; managers at all levels of the hierarchy must possess the skills to create satisfying and motivating work environments for their employees. A wealth of personnel research shows that people oriented skills—the abilities to communicate, counsel, train, and develop—are significant factors that distinguish successful managers from less successful managers.

Managing the personnel function, however, is a shared responsibility. The obligation to make maximum use of human resources is divided between two separate units: the organization's management team and the personnel department. Working together, managers and personnel administrators create objectives, write policies, and implement programs designed to satisfy organizational needs for competent, qualified personnel

and human needs for security, job satisfaction, and personal growth.

In this chapter, we will discuss how the personnel department is typically organized and managed, examine the working relationships between managers and personnel officials, and discuss common organizational problems, giving alternative methods for keeping these problems at a minimum.

Examining the functions of management in addition to the attributes common to all organizations will help you understand the nature of the personnel function. In this way, the role of personnel administrators and the relationship of the personnel department to other organizational elements may be more fully recognized and understood.

MANAGEMENT FUNCTIONS

Managers perform an extremely wide variety of activities; endless books have been written about what managers do and should do to become effective. While each author approaches management in a different way, most writers agree that the duties and responsibilities of managers may be grouped into a small number of separate yet related functions:[1]

Planning

Planning is the process of "deciding what objectives to pursue during a future time period and what to do in order to achieve those objectives."[2] The phrase "the primacy of planning" underscores the fact that planning must precede all other management functions if the organization is to successfully achieve its objectives. For example, it would be a futile exercise for an organization to hire and train new employees unless the products and services to be offered in the future had been determined as well as what human skills and abilities would be needed to produce those products and services.

Strategic plans are long-range, generally spanning three or more years. Strategic plans usually involve major decisions about the direction the firm will take and the strategies it will use. Operating plans typically coincide with the company's fiscal year, including annual goals that help accomplish broader, strategic objectives. Short-range or operational plans are activities of less than one year's duration. Strategic, operational, and short-range plans must be integrated. For example, strategic plans may include a 20 percent

increase in production and sales within five years; the operating plan may include the construction and start-up of a new plant and the hiring and training of new personnel so that the strategic plans may be achieved. Common short-range examples include, weekly, monthly, and quarterly production, sales, and inventory schedules.

While all managers plan, managers at different levels generally plan for different time periods. Strategic planning is usually the responsibility of top management—the board of directors, president, vice-president group, and perhaps a long-range planning committee. The job of creating and implementing operating plans is often performed by middle managers such as plant managers, regional sales managers, and department heads. First level supervisors such as plant foremen, and an occasional forelady, office managers, and accounting supervisors usually receive the lion's share of developing and carrying out short-range plans.

Organizing

"Form follows function" is an often-cited architectural axiom. An office building, for example, should be designed according to the purposes it must serve. This principle also holds true for organizations. Once goals and objectives have been defined, a structure must be developed enabling the organization to accomplish its purposes as effectively as possible. Organizing involves three broad activities: First, jobs must be designed so that the necessary work may be performed. Second, individual jobs must be grouped into logical and manageable units. This process results in departments

---

1. Leslie W. Rue and Lloyd L. Byars, *Management: Theory and Application* (Homewood, IL: Richard D. Irwin, Inc., 1977), p. 7. For a discussion of other management functions, see Richard M. Hodgetts, *Management: Theory, Process and Practice* (Philadelphia: W. B. Saunders Company, 1979), p. 64.

2. Rue and Byars, *Management: Theory and Application*, p. 7.

such as engineering, marketing, manufacturing, and personnel. Third, individuals are assigned responsibilities and delegated authority to perform their jobs and accomplish objectives.

Because organization managements continually alter their directions and adopt new goals and objectives, reorganization and job redesign strategies must generally be implemented to ensure new goals are effectively met. Each time, the structure is modified to accommodate new purposes.

Staffing

In a board sense, staffing involves determining future needs, and recruiting, selection, and training the organization's work force. Because people ultimately determine the success or failure of an organization, staffing is a critical element in the overall personnel management function. Most of the duties and responsibilities involved in the staffing function lie within the domain of the personnel department.

Motivating

Perhaps since the beginning of organized activity, managers and supervisors have pondered methods and techniques for extracting the maximum output from their workers. Ages ago, efforts to gain optimum employee productivity were crude indeed—whips and threats of death were sometimes used by slave drivers and overseers to bring about the greatest efforts by their laborers.

Even today, motivating employees is a major issue for managers at all levels. While the carrot has largely replaced the stick, there is little agreement among stu-

dents, teachers, and practitioners of management about what form the carrot should take. Throughout this book, we will touch upon several individual techniques in use by organizations today to enhance worker motivation. Personnel administrators are often involved in designing and implementing these techniques. Some of these include redesigning the job to bring about greater challenge and satisfaction, training and development exercises, organization development, career management, monetary incentive plans, and employee counseling.

Controlling

By necessity, management generates a great number of plans, objectives, performance standards, policies, rules, and procedures to define acceptable employee behavior and create an atmosphere of organization and coordination. However, managers must create *control mechanisms* to ensure that these expectations are being met. A control mechanism is a simple three-part process: (1) establishing standards (goals, performance objectives, policies, etc.), (2) comparing actual performance to standard, and (3) correcting deviations from standards. To illustrate, assume a business school professor is expected to achieve an overall rating of "good" on course evaluation questionnaires completed by students who have taken the course. If the professor actually receives an overall rating of "below average," the department chairperson would discuss the matter with the professor and develop a plan to improve the course ratings. In reality the control process is not this simple. Objective performance data are often nonexistent. Timely, valid performance information lies at the heart of the control system, and personnel administrators play a key role in developing relevant and usable performance related information systems.

━━━ ORGANIZATIONS ━━━

Employees at all levels—managers, administrators, office workers, and blue-collar employees—perform their jobs in organizations. Forming the economic base of every society, organizations produce myriad goods and services demanded by consumers. Under the capitalistic system, common forms of business organizations include proprietorship, partnership, and incorporation.[3] Regardless of the type of business enterprise or economic system in which it exists, a common definition will generally describe the essence and purpose of all organizational forms: An organization is a group of people bound together in a formal relationship to achieve organizational goals.[4]

By "group of people" we mean the organization's total human resource group—made up of many individual large and small work units and departments which perform separate functions and activities. The term *formal relationship* indicates that the way people behave and interact is influenced and guided by different control mechanisms: policies, standards, rules, and regulations. In addition, the formal status of a supervisor or manager indicates that this employee has been delegated to control and direct the behavior of subordinates. Finally, all organizations are created and operated to meet certain "organization goals." Business enterprises generally strive to meet a number of purposes: profit, growth, market share, innovation, adaptability, employee welfare, and social responsibility. Government organizations also work toward multiple goals: recreation, medical care, defense, and transportation.

No two organizations are exactly alike; each organization is set apart from the other. But every organization—whether it be a worldwide corporate conglomerate headquartered in New York City or a twenty-employee countyseat in southeast Idaho—assumes the same set of characteristics during its creation and the ultimate pursuit of its goals. Although authors use various labels to describe these elements, four are generally mentioned:

Job Design

Job design decisions are an integral part of creating and maintaining an effective organization. Job design focuses on the three interrelated areas: (1) job content, (2) job functions, and (3) the interpersonal relationships required by the job holder.

Departmentalization

Departmentalization is the process of combining jobs into work units and grouping similar work units. For example, within a school of business departments may be entitled management, marketing, accounting, finance, or economics.

Perhaps the most prevalent type of departmentalization is functional departmentalization. In this form, organizations are departmentalized by major work activ-

---

3. Detailed discussions of the various forms of business organizations may be found in any introductory business book.

4. Henry L. Sisk, *Management & Organization* (Cincinnati: Southwestern Publishing Co., 1977), p. 169.

FIGURE 2–1: *Departmentalization*

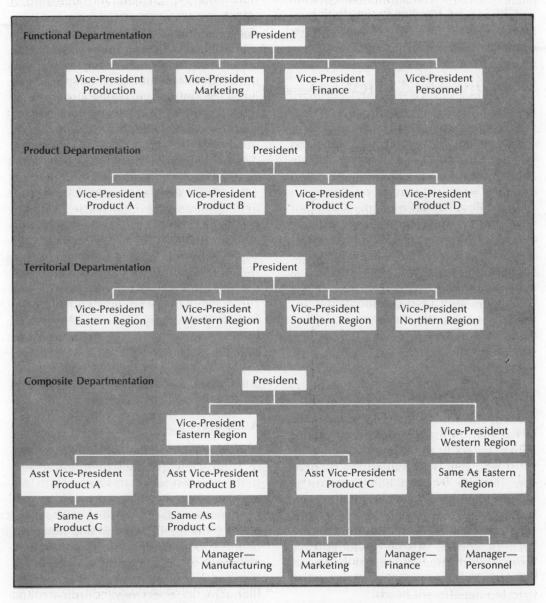

ities. For example, in a manufacturing firm, typical functions include marketing, manufacturing, engineering, finance, and personnel. Another way to departmentalize is product departmentalization, whereby the organization is divided by major product lines. To illustrate, General Motors Corporation is divided into three major product groups: Car and Truck Body and Assembly Group, Automobile

Components Group, and Household Appliances Group. The automobile division is further divided into Pontiac, Chevrolet, Buick, Oldsmobile, and Cadillac divisions. Departmentalizing an organization by product is often referred to as divisionalization.

A third method is territorial departmentalization, a common technique for large, geographically dispersed companies. Under this form, the organization is divided into territorial units that generally operate autonomously from one another. As an example, large, nationwide retailers such as Sears, Roebuck & Company, K-Mart, or the Gulf Oil Corporation are most likely organized into north, south, east and west operations. Finally, most large organizations combine several forms of departmentalization into what may be called a composite form of departmentalization. Figure 2–1 illustrates the forms of departmentalization.[5]

Span of Control

Span of control is sometimes referred to as the span of management; the *span of control* refers to the number of subordinates who report directly to the supervisor. The key word in our definition is directly. Some may suggest that a plant manager is responsible for the plant's entire human resource group, but the span of control actually includes only those subordinates who report directly to the manager. This probably includes less than ten department heads.

___

5. A discussion of other forms of departmentation and the advantages and disadvantages of each form is contained in James A. F. Stoner, *Management* (Englewood Cliffs, NJ: Prentice-Hall, Inc., 1978), pp. 224–32.

The span of control is generally large at the operative level of the organization and shrinks considerably for middle and top management groups. For example, it is not unusual for a first-line manufacturing supervisor's span of control to number thirty or forty blue-collar employees or more. A middle manager's span may include nine or ten, and a top manager's span may include five, six, or seven executives.

How large should the span of control be? The characteristics of the supervisory-subordinate work group play a major role in determining the optimal size. The optimal size is, simply put, neither too large nor too small. A large span increases the supervisory-subordinate ratio and in turn reduces overall supervisory salaries. But too great a span may reduce the time a supervisor can spend with each subordinate and decrease the effectiveness of both the manager and the subordinates. Thus, management is faced with weighing the advantages and disadvantages of creating spans of various sizes.

Authority

Authority refers to the right a manager has to control the activities of subordinates. In the simplest sense, this amounts to telling other people what to do: setting performance standards, creating work schedules, changing the content and functions of the subordinates' jobs, or sending an employee to a training program. *Authority* is necessary for managers throughout the hierarchy to effectively coordinate and control human behavior so that goals and objectives may be achieved.

While viewpoints differ on the concept of authority, the most popular approach is the classical, or "top-down," theory of authority.[6] This theory proposes that authority evolves from the constitutional right to private property and is delegated—or passed downward—through the organization's board of directors, to each management level, and finally, to the operative employee group. As illustrated in Figure 2–2, authority flows through the organization, creating a continuous link of supervisory-subordinate work groups. This *chain of command* reflects how the organization is structured and shows "who has authority over whom."

The extent to which authority is delegated, or dispersed, throughout the organization may be explained by the concepts of centralization and decentralization. Under *centralization,* upper level management retains major decision–making authority, creating all major policies and programs, and reserving the authority to make significant changes. The armed forces is a good example of centralized authority because the top brass in each branch make major goal and policy decisions for the entire structure. In the U.S. Army, generals and colonels create goals and write policies; majors, captains, and lieutenants are responsible for achieving goals and implementing policy. In business firms, centralization is common in small and medium-sized enterprises. The president and top management team delegate little authority and often make all major—and sometimes minor—decisions.

With *decentralization,* significant deci-

FIGURE 2–2: *Span of Control and Chain of Command*

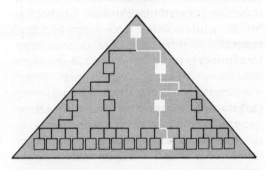

sion-making authority is delegated throughout the organization to lower management levels. As more and more authority is delegated, the organization becomes decentralized and middle and first level managers make more decisions and more important decisions. To illustrate, a large bank with several branches throughout the state may decide to decentralize operations, giving branch managers more decision-making authority. Decisions that may be affected might include:

● A branch loan officer making personal loans up to $25,000 without home office approval.

● A branch manager participating with top management in setting annual goals.

● A branch manager deciding which service hours will best serve that branch's customers.

● A branch personnel officer developing effective procedures for acquiring new personnel.

Closely related to decentralization is the *profit center* which is an independent, autonomous organizational unit that earns a satisfactory profit and return on investment. Because they are held ac-

---

6. An opposing view concerning the creation of authority is labeled the acceptance theory of authority. This theory, developed by Chester Barnard, suggests that a supervisor's authority must be first accepted by a subordinate before it becomes legitimate. See Chester I. Barnard, *The Functions of the Executive* (Cambridge, MA: Harvard University Press, 1938), pp. 161–84.

countable for profits, profit center managers retain a great deal of authority in operating their organizations. Many large manufacturers with multiple product lines operate each product division as a separate profit center. Prime examples include the General Electric and General Motors corporations. At General Motors, each automobile division is a profit center where top divisional managers are given an annual operating budget, goals, objectives, and broad decision-making powers.

No organization is purely centralized or decentralized; managers and administrators at all levels make some decisions. Rather, the concepts should be thought of in relative terms: the army is relatively centralized; whereas, General Motors is relatively decentralized.

Types of Authority

In every large, complex organization, several different kinds of authority exist. The most basic is called *line authority*, which empowers the supervisor with the right to command subordinates. Thus, every manager possesses line authority. A related organizational concept is *line function*, which is directly responsible for the achievement of organization goals. In a typical manufacturing enterprise, line functions include production and sales. In a university, teaching is a line function and the faculty are line personnel.

Staff authority is supportive and may be defined as the right to advise and provide service to other organizational members. Individuals who provide staff services generally fall into one of two categories: personal staff or specialized staff. A *personal staff member* is an individual who

assists a manager in carrying out duties and responsibilities. This staff member is often a personal assistant to one individual. A *specialized staff* generally refers to a staff department which provides specialized services for the entire organization. Staff department members are often technical experts in a relatively narrow field; staff personnel are sometimes referred to as "specialists," while line managers are called "generalists." Specialized staff departments include engineering, research and development, purchasing, quality control, legal, finance, and personnel-industrial relations.

When a specialized staff member acts in a purely advisory role, this advice can, in theory, be accepted or rejected by the individual to whom the advice is being given. Perhaps an example will clarify this point. Assume the vice-president of sales of a large insurance company (a line manager) asks the training and development director to draw up recommendations for a sales training course for newly hired sales personnel. Over the next four or five weeks, the training director puts together a course outline which includes topics to be covered, potential instructors, costs, and a plan for evaluating the course. The training director then presents the plan to the sales executive who may approve the plan, reject it outright, or ask for modifications in certain areas. Of course, continual rejection of staff advice can greatly harm line/staff relations. Later in the chapter, we will discuss other factors which have a negative impact on line and staff relationships and explore some steps for strengthening the relations between line and staff personnel.

In addition to providing advice and service to other organizational members, staff personnel are also granted authority to create and implement policy, and control certain activities. This authority is referred to as functional authority and may be defined as authority over a particular function or activity. *Functional staff authority* gives staff personnel the power to regulate certain policies, procedures, and goals of other departments throughout the organization. Examples of functional staff authority include:

Type of Staff Department	Exercise of Functional Staff Authority
Personnel	Require orientation training for all new employees
Legal	Approve organization's legal contracts
Purchasing	Determine purchasing procedures
Quality Control	Set and enforce quality tolerance limits on manufactured goods
Accounting	Determine financial and accounting procedures

A staff member may actually possess all three types of authority: line, staff, and functional staff authority. The head of the quality control department has line authority over subordinates. The exercise of staff authority may involve giving advice to manufacturing superintendents on how to reduce the error rate via certain preventive maintenance procedures. Finally, most quality control officials can immediately stop a manufacturing process if the finished part or product fails to meet certain quality standards. This is an example of functional staff authority.

PERSONNEL DEPARTMENT FUNCTIONS

As a specialized staff unit, the primary task of the personnel department is to ensure that the organization's human resource group is utilized and managed as effectively as possible. Personnel administrators help design and implement policies and programs that strengthen human skills and abilities and thus improve the organization's overall effectiveness. No longer are personnel officials second class citizens as they were once perceived to be. Top managers and executives have learned—sometimes the hard way—that inattention to personnel relations and the neglect of sound personnel programs are often direct causes of poor labor-management relations, excessive absenteeism and turnover, law suits charging discrimination, and substandard productivity. More and more today, leaders of public and private organizations recognize that people are the organization's key resource and acknowledge the personnel department's role in developing human resources.

Personnel Roles

To acquire, strengthen, and retain an organization's human resource group, personnel administrators must perform all of the personnel department's contemporary roles: to create and implement policy, to offer advice, to provide services, and to exert control. In performing their jobs, personnel administrators apply specialized, expert knowledge in a variety of ways and use different kinds of authority in doing so. Let us more fully examine the multiple roles of the personnel staff.

POLICIES

Policies are guides to management thinking and help management achieve the organization's personnel objectives. Policies help define what is acceptable and unacceptable behavior and state the organization's position on an issue. Top personnel officials—the vice-president of personnel or personnel department heads—are generally responsible for policymaking. In regard to major or critical personnel matters—such as equal employment or management development—the policies may be drafted by a personnel committee for approval by the chief executive officer. Personnel committees generally include members from both line and staff departments. Line managers not only bring knowledge and experience to the personnel committee, but are more likely to support the policies they help create.

POLICIES SHOULD BE IN WRITING AND COMMUNICATED To be maximally effective, personnel policies should be in writing and communicated to all employees. To ensure employees are familiar with personnel policies, many companies—particularly large firms and government organizations—publish a personnel policy manual. Each manager receives a copy of the manual with instructions to review it in detail with all new employees. Manual updates may be posted on bulletin boards and supervisors may be required to discuss policy revisions with their employees. A well written and communicated policy manual can be a valuable aid not only in orienting new employees, but also in settling differences of opinion between supervisors and subordinates.

Another document often used to communicate personnel policies is the employee handbook. The handbook normally outlines all of the conditions of employment and typically is given to new employees. As an example, the employee handbook of a large southeastern hospital includes policies regarding equal employment opportunity, probation periods for new employees, work scheduling, attendance, personal conduct, safety, wage and salary administration, merit reviews, discipline, promotion and transfer, and termination.

POLICIES ARE IMPLEMENTED THROUGH PERSONNEL PROCEDURES In general, policies are broad statements which express the organization's principles and philosophy toward its human resource group. Intentionally broad so that they may be applied to various situations, policies do not include detailed statements describing specifically how the policy is to be implemented. Policies are implemented by procedures, or the chronological steps for carrying out a policy. Generally, procedures are written to implement policies in most personnel activities. For example, an organization's policy on management and staff level promotions may state that "the company upholds a strong policy of promotion from within and promotions are made solely on the basis of performance and promotability." Procedures that may be used to implement this policy include:

Job vacancies will be posted so that all interested personnel may apply.

The supervisor of the vacant job, and the immediate section superior, will review the personnel records of all applicants.

All employees qualified for the promotion will be interviewed by both supervisors and will undergo a series of tests designed to predict performance in the new job.

The supervisors will make the promotion decision based upon past performance, the interview, and predicted performance.

Generally, personnel administrators formulate and implement personnel policies and procedures through the use of functional staff authority. Therefore, managers and administrators must abide by the policies and procedures approved by top management. Of course, policies and procedures must be flexible, and there may be a valid reason for not following a particular policy. Referring to our previous example concerning promotion from within, management may find that no employees are qualified for a vacant job. In this case, management is forced to depart from the written policy and go outside for a qualified individual.

ADVICE

Over the past several decades, management has become increasingly complex. A restrictive legal environment, sophisticated technologies, a restive labor force, and demands by various societal groups for more "socially responsible activities" are a few of the pressures felt by modern managers. While coping with complex issues and problems, managers often turn to staff experts for advice and counsel. Some questions which personnel staff members may answer include:

- How do I deal with an employee who I suspect is on drugs?
- How do I meet my equal employment goals without raising cries of "reverse discrimination?"

- How do I tell a high-achieving employee that the budget won't allow a merit increase this year?
- How do I counsel a manager who is suffering a mid-career crisis?
- How do I fire an employee who has been with the company for twenty five years but can no longer perform?
- How can I increase employees' morale?

As mentioned earlier, personnel staff advice may be accepted or rejected. This is generally an unwritten condition that underlies the giving of advice and the use of staff authority. Line managers who feel advice is not sound have the prerogative to disregard it. Of course, the rejection of staff advice will be inversely proportional to the quality of advice and confidence in staff experts. Thus, all staff members have an obligation to ensure their advice is sound, objective, fair, and will contribute to both organizational and personal goals.

SERVICE

The service activities of the personnel department generally refer to the permanent human resource programs and activities that aid line managers and administrators in performing their jobs. Separating service activities from other personnel responsibilities such as policymaking, advice, and control is difficult. The personnel department—like each staff unit—exists to serve other organizational units, and practically all personnel activities may be broadly labeled as some form of service. On the other hand, certain personnel functions clearly conform to the term *service:*

- recruiting, selection, and placement programs
- equal employment opportunity activities
- administering employee benefits programs
- employee training and development programs
- personnel research
- company recreation programs
- labor relations activities
- counseling programs
- employee suggestion programs

An important part of the personnel department's service role is to provide decision makers with innovative tools and techniques that help solve human resource problems and result in a greater utilization of human resource skills and abilities.[7] In recent years, studies in organizational behavior and industrial psychology have led to programs that have successfully enhanced employee productivity, reduced absenteeism and turnover, and eliminated blue-collar and white-collar boredom. Research shows that many innovative human resource programs have led to a significant improvement in the quality of working life and enhancement of organizational profits. Most of these programs, such as job enrichment, flexible working hours, compressed workweek, and organizational development, are fully discussed in this text.

CONTROL
Like the quality control department that

exists in every manufacturing concern, the personnel department performs important control and audit functions. For example, a written policy on affirmative action is ineffectual unless decision makers are aware of the policy and adhere to it. Personnel administrators are responsible for monitoring personnel goals and guidelines to ensure they are being achieved. Common control and audit activities include:

- Collection and analysis of hiring, selection, placement, and promotion data to ensure that equal employment opportunity laws and policies are being observed.
- Analysis of performance appraisal records to determine if required appraisals are being conducted in an objective, unbiased manner.
- Implementation of an exit interview program to determine and control the causes of employee turnover.
- Analysis of statistics concerning absenteeism, grievances, and accidents to determine where these problems are most critical and what may be done to reduce them.

Because of the nature of these activities, personnel staff members generally possess functional authority to carry out control and audit functions. Line managers and other staff units must cooperate with personnel officials in carrying out these activities. Personnel staff members must ensure that decision makers fully understand all personnel policies, procedures, and standards so that resentment and conflict are not created when control activities are performed. Further, personnel administrators must use diplomacy

---

7. See Fred K. Foulkes and Henry M. Morgan, ''Organizing and Staffing the Personnel Function,'' *Harvard Business Review* (May–June 1977): 142–54.

and tact when bringing pressure on managers to conform with personnel guidelines. Harmonious relationships between the personnel department staff and other organizational units will ensure compliance with guidelines with a minimum of stress and disruption to the organization.

MANAGEMENT/ PERSONNEL INTERACTION

What makes a personnel department truly effective? Why are some personnel staffs highly influential in bringing about greater organizational effectiveness while others seem to flounder and cause more problems than they solve?

Technical skills and abilities, education, experience, and an appropriate philosophy about people and work are all important factors in creating an effective personnel staff. However, the influence of personnel administrators is significantly diminished unless the personnel staff has the ability to create and maintain close, cooperative working relationships with other line and staff units. Regardless of the technical expertise of the personnel staff, the absence of cooperation and coordination between personnel officials and line managers will result in a powerless, largely ineffective human resource function.

Sources of Conflict

Many personnel managers attest that poor interdepartmental relationships are sources of dissatisfaction in their jobs. While the personnel executive's status, power, and influence have increased sig-

nificantly in recent years, so have the unwelcome aspects like conflict, stress, and antagonism. Primary sources of interdepartmental hostility are described below.

TERRITORIAL ENCROACHMENT

In carrying out their jobs, personnel administrators sometimes appear to be invading or *encroaching on the territory* of other organizational decision makers. Line and staff administrators must conform to personnel policies, procedures, rules, and regulations; often they perceive this as erosions of their authority. Because each manager is ultimately responsible for achieving specific goals, undesired or poor policy advice or service from a staff unit cannot be used as an excuse for unsatisfactory performance. For example, a manufacturing manager may feel strongly that the conservative wage and salary administration program developed by the personnel staff is hindering recruitment and retention of qualified employees. Attempting to blame productivity and turnover problems on personnel would be unwise for the line manager who must assume responsibility for labor problems in manufacturing.

PERCEPTIONS OF AUTHORITY

In theory, distinguishing between staff or advisory authority and functional staff authority and giving examples of each is not difficult. In practice, however, there is often widespread confusion over the type of authority a staff member has in carrying out a particular function. What a personnel administrator views as functional staff authority, a line manager may perceive as purely advisory authority. This confusion is particularly common in the training and development of employees. For example, a personnel director may see the need for a training program to improve the counseling skills of first-line supervisors and arrange to develop and schedule such a course. The training administrator may then try to sign people up using functional staff authority. The supervisor's bosses, however, may view the program as a service activity which can be accepted or rejected.

SOLUTIONS TO PROBLEMS

Personnel administrators are often called upon to assist in reducing a variety of human resource problems. Generally, these people problems can be approached from several different perspectives, which—unfortunately—do not lend themselves to an objective, straightforward analysis. Consequently, comparison of different approaches to problem solving is difficult; a decision maker's approach to a particular problem is often formed by past experiences, attitudes, values, and beliefs. The greater the differences in attitudes and values of line and staff personnel, the greater the potential for conflict over how organizational problems may be most effectively solved.

A common organizational problem may illustrate this dilemma: Assume a keypunch supervisor has high absenteeism among his keypunch operators and requests assistance from a personnel administrator. Feeling the negligent employees are shiftless, the supervisor may suggest that the best way to eliminate the problem is to crack down on a few serious offenders. On the other hand, believing keypunch work is boring and routine, the personnel specialist may decide employees stay away from work because keypunching holds no challenge or responsibility. Thus, the personnel administrator may want to solve the problem by enriching the job and giving employees more decision-making responsibility; by making it more rewarding for employees to come to work rather than stay away. But if neither the supervisor nor personnel member places much value in the other's proposal, conflict will result. Or, one party may begrudgingly give in and agree to the other's plan; ill feelings result from this sort of win or lose situation.

PERSONAL CONFLICTS

Often differences in the sex, age, experience, and education of line and staff members result in personality conflicts. Also, resentment and conflict may result from age and educational differences that sometimes set the line and staff employee apart. As one management author stated,

> . . . it is common to find that the line executive is the older person who came up the hard way. If he or she has a college degree, many of the hours may have been earned through correspondence study or night classes. Conversely, the staff counterpart is often a younger executive, perhaps with a master's degree in market research, who has many "bright ideas" about how to improve sales. The line executive sees the young person as lacking in practical experience. The staff executive sees the older person as unwilling to try new ideas.[8]

Although somewhat dated, Melville Dalton's classic research in three industrial plants reflects the antagonism that still exists between line and staff units today:

> Explaining the relatively few cases in which his staff had succeeded in "selling ideas" to the line, an assistant staff head remarked, "We're always in hot water with these old

---

8. Richard M. Hodgetts, *Management: Theory, Process, and Practice* (Philadelphia: W. B. Saunders Co., 1979), p. 121.

guys on the line. You can't tell them a damned thing. They're bull-headed as hell! Most of the time [when] we offer a suggestion it's either laughed at or not considered at all. The same idea in the mouth of some old codger on the line'd get a round of applause. They treat us like kids."

Line officers in these plants often referred to staff personnel (especially members of the auditing, production planning, industrial engineering, and industrial relations staffs) as "college punks," "slide rules," "crackpots," "pretty boys," and "chair-warmers."[9]

Reducing Conflict

Interdepartmental strife should not be accepted as a natural part of organizational life. Many organizations make deliberate efforts to maintain close, harmonious relationships among their departments and work units. Recognizing that some interdepartmental conflict is an inevitable by-product of organizational life, such organizations take definite steps to keep conflict at manageable levels. On the other hand, many social scientists agree that *some* conflict is healthy as it results in innovation and creativity. Ways to keep line/staff conflict at a minimum are described below.

SPHERES OF RESPONSIBILITY

When embarking on any type of line/staff relationship, questions concerning authority and responsibility will inevitably be raised. Working jointly, line and staff personnel must agree on whether a staff member's role carries advisory or functional staff authority. A staff member acting purely in an advisory capacity cannot order implementation of recommenda-

tions. On the other hand, decision makers must recognize that personnel policies and procedures and audit and control activities normally carry functional staff authority and that all managers and administrators are obliged to carry them out.

Line and staff personnel must agree on the division of responsibilities for implementing human resource programs because most, if not all, human resource activities involve a partnership between the personnel staff and other line and staff units. As an example, the implementation of programs to rehabilitate troubled employees addicted to drugs or alcohol may involve the following steps:

1. Creating personnel policies concerning troubled employees.

2. Creating procedures for implementing rehabilitation programs.

3. Pinpointing troubled employees at work.

4. Persuading troubled employees to seek assistance.

5. Channeling troubled employees to the proper rehabilitation specialists, and

6. Monitoring postrehabilitation activities to ensure employees' performance is satisfactory.

Usually, the personnel staff is responsible for steps 1, 2, 5, and 6 while supervisors are responsible for performing steps 3 and 4. Personnel also trains line supervisors to understand and use the program. Regardless of the nature of the human resource activity, the division of responsibilities between the personnel staff and other units must be made clear.

---

9. Melville Dalton, "Conflicts Between Line and Staff Managerial Officers," *American Sociological Review* 15 (1950): 342–51.

OPEN COMMUNICATION

Personnel administrators must maintain open lines of communication. One way is through regular meetings with other departments to discuss human resource problems and consider ways in which the personnel staff may help reduce these problems. These meetings may also serve as sounding boards to discuss interdepartmental conflicts and problems between the personnel staff and other units.

Another mechanism that may facilitate communication is mixed membership on committees and task forces. Personnel officials should invite line and staff departments to participate on committees which affect the entire organization, like the grievance committee, wage and salary review committee, management development committee, employee suggestion program committee, and employee disciplinary committee. Personnel staff members should seek membership on the committees and task forces of other departments that focus on human resource issues. A manufacturing plant manager, for example, may create a task force to study turnover and absenteeism and recommend solutions to these problems. In this case, inputs from a personnel staff member should prove valuable. By joining committees and task forces, personnel staff members build stronger ties with other departments and become more familiar with their problems and working cultures. Further, other line and staff units gain a greater appreciation for the problems of the personnel staff and learn how personnel activities may enhance organizational effectiveness.

TEMPORARY PERSONNEL ASSIGNMENTS

Years ago, a transfer to personnel was a "one-way ticket to oblivion."[10] The personnel department was viewed as a collection of burned-out administrators who spent their days straightening the files and arranging company picnics. This archaic view of the personnel function has largely disappeared today. Many companies are finding that a temporary assignment in personnel not only broadens the human resource skills and abilities of line managers, but also gives personnel specialists a better perspective on the problems the organization faces:

> In many companies the personnel director's responsibilities have become so complex that they can only be shouldered by topflight business managers who have the backing of the chief executive. The people who do the job like to say that in the years to come, a tour of duty in the personnel department (more likely the division of human resources) will be mandatory for any executive who aims to be chairman. Though that may prove to be an exaggeration, it is true that more companies are transferring up-and-coming executives into personnel for a while, en route to greater things. Dow Chemical's Herbert Lyon says it's a good thing for personnel departments to have a mix of professional experts, who have worked exclusively in personnel, and generalists who are brought in for a tour of duty from other parts of the company. IBM's Walton Burdick agrees and adds that in his view the professional personnel types—of whom he is one—benefit even more than the generalists from having a mix. "It gives the specialists a better sense of what's really going on out there," he explains.[11]

AGENTS OF CHANGE

Personnel administrators' activities often impact on the way other people perform their jobs. Frequently, new personnel pol-

---

10. Meyer, "Personnel Directors," p. 84.
11. Ibid., p. 140.

icies, procedures, and programs add to or alter the duties and responsibilities of decision makers throughout the organization. New grievance procedures, equal employment opportunity programs, or performance appraisal procedures are examples of the changes the personnel staff may bring to an organization. Because the personnel staff is often involved in changing the way the organization functions, personnel administrators also take on an important role: *agents of change.* This role demands that personnel administrators understand how to introduce change successfully and how to keep employee resistance to change at a minimum. Many practicing managers will testify that the implementation of a change program is as important as the program itself, and that many new programs and policies have failed because the change was brought about in an unplanned, haphazard manner.

One popular model for managing the organizational change process is Kurt Lewin's *"unfreezing-changing–refreezing"* model.[12] Lewin suggested that change will be resisted unless employees are ready and motivated to change. This unfreezing process underscores the importance of ensuring that employees see a need for change. The changing process involves the actual implementation of a new program, policy, or technique. Employees may be given authority and responsibility for a new duty and receive training to perform the new part of their jobs effectively. The final stage—*refreezing*—provides reinforcement to ensure new attitudes and behaviors become a permanent part of employees' behavior.

---

12. Kurt Lewin, "Frontiers in Group Dynamics: Concept, Method, and Reality in Social Science," *Human Relations,* Vol. 1, No. 1 (1947): 5–41.

To illustrate, assume that an organization wants to increase employee output and decides to switch from a fixed daily wage system to a piecework incentive system. The change process may be conducted as follows:

Unfreezing: In labor-management meetings, employees receive complete details of the program before it is implemented. All questions are answered and fears are put to rest. Employees are shown, in detail, that they will make just as much—and possibly more—money with the new system. Management states that the goal is to increase productivity and reward employees who achieve this goal.

Changing: New procedures are implemented and employees are informed of the effective date of the new pay system.

Refreezing: After implementation of the new system, management communicates with employees to ensure all problems are resolved and questions are answered. Employee support of the new system is appreciated and encouraged. Productivity records are closely analyzed to ensure the new system is achieving expected results.

SELLING PERSONNEL PROGRAMS

In working with other organizational units, personnel administrators must often sell their ideas and programs to decision makers, particularly when they are giving advice which does not carry functional staff authority. Successful personnel staff members are persuasive and effectively communicate the value of their ideas and suggestions. While the importance of technical skills cannot be overstated, an idea, suggestion, or program must be sold and working before it has any true value. Some factors that help personnel administrators be more effective salespeople:

- Appreciating the real-life problems of other managers and administrators and recognizing that many obstacles must often be overcome before a personnel program is successful.

- Learning and speaking the jargon that characterizes various functional specialties. For example, when discussing a new training program for manufacturing supervisors with the plant manager, important terms may be: economic order quantity, Gantt chart, flow process chart, resource allocation, inventory control, and quality control limits.

- Showing how personnel activities affect the bottom line. Decision makers are more likely to heed the advice of a staff specialist if it can be clearly shown how organizational change will result in greater profits through an increase in revenues or decrease in operating costs. Personnel administrators should prepare a *cost-benefit analysis* when proposing a new human resource program or changing an existing one. Admittedly, this is often difficult to do, as many personnel activities are very difficult to quantify in terms of dollars and cents. For example, placing an economic value on a new employee orientation program or employee counseling project would involve subjective and highly debatable estimates. Other personnel activities, however, lend themselves to quantification and the impact on the bottom line may be estimated with a fair degree of accuracy. Whenever

possible, costs and benefits for personnel activities and programs should be developed, analyzed, and discussed with decision makers who will be affected by the impending changes.

- Employing the *completed staff work* concept when making recommendations to decision makers. Completed staff work involves presenting a recommendation for a new policy, program or procedure to decision makers in such a way that it may be approved or disapproved. By working out all details prior to the presentation the staff members save the decision-making sector from spending an inordinate amount of time in meetings and conferences. Of course, good oral communication skills are particularly valuable in presenting completed staff work, and many personnel administrators make effective use of flip charts, overhead transparencies, and slides when making presentations and selling their ideas to middle and top management.

PERSONNEL DEPARTMENT ORGANIZATION

Typically, the personnel staff is organizationally located in the personnel, industrial relations, or employee relations departments. We shall use the common term *personnel department* throughout this book to refer to the organizational unit that assumes responsibility for human resource programs and activities.

Jobs

The personnel department normally contains clerical/support, professional, and managerial jobs. Clerical/support employees include clerks, typists, receptionists, and lower level administrative assistants. Professional employees are specialists in a narrow field such as counseling, employee development, testing, or labor relations. These individuals often possess college degrees in business administration and may have concentrated their studies in personnel or human resources. Lower level employees are occasionally promoted to professional positions and are given both on- and off-the-job training to help them perform successfully in their new roles. The managerial staff leads and motivates the clerical/support and professional employees and coordinates the organization's personnel programs and activities. Top level personnel managers formulate personnel policies and create major personnel programs.

STRUCTURE

Almost without exception, the personnel department is organized by function. We will briefly examine the personnel depart-ment structure in three different kinds of organizations:

THE COMPANY WITH 2,000 EMPLOYEES OR LESS In the small plant or office, the personnel manager performs the full range of personnel activities with the assistance of a small clerical/support staff. Normally the personnel manager reports directly to the president. The structure of a small company is illustrated in Figure 2–3.

THE MEDIUM-SIZED COMPANY WITH 2,000 TO 4,000 EMPLOYEES The personnel structure of the medium-sized company will contain individual work groups organized around separate personnel functions. A personnel manager will head each group and provide leadership to the professional and clerical/support employees. The personnel department may be headed by a vice-president of personnel who reports to the president. The personnel structure for a medium-sized organization is shown in Figure 2–4.

THE LARGE MULTIDIVISIONAL COMPANY WITH OVER 4,000 EMPLOYEES Large corporations have divisions in many states and foreign countries. Each division is usually run independently as a decentralized profit center. Division managers have their own

FIGURE 2–3: *The Personnel Department Structure in a Small Company*

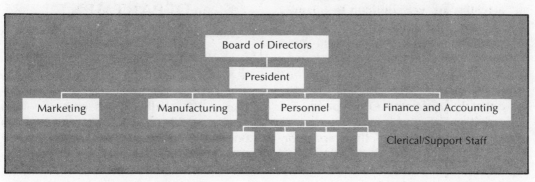

FIGURE 2–4: *Personnel Department Structure in a Medium-sized Company*

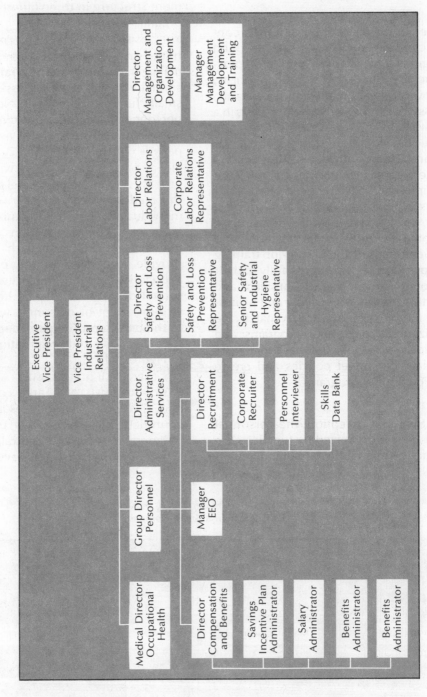

SOURCE: Allen R. Janger, *The Personnel Function: Changing Objectives and Organization, Report 712* (New York: The Conference Board, 1977), p. 71. Used with permission.

staff services—for example, engineering, accounting, finance, legal, and personnel—under their control. The corporate personnel staff, however, generally creates major personnel policies and programs for recruiting, management development, equal employment, and wage and salary policies that are put in operation by the divisional personnel managers. In this way, consistency in personnel activities across all divisions is achieved while allowing each division's personnel manager enough flexibility to manage the division's personnel program. The relationship between the corporate personnel staff and each division personnel manager is illustrated in Figure 2–5.

In summary, the personnel department's overall effectiveness depends on its ability to create successful human resource programs and maintain cooperative working relationships with other departments. Personnel staff members who work closely each day with managers must possess a thorough knowledge of management responsibilities and functions (planning, organizing, staffing, motivating, and controlling). Potential conflict between the personnel staff and other units may be caused by territorial encroachment, misunderstanding the nature of the personnel staff's authority, different viewpoints over how to solve problems, and personal characteristics of line and staff members. Personnel staff members should take positive steps to minimize the likelihood of serious conflicts with other departments. Both line and staff members must agree on the nature of the staff authority and how responsibil-

FIGURE 2–5: *Corporate Personnel Staff and Division Personnel Managers*

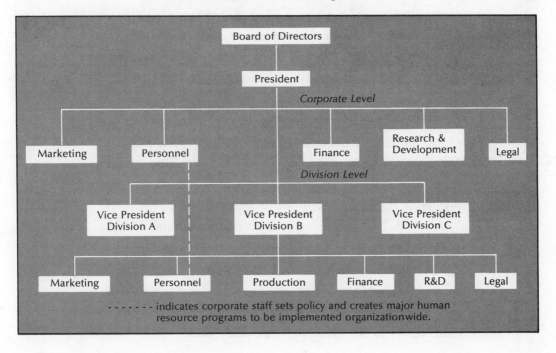

ities will be divided. Because one of their tasks is to implement new policies, programs, and procedures, personnel administrators must know how to introduce change successfully and minimize employee resistance to change. One popular change model is the unfreezing–changing–refreezing model which involves unfreezing old attitudes and habits, implementing the change, and providing reinforcement to freeze new attitudes and behaviors.

The Solution

Mary Brice has some real problems with irate Production Manager Carl Mead. In order for the company's affirmative action program to operate successfully, the entire management team—particularly the top management structure—must support the endeavor. Mead's backing is critical as he commands the largest department.

While Brice has functional authority to create and implement the affirmative action program, this does not mean that resistance will not be felt. Perhaps resistance could have been minimized if Brice had invited the participation of line managers during the creation of the program. She could have formed a task force to develop the program and invited the participation of top managers from all line and staff units.

Brice could also estimate the impact of the program on the bottom line to illustrate the program's effect on profits. She could show how much discrimination has cost the company thus far in legal settlements and estimate how much continued discrimination might cost in future legal action.

In the end, all managers must be held accountable for implementation of the program. Each manager should have affirmative action goals to reach and failure to reach these goals should result in a close examination of the reasons why they were not met. If Mead continually resists the program, he must answer to the president—not Mary Brice.

═══ KEY TERMS AND CONCEPTS ═══

Planning	Staff Authority
Control Mechanism	Functional Staff Authority
Departmentalization	Personal Staff
Span of Control	Specialized Staff
Chain of Command	Profit Center
Centralization	Territorial Encroachment
Decentralization	Agents of Change
Line Authority	Unfreezing—Changing—Refreezing Model
Line Function	Completed Staff Work

═══ FOR REVIEW ═══

1. What are the functions of management?

2. What elements are common to all organizational forms?

3. What different kinds of authority exist?

4. What are the major roles performed by personnel administrators and managers?

5. What factors lead to conflict between the personnel staff and other organizational units?

6. What strategies may be employed to reduce conflict between the personnel staff and other organizational units?

7. How do personnel department structures vary for small, medium, and large organizations?

═══ FOR DISCUSSION ═══

1. The personnel manager of a small metals manufacturer has noticed that one production supervisor has frequently violated safety rules and looks the other way when his employees do the same. The personnel department monitors the plant's safety program. Does the personnel manager have the authority to discipline the supervisor? What should the personnel manager do?

2. According to theory, managers plan, organize, staff, influence, and control. How relevant are these functions for personnel managers? Personnel specialists?

3. Do you agree with the notion that line managers should have experience in personnel? Should personnel administrators have experience in line functions? What problems would this line/staff training arrangement create?

4. Your organization has decided to hire and train more minorities into staff and management positions. As the personnel manager, how would you sell the notion of equal employment opportunity to managers throughout the organization? Would you expect to find resistance?

5. What skills and abilities are needed for success as a personnel manager of an organization of 150 employees? A personnel vice-president for a multidivisional corporation employing 20,000 employees? How do the requirements differ?

6. As a recent college graduate with a degree in management, you have been offered two jobs: a first-line manufacturing supervisor in a large automobile manufacturer and a personnel training specialist with a medium-sized grocery chain. Aside from the obvious need to develop different technical skills and abilities, what other kinds of differences would these jobs involve? Which job do you feel you would prefer? Why?

SUPPLEMENTARY READING

Burack, Elmer H., and Miller, E. L. "A Model for Personnel Practices and People." *The Personnel Administrator* 24 (1979): 50–56.

Famularo, Joseph J. *Handbook of Modern Personnel Administration.* New York: McGraw-Hill, Inc., 1972.

Foulkes, Fred J., and Morgan, Henry M. "Organizing and Staffing the Personnel Function." *Harvard Business Review* 55 (1977): 152.

Hollingsworth, Thomas A., and Preston, Paul. "Corporate Planning: A Challenge for Personnel Executives." *Personnel Journal*, August 1976, pp. 386–89.

How to Develop A Company Personnel Policy Manual. Chicago: The Dartnell Company (no date).

Meyer, Herbert E. "Personnel Directors Are the New Corporate Heroes." *Fortune,* February 1976, p. 88.

Myers, Charles, and Turnbull, John. "Line and Staff in Industrial Relations." *Harvard Business Review,* October-November 1969, pp. 1–12.

Staats, Elmer B. "Personnel Management: The Starting Place." *Public Personnel Management* 5 (November-December 1976): 434–41.

For Analysis: Armadillo Auto Parts Company

The Armadillo Auto Parts Company in Dallas, Texas, is an auto parts remanufacturer—a firm which rebuilds worn-out auto parts for resale. Starters, generators, and carburetors are the principal accessories in the Armadillo line. The rebuilt auto parts are marketed to auto supply wholesalers and retailers across the country and Canada. Armadillo has a reputation for quality products and has built a favorable reputation in the rebuilt auto parts industry.

Armadillo enjoyed booming sales during the latter part of the 1970s as inflation and the skyrocketing cost of new automobiles forced drivers to keep and fix up their cars rather than trade them in. As a result, Armadillo increased its work force from 122 employees in 1973 to 270 in 1981. During that period, however, the personnel department increased its staff only by two clerks; the total personnel staff numbers seven. As the personnel manager, Mary Reston was primarily responsible for recruiting, hiring, orientation, wage and salary administration, safety, and labor relations. She delegated as much work as she could, but hesitated delegating too much because her staff was largely untrained in personnel decision making. Her staff performed primarily support services such as typing, filing, correspondence, and so on. Mary felt severely overworked and on several occasions requested the addition of a professional staff member to assist her in her duties. Her requests were repeatedly turned down for budgetary reasons.

Reston took a seat in the conference room that adjoined the president's office. A few minutes after her arrival, Jake Armstrong, president of the auto parts company, sat down next to Reston with a folder full of papers.

"Mary, I made a big decision a few days ago. I finally decided to buy Acme Transmission Rebuilders, an auto parts

remanufacturer like us. I clinched the deal yesterday. Of course, I think everyone around here knew I wanted to buy Acme for a long time; I'm making the formal announcement of the purchase this afternoon. I've also decided to expand our facilities here and move Acme's equipment and personnel from Fort Worth to our location. I think the economies of scale from locating under one roof will bear out over the long run. Of course, a lot of organizational changes will have to be made, but we've really got to look closely at how we restructure the personnel function. I have a copy of Acme's organization chart for personnel. Study it closely and let me know your ideas for combining your staff with their existing personnel staff.

Reston asked, "What about the personnel budget? Are we going to be able to hire more professional personnel? With the size of our work force doubling overnight, there's no doubt we'll need more help from experienced personnel people."

Armstrong responded, "Yes, I've thought of that. Of course, the personnel staff and budget will be increased. But our accounting people tell me we're going to have to play it pretty close to the belt for a while. Acme was in a weak financial position, and we've got to tighten up wherever we can."

Based on the following exhibits,

1. *Draw an organization chart for the Armadillo personnel department based on the proposed merger with Acme Transmission. What factors will determine the specific form the new personnel department will take?*
2. *How may the personnel manager determine when additional staff—particularly professional staff—are necessary?*

EXHIBIT I: *Armadillo Auto Parts Company*

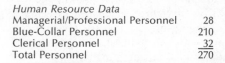

Human Resource Data

Managerial/Professional Personnel	28
Blue-Collar Personnel	210
Clerical Personnel	32
Total Personnel	270

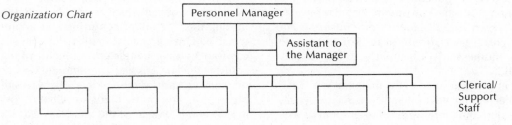

Organization Chart

EXHIBIT 2: *Acme Transmission Rebuilders, Inc.*

Human Resource Data

Managerial/Professional Personnel	34
Blue-Collar Personnel	227
Clerical Personnel	44
Total Personnel	305

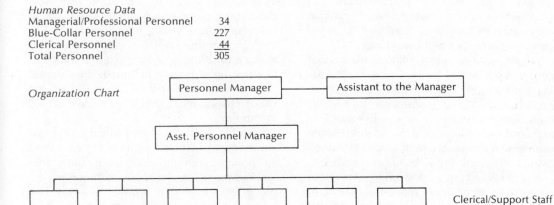

Organization Chart

════ **SELECTED PROFESSIONAL READING** ════

What the Chief Executive Expects of the Personnel Function

J. A. HENDERSON

I have been on both sides of the question: "What does the chief executive officer expect from the personnel function?" My views on the subject have not changed since I moved from personnel into general management, but my sense of urgency has. I think the future

Reprinted from the May 1977 issue of *Personnel Administrator*, 30 Park Drive, Berea, Ohio 44017, $26 per year.

poses some new and more difficult challenges that relate directly to those expectations. But perhaps some history is necessary to put the future into proper perspective.

After four or five years of adjustment and changeover from the wartime production of World War II, our country entered a prolonged period of business prosperity that may one day be known as the Golden Age of Business. For roughly 20 years, from 1950 to 1970, the climate for business in this country was unusually good.

Let's look at some of the major factors. First, the economic environment was relatively stable although there were some ups and downs in the '50s. The economy was characterized by a generally high rate of real economic growth and, of particular importance, virtually no inflation. This, in turn, led to nearly full employment, uninterrupted annual gains in disposable income and, therefore, a rising consumer affluence and confidence.

Second, this economic climate meant that corporations looked forward to generally rising demand and growth. International growth opportunities added to domestic prosperity. Profit margins and cash flow were relatively high and expansion could be financed while maintaining reasonable debt levels. The stock market reflected these business conditions and generally was in a rising mode. Many people were beneficiaries of this trend, which, in turn, led to even more consumer affluence.

The political and social environment was also favorable. Businessmen were generally accepted as leaders, the best problem solvers of our society and as people to be trusted.

Finally, the people in our businesses and in the society by and large believed in hard work and security. The older people of the working group had experienced the Great Depression of the '30s first-hand. That depression left its mark in terms of an overriding concern for savings, for security and a good job.

The younger working generation in the '50s and '60s had experienced World War II and, as a result, were part of the greatest effort of all time—to defeat the Axis. Out of that effort came a faith and pride in our country. Since most had firsthand experience with the military establishment, they were conditioned to accept a big organization geared to achieve national objectives. So the society and the workforce were, in general, ready to accept the leadership of business management.

Near the end of this 20-year period, however, trends began which have culminated in making the '70s rather confusing and unpredictable. One of the most dramatic changes came about in the people environment. Young adults in the late '60s had a far different view of our society than did their elders. The waves of protest touched off by the Watts Ghetto riots in 1965 and later against the Viet Nam War set the tone of confrontation and open revolt against many of our institutions.

These youngsters were a product of the best educational system in the world. Although there were certainly a handful of radicals, in retrospect these young people were impressive. Their education had taught them to question the institutions of our society and the values that older people accepted. They placed human values above material ones and felt that major change must be made in most of our institutions.

Business leadership, in particular, did not come off well in their eyes. They saw rivers and air polluted, an industrial community that ignored the black, the Mexican-American, the Indian and even the female. Business had become complacent about the way it served the customer—unreasonably high prices and, in some cases, inferior or even dangerous products.

Unfortunately, business leadership did not respond well, perhaps because the young people often used confrontation as a tactic. Real communication never took place. These young people soon convinced enough of their elders that the credibility of business leadership declined rapidly and the role of the businessman as a leader and respected citizen diminished. The consumer revolt was on.

Although there were attempts, business as a whole did not police itself and it was inevitable that the government would be drawn into the picture in response to voter pressure. More regulatory agencies and congressional committees were formed. The social/political environment changed greatly in just a few years.

Simultaneously, we experienced major changes in our economy. In 1969 and 1970, the economy experienced its first recession in nine years, rebounded to very strong growth in 1972 and 1973 and then spiraled into recession. Basic inflationary trends were set off which have not yet been arrested.

These wide swings in the economy in the face of inflationary pressures were very difficult for business to handle. Planning was particularly perplexing. I think most of us believed that this uncertain period was temporary, that long term and favorable business conditions would resume and, therefore, planning for expansion continued, despite the lower profit margins from inflation. Since this investment in fixed assets and working capital could not be financed out of cash flow from operations, funds were borrowed.

The result has been that the nation's industry has undergone a major and significant change in its capital structure. The efforts of the Federal Reserve System to combat inflation and offset larger and larger federal budget deficits resulted in restricted credit availability and a dramatic increase in interest rates. In 1965, the prime interest rate was four-and-a-half percent while in 1973 it reached 12 percent.

After several years of this instability, I think we can piece together a clearer picture of what we face in the future. We can expect periodic recessions along with periods of moderate growth. The upward and onward growth rates of the '60s are a thing of the past. Unfortunately, we also appear to have institutionalized inflation and unemployment in our economy. Higher unemployment will slow the rate of economic growth in time of prosperity and inflation will continue to keep corporate profit margins under severe pressure. The energy crisis will continue to keep the inflationary pressure with us.

Therefore, the corporation, already at a very high debt level, will have difficulty in affording capital investment to modernize plants and equipment and invest in new technology.

Over capacity which has resulted from the heavy investment of the '60s and early '70s will be with us for some time, making it difficult to raise prices to preserve margins. The profit squeeze will continue.

We can expect little relief from government in the form of reduced regulation or reduced taxes. In fact, governmental pressures are likely to go in the other direction. The regulatory commissions are still at work but under increasing attack from all sides. There is a trend toward ever-increasing use of the judicial branch as a final arbitrator of all complaints and this slows the process of government. The outlook is likely for increasing government involvement in business rather than less, at least until business succeeds in establishing some credibility in the eyes of society.

If this is the environment of the future, it means a whole new orientation for business.

For many companies, the focus must shift from growth to survival. Business leadership, in general, faces a major task of getting its financial structure in shape. This can only happen if we make major gains in internal efficiency and productivity and this is largely a job of cost cutting. We can expect no outside help. If we cannot do it ourselves, then our country may face a combination of decline in our standard of living and fundamental changes in our economic and social system.

I feel it is imperative that we make those changes ourselves. Where business has turned to government or government has intervened, the results are not impressive. Unfortunately, the period of the '50s and '60s have made the task of cutting costs more difficult. Those of us who managed in this period have not been trained in such an effort nor are we experienced. Growth has helped us hide inefficiency and tolerate high overhead.

I think it is very important that we understand how we got to this point in order to comprehend the changed emphasis of both top management and the personnel department. I have always viewed top management and the personnel function as a partnership. Management is, after all, people. At Cummins the personnel head has always reported to the senior operating officer and has been a part of all major decisions. He is one of our most important officers and is paid accordingly. I believe this will be the only way a company can operate effectively in the future. The personnel head must be one of the very best people in the company—confident, courageous, warm and perceptive.

The job ahead for both top management and the personnel department can be summed up very simply as: fewer people, better people and leadership. That is, fewer people to do a given amount of work, thereby increasing productivity and ultimately cash flow. Better people, in order to cope successfully with a less favorable environment and find new ways to do the job, and leadership, in order to make major change in the way we do business. Management can be static; leadership is making change.

I'd like to examine these points and the role personnel plays in each. First, fewer people. When you run a five year or longer projection of cash flows in an inflationary environment, you realize that each single person is a very costly asset. If manpower can be held or reduced, margins increase very sharply in such a projection.

I'm not referring only to direct labor. In staff groups, salary and wages account for a very high percentage of the total cost of that department. In an inflationary environment, that cost escalates rapidly. A young executive making $20,000 today, will be making $52,000 in 10 years if he or she receives a 10 percent increase per year. If inflation is five to eight percent, then two to five percent per year for merit or promotion would not be unrealistic *under past standards*.

We have built such expectations during the '60s. Our people say they expect to stay even with inflation *and* make gains. There seems to be a feeling that "we have a *right* to our compensation growth." The fact is, most likely we cannot sustain such a high level of individual compensation growth in future years. Certainly we will be unable to do so unless we can increase productivity. But I can conceive of a highly productive organization with a relatively

few (by past standards) well trained, highly flexible, and, therefore, well paid people.

There is not only the direct wage or salary increase; union pressures have brought a very high level of fringe benefits for both hourly and salaried people. I can remember in 1964 using a figure of 17 percent of direct labor for fringe benefits and in 1975 we used 33 percent. There is talk in some companies of 50 percent in the near future. The amount of worry and administrative and overhead costs concerned with fringe benefits are much higher than for direct labor, as we all know. Most of these benefit systems are patchwork which have grown from the process of collective bargaining over the golden years and need overall re–examination. Changes will be difficult in the bargaining process, of course.

I personally had a rude awakening when we were asked to project our pension costs in the future. In 1970 we paid approximately $2 million a year and in 1975, after negotiations, it was $10 million. We then projected pension costs for 20 years. We made a modest inflationary assumption of five percent and a benefit level which only stayed even with inflation. Most important, we held our growth and head count level at *no* additional people. In 1995, the pension cost of the corporation at these modest assumptions will be $42 million, 20 times as great as 1970 and virtually equal to our before tax profits of 1974.

When you look at this escalation in cost, you can't help but reach the conclusion that a commitment to hiring a single person is a commitment to greatly increased costs. Each opening must be critically examined with a return of investment justification. We can no longer regard people as a relatively inexpensive and therefore expendable asset as we have.

Second, we must take a fundamental look at organizational concepts that have long been accepted. American business was one of the first to break the job down into its simplest elements under the influence of Frederick Taylor. This happened at a time of rapid industrial growth and was particularly suited to the growth of our society at the time. Many of the people entering our workforce were immigrants who did not handle the language well. A very simplified job which they could understand and which they were grateful to have was an obvious solution. But, it has also built a massive overhead in the form of staff support and a military hierarchy-type structure. Setters, inspectors, engineers, salvage men, material expeditors, maintenance men and a seemingly endless group of other specialists have been built in as support—as well as several layers of management. This factory-type organization influences organization throughout industry—even in staff groups.

We are all familiar with the work of the behavioral scientists. Some very important concepts—that are really quite logical—have been agreed upon:

- Most people are able and willing to do more than they have been asked to do.

- Achievement, recognition for that achievement, the work itself and the responsibility and opportunity for personal growth that the work offers are most important.

- Identification with the goals and success of an organization is important.

Several experimental operations are underway—we have some in Cummins. They show promise of operating with far less supervision and overhead and at equal levels of quality and output. They also are looked upon with suspicion. In part, this is because some over-zealous behavioral scientists and their followers got caught up in the jargon, sold the concept as a way to increase employee happiness and turned busy managers off. Probably more important, they threaten, because the traditional role of the supervisor to the people is dramatically changed.

There is definitely promise in these organizational efforts of far more productivity and effectiveness than American business has achieved to date. The task of applying these to established plants and staff groups will be very difficult, but now also very vital, as business seeks higher productivity to do the same work with fewer people, or more work with the same people.

There is a third and important element to the future that appears a little farther over the horizon, but nevertheless is on its way. The manufacturers of computing and tele–communications equipment believe they have equipment which provides a dramatic increase in capacity at far lower costs. Digital storage devices and data transmission have been lessening in cost and very sophisticated programs are now taking shape to manage information. Though it takes a million bits to store in digital form what's on an $8\frac{1}{2} \times 11$ piece of paper, this may well not be a cost problem in the future, we are told. The enthusiasts see a logical extension of this technology as creating virtually a paperless system except for selected output people need on an exception basis. We already have typewriters tied to computers to improve typing efficiency and transmit the material to other typewriters and terminals. Information costs can be very high, but these changes give promise, at last, of a major reduction in clerical and staff costs and travel. If not a cost reduction, then far better management information on a real time basis which means a greatly altered way of operating. Anyone who has attempted to change the ways of an office in only a small way can appreciate what kinds of problems we will have in assimilating this change that is evidently not far in the future.

If we are to hold or reduce manpower, then what things must the personnel department do? First, it must perform a greatly expanded manpower planning and organization analysis function. It must thoroughly understand all aspects of the business and how it operates. It must be able to spot situations where there is excessive overhead, ill-designed job content, overlap of responsibility, lack of proper motivation, opportunity to combine functions and the like, and have the credibility to convince line managers to investigate these areas. This is an action concept rather than one of pure reaction.

Second, the personnel department must become expert in solving the problems of organization re-design that eliminate needless overhead and become the change agent or expert. Implied in this is the ability to effect major change *and* solve the people problems.

Finally, it must be numbers-oriented. It must project future costs and reduce them by straightening out and cost-reducing overlapping benefit schemes. If we are to reduce people, it must be largely by attrition. Personnel must project and plan attrition levels and devise new compensation methods—such as early retirement—to increase it and it must measure productivity in new ways and project what a corporation can afford in compensation as it relates to this productivity.

In addition to fewer people, we identified *better people* as a need for the corporation. Peter Drucker has said that people now must work "smarter, not harder". The companies that have the ablest people at all levels, and working in the proper environment, will cope best with the future because personal creativity, willing effort and the capacity for innovation will be the highest order.

Again, the '50s and '60s did not prepare us for this effort. Business was good. We could afford to hire and promote persons of relatively *limited* ability to innovate or manage people effectively—and we often did. Seniority and loyalty counted more than they should have. Also, too often we put up with individual behavior which should not have been tolerated. It is still far too easy for an able person in a major U.S. corporation to get crossways with an arbitrary boss who has perhaps been threatened and find him or herself sidetracked or even fired.

Corporations have used the percentage of projected growth as the percent of people to add in the past. In too many cases this has produced far too great a growth in people—and produced bureaucracy which slows decision making and dulls innovation. Organizations have lost their warmth and sense of community. There is little personal attention or interest in the individual. The sense of belonging people felt in small organizations is missing. Supervisors carry their worries in their sleeve—and don't interact with their people.

For the most part, we have not yet tapped minority or female sources of talent as we should. There is, of course, now federal legislation to give impetus to this effort—but we have allowed ourselves to become cut off from these sources of talent—and missed an opportunity to broaden and enrich our management teams.

Largely for these reasons, business often hasn't attracted and retained the most able people. We will require the most able people to solve our future problems and it is possible we will be seeking outstanding talent at the very time we are striving to do the job with fewer people. It will not be inconsistent to do this, but it will be difficult to explain.

Again, better people are required at *all levels*. If business conditions warrant hiring into our shop or clerical forces, then the same care should go into their selection as for managerial level people. This has been overlooked, but organization changes will require able people there, too.

The role of the personnel department in attracting and holding better people is again an active one. First, it must re-define and re-examine hiring standards for all sources of people, shop, office and salaried, and maintain an active search for talent at all of these levels—including minorities and women.

Second, it must make sure it understands the capabilities, situation and feelings of each *individual* in the organization. The emphasis is upon the individual and not the organization. This is a big order and if problems are encountered—personnel must have the clout to force action.

Third, the personnel department must have a role in selection, both hiring and promotion, and then have the objectivity and courage to recommend employment or advancement for those able individuals who might not be selected by popular vote of the high seniority people.

Finally, the personnel department should be developing salary and compensation systems which allow for organization change. In the successful corporations, we will see smaller, flatter organizations with more highly trained, capable people in both the office and shop—and we must compensate those taking on increased responsibility. Job evaluation systems must be capable of rewarding innovation and flexibility rather than seniority, working conditions or number of people supervised.

The final area which we identified for the future was leadership. Here, we are talking about top management—but there is a vital role for personnel, too.

There are several aspects to leadership that I would like to mention. I want to emphasize that I am not talking only about company presidents—but leaders of units within a company, too—in other words, the key management members.

First, we have discussed the decline in business credibility. I was at a Board Meeting recently when a statement by a major company head was quoted and none of the persons at the table, all of whom were businessmen, believed it. This lack of credibility is particularly obvious in relation to government. Too often our business spokesmen take a position in opposition to *all* government regulation or *all* social programs or put the blame for business problems at the government's doorstep. This does not ring true to the reader or listener and is not the way business decisions are made. We consider facts and alternatives and select the most practical course of action. Business decisions aren't made from an idealogical base. It appears that too often our business leaders are not at home in the world of ideas and cannot relate to the society as a whole on which they are dependent for the ultimate success of their companies.

A second aspect of leadership is the moral or ethical tone that key members of management set for their organizations. What appears to be concern only for business or personal success, no matter what the means, has surfaced in recent years in a number of companies. The leadership we require must be of the highest personal integrity, genuinely concerned about each person in the company, intolerant of bureaucracy and have a healthy suspicion of the chain of command. Quality, integrity, openness and a capacity to relate to and to *listen to* customers, to employees, to society, to government, are vital.

Finally, of course, the key to the future will be the capability to effect the changes we have discussed. A leader who makes change effectively must gain organization acceptance and change the concept which the organization has of what is acceptable performance and what, indeed, it is possible to accomplish. The leader has a sensitive job of selecting goals and objectives that stretch and require innovation and hard work, but which are achievable and within the capability of the organization. The ultimate goals must be accepted by the organization or the result is that the organization will reject it—either by inaction or perhaps by departing. The leader must give direction, achieve commitment and impart confidence and spirit. He or she must work to re-establish the sense of community, of shared goals, of everyone having a part in success.

The role of the personnel department in the process of leadership is vital. First, there is the rare but occasional opportunity to vote in the selection of corporate leadership, or key management personnel. Be prepared. You are helping to select your own leadership. An understanding of how a prospective officer or management member conducts himself or herself in a variety of situations, not just business, is vital. How is he or she perceived by peers, subordinates, the community? Is there a basic moral guidance system in the prospective leader? Is he or she concerned about people and willing to try new ideas?

Second, the personnel head should be a close advisor in the process of change. The personnel head must provide guidance as to whether the change is accepted—is too fast or too slow. He or she must sense attitudes and how to make the leadership more effective. This input is absolutely vital to the chief executive and to key management members, who are inevitably isolated.

The business environment has changed and the future is not favorable by past standards. A large number of companies have a major task to get their financial structures in shape and all companies must look very hard at their productivity and, therefore, their people. In general, a tougher, more complete leadership job must be done. The environment will be difficult, but in some ways, more predictable. Three areas—fewer people, better people and leadership—are vital for the future of business.

I am a firm believer in a partnership between personnel and the top manager. The personnel director must tread the delicate line of maintaining close contact with top management and with the people. In many ways what I've described is not new. Personnel people have advocated much of this for years. However, as we have seen, it simply wasn't vital to business success in the past. Now it is. I predict far more top management interest and concern. The time spent on people matters has already risen dramatically in our company and I expect that trend to continue.

Job analysis requires questioning employees about all phases of their jobs.

3

JOB ANALYSIS

Job Analysis Methods and Implementation

Job Analysis Problems

Job Descriptions

The Problem: Cateon Company

In the Cateon Company cafeteria Shari Mosely approached her co-worker, Pat Cohen, who is obviously upset.

Mosely: What's new?

Cohen: Nothing much; how about you?

Mosely: I'm fine, but you have been down all day.

Cohen: Well, I don't understand some things around here.

Mosely: Like what?

Cohen: I've been here for almost a year, and I've learned my job. Also, I changed our system of inputting price changes into the computer.

Mosely: I know! Our whole department knows that things have gone easier since you came here.

Cohen: Well, yesterday I found out that Jane Heath, a new account auditor over in the western division, makes a lot more money than I do.

Mosely: I don't believe it! I've been here six years and I know we do a better job than they do.

Cohen: She even told me everything she does—and she doesn't even balance the over-the-counter tabs.

Mosely: Let's go ask Mary Quinn.

Cohen: I did . . . she said we aren't supposed to compare paychecks and that Herden and personnel make those decisions. Then Herden told me he doesn't decide starting salaries; he can only recommend merit increases.

Mosely: Well then, I guess there is nothing we can do.

Cohen: *It just isn't fair. Maybe I'm not doing everything*
I should, but I'm doing more than the man who
was here before me . . . I just don't know.

Job analysis refers to the method by which management systematically investigates the tasks, duties, and responsibilities of an organization's jobs. This includes investigating the levels of decision making by people within those jobs, the skills people need to do these jobs adequately, the autonomy of the jobs involved, and general mental effort. Machines which must be operated, reports completed, and specific financial or other responsibilities should be included in the analysis of jobs. Also examined in the analysis are the working conditions of the job, such as levels of temperature, light, offensive fumes, noise, and other difficult conditions.

Job analysis is, perhaps, one of the oldest personnel functions in existence. While many organization managements perform the systematic investigation which is called job analysis, other organizations call their systems of job analysis job reviews or job classifications. Whether or not the exact term *job analysis* is used by the organization is not important, because management will perform job analysis whether indirectly through other techniques, or in a direct, intentional job analysis program.

Before discussing job analysis in more detail, many related terms used in personnel should be carefully defined:

task—a distinct work activity which has an identifiable beginning and end. Example: Hand sorting a bag of mail into the appropriate boxes.

duty—several tasks which are related by some sequence of events. Example: Pick up, sort, and deliver incoming mail.

position—a collection of tasks and duties which are performed by one person. Example: Mail room clerk prepares outgoing mail, sorts incoming mail, operates addressing machine, postage machine, and related equipment.

job—one or more positions within an organization. Example: Three mail clerks have the same job but different payroll positions.

job family—several jobs of a similar nature which may come into direct contact with each other or may be spread out throughout the organization performing similar functions. Example: Clerical jobs located in different departments.

job analysis—a systematic investigation into the tasks, duties, and responsibilities of a job.

job description—a written summary of tasks, duties, and responsibilities of a job.

job specification—the minimum skills, education, and experience necessary for an individual to perform a job.

job evaluation—the determination of the worth of a job to an organization. Job evaluation is usually a combination of an internal equity comparison of jobs and an external job market comparison.

job classification—the grouping or categorizing of jobs on some specified basis

FIGURE 3–1: *Job Analysis*

Personnel data gathering ⟶	Personnel end product ⟶	Organization usage
Job Analysis	Job Descriptions	Recruitment Selection Orientation Training Performance Appraisal
	Job Specifications	Recruitment Selection Promotions Transfers
	Job Evaluation	Compensation System Wage Surveys

such as the nature of the work performed or the level of pay. Classification is often utilized as a simplified method of job analysis.

Job analysis is a key personnel function which gathers information to be utilized in one or more other important functions such as writing job descriptions, determining specifications, or making job evaluations. The importance of a good job analysis procedure is demonstrated by Figure 3–1. How information is collected and objectively utilized by the personnel department and the organization is of critical importance because it affects many areas which directly involve employees, such as pay and work assignments. Thus, job analysis procedures may indirectly affect the level of employee satisfaction and productivity.

The federal government and the courts have encouraged the use of job analysis and job descriptions so that organizations have objective, specific methods of determining their basic personnel decisions. The government's *Uniform Guidelines on Employee Selection Procedures* state:

Job analysis. A description of the method used to analyze the job should be provided (essential). A complete description of the work behavior(s) and, to the extent appropriate, work outcomes and measures of their criticality and/or importance should be provided (essential). The report should also describe the basis on which the behavior(s) or outcomes were determined to be important, such as their level of difficulty, their frequency of performance, the consequences of error or other appropriate factors (essential). Where jobs are grouped or compared for the purposes of generalizing validity evidence, the work behavior(s) and work product(s) for each of the jobs should be described, and conclusions concerning the similarity of the jobs in terms of observable work behaviors or work products should be made (essential).[1]

A job analysis is seldom the end product; instead, it provides the input to systematically obtain end products. A job analysis determines the minimum and

---

[1] "Uniform Guidelines on Employee Selection Procedures (1978)," *Federal Register* (August 25, 1978): 38302, 38306.

desirable qualifications necessary to perform in a job. Obviously, this information is crucial in putting together a recruitment plan. In the selection process the employees' relative abilities and skills must be evaluated. A job analysis indicates what tasks, duties, and responsibilities the job will entail, how repetitive it may be, or the amount of independence required in the job. Using job analysis information during the interviewing procedure, the personnel person can compare and evaluate the qualifications of the individual being considered for the job.

Once hired, the new employee needs to be oriented to the organization as quickly as possible. A job analysis lists what must be learned to complete the job successfully for the new employee. Often management will give the new employees such information at the initial hiring. A complete job analysis program will reveal if a new employee, lacking in one or two skills, needs additional training in certain areas to complete the job successfully. This can usually be discerned by comparing the employee's past work history and training to the tasks specified in the job analysis.

Job analysis information can also help management determine an equitable pay system. Almost all organizations desire to base a pay system on the relative value of each job to the organization. Difficult jobs, those which require more specific training and abilities, or those which are more hazardous, should receive more pay than less difficult jobs. Through job analysis, management can find out exactly what tasks are performed on each job, and can compare individual tasks for similar jobs across the organization, such as record-keeping, machine operation, or specific knowledge of operations. The process

of performance appraisal—determining how well employees have performed their jobs in the past—and if they should be considered for promotion can be facilitated by a good job analysis system which evaluates specific tasks employees perform. Job analysis can provide information about each job's specific duties and responsibilities, and decide which duties and responsibilities should be considered in an evaluation.

A good job analysis system is an important key to the personnel function. The primary focus of the personnel function is to maintain a high level of employee productivity and efficiency. Job analysis affects most areas of employment, and therefore, will indirectly affect factors such as performance appraisal, compensation, and training, which are most likely to affect employee performance and productivity.

PROGRAM IMPLEMENTATION

The creation and implementation of a job analysis program will vary from firm to firm. Nonetheless, most organizations follow a standard format in conducting a job analysis. The steps that are generally included in most job analysis programs are:

Step 1—Job Analysis Committee

The first step in a job analysis implementation should be the designation of a committee to oversee and make critical decisions during the job analysis program. Working with the personnel department and job analyst, the committee will review information concerning each job within the organization. The committee will make difficult decisions comparing different job factors such as relative responsibility or working conditions.

Committee membership should include all the major departments to be studied in the job analysis system. That is, if jobs to be analyzed are from six different areas then these six departments should have representatives on the committee who understand their departments' jobs and procedures. The committee should include personnel staff members who will collect and evaluate job analysis information on a firsthand basis. All of the people assigned to this committee should understand the standard operating procedures within the organization, and be able to work well together.

The quality of the job analysis will depend upon the accuracy of the information gathered by the job analyst, the consistency and objectivity of the job analyst's evaluation of the information, and the ability of the committee members to give input and make critical, comparative decisions when necessary. In this first step the committee should decide the end products of the job analysis. That is, will the information be used to write job descriptions, will the analysis be the basis for a system of job evaluation, or will it be used to determine minimum specifications for jobs in the organization? Possibly these different end products will all be desirable to the organization.

The committee needs the coooperation of employees and supervisors in the information-gathering process. One reason for having each department represented in this process is to allow committee members to report back to their departments about how the job analysis

will proceed and to reassure fellow employees that it is being done accurately and fairly.

Step 2—Information Collection

Basically, at this point the committee must decide whether information will be collected by individuals within the organization through a method which they will devise, or if a standardized method of job analysis will be utilized. Standardized methods of job analysis have the advantage of being previously tested and utilized, which increases their general validity. However, most also contain the disadvantage of not being specifically designed for use by any one organization.

U.S. DEPARTMENT OF LABOR

The United States Department of Labor (DOL) has developed a standardized method for job analysis with four major job categories that relate to worker performance:[2]

1. worker function—the worker function describes what the worker does in relation to people, data, and things: see Figure 3–2.

2. work fields—the methods by which workers carry out the technological, sociological, or scientific requirements.

3. equipment utilization—the tools, machines, and equipment which must be utilized.

4. products and services—the materials worked on, products produced,

---

[2]U.S. Department of Labor, Manpower Administration, *Handbook for Analyzing Jobs* (Washington, DC: U.S. Government Printing Office, 1972), pp. 340–51.

knowledge assembled, or other services rendered.

One advantage of the DOL method of job analysis is the utilization of the U.S. Employment Services' *Dictionary of Occupational Titles* (DOT). The DOT classifies jobs based on general field of work, tasks performed, and the relationship of the job to data, people, and things. Each job title in the DOT system is given a six-digit code. The first digit indicates the general occupation:

DOT 1st Digit	Occupation
0, 1	Professional, technical, managerial occupations
2	Clerical, sales
3	Service
4	Farming, fishery, forestry
5	Processing
6	Machine trades
7	Bench work
8	Structural work
9	Miscellaneous

The second and third digits provide a finer breakdown with respect to industry and function. The last three digits of the code are derived from the work function code as illustrated in Figure 3–2. A tax accounting job is coded:

160.162

"1" indicates professional	"1" indicates data coordinating function
"60" indicates accounting field	"6" indicates speaking–signalling people contact
	"2" indicates operating–controlling level of things

The DOL system is primarily of use to smaller firms where personnel specialists can quickly classify each of their jobs and utilize the DOT job descriptions. In other firms, specialists use the DOT system simply as a starting point, modifying the standardized descriptions to fit their jobs. The greatest asset of the DOT is its acceptance by federal employment agencies. The Uniform Guidelines on Employee Selection Procedures (1978) state that "it is desirable to provide the user's job title(s) for the job(s) in question and the corre-

FIGURE 3–2: *Worker Function Scales from DOT*

Data (4th Digit)	People (5th Digit)	Things (6th Digit)
0 Synthesizing	0 Mentoring	0 Setting Up
1 Coordinating	1 Negotiating	1 Precision Working
2 Analyzing	2 Instructing	2 Operating-Controlling
3 Compiling	3 Supervising	3 Driving-Operating
4 Computing	4 Diverting	4 Manipulating
5 Copying	5 Persuading	5 Tending
6 Comparing	6 Speaking-Signalling	6 Feeding-Offbearing
	7 Serving	7 Handling
	8 Taking Instructions-Helping	

SOURCE: U.S. Department of Labor, *Dictionary of Occupational Titles,* 4th ed. (Washington: United States Government Printing Office, 1977).

sponding job title(s) and code(s) from U.S. Employment Services' *Dictionary of Occupational Titles*."[3]

POSITION ANALYSIS QUESTIONNAIRE

The *Position Analysis Questionnaire* (PAQ) is another standardized method of job analysis. The PAQ[4] includes 194 job elements which are divided into 27 job dimensions and 6 overall job divisions. The six major divisions within the PAQ method are:

information input—how workers get information to do their jobs

mental processes—decision making, planning, organizing

work output—tools, machines, physical activity of the job

relationships—co-workers, supervision given, customer relationships, etc.

job content—working conditions of the job, including hours, physical conditions

other job characteristics

The authors of the PAQ system identify the job elements within the different dimensions which describe job families most common to organizations. The PAQ system requires that workers or supervisors are familiar enough with the job being analyzed to check to what degree each of the 194 job elements exist on that job. Figure 3–3 shows one page from the Position Analysis Questionnaire—the information input area.

The PAQ system has the obvious advantage of being quantitative in nature. Also,

this system has the advantage of being standardized, i.e., each job is being looked at in a consistent method; thus, the same elements of each job are being examined by the job analyst. Having a quantitative system such as the PAQ system is helpful because it enables the job analyst to easily differentiate between jobs, to compare the point totals of one job to another and, therefore, assign jobs to different pay grades.

FUNCTIONAL JOB ANALYSIS

A modification of the DOL method has been made by Sidney A. Fine, a former member of the Employment Services Division of the U.S. Department of Labor. Fine has created a standardized job analysis system which he terms *Functional Job Analysis (FJA)*.[5] The FJA method is similar to the DOL method with some improvements; additional scales are utilized which measure: 1) worker instructions (see Figure 3–5); 2) educational development; 3) reasoning development; 4) mathematical development; and 5) language development. The DOL and FJA systems, like the PAQ system, have the advantage of being quantitative in nature. They also are organized, pretested, and can be used systematically throughout the organization to complete a job analysis. However, like all standardized methods, they have the disadvantage of being generally broad, and not directly relating to the specific behaviors required on jobs within any one organization.

INTERNAL METHODS

An alternative for management is to de-

[3]*Uniform Guidelines* pp. 38304, 38306.

[4]Ernest J. McCormick, Paul R. Jeanneret, and Robert C. Mecham, "A Study of Job Characteristics and Job Dimensions as Based on the Position Analysis Questionnaire (PAQ)," *Journal of Applied Psychology* (August 1972): 347–68.

[5]Sidney A. Fine and Wretha Wiley, *An Introduction to Functional Job Analysis: A Scaling of Selected Tasks from the Social Welfare Field*, Methods for Manpower Analysis No. 4 (Kalamazoo, MI: W. E. Upjohn Institute for Employment Research, 1979), pp. 3–20.

FIGURE 3–3: *Position Analysis Questionnaire Page*

1 INFORMATION INPUT

1.1 Sources of Job Information

Rate each of the following items in terms of the extent to which it is used by the worker as a source of information in performing the job.

	Extent of Use (U)
NA	Does not apply
1	Nominal/very infrequent
2	Occasional
3	Moderate
4	Considerable
5	Very substantial

1.1.1 Visual Sources of Job Information

1 __4__ Written materials (books, reports, office notes, articles, job instructions, signs, etc.)

2 __4__ Quantitative materials (such as graphs, accounts, specifications, tables of numbers, etc.)

3 __1__ Pictorial materials (picturelike materials used as sources of information, for example, drawings, blueprints, diagrams, maps, tracings, photographic films, X-ray films, TV pictures, etc.)

4 __NA__ Patterns/related devices (templates, stencils, patterns, etc., used as sources of information when observed during use; do not include here materials described in item 3 above)

5 __1__ Visual displays (dials, gauges, signal lights, radarscopes, speedometers, clocks, etc.)

6 __1__ Measuring devices (rulers, calipers, tire pressure gauges, scales, thickness gauges, pipettes, thermometers, protractors, etc., used to obtain visual information about physical measurements; do not include here devices described in item 5 above)

7 __NA__ Mechanical devices (tools, equipment, machinery, and other mechanical devices which are sources of information when observed during use or operation)

8 __NA__ Materials in process (parts, materials, objects, etc., which are sources of information when being modified, worked on, or otherwise processed, such as bread dough being mixed, workpiece being turned in a lathe, fabric being cut, shoe being resoled, etc.)

9 __NA__ Materials not in process (parts, materials, objects, etc., not in the process of being changed or modified, which are sources of information when being inspected, handled, packaged, distributed, or selected, etc., such as items or materials in inventory, storage, or distribution channels, items being inspected, etc.)

10 __NA__ Features of nature (landscapes, fields, geological samples, vegetation, cloud formations, and other features of nature which are observed or inspected to provide information)

11 __NA__ Features of environment created by people (structures, buildings, dams, highways, bridges, docks, railroads, and other altered aspects of the indoor or outdoor environment which are observed or inspected to provide job information; do not consider equipment, etc., that an individual uses during work, which are covered by item 7).

SOURCE: Adapted from the Position Analysis Questionnaire: Visual Sources of Job Information. PAQ Services, Inc. Logan, UT. Used with permission.

velop an information gathering system specific to the organization. This could include several different methods of collecting the information. One method would be direct observation of the jobs being performed, where job analysts observe all of the different jobs within an organization. If six or seven individuals, for example, performed the same job, the analyst would only observe the two indi-

FIGURE 3–4: FJA Scales for Controlling the Language of Task Statement

THINGS

3a. Precision Working,
b. Setting Up,
c. Operating-Controlling II
2a. Manipulating,
b. Operating-Controlling I,
c. Driving-Controlling,
d. Starting Up
1a. Handling,
b. Feeding-Offbearing,
c. Tending

DATA

6. Synthesizing
5a. Innovating,
b. Coordinating
4. Analyzing
3a. Computing,
b. Compiling
2. Copying
1. Comparing

PEOPLE

7. Mentoring
6. Negotiating
5. Supervising
4a. Consulting,
b. Instructing,
c. Treating
3a. Coaching,
b. Persuading,
c. Diverting
2. Exchanging Information
1a. Taking Instructions-Helping,
b. Serving

NOTES: 1. Each hierarchy is independent of the other. It would be incorrect to read the functions across the three hierarchies as related because they appear to be on the same level. The definitive relationship among functions is within each hierarchy, not across hierarchies. Some broad exceptions are made in the next note.

2. Data is central since a worker can be assigned even higher data functions although Things and People functions remain at the lowest level of their respective scales. This is not so for Things and People functions. When a Things function is at the third level, e.g., Precision Working, the Data function is likely to be at least Compiling or Computing. When a People function is at the fourth level, e.g., Consulting, the Data function is likely to be at least Analyzing and possibly Innovating or Coordinating. Similarly for Supervising and Negotiating. Mentoring is some instances can call for Synthesizing.

3. Each function in its hierarchy is defined to include the lower numbered functions. This is more or less the way it was found to occur in reality. It was most clear-cut for Things and Data and only a rough approximation in the case of People.

4. The functions separated by a comma are separate functions on the same level, separately defined. The empirical evidence did not support a hierarchical distinction.

5. The hyphenated functions, Taking Instructions-Helping, Operating-Controlling, etc. are single functions.

6. The indented functions in the Things hierarchy are machine oriented as opposed to the hand or hand tool oriented functions (Handling, Manipulating, or Precision Working). They can be considered as parallel hierarchies.

SOURCE: Sidney A. Fine, Ph.D. Advanced Research Resources Organization, Washington, D.C. Used with permission

FIGURE 3–5: *Worker Instructions Scale*

The Worker Instructions Scale defines *responsibility* in terms of the mix of specifications (that which is prescribed) and judgment (that which is specifically left to discretion) assigned to the worker. This can range across several levels depending on the activity(ies).

Level 1

Inputs, outputs, tools, equipment, and procedures are all specified. Almost everything the worker needs to know is contained in the assignment. The worker is to produce a specified amount of work or a standard number of units per or day.

Level 2

Inputs, outputs, tools, and equipment are all specified, but the worker has some leeway in the procedures and methods used to get the job done. Almost all the information needed is provided in the daily assignment. Production is measured on a daily or weekly basis.

Level 3

Inputs and outputs are specified, but the worker has considerable freedom as to procedures and timing, including the use of tools and/or equipment. The worker may have to refer to several standard sources for information (handbooks, catalogs, wall charts). Time to complete a particular product or service is specified, but this varies up to several hours.

Level 4

Output (product or service) is specified in the assignment, which may be in the form of a memorandum or of a schematic (sketch or blueprint). The worker must work out ways of getting the job done, including selection and use of tools and/or equipment, sequence of operations (tasks), and obtaining important information (handbooks, etc.). The worker may either do work or set up standards and procedures for others.

Level 5

Same as (4) above, but in addition, the worker is expected to know and employ theory—the whys and wherefores of the various options that are available for dealing with a problem—and can independently select from among them. Reading in the professional and/or trade literature may be required in order to gain this understanding.

Level 6

Various possible outputs are described that can meet stated technical or administrative needs. The worker must investigate the various possible outputs and evaluate them in regard to performance characteristics and input demands. This usually requires creative use of theory well beyond referring to standard sources. There is no specification of inputs, methods, sequences, sources, or the like.

Level 7

There is some question as to what the need or problem really is or what directions should be pursued in dealing with it. In order to define it, to control and explore the behavior of the variables, and to formulate possible outputs and their performance characteristics, the worker must consult largely unspecified sources of information and devise investigations, surveys, or data analysis studies.

Level 8

Information and/or direction comes to the worker in terms of needs (tactical, organizational, strategic, financial). The worker must call for staff reports and recommendations concerning methods of dealing with them. The worker coordinates both organizational and technical data in order to make decisions and determinations regarding courses of action (outputs) for major sections (divisions, groups) of the organization.

SOURCE: Adapted from scale developed by Sidney A. Fine, Ph.D. Advanced Research Resources Organization, Washington, D.C. Used with permission.

viduals who perform that job best. While observing the individuals performing different jobs, the analyst would try to note all the different tasks involved, the decisions being made, the skills necessary, the interpersonal relationships utilized, etc. The problem with direct observation is that it can only be used in repetitive, manual jobs and most jobs today contain a large percentage of mental activities. That is, the analyst would not learn much from observing a bookkeeper who enters figures into different books all day. Also, the observation method has another disadvantage of being quite obvious to the employees, who may resent the observation. Others may increase their normal work output while they are being observed. This is often referred to as the Hawthorne effect, first discovered in the early Hawthorne Studies of human motivation.[6]

Another alternative is for job analysts to perform all the different tasks necessary to complete each job in order that they may determine each job's requirements. Obviously, this is quite limited in scope as many analysts could successfully perform only a few jobs within the organization.

A more common alternative would be to interview either the employee or the immediate supervisor of each job. Depending upon the job situation, the cooperation of employees, and other factors, the interviewer will have a difficult time objectively collecting job information, unless it is possible to learn much about the job ahead of time in order to ask the pertinent questions. If the interview technique is selected, several suggestions will help the analyst:

[6]Alex Carey, "The Hawthorne Studies: A Radical Criticism," *American Sociological Review* 32, no. 3 (1967): 403–16.

- Consult the supervisor of the job before selecting which persons to interview. If six or eight individuals perform the same job, ask the supervisor which two individuals perform the job best and would be able to interview accurately.

- Make sure the interviewee understands the purpose of the job analysis; many times employees fear that the interview will be used against them or to increase the scope of their jobs. Gain rapport with the employee as soon as possible and express the stated goals of the job analysis program before the interview begins. Often it will be necessary to emphasize that there will be no increase in work load and/or reduction in pay as a result of this job analysis.

- Structure the interview as much as possible; decide what questions will be asked of all employees before any interviews begin. This will assure a standardization of format and comparability of information gathered. Also, it will help keep the interviews from developing into bull sessions or complaint sessions with employees.

- Complete a rough draft of the interview, and then go back to the employee to verify that this interpretation of the employee's statements is correct. After verification from the employee, contact the supervisor to check the accuracy of the information.

The primary disadvantage of the interview technique is that the analyst must spend a great deal of time with each employee. Often the employees will not be able to carefully frame their responses since they are on the spot during an interview. Also, comparison of information is difficult as information is gathered from different interviews. Even structured interviews result in a lack of standardized information being received, especially if more than one analyst is utilized.

Possibly the best method of developing an in-house job analysis information gathering system is by using the written questionnaire. A job analysis questionnaire system is faster and easier than the interview system. Usually less expensive, the use of the questionnaires almost always results in standardized, specific information about the jobs in an organization. Whenever information gathered through the written questionnaire system is not sufficient, follow-up interviews can be scheduled with certain employees. Thus, the advantage of the interview system—exploring specific questions which the analyst is unclear about or receiving additional information not in the standardized questions—can be achieved with the questionnaire system. Usually only 5 percent or less of the standardized questionnaires require follow-up interviews.

JOB ANALYSIS QUESTIONNAIRES Figure 3–6 includes a sample of a job analysis questionnaire which has been used in service and production oriented organizations. When compiling a questionnaire, we suggest that you:

- Review questionnaires used by organizations, professional groups, or university researchers. By reviewing other questionnaires, often you can put together your own questionnaire in a relatively short period of time. Many items on other questionnaires may not occur to you before the process begins; thus, you can learn from other analysts' experiences.

- Keep it short. Most individuals do not like completing questionnaires. Thus, the longer the questionnaire, the less attention will be paid to the items during its completion.

- Have each questionnaire completed. Questionnaires which must be completed at home often are not given the earnest effort. As important to the organization as job analysis is, it should be done on company time so that employees have adequate time to provide the information, and do not look upon this as an extra burden they must bear.

- Categorize answers. Structure questions so that the responses can be categorized as much as possible. Whenever possible, design closed-end questions; have employees check one of several responses or indicate numbers or percentages for responses whenever possible. This avoids gathering information which is hard to compare or cannot be used by the analyst.

- Test the questionnaire with several trusted employees. Many times the analyst will find that questions may be vague and misleading, or that important aspects of the jobs have been omitted.

- Include one open-end question. Always include at least one open-end question which allows the employee to give any additional information that has not been transmitted in the rest of the written questionnaire. This may facilitate communication about particular qualities of some jobs.

FIGURE 3–6: *Job Analysis Questionnaire*

1. Employee's Name: _____ Date Completed: _____

   Position Title: _____ Department: _____

   Title of Immediate Supervisor: _____

2. List the names and job titles of persons that you supervise, and the percentage of time spent in supervision.

Name	Title	Hrs. Per Day/Week Supervising
_____	_____	_____
_____	_____	_____

3. What is the lowest grade of grammar school, high school, or college that should have been completed by a person starting in your position?

   _____

4. What special type of training, skill, or experience should a person possess before starting in your position?

   _____

5. What training or experience have you received in your position, and how long would it take the average person to perform this work satisfactorily without close supervision?

   _____

   _____

6. What machines or equipment do you operate in your work and for what percentage of your time per day, week, or month?

Machine	%	Period
_____	_____	_____
_____	_____	_____

7. What do you consider to be the most important decisions that you alone make in the course of your work, and what percentage of your time is devoted to making such decisions?

   _____

   _____

   _____

8. What responsibility do you have for handling money, securities, inventory, or other valuables, and what is your estimate of their worth?

Responsibility	$ Worth per Week
_____	_____
_____	_____

FIGURE 3–6: *continued*

9. What responsibility do you have in dealing with customers or other persons outside the company?

Person Contacted	Position	Nature of Contact	Frequency of Contact
_____	_____	_____	_____
_____	_____	_____	_____
_____	_____	_____	_____

10. What unusual aspects about your work and your work surroundings (working conditions, hours, out-of-town travel, physical requirements, etc.) should be included in a description of your job?

_____

_____

_____

11. What activities do you perform only at stated periods (weekly or monthly) or at irregular intervals?

Activity	Purpose	Interval
_____	_____	_____
_____	_____	_____
_____	_____	_____

12. List the specific duties you perform in the usual course of your daily work, and approximately what percentage of your workday is spent in each activity. (Please try to use active verbs such as type, file, interview, etc. On the following page you will find a sample list of duties that may be helpful in preparing your answer to this question).

_____

_____

_____

13. Discuss any considerations *not covered* in this questionnaire that you would consider important in writing a description of your job.

_____

_____

_____

THANK YOU FOR FILLING OUT THE QUESTIONNAIRE.

Step 3—Review Information

Regardless of the method that has been selected by the analyst to collect information, the next step will be to assemble and review that information with the employees and the job analysis committee. After writing a first draft of the standardized information collected, the analyst will need to make sure that the analysis is factually correct, complete, and a clear picture of the job being portrayed. After checking with the employees and supervisors involved in gathering information, the analyst must take these first drafts to the job analysis committee which begins to review each analysis to make sure it is objective and comparable. That is, the information must not only be accurate and complete, but also easily comparable from one job to another. Establishment of standardized categories of information about the jobs, such as work environment, decision making required, and supervision, make comparisons between jobs easier. The more effort put into these first drafts of job analysis, the easier it will be to determine the desired end products.

Step 4—End Products

The fourth step involves the completion of whatever end products are desired by management. For example, job analysis data may be used to write job descriptions or job specifications, to conduct a job evaluation for wage and salary purposes, to determine training and development needs, or to create tests for employee selection.

Step 5—Future Use and Updating

The last step in the job analysis system will be to determine how the information will be stored for future use. The personnel department should have access to this information in case additional end products are desired. Also, the job analysis committee will need to determine how to update the information periodically as information gathered in the job analysis process is only accurate at the current time. Daily changes will occur as supervisors train employees to accept more responsibility, additional tasks are developed, or organizational changes are made. Updating the information in the job analysis program maintains its accuracy and guarantees its usefulness in the future.

JOB ANALYSIS PROBLEMS

Any job analysis effort by an organization will run into certain problems regardless of the size of the organization, its employee relations, and the abilities of those performing the analysis. One of the most common problems is employees' fear. Often they see a job analysis as a threat to their current jobs and/or pay levels. In the past job analysis has been used as a means of expanding jobs while reducing the total number of employees. Job analysis has also been used to increase production rates and, therefore, decrease employees' net pay. Organizations must overcome employees' fears so that employees and their supervisors give accurate input into the job analysis program.

One of the most successful methods of placating employees' fears is to involve employees or their representatives in as many aspects of the job analysis program as possible. Before the program begins, employees should be told its purposes, who will be initiating it, how they will be affected, and why their input is critical. Management may want to make a written commitment that the organization will not terminate any employees, lower the pay of any employees, or decrease the total number of jobs due to the job analysis results. These measures may enable the job analysts to perform their functions accurately and get complete information from employees. It is unfortunate for job analysts that in past years job analysis has been used improperly.

A second problem of job analysis is the need for updating the information. While the current job analysis is being completed, jobs will be changing as the organization changes. As employees expand in their jobs, as work is reassigned within a department, as supervisors develop, it will be necessary to change the content of jobs. The problem, then, becomes how to keep the job analysis information current. One answer is an annual review of the job analysis information. Usually the personnel department will send job analysis information to supervisors asking them to note any changes that have been made in jobs during the past year. The second common method is to have managers submit proposed changes in jobs, or reclassifications. The management proposal technique is especially necessary when the reclassification may directly result in a change in pay. Both of these systems have their problems. The annual review is quite time consuming as every job must be reanalyzed each year. Also, when jobs are reviewed annually, employees will sometimes expect their jobs to be reclassified with accompanying pay increases.

Another problem with an annual review is that whenever the content of a job is substantially increased only a week or two after the initial job analysis, employees in that job may be underpaid for the next forty or fifty weeks. Finally, the annual review looks at all jobs, even those which have not changed. Possibly 90 percent of the jobs do not need to be reexamined; only the 10 percent that have changed during the year need to be reexamined. Constant updating by managers implies that only those jobs which need to be changed will be looked at. Also, the management proposal technique will obviously be more current and employees will not have to wait for months before the annual review to have their jobs reclassified with a possible change in salary or other benefits. A primary disadvantage of this technique is that management often tends to forget to keep up with changes. Thus, employees get frustrated, feel underpaid, or don't realize what must be done to have their jobs reclassified.

If management constantly updates job descriptions as they are changed, this is a better technique that the annual review. The two systems may be combined in some form, such as having biennial reviews with constant submission by managers who want to reclassify jobs. Unfortunately these combination systems contain the advantages as well as the disadvantages of the two techniques. Such combination systems are less common than using one technique or the other.

A fourth common problem with the job analysis process occurs when a job is held by only one or two incumbents; often the analysis is of the person's performance and not the job specifications. The analyst must look at what the job should entail and not how well or how poorly the incumbent is performing the job. As the requirements for a job increase, the description needs to be updated.

One problem commonly occurs when job analyses are the basis for job descriptions which are handed out to employees for the first time. Employees often feel that the description is a contract describing what they should and should not do on the job. When asked to do extra work or an unusual task once in a while, employees may respond, "It's not in my description," and therefore, do not perform the new task. Management can change job descriptions by assigning added tasks to employees; however, if a task is only done annually or may never be repeated, changing the job description for a single situation is unnecessary. Many nonunion organizations use *elastic clauses* in their job descriptions. An elastic clause like "performs other duties as assigned" will allow supervisors to assign employees duties different from those they normally perform without changing their job descriptions.

JOB DESCRIPTIONS

The most common end product of a job analysis is a written job description. One of the oldest personnel tools, job descriptions have received renewed interest in recent years due primarily to governmental guidelines. Job descriptions have no exact format and are often used for many different purposes by organizations.

Uses

The purposes for writing and utilizing job descriptions fall in three general areas:

EMPLOYMENT AND COMPENSATION

RECRUITMENT Job descriptions may be used to develop recruitment ads in newspapers and other publications and to provide applicants with additional information about the job openings.

INTERVIEWING Job descriptions are often used when they include job specifications as a means of providing the interviewer with concise, accurate information about the job so that the interviewer may better match the applicant to the job opening, and make sure that the minimum qualifications of the job are met by the applicant.

ORIENTATION New employees may be given job descriptions to spell out job demands and areas to be evaluated later.

TRAINING Some organizations will use job descriptions to specify the training an employee needs to accurately perform a job, and therefore, the type of training new or current employees may need to keep them productive.

JOB EVALUATION Job descriptions often specify comparable factors in the job evaluation process so that the job evaluator can compare components of the various jobs and make internal pay comparisons.

WAGE COMPENSATION SURVEY Job descriptions give the personnel administrator the opportunity to estimate whether wages being paid for a job in the organization are equitable to similar jobs in other organizations within the community or around the country. Thus, job description provides information for internal comparisons through job evaluation, and external comparisons through survey analysis.

PERFORMANCE APPRAISAL Job descriptions may specify what areas an employee will be evaluated on during performance appraisal. If employees are told which areas and duties they are responsible for performing, then those are the duties and responsibilities on which they should be evaluated.

LEGAL REQUIREMENTS

FAIR LABOR STANDARDS ACT, 1938 Amended in 1974, the act created the initial demand for job descriptions and made them popular in the 1940s. The act specifies, among other things, that employees will be paid minimum wage. Also, the Fair Labor Standards Act set a forty-hour workweek for this country by dividing employees into two categories—exempt or nonexempt. Nonexempt refers to those employees who must be paid time and a half when they work over forty hours per week. Exempt employees are those who are not paid overtime wages. Thus, the organization must determine whether each job is exempt or nonexempt through job analysis or by analyzing the job descriptions. Basically, exempt positions are those which are managerial, supervisory, technical, or professional. There are also statutes similar to the national Fair Labor Standards Act in most states.

EQUAL PAY ACT, 1963 This act requires that organizations give "equal pay for substantially equal work requiring equal skill, effort, responsibility, and working conditions." Job descriptions may be a good organization defense against discrimination cases filed under the Equal Pay Act. Descriptions can be used to show that jobs are not substantially equal in terms of skill, effort, responsibility, or working conditions, and, therefore, can be paid at different rates.

TITLE VII OF THE 1964 CIVIL RIGHTS ACT Job descriptions are one of the organization's best defenses against unfair discrimination claims made under the Civil Rights Act. This is thoroughly discussed in George Wendt's article at the end of Chapter 5.

OCCUPATIONAL SAFETY AND HEALTH ACT (OSHA) OF 1970 Job descriptions are required to specify "elements of the job that endanger health, or are considered unsatisfactory or distasteful to the majority of the population," by OSHA. Again, providing this description to employees as an advance notice is a good defense in legal matters concerning employees.

COLLECTIVE BARGAINING DEMANDS

A long-standing union demand is "equal pay for equal work." Thus, job descriptions specifying work to be performed often stipulate pay for specific duties. Such pay considerations have been a critical area in labor negotiations for many years.

Elements of the Job Description

While there is no universal format for job descriptions, most have certain common features. A list of job duties is one element found in all job descriptions. Most will contain some identification, a brief job summary, and often job specifications. However, it is also common practice to list specifications on separate forms used only for personnel work.

JOB IDENTIFICATION

Job identification usually includes the title of the job, the department, and the title of the immediate supervisory position. The identification may also include the status of the job (exempt or nonexempt), the pay grade, or pay range. The DOT code may be included in the identification.

JOB SUMMARY

A job summary is basically one to three lines which give the essence of the job.

Job summaries usually start with an action phrase such as supervises, coordinates, or directs. Job summaries should either emphasize the most common function, the primary output, or objective of the job.

JOB DUTIES

Job duties and responsibilities are the heart of the job description. There are primarily two formats for the duties section: One is a paragraph narrative job description. The problem with the paragraph format is that it is not as easy to scan or to realize which functions are important. A more popular form is grouping tasks of a job and separating those tasks and listing them. The tasks might be grouped by functional categories such as supervision given, decision making, reporting requirements, organization of work, physical demands, financial accountability.

JOB SPECIFICATIONS

Job specifications, or minimum qualifications as they are sometimes called, essentially give the qualifications which job applicants must possess to be considered for the job. Since the passage of the Equal Pay Act in 1963, it is common to divide job specifications according to the areas of skill, effort, responsibility, and working conditions. Job specification skills might include required education, experience, special training, manual skills, or specific certification required for the job. Effort as a job specification would include specific physical effort which the job holder must be able to perform, ability to handle emotional stress situations, or experience in a supervisory position. Responsibility as a job specification may include reporting responsibility, supervisory responsibility for inventory maintenance or equipment readiness, or financial responsibility such as making up shortages in a cash drawer.

The job specification may include working conditions such as hours the employee must be available to work, sick leave or vacation policy, and other unusual conditions such as high levels of noise, fumes, or other hazardous conditions.

Figures 3–7 and 3–8 are sample job descriptions. The quality control job description contains a particularly good example of the job identification element. The identification not only includes the usual information such as job title, department, and title of immediate supervisor, but also the Job Code—which refers to the DOT job number. The exempt status indicates a salaried position that does not pay overtime wages. The job identification information indicating a date on which the description was approved and who approved it eliminates future questions or conflicts concerning accuracy or completeness. Pay grades are given so that employees or applicants can estimate the pay range for each job and the levels within the organization. The 751 points refers to evaluation points; if the point total is close to the next highest pay grade, then future reclassifications may move it up into the next highest pay grade. The estimated time spent on each duty appears in parentheses.

The word processing secretary's job description contains a job specification element which allows the interviewer to easily and objectively decide if the applicant meets the specification. While a specification may not always be quantitative in nature, whenever possible, it should be. The first three specifications for the word processing secretary are examples of measurable or verifiable qualifications. The interviewer can verify that a person has a high school degree or college experience and measure an appli-

FIGURE 3–7: *Job Description*

Chief Quality Control Engineer	
Job Title	Job Code
Manager of Quality Control	*Quality Control*
Title of Immediate Supervisor	Department

7	*Louisville*	*Exempt*	*August 12, 1982*
Bldg.	Plant	Status	Date

Robert Myers	*12* *751*
Approved by	Grade Points

SUMMARY

Supervises six salaried quality control personnel; plans, organizes, coordinates, and administers manufacturing activities.

JOB DUTIES

1. Establishes and maintains supplier contacts to assist in solving quality problems by evaluating contacts' quality capabilities, facilities, and quality systems. (10%)
2. Establishes and reviews goals, budgets, and work plans in the areas of quality, cost schedule attainment, and operator/equipment utilization. (10%)
3. Reviews product and process designs, identifying problems which might result in customer dissatisfaction or failure to meet established goals or allocated costs. (20%)
4. Specifies quality control methods and processes to support quality planning. Provides cost estimates and procures necessary tools and equipment to support overall project schedule. (10%)
5. Supplies input to manufacturing engineers on producibility and other quality matters. (20%)
6. Provides feedback on quality levels and costs during test runs and during production to measure system effectiveness. (10%)
7. Supervises six to eight salaried personnel assigned to the quality control engineering area. Trains new personnel in proper procedures and policy. Completes performance appraisals of subordinates. (20%)

cant's typing and filing ability with valid tests. The fourth and fifth specifications are important but are more vague and subjective—thus subject to interviewer bias.

In summary, everyone benefits from sound job analysis practices: Employees are hired and paid according to their qualifications, duties, and responsibilities; they are treated fairly and openly. The firm benefits by keeping good, productive employees. Because difficult personnel decisions regarding promotion and pay are made more objectively on a job related basis, legal problems with employees are decreased.

FIGURE 3–8: *Job Description*

Job Title: *Word Processing Secretary*
Department: *Branch Administration*
Position of Immediate Supervisor: *Branch Administrative Manager*

I. GENERAL SUMMARY OF RESPONSIBILITIES:

Types, edits, and distributes various correspondence to clients and internal staff. Transmits and proofs various essential status reports for day to day operations.

II. SPECIFIC JOB RESPONSIBILITIES:

Types daily correspondence and sales orders from nine representatives from machine dictation and hard copy. (40%)

Proofreads and prepares final copies for distribution. (10%)

Receives handwritten copies and maintains priority file of reports and correspondence. (5%)

Types special projects, such as proposals, quotations, systems analyses, and office surveys for marketing department. (20%)

Transmits computer programs via magnetic card typewriter and other telecommunication equipment. (10%)

Logs and maintains records of completed staff and client work. (4%)

Receives and assigns priority to special client and staff requests and special projects. (5%)

Serves as backup for receptionist. (5%)

Performs other duties as assigned. (1%)

III. JOB SPECIFICATION:

High school diploma required, with one or two years of college preferred.

Training or one year's experience on magnetic card typewriter. Type 50 wpm.

Able to file ten documents per minute without error.

Must be able to consistently produce accurate, professional quality documents.

Ability to work well with people in developing proposals essential.

Pressure from the federal government and the courts has encouraged many organizations to develop a job analysis program. Implementation of job analysis begins with the selection of a job analysis committee composed of representatives from all major departments in the organization. This committee gathers information about each job, reviews the information, and develops job descriptions, job specifications, or job evaluation programs—all of which are updated periodically. Job descriptions are used for recruitment, selection, orientation, training, and performance appraisal. In addition to being used in recruitment and selection, job specifications are useful in making promotion and transfer decisions. Job evaluations help management determine the pay levels and value of jobs within the organization.

The Solution

Cateon Company cannot stop Shari Mosely and Pat Cohen from comparing their work performances and pay. However, Cateon management could minimize perceptions of inequity by treating employees fairly. Several points in the conversation between Mosely and Cohen suggest possible areas of improvement. First, Cohen has apparently made significant improvements in her work, which could justify a merit increase. However, Herden has not made such a suggestion, either because there is no system to do so or he leaves that to the supervisor, Mary Quinn. She says only that employees should not compare paychecks. More importantly, Quinn does not address the important questions, such as how the organization determines pay levels.

If a documented job analysis led to job descriptions and an objective evaluation system of pay, then she should explain that to Cohen. Quinn might investigate and find there is a good reason that Heath is paid more. When an employee finds that another employee in a similar position, with less seniority and fewer duties, is paid more, some explanation should be given. Quinn may find out that a reclassification of Cohen's job is in order. Finally, there is a hint of sex discrimination; Cohen's predecessor was a male. Quinn should investigate if and why the male employee was paid more than Cohen.

KEY TERMS AND CONCEPTS

Job	Task
Job Analysis	Duty
Job Descriptions	Position
Job Evaluation	DOT
Job Specifications	FJA
Job Classification	PAQ
Job Family	Elastic Clause

FOR REVIEW

1. Define the practical relationship between job analysis, job descriptions, and job specifications.

2. What information is necessary to develop job descriptions? What are some of the qualities of a well-constructed job description?

3. How can a firm benefit from having a complete and accurate system of job descriptions and job specifications?

4. Outline the advantages and disadvantages of the various methods of job analysis.

5. How do governmental influences affect the process of job analysis?

6. If an organization has no formal system of job analysis, how might the objectives of job analysis be obtained?

FOR DISCUSSION

1. If you were a personnel specialist in a company which was introducing job analysis, how would you reassure employees who felt threatened?

2. When faced with the problem of updating job analysis information, would you favor an annual review or reclassification? Explain why.

3. Describe the methods you would use to gather job information in a bank, a small manufacturer, or a newspaper.

4. Discuss how job analysis could or could not resolve the following problems: An employee who produces less than others doing the same job. An employee who complains about a dirty work environment. An employee who feels passed over when promotions are announced.

5. As a personnel manager you must describe job analysis to employees. Which ideas would you stress for blue-collar workers? For white-collar workers?

SUPPLEMENTARY READING

Archer, W. B. *Computation of Group Job Descriptions from Occupational Survey Data.* San Antonio: USAF, Personnel Research Laboratory, 1966.

Carrell, M. R., and Dittrich, J. E. "Employee Perceptions of Fair Treatment." *Personnel Journal,* October 1976, pp. 523–24.

————. "Equity Theory: The Recent Literature, Methodological Considerations, and New Directions." *Academy of Management Review* 3 (1978): 202–10.

Dunnette, M. D. *Personnel Selection and Placement.* Belmont, CA: Wadsworth, 1966.

Farrell, W. T.; Stone, C. H.; and Yoder, D. *Guidelines for Sampling in Marine Corps Task Analysis.* Evaluation of Marine Corps Task Analysis Program, TR No. 11. Los Angeles: California State University, 1976.

Fine, S. A. "Functional Job Analysis: An Approach to a Technology for Manpower Planning." *Personnel Journal,* November 1974, pp. 813–18.

————. *Functional Job Analysis Scales: A Desk Aid.* Kalamazoo: W. E. Upjohn Institute for Employment Research, 1973.

————, and Wiley, W. W. *An Introduction to Functional Job Analysis.* Kalamazoo: W. E. Upjohn Institute for Employment Research, 1974.

Flanagan, J. C. "The Critical Incident Technique." *Psychological Bulletin* 51 (1954): 327–58.

Marquardt, L. D., and McCormick, E. J. *Attribute Ratings and Profiles of the Job Elements of the Position Analysis Questionnaire (PAQ).* Department of Psychological Sciences, Report No. 1. West Lafayette: Purdue University, 1972.

McCormick, E. J. *Job Analysis: Methods and Applications.* New York: AMACOM, 1979.

————; and Ammerman, H. L. *Development of Worker Activity Checklists for Use in Occupational Analysis.* San Antonio: USAF Personnel Research Laboratory, 1960.

————; Jeanneret, P. R.; and Mecham, R. C. "A Study of Job Characteristics and Job Dimensions as Based on the Position Analysis Questionnaire (PAQ)." *Journal of Applied Psychology* 56 (1972): 374–86.

Mecham, R. C., and McCormick, E. J. *The Rated Attribute Requirements of Job Elements of the Position Analysis Questionnaire.* Department of Psychological Sciences, Report No. 1. West Lafayette: Purdue University, Occupational Research Center, 1969.

Moore, B. E. *Occupational Analysis for Human Resource Development.* Washington, DC: Department of the Navy, Office of Civilian Manpower Management, 1976.

Primoff, E. S. *How to Prepare and Conduct Job-Element Examinations.* U.S. Civil Service Commission, Technical Study 75–1. Washington, DC: U.S. Government Printing Office, 1975.

Stone, C. H., and Yoder, D. *Job Analysis*. Long Beach: California State College, 1970.

U.S. Civil Service Commission. *Job Analysis: Developing and Documenting Data, A Guide for State and Local Governments*. Washington, DC: U.S. Government Printing Office, 1973.

U.S. Department of Labor. *Dictionary of Occupational Titles*. 4th ed. Washington, DC: U.S. Government Printing Office, 1977.

_____. *Task Analysis Inventories*. Washington, DC: U.S. Government Printing Office, 1973.

Yoder, D., and Heneman, H. G., Jr., eds. *ASPA Handbook of Personnel and Industrial Relations*. Washington, DC: Bureau of National Affairs, Inc., 1979.

For Analysis: The Outside Consultant

A southern manufacturing company employing about four hundred persons has always utilized commonly accepted personnel techniques. Standard operating procedures and job descriptions were first written about twenty years ago. Since then, the personnel department has updated the descriptions and procedures each year. The firm has a compensation system which compares job descriptions, ranks each job, and then assigns a pay grade to each job.

Today, James Magre, company president, is considering whether to hire an outside personnel consultant to review the firm's operation. About two months ago a female employee filed a pay discrimination suit which has not yet come to trial. The firm's attorney and personnel director feel good about the company's defense. However, one statement made by the attorney is bothering Magre. "You cannot rule out the possibility of losing the case. Your personnel system is not that airtight."

A good friend of Magre's has suggested the name of a personnel consultant "who is not cheap, but very competent."

Questions:

1. *If you were James Magre, what additional information would you seek?*
2. *When should Magre take action?*
3. *What criteria should be important in this decision process?*

SELECTED PROFESSIONAL READING

When the Traditional Job Description Is Not Enough

DONALD E. KLINGNER

Most personnel managers agree that job descriptions are an important part of the personnel function. Job descriptions are the basis for many other personnel activities, such as human resource planning, recruitment, and position management. Yet these same personnel managers may also admit to one another that the traditional job description is not related to the most basic need of the organization and its employees: improving productivity.

This dilemma is important because it affects the way personnel managers view their jobs and the way other organizational managers view the personnel function. It can be clarified by answering these questions:

What are the traditional purposes of job analysis and evaluation?

What organizational and employee needs are not met by traditional job analysis and evaluation methods?

What can be done to improve job description and evaluation?

How will this affect managers, employees and personnel managers?

PROBLEMS WITH TRADITIONAL METHODS

Below is an example of a traditional job description. Note that it specifies the organizational unit to which this position is responsible, the general duties performed by the incumbent and the minimum qualifications required for eligibility.

FIGURE 1: *Typical Job Description*

Administrative Assistant
Responsibilities: Works under the direction of the supervisor, operations control section

Duties:
  Types correspondence and reports
  Compiles reports
  Maintains inventory of supplies
  Arranges meetings and conferences for the supervisor
  Handles routine correspondence
  Other duties as assigned

Qualifications:
  High school degree or equivalent
  Type 40 wpm
  Two years' experience in a secretarial position, or equivalent education

---

Condensed from "When the Traditional Job Description Is Not Enough" by Donald E. Klingner. Reprinted with permission *Personnel Journal*, Costa Mesa, CA, April 1979.

This job description is deficient in two respects: it does not specify the performance expected of the employee, and it does not specify the linking or enabling relationship between standards, skills and minimum qualification.

This job description lists the general duties performed by any number of administrative assistants. Because it applies to a range of positions, it is necessarily vague concerning the nature of the typing, reports, meetings, and correspondence involved. The employee may be working in a foundry, a personnel office or a chemical supply house. In each case, specific duties will differ. The last entry, "other duties as assigned," leaves the job description open to any additions the supervisor may propose.

Second, there are no clues provided concerning the conditions under which the job is to be performed. Is an electric typewriter available or not? How large is the filing system, and is it current and accurate? How much correspondence is there to answer? Do all duties occur continuously, or do some require more work at certain times? What guidelines or instructions are available to aid the employee? What working conditions make task performance easier or harder?

Most critically, there are no standards set for minimally acceptable employee performance of each of the job's duties. This omission is basic to the distinction between job evaluation and performance evaluation. The former is the process of evaluating job worth, while the latter is the process of measuring the performance level of an employee in that job. While this distinction is accepted by most personnel managers, most managers and employees feel that in practice it is difficult to separate an abstract "job" from the concrete performance of its incumbent. The above job description does not specify the quantity, quality of timeliness of service required, nor does it set these standards in the light of varying conditions. For example, it may be easier for a salesperson to increase sales 10 percent annually in an industry growing by 20 percent annually. It is more difficult to achieve the same sales increase in a declining market.

Moreover, traditional job descriptions specify a general set of minimum qualifications for each position. If jobs have been classified according to the type of skill required, these minimum qualifications may be based on skills required to perform duties. In general, however, traditional methods blur the following logical sequence of relationships between tasks, standards, skills and qualifications:

- Each job task must be performed at certain minimal standards for the organization to function

- Certain skills, knowledge and abilities enable the employee to perform a task up to standard

- Certain minimum qualifications ensure that the employee will have these skills, knowledge and abilities.

These two problems reduce the usefulness of job descriptions to organizational planners, program managers, and employees.

Organizational planners are handicapped because such traditional job descriptions describe only the personnel inputs into a job and not the resultant outputs. That is, they do not specify how many employees would be needed to produce outputs at a given level of quantity, quality or timeliness. Because traditional job descriptions do not lend themselves to open systems analysis or contingency planning, they do not meet the increasing need to measure program outputs relative to inputs, rather than measuring only inputs. Legislators and executives are less willing to assume, as they may have in the past, that an agency will provide 10 percent more services if it is allocated 10 percent more employees. Output-oriented job descriptions are analogous to program budgets, while traditional job descriptions resemble input-oriented line-item budgets. Clearly, the line-item approach is useful for control purposes, while the program approach is more useful for productivity improvement.

Managers, in their turn, are handicapped

because they cannot readily use such job descriptions for recruitment, orientation, management by objectives (MBO) goal setting or performance evaluation. If new employees are recruited on the basis of the brief description of duties and qualifications given in the traditional job description, then extensive interviewing by managers may be needed to select those applicants most qualified for a particular job. Orientation will require clarification of the job description to fit the particular organizational context, and it may be incomplete because of other demands on the manager's time. If the organization uses MBO goal setting and evaluation procedures, these will occur independently of the position's job description. This means that job descriptions will be used only by the personnel department for human resource planning, recruitment and position management, while managers will control and evaluate employee performance by an unrelated set of MBO procedures. If MBO is not used, then performance evaluation will probably be based on employees' job-related personality traits rather than on outputs.

Employees are generally unable to use traditional job descriptions for orientation, performance improvement or career planning. Because they give only a brief description of duties, employees must wait to learn about working conditions and standards until they have been hired. Yet this may be too late; unclear or inequitable psychological contracts are a cause of much unrest between employees and organizations. Evaluating employees without giving them clear performance expectations is a sure way to increase anxiety and frustration. Lastly, employees cannot use traditional job descriptions for career/life planning, because they do not specify how increases in minimum qualifications are related to increases in skills required for satisfactory task performance. It is easiest for employees to accept the qualifications for a position, and to strive to meet them through upward mobility programs, if these linkages are more apparent.

Personnel managers, and the personnel management function itself, are most seriously affected by the limited usefulness of traditional job descriptions. Because traditional job descriptions are not suited to cataloguing and managing positions, they are regarded as irrelevant to productivity improvement by program planners, managers and employees. Inevitably, they tend to be regarded in the same light as inventories of office equipment or the updating of civil defense plans—something which must be maintained as a bureaucratic necessity, but which is not a useful tool for accomplishing primary organizational or employee goals. This perceived uselessness of job descriptions affects other personnel activities as well. If personnel managers consider job descriptions one of the most important personnel activities, and if job descriptions are in fact useless for managers and employees, it follows logically that other personnel activities are equally unimportant. This logic is frequently used to belittle performance evaluation, job analysis, training demand surveys and other items of the personnel manager's stock in trade.

Therefore, the primary result of these deficiencies in traditional job evaluation is to divorce personnel management from those organizational activities which are concerned with inputs, outputs and environmental relationships—primarily program planning, budgeting, and program evaluation. As a result, personnel management is viewed as a series of low-level, operational techniques which are used mainly for organizational maintenance purposes.

HOW TO IMPROVE JOB DESCRIPTIONS AND EVALUATION

Obviously, job descriptions would be more useful if they clarified the organization's expectations of employees and the linkages between tasks, standards, skills and minimum qualifications. These improved, results-oriented job descriptions (RODs) would contain the following information:

Tasks: What behaviors, duties or functions are important to the employee's job?

Conditions: How often is a task done? What conditions make the task easier or harder to complete? What written or supervisory instructions are available to aid the employee in performing a task?

Standards: What objective performance expectations are attached to each task? These standards of quantity, quality and timeliness should relate meaningfully to organizational objectives.

SKAs: What skills, knowledge and abilities are required to perform each task at the minimally acceptable standard?

Qualifications: What education and/or experience (length, level and type) are needed to ensure that employees will have the necessary SKAs for task performance?

Three examples of results-oriented job descriptions are shown in Figure 2.

These RODs provide clearer organizational expectations to employees. They encourage supervisors and employees to recognize that both standards and rewards can be contingent upon conditions. For example, a secretary can type neater copy more quickly on an electric than on a manual typewriter. In the second example, an increase in the local crime rate might cause a temporary increase in each probation officer's caseload from 60 to 75 clients. If this happens, it could be expected that the quality, length or frequency of weekly visits would be reduced and that the judge would accept fewer than 75 percent of their presentence recommendations. In the third example, standards might vary with the total sales volume of the company, the experience of the salesperson or market conditions.

SKAs are tied to task performance, and minimum qualifications are related to them using content or face validation methods. As performance standards vary, it is probable that SKAs would vary in corresponding fashion as would minimum qualifications. For example, a probation officer handling more difficult cases and

working without direct supervision would need more skill in counseling probationers and writing presentence investigation reports. This would probably require more experience, more related education or a more successful counseling record.

HOW DO RODS AFFECT ORGANIZATIONS?

Results-oriented job descriptions focus on performance standards, the conditions that differentiate jobs and the linkages between standards, SKAs and qualifications. In so doing, they resolve many of the problems attributed to traditional job descriptions:

● They give the program planner a means of relating personnel inputs to organizational outputs

● They give managers a means of orienting new employees to performance expectations, setting MBO goals and evaluating employee performance objectively

● They give employees a clearer idea of organizational performance improvement expectations and of the minimum qualifications for promotion or reassignment

● They increase the impact of personnel managers on organization and employee productivity, rather than merely on position management and control.

While they are useful for these purposes, RODs appear to have some serious disadvantages: 1) changes in conditions and standards require constant rewriting of RODs, 2) each position requires a different ROD, 3) some positions do not have measurable performance standards and 4) RODs cannot be used to classify jobs for human resources planning purposes or to evaluate them for pay comparability purposes.

First, it is inevitable that conditions affecting task performance will change. Won't this require that RODs be rewritten frequently to specify these changed conditions and standards, thereby causing an unmanageable paperwork load for supervisors and the person-

FIGURE 2: *Results-oriented Descriptions*

Typist/Receptionist

Tasks	Conditions	Standards
Type letters	When asked to by supervisor; using an IBM Selectric typewriter; according to the office style manual	All letters error-free; completed by 5 p.m. if assigned before 3 p.m.
Greet visitors	As they arrive, referring them to five executives with whom they have appointments	No complaints from visitors referred to the wrong office, or waiting before being referred

Skills, knowledge and abilities required:

Ability to type 40 wpm

Ability to use Selectric typewriter

Knowledge of office style manual

Courtesy

Minimum qualifications:

High school diploma or equivalent

Six months' experience as a typist, or an equivalent performance test

Juvenile Probation Officer

Tasks	Conditions	Standards
Meet with probationers weekly to assess their current behavior	Caseload of not more than 60 appointments scheduled by receptionist; supervisor will help with difficult cases; use procedures stated in rules and regulations	All probationers must be seen weekly; those showing evidence of continued criminal activity or lack of a job will be reported to supervisor
Prepare presence reports on clients	When requested by the judge; average of 5 per week, per instructions issued by judge; supervisor will review and approve	Reports will be complete and accurate as determined by the judge, who will accept 75% of pre-sentence recommendations

Skills, knowledge and abilities required:

Knowledge of the factors contributing to criminal behavior

Ability to counsel probationers

Ability to write clear and concise probation reports

Knowledge of judge's sentencing habits for particular types of offenders and offenses

Knowledge of law concerning probation

Minimum qualifications:

High school diploma or equivalent; plus four years' experience working with juvenile offenders, or a B.S. degree in criminal justice, psychology, or counseling

Able to pass a multiple choice test on relevant probation law

Possess a valid driver's license

Salesperson

Tasks	Conditions	Standards
Sell plumbing fixtures	Over an 11-state area; to hardware retailers	Annual sales of $250,000
Retain current customers	375 existing customers	95% of current customers reorder each year

Skills, knowledge and abilities required:

Knowledge of plumbing fixtures

Knowledge of contractors and purchasers

Ability to sell

Ability to work independently

Minimum qualifications:

High school diploma or equivalent

Two years' experience selling plumbing fixtures

Proven sales record (equivalent territory and sales volume)

nel department? On the other hand, most communication between employees and supervisors concerns unforeseen changes in organizational goals, employee tasks, environmental conditions and performance standards. Integrating RODs into the organizational planning and evaluation system does mean an increase in time spent on writing job descriptions, but it may not mean an increase in time spent on organizational communications. What will occur, in fact, is a new focus of communications on those changes in goals or conditions which affect employee performance standards. Moreover, most organizations do not change objectives frequently. The use of a new job description method will not in itself increase the rate of organizational change.

Second, much of the previous analysis has emphasized that different positions within a job will have different conditions and standards. Won't this lead to a proliferation of different position descriptions for similar positions? The answer to this question depends on the position. It will not do so where groups of employees perform similar tasks under similar conditions. It will where they do not. For example, a group of claims examiners who were assigned clients on a random basis, using identical methods and equipment and having equal experience, could be expected to evaluate claims according to the same standard. But if employees worked in different locations, had different tasks and used different equipment, then their standards would differ. While some increase in the number of position descriptions would occur under RODs, there would not be a separate description for each position.

Third, many supervisors and job analysts consider it difficult to establish individual performance expectations where groups of employees must work closely together. There are two possible responses to this problem: 1) to establish (as part of the conditions statements attached to a task) the nature and extent of mutual expectations which one position's successful task completion requires of others or 2) to develop work group performance expectations which assume that mutual interdependencies exist. The first solution, while cumbersome to develop or revise, may be useful in clarifying the key points on which work group members need to build communications and trust. The second solution, while it ignores interdependencies explicitly, is more often more useful in group incentive situations (project teams), where it is difficult to evaluate the relative effectiveness of individual members' contributions in the absence of a completed product or service.

The last objection is the most serious from the personnel manager's viewpoint. Job descriptions are used not only to clarify expectations for each position, but also to classify jobs for human resource planning purposes and to evaluate them for pay comparability purposes. How could these vital functions be accomplished using RODs? The answer is to continue using those aspects of traditional job analysis that are necessary for these purposes. Personnel managers could continue to group jobs into occupational classes based on the type of work performed. Traditional job evaluation methods could then be used to determine the pay ranges appropriate to each position, and employee performance relative to objectives specified in the ROD would be used to "fine-tune" the system within pay ranges. This would give managers some other basis besides seniority for awarding or withholding within-grade increases, and would also resolve the conflict over the relative importance of job evaluation and performance evaluation in setting pay.

By correlating skills, knowledge and abilities to tasks and validating minimum qualifications as enablers to task performance, linkages could be established between positions to aid in career/life planning, promotion assessment and upward mobility. Here again, the relationship between RODs and traditional evaluation methods would be complementary. Traditional methods would show an organization's job structure, and clusters of RODs (grouped by occupation) would show how increasing qualifications were related to SKAs and SKAs to task performance.

Adopting RODs means that organizations will use two types of job descriptions—traditional and performance-oriented. There is a justifiable tendency to reject proposed solutions that are more complicated than current techniques. However, this tendency also reflects a desire to return to an era when personnel management techniques were simpler and more uniform than they are today. Yet our experience usually shows that diverse techniques are necessary. Most authorities recommend different performance evaluation methods for different purposes (i.e., performance improvement or reward allocation). They also recommend a variety of selection methods such as performance tests, biodata review or probationary appointments, for different types of positions. Because job analysis and evaluation are used for several different purposes—performance improvement chief among them—we need to accept the use of different methods.

The Western Electric assembly line requires workers with highly-specialized skills.

4

JOB DESIGN AND ALTERNATE WORK SCHEDULES

Job Specialization

Job Design and Motivation

Modern Job Design

Compressed Workweeks

Discretionary Workweeks

The Problem: Well Paid or Challenged?

*Riding home on the bus, Mary Anne Kozak sat next to a
former high school classmate, Susan Franz. The two friends
discussed classmates, family, and eventually the discussion
turned to jobs:*

    Kozak: "Why haven't I seen you on this bus before?"

    Franz: "This is my first day on the 8 to 5 shift; I work at
            Banes Engines."

    Kozak: "Yeah? What do you do there?"

    Franz: "I test starters for engines. It's really dull, but I
            make over eight dollars an hour."

    Kozak: "Wow! That's great. Wish I made that much."

    Franz: "Why? Where do you work?"

    Kozak: "Oh, I work at Ryan's Pet Store."

    Franz: "Cashier?"

    Kozak: "Yeah, and I take care of the pets and keep the
            books. I really like it. We get a lot of kids in the
            store, and I really like pets. Mr. Ryan is really
            super, too."

    Franz: "I'd really like that; I've always enjoyed animals,
            and Ryan's seems like a friendly place whenever I've
            been in there."

    Kozak: "You wouldn't like it. You're making twice as much
            money as I am, and you probably even get
            benefits."

    Franz: "Yeah, four weeks paid vacation, and the company
            pays our Blue Cross/Blue Shield and reimburses
            tuition. But I really dread going in to work. All I
            see is ninety-six starters every day. I don't even

*have time to talk to anyone except at lunch. If I
didn't need the money so bad, I'd look for a job
like yours."*

What employees actually do on the job, the design of their work, has great impact on their satisfaction, productivity, and many other factors. In the past, it seemed as though most jobs were designed for idiots; they included simple, repetitive, and dull tasks. Today's more educated and creative workers demand interesting, challenging jobs. These same workers are questioning why jobs must be scheduled nine to five, forty hours per week. Alternatives to nine to five work schedules such as flextime and four–day work-weeks, lower overtime costs and result in less absenteeism and tardiness.

DESIGNING JOBS

One of the most important concerns of personnel managers in the past several years has been employee productivity and satisfaction. Personnel officers have realized that a critical factor affecting these areas is the type of work performed by the employee. Job design determines what work is done and, therefore, greatly affects how an employee feels about a job, how much authority an employee has over the work, how much decision making the employee has on the job, and how many tasks the employee has to complete. Managers realize that job design determines their working relationship with their employees and the relationship among employees themselves. Job design

determines if social relationships exist on the job, as well as the relationship between the employee and the work.

Job design is defined as the content, functions, and relationships of jobs directed toward the accomplishment of organizational purposes and satisfaction of the personal needs of individual job holders.[1] The content of the job includes several aspects: 1) variety of tasks performed; 2) autonomy over one's own work; 3) routineness of tasks performed; 4) difficulty level of the duties performed; 5) task identity or the extent to which the whole job is performed by the person involved.[2] The functions of the job include the work methods utilized, and the coordination of the work, responsibility, and authority of the job. The relationships of the job refers to work activities shared by the job holder and other individuals in the organization.[3]

Figure 4–1 demonstrates that total job design is of great importance to both the individual and the organization. The design of the job determines how and to what extent tasks are accomplished by the job holder. Therefore, the worker's satisfaction with the job situation—that is, the work itself—is at stake. The workers'

1. John Ivancevich, Andrew Szilagyi, and Marc Wallace, Jr., *Organizational Behavior and Performance* (Santa Monica, CA: Goodyear, Inc., 1977), pp. 141–42.
2. Ibid., p. 141.
3. Ibid., p. 142.

FIGURE 4–1: *A Framework for Job Design*

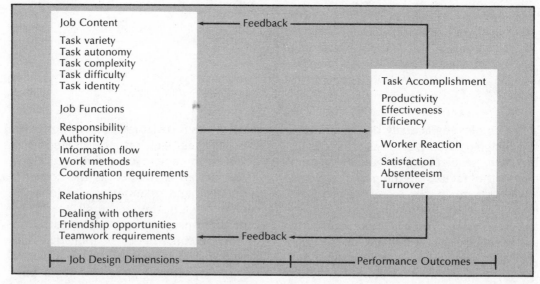

From *Organizational Behavior and Performance,* 2nd Edition by Andrew D. Szilagyi and Marc J. Wallace (p. 149) Copyright © 1980 by Goodyear Publishing Company. Reprinted by permission.

favorable reaction to job design means greater accomplishment and job satisfaction, less absenteeism, fewer grievances, and less frequent turnover.

How should jobs be designed? While this question has been discussed widely since the Industrial Revolution, traditional approaches to job design have been seriously questioned in recent years. Some job design problems in the last twenty-five years have been caused by workers who are increasingly dissatisfied with jobs designed for robots or mindless machines. Henry Ford described his assembly line process as "a haven for those who haven't got the brains to do anything else." Ford's assembly line is an excellent example of the job design method known as job specialization.

Job Specialization

Job specialization is characterized by jobs

designed with very few tasks which are repeated often during the work day, and require few skills and little mental ability on the part of the workers. Job specialization was the primary component of the scientific management approach developed by Frederick Taylor who described management's role in job design as a three-step process:[4]

Step 1: The manager determines the "one best way of performing the job."

Step 2: The manager hires individuals according to their particular abilities which match the particular needs of the job design. The emphasis here would be to hire a stronger man for carrying heavy loads, an intelligent work-

---

4. F. W. Taylor, *The Principles of Scientific Management* (New York: Harper and Row, 1947).

er for the bookkeeping jobs, etc.

Step 3: Management trains workers in the one best way the job should be performed. Management decides how the job should be done. All planning, organizing, and controling of the job is done by the manager.

Scientific management, which has been quite popular in this country for years, has many advantages. First, the owner/manager can hire unskilled labor for almost all operative jobs in the organization. Since highly specialized jobs are designed for people with very little ability or experience, most members of the total work force can perform a great percentage of the lower level jobs in a company. The second advantage is that unskilled workers are among the lowest paid members of the work force. This was particularly true in the early 1900s when unskilled labor was moving from the agricultural to the industrialized sector of society and few unions protected unskilled workers.

A third advantage is that workers tend to make very few errors or mistakes on simple, routine jobs. There are also very few chances for mental errors since managers organize the work flow so that the employee makes few decisions. A fourth advantage of the highly specialized jobs is that the average cost per unit decreases as jobs become highly specialized. As Henry Ford discovered, it is far more cost efficient to build cars on an assembly line where workers are trained to perform one or two simple, routine tasks, than to hire engineers or mechanics who could assemble a complete automobile. This principle of reduced average cost per labor dollar spent has long motivated managers who designed highly specialized jobs.

JOB DIMENSIONS

The degree to which a job is highly specialized can be determined by measuring two dimensions of the job: the first dimension is the *scope*—how long it takes a worker to complete the total task. For example, an assembly line worker for Henry Ford might have taken five minutes to add a wiring harness to an automobile as it moved down the assembly line. After the wiring harness was added to one automobile, the next car moved down the line and the worker had five minutes to add a harness to that car. Thus, the scope of the job, or the job cycle, was five minutes.

The second dimension measuring specialization is the *depth* of the job. This dimension is more difficult to determine because it cannot be measured in easily identifiable terms. The depth of the job refers to how much planning, decision making, and controling the worker does in the total job. For example, to what extent can a worker vary the methods utilized on the job? How many decisions can the worker make without supervisory approval? If various techniques and tools are determined solely by management, then the job is said to be very shallow or have very little depth. At the other end of the continuum, a job in which a worker performs almost completely independently contains great depth, or a great deal of autonomy.

A worker's *relative ability* is the amount of general ability which can be utilized on the job. Unskilled jobs can be filled successfully by more people since their general abilities can be utilized. Figure 4–2 illustrates that a highly specialized job has a very short *job cycle* with very little

FIGURE 4–2: *Job Specialization Effect on Workers' Abilities*

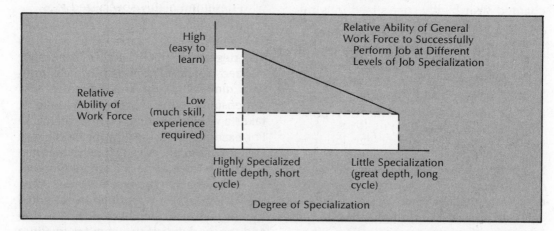

depth, and that as jobs became less specialized fewer persons have the ability, experience, or knowledge required to perform them.

SPECIALIZATION PROBLEMS

Why, then, is job specialization not regarded as the primary means of designing jobs? Probably the most comprehensive answer to this question was given by Walker and Guest's mid-1950s study, titled *The Man on the Assembly Line*. They found that the automobile industry was probably the epitome of job specialization in this country. Walker and Guest heard several complaints from employees about their highly specialized jobs:[5]

REPETITION Employees performed a few tasks which had to be repeated many times a day. This quickly led the employee to become very bored with the job. There was no challenge to the employee to learn anything new or to improve the job.

MECHANICAL PACING Employees were restricted by the assembly line which made

them maintain a certain regular pace of work. That is, employees could not take a break when they needed to, or simply divert their attention to some other aspect of the job or another individual. Instead, their constant attention and effort had to be maintained at a certain speed which is often too fast for some employees, too slow for others.

NO END PRODUCT Employees found that they were not producing any identifiable end product; consequently, they had little pride and enthusiasm in their work.

LITTLE SOCIAL INTERACTION Employees complained that because the assembly line required constant attention, there was little chance to interact on a casual basis with other employees. This made it difficult for employees to develop any type of social relationship with other employees.

NO INPUT Employees complained that they had little chance to choose the methods by which they performed their jobs, the tools which they used, or the work procedures. This, of course, created little interest in the job because there was nothing which they could improve or change.

---

5. C. R. Walker and R. H. Guest, *The Man on the Assembly Line* (Cambridge, MA: Harvard University Press, 1952).

Why had employees become disenchanted with highly specialized jobs following World War II when they were happy to perform these jobs in prior years? While there is no certain answer, several events following the war changed employees' job outlooks:

● Prior to World War II employees often were faced with a very lean job market. They often realized that any job which would allow them to maintain a reasonable standard of living had to be a good job because jobs were scarce. On the other hand, employees found when there were several jobs available, they no longer had to be satisfied with a boring, unchallenging job.

● The general pay scales offered by firms had increased substantially from the early 1900s to the 1950s and had created a true middle class. This enabled employees to choose jobs for reasons other than simply income. While pay was still primary, other factors such as the challenge, autonomy, nature, and working conditions of the job were also weighed when comparing jobs.

● The education level of employees had risen quickly in the post-World War II period, and that level has continued to rise every year since. A much larger proportion of the total work force in our society is educated beyond the elementary levels which were average for the industrial employee in the last century. Often a more highly educated employee expects a challenging and rewarding career and is not happy with a boring job which requires little mental effort or ability.

● The increase in service jobs also was a contributing factor to the employee disenchantment with specialized jobs. From the 1920s to the 1960s more jobs were available in service producing organizations such as hospitals, educational institutions, the hotel-motel–restaurant industry, professional jobs, etc. While many service jobs are highly specialized, the proportion in service industries is usually less than in the manufacturing industry. Also, the jobs which were not specialized increased during those years; employees had the opportunity of obtaining nonspecialized jobs which were more interesting and challenging to them.

The Walker and Guest study outlined a problem of the 1950s and 1960s which is still a problem today. Industrial engineers developed a job design approach which emphasized human engineering, often referred to as ergonomics, which treated the worker as part of the production function. The worker was to be trained to perform a specifically defined task, which required no decision making.

Job Design and Motivation

The second major job design approach emphasizes the human factors involved in jobs. This human relations approach recognizes the need to design jobs which are interesting and rewarding. Unmotivated employees have low levels of productivity, low interest in the quality of their products or services, high levels of absenteeism and grievances, and are apt to leave the organization whenever a better alternative is presented to them. Today, management has found that the increased

FIGURE 4–3: *Advantages of Major Job Design Approaches*

Specialization Intense Jobs	*Motivation Intense Jobs*
High productivity of unskilled workers	High productivity of challenged workers
Less training time required	Less absenteeism
Easy to replace workers	Less turnover
Few mental work errors	Higher product quality
Greater manager control of operations	More employee ideas, suggestions
	Greater employee job satisfaction

cost of employee absenteeism, turnover, and decreased productivity, may outweigh the advantages of highly-specialized jobs. The problem is to balance the motivation and specialization aspects of each job. Thus, job performance is determined by the employee's motivation and relative ability to perform the job.[6] Employees' jobs must necessitate high levels of ability and motivation so that they can give high level performances.[7]

Designing jobs interesting enough to motivate employees, yet simple enough so that most members of the work force have the ability to perform them efficiently is quite a task. Personnel managers and industrial engineers today attempt to design motivating jobs which have high levels of specialization. The usual result is that jobs which are specialized have motivation factors provided by other means. Often the other means must be created by the personnel office in the form of social functions, sports programs, or contests for employees. Such techniques do not replace the motivation employees lose when assigned to highly specialized jobs.

DESIGN PROBLEM SOLUTIONS

Since the Walker and Guest study, organizations throughout the world have been grappling with the problem of job design.[8] The primary choice is usually a motivated work force or high productivity achieved through highly specialized jobs. Employee productivity is the criterion the firm usually considers most important when designing jobs. The advantages of jobs designed to be highly motivating are apparent; however, it is often harder to measure the dollar value of lower absenteeism or higher quality.

Productivity is defined as the ratio of some measurable unit of output to some unit of input.[9] To evaluate productivity, an organization must measure two variables: output produced by an employee and the input given by the employee. Productivity is a measure of efficiency, or the amount of work employees accomplish during each workday. A familiar productivity measure is miles per gallon; how many miles an automobile can be driven for each gallon of gasoline it uses is a measure of that automobile's productivity.[10] When measuring productivity, the de-

---

6. Ernest J. McCormick, *Job Analysis: Methods and Applications* (New York: AMACOM, 1970), pp. 273–74.

7. James L. Gibson, John M. Ivancevich, and James H. Donnelly, Jr., *Organizations* (Dallas: Business Publications, Inc., 1979), p. 282.

8. Walker and Guest, *The Man on the Assembly Line.*

9. Mitchell S. Novit, *Essentials of Personnel Management* (Englewood Cliffs, NJ: Prentice-Hall, Inc., 1979), p. 178.

10. Ibid., pp. 178–79.

nominator is usually the number of hours worked. The numerator changes according to the work being accomplished; it is the unit by which employees' production is measured: the units produced per hour, the customers served per day, or the clients contacted per week. In measuring plant output, labor-hour equivalents should be used in measuring productivity. Products should be expressed in terms of the hours required to produce them. This is preferred to using dollar measures which change quickly as costs and inflation change their values.[11]

Often managers rely on productivity measures to indicate the efficiency of their departments. Supervisors interested in direct productivity of employees may disregard other indices which increase unit cost such as absenteeism, turnover, or product quality. Thus, the advantages of highly specialized jobs are overemphasized when only the direct productivity of specialization is measured. In recent years, however, managers have begun to include the indirect costs of job specialization in productivity estimates.

How much does turnover cost an organization? Administrators have only begun to accurately measure the cost of turnover. One late seventies cost estimate for a firm losing a college graduate who was on the job for two years was $2,000 or more.[12] Absenteeism costs have been measured more frequently in recent years as it is easier to directly measure absenteeism costs than the costs of turnover, loyalty, or tenure.

During the 1950s and 1960s, personnel managers began realizing that highly specialized jobs were greatly increasing total personnel costs.[13] Therefore, alternative solutions to the problems of job specialization were explored. Many of the first programs designed to ease the boredom of specialized jobs are still in existence. Some of the techniques considered highly effective by many organizations, are considered ineffective by other organizations, and partially effective by still other organizations. There is no easy solution to the problem of motivating employees with highly specialized jobs. Nor is there any way to design jobs which will be highly motivating and maintain maximum levels of productivity.

PAY INCREASES One of the most common techniques to solve a lack of employee motivation is a round of pay increases. Managers and personnel officials have turned to the pay increase as a solution to many problems for decades. The pay increase gives an employee a greater sense of worth, more take-home pay, and more reason to stay with the organization in a job which may be boring or unchallenging.

How successful is the pay increase at solving motivational problems? The answer expressed by most personnel officers and managers is "not very." A good example of why pay increases do not solve employees' problems was demonstrated by the experience of a midwestern manufacturing firm. During the last ten years, the firm's absentee levels were close to 20 percent. Management decided that a major pay increase would make employees feel that their work was highly valued and they would decrease absenteeism, which was the organization's

11. Leon Greenberg, *A Practical Guide to Productivity Measurement* (Washington, DC: Bureau of National Affairs, Inc., 1973).

12. Robert Sutermeister, *People and Productivity* (New York: McGraw-Hill, 1979), pp. 57–68.

13. Ibid.

greatest problem. The absenteeism level dropped the first six months after the pay raise. However, one year later it was higher than ever before. Why such a reaction? Possibly because once they reach comfortable income levels, today's employees value their leisure time much more than their fathers and grandfathers did. With a higher wage scale employees can work fewer hours to maintain the same level of income! After a few months of working regularly for increased wages employees realized that even though they are faced with the same routine job, now they could work fewer hours to maintain the same life–style. Therefore, the employee in a highly specialized, unchallenging job, weighs the increased income which can be earned by fewer absences against the lack of opportunity to get away from the job.

JOB ROTATION Another technique designed to enhance employee motivation is *job rotation*, or periodically assigning employees to alternating jobs or tasks. For example, an employee may spend two weeks attaching bumpers to vehicles and the following two weeks making final checks of the chassis. During the next month the same employee may be assigned to two different jobs. Therefore, the employee would be rotated among four different jobs. The advantage of job rotation is that employees do not have the same routine job day after day. Instead, they are only placed on the same exact job for short periods.

Does job rotation solve the problem of boringly repetitious jobs? No, job rotation only addresses the problem of employees being assigned to jobs of limited scope; the depth of job does not change. The job cycle of the actual daily work performed has not been lengthened or changed in any manner. Instead, employees are simply assigned to different jobs with different cycles.

In practice, because job rotation does not change the basic nature of the jobs, it is criticized as nothing more than having an employee perform several boring and monotonous jobs rather than being assigned to the same one.[14] Some employees dislike job rotation more than being assigned to one boring job. They state that at least when they are assigned to one job they know exactly where to report and what work to expect each day. Workers quickly realize that job rotation is not increasing their interest in their work.

Why then is job rotation still in common practice? While job rotation seldom addresses the lack of employee motivation, it does give managers a means of coping with frequent absenteeism and turnover. Thus, when absenteeism or turnover occurs in the work force, managers can quickly fill the vacated position because each employee can perform several jobs.

Job rotation is often effectively used as a training technique for the new, inexperienced employees.[15] Rotation also helps develop managerial generalists because it exposes them to several different operations.[16]

JOB ENLARGEMENT A third potential means of increasing employees' satisfaction with routine jobs is *job enlargement*, or increasing the tasks performed—the scope of the job. Job enlargement, like

---

14. Gibson, Ivancevich, Donnelly, *Organizations*, p. 285.

15. Paul Greenlaw and William Biggs, *Modern Personnel Management* (Philadelphia: W. B. Saunders, 1979), pp. 273–75.

16. Ibid.

job rotation, tries to eliminate short job cycles which create boredom. Unlike job rotation, job enlargement actually increases the job cycle. When a job is enlarged, the tasks being performed are either enlarged or several short tasks are given to one worker. Thus, the scope of the job is increased because there are many tasks to be performed by the same worker. Job enlargement programs change many methods of operation in contrast to job rotation where the same exact work procedures are used by different people who rotate between work stations. Although it actually changes the pace of the work and the operation by reallocating tasks and responsibilities, job enlargement does not increase the depth of a job.

The focus of designing work for job enlargement is the exact opposite of that for job specialization. Instead of designing jobs to be divided up into the fewest number of tasks per employee, a job could be designed to have many tasks for the employee to perform. An enlarged job requires a longer training period because there are more tasks to be learned. Worker satisfaction should increase because boredom is reduced as the job scope is expanded.[17] Job enlargement programs are successful only if workers are more satisfied with jobs which have a longer scope; if so, they are less prone to resort to absenteeism, grievances, slowdowns, and other means of displaying job dissatisfaction.

An early job enlargement program at Maytag Company is a good example of this job design approach. Maytag undertook fifteen job enlargement projects during a three-year period. At the conclusion,

Maytag managers observed:[18]

- Quality of production was improved.
- Production costs were lower.
- Employees reported higher job satisfaction. They especially preferred the slower work pace which resulted from an enlarged job that did not have as repetitious a cycle and required a greater variety of skills.
- The company also benefited by greater efficiency stemming from reduced materials handling and a greater stability of production standards being met.

While job enlargement is still considered a valid means of addressing specialization problems, it has been augmented by a more sophisticated technique known as job enrichment. Most modern management redesign projects are termed job enrichment, therefore, rather than job enlargement. However, the two concepts have distinctly different definitions and applications.

JOB ENRICHMENT Commonly, *job enrichment* refers to a program which is designed to increase worker satisfaction derived from the work itself. Job enrichment changes the nature of the work to increase the scope and depth of a job. In a job enrichment program the worker decides how the job is performed, planned, and controlled, and makes more decisions concerning the entire process. The job enrichment approach to boring jobs is to give the individual employee more autonomy in that job. Employees decide

17. Gibson, Ivancevich, Donnelly, *Organizations*, p. 285.

18. M. D. Kilbridge, "Reduced Costs through Enlargement: A Case," *Journal of Business* (October 1969): 357–62.

how the job will be performed and receive less direct supervision on the job. As a result, the employee receives a greater sense of accomplishment as well as more authority and responsibility.

Job enrichment programs are usually quite comprehensive; by their nature they must involve large portions of the total work force in an organization. When one job is enriched, typically the previous functions of supervisors and other employees are altered to allow for the increased responsibility of the enriched job. Therefore, enrichment programs usually require a great deal of planning by top level management, retraining of employees, and implementation by managers who give up some of their authority and responsibility.

Job enrichment programs often require a substantial change in the individual manager's leadership style and personal philosophy of management. Managers who have developed tight control over the operations within their areas must allow workers to make more decisions. A critical aspect of a successful job enrichment program, therefore, is the ability of top level managers to convince supervisors and lower managers that the job enrichment program is in the best interest of the company, and that their employees are able to take on increased responsibility and authority.[19]

Union Response to Job Enrichment. Labor leaders have been particularly skeptical of job enrichment programs in recent years; typical responses ranged from mild skepticism to total opposition. Such negative feelings are not completely unjustified. In the past, unfortunately, managers have introduced programs under the guise of "job enrichment" which increased work standards for employees, or decreased jobs by increasing the work each employee performed. Since most job enrichment programs result in employees taking on additional responsibilities, determining whether a program will result in increased job autonomy or simply increased work loads is difficult. A premier labor leader stated what many of his colleagues believe:[20]

> . . . studies tend to prove that workers' dissatisfaction diminishes with age. That's because older workers have accrued more of the kinds of job enrichment that unions have fought for—better wages, shorter hours, vested pensions, a right to have a say in the working conditions, a right to be promoted on the basis of seniority and all the rest. That's the kind of enrichment that unions believe in.[21]

Employees of nonunionized firms may also have good reasons to distrust job enrichment programs. Too often, when such a program is begun, supervisors begin to use it as a whip for increasing employee work loads while making only token changes in actual responsibility and authority. Thus the actual depth of the job is barely increased while employees find themselves working harder—possibly too busy to notice or complain about their increased work loads. Fortunately, job enrichment programs can be quite successful. In fact, job enrichment may include the best and the worst of the programs designed to increase worker satisfaction.

AUTONOMOUS WORK GROUPS Job enrichment may involve *autonomous work*

---

19. Novit, *Essentials of Personnel Management,* p. 183.

20. William W. Winpisinger, "Job Satisfaction," *AFL-CIO American Federationist* 80, no. 2 (1973): 9–10.

21. Ibid.

groups; this managerial technique has been successful in recent years. Generally, when an autonomous work group is created, the group manages itself and controls the planning and decision making within the group. Members may elect their own leader or decide not to have a leader but to make decisions jointly. Typically the group sets its own work schedules and even sets its own quantity and quality output levels.[22]

An early example of the autonomous work group is Sony Corporation in Japan which first utilized work groups in the production of television sets. In the Sony experiment, rather than assembling television sets on a traditional assembly line, Sony tried autonomous work groups which selected their own leaders, set their own hours of work, and determined their own standards of efficiency and discipline. Each group was required to produce a certain number of completed units each week, and was responsible for its error rate; the cost of deficient units was deducted from the group's paychecks. Sony's experiment was quite successful in increasing quality and productivity as well as reducing employee absenteeism and other common morale problems.

WORK SIMPLIFICATION Work simplification is the process of designing routine tasks so that employee-controlled machines can perform them. Twenty-five years ago, *work simplification* would have been referred to as automation; however, today this term has acquired negative connotations. Employees see automation as either a means of doing away with their jobs, or of making them slaves to expen-

sive, complex machinery. While the same is true of work simplification, this term is accepted by unions and employees. Because it frees them from boring tasks, employees and their bargaining officials find work simplification desirable.

The concept of work simplification can be traced to Taylor's scientific management approach and time and motion studies. The basic approach is one of structuring jobs to remove less demanding tasks which can be performed by machines. For example, the objective of a work simplification approach is to make jobs more productive and meaningful by eliminating duplicate tasks that are not really necessary or challenging to human beings.[23]

Work simplification, like job rotation programs, is often combined with other job design methods. An example of this occurred at Cummins Engine Company in Columbus, Indiana, where work simplification was combined with job enrichment to increase employees' productivity, decision making, and morale. At Cummins, employees developed new work methods to eliminate repetitive tasks and unnecessary handling of parts. In addition, employees were given the authority to determine rates of production. During this process a team consisting of a supervisor and five employees was able to reduce the fabrication cost of an item from $6 to $4 simply by redesigning the work and simplifying it.[24]

Modern Job Design

In management today, the problem of designing jobs which are both motivating and specialized is a common one. When

---

22. Richard Woodman and John Sherwood, "A Comprehensive Look at Job Design," *Personnel Journal* (August 1977): 384–86.

23. Ibid., p. 386.
24. Ibid.

implementing a program designed to increase the motivation and productivity of employees, management should consider the following:

- Is the problem one which can be addressed by enlarging the scope of most employees' jobs? Often jobs traditionally designed to be very routine and dull can, in fact, be improved simply by giving employees more and varied tasks to perform. Job rotation and job enlargement usually require minimal management, planning, and cost. More complete programs increase not only the scope of the job, but more importantly, the depth to make the job more motivating to employees. These are usually more expensive to develop and implement. Job enrichment, autonomous work groups, and work simplification which may involve greater cost and time, often reap greater returns.

- Any job design program should have two objectives: an increase in the general morale of employees which will bring greater productivity and lower costs to the organization, and an increase in employee job satisfaction because jobs are more interesting and challenging. Top management's and employees' program objectives must be given equal weight because both must cooperate completely if such a program is to succeed.

- Employees satisfy different needs on their jobs. Any job designer must consider that not all employees want increased responsibility and authority or an increased scope. A certain portion of the work force prefers specialized jobs so that they can easily learn their jobs, become proficient, and not worry about their security because they know they can be productive employees in the future. These employees often find personal achievement and growth outside the organization and do not seek high levels of autonomy and achievement through their jobs.

- Before considering a job design program, an organization should carefully investigate the exact causes of employee problems. The design of the work may not be at the heart of employee problems; it may be caused by poor supervision, lack of advancement, poor working conditions, or low pay.

- Finally, when embarking upon a job design program, management should tap its greatest source of ideas and knowledge: its employees. This was exemplified by Sony, Cummins Engine, and Maytag.

ALTERNATE WORK SCHEDULES

For decades, managers and union representatives have ignored work scheduling alternatives. The major trend from the early 1900s until recent years was a slow and quiet evolution toward a shorter workweek. This trend was accompanied by an increase in the general standards of living of employees with increased interest in leisure time activities.[25] After the Fair Labor Standards Act of 1938, Ameri-

25. John W. Newstrom and Jon L. Pierce, "Alternative Work Schedules: The State of the Art," *The Personnel Administrator* (October 1979): 19.

can workers defined the standard work week as eight hours a day for five days a week, or 5/40.

A problem of job design often called the "quality of work life" accelerated from the 1950s to the present. During this time, workers often enjoyed a higher standard of living, which enabled them to have more income to enjoy their increased leisure time; with increased employment opportunities they had a wider selection of jobs to choose from which could provide them with decent standards of living. Therefore, workers began looking for alternatives to the jobs which they were not satisfied with, whereas in previous decades they had been happy simply to have a job. Managers tried many alternative solutions to the problem of jobs that by design were routine and boring. Some systems helped, some completely cured the problem, but in many cases, everyone had to admit that some jobs were simply more productive when highly specialized. In recent years, a new approach to job boredom has been taken by organiza-

tions. This approach does not change the nature of the work; instead, the worker is given an alternative work schedule. With alternate work schedules, the actual work does not change, but the change in work scheduling provides motivational benefits. Common forms of alternate work schedules include the four-day workweek, flextime, and part-time work.

Compressed Workweeks

Compressed workweeks are work schedules with fewer than five workdays a week; the hours worked per day are increased so that the hours worked per week still total forty. The most common compressed workweek is the four-day workweek. Perhaps the oldest alternate work schedule, the four-day week has been discussed and tried in organizations for a number of years. Managers of large manufacturing organizations report substantial savings by reducing start-up time and increasing energy conservation as well as the savings typically gained from

FIGURE 4–4: *Topology of Work Schedule Alternatives*

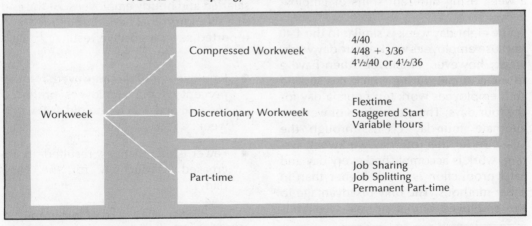

SOURCE: Adapted from J. W. Newstrom and J. L. Pierce, "Alternative Work Schedules: The State of the Art." Reprinted with permission from the October 1979 issue of the *Personnel Administrator* copyright, 1979, The American Society for Personnel Administration, 30 Park Drive, Berea, Ohio 44017.

increased employee morale, where the four-day week is utilized.

4/40

The usual *four-day workweek* is four ten–hour days. Sixty percent of all compressed workweeks fall into the 4/40 category. In practice, some of the forty-hour work-weeks have actually become four nine–hour work periods as employees trade off coffee breaks and clean up time for extra hours off. With this scheme, managers believe they are getting as much work accomplished in four nine-hour days as they might in a 5/40 workweek because they save start-up time and maintenance which is often scheduled for the fifth day of work.[26]

With the 4/40 workweek, administrators primarily use one of two approaches: First, the company operates only four days a week, thus for three days each week there are no energy or start-up costs, and maintenance can be accomplished. In the second approach employees only work four days per week, but the organization actually operates seven days a week using different shifts of employees.

The eight-day week is similar to the 4/40 because employees work a four-day work-week; however, employees then have a four-day break during which the second shift employees work ten hours a day for the four days. Thus, two shifts of workers alternate four-day cycles through the year. Under this four-day workweek system, work is accomplished every day and total production is much higher than in other methods. The only disadvantage to the employee is that normal weekends and holidays must often be worked during the four-day work shift.[27]

4/48 AND 3/36

An alternative to the 4/40 compressed workweek is a week which rotates four–day shifts and three-day shifts. In this technique, employees who work four twelve-hour days are off three days. Then they work three twelve-hour days, followed by a four-day layoff. Employees then work forty-eight hours one week and thirty-six hours every other week. For forty-eight-hour weeks they automatically receive eight hours of overtime pay. This compressed workweek system requires two crews of employees for each shift. One crew will work from 9 P.M. to 9 A.M. as the night shift, while the day crew works 9 A.M. to 9 P.M. In total then, four shifts of employees will work twelve-hour days with three-day workweeks alternating with four-day workweeks throughout the year.[28]

One of the first organizations to alternate three- and four-day workweek schedules was Monsanto Company, where this program was designed by a committee of salaried and hourly employees. At the end of a six-month trial period, the four crews reported several positive results:[29]

● Employee morale improved. Ninety percent of the employees preferred the 4/48 and 3/36 to the old 4/40 work-week.

● Fewer shift changes resulted in increased productivity for the company.

26. "Flexible Work Schedules," *Small Business Report* (October 1978): 24–25.

27. Newstrom and Pierce, "Alternative Work Schedules," pp. 19–20.
28. "Flexible Work Schedules," pp. 24–25.
29. Ibid., pp. 25–26.

- Absenteeism decreased significantly and continued to decrease during the trial period.
- Turnover was reduced by almost 50 percent.
- There were no communication problems since both supervisor and work crew rotated together. No fatigue problems were reported and safety and quality records supported this observation. (Often this is not the case in four-day workweeks.)

The increased overtime cost was offset by the elimination of shift differentials which had previously been paid for rotating shifts. Thus, the organization benefited significantly, as did employees, without incurring many additional costs.[30]

4½/40 OR 4½/36

A third method of compressed workweek is the four and one-half day workweek. The four and one-half day workweek has been utilized with various total hours worked: Some administrators favor working nine hours Monday through Thursday and a half a day on Friday, a forty-hour week. Their employees enjoy having scheduled time off for personal use. In other organizations employees work eight-hour days Monday through Thursday and work only a half day on Friday whenever scheduled production levels have been reached. Thus, employees are motivated to complete their work in thirty-six hours. This incentive approach is particularly useful in organizations which produce individual orders and know which orders need to be finished by the end of the week or by a certain day.

A four and one-half day week has been

---

30. Ibid.

successfully implemented in a small printing firm in a midwestern city. Previously employees threatened to unionize because among other grievances, they simply did not have enough free time to take care of personal business after work or on weekends. Management offered employees the incentive of leaving by noon each Friday that all the work scheduled for the week was completed. By leaving at noon on Friday, the employees had time to shop and do other chores. After only a few months, morale increased significantly as absenteeism, grievances, and quality problems decreased. Employees were satisfied that they had the time necessary to complete their personal errands. This type of compressed workweek is very effective in manufacturing firms that cannot easily redesign their jobs to make them more rewarding to employees.

Discretionary Workweeks

Each of the three varieties of *discretionary workweeks* offers employees greater freedom in regulating their own lives. Retail stores, service agencies, and some manufacturers have met the demands of business with more satisfied, more productive employees working varied schedules.

FLEXTIME

Second in popularity to the four-day workweek, *flextime* or flexitime provides a true alternate work schedule for employees who may follow different schedules of work each day of the workweek. Flextime has been particularly beneficial to service organizations such as retail outlets, banks, savings and loan associations, and insurance companies.

Almost every survey now in existence shows companies reporting more advantages than

FIGURE 4–5: *Flexible Work Schedules*

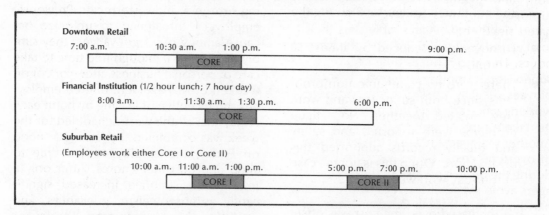

disadvantages to flexible work schedules, regardless of type. Savings in employee turnover, absenteeism, and tardiness, are reported so often and over such long periods of time that these advantages must be considered valid attributes of flexible schedules.[31]

In a typical flextime system, the employer establishes a core time when all employees must work; for example, from 10:30 A.M. to 1:00 P.M. for a retail outlet where most customers come in during their lunch breaks. As Figure 4–5 demonstrates, the employer also establishes the total hours of operation during which the employee must work. Normally, the employee must work the core hours within the total eight hours worked. If the core time is not worked, then the employee does not get credit for the workday; usually an employee does not arrive at work at all if the core time cannot be worked. For service organizations, core time would be a time during which most customers arrive, such as lunchtime for downtown retail organizations, or five-to–nine for suburban shopping locations. The employee may choose a different starting time and stopping time each day of the week, as long as the core time is worked and the total hours worked are within the hours during which the organization is open. The organization may alternate core times for different days of the week if this is necessary to meet customers' demands.

Most employees both here and overseas favor flextime operations. Employees particularly like the control flextime gives them over their personal lives. They can better schedule leisure time activities and family responsibilities, and take care of personal business during normal work hours. Other flextime advantages appreciated by employees include reduced commuting time and faster accomplishment of shopping and other retail and service outlet business during slack times. Women, in particular, enjoy the advantages flextime gives them since many times they are responsible for school age children.[32]

Organizations which have experimented with flextime report many advantages to the system: improved employee morale, significantly increased produc-

---

31. Ibid., p. 23.

32. Ibid., pp. 23–26.

tion, and decreased absenteeism and turnover. Tardiness is completely eliminated since employees simply start their total workday later and still work the same hours. This also reduces time keeping by supervisors. Employers report that employees usually arrive ready to begin working since any personal problems can be taken care of before they came in. Another major advantage is the reduction of overtime costs. By setting core hours during the busiest periods of the day managers avoid scheduling overtime or hiring part-time employees to help handle these busy periods. Quite often, retail and service organizations must actually over staff to be sure an adequate number of employees is available during a rush period. This is necessary to a much lesser degree under a flextime system.[33]

An American Management Association survey of nongovernmental organizations with fifty or more employees found almost 13 percent used some form of flextime in 1977. Over one out of ten manufacturers and two out of ten finance and insurance companies use some form of flextime; other types of industry vary within these figures. The companies using flextime have more than doubled since 1974. Organizations responding to the AMA survey reported these advantages to their flextime systems:[34]

Raised employees' morale	Almost always
Reduced tardiness	84%
Eased employees' commuting	75%
Reduced absenteeism	75%

Made recruiting easier	65%
Reduced turnover	50%
Increased productivity	50%

Managers also reported that in many cases the quality of work during flextime was higher because employees became task oriented since they were not watching a time clock. However, administrators also found that supervision was far more difficult with the flextime system because of the staggered employee hours and fractured internal communications. Production managers had difficulty in using flextime due to interrelatedness of the work which required almost all employees to work together. In summary, AMA's survey reported thirteen major successes with flextime for each failure.[35]

Union leaders have been negative about flextime; to some extent, their reaction is typical for any new scheduling scheme devised by management. However, labor spokesmen do have several specific concerns about flextime. They contend that flextime increases the employee's intensity and productivity but not the weekly wage. How can this occur? Often employees working flextime spontaneously decide to stay in order to finish a job and voluntarily offset these hours worked by taking off time during a slack period of the day. Thus, the company's overtime costs are significantly reduced because the total hours worked per week do not exceed forty. Also, employees may simply work more effectively when they are on the job because they arrive psychologically prepared to work. Therefore, unions may not favor flextime because employees' overtime pay has been reduced and management is receiving the same amount of work as before. Under

33. Keith Bernard, "Flextime's Potential for Management," *The Personnel Administrator* (October 1979): 51–54.
34. "Flexible Work Schedules," p. 24.

35. Ibid., p. 25.

those conditions, continued union opposition to flextime is predictable.[36]

STAGGERED START

A second type of discretionary workweek system involved the *staggered start* management option, under which the employee chooses one of several alternative starting times and works a normal workday. Management determines how many employees will be needed at different hours during the day and defines different options from which employees may choose. Some managers prefer a group stagger start system under which the entire work group that needs to work together to be productive works the same hours during the work day. The staggered start system is not entirely new; it was first introduced in 1926 when New York City experimented with a similar system as a means of reducing rush hour traffic congestion.[37]

A staggered start system obviously does not have the many advantages of a flextime discretionary workweek. Employees do not control their workdays as they do under flextime. The primary advantages of a staggered start system are that employees reduce their commuting time, and supervisors may allow employees to choose different starting times as an incentive in work performance.

VARIABLE HOURS

The *variable working hours* system is similar to flextime in that employees have a wide latitude in defining their hours to be worked. Under a variable system, employees contract with their supervisors to work for a specified time each day, week, or month, with the possibility of varying schedules on a daily basis whenever agreeable to both parties. This system does not include the core time component of the flextime system and avoids many of the communication problems flextime creates between employees and supervisors in organizing work on a daily basis.[38]

The variable working hours system removes from the flextime system employees' ability to daily choose their starting and ending times. This control over personal and work hours is a major factor in the success of flextime systems. However, if a flextime system simply creates too many communication and organization problems for supervisors, the variable work hour system does give employees the latitude they need in scheduling their leisure time and family responsibilities. Under the variable system, the employee can still arrive at school on time to pick up children or attend continuing education classes at a nearby university.

DISCRETIONARY WORKWEEK APPLICATIONS

The Berol Corporation of Danbury Connecticut, has been using a flextime program since 1973 for its clerical and manufacturing employees who may follow any work schedules as long as they are present for the core hours. The company requires only that each department conduct its work flow as usual. For example, the customer service department must be at least minimally staffed from nine to five each working day; staffing arrangements are left up to the employees of the department. Since 1973, Berol Corporation has reduced absenteeism by 50 percent, eliminated tardiness, and decreased excused

36. Maureen McCarthy, "Trends in the Development of Alternative Work Patterns," *The Personnel Administrator* (October 1979): 25–27.
37. Newstrom and Pierce, "Alternative Work Schedules," pp. 20–21.

38. Ibid. pp. 20–22.

leave days by 80 percent. Berol reports that overall job performance has improved and that flextime is a major reason for employee job satisfaction and work performance.[39]

The program initiated by the Colorado Springs Division of Hewlett Packard is an example of flexible starting time. Under the Hewlett Packard system, day shift employees may come to work any time between 6:30 and 8:30 A.M. and night shift from 3:30 to 5:30 P.M. Eight and one-half hours later they leave. While very little hard data is available from firms which have experimented with flexible starting times, Hewlett Packard reports that 97 percent of their employees favor this system.[40]

Part-time Work

In the past decade, part-time work has become a very popular innovative work scheduling alternative. The tremendous influx of women into the job market has increased the supply of part-time workers, as have family members looking for second incomes to keep pace with inflation. At the same time, managers have only begun to realize the benefits— higher enthusiasm and lack of boredom—which part-time employees bring to specialized jobs.

JOB SHARING

In recent years, *job sharing* has evolved as an opportunity for career part-time employment. Job sharing generally refers to dividing full-time jobs into two or more part-time positions, often without particular regard for how the full-time job is divided. In personnel work, the term generally means two employees hold a position together, whether as a team jointly responsible for the position or as individuals responsible for only half of the position. "Leisure sharing" refers to a couple sharing a single position because they prefer the increased leisure time two household members gain by sharing a job. In this way both of them can pursue careers.[41] Job sharing as an alternate work scheduling technique provides the organization with several possible advantages: increased productivity, a greater pool of qualified applicants, and reduced costs. The most common result is an influx of new energy and enthusiasm brought to the job by a second person. The company often gets more than twice the talent in increased stimulation from having two workers perform the same job.[42]

When job sharing was studied in the mass assembly department of a southeastern manufacturing firm, the scrap ratio was 12 percent lower and output 7 percent higher for the shared job positions. Finding four hours to be far less tiring than eight, workers were able to work at a faster pace. Also, fatigue caused errors were greatly reduced.

The supervisor of a Wisconsin State telecommunications department felt that the primary advantage of job sharing is that employees working a few days a week, or four hours a day, simply are more charged up and enthused about their jobs than full-time workers. Many times the expenses of training, hiring of temporary workers, and overtime are

39. "Flexible Work Schedules," pp. 20–21.
40. Bernard, "Flextime's Potential for Management," pp. 51–53.
41. Grett S. Meier, *Job Sharing* (Kalamazoo: W. E. Upjohn Institute, 1978): pp. 1–3.
42. Michael Frease and Robert Zawacki, "Job-Sharing: An Answer to Productivity Problems?" *The Personnel Administrator* (October 1979): pp. 35–37.

reduced. Training costs are often reduced because one job sharing employee can give on-the-job training to the other. Turnover costs are often reduced since job sharers with hours specifically tailored to their personal needs are less likely to give the job up for another one.[43]

Job sharing has disadvantages; obviously, communication problems may increase between job sharing partners and between them and other members of the work force. Job sharing may make it difficult to affix responsibility to a particular individual. Benefit costs to the organization may increase, particularly if the Social Security (FICA) tax or state taxes for unemployment insurance cannot be prorated. Companies employing job sharers whose incomes exceed the FICA ceiling may pay additional FICA taxes. However, benefit costs usually decrease because the two part-time employees do not receive all the benefits of full-time employees. Perhaps the greatest obstacle to job sharing is that surveys show job sharing is not positively viewed by managers. Generally they feel that job sharers do not take the shared job seriously enough, or lack the full-time commitment to a job that a full-time employee would have.[44]

Administrators considering job sharing should look carefully at several factors:

Eligibility Rules: Management must determine the optimal number of job sharers to be allowed in proportion to the total number of employees to minimize communication problems. Also they must determine if job sharing will be available to current employees and/or outside applicants. Management should also determine which jobs are to be included in

the sharing program and how high up the organization job sharers will be able to function effectively.

Job Descriptions: Managers will need complete and accurate job descriptions in order to plan for two employees to perform the same task or tasks which are easily divisible between two.

Interview Process: While interviewing, managers will want to be aware of the possibility of matching partners for job sharing so that fewer communication and personality problems will arise.

Fringe Benefits: Management must determine equitable allocation of fringe benefits to job sharers. Most companies find that prorating benefits in proportion to salary is a preferable solution.

Performance Appraisals: Administrators will need to consider whether normal performance appraisal techniques are applicable for job sharers.

Promotion: Management must determine if job sharers are eligible for promotion, and to what extent their experience grants them the same amount of seniority as full-time employees.[45]

JOB SPLITTING

A second method of part-time work scheduling is *job splitting,* where the tasks of a single job are divided into two entirely separate part-time positions. The employees do not perform the same duties as they would under job sharing; instead, the part-time employees may work the same days but on different tasks. Managers have found job splitting has most of the advantages of job sharing since employees are still performing in a part-time mode and have definite respon-

43. Ibid.
44. Ibid., p. 37.

45. Meier, *Job Sharing,* pp. 153–54.

sibility for different sets of tasks and duties. Job splitting is sometimes referred to as job sharing since the latter has a wider usage and often includes situations where two or more employees work one full-time job.

PERMANENT PART-TIME

The final major method of part-time work scheduling is the time-tested *permanent part-time* category. In recent years, retail and service organization administrators have found that permanent part-time workers have advantages for these organizations. Permanent part-time employees can be hired at lower salaries and often do not have the morale problems of full-time employees. Further, employees performing permanent part-time work during peak demand hours do not work during slack hours. Therefore, organizations catering to the general public find permanent part-time work schedules more beneficial than full-time schedules. Usually managers find they need both types of schedules, as technical or administrative positions cannot be adequately performed by part-time employees. Frequently, permanent part-time positions are restricted to entry level positions such as clerks, tellers, clerical operatives, or sales representatives.

FIGURE 4–6: *Comparison of Alternate Work Schedules*

	Scheduling Method			
Employee Advantages	4-Day Week	Flextime	Job Sharing	Permanent Part-time
Reduced commuting time	U	A	P	P
Less boredom on specialized jobs		P	U	U
Greater latitude in setting hours		A	P	P
Easier to complete personal business	A	A	A	A
Organization Advantages				
Decreased benefit costs			P	U
Increased energy conservation	U			
Less start-up time	U			
Decrease in tardiness		A	U	U
Less absenteeism	P	U	U	U
Decrease in wages		U	U	U
Disadvantages				
Fatigue	U			
Communication problems		P	P	P
Interrelated work problems		A	P	P
Poorer customer relations		P	P	P

Key: P—Possibly
U—Usually
A—Always

DISADVANTAGES OF ALTERNATE WORK SCHEDULES

The work schedule alternatives just discussed are only the beginning of a trend toward new and varied work schedules. Realizing that they cannot redesign all jobs to make them more challenging or interesting, managers use different scheduling techniques to give employees increased freedom to plan work or leisure time. The three major work scheduling alternatives—compressed workweek, discretionary workweek, and part-time work—have been successful for the most part. As Figure 4–6 indicates, the advantage of alternate work schedules is a substantial gain in employees' satisfaction with their jobs and work environment. However, there have been disadvantages associated with alternate work scheduling:

EMPLOYEE RESISTANCE to a different type of scheduling occurs simply because traditionally-oriented employees resist change of any type. Uncertain of what the new system will bring, and at least partially satisfied with the current system, many employees resist possible changes in their basic life–styles.

COMMUNICATION PROBLEMS are possibly the most common disadvantage encountered by any company using alternative work schedules. Inconsistent work hours change common communication patterns; at times some employees may be inaccessible for group meetings or casual discussions. This problem can be minimized by proper management planning

FIGURE 4–7: *Future Work Week?*

1925	1965	2005
"A six day week, are you crazy? It will never happen!"	"A four day week, are you crazy? It will never happen!"	"A two day work week, are you crazy? It will never happen!"

and correct implementation of the particular work schedule alternative which has been adopted.

FATIGUE has been a major complaint of some employees on compressed workweek schedules. Obviously, many compressed workweek schemes which involve longer days and mental and physical fatigue may become a real hardship on employees. While many employees may not complain of fatigue directly, the later hours of the workday must be carefully monitored to make sure that fatigue is not becoming a major cause of increased injuries or decreased productivity during a compressed workweek schedule.

INTERDEPENDENCE OF JOBS creates real problems for flextime or part-time alternative work scheduling schemes. In fact, highly interdependent jobs such as assembly line operations probably make these alternative work scheduling procedures simply impractical. Primarily, flextime and other discretionary workweek programs have been utilized by service or small manufacturing organizations which do not have highly interdependent jobs.

In summary, employees' job satisfaction may be increased by changing the design of their jobs or implementing alternative work schedules. Job design changes involve modifying the content, functions, or relationships of jobs. Alternate work schedules include compressed, discretionary, and part-time workweeks. From the fifties through the seventies, job enrichment and job enlargement programs were viewed as the answers to job design problems; recently alternative work schedules have become increasingly popular with management. Employees should participate in planning a changeover to a new workweek in order that employees understand the new system and work to make it successful. Redesigning jobs and altering work schedules may increase employee morale and productivity, as well as decrease absenteeism, turnover, and other problems.

FIGURE 4–8: *1979 Alternate Work Pattern Experiences of 250 Firms*

Position	Flexitime	Part Time Options	Flexible Schedules	Increased Vacation/ Sabbatical
Implemented	14%	19%	7%	6%
Beginning Implementation	3	3	2	2
Serious Consideration	6	12	5	4
Preliminary Consideration	11	16	10	9
Not Considered	66	50	76	79
Total	100%	100%	100%	100%

From Lois Copperman, "Alternative Work Policies in Private Firms." Reprinted with permission from the October 1979 issue of the *Personnel Administrator* copyright, 1979, The American Society for Personnel Administration, 30 Park Drive, Berea, Ohio 44017.

The Solution

Susan Franz's job at Banes Engines and Mary Anne Kozak's position at Ryan's Pet Store illustrate classic job design differences. One job is designed to be quite specialized, with a great deal of mechanically paced routine. The other is designed to give the employee mental as well as physical freedom on the job. The lower-paid job involved more decision making and responsibility than the assembly job.

Job satisfaction and motivation levels expressed by the two employees are typical; they realize that pay and interesting work are both important factors. Each may realize that neither of them has the best of both worlds.

═══ KEY TERMS AND CONCEPTS ═══

Job Design	Four-day Workweek
Job Rotation	Flextime
Job Enrichment	Staggered Start
Job Enlargement	Job Sharing
Work Simplification	Job Splitting
Autonomous Work Groups	Permanent Part-time Work
Motivation Intense Job	Variable Hours
Specialization Intense Job	Compressed Workweek
Depth of a Job	Discretionary Workweek
Scope of a Job	Relative Ability
Productivity	Job Cycle

═══ FOR REVIEW ═══

1. In what types of organizations could flextime be most effective? Why?

2. Why are employees increasingly becoming dissatisfied with specialized jobs?

3. Why is it difficult to design highly motivating jobs which can be easily learned by most people?

4. What can be gained by using part-time workers instead of full–time workers?

5. Why might working spouses prefer a flextime schedule to a four–day workweek?

FOR DISCUSSION

1. Discuss the factors involved in redesigning jobs in an auto assembly plant or an insurance agency. Which company would be easier to redesign?

2. Would you prefer to work flextime, or a four-day, five-day, or eight-day week if you had an assembly line job? If you were a computer programmer? If you were a Fuller Brush salesperson?

3. If you managed a fast-food franchise, would you raise salaries or rotate, enlarge, or enrich jobs to decrease turnover and absenteeism? Explain your choice.

4. Do you believe that blue-collar employees on flextime can be trusted to keep track of their own hours? Can white-collar workers? What factors would influence both groups?

5. How would you decide which work schedule would be most efficient in a car wash, an accounting firm, a gas station, a veterinarian's office?

SUPPLEMENTARY READING

Anderson, J. W. "The Impact of Technology on Job Enrichment." *Personnel*, 1970.

Carrell, M. R. "How to Measure Job Satisfaction." *Training*, November 1976, pp. 25–27.

Conant, E. H., and Kilbridge, M. D. "An Interdisciplinary Analysis of Job Enlargement: Technology, Costs, and Behavioral Implications." *Industrial and Labor Relations Review* (1965): 377–95.

Cummings, L. L.; Schwab, D. P.; and Rosen, M. "Performance and Knowledge of Results as Determinants of Goal-Setting." *Journal of Applied Psychology* (1971): 526–30.

Davis, L. E., and Cherns, A. B., eds. *The Quality of Working Life*. New York: The Free Press, 1975.

Fein, M. "Job Enrichment: A Reevaluation." *Sloan Management Review* (1974): 69–88.

Ford, R. N. "Job Enrichment Lessons from AT&T." *Harvard Business Review* (1973): 96–106.

Foy, N., and Gadon, H. "Worker Participation: Contrasts in Three Countries." *Harvard Business Review* (1976): 71–83.

Golembiewski, R. T.; Fox, R. G.; and Proehl, C. W. "Flexitime = The Supervisors' Verdict." *The Wharton Magazine*, Summer, 1980, pp. 43–47.

Hackman, J. R., and Oldham, G. R. "Motivation through the Design of Work: Test of a Theory." *Organizational Behavior and Human Performance* (1976): 250–79.

Hulin, C. L. "Individual Differences and Job Enrichment—The Case Against General Treatments." In Maher, J. R., ed., *New Perspectives in Job Enrichment*. Princeton, NJ: Van Nostrand Reinhold, 1971.

Lawler, E. E. "Job Design and Employee Motivation." *Personnel Psychology* (1969): 415–44.

Rush, H. M. *Job Design for Motivation*. New York: The Conference Board, 1972.

Suojanen, W. W.; Swallow, G. L.; and McDonald, M. J. *Perspectives on Job Enrichment and Productivity*. Atlanta: Georgia State University, 1975.

Umstot, D. D.; Bell, C. H.; and Mitchell, T. R. "Effects of Job Enrichment and Task Goals on Satisfaction and Productivity: Implications for Job Design." *Journal of Applied Psychology* (1976): 379–94.

For Analysis: Design or Scheduling Problem?

Barsotti and Smith, Inc., a medium-sized manufacturing plant employing slightly over three hundred persons, recently encountered turnover and absenteeism problems. Located in a small midwestern town of about twenty thousand, the firm produced tractor parts.

Only two years earlier Barsotti and Smith had moved from Cleveland, Ohio, because of market considerations and union problems. Management believed that a midwestern location would greatly lower transportation costs since most customers were located further west. They also hoped that nonunion labor costs would be lower. About fifty employees decided to relocate in the Midwest. While the projected cost savings had materialized, the first two years brought unforeseen problems; absenteeism and turnover greatly disrupted production, and delivery dates were not being met.

President Jay Barsotti asked the Plant Manager Lorenzo Taylor and Personnel Director Kate Merz to meet with him to discuss the situation:

Barsotti: "At first I thought these high levels of turnover and absenteeism were temporary problems of adjusting to a new location, But, my God, two years! What is causing this?"

Merz: "I'm getting good workers. Most are thankful to get jobs in this area so they don't have to commute to a city or leave their families."

Taylor: "I really don't understand it. Like she said, they're good workers. They don't loaf on the job or steal parts; they aren't even tardy! But after a few months they're absent a lot and then, they usually quit."

Merz: "We've had 70 percent turnover these first two years."

Barsotti: "Are they going somewhere else to work?"

Merz: "I don't think so. We are the largest employer in the county, and we pay better than anyone."

Barsotti: "Are they any different than the employees we had in Cleveland?"

Taylor: "Yes, almost all of them are working wives and young men just out of high school. In Ohio we had almost all middle-aged or older men."

Barsotti: "Well, maybe the turkeys don't like the work."

Merz: "They seem to . . . most say they like working in small groups and electing their own supervisors."

Barsotti: "Well, maybe we should just wait and see. . . ."

Merz: "No, it's almost April, and the last two Aprils have been our worst turnover months."

Barsotti: "Any suggestions?"

Taylor: "Well, a couple workers have asked if they could work at night, but we don't need a second shift, and it would be too expensive to operate sixteen hours a day."

Barsotti:	"We'd go broke fast. . ."
Merz:	"I've had a lot of women apply for part-time work, but we've always hired only full-time. Now that we're running out of applicants . . .
Barsotti:	"No! We tried part-time people five years ago; they don't have any loyalty."
Merz:	"Well, we have had people who quit last year ask to be rehired; most had good records."
Barsotti:	"I hate to bring back people who let us down once. We never did that in Ohio. Well, you two come up with something by Monday, when we meet again to decide what to do."

Questions:

1. How could the organization determine what factors may be causing the high turnover and absenteeism?

2. What needs might the new work force have that are different from those of the Cleveland employees?

3. Describe some work scheduling techniques that might be suggested to Barsotti.

This female road construction worker typifies new work roles for men and women.

5

FEDERAL EMPLOYMENT GUIDELINES AND LAWS

Major Federal Employment Legislation

Affirmative Action Programs

Equal Employment Opportunity Commission

Significant Court Cases

The Problem: Wirtz, Secretary of Labor *v.* Basic, Inc.
256 F.Supp. 786 (1966)
U. S. District Court of Nevada

Three laboratory analysts at Basic, Inc., Jo Ann Barredo, Ann Jones, and Byron O'Dell, were involved in a dispute. Jones was hired in 1953 and Barredo was hired in 1959; both were trained by Chief Chemist Red Thompson. O'Dell was hired in 1962 and trained by Thompson, Barredo, and Jones. Only O'Dell had laboratory experience; he had thirteen years' experience. Essentially, all three ran simple standardized chemical tests in accordance with the company's testing manual. Given the title shift analyst, O'Dell worked a swing shift (after 5:00 P.M.) for alternate two-week periods and received a higher hourly pay rate every week than Barredo or Jones.

After passage of the Equal Pay Act of 1963, which prohibited pay discrimination on the basis of sex, Thompson discussed the necessity of equalizing the pay of the laboratory analysts. No action was taken, and Thompson resigned in 1964.

▰ FEDERAL LEGISLATION ▰

From the mid-1960s through the mid–1970s personnel administrators were bombarded with federal legislation and court cases involving the recruitment and selection of employees. In reflecting the mood of society, Congress and the courts initiated reforms to ensure that individuals have equal chances of being selected for employment and that they will be treated equally once they are hired. Special emphasis was given to veterans and minorities who had experienced discrimination in past decades.

Equal Pay Act of 1963

Due to many publicized cases of female employees being paid substantially less than their male counterparts while performing identical work, the *Equal Pay Act of 1963* was passed by Congress. The act requires organizations of all sizes to pay men and women substantially the same wages for *substantially equal* work. Substantially equal refers to approximately equal "skill, effort, responsibility, and working conditions." As defined in the courtroom, substantially equal is the basis upon which jobs should be compared. In practice this means that jobs do not have to be identical to be paid the same basic wage; neither do employers have to pay each different job a different wage. They can pay equal wages for substantially equal work. The Equal Pay Act is administered by the Wage and Hour Division of the U.S. Department of Labor.

The Equal Pay Act has had wider application than any other employment legislation because the act does not stipulate a statutory minimum number of employees; the act applies to all organizations. Unlike the Civil Rights Act and other employment acts which specified a minimum work force requirement for organizations included under the terms of the acts, the Equal Pay Act applies to any firm which has two or more employees.[1]

Of particular importance are the exceptions allowed by the Equal Pay Act; differences in pay can be based on seniority, merit, quality of work, or quantity of work. Therefore, paying different wages to men and women performing the same job can be justified by these differences.

This act has caused many organizations to develop a wage and salary system based upon formal job evaluation plans. Under such plans employees are paid according to the jobs they are performing and not other factors such as sex or supervisory bias. Organizations which adopt or amend their wage and salary plan cannot, according to the Equal Pay Act, reduce the wage rate of any employee in order to comply with the act.[2]

Civil Rights Act of 1964

The primary federal law that regulates employment practices is the *Civil Rights Act of 1964,* an act passed while the nation mourned the death of John F. Kennedy. Only months before his assassination the nation had witnessed civil rights demonstrations throughout the country as minorities demanded recognition of their civil rights. The act requires employment and compensation of employees without discrimination:

> *Title VII, Section 703 of the Civil Rights Act of 1964* It is unlawful for an employer to discriminate against an individual with respect to his compensation, terms, conditions, or privileges of employment because of such individual's race, color, religion, sex, or national origin; or to limit, segregate, or classify his employees in any way which would deprive or tend to deprive any individual of employment opportunities or otherwise adversely affect his status as an employee, because of such individual's race, color, religion, sex, or national origin.

The act also established the *Equal Employment Opportunity Commission (EEOC).* The EEOC was given the authority

---

1. George Wendt, "Should Courts Write Your Job Descriptions?," *Personnel Journal* (September, 1976): 442–44.

2. Ibid., pp. 443–50.

to investigate employee complaints of job discrimination. Where the EEOC finds such complaints justified, it cannot directly order organizations to take employment action; however EEOC can bring suit in federal courts against employers. Under Title VII, the EEOC is empowered to investigate employees' complaints and act as their attorney. The employer is obligated to show personnel records and other requested material to the EEOC. In addition, all employee applications must be kept for three years in case they should be needed in an EEOC complaint or other action.

Typically, a discrimination complaint is processed in this manner:

Step 1: The employee's inquiry is filed with the EEOC or a state commission dealing with human rights. The employee is interviewed by a professional who ascertains all facts of the case. The EEOC then reviews the facts and determines if the case warrants further investigation.

Step 2: If the EEOC finds that there may be *probable cause*—the reasonable possibility—of discrimination, the commission requests the employer's records. These records may include application blanks, interview results, or test results. The EEOC then determines if there was probable cause for the complaint.

Step 3: The EEOC arranges a *conciliation meeting* with the employer to discuss the employee's complaint if the EEOC feels that it has probable cause. The purpose of the conciliation meeting is to arrive at a mutual agree-

ment which will satisfy both the employer and aggrieved employee. If this is not possible, then the EEOC weighs the severity of the complaint and discusses alternative actions with the employee.

Step 4: Without any satisfactory conciliation agreement, the EEOC may issue a right to sue to the complainant indicating that the commission does not feel that the case should be taken to court. Therefore, the complaining employee does have the right to sue with a private attorney. Many times this is an indication that the EEOC does not feel that the complainant has a strong case. The alternative of sending the complainant a right to sue is for the EEOC to take the case of the complainant to court. Title VII covers attorney fees for complainants if the EEOC takes the case to court.

COURT PROCEDURES

If the discrimination complaint is taken to court, the case proceeds in a similar fashion to the *McDonnell-Douglas* v. *Green* case.[3] The complainant must generally prove:

Minority or female status: In most cases this is not difficult. However, proving that one is of American Indian or Hispanic origin may be difficult in some situations.

Qualification for the position: The complainant must demonstrate minimum qualifications for the position specified

3. McDonnell Douglas Corp. v. Green, 441 U.S. 792 (1972), SEPD.

in the employer's position announcement or recruitment ad.

Failure to be hired: Usually this is easily proven except in cases of ongoing recruitment where the complainant may still be under consideration for selection.

Someone less qualified was hired: This is often a difficult and debatable aspect of a discrimination case. Using the company's own records, the complainant must prove that he or she is better qualified than the person hired who is not a minority or female. In other words, the complainant cannot claim discrimination if the employer hires one minority instead of another minority since both are equally protected under the Civil Rights Act.

The organization may generally prove as a defense:

- That the employee did not have the requisite *bona fide occupational qualification (BFOQ):* Title VII provides that an employer could hire employees in certain instances where religion, sex, or national origin is a bona fide occupational qualification if it is reasonably necessary to the normal operation of the organization. BFOQ is a vague and seldom-used defense for discrimination cases. An example of a BFOQ might be a firm hiring a male to serve as a men's room attendant; or a church refusing to hire someone of a different religion to serve as a minister. The courts have ruled that it is not a BFOQ for flight attendants to be female. Title VII also states that an organization must make reasonable accommodation for em-

ployees of specific religious beliefs or with handicaps. However, exactly how much is reasonable accommodation is subject to interpretation.

- That it was a business necessity not to hire the complainant: If safety or profitability require hiring a specific person, then discrimination could be defended under the Title VII. For example, if a company hired an individual to work specific hours during the week, and after being hired the individual could not work those hours due to personal circumstances, management may claim a *business necessity* as a defense. Another example is a dress shop which claims that it is a business necessity to hire young females as salesclerks so that they may relate to the public they are serving.

- That the person hired is better qualified for the job than the complainant: This is the most common defense for an organization charged with employment discrimination. Personnel records should prove that the results of the tests or interviews indicated that the person hired was better qualified than the complainant. Personnel departments with standardized and documented records, using proper selection techniques, have a strong defense. If, however, their defense is based solely upon what they remember about a case or believe occurred, then they have a weak defense in most cases.

The EEOC usually hears complaints from applicants who were discriminated against in the process of hiring or promotion, not in matters of unequal pay. Under Title VII, employment discrimination refers to much more than the initial hiring process; it encompasses "terms, conditions, or privileges of employment" and includes selection, promotion, transfers, or employee training. Therefore, all organizational decisions which relate to an employee's job classification are included under the Civil Rights Act.

The Equal Employment Opportunity Act of 1972

In 1972 the Civil Rights Act of 1964 was amended by the Equal Employment Opportunity Act. The amendment effectively changed Title VII of the 1964 Act to include all private employers and labor unions with fifteen or more employees or members, state and local governments, and public and private educational institutions. More importantly the Equal Employment Act considerably strengthened the 1964 Act by giving the EEOC power to bring suits directly to federal courts when conciliation efforts had proven unsuccessful. Previously, the EEOC did not have such power and relied upon employers to voluntarily comply with conciliation efforts. State and local EEOC offices were established to provide local level counseling for complainants who feel they have suffered discrimination.

Age Discrimination and Employment Act of 1967

This act makes discrimination against individuals between the ages of 40 and 70 illegal in companies with twenty-five employees or more. Under the act employers cannot refuse to hire or discriminate in compensation, terms of employment, or other conditions or privileges of employment due to an individual's age. Like the

Equal Pay Act, the employer cannot reduce the wage of any employee in order to comply with the Age Discrimination Act of 1967. The act is administered by the Wage and Hour Division of the U.S. Department of Labor.

One effect of this law is that fewer positions will open due to retirement each year. As an example, Sears, Roebuck and Company surveyed employees who were eligible for retirement. The results indicated that Sears would have 7,790 fewer job openings that year with a resulting 33,240 fewer promotions and transfers within the company. Fewer promotions and transfers in lower levels of the company will make it increasingly more difficult for young employees to move up the organization ladder during the 1980s.[4]

Employers will have to carefully develop performance appraisal systems to support any actions taken against employees who are between 40 and 70. This problem may further be aggravated by the possible passage of an open retirement system which has been proposed in Congress in recent years. Open retirement would remove the age limit of 70 or increase it to 75 or even 80. A high retirement age would remove from Social Security rolls and government relief programs individuals eligible for payments, who prefer to work.

Vocational Rehabilitation Act of 1973

Under the Vocational Rehabilitation Act of 1973, employers with government contracts of $2,500 or more must have approved affirmative action programs for the handicapped. Programs include special recruitment efforts for the handi-

4. Lawrence A. Wangler, "The Intensification of the Personnel Role," Personnel Journal (February, 1979): 111–19.

FIGURE 5–1 *Affirmative Action Compliance Survey*

COMPLIANCE SURVEY

AFFIRMATIVE ACTION YEAR FROM: _____ , 19____ TO _____ , 19____

COMPANY NAME: _____

ADDRESS: _____ Phone: (Area Code ____) _____

FACILITY COVERED BY PLAN: _____

ADDRESS: _____ Phone: (Area Code ____) _____

JOB CATEGORIES	TOTAL	PRESENT WORKFORCE										JOB VACANCIES DURING PAST YEAR HOW FILLED				% AVAIL-ABILITY		UNDER UTILI-ZATION (Yes/No)		PROJECTED OPENINGS	GOALS					
		MALE					FEMALE														CURRENT YEAR				ULTIMATE	
		White	Black	Hispanic	Asian/ P.I.	Am. Ind. Ak. Nat.	White	Black	Hispanic	Asian/ P.I.	Am. Ind. Ak. Nat.	Total	Male	Fem.	Min.	Fem.	Min.	Fem.	Min.		Hires		Promotes		%/Year	
																					Fem.	Min.	Fem.	Min.	Fem.	Min.
OFFICIALS AND MANAGERS																										
PROFESSIONALS																										
TECHNICIANS																										
SALES WORKERS																										
OFFICE AND CLERICAL																										
CRAFTSWORKERS (Skilled)																										
OPERATIVES (Semi-Skilled)																										
LABORERS (Unskilled)																										
SERVICE WORKERS																										
TOTALS																										

EQUAL EMPLOYMENT OFFICER NAME _____

SIGNATURE _____ DATE _____

SOURCE: *Affirmative Action and Equal Employment, A Guidebook for Employers,* Vol. 2, U.S. Equal Employment Opportunity Commission, (Washington, DC: U.S. Printing Office, 1974), p. 25.

capped as well as procedures to promote and develop the handicapped within the organization. Employers are also required to make environmental changes such as adding ramps to make their businesses more accessible to the handicapped. The act is administered by committee members from the Civil Service Commission, the Administration of Veterans' Affairs, the U.S. Department of Labor, and the U.S. Department of Health and Welfare. Handicapped individuals who feel that their rights have been violated under the act may file complaints with the U.S. Department of Labor.

Vietnam Era Veterans Readjustment Act of 1974

This act was a special effort to help Vietnam War veterans who had particular difficulty in securing jobs when they returned to this country. The *Vietnam Era Veterans Readjustment Act of 1974* requires all organizations holding government contracts of $10,000 or more to hire and promote veterans of the Vietnam era. The act is administered by the Veterans Employment Service of the U.S. Department of Labor. Employers holding government contracts are required to list their job openings with local state employment offices in order that these offices may contact unemployed veterans as well as other individuals. One side effect of the act has been a demonstrated increase in job openings listed by state employment offices which has increased their effectiveness in many communities.

▬ FEDERAL GUIDELINES ▬

By Executive Order 11246, President Lyndon B. Johnson created what is known today as *affirmative action*. Since 1965 this order has been amended several times by later presidents. An *executive order* is not a law and, therefore, does not have the wide impact of federal laws such as the Civil Rights Act of 1964. It directly affects only governmental agencies and organizations which are contractors or subcontractors of federal government programs. However, organizations may be ordered by a court to develop an affirmative action plan, approved by the EEOC or local rights commission. Unlike the previously discussed laws passed by Congress, which may be referred to as *neutrality laws* because they only require that organizations obey them, executive orders relating to affirmative action require that the certain organizations take specific positive actions to improve the employment opportunities of minorities.

Affirmative Action Program Development

Development and administration of an affirmative action program usually requires that you:

● Give a copy of the equal employment opportunity policy which specifies a commitment to equal employment opportunity and affirmative action to all employees and to all applicants. Reaffirm these commitments in all ads and employee notices.

● Give a specific, top-ranking organization official the authority and responsibility for affirmative action program implementation. This manager or coordinator should have the authority to secure necessary information and demand assistance in developing and carrying out an affirmative action plan. This person must receive complete support from top management to engender cooperation from lower level employees who may not place affirmative action problems at the top of their daily work routine.

● Complete a *work force analysis* of the organization. The first step in completing a work force analysis is to do a "head count" of the employees in the organization by number and percentage of minorities and females in each major job classification. Then determine if the organization has *underutilization of minorities* and females in any job classification. For example, in Figure 5-1 there are three areas in which the organization has underutilization of females and minorities. Underutilization can be defined as having fewer minorities or women in a particular job category than would be found in the relevant labor market. Compare your own employment figures with those of the Standard Metropolitan Statistical Area (SMSA). These data are available from the local U.S. Department of Labor office. The work force analysis should also identify any concentration of minorities or females in a particular job category. A concentration refers to more of a particular minority group located in a job category than would be expected when compared to the labor market figures. The next step of the work force analy-

sis is to determine which job categories have an underutilization or concentration of minorities or females. If either underutilization or concentration occurs, then management must take affirmative actions in order to end

FIGURE 5–2: *Equal Employment Opportunity Commission Description of Job Categories*

Officials and Managers—Occupations requiring administrative personnel who set broad policies, exercise overall responsibility for execution of these policies, and direct individual departments or special phases of a firm's operations. Includes: Officials, Executives, Middle Management, Plant Managers, Department Managers, and Superintendents, Salaried Foremen who are members of Management, Purchasing Agents and Buyers, and Kindred Workers.

Professional—Occupations requiring either college graduation or experiences of such kind and amount as to provide a comparable background. Includes: Accountants and Auditors, Airplane Pilots and Navigators, Architects, Artists, Chemists, Designers, Dietitians, Editors, Lawyers, Librarians, Mathematicians, Natural Scientists, Registered Professional Nurses . . . and Kindred Workers.

Technicians—Occupations requiring a combination of basic scientific knowledge and manual skill which can be obtained through about 2 years of post high school education, such as is offered in many technical institutes and junior colleges, or through equivalent on-the-job training. Included: Computer Programmers and Operators, Draftsmen, Engineering Aides, Junior Engineers, Mathematical Aides, Licensed, Practical or Vocational Nurses . . . and Kindred Workers.

Sales—Occupations engaging wholly or primarily in direct selling. Includes: Advertising Agents and Salesmen, Insurance Agents and Brokers, Real Estate Agents and Brokers, Stock and Bond Salesmen, Demonstrators, Salesmen and Sales Clerks, Grocery Clerks and Cashier-Checkers, and Kindred Workers.

Office and Clerical—Includes all clerical-type work regardless of level of difficulty, where the activities are predominantly nonmanual though some manual work not directly involved with altering or transporting the products is included. Includes: Bookkeepers, Cashiers, Collectors (Bills and Accounts), Messengers and Office Boys, Office Machine Operators . . . and Kindred Workers.

Craftsmen (Skilled)—Manual workers or relatively high skill level having a thorough and comprehensive knowledge of the processes involved in their work. Exercise considerable independent judgment and usually receive an extensive period of training. Includes: The Building Trades, Hourly Paid Foremen and Leadmen who are not members of management, Mechanics and Repairmen, Electricians, Engravers, Job Setters (Metal), Motion Picture Projectionists . . . and Kindred Workers.

Operatives (Semiskilled)—Workers who operate machine or processing equipment or perform other factory-type duties of intermediate skill level which can be mastered in a few weeks and require only limited training. Includes: Apprentices (Auto Mechanics, Plumbers, Bricklayers, Carpenters, Electricians, Machinists, Mechanics, Building Trades, Metalworking Trades, Printing Trades, etc.) Operatives, Attendants (Auto Service and Parking), Blasters, Chauffeurs, Deliverymen and Routemen, Dressmakers and Seamstresses (Except Factory), Dryers, Furnacemen, Heaters (Metal), Laundry and Dry Cleaning Operatives, Milliners, Mine Operatives and Laborers, Motormen, Oilers and Greasers (Except Auto) . . . and Kindred Workers.

Laborers (Unskilled)—Workers in manual occupations which generally require no special training. Perform elementary duties that may be learned in a few days and require the application of little or no independent judgment. Includes: Garage Laborers, Car Washers and Greasers, Gardeners (Except Farm) and Groundskeepers, Longshoremen and Stevedores, Lumbermen . . . and Kindred Workers.

Service Workers—Workers in both protective and nonprotective service occupations. Includes: Attendants (Hospital and Other Institutions, Professional and Personal Service, including Nurses Aides, and Orderlies), Barbers, Charwomen and Cleaners, Cooks (Except Household), Counter and Fountain Workers, Elevator Operators, Firemen and Fire Protection, Guards . . . and Kindred Workers.

SOURCE: *Instructions for Filing Employer Information Report EEO-1*, U.S. Equal Employment Opportunity Commission, (Washingon, DC: U.S. Printing Office, 1965), pp. 1–12.

discriminatory activities which caused the underutilization or concentration.

● Establish goals and timetables. Once the managers have determined where an organization may have discriminated in the past, then specific goals and timetables to improve performance in those job categories can be developed. Determine if any discrimination barriers may have limited minority and female participation in certain job categories and also determine how to ensure that sufficient minorities and females will be hired in the future. As Figure 5-1 illustrates, the goals should be specific numbers and percentages to be hired in specific job categories and the timetable should set dates when these goals should be accomplished.

● Develop recruitment plans. This may include advertising at colleges and universities which traditionally have large minority and female enrollments. Present minority and female employees are usually good sources of information about reaching interested female and minority applicants.

REQUIRED RECORDS

Adequate and complete records must be kept to meet EEOC requirements. Even if the organization's statistics show no problems with underutilization or concentration, these records can provide possible defense in court cases or be kept for compliance reviews by federal agencies. The U.S. Equal Employment Opportunity Commission recommends these records

and supporting data be kept for affirmative action purposes:[5]

1. Most recent SF-100 (EEO-1) report and previous three years' reports.

2. Number of applications for each major job grouping and hires by sex and minority group for the last twelve months. (Form P).

3. Chronological list of all hires by name, sex, minority group, job, rate of pay, and recruitment source for the last twelve months. (Form P).

4. If there is a college recruitment program, list of schools, date, name, sex, minority group of those interviewed, indicating those to whom offers were extended and disposition. (Form P).

5. List of all promotions and transfers giving date, name, sex, minority group, previous job department and pay, and new job department and pay, for last twelve months. (Form Q).

6. List of all terminations by department for past twelve months, giving name, sex, minority group, job and department, date of hire, date of termination, and reason. (Form S).

7. List of various ongoing or completed training programs during past twelve months, with name, sex, minority group of participants, date of completion, and job and pay before and after training. (Form R).

8. Copies of any agreements pursuant to investigations of charges of dis-

5. U.S. Equal Employment Opportunity Commission, *Affirmative Action and Equal Employment, A Guidebook for Employers* (Washington, DC: U.S. Government Printing Office, 1974) pp. 47–48.

crimination by federal, state, or local agencies and copies of any outstanding charges and present status.

9. Copies of all current labor agreements.

10. Seniority lists or computer printouts showing all employees by name, sex, minority group, date of hire, other job related dates, original job, date of last promotion, present job and EEO-1 category, rate of pay, and if available, education and/or special training. Data must be provided in seniority order within departments, along with all interpretative materials including organization charts, promotional sequences, and lines of progression. Those on layoff status should be designated.

11. Affirmative action plan goals along with current status of attainment.

12. Material on testing.

13. Written job descriptions and qualifications.

PROGRAM IMPLEMENTATION

Unfortunately, many managers and employees still do not recognize the importance of antidiscrimination laws and their impact on organizations. Often EEO coordinators and affirmative action program managers do not get complete cooperation from department heads and employees. Sometimes coordinators must resort to coercion to get information and assistance from employees.

The affirmative action program manager may find it more productive to implement three basic strategies: First, try to make the recruitment and selection of employees more job related rather than trying to change employees' attitudes toward the recruitment and selection of minorities and females. Second, encourage participation in the design and implementation of the program from all levels of management. Third, relate organizational goals to each department's goals and timetables.[6] A specific letter of instruction to department heads concerning goals and timetables may help to accomplish this third objective. (See Figure 5-3.)

Uniform Guidelines on Employee Selection Procedures

After 1966 federal agencies began issuing separate, sometimes conflicting, guidelines which led to enforcement problems as well as severe criticism from private industry. The early guidelines were complex and difficult for practitioners to understand. One consequence of the confusion was the abandonment of employment testing which was believed to be greatly limited by the early guidelines. In some cases subjective selection procedures were often adopted and minority candidates hired to avoid charges of noncompliance.[7]

On August 25, 1978, the Uniform Guidelines On Employee Selection Procedures were adopted by four federal agencies: the Equal Employment Opportunity Commission, Civil Service Commission, U.S. Department of Labor, and U.S. Department of Justice. In order to comply with suggested practices and avoid potentially

6. David Brookmire, "Designing and Implementing Your Company's Affirmative Action Program," *Personnel Journal* (April 1979): pp. 232–37.

7. C. Paul Sparks, "Guidance and Guidelines," *The Industrial-Organizational Psychologist* 14, no. 3 (May, 1977): 30–33.

FIGURE 5–3: *Goals and Timetables Instructions*

Each manager will establish goals and timetables to rectify underutilization of minorities and women. Clearly, this is the heart of each unit's affirmative action program. Goals should be significant, measurable, and attainable given the commitment of the organizational unit and its good faith efforts. The internal work force utilization analysis and the analysis of the relevant external labor area provide the basic data on which goals and timetables are formulated, in combination with the company's goals and timetables. Parameters for goal and timetable determination are:

1. Goals and timetables will be determined for women and minorities separately.
2. In establishing timetables to meet goals, each organizational unit will consider the anticipated expansion, contraction, and turnover of its work force.
3. Specific goals and timetables for women and minorities will be established for each category of employment (e.g., office, factory, apprenticeship, college, professional).
4. Specific goals and timetables for women and minorities will be established for each promotional category (e.g., hourly to exempt, office, factory, professional).
5. The nature of the goals and timetables established are a function of:
    a. The degree of underutilization within the specified job family.
    b. The scope of the relevant recruitment area.
    c. The availability of qualified or qualifiable minorities and women in the area.
    d. The number of job openings available, determined by turnover, expansion, etc.
    e. The commitment of the organizational unit to correct underutilization of minorities and women.
    f. The AAP and EEO policy of the company.
6. The one year and five year goals will be recorded on Form XX, by completing Columns 37-61 per the instructions.

SOURCE: Adapted from *Affirmative Action and Equal Employment, A Guidebook for Employees,* U. S. Equal Employment Opportunity Commission, (Washington, D.C.: U.S. Government Printing Office, 1974), p. A-14.

costly litigation, managers, as well as personnel practitioners, should be familiar with the guidelines' basic principles.

SIGNIFICANT SECTIONS

The more significant sections are included below with explanations:

SECTION 2. (B) EMPLOYMENT DECISIONS: These guidelines apply to tests and other selection procedures which are used as a basis for any employment decision. Employment decisions include—but are not limited to—hiring, promotion, demotion, membership (for example, in a labor organization), referral, retention, and licensing and certification to the extent that licensing and certification may be covered by federal equal employment opportunity law. Other selection decisions, such as selection for training or transfer, may also be considered employment decisions if they lead to any of the decisions listed above.

Remember that guidelines apply to tests of the paper and pencil variety and "other selection procedures." Thus, any reference check, interview, application blank, or other selection instrument utilized by an organization is included. In recent years, due in part to the guidelines, the use of written tests has declined and the use of interviews in selection has increased. Ironically, the interview, which may be subject to even more personal bias, is just as vulnerable to EEO pressures.[8]

SECTION 3. DISCRIMINATION DEFINED: Relationship between use of selection procedures and discrimination. Procedure having adverse impact constitutes discrimination unless justified. The use of any selection procedure which has an adverse impact on the hiring, promotion, or other employment or membership opportunities of members of any race, sex, or ethnic group will be considered to be discriminatory and inconsistent with these guidelines, unless the procedure has been validated in accordance with these guidelines, or the provisions of section 6 below are satisfied.

In this section the guidelines link discrimination directly to adverse impact. *Discrimination* occurs when an individual who has an equal probability of being successful on a job does not have an equal probability of getting the job.

An *adverse impact* on an employment practice causes members of any race, color, sex, religion, or national origin to receive unequal consideration for employment. If an employer's selection procedure, such as an interview, results in an applicant not having an equal chance to be hired or promoted, then that procedure caused the organization to discriminate against that applicant. A selection procedure or policy which adversely impacts on the employment opportunities of any race, sex, or ethnic group is illegal under Title VII.

Section Three points out that a properly validated selection procedure is not discriminatory. *Validity* in testing occurs whenever a test actually measures what it is intended to measure. If a test is valid,

then the employer knows that it is directly measuring the applicant's ability to perform the job and is not measuring something else or influenced by personal bias. For example, a person measuring a tree with a yardstick and finding it to be 34 inches high, feels that is a valid measurement. The yardstick could not actually measure a friend's ability to correctly estimate the height of the same tree. The friend's point of view—size and proximity to the tree—influences the guesstimate. The same type of influence occurs when individuals' "points of view" consciously or unconsciously influence decisions concerning job applicants. Since there were no yardsticks available to measure the validity of employment tests, the guidelines use standards for test validity:

SECTION 5. GENERAL STANDARDS FOR VALIDITY STUDIES: A. Acceptable types of validity studies. For the purposes of satisfying these guidelines, users may rely upon criterion–related validity studies, content validity studies or construct validity studies in accordance with the standards set forth in the technical standards of these guidelines.
B. Criterion–related content, and construct validity. Evidence of the validity of a test or other selection procedure by a criterion–related validity study should consist of empirical data demonstrating that the selection procedure is predictive of or significantly correlated with important elements of job performance. Evidence of the validity of a test or other selection procedure by a content validity study should consist of data showing that the content of the selection procedure is representative of important aspects of performance on the job for which the candidates are to be evaluated. Evidence of the validity of a test or other selection procedure through a construct validity study should consist of data showing that the procedure measures the degree to which candidates have identifiable characteristics which

---

8. Robert Gatewood and James Ledvinka, "Selection Interviewing and EEO: Mandate for Objectivity," *The Personnel Administrator* (May, 1976): 15–18.

have been determined to be important in successful performance in the job for which the candidates are to be evaluated.

Criterion-related validity can be established by collecting data from job applicants and employees. This form of validation correlates test scores to employees' success on the job. There are many criteria or measures of employee productivity which may be used such as absenteeism, sales levels, supervisory evaluations, or quantity of production. Two primary methods of establishing criterion-related validity are predictive validation and concurrent validation.

Predictive validity is preferred by the EEOC and usually the most difficult to determine. A predictive validity study requires testing the entire pool of job applicants, hiring them, and then correla-

ting their test scores with their criterion scores.

For example, to determine the validity of a test given to applicants for sales representative positions, all applicants during the previous month are tested. The applicants are then hired, given equal training, and assigned to sales routes. After one year, the total commission sales of the new employees (the criterion of job success) are correlated with their test scores. A resulting validity coefficient, r* = .67, would be significantly high and demonstrate that the test is valid for sales representatives because individuals' test performances relate to the criterion of job performance.

If the comparison of the applicants' test scores with their criterion scores produces a high correlation, then the organization may use the test for future appli-

FIGURE 5–4: *Model of Predictive Validity*

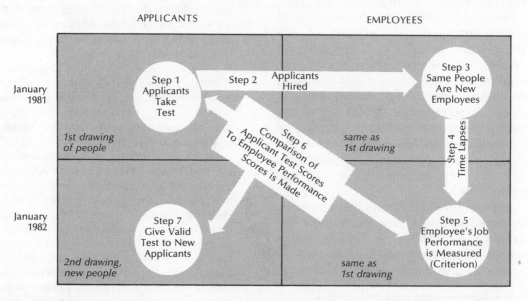

*r is a correlation coefficient which can vary from −1 to +1 with .67 being a high correlation. A validity coefficient is a correlation with one of the two variables being a test and the other being a job performance criterion.

FIGURE 5–5: *Model of Concurrent Validity*

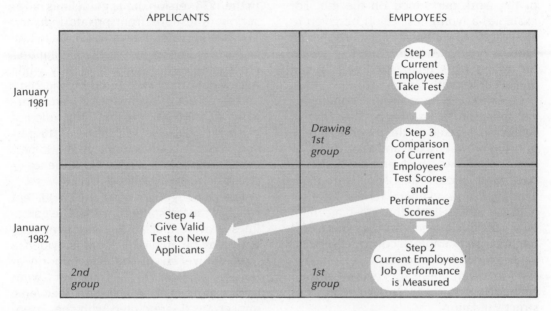

cants because it has evidence that the test is a valid predictor of employee performance.

Concurrent validity is quite similar to predictive validity in that test scores are compared to job performance measures. However, as concurrent indicates, this study collects both sets of scores at the same time. This is accomplished by testing current employees, for whom the organization has performance scores such as supervisory ratings. The major difference between the predictive and concurrent methods is that the predictive method tests applicants where the concurrent method tests present employees. This difference is very important because with the predictive method the firm can get test scores from the total range of individuals who might apply for the job. However, the concurrent method tests only those individuals who have been kept as employees. The concurrent method then

does not include the total range of applicants: the applicants who were not hired; those who were fired as employees; and those very good employees who were promoted. The predictive method compares present applicants to future applicants whereas the concurrent method compares present employees to future applicants.

For practical reasons the concurrent method is more preferable than the predictive method. One important reason is that administrators do not like to hire all applicants, some of whom very likely will fail as employees. Another reason is time. The concurrent method can be completed within a few weeks; because of the time lapse requirement the predictive method requires at least six months to a year.

Content validity is a nonempirical (not data based) approach to validation. In a content validation study the organization shows, often through job analysis, that the content of the test is actually a sample of the work performed on the job. For example, a typing test could be given to applicants for clerical positions which require typing. Another example would be testing bank teller applicants' speed and accuracy with figures.

Construct validity is another nonempirical approach to validation. This type of validation is based on the theoretical relationship between a test and a construct, or characteristic which an employee should have to be successful. Giving store manager applicants a general IQ test because management believes they need a certain level of intelligence to be successful might be an example of construct validity. Sales clerks being given "personality" tests to determine if they will work well with customers could be considered construct validation.

In general, the EEOC gives greatest preference to the predictive validity method and the least to construct validity. Both empirical methods, predictive and concurrent, are stronger validation methods because they involve empirical data collection and statistics which are not discriminatory. Content validity is at least a direct test of individuals' ability to perform some—usually not all—of the tasks required on the job. Construct validity is often management's last choice and may be hard to defend in court.

SECTION 4. D. ADVERSE IMPACT AND THE "FOUR-FIFTHS RULE": A selection rate for any race, sex, or ethnic group which is less than four-fifths (4/5) (or eighty percent) of the rate for the group with the highest rate will generally be regarded by the federal enforcement agencies as evidence of adverse impact, while a greater than four-fifths rate will generally not be regarded by federal enforcement agencies as evidence of adverse impact.

The *four-fifths rule* or "80 percent" rule in the 1978 version of the guidelines raises serious questions from private industry. The rule provides a quantitative definition of adverse impact, not a legal definition.[9] For example, if eight out of fifty white male applicants were hired (16 percent) and three out of twenty black male applicants (15 percent), the four-fifths rule has been met because four-fifths of 16 percent (12.8 percent) is less than the 15 percent hiring rate for blacks. No evidence of adverse impact would be present.

The word "generally" in the 80 percent rule has caused some concern. The guidelines provide that a more stringent standard may be applied if there is evidence the employer has discouraged minority or female applications.[10] Employers who want a more explicit definition of adverse impact are disappointed with the extensive use of the term *generally*.[11] "The fact that an employer has met the 'four-fifths' rule does not rule out the possibility of a federal agency finding adverse impact."[12]

SECTION 1. B. PURPOSE OF GUIDELINES: These guidelines do not require a user to conduct validity studies of selection procedures where no adverse impact results. However, all users are encouraged to use selection procedures which are valid, especially users operating under merit principles.

SECTION 4. C. THE BOTTOM LINE PROVISION: If the information called for shows that the total selection process for a job has an

9. "Uniform Guidelines on Employee Selection Procedures (1978)," *Federal Register* (August 25, 1978): 38291.

10. William A. Simon, Jr., "A Practical Approach to the Uniform Selection Guidelines," *The Personnel Administrator* (November, 1979): 75–80.

11. David E. Robertson, "New Directions in EEO Guidelines," *Personnel Journal* (July, 1978): 360–62.

12. Simon, pp. 78–80.

adverse impact, the individual components of the selection process should be evaluated for adverse impact. If this information shows that the total selection process does not have an adverse impact, the federal enforcement agencies, in the exercise of their administrative and prosecutorial discretion, in usual circumstances, will not expect a user to evaluate the individual components for adverse impact, or to validate such individual components, and will not take enforcement action based upon adverse impact of any component of that process, including the separate procedure that is used as an alternative method of selection.

This section of the guidelines permits one component of the selection process to have adverse impact if the total selection procedure does not produce adverse impact. If an employer's selection process meets the 80 percent rule but the interview, as one of several components, violates the 80 percent rule, the federal government usually will not take action or require validation of the interview process as part of the entire selection procedure. This *bottom line provision of the guidelines* allows employers to review only their bottom line figures—the total number and percentage hired in each applicant category and not each step in the selection process which would be time consuming.

SECTION 4. INFORMATION REQUIRED: Information on impact.—A. Records concerning impact. Each user should maintain and have available for inspection records or other information which will disclose the impact which its tests and other selection procedures have upon employment opportunities of persons by identifiable race, sex, or ethnic group as set forth in subparagraph B below in order to determine compliance with these guidelines. Where there are large numbers of applicants and procedures are

administered frequently, such information may be retained on a sample basis, provided that the sample is appropriate in terms of the applicant population and adequate in size.

The guidelines require that certain records be kept by employers. Private employers must complete the EEO-1 form annually; it includes the number of applicants and employees by minority group and sex. The format is quite similar to that required in affirmative action reports.

The employer must indicate on the EEO-1 form if the selection process for any job has had an adverse impact on any minority/female group which constitutes 2 percent of the relevant labor force.[13] This section means that employers are not required to maintain records for minority groups which constitute less than 2 percent of the relevant labor force. Therefore, some employers will only be concerned with adverse impact against females and blacks since many sections of the United States do not contain 2 percent of other minority groups.

Court Cases
RACIAL DISCRIMINATION
Griggs v. *Duke Power Co.*
401 U.S. 424 (1971)
Supreme Court of the United States

The question at issue was if the Civil Rights Act of 1964, Title VII, prohibits employers from requiring that applicants have a high school education or pass a standardized, general intelligence test. Neither condition of employment was shown to be significant for successful job performance. Both requirements disqualify black applicants at a substantially higher rate than white applicants, and the job

13. Simon, p. 77.

FIGURE 5–6: ***Equal Employment Opportunity Commission Employer Information Report EEO-1***

Standard Form 100
(Rev 12-76)
Approved GAO B 180541 (R0077)
Expires 12-31-78

EQUAL EMPLOYMENT OPPORTUNITY

EMPLOYER INFORMATION REPORT EEO-1

Joint Reporting Committee

- Equal Employment Opportunity Commission
- Office of Federal Contract Compliance Programs

Section A — TYPE OF REPORT

Refer to instructions for number and types of reports to be filed.

1. Indicate by marking in the appropriate box the type of reporting unit for which this copy of the form is submitted (MARK ONLY ONE BOX)

(1) ☐ Single-establishment Employer Report

Multi-establishment Employer:
(2) ☐ Consolidated Report
(3) ☐ Headquarters Unit Report
(4) ☐ Individual Establishment Report (submit one for each establishment with 25 or more employees)
(5) ☐ Special Report

2. Total number of reports being filed by this Company (Answer on Consolidated Report only) ______

Section B — COMPANY IDENTIFICATION *(To, be answered by all employers)* — OFFICE USE ONLY

1. Parent Company
   a. Name of parent company (owns or controls establishment in item 2) omit if same as label — a

Name of receiving office | Address (Number and street) — b

City or town | County | State | ZIP code | b. Employer Identification No.

2. Establishment for which this report is filed (Omit if same as label)
   a. Name of establishment — c

Address (Number and street) | City or town | County | State | ZIP code — d

b. Employer Identification No. (If same as label, skip.)

3. Parent company affiliation (Multi-establishment Employers Answer on Consolidated Report only)
   a. Name of parent—affiliated company | b. Employer Identification No.

Address (Number and street) | City or town | County | State | ZIP code

Section C — EMPLOYERS WHO ARE REQUIRED TO FILE *(To be answered by all employers)*

☐ Yes ☐ No 1. Does the entire company have at least 100 employees in the payroll period for which you are reporting?

☐ Yes ☐ No 2. Is your company affiliated through common ownership and/or centralized management with other entities in an enterprise with a total employment of 100 or more?

☐ Yes ☐ No 3. Does the company or any of its establishments (a) have 50 or more employees AND (b) is not exempt as provided by 41 CFR 60-1.5, AND either (1) is a prime government contractor or first-tier subcontractor, and has a contract, subcontract, or purchase order amounting to $50,000 or more, or (2) serves as a depository of Government funds in any amount or is a financial institution which is an issuing and paying agent for U.S. Savings Bonds and Savings Notes?

NOTE: If the answer is yes to ANY of these questions, complete the entire form, otherwise skip to Section G.

in question was formerly filled by only white employees.

The Duke Power Company contended that its general intelligence tests were permitted by the Civil Rights Act because the act authorizes the use of any professionally developed test that is not designed, intended, or used, to discriminate. The EEOC, however, contended that the Civil Rights Act and Congress intended only job-related tests to be authorized.

The court noted that neither the high school completion requirement nor the general intelligence test had been shown to be directly related to successful performance of the jobs for which they were required. A company official had testified

FIGURE 5–6: (Continued)

Section D — EMPLOYMENT DATA

Employment at this establishment--Report all permanent, temporary or part-time employees including apprentices and on-the-job trainees unless specifically excluded as set forth in the instructions. Enter the appropriate figures on all lines and in all columns. Blank spaces will be considered as zeros.

JOB CATEGORIES	OVERALL TOTALS (SUM OF COL B THRU K) A	MALE						FEMALE				
		WHITE (NOT OF HISPANIC ORIGIN) B	BLACK (NOT OF HISPANIC ORIGIN) C	HISPANIC D	ASIAN OR PACIFIC ISLANDER E	AMERICAN INDIAN ALASKAN NATIVE F	WHITE (NOT OF HISPANIC ORIGIN) G	BLACK (NOT OF HISPANIC ORIGIN) H	HISPANIC I	ASIAN OR PACIFIC ISLANDER J	AMERICAN INDIAN OR ALASKAN NATIVE K
Officials and Managers											
Professionals											
Technicians											
Sales Workers											
Office and Clerical											
Craft Workers (Skilled)											
Operatives (Semi-Skilled)											
Laborers (Unskilled)											
Service Workers											
TOTAL											
Total employment reported in previous EEO-1 report											

(The trainees below should also be included in the figures for the appropriate occupational categories above)

| Formal On-the-job trainees | White collar | | | | | | | | | | | |
| | Production | | | | | | | | | | | |

1. NOTE: On consolidated report, skip questions 2-5 and Section E.
2. How was information as to race or ethnic group in Section D obtained?
   1 ☐ Visual Survey   3 ☐ Other — Specify ....
   2 ☐ Employment Record   ....
3. Dates of payroll period used –

4. Pay period of last report submitted for this establishment

5. Does this establishment employ apprentices?
   This year? 1 ☐ Yes 2 ☐ No
   Last year? 1 ☐ Yes 2 ☐ No

Section E — ESTABLISHMENT INFORMATION

1. Is the location of the establishment the same as that reported last year?
   1 ☐ Yes 2 ☐ No 3 ☐ Did not report last year 4 ☐ Reported on combined basis

2. Is the major business activity at this establishment the same as that reported last year?
   1 ☐ Yes 2 ☐ No 3 ☐ No report last year 4 ☐ Reported on combined basis

3. What is the major activity of this establishment? (Be specific, i.e., manufacturing steel castings, retail grocer, wholesale plumbing supplies, title insurance, etc. Include the specific type of product or type of service provided, as well as the principal business or industrial activity.)

OFFICE USE ONLY

e.

Section F — REMARKS

Use this item to give any identification data appearing on last report which differs from that given above, explain major changes in composition or reporting units, and other pertinent information.

Section G — CERTIFICATION (See instructions G)

Check one
1. ☐ All reports are accurate and were prepared in accordance with the instructions (check on consolidated only)
2. ☐ This report is accurate and was prepared in accordance with the instructions.

Name of Certifying Official	Title	Signature		Date
Name of person to contact regarding this report (Type or print)	Address (Number and street)			
Title	City and State	ZIP code	Telephone Area Code	Number	Extension

All reports and information obtained from individual reports will be kept confidential as required by Section 709 (e) of Title VII.

SOURCE: *Mission, 5*, U.S. Equal Employment Opportunity Commission, (Washington, DC: U.S. Printing Office, 1977), p. 13.

that the requirements were chosen because the company believed they would improve the quality of the work force. The court stated that if an employment practice which excludes blacks cannot be shown to be related to job performance, it is prohibited by the Civil Rights Act.

The Civil Rights Act does not command that any person be hired simply because of former discrimination or minority group membership. The act does try to remove artificial, arbitrary, and unnecessary barriers to employment which discriminate on the basis of race, color, religion, sex, or national origin.

In this landmark case regarding Title VII of the Civil Rights Act, the Supreme Court's decision provided critical direction to the interpretation of the act. The decision established that (1) the employer must prove that any employment requirement is job related; (2) the absence of discriminatory intentions does not absolve an employer who has discriminated in practice; (3) even professionally developed, widely adopted tests must be shown to be significantly related to an applicant's ability to successfully perform on the job.

REVERSE DISCRIMINATION
United Steelworkers v. Weber
443 U.S. 193 (1979)
Supreme Court of the United States

Weber alleged that the filling of craft trainee positions under the affirmative action program, which reserved 50 percent of the openings for blacks, had resulted in junior black employees receiving training in preference to more senior white employees. Weber contended that Congress intended in Title VII to make it illegal to "discriminate . . . because of . . . race" in hiring, promotions, transfers, and the selecting of apprentices for training programs. This is seen as a literal interpretation of the Civil Rights Act.

The court noted that while the argument made by Weber was "not without force," it did not consider the spirit of the 1964 Civil Rights Act. Congress' primary concern was with "the plight of the Negro in our economy." Prior to the act, blacks were largely relegated to unskilled and lower level jobs. Congress intended to open employment opportunities for blacks in occupations previously closed to them. Given the legislative history of the Civil Rights Act, the court contended that it could not agree that Congress intended to prohibit the private sector from accomplishing the goal of the act. The court noted that it is a "familiar rule, that a thing may be within the letter of the statute and yet not within the statute, because [it is] not within its spirit, nor within the intention of its makers."

The court concluded that the adoption of the affirmative action plan falls within the area of discretion left by Title VII to the private sector to adopt plans designed to eliminate conspicuous racial imbalance.

The Weber case is viewed by many to be the landmark *reverse discrimination* case. In effect, it may have voided the concept of reverse discrimination in employment practices when a firm is following an approved affirmative action plan. The concept of reverse discrimination had been the major issue in a 1978 Supreme Court decision in *Bakke* v. *University of California*.[14] In that case, Bakke, a white male, claimed reverse discrimination when denied admission to the University of California at Davis Medical School. Bakke had been denied admission even though he had scored higher on tests than some of sixteen minority students who were admitted because the school had reserved sixteen positions for them. In a five-to-four decision the Supreme Court

---

14. Bakke v. University of California (1978).

ruled that Bakke should be admitted even though race could be considered in a school's admission plan. The vagueness of the Bakke decision may have encouraged the Supreme Court to hear the Weber case the following year in order to address the question of reverse discrimination.

The Weber decision established that: (1) the Civil Rights Act cannot be literally interpreted, but must be considered in light of its historical perspective; (2) Title VII permits employers to establish race conscious affirmative action plans, although it does not require them to do so; and (3) such affirmative action plans can require that a certain number or percentage of positions be filled by minorities or women.

AGE DISCRIMINATION
Coates v. *National Cash Register Co.*
433 F.Supp. 655 (1977)
U.S. District Court (WD of Va.)

In 1975 the National Cash Register Company (NCR) reduced its staff of field engineers due to deteriorating economic conditions. The Age Discrimination and Employment Act states that it is unlawful for an employer to discharge or to discriminate against any individual "because of such individual's age."

NCR stated that its decision to discharge certain individuals was not based on age, but on the training of the individuals. The court found the evidence in the case established that the relative training levels of NCR employees were directly related to the age of the employees. Therefore, by using the training level as the basis of the discharge decision, NCR indirectly discharged the plaintiffs because of their ages. The age discrimination need not be direct or intentional; the

court held that the plaintiffs were discharged "because of their ages."

The Coates case clearly determined that the Age Discrimination and Employment Act of 1967 has "teeth" since: (1) the court held that just because an employer's action does not directly discriminate on the basis of age, if age is a "determining factor," the employer may be guilty of age discrimination; (2) individuals who have been subjects of age discrimination may be awarded back wages, reinstatement, and damages for pain and suffering.

SEX DISCRIMINATION
EEOC v. *Multiline Cans, Inc.*
73-223 (1974)
U.S. District Court (MD of Fla.)

The defendant, Shirley Duggan, filed a grievance against the company alleging a violation of the collective bargaining agreement. Her grievance was submitted to arbitration on the issue of "whether the company violated Article 23 of the agreement when it refused to place the grievant on the job of lift truck operator." The arbitrator's decision was against Shirley Duggan.

The defendant, Multiline Cans, Inc., asserts that the arbitration decision was based on the identical issues that Shirley Duggan then alleged to the EEOC and, therefore, barred any further action. The EEOC argued that as an enforcement agency of the United States, it is not barred by a private contractual arrangement. The EEOC also argued that previous Court of Appeals decisions contended that an arbitration award is only proper where the contract and arbitral process involved adequately safeguarded the public interest in Title VII to eliminate discrimination in employment.

The court found that the collective bargaining agreement, which was in effect at the time of Ms. Duggan's grievance, did not place upon the employer an obligation similar to that imposed by Title VII. Nowhere in the agreement was there any expressed prohibition against sexual discrimination. Thus, the issue of sex discrimination raised in the EEOC's suit was beyond the arbitrator's power of decision. Also the U.S. Court of Appeals for the Fifth Circuit in *Hutchings* v. *United States Industries, Inc.* held that the invocation of arbitration under a collective bargaining agreement does not bar an employee from seeking Title VII relief in federal district court. This suit established that barring women from jobs solely on the basis of sex, and not physical ability, is discriminating.

In summary, federal legislation and court cases have greatly influenced the recruitment and selection of personnel.

Through interpretation of legislation and precedent cases, the U.S. Supreme Court and lesser courts have affected personnel policy creation and implementation since the mid-sixties. Because the burden of proof in legal cases is on the employer, administrators have utilized job analysis to document that their pay systems are providing equal pay for equal work. Employers must also be able to prove that their selection techniques validly and accurately predict future employee behavior. Subsequently, management has required that all employees who may be part of the recruitment and selection process be carefully trained to avoid accidental or intentional discrimination charges. While affirmative action programs are not required of all employers, many have voluntarily implemented such programs to ensure that their organizations have the minority representation required for federal contract eligibility.

The Solution

Wirtz, Secretary of Labor *v.* Basic, Inc. *illustrates why Congress saw the need for the Equal Pay Act. Company officials made an arbitrary, undocumented decision to pay a male a higher wage than females doing the same work.*

The U.S. District Court of Nevada noted that "Application of the equal pay standard is not dependent on job classification or titles but depends rather on actual job requirements and performance." Equal does not mean identical, and insubstantial differences in the skill, effort, and responsibility requirements of particular jobs should be ignored. The job requirements should be viewed as a whole. The court commented that as a shift analyst, O'Dell was entitled to a different rate of pay which he was not entitled to on the day shift. Inasmuch as Barredo and Jones are doing equal work, the wage rates of both were raised to equal O'Dell's.

KEY TERMS AND CONCEPTS

Equal Pay Act of 1963
Substantially equal work
Civil Rights Act of 1964, Title VII
EEOC
Probable Cause
Conciliation Meeting
Affirmative Action
Neutrality Laws
BFOQ
Age Discrimination Act of 1967
Vocational Rehabilitation Act of 1973
Vietnam Era Veterans Readjustment
   Act of 1974
Executive Order 11246

Work Force Analysis
Underutilization of Minorities
Discrimination
Adverse Impact
Criterion-related Validity
Predictive Validity
Content Validity
Concurrent Validity
Construct Validity
Four-fifths Rule
"Bottom line" Provision of
   the *Guidelines*
Reverse Discrimination

FOR REVIEW

1. Why does the Equal Pay Act have wider applications among organizations than other federal legislation?

2. Which organizations are affected by the Civil Rights Act? What is its primary purpose?

3. Why should young employees today be concerned with the Age Discrimination Act and open retirement?

4. How can a firm get cooperation from managers in implementing an affirmative action program?

5. What should managers have learned from the *Griggs* v. *Duke Power Co.* and *United Steelworkers* v. *Weber* cases?

FOR DISCUSSION

1. Do you favor a higher retirement age to ease the burden on the

Social Security System or early retirement to create advancement opportunities? Why? Will you most likely make the same decision in forty years?

2. Enumerate various jobs you have seen handicapped workers performing and discuss jobs handicapped workers could perform.

3. Cite examples of reverse discrimination by local employers. How could reverse discrimination be defended in each case?

4. If you believed you were discriminated against, under what circumstances would you contact the local EEOC or let the situation ride? Why?

5. What has your community done to help Vietnam Vets secure employment? What else could be done?

SUPPLEMENTARY READING

Dyer, Frank J. "An Alternative to Validating Selection Tests." *Personnel Journal* 57 (April 1978): 200–203.

Ebel, Robert L. "Comments on Some Problems of Employment Testing." *Personnel Psychology* 30 (Spring 1977): 55–64.

Famularo, Joseph J., ed. *Handbook of Modern Personnel Administration*. New York: McGraw-Hill, 1972, Part IV.

Feild, Hubert, and Bayley, Susan. "Employment Test Validation for Minority and Nonminority Production Workers." *Personnel Psychology* 30 (Spring 1977): 37–48.

Guion, Robert M. " 'Content Validity' in Moderation." *Personnel Psychology* 31 (Summer 1978): 205–213.

Hoyman, Michele, and Robinson, Ronda. "Interpreting the New Sexual Harrassment Guidelines." *Personnel Journal* 59 (December 1980): 996–1000.

Koen, Clifford. "The Pre-Employment Inquiry Guide." *Personnel Journal* 59 (October 1980): 825–29.

Ledvinka, James, and Schoenfeldt, Lyle F. "Legal Developments in Employment Testing: Albemarle and Beyond." *Personnel Psychology* 31 (Spring 1978): 1–14.

McCormick, Ernest J., and Tiffin, Joseph. *Industrial Psychology*. 6th. ed. Englewood Cliffs, NJ: Prentice-Hall, 1974.

Principles for the Validation and Use of Personnel Selection Procedures. Washington, DC: Division of Industrial-Organization Psychology, American Psychological Association, 1975.

For Analysis: EEOC *v.* Local 638
12 F.E.P. 715 (S.D.N.Y. 1975)

In cases involving possible employee discrimination like EEOC
v. Local 638 *elementary statistics are often used to resolve
the situation. This case is a good example of why personnel
officers need a basic understanding of simple statistical
techniques.*

    *An examination was given by Local 638 for interested
apprentices to determine if they had reached journeymen
status. Fifty black apprentices took the exam—none passed;
280 white apprentices took the exam and only 34 passed. To
determine whether any statistically significant difference existed
between black or white test results, the Chi-Square (X^2) Test
was utilized.*

    *In this case, the null hypothesis—a hypothesis that an
observed difference is due to chance alone—was that there
was no significant difference in the test results of blacks and
whites on the journeyman examination. The alternate
hypothesis was that there was a difference in the performance
of blacks and whites on the journeyman examination.*

Questions:

1. *Which hypothesis is supported by a Chi-Square Test?*

2. *Do you see any problems in using the Chi-Square Test in
   this type of case?*

3. *If you were the judge in this case, what would you
   decide?*

SELECTED PROFESSIONAL READING

Should Courts Write Your Job Descriptions?

GEORGE R. WENDT

The Equal Pay Act of 1963 has wider applications among employers than any other piece of fair employment legislation because it has no statutory minimum on firm size based on number of employees in the firm. This is unlike the Civil Rights Act of 1964 as amended in 1972, the Age Discrimination in Employment Act of 1967 and many state statutes in the fair employment field. It is like, however, the Civil Rights Acts of 1866, 1870 and 1871, which are being interpreted by the courts as covering employment situations. In practical terms, the Equal Pay Act applies if a firm has two or more employees.

Through 1972 education amendments to the Equal Pay Act, coverage of the equal pay provisions was extended to executive, administrative, professional and outside sales personnel. But such employees still remain exempt from the minimum wage and overtime provisions of the original Fair Labor Standards Act of 1938. In May, 1974, seven million state, federal and other employees were added to coverage under the Equal Pay Act. Since then the U.S. Department of Labor may also recover damages equal to back pay awards (up to two years), whereas before only individual complainants under civil suit could recover both back pay and damages.

It is well to keep in mind that the Equal Pay Act was in the first instance an amendment to the Fair Labor Standards Act. But standing alone it is receiving increasing attention through litigation. Finally in 1974, the case of *Corning Glass Works* v. *Brennan* was heard. This case reached the Supreme Court through the consolidation of conflicting opinions presented by the Second and Third Circuit Courts of Appeals. However, over the years, the Fifth Circuit Court of Appeals has heard more precedent-setting cases on equal pay matters than any other Circuit. These cases include *Weeks* v. *Southern Bell Telephone and Telegraph Company*, *Hodgson* v. *Brookhaven General Hospital* in 1970, *Hodgson* v. *American Bank of Commerce* in 1974 and *Brennan* v. *Victoria Bank and Trust Company* in 1974. In yet another case (*Orr* v. *MacNeill & Son, Inc.*) of the Fifth Circuit in April, 1975, the issues are clearly equal pay even though suit was brought under the Civil Rights Act of 1964 as well. The latter case is important because it concerns exempt managerial employees.

An increasing number of cases under the Equal Pay Act have arisen in U.S. district courts which involve banks, hospitals, school systems, universities and retailers. The Act prohibits pay differences because of sex and, thus, has a limited definition of sex discrimination. Sex discrimination covered by the Civil Rights Act of 1964 (Title VII) is considerably broader and may include acts of hiring, promotion, dismissal and constructive discharge, job assignment, seniority, fringe benefits and pay matters. Frequently the two acts are related and intertwined as they apply to given situations.

These things seem very clear. However, courts have gotten into the business of writing job or position descriptions, as well as detailed examinations of job content and, in actuality, accomplished job evaluations. To do this they have depended heavily on the basic principles of scientific job evaluation systems to reach their decisions. Equally clear is the heavy reliance of the Equal Pay Act itself on the principles of modern job evaluation. Our purpose here is to examine some of these relationships and to suggest ways of keeping the courts out of the average personnel department or industrial engineering department.

The courts have become involved in job evaluation because the Equal Pay Act describes equal jobs in the four component factors of modern job evaluation systems: skill, effort, responsibility and working conditions.

The case of *Corning Glass Works* v. *Brennan* did establish for all courts the marriage of scientific job evaluation and the Equal Pay Act. In brief outline, the court ruled that higher base rates on a second shift where all males performed the same job as females performed at a lesser rate on a first shift was sex discrimination, even though the differences were an historical accident going back almost fifty years. The court held further that to allow women to work the second shift at their current base rates plus a night shift differential, which the men on the second shift received as well, did not cure anything and would still be sex discrimination. Finally, the court held that even after rates for all sexes on all shifts were equalized, paying out-of-range red circle rates only perpetuated the very condition that the case was about. The court took great pains to examine and determine that the time of day a person works does not constitute a difference in working conditions, one of the four conditions which must be met to have equal jobs. There were never any claims in this case that different sexes were performing different work.

The Equal Pay Act does allow exceptions which are common in industry and commerce. Payments may be different for the same work if such differences are based on seniority, merit, piecework, or factors other than sex. Were it not so, nearly every wage and salary plan in use would have to be scrapped.

Another key phrase in the act which is raised repeatedly in litigated cases requires that employers "shall not, in order to comply with the provisions of this subsection, reduce the wage rate of any employee." This means that lower wages must be raised, not the higher wages reduced. On top of back wages which may be determined as owing, damages equal to the dollars of back pay due are allowed by statute. Courts will sometimes award attorney's fees and courts costs as well.

The concept of "substantially equal" has arisen in court decisions. That is, the "equal" skill, effort and responsibility under similar working conditions of the statute has been defined as substantially equal in the court room. This means jobs do not have to be precisely the same, or identical.

The substantially equal concept widens the areas for disagreement between litigants. But it is consistent with the marriage of the law and modern job evaluation. Modern job evaluation has, since its inception, recognized the substantially equal concept in that any one job may fall within a range of points or money values; yet it is classified in the same job grade as any number of other similar kinds of jobs— similar meaning requiring similar amounts of effort, skill and responsibility. It is unlikely that any two job analysts working independently would rate all the factors to the same degree for any one job, but it is also unlikely they would disagree on what grade a particular job will merit. Job evaluation rates the factors within a job, *not* the person doing the job.

Neither do similar job titles make equal jobs, or make jobs equal. An assembler of electronic components on printed wiring boards does not do the same thing as an assembler of steel office furniture does. Providing nursing care in an intensive care unit of a hospital is not the same thing as providing nursing care in the surgical unit of the same hospital, nor is it the same as being a nurse in a convalescent home. Different sexes carrying the same job titles does not mean substantially equal work either, as *Orr* v. *MacNeill and Son, Inc.*, demonstrated in 1975, at the appeals court level. Relying on the substantially equal doctrine, the appeals court panel found that a female accounting manager in a 40-employee insurance agency did not perform work equal to managers of underwriting or claims who happened to be males. There are employers who use job titles very loosely as a way of providing psychic income to employees. The department manager of one department may be paid twice as much as the manager of another. When divergencies are that wide (not so in *Orr* v. *Mac-Neill*) somebody is trying to fool somebody. Such situations can cause hard feelings.

Over the years banks have advanced several cases into appellate courts on issues primarily centering on tellers. In 1975, banks with fifty employees, rather than 100, came under revised EEO-1 reporting requirements.

The Southern District of Texas has dealt with three different banks in cases which have been appealed to the Fifth Circuit Court. Judge Thornberry may well be the nation's judicial expert on equal pay matters, having heard nearly all the appeals in this circuit over the years. In nearly all cases the issues are divided on whether male and female tellers are performing substantially equal work. Hiring rates have been examined when they have been different, performance review systems have been questioned, the presence of training programs has been assessed and the value of extra duties performed has been dealt with. The general theme in all the cases is that male and female tellers do not perform work that is different enough to qualify for unequal rates of pay, despite claims to the opposite.

Companies concerned with union contracts most frequently protect employees from working out of grade by paying for the highest skill or responsibility factors present within a job even though the duties may be performed only infrequently. It is a way to avoid arguments with the union. Since banking is not a heavily unionized industry, it is through court actions, rather than contract negotiations or arbitration cases, that some of this concept carried over into banking. Banks have in particular pushed the issue that males in training programs constitute a difference.

About the only thing missing in the various court evaluations of job content is specific reference to the "degrees" that various factors may be present in a job. Court cases usually deal in the frequency of occurrences—that is, how often catherizations may be performed in a week or how often the lifting of heavy objects might be required. While degrees in job evaluation may include frequencies of performing specific duties, more often, degrees refer to the depth or extent of exposure to certain factors within a job. Thus, frequency of lifting certain objects and their weight as a measure of physical demand makes sense, but frequency makes no sense when dealing with education, experience, equipment, effects of errors and so on. For these factors, it is time, accountability and judgment that play an important part.

It should not be assumed that employers involved in the cases outlined did not have position descriptions or job evaluations. In most cases they did. But, courts will rewrite descriptions and re-evaluate jobs when necessary. They will also write job descriptions if employers will not.

When employers opt for scientific job evaluations and it is done properly, several fair employment and industrial relations concerns will be attacked simultaneously:

1. Scientific job evaluation (point analysis or factor analysis) is geared to preventing or dissolving historic or systemic inequalities between jobs requiring substantially equal skill, effort and responsibility under similar working conditions. Such inequalities may have a base in past economic conditions, in traditional assumptions about what men should do and what women should do, in changing technology and methods, or in very rapid growth and urgency to get the product out or provide the service.

2. Scientific job evaluation can be debased by a management which uses such a system to provide psychic income (providing fancy titles, for example) or plays favorites and rates individuals rather than jobs. Job evaluation should not reflect a need to upgrade some jobs and downgrade others or create new levels of supervision.

3. Equity among jobs within a firm is necessary as well as equity among firms in similar industries and in the labor market.

Systematic job evaluation permits employers to participate intelligently in area wage surveys and, in turn, to get results of such surveys. Suzie's unhappiness with wages may come from knowing what Frank at the next desk is earning and from knowing what Lynn at the company down the street is being paid.

4. Good job descriptions and position evaluations are very helpful for government contractors and subcontractors who must prepare workforce utilization analyses as required by Revised Order #4. Lines of progression should be fairly evident when job grades exist.

5. Good job evaluation systems will make the preparation of the Employer Information Report (EEO-1) much easier for those companies needing to make this report.

6. The first equal pay case involving exempt managerial employees heard in April 1975, may open the door for more such cases, even though the complainant lost the case.

7. Beware red-circle rates of pay. Perhaps such people should be promoted or new position descriptions created.

8. In inflationary times, the problem of hiring new personnel at rates of pay the same or even more than what is currently being paid employees with service on a particular job and longevity with the employer is often raised by incumbents. So long as the rates paid are within established ranges for the job, the incumbent does not have a case under the Equal Pay Act. However, if it were to happen that all new males hired for a particular job received more pay than all females on that same job, then a pattern of discrimination emerges. It is precisely such patterns the investigators are attempting to devote more time and effort to.

9. Because jobs change, position descriptions and job evaluations must be audited from time to time.

10. To make job descriptions and job evaluations a valuable program, they must have performance and salary evaluations (either separate or together) as part of a total wage and salary administration plan. Performance and salary evaluations each operate with their own guidelines as to frequency, factors to be evaluated, amounts of increments, reasons for denying increments, bases for dismissal or transfer and so on.

A Labor Department compliance officer related the story of an employer who was so proud of his equal pay record because he was paying all the women in a particular job more than the men. Since that is not the intent of equal pay laws, adjustments had to be made. Equal pay for substantially equal effort, skill and responsibility under similar working conditions should generally mean mixed rates of pay among men and women on any one job, given allowances for differences justified by seniority, merit, or quantity and quality of output produced. When it is all put together scientifically, it should mean the courts can get out of the job description and job evaluation business.

Filling out an application is often the first step toward employment.

6

PERSONNEL RECUITMENT

===== *Labor Market Information* =====

===== *Cost/Benefit Analysis* =====

===== *Recruitment Sources* =====

===== *Methods of Recruitment* =====

===== *Successful Recruitment* =====

The Problem: College Recruiting

Nina Combs returned from a three-day recruitment trip to four college campuses. She interviewed eighty-eight college seniors but found few promising candidates to fill her firm's needs for fifteen computer programmers. For the last seven years she has made many, many recruitment trips to college campuses, and can only recall five cases where she was able to hire programmers from a campus interview. "Why only five?" she asks herself.

Combs is a recruiter/interviewer for the large west coast branch of a national insurance firm which employs almost four thousand employees in California alone. The office is located in a small town about two hundred miles from the nearest large state university. Combs has had countless interviews with college seniors who either are not qualified for the job, are not mature enough, or end up taking a similar job in a large city. In the end, the firm has gotten by with the few programmers it has working overtime. Many are loyal employees from the local area who are happy there. But recruiting trained applicants has always been a problem for the company.

The future does not hold much promise. Combs realizes that the demand for programmers is increasing faster than the supply. Yet, her supervisor, Ned Beckmann, told her only last week she must increase her campus recruiting trips because by next year the number of vacant programmer positions will increase to twenty-five.

Every organization regardless of size, product, or service must recruit applicants to fill positions. While there are few really new techniques in the recruitment field today, recent emphasis on different recruitment methods and legal considerations have given personnel specialists a renewed interest in recruitment.

Recruitment is the process of acquiring a pool of applicants, who are available and qualified to fill positions in the organization. Most often personnel administrators will only actively recruit as positions become vacant. Through direct application by individuals and by walk-in applicants, an organization can maintain a large pool of available and qualified applicants without much additional recruitment effort. However, due to federal guidelines and the increasing need to hire the very best applicants, today administrators find it necessary to recruit even when they do have a large number of available and qualified applicants.

The most available group of people that organizations can recruit is, of course, the unemployed who can be contacted through direct application, employment agencies, or by media advertisements. In the 1980s organizations most likely will continue a trend which began in the 1970s, to develop additional sources of recruitment previously not utilized.

Part-time employees are a good example of a recently-developed recruitment source. In past years some managers believed that part-time employees were not loyal to the organization and that they did not produce at the level of full-time employees. However, organizations have recently found that part-time employees are very productive and that there are qualified applicants who wish to work on a part-time basis. Due to a decrease in benefit costs and lower wages, the part-time employees are less expensive to the organization; if the part-time employees can produce at the same level as full-time employees, they become an attractive alternative. Administrators have also found that frequently part-time employees have a greater enthusiasm for jobs that are traditionally boring and routine because they do not face constant repetition, day after day, for long periods of time. As Figure 6–1 indicates, more people are joining the labor force each year, many of them through part-time work.

Underemployed individuals are another group of applicants which organizations realize can be successfully recruited. Due to a better-educated work force and a shortage of better paying positions in many parts of the country and many occupations, some full-time employees feel that they are underemployed because their jobs are unrelated to their interests and training. In fact, these people are not looking for jobs actively in many cases, but they can be recruited by another organization because they would prefer jobs which are more in line with their training and skills. When firms actively recruit employees of other organizations this is termed *pirating*. Administrators may hear of an employee at a competitive firm or a firm in a related industry and become aware of that individual's ability. They steal or pirate an individual away from the present employer by offering a more attractive salary, better working conditions, or other benefits. In some industries and for some large firms pirating individuals from other organizations is preferred to hiring recent college graduates because trained, experienced persons can more quickly become productive and successful.

FIGURE 6–1: *Labor Force and Participation Rates, 1960 to 1978*

[Persons 16 years old and over. Labor force data are annual averages of monthly figures. Includes Armed Forces. Rates are based on total population of each specified group as of July and represent proportion of each specified group in labor forces. See also *Historical Statistics, Colonial Times to 1970*, series D 29–41]

RACE, SEX, AND AGE	TOTAL LABOR FORCE (millions)							PARTICIPATION RATES (percent)						
	1960	1965	1970	1975	1976	1977	1978	1960	1965	1970	1975	1976	1977	1978
Total	72.1	77.2	85.9	94.8	96.9	99.5	102.5	59.2	58.8	60.3	60.9	61.2	61.8	62.7
White	64.2	68.6	76.4	83.9	85.7	87.9	90.2	58.8	58.5	60.2	61.1	61.5	62.1	62.9
Male	44.1	45.9	48.8	51.6	52.2	53.1	53.9	82.6	80.4	79.7	78.1	77.9	78.0	78.0
Female	20.1	22.8	27.5	32.3	33.5	34.8	36.3	36.0	37.7	42.0	45.4	46.3	47.4	48.8
Black and other	7.9	8.6	9.5	10.9	11.3	11.7	12.4	63.0	62.1	61.1	58.8	59.1	59.5	61.2
Male	4.8	5.1	5.5	6.1	6.2	6.4	6.7	80.1	77.4	74.7	70.4	69.7	69.8	70.8
Female	3.1	3.5	4.0	4.8	5.1	5.3	5.7	47.2	48.1	48.9	48.7	49.7	50.5	52.8
Male	48.9	50.9	54.3	57.7	58.4	59.5	60.5	82.4	80.1	79.2	77.3	76.9	77.0	77.2
16–19 years	3.2	3.8	4.4	5.1	5.2	5.3	5.4	58.6	55.7	57.5	60.2	60.3	61.8	62.7
16–17 years	1.3	1.6	1.8	2.1	2.1	2.1	2.2	45.9	44.1	46.7	48.5	48.4	50.0	51.5
18–19 years	1.8	2.3	2.6	3.1	3.1	3.2	3.2	73.1	68.3	68.8	72.1	72.1	73.5	74.0
20–24 years	4.9	5.9	7.4	8.2	8.4	8.6	8.8	88.9	86.2	85.1	84.6	85.2	85.3	85.6
25–34 years	10.9	10.7	12.0	14.5	15.0	15.5	15.9	96.4	96.0	95.0	94.2	94.2	94.2	94.3
35–44 years	11.5	11.5	10.8	10.6	10.7	10.9	11.3	96.4	96.2	95.7	94.8	94.6	94.9	94.6
45–54 years	9.6	10.1	10.5	10.5	10.4	10.2	10.2	94.3	94.3	92.9	91.1	90.6	90.3	90.4
55–64 years	6.4	6.8	7.1	7.0	7.0	7.0	7.1	85.2	83.2	81.5	74.8	73.5	73.0	72.5
65 yr. and over	2.4	2.1	2.2	1.9	1.8	1.8	1.9	32.2	26.9	25.8	20.8	19.4	19.3	19.7
Female	23.2	26.2	31.6	37.1	38.5	40.1	42.0	37.1	38.8	42.8	43.7	46.8	47.8	49.3
16–19 years	2.1	2.5	3.3	4.1	4.2	4.3	4.5	39.1	37.7	43.7	49.0	49.8	51.3	53.8
16–17 years	.8	1.0	1.3	1.7	1.7	1.7	1.9	28.6	27.5	34.6	40.0	40.6	41.9	45.2
18–19 years	1.3	1.6	1.9	2.4	2.5	2.6	2.6	51.0	48.6	53.4	58.1	58.9	60.4	62.2
20–24 years	2.6	3.4	4.9	6.1	6.3	6.6	6.9	46.1	49.7	57.5	63.9	65.0	66.4	68.2
25–34 years	4.2	4.3	5.7	8.5	9.2	9.9	10.6	35.8	38.5	44.8	54.3	56.9	59.2	62.0
35–44 years	5.3	5.7	6.0	6.5	6.8	7.2	7.6	43.1	45.9	50.9	55.6	57.6	59.4	61.3
45–54 years	5.2	5.7	6.5	6.7	6.7	6.7	6.8	49.3	50.5	54.0	54.3	54.6	55.5	56.8
55–64 years	3.0	3.6	4.2	4.2	4.3	4.4	4.5	36.7	40.6	42.5	40.6	40.7	40.6	41.1
65 yr. and over	1.0	1.0	1.1	1.0	1.1	1.1	1.1	10.5	9.5	9.2	7.8	7.8	7.6	7.8

SOURCE: U.S. Bureau of Labor Statistics, *Special Labor Force Reports.* (Washington, DC: U.S. Government Printing Office, 1979) p. 18–26.

LABOR MARKET
INFORMATION

An organization's recruitment efforts must compare favorably with its competitors' recruitment strategies. The firm's personnel department must realize that it is competing with other organizations in the local area for the same good job applicants. In most instances, some type of wage survey is utilized to maintain labor market information for the local area. Most professional organizations will conduct surveys for not only the local area but regional and national areas as well.

Professional positions require a greater regional and national emphasis because individuals seeking professional jobs are often more willing to relocate to take interesting jobs. Within the strictly local labor market the firm could either compile its own survey of wages and positions or use published surveys for semiskilled and unskilled jobs as well as clerical and other positions. A number of published surveys can be obtained from union groups, academic groups, and government sources. Local offices of the U.S. Employment Service are probably the most commonly utilized labor market information source. The survey information available at these local offices is free to organizations and presented in a comprehensive, professional manner. The cost of personally compiling survey information for different jobs is quite prohibitive even if it could be done completely and professionally. The fact that the U.S. Employment Service does the same surveying throughout the country and has comparative information for different localities makes it an attractive source of survey information.

Figure 6–2 illustrates U.S. Employment Service data for individuals in the different categories of labor and provides important statistics. One popular statistic is the *unemployment rate*. Changes in the

FIGURE 6–2: *U.S. Employment Service Information*

Categories of Labor:

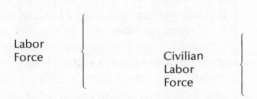

People under 16 or institutionalized
Armed Forces
Employed individuals (work for pay or profit more than 15 hours/week)
Unemployed individuals (actively seeking work)
Labor reserve (individuals who choose not to work; housewives, students, etc.)

Important Labor Statistics:

$$\text{Unemployment Rate} = \frac{\text{Unemployed}}{\text{Employed} + \text{Unemployed}}$$

$$\text{Civilian Labor Force Participation Rate} = \frac{\text{Employed} + \text{Unemployed}}{\text{Employed} + \text{Unemployed} + \text{Labor Reserve}}$$

$$\frac{\text{Total Labor Force}}{\text{Participation Rate}} = \frac{\text{Armed Forces} + \text{Employed} + \text{Unemployed}}{\text{Labor Reserve} + \text{Armed Forces} + \text{Employed} + \text{Unemployed}}$$

unemployment rate over a period of time can help a firm determine the labor market conditions of a local area. However, the *labor force participation rate* is also an important statistic for an area which should be understood and utilized in the recruitment process. In the last decade for several years when the government claimed the total number of employees working had increased, labor unions indicated that the unemployment rate has increased.[1] Actually, both statements can be true for the same period of time because in reality, many persons who were part of the *labor reserve* have decided to join the labor force. Due to inflationary pressures, housewives, students, and retired individuals have taken jobs in order to supplement family incomes. The result is that while more individuals are employed, at the same time the number of unemployed in an area increases due to layoffs and other economic conditions, thus the resulting unemployment rate increases even though more individuals are working in a labor market area.

Just as important as knowing the size of the labor market is knowing the going wage rates for the labor market. The recruiter must be able to make attractive, competitive offers to job applicants. As Figure 6–3 illustrates, the U.S. Employment Service provides wage and salary information which a recruiter can utilize To make the firm competitive in the local market and in the regional and national market for professional and technical jobs.

The beginning step in the actual recruiting process is to determine the relevant labor market and its related information.

The relevant labor market will determine which strategy and method of recruitment a firm will utilize. Recruiting methods are quite diversified in their expense and operation. Which one an organization chooses for its particular jobs is greatly affected by the survey information available to the organization.[2]

Operation of the Labor Market

Economists will claim that the labor market operates in very predictable patterns: to get more individuals into the labor supply, a firm should offer higher wages as an incentive. This economic principle assumes that applicants are aware of the wages and benefits offered by different organizations. The principle also assumes that a wage and benefit comparison will be the basis of accepting or rejecting job offers. In reality, the labor market does not operate according to the simple economic model of wage levels and labor supply. Instead, most applicants who are looking for jobs or who consider themselves underemployed are not aware of the labor market in their area. Often they have only general notions, at best, of what the going wage rates are, unless they are in a heavily unionized or specialized field. Even if they do know the going wage rates for their jobs, they have a difficult time comparing benefit plans of different organizations. In fact, many do not even consider the benefit plans when comparing organizations. Faced with a lack of information, applicants often concentrate on the nature of the work, whether it is pleasant and desirable, the gross salary, and perhaps, opportunities for promotion.

1. Mitchell S. Novit, *Essentials of Personnel Management* (Englewood Cliffs, NJ: Prentice-Hall, 1979), pp. 60–64.

2. Paul Greenlaw and William Biggs, *Modern Personnel Management* (Philadelphia: W. B. Saunders, 1979), pp. 121–27.

FIGURE 6–3: *Average Hourly Earnings of Maintenance, Toolroom, Powerplant, Material Movement, and Custodial Workers, by Sex, Louisville, Kentucky—Indiana, November 1979*

Occupation, sex, and industry division	Number of workers	Average (mean) hourly earnings
MAINTENANCE, TOOLROOM, AND POWERPLANT OCCUPATIONS—MEN		
MAINTENANCE CARPENTERS	201	$ 8.38
MANUFACTURING	155	9.51
MAINTENANCE ELECTRICIANS	586	9.68
MANUFACTURING	507	9.78
MAINTENANCE PAINTERS	121	7.89
MANUFACTURING	74	9.35
MAINTENANCE MACHINISTS	473	9.78
MANUFACTURING	456	9.79
MAINTENANCE MECHANICS (MACHINERY)	560	8.86
MANUFACTURING	487	8.82
NONMANUFACTURING: PUBLIC UTILITIES	71	8.19
MAINTENANCE MECHANICS (MOTOR VEHICLES)	598	8.53
MANUFACTURING	143	8.39
NONMANUFACTURING	455	8.57
MAINTENANCE PIPEFITTERS	443	9.75
MANUFACTURING	443	9.75
MAINTENANCE SHEET-METAL WORKERS	88	10.53
MANUFACTURING	88	10.53
MILLWRIGHTS	257	10.07
MANUFACTURING	257	10.07
MAINTENANCE TRADES HELPERS	59	7.64
MANUFACTURING	29	7.61
TOOL AND DIE MAKERS	349	9.61
MANUFACTURING	349	9.61
STATIONARY ENGINEERS	115	8.93
MANUFACTURING	71	9.53
BOILER TENDERS	214	6.74
MANUFACTURING	151	8.27
MATERIAL MOVEMENT AND CUSTODIAL OCCUPATIONS—MEN		
TRUCKDRIVERS	2,424	7.83
MANUFACTURING	491	7.07
NONMANUFACTURING	1,933	8.02
PUBLIC UTILITIES	856	10.23

Occupation, sex, and industry division	Number of workers	Average (mean) hourly earnings
MATERIAL MOVEMENT AND CUSTODIAL OCCUPATIONS—MEN—CONTINUED		
TRUCKDRIVERS—CONTINUED		
TRUCKDRIVERS, LIGHT TRUCK	263	$3.75
MANUFACTURING	52	5.25
NONMANUFACTURING	211	3.38
TRUCKDRIVERS, MEDIUM TRUCK	1,015	7.88
MANUFACTURING	186	6.67
NONMANUFACTURING	819	8.15
TRUCKDRIVERS, HEAVY TRUCK	160	7.34
MANUFACTURING	84	8.15
TRUCKDRIVERS, TRACTOR-TRAILER	881	9.36
MANUFACTURING	128	7.44
NONMANUFACTURING	753	9.69
SHIPPERS	79	6.71
MANUFACTURING	43	6.52
RECEIVERS	290	7.42
MANUFACTURING	196	8.17
NONMANUFACTURING	94	5.87
SHIPPERS AND RECEIVERS	58	5.88
NONMANUFACTURING	39	5.15
WAREHOUSEMEN	511	5.80
MANUFACTURING	229	5.80
NONMANUFACTURING	282	6.80
ORDER FILLERS	918	5.91
NONMANUFACTURING	622	5.45
SHIPPING PACKERS	218	6.09
MANUFACTURING	144	6.77
MATERIAL HANDLING LABORERS	1,292	6.59
MANUFACTURING	1,040	6.92
NONMANUFACTURING	252	5.21
FORKLIFT OPERATORS	2,004	7.15
MANUFACTURING	1,688	7.30
NONMANUFACTURING	316	6.33
POWER-TRUCK OPERATORS (OTHER THAN FORKLIFT)	232	8.12

Occupation, sex, and industry division	Number of workers	Average (mean) hourly earnings
MATERIAL MOVEMENT AND CUSTODIAL OCCUPATIONS—MEN—CONTINUED		
GUARDS	1,397	$4.12
MANUFACTURING	323	7.21
NONMANUFACTURING	1,074	3.17
PUBLIC UTILITIES	26	7.26
GUARDS, CLASS A	184	7.85
MANUFACTURING	185	7.90
GUARDS, CLASS B	1,202	3.50
MANUFACTURING	138	6.29
NONMANUFACTURING	1,064	3.14
JANITORS, PORTERS, AND CLEANERS	1,613	4.93
MANUFACTURING	743	6.74
NONMANUFACTURING	873	3.39
PUBLIC UTILITIES	67	6.28
MATERIAL MOVEMENT AND CUSTODIAL OCCUPATIONS—WOMEN		
RECEIVERS	32	6.87
MANUFACTURING	28	6.92
ORDER FILLERS	267	3.69
NONMANUFACTURING	244	3.59
SHIPPING PACKERS	75	4.23
MATERIAL HANDLING LABORERS	68	6.50
FORKLIFT OPERATORS	37	6.83
MANUFACTURING	31	7.13
GUARDS	103	3.67
GUARDS, CLASS B	95	3.33
JANITORS, PORTERS, AND CLEANERS	1,429	3.90
MANUFACTURING	312	6.96
NONMANUFACTURING	1,119	3.85

SOURCE: *Area Wage Survey: Louisville, Kentucky–Indiana, Metropolitan Area, November 1979*, U.S. Department of Labor, Bulletin 2050–66, April 1980, p. 13.

There is a tendency for nonexempt personnel to informally seek jobs through newspapers and friends. Typically, nonexempt individuals do not know what the labor market wage rate is. If they quit one job before finding a new job, they are more pressured to accept the next offer they receive. Nonexempt personnel also tend to stay in one labor market area rather than being mobile and looking for jobs in other labor markets.

Exempt personnel generally know more about the market and have a better idea about the going wage rates. They tend to compare benefits of organizations to some degree. Usually exempt personnel have a broader geographic market, are willing to relocate, and to interview in other geographic areas. Membership in professional organizations which do national and regional wage surveys helps exempt personnel keep abreast of the job market. Typically, exempt personnel will stay in their jobs until they find more desirable jobs; thus they are not pressured to take the first new job that is offered to them.

COST/BENEFIT ANALYSIS === OF RECRUITMENT ===

The basic goal of recruitment is to locate at the least cost, qualified applicants who will remain with the organization. Therefore, underqualified individuals who will later be terminated should not be hired; neither should overqualified individuals who will experience frustration and leave the organization.[3]

A cost/benefit model illustrates the decision-making aspects of recruitment and stresses the economic implications of selection decisions. In the recruitment and selection process four outcomes are possible for each individual applicant: quadrants I and III of Figure 6-4 indicate correct decisions to hire applicants who eventually become successful employees, or not to hire applicants who would have eventually become failures as employees. In quadrants II and IV, however, management makes incorrect decisions. In quadrant IV an employee was not adequate on the job. In quadrant II management rejected an applicant who could have been successful as an employee.[4] The incorrect decision in quadrant IV is referred to as a *false positive* because management was positive about an applicant who turned out to be unsuccessful. In quadrant II the incorrect decision is termed a *false negative* because administrators were negative about an applicant who would have been successful.

In quadrants I and III the managers scored a "hit" in correctly predicting the future performance of the applicant. Of course, management desires to maximize its rate of correct decisions, or *hit rate,* which is its percentage of correct predictions about future performances of employees. In order to accomplish a cost/benefit analysis of the recruitment program, several estimates must be made. The cost of the two types of errors that can be made in recruitment selection process should be considered. The actual dollar costs include advertising of positions, reviewing applications, interviewing applicants, and testing a large group of applicants. Also the cost of orientation and training of new applicants due to the

---

3. Ibid., pp. 126–27.

4. Lawrence J. Peters and R. Hall, *The Peter Principle* (New York: Bantam Books, Inc., 1969).

FIGURE 6–4: *Outcomes of the Recruitment/ Selection Process*

Applicant/ Employee Performance	Selection Decision	
	Reject	Hire
Successful Applicant/Employee	II Incorrect Decision (False Negative)	I Correct Decision (Hit)
Unsuccessful Applicant/Employee	III Correct Decision (Hit)	IV Incorrect Decision (False Positive)

$$\text{"Hit Rate"} = \frac{\text{Hits (I + III)}}{\text{Hits (I + III) + False Negatives (II) + False Positives (IV)}}$$

false positive decisions must be included.

Perhaps more important than direct costs are the potential costs which cannot be easily measured in dollars. False positives include the potential costs of an employee becoming disenchanted with the organization and spreading low morale. The costs associated with false negative decisions are also very difficult to estimate. Organizations often do not know except in extremely costly situations how much potential they have lost when they rejected an employee who could have been a successful employee. For example, what did it cost the professional baseball team which rejected the Cy Young Award winner, Tommy John?

Generally, the firm should develop a cost/benefit analysis to weigh the alternative of recruiting more individuals, which increases recruiting costs, against the cost of recruiting fewer individuals and possibly not locating a successful employee. A training program can be developed which would identify the potential employment capabilities of negative and false positive applicants.

A perfect recruitment selection process, of course, would identify which of the four quadrants an applicant falls into and enable the recruiter to choose only those applicants who would be successful employees. Managers can estimate the success of their recruitment by looking at their hit rates and how the rates have changed. The most important cost/benefit analysis associated with recruitment focuses on the sources of recruitment. As illustrated in Figure 6–5, each source will produce a different percentage of successful job candidates at differing costs. Managers can easily relate the costs of using a source to the number of applicants located. The disadvantage of compiling direct dollar recruitment costs in this manner is that there is no accounting for the costs to an organization of losing a star performer, because one source of recruitment was not utilized. However, that type of unusual situation should not discourage cost-benefit analysis of re-

FIGURE 6–5: *Characteristics of Hires by Source*

	Percent of Total Hires	Efficiency Rating (Ratio of Hired/Interviewed)	Mean Age	Cost Per Hire
Company transfers	43.7%	.442	35.2	$ 387
Employee referrals	18.8	.358	33.4	350
Ad responses	9.6	.187	32.4	1,398
Write-ins	8.5	.245	32.9	520
Employment agencies	4.6	.162	32.4	3,006
Field trips	4.2	.194	34.2	2,142
Futures (early promotions)	3.1	.252	34.6	456
Walk-ins	2.6	.207	21.4*	203
Miscellaneous	2.9	.268	30.4	484
College hires	2.0	.157	25.2	833
Total or mean	100.0%	.297	33.5	$ 705

*The mean "age" is misleading in the walk-ins source because of small samples, irregular distribution, and the interval method of calculation. The typical walk-in was nearer 25 years old with about four years' experience.

SOURCE: Adapted, by permission of the publisher, from *The Recruitment Function*, by Roger H. Hawk, © 1967 by American Management Association, Inc., p. 179. All rights reserved.

cruitment. Many dollars can be saved by an efficient, successful recruitment program.

RECRUITMENT SOURCES

Once management has determined an organization's staffing requirements by estimating job openings to be filled, the recruitment process begins. The first decision to be made in the recruitment process is whether a particular job opening should be filled by someone already employed or by an applicant from outside. Normally, firms recruit both internally and externally. In each case the advantages of recruiting outside the organization must be weighed against the advantage of recruiting inside the organi-

zation before the recruitment process is determined.[5]

Internal Applicants

As summarized in Figure 6–6, there are several advantages to recruiting within the organization. Probably of greatest importance is the increased morale factor for employees who believe that the organization will reward successful performance and that they will be recruited for higher positions. The lack of possible promotion and advancement within an organization can be a major cause of employee turnover and dissatisfaction.

Managers recruiting within the organization have the advantage of using accurate personnel data maintained by the

5. Ibid.

FIGURE 6–6: *Advantages of Internal and External Recruiting Sources*

Internal Applicants	External Applicants
Increased morale of all employees	Applicant pool is greater
Knowledge of personnel records	New ideas, contacts
Chain effect of promotion	Reduces internal infighting
Need to hire only at entry level	Minimizes Peter Principle
Usually faster, less expensive	

company. Interviews with supervisors and employee performance records can be added to the applicant's file during the recruitment process. At best, the organization can only guess at the completeness and objectivity of information about applicants received from other organizations. Only after years of interaction with the other organizations can a personnel officer begin to measure the accuracy of other organizations' personnel files.

A promotion within the organization often leads to an applicant vacating a position which is then filled from within the organization. This chain effect on promotion means that not only one position is filled within the organization but two or more positions often will be filled when internal recruitment is utilized. Thus chain effect promotion has a positive effect on employee morale because it positively affects several employees.

When organizations promote from within, in most situations only entry level vacancies are filled from the outside. The advantage of this approach is that it is not necessary to experiment with unknown entities at high levels in the organization; individuals have a chance to prove themselves at lower positions within the orga-

nization and be rewarded for successful performance by promotion. Internal recruitment also can be faster and less expensive than external recruitment. Therefore, because an organization utilizes its own records and sources of testing, internal recruitment can save money and time.

External Applicants

The greatest advantage of recruiting from the outside is that a greater number of applicants can be recruited. This should lead to a larger pool of more qualified applicants than could normally be recruited internally. Outside applicants should bring new ideas, work techniques, production methods, or training to the organization which result in new insights into profitability.

External applicants also may have contacts which internal employees do not have. In sales, research and technology, and purchasing, for example, good external contacts are critical and the recruitment of outside applicants with these contacts may be very helpful.

Recruitment of outside applicants for mid-level and higher positions will eliminate infighting by employees jockeying for promotion. Wherever infighting is severe, organizations begin to do more external recruiting to decrease internal dissension.

In recent years organizations have sought applicants from the outside to minimize promoting employees to levels where they are unable to perform successfully. Referred to as the *Peter Principle*, this theory has been validated as more and more managers have promoted employees who cannot perform as expected once promoted.[6] This may be a self-fulfilling prophecy for policymakers who blame the Peter Principle for their own lack of good internal recruitment methods or inept selection of employees. However, any firm where promotions are made exclusively from within will experience the Peter Principle to some extent.

One common method of avoiding the Peter Principle and the resulting dissatisfied employee is the use of temporary or acting position titles. The employee is promoted to acting department head for an unspecified period of time. If the employee is not capable of performing the job, a permanent department head can be recruited. Thus, the employee does not suffer the embarrassment of failing to handle the position; nor is a demotion or termination made part of the employee's permanent record. Whenever an acting department head proves capable, that employee can be made permanent department head.

Whether employees are recruited from within or the outside should be determined by the availability of qualified employees within the organization, the size of the organization, and the desire to keep up with ideas and methods within other organizations. Employees should realize that external recruitment does not indicate that no one is qualified to fill the position internally. It indicates the need for fresh ideas and new approaches to old problems.

METHODS OF RECRUITMENT

The most common methods of internal

6. *Employee Promotion and Transfer Policies, PPF Survey No. 120* (Washington, DC: Bureau of National Affairs) Inc., 1978), pp. 2–4.

recruiting are bidding positions and job posting. The bidding process is common with unionized organizations; when an opening exists, qualified employees are notified that they may bid on the position if they wish to be considered for it. The employee with the most seniority receives the promotion. This structured process is usually specified in the union contract; promotions are almost entirely based upon seniority.

Job Posting

One of the most popular methods of filling positions within organizations is *job posting*. According to a government survey of employee promotion policies, job posting is the most common method of notifying employees of current openings. Clerical and blue–collar positions were posted on bulletin boards much more frequently than professional job openings.

An effective, useful management tool, job posting can create severe employee morale problems if not handled properly. Managers should consider several aspects of the job posting process. First, the job posting procedure should be clearly specified to the employees and should be followed to the letter each time a position is open. If the procedure varies according to the job or the particular employee applying for a position, employees may suspect that employer subjectivity is unfairly entering into the process.

Job specifications should include the years of experience, skills, or training employees must have to apply for the posted position. The more specifications the posted position has, the fewer applicants there will be. This will make the decision process easier for management, assuming that strict seniority will not be used as the only criteria and other factors such as an employee's personnel record, results of interviews, etc. will be considered. When only a few job specifications are included in the posted position, then the personnel specialist will have a larger number of applicants to review during the selection process.

Job posting procedures should specify the exact time period posted positions will remain open. For example, a position may remain open fourteen working days after it is first posted, and applications will be taken until 4:30 P.M. on the fourteenth day. Also the procedure should specify that employees on vacation, or laid off will be notified by mail or employee publication of posted positions. The exact media to be used in the job posting process, that is, bulletin boards, employee newspaper, etc., should not only be specified, but consistently used and not changed unless employees are notified prior to any change.

An employee may apply for a posted position through the personnel department or a supervisor. If the employee applies directly to the personnel department, then supervisors feel that the chain of command has not been used. On the other hand, employees going through their supervisors sometimes feel that their supervisors may not wish them to receive the positions. A common compromise is to have employees submit written applications for a posted position to the personnel department with a copy to the supervisor.

Perhaps the most important function of the organization's personnel department in the job posting process is ensuring that employees receive adequate positive feedback once a position decision is made. For example, when nine applicants apply for a posted position, and one is accepted, the eight rejected employees, who are good employees but just not as good as the promoted employee, feel depressed and somewhat rejected. While no amount of communication will entirely eliminate this rejected feeling, it is imperative that the rejected employees receive positive feedback. If this is not done, the morale of one employee may increase while the motivation of eight other good employees significantly decreases. Rejected employees should be given positive feedback about their qualifications, and their promotion potential within the organization; they may need guidance about what positions they should apply for in the future, what strengths they should emphasize, and what weaknesses should be overcome before they again apply for a position.

If properly utilized, job posting helps employees feel that they have some control over their own futures in the organization. Job posting often uncovers employee talent which supervisors would not voluntarily reveal in order to keep good employees. While it is certainly selfish for a supervisor to not recommend a good employee for promotion, supervisors may believe that the undue pressure on the department created by a good employee's loss outweighs the morale gained by having an employee promoted outside the department. Job posting will also avoid the recommendation of an employee for promotion to an undesired position. When a promotion is offered, the employee may feel obligated to accept it or risk possibly never being asked again. Through job posting, employees who are not interested in positions do not apply, and the problem is avoided.

Direct Applications

For most organizations, direct applications by mail or individuals applying in person is the largest source of applicants. In the case of blue-collar jobs, walk-ins are often called *gate hires*. Direct applications can provide an inexpensive source of good job applicants to the organization, especially for entry level, clerical, and blue-collar jobs. In recent years direct applications from recent college graduates have been used to fill other entry-level positions.

The usefulness of direct applications will often depend upon the image the organization has in the community and, therefore, the quality of applicants who will directly apply to the organization. The size of an organization and its reputation determines whether applicants will seek out the organization rather than respond to other recruitment methods. Only the largest, well-known organizations in the labor market will receive a great quantity of direct applications. Organizations which receive many direct applications must develop an efficient means of screening those applications and keeping a file of current applications of qualified candidates. While the cost of recruitment is low if large numbers of applications are received, the cost of screening and maintaining a file of applicants can become quite high. Medium-sized and smaller firms do not receive a large enough volume of direct applications to fill all their positions with available and qualified candidates without further recruitment methods.

Employee Referrals

In recruiting for exempt and nonexempt positions, employee referrals are one of the best means of recruiting applicants. Employees can be encouraged to help their employers locate and hire qualified applicants by rewards, either monetary or otherwise, as well as recognition for those who assist the recruitment process.

Employees who recommend applicants place their own reputations on the line; therefore, they are usually careful to only recommend qualified applicants. When recommended applicants are hired, employees take an active interest in helping new employees be successful in their jobs.

Obviously, employee referrals are a quick and relatively inexpensive means of recruitment. In skilled, technical, or professional positions, employee referrals can help the organization pirate successful employees from other companies. Newly-recruited employees from other organizations often add new insights to the organization or new clientele to the organization.

DISADVANTAGES OF REFERRALS

Some administrators avoid employee referrals because inbreeding and nepotism can cause employee morale problems, as well as a lack of successful and productive employees in future years. For example, friends of an employee rejected for promotion, will also feel rejected. Naturally, employees who recommend applicants are dissatisfied when their applicants are not hired; they may show their dissatisfaction by not cooperating with the new employee. Typically, employee referrals do not help an organization recruit qualified minority candidates to meet EEO/AA requirements.

In past years a number of "old boy network" referrals filled entry-level through top-level positions in some organizations with friends and relatives. This hiring of former college friends or neighborhood associates leads to a distorted mix of employees and usually an underrepresentation of minority groups in various job categories.

Before taking advantage of the relatively inexpensive and easy method of recruiting employees through employee referrals, administrators should minimize possible problems by:

- Establishing specific policies barring nepotism.
- Conducting objective recruitment procedures which will ensure compliance with EEO/AA guidelines.
- Ensuring that decisions regarding the hiring of applicants and their salaries are kept confidential. This process should always be confidential, but it is even more important when applicants are referred by current employees.

Campus Recruiting

While the popularity of recruiting job applicants on college campuses has decreased from the early 1960s, it is still heavily utilized. Campus recruiting can be divided into two major sources:

- The trade school or school providing specialized education such as engineering or auto mechanics where recruitment is somewhat easier for organizations because the student product is more uniform than that typically found on the four-year campus.
- The four-year college presents a wide variety of individuals with varying edu-

cation and skill levels. Compared to other sources of recruitment, the college campus recruitment process is very expensive and time-consuming for the organization. Usually the campus recruiter finds it very difficult to conduct in-depth, accurate interviews in the recruiting session. Often students who arrange for interviews later cancel or find that they are really not interested in the company or position after the interview has begun. Use of campus recruiting is dependent upon the condition of the economy and the job market.

In recent years managers have reassessed whether positions requiring college graduates might be filled with less educated applicants. A primary reason for this is the high turnover of college graduates, particularly in jobs which are not directly related to their majors. A history major, for example, may take a job selling industrial equipment. Another example would be the hot shot MBA who takes a trainee position with a major manufacturing organization only to find that after two years the position is less and less attractive as the daily routine begins to be unbearable. Thus, with deflated egos and the sudden awareness that what they are doing is sometimes more important than how much they are being paid or where they are doing it, recent college graduates resign to seek jobs more compatible with their interests. Campus recruiters report a variety of special problems encountered while recruiting the recent graduate. A recent national survey of personnel departments which hired large numbers of college graduates questioned why recent college graduates are turned down flat after the initial campus interview. The following reasons were given in order of their occurrence:[7]

1. Poor personality and manner, lack of poise, poor presentation, no self–confidence, timid, hesitant approach, arrogant, conceited

2. Poor scholastic record without reasonable explanation for low grades

3. Poor personal appearance and careless dress

4. Lack of enthusiasm and interest, no evidence of initiative

5. Lack of goals and ambition, indecisive, does not know interests

6. Poor speech habits and expression

7. Unrealistic salary demands, more interested in salary than opportunity

8. Lack of maturity, no leadership potential

9. Lack of extracurricular activities without adequate reason

10. Lack of preparation for the interview, failure to get information about the company resulting in inability to ask intelligent questions

11. Lack of interest in the company and the type of job open

12. Excessive interest in security and benefits, "What can you do for me?" attitude

13. Objection to travel or moving out of town to branch office

14. Immediate or prolonged service obligations

15. No vacation jobs or work experience, did not help to finance education

---

7. Frank S. Endicott, *The Endicott Report* (Evanston, IL: Northwestern University, 1977), pp. 10–11.

Therefore, campus recruiting is expensive, difficult for the recruiter, and often unproductive; even where recruitment is successful, it may lead to a high percentage of turnover by college graduates. In recent years the supply of college graduates in many fields far exceeded the demand for positions in those fields. In fact, the supply for college graduates in general exceeds the demand for graduates. Except in specialized fields such as engineering, accounting, business, health sciences, and computer sciences, this trend probably will continue during the 1980s. Both organizations and college graduates are turning to other recruiting methods. Students should continue to use the university's placement office; however, they should not count on it to find them a job because some personnel specialists would rather hear from applicants directly through resumes or personal references.

Private Employment Agencies

While personnel departments have increased their use of private employment agencies in recent years, some will only use private agencies as a last resort, for the expense involved is usually prohibitive. Sometimes, the employer pays 10 percent of the applicant's first-year salary as a fee to the agency. In recent years with the pressure to recruit the best applicants from the hundreds of applicants who meet EEO/AA guidelines, the use of private agencies had increased. In some cases, a good employment agency can save the personnel office valuable time by screening out unqualified applicants and locating qualified applicants. Effective agencies may actually save the organization money by reducing recruitment and selection costs. Use of private employment agencies does not relieve personnel departments of any requirements under federal employment laws. Only two or three competent agencies should be used by one organization; one specific agency should be used for a position when that agency typically has a good number of qualified applicants for that type of position. A *source trust* should be developed with a particular agency counselor so that unqualified applicants are not sent from the agency. A counselor who has the business of the organization will work harder to retain repeat business than one trying to simply fill one immediate opening. Repeated contacts will help the counselor acquire a better understanding of the company and its requirements.[8]

Personnel managers should limit the applicants they allow an agency to send to four or five; this will keep them from being flooded with marginal applicants who probably could have been located without the agency. Limited to only four or five applicants, the counselor will do a better job of screening and send only the people who have the best opportunity to be hired so that the agency could receive its fee.

Advertising

A popular recruitment technique is employment advertising; in past years it has been primarily associated with newspaper classified ads. Many factors make advertising an attractive recruitment method. First, employers can attract employees

from a wider geographic area than their immediate vicinity with advertising. This has become necessary as employers seek to recruit through techniques other than the old boy network or gate hires. Second, many organizations find that they must recruit from nontraditional sources in order to meet EEO/AA guidelines. Third, employers have found that attractively designed and professionally developed recruitment advertising can be successful in attracting good applicants. Thus, personnel specialists have found that advertising can be just as important a tool in their field as in product marketing. Some larger organizations have been increasing their use of professional advertising agencies in recent years.

Personnel recruiters can develop successful recruitment advertising for local newspapers as well as trade and professional publications by incorporating the elements of a recruitment ad outlined in Figure 6–7. Often an organization using advertising is not really trying to recruit the unemployed person who will diligently follow up on most ads, but rather the underemployed person who, if given the right opportunity, would welcome a change of jobs. To recruit this employee, the ad must be attractive enough to stimulate the employee to respond.

For the job seeker, the number of recruitment ads in a local newspaper is not a reliable indicator of actual job opportunities. *Fortune* magazine editors closely scrutinized ads in a New York state newspaper and found that within a metropolitan area of about 273,000 people the classified ad section contained 228 employment ads. Of the 228 ads, only 131 or 57 percent offered full-time jobs in the immediate area. These ads included eight jobs offered through *blind ads,* which

---

8. Erwin S. Stanton, *Successful Personnel Recruiting and Selection* (New York: AMACOM, 1977), pp. 53–55.

FIGURE 6–7: *Elements of a Recruitment Ad*

A. Key:

1) Attracts attention of readers with training or experience indicated. 2) Screens out unqualified people. 3) Identifies ad as recruitment ad. ("Key" not always necessary for display ad in recruitment section of publication.)

B. Headline:

1) Attracts reader, motivates to read ad. 2) Summarizes ad message. 3) Screens out nonqualified.

C. Main subhead:

1) Supplements headline. 2) Reinforces impact, and/or 3) Introduces a second motivating factor. (Not all ads need subheads.)

D. Illustration:

1) Gains reader's attention. 2) Supports headline, and/or 3) Visually defines job, field, or industry, and/or 4) Supplements ad message with nonverbal information (e. g., example shown demonstrates affirmative action). Not all display ads need illustrations.

E. Display type:

1) Creates impact and visibility.
2) Makes headline easy to read.
3) Enhances attractiveness of ad.

F. White space:

1) Isolates elements of ad for greater visual impact. 2) Enhances attractiveness and readability by avoiding cramped appearance.

G. Body copy (or text):

1) Supports main message. 2) Expands on points made in headline and/or subhead. 3) Provides information on opportunities, company, and field to motivate reader action.

H. Body type:

Presents text of ad in readable form.

I. Subheads:

1) Divide text for better readability. 2) Maintain reader interest in message, or 3) Introduce particular section of ad.

J. Job specifications:

(Unique to recruitment ads) 1) Identify as recruitment ad. 2) Describe job openings and requirements (Sometimes simply a listing of job titles).

K. Contact information:

Provides source for further information, where to forward resume, etc.

L. Affirmative action line:

Assures potential applicants of company's compliance.

M. Logo:

Company's official signature. 1) Identifies organization. 2) Attracts reader's attention if company is well known. 3) Builds company image.

SOURCE: *Recruitment Manual* 1976–77, (New York: Deutsch, Shea and Evans, Inc.). Used by permission.

briefly describe a job at an unnamed organization giving a box number to which an applicant must mail a letter. Only 42 out of 228 ads offered full-time jobs in the area to unskilled or semiskilled workers.[9] In recent years the number of employment ads in local newspapers had become less indicative of the local economy since more companies are advertising positions not previously advertised. Some of these companies are advertising due to the increased success they have had with advertising of positions, others to comply with federal employment guidelines.

OVERTIME AND ══ TEMPORARY HELP ══

The two most immediate sources of additional labor are current employees who work overtime and temporary employees.

9. Herbert E. Myer, "Jobs and Want Ads: A Look Behind the Words," *Fortune* (November 20, 1978): 88–96.

FIGURE 6–8: *Typical Recruitment Advertisements*

MERCHANDISER

Excellent opportunity for progressive, self-starter with retail experience. Merchandising experience preferred; stock clerk experience essential. Challenging and creative full time work in modern Taylor Drug Store. Apply to:

Manager
Taylor Drug Stores Inc.
Columbus Center

PHARMACIST

Louisville based chain seeks pharmacist for full line drug store in East Central Indiana. Excellent opportunity, complete benefit package and salary to $22,000. Apply:

Director of Professional Relations
P.O. Box 1884
Louisville, KY 40201

SECRETARY, EXECUTIVE

EXECUTIVE SECRETARY

Secretary to key executive of company. Must have good organizational and communicative skills. Excellent shorthand and typing plus 5 to 7 years secretarial experience.

Send resume to:
Personnel Administrator
GLENMORE
DISTILLERIES CO
P.O. Box 900
Louisville, Ky. 40201
Equal employment opportunity employer. Male/Female

DIRECTOR
TRAFFIC & DISTRIBUTION

Glenmore Distilleries Company, a fast growing Company in the alcoholic beverage industry, needs a take-charge, results-oriented person to direct all areas of transportation and distribution, reporting directly to corporate First Vice President.

Responsible for selection of most efficient transportation for movement of all raw materials, finished products and supplies including evaluation of costs and performance, operation of Company truck fleet, and selection of transportation of all import and export products. Must also be able to monitor complete warehousing operation.

Successful candidate must have a B.S. in Transportation/Traffic plus eight (8) years experience in intermodalism and international transportation with a minimum of four (4) years as a General Traffic Manager. FMC/ICC Practitioner desirable.

Salary and benefits are highly competitive. Location at Corporate Headquarters in Louisville, Kentucky. Relocation costs paid.

Send resume in confidence to:

Personnel Administrator
GLENMORE DISTILLERIES COMPANY
P. O. Box 900
Louisville, Kentucky 40201

AN EQUAL OPPORTUNITY EMPLOYER

BOTTLING
ENGINEER

Immediate opening for hard-working, results-oriented manager to direct and coordinate activities for design, construction and maintenance of equipment and machinery in our Owensboro bottling plant. This position reports directly to the Vice President—General Manager.

Bachelor's Degree in Engineering plus a minimum of three (3) years experience as a graduate engineer, one of which must have been in a supervisory capacity.

Salary and benefits are highly competitive. Major relocation costs paid.

Send resume in confidence to:

Peronnsel Administrator
GLENMORE
DISTILLERIES
COMPANY
P. O. Box 900
Louisville, Kentucky 40201

AN EQUAL OPPORTUNITY EMPLOYER

Used with the permission of Taylor Drug Stores, Inc. and Glenmore Distilleries Company.

Assigning overtime to employees is an obviously attractive alternative because it is a short-term addition rather than a permanent staff increase. Choosing overtime means that experienced, knowledgeable employees who do not require any additional training or orientation on the job will be used. However, overtime also means additional fatigue for employees who have already worked their full shift and usually the expense of time-and-a–half or double time pay.

Temporary help may be less costly than hiring new permanent employees, particularly in cases where seasonal demands are great or for an unforecasted temporary absence of key personnel. In office administration, accounting, and engineering, temporary help can quickly be trained to be productive on the job with little inefficiency due to start-up costs.

These two alternatives have become even more attractive in recent years since organizations have found the cost of

FIGURE 6–9: *SCAT Example: Cost of Staffing Alternatives*

Hour	Option						Least Cost Alternative
	Overtime		Hire		Temporary Help		
	Total Cost	Efficiency	Total Cost	Efficiency	Total Cost	Efficiency	
1	8.36	.91	40.90	.31	8.77	.21	
2	16.78	.90	50.37	.33	17.48	.23	
3	25.19	.90	59.75	.34	26.13	.24	
4	33.60	.90	69.04	.36	34.72	.25	
5	42.00	.90	78.23	.38	43.26	.27	
6	50.40	.90	87.33	.39	51.73	.28	
7	58.80	.90	96.33	.40	60.15	.29	
8	67.19	.91	105.23	.42	68.52	.31	Overtime
9	75.03	.99	114.04	.44	76.82	.32	
10	82.94	.98	122.76	.45	85.06	.33	
11	90.91	.97	131.38	.46	93.25	.35	
12	98.95	.96	139.91	.48	101.38	.36	
13	107.04	.95	148.34	.50	109.45	.37	
14	115.19	.94	156.67	.51	117.46	.39	
15	123.41	.93	164.91	.52	125.42	.40	
16	131.69	.92	173.06	.54	133.34	.41	
17	139.47	1.00	181.11	.56	141.42	.42	
22	179.63	.94	219.95	.63	180.12	.46	Overtime
23	187.84	.93	227.43	.65	187.80	.46	Temporary Help
67	558.28	.97	495.62	.93	495.95	.74	Temporary Help
68	566.31	.96	501.27	.93	502.42	.74	Hire

SOURCE: Marc J. Wallace, Jr., "A Planning Model for Short-Run Staffing Decisions," *Proceedings of the 36th Academy of Management Meeting,* 1976. Used with permission.

recruiting and selecting employees under mandated federal guidelines much more expensive than in past years. While many factors must be considered in determining whether to use temporary help or overtime, most of them can be adopted to a quantitative model with the primary decision being cost efficiency. One such model called *Staffing Cost Analysis Technique* (SCAT) has been developed. A SCAT model utilizes the simple, quantitative technique of break-even analysis in deciding whether to hire new full-time employees, assign current employees overtime, or hire temporary help. With assistance from Manpower Temporary Services which employs one-half million workers, the SCAT model was designed as a cost minimization technique.[10]

The SCAT model indicates that in most situations requiring an additional work force, the overtime alternative is the least expensive when a few additional hours of labor are needed. The overtime option also avoids recruitment and selection overhead costs connected with newly-hired employees as well as the fee paid to the temporary service agency. However,

10. Marc Wallace, Jr., "A Planning Model for Short-run Staffing Decisions," *Proceedings of the Southern Management Association Meeting,* Atlanta, Georgia, 1977.

the overtime option involves the disadvantage of higher salary costs and fatigue of employees. Also, management may be constrained by the number of overtime hours it can utilize.

The temporary help alternative usually becomes the most cost efficient when the total number of hours required increases. As Figure 6–9 indicates, the temporary help alternative becomes the most cost efficient when twenty-three additional hours were required. The major cost advantage of the temporary help alternative is that the employer avoids the cost of recruitment and selection of permanent employees; the disadvantage is the fee for the temporary help service agency. At some point in terms of hours required by the organization, the temporary help alternative becomes more costly than to use permanent, additional employees. In Figure 6–10, the new hire alternative becomes most cost efficient when sixty–eight hours of additional labor are required.[11]

SUCCESSFUL RECRUITMENT

Successful recruitment begins when the personnel specialists in an organization accurately forecast personnel needs. By constantly attracting applicants and maintaining a supply of qualified candidates, personnel specialists are able to fill vacant positions as quickly as possible. Their recruitment ads and recruiters' interviews should describe the position and company realistically so that applicants can

decide if their job expectations can be met at that company.

Realistic and Hard Sell Techniques

Traditionally, job candidates were attracted by hard sell speeches about the virtues of the organization. Recruiters would extol the organization's excellent pay, benefits, and fast promotion. For example, recruiters would tell applicants that the positions they were recruited for were only stepping stones, that they would find the work challenging, and that co-workers would be interesting and helpful. Recent college graduates would accept such positions with high expectations of interesting, challenging work, and a fast track to the top. Within a few months the new employee would become disillusioned and feel misled by the organization. Disillusioned employees would leave feeling that other organizations may offer better situations or, at least, honest management.

An alternative approach to selling the organization to job candidates is to be realistic about the job.[12] The primary advantage of a realistic approach is that employees do not experience great differences between what they were told during the job interview and what they actually find themselves doing after they are hired. Even if they do not find the job to be as challenging as they had hoped for, these employees do not feel like they were intentionally misled due to a recruiter's need to quickly fill a position. Creating a successful job match between what management expects from the employee and what the employee expects from

---

11. Ibid.

12. John P. Wanous, "Tell it Like It Is at Job Previews," *Personnel* (July-August, 1975): 50–59.

management, can severely reduce both absenteeism and turnover of recently hired employees.[13] This realistic approach is successful because both parties know beforehand what they expect of each other and what is expected of them; therefore, they try to make the job match a successful one.

Forecasting Future Personnel Needs

Personnel specialists constantly determine what positions will be needed at all levels in the future and how many qualified employees will be available to fill those positions. This process is *personnel planning*. The personnel recruiter anticipates the company's needs, training time required, and employee turnover. As Figure 6–10 indicates, the recruiter for entry level positions can estimate the number of applicants needed in order to fill several positions. This process can be used for each different distinct type of entry level position, thus, four or five different estimates may be made. For example, if a firm typically hires a large number of entry–level clerical workers or sales representatives during the year, these estimates can minimize the time such positions are left open due to a lack of qualified trainees. Future personnel needs planning balances the long-run demand for employees and long-run supply of internal and external applicants. Thus, current adjustments in training, transferring employees and external recruitment can minimize severe personnel shortages in future years.

Figure 6–11 depicts planning for future

---

13. John P. Kotter, "The Psychological Contract: Managing the Joining-Up Process," *California Management Review* XV, no. 3 (1973): 91–99.

FIGURE 6-10: *Determining Entry Level Applicants Needed*

Available and Qualified Applicants Needed Annually	= (Current + Future Positions Needed)
	×
	Turnover Rate
	×
	Ratio of Applicants Needed to One Applicant Being Hired $\left(\dfrac{\text{Applicants}}{\text{Hired}}\right)$

Example:

Applicants Needed Annually	= 40 Entry Level × .50 Turnover Rate Clerical Positions

$$\times \frac{3}{1} \text{ Applicants Hired} = 60$$

If training programs begin on the first of each month, then:

$\dfrac{60 \text{ Applicants}}{12 \text{ Months}}$ = 5 applicants needed to start each training program

personnel needs. First, the future customer demands are estimated by examining the market for products and services, the competition, and long-term growth potential. Once customer demand is estimated, then decisions must be made regarding financial resource availability, which determines the two critical inputs in the organization process, capital, and materials. Once financial determinations are made, the level of operation must be decided. Management estimates the level of operation which will be required in future months and years so that it can economically purchase materials and capital. Sometimes overlooked is an estimate of the level of operation and its effect upon personnel needs. Estimating the level of operation is critical to personnel planning

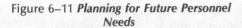

Figure 6–11 *Planning for Future Personnel Needs*

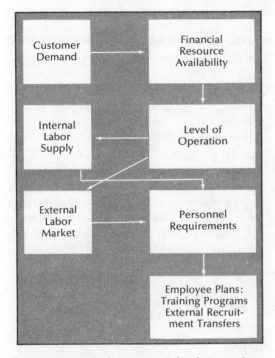

because it involves not only the number of employees needed but the different types of employees required for current and future positions.

The next step in the planning process is to look at both the internal and external labor supplies. By looking at past patterns of promotion, transfers, and employee turnover it is possible to forecast what type of qualified employees will be available to fill future positions. When these internal supply levels are matched against the future demand for employees, then expected overages and shortages can be determined. At the same time demand excesses or supply shortages in the external labor market must be predicted, as well as if employees with the necessary background and skills will be available externally and at what cost. These cost considerations can then be compared against the alternative of training and promoting internal employees at a more rapid pace to fill future vacancies rather than going into the external labor market. Therefore, once internal and external supplies of labor and the company's demand for labor are estimated personnel requirements can be determined.

Through quantitative and qualitative personnel planning, specific future employment plans will develop within an organization. Such plans include beginning or increasing specific training programs to provide more internal employees with certain skills and expertise, as well as transferring employees to decrease the employees in areas predicted to be overstaffed. Other plans include greater recruitment from the external labor market of employees who can be given experience to fill future vacancies which will not be filled internally.

The goals of the personnel planning process must be both quantitative and qualitative. Quantitatively, the right number of available and qualified employees must be ready to assume positions when they are needed in the future, at the least cost to the organization. Qualitative factors include the morale of current employees who are overqualified for some future jobs and/or underqualified for others. This problem, of course, can be avoided through proper personnel planning techniques. A major goal of human resource planning is to have employees available to quickly fill positions rather than leaving positions unfilled for long periods of time or hiring incompetent employees. Personal planning is the heart of the recruitment process because it sets the recruitment pace within an organization. For example, if a firm's future employment plans show there will be a severe shortage of skilled technicians for next year's product expansion, personnel recruiters should develop plans either internally or externally to minimize the time and cost of filling these positions. Just as in the case of entry-level positions in Figure 6–10, personnel planning can estimate the number of qualified, available applicants that need to be recruited for all levels throughout the organization.

In summary, administrators often find that internal recruiting is cheaper and faster than recruiting externally and that it increases employee morale. External applicants, however, bring new ideas and contacts to the organization as well as minimize internal problems such as em-ployees jockeying for promotions and the Peter Principle. Various recruiting methods include: posting jobs, accepting direct applications, considering employees' referrals, recruiting on campuses, using state or private employment agencies, and advertising. Competent recruiting requires an understanding of current market conditions for all types of labor, determining which recruiting methods best reach applicants, and planning for future personnel needs. Having critical positions unfilled for long periods or selecting unqualified candidates for critical positions can be quite costly; break-even analysis can help personnel recruiters decide either to hire new permanent employees, assign overtime, or acquire temporary help.

The Solution

Nina Combs is asking herself some very valid questions; with the firm's poor campus recruiting record, she should press the issue with Ned Beckmann. At least she should suggest that some form of cost/benefit analysis be performed. Such an analysis might show that rather than continuing campus recruiting the firm would benefit more by sending some of its current employees to a training facility or university. This may incur a greater short-run expense; however, if these employees indicate their intention of staying with the firm, the long-run may provide cost savings.

Beckmann might question how Combs is arranging and conducting her campus interviews. Has she reviewed wage surveys and benefit plans to ensure that the firm is making competitive offers? Is she a competent interviewer? Perhaps

Combs' performance should be closely monitored to ascertain whether she is partially responsible for the unsuccessful campus recruiting efforts.

KEY TERMS AND CONCEPTS

Underemployed
Pirating Employees
Unemployment Rate
Labor Force Participation Rate
Labor Reserve
Hit Rate
False Negative

False Positive
Peter Principle
Job Posting
Gate Hires
Source Trust
Blind Ads
Personnel Planning

FOR REVIEW

1. Discuss exempt and nonexempt applicants' knowledge of labor markets.
2. What are the advantages of recruiting applicants from within the organization? External to the organization?
3. Why might a recent college graduate be quickly rejected during a campus interview?
4. Has media advertising increased as a recruitment technique in recent years? Why?
5. Why might hiring temporary help be preferable to assigning overtime or hiring new employees?

FOR DISCUSSION

1. If you were an underemployed MBA, what steps would you take to find a more satisfactory position?
2. From an inexperienced job applicant's point of view, which recruitment method is most attractive? From the point of view of an applicant with twenty years' experience?
3. A number of books like Richard Bolles's *What Color Is Your Parachute?* suggest that applicants strenuously prepare for job interviews. What steps do these books suggest? If you were interview-

ing job applicants, how would you know which applicants had prepared for the interview?

4. As the president of a small company, you must explain why you've chosen a new public relations head from the outside, rather than promoting one of the two women in the public relations office; each has been with the company for fifteen years. What reasons could you give?

5. Describe the type of speech you would make to a group of high school students during a career day program, telling them how your company views personnel recruitment.

SUPPLEMENTARY READING

Byham, William C. "Common Selection Problems Can Be Overcome." *The Personnel Administrator* 23 (August 1978): 42–47.

Chicci, David L., and Knapp, C. L. "College Recruitment from Start to Finish." *Personnel Journal* 59 (August 1980): 653–57.

Cross, Frank, *Recruitment Advertising*. New York: American Management Association, 1968.

Dennis, Terry L., and Gustafson, David. "College Campuses versus Employment Agencies as Sources of Manpower," *Personnel Journal*, August 1973, 720–24.

Doeringer, Peter B., ed. *Programs to Employ the Disadvantaged*. Englewood Cliffs, NJ: Prentice-Hall, Inc., 1969.

Guion, Robert M. "Recruiting, Selection, and Job Placement." In Dunnette, Marvin D., ed., *Handbook of Industrial and Organizational Psychology*. Chicago: Rand McNally, 1976, pp. 777–828.

Jaquish, Michael P. *Recruiting*. New York: John Wiley and Sons, Inc., 1968.

For Analysis: Ostermiller, The Accountant

Julian Fairchild, president of Acme Quonset Huts, decided last June that the firm's three person accounting staff must be increased to four. He knew that there were only six other non-production employees in the company, and believed that none of them was interested in accounting.

The local university offered a full accounting program, so Fairchild called the placement director and asked for the names of all recent accounting graduates who were in the job market. After making several phone calls, four interviews were arranged. Two weeks later Fairchild offered the job to Eudora Goodstore who had ten days to reply.

Two days after making the offer Fairchild mentioned Goodstore and the offer to Wendell Hardy, the personnel officer. Hardy became very upset because he knew nothing about hiring an additional accountant. After much discussion Fairchild agreed to list the position under normal procedures, even though he felt it was a waste of time because the job required an accounting degree and he already had a good candidate in Goodstore.

One week after Goodstore was given the job offer, she called Fairchild at 10:00 a.m. to accept it. At 9:00 a.m. that same day Sandy Ostermiller, a production employee for three years came to Hardy's office to discuss the accounting position:

Ostermiller: "I noticed that an opening for an accountant position was advertised in yesterday's paper."

Hardy: "Yes, I am very proud of that because, off the record, old man Fairchild did not want to list it. He thinks this place is still in the 1950s with seven employees."

Ostermiller: "Well, good! My best friend, Emily Laurel, and I are considering applying."

Hardy: "You can't—you must have an accounting
                degree."

Ostermiller: "That's why we're so excited about it. Next
                week we both finish summer school at U of T,
                where we're accounting majors."

Hardy: "That's really good news. We like to give our
                own employees a chance to move up—here are
                two applications."

Ostermiller: "Well, that is what we thought, but we didn't
                know the policy about promoting people from
                inside."

Hardy: "To tell the truth, there isn't a written policy
                or anything. In my five years here, I've just
                always given our own people first chance at a
                job if they are qualified. As soon as I can, I'll
                tell Fairchild, I know he will be happy that
                you two have worked so hard at night school."

Ostermiller: "Thank you. We both like it here, but we
                really don't want to work on the line for thirty
                more years."

Hardy: "Very good! Bring back the applications as soon
                as possible."

Questions:

1. What has caused this difficult situation?

2. How can such future problems be avoided?

3. If Goodstore is hired, can the firm be sued for
   discrimination?

4. If you were Hardy, how would you handle this situation?

SELECTED PROFESSIONAL READING

The State Employment Service: An Aid to Affirmative Action Implementation

WILLIAM S. HUBBARTT

There is little doubt that the federal government's mandates for affirmative action and equal employment opportunity have added a new dimension to the job of the personnel or industrial relations manager. A number of recent articles appearing in *Personnel Journal* have suggested ideas for establishing equal employment opportunity goals[1] or corporate strategies and talent sources[2] which may assist the personnel manager in developing an effective EEO program.

The federal compliance agencies which monitor and enforce the EEO/AA clauses in government contracts, have, at times, directed the personnel manager to the state employment office for assistance in meeting affirmative action goals.[3] Now, the Vietnam Era Veterans Readjustment Act of 1974 includes disabled and Vietnam Era veterans as a group covered by affirmative action. This same law also requires certain government contractors to list job openings with the local office of the state employment security agency.

THE ROLE OF THE SERVICE

While some recruiters have experienced difficulty in obtaining complete satisfaction from the state employment office, others have made a special effort to take advantage of the no-cost services offered by the state employment

1. James M. Higgens, "The Complicated Process of Establishing Goals for Equal Employment Opportunity Programs," *Personnel Journal*, Dec. 1975.

2. John Iacobellie and Jan Muczyk, "Overlooked Talent Sources and Corporate Strategies for Affirmative Action," Parts I and II, *Personnel Journal*, Oct. and Nov., 1975.

3. Evelyn Idelson, "Affirmative Action and Equal Employment, Vol I and II," Equal Employment Opportunity Commission, Washington, D.C., 1974.

agencies. This article explores some of the services provided by the State Employment Security Agencies (SESAs) that may be useful to a company's program of equal opportunity employment. Then, there are some suggestions on how to use the state employment office with a minimum of difficulty.

The State Employment Security Agencies generally have two functional divisions. One division administers the system of unemployment insurance benefits and the other division provides employment services. It is the job service or state employment service office which has the basic role of providing job placement services matching workers with jobs and the collection and dissemination of labor market information. Both of these services can provide a useful contribution to an affirmative action plan. A key point to remember is that the "service" function of the state employment office should be distinguished from the "monitoring and enforcement" function of the compliance agencies.

The nature and level of services provided by the state employment offices varies from state to state and even from community to community. A survey was conducted in order to have a more detailed look at what services are provided. Using a survey questionnaire, the SESAs were queried regarding the variety and nature of employment services which are provided to meet the special needs of firms operating with affirmative action plans.[4]

4. William Hubbartt. "The Role of the State Employment Security Agencies in Servicing Firms with Affirmative Action Plans," an unpublished research seminar paper at Loyola University of Chicago, Institute of Industrial Relations, November, 1976.

Condensed. Reprinted with permission, *Personnel Journal*, Costa Mesa, CA, copyright June, 1977.

SCOPE OF THE SURVEY

All fifty three state employment agencies were surveyed. Thirty-three responses were received with twenty-eight returning questionnaires resulting in a response rate of 55 percent. Customary employment service terminology was used to identify the types of services provided. While the findings of the survey represent a good overview of the subject area, they cannot be construed as universal because of the incomplete response rate and differing administrative priorities of the various agencies.

JOB PLACEMENT SERVICES

As an affirmative action employer, one of the objectives is to recruit, employ, and upgrade the status of minorities and females. To achieve this, the affirmative action plan normally details numerical goals and recruiting strategies which may include the use of the state employment service. A frequent situation may occur in which the personnel manager contacts the state employment office to request the referral of qualified minority and female applicants. A potential dilemma then arises. The state employment office (or any other type of public or private employment agency) is subject to Title VII of the Civil Rights Act of 1964 and cannot legally accept a job order which indicates a "preference" for a particular sex or ethnic group except in the case of an approved BFOQ. In fact, in a recent decision, a state employment agency was held by the EEOC to have discriminated because it failed to refer a white applicant to an employer due to the employee's affirmative action obligations.[5]

So, how can the state employment office assist you in affirmative action recruiting? A look at the survey results provides some guidance: 58 percent of the responding SESAs have developed a policy regarding affirmative action services; 57 percent indicate on their job

orders that the employer has an affirmative action plan. This alerts the SESA interviewing staff to your special needs. Further, over 70 percent of the survey respondents indicated that local employment offices will attempt to refer target group applicants without excluding other qualified job seekers. Over 60 percent of the responding agencies also described affirmative efforts which are made to recruit target group applicants. Such extra recruiting efforts included call-in and referral of qualified applicants already on file and developing recruitment contacts with schools, civic groups, social organizations, and other local sources of target group applicants.

In most metropolitan areas, the SESAs operate a computerized system called job bank which provides a daily list of job openings to all the state employment offices in the area. Some states even operate statewide job banks. The chief advantage for the affirmative action plan is that job openings listed with the employment service job bank are exposed to a large pool of available job seekers. Accordingly, there is a greater potential for reaching the target group populations.

TECHNICAL SERVICES

In addition to recruitment and job placement, many of the state employment agencies provide a variety of technical services which may be useful contributions to the affirmative action plan; 79 percent of the survey respondents indicated that one or more of such services were available to firms. The survey responses are charted and described (see graph of SESA functions).

Labor Market Information—All SESAs provide labor force data designed for affirmative action plans, additional details are described in a subsequent part of this article.

Positive Recruiting—This service is best suited for recruiting a large number of workers. An employer can recruit directly from an employment service office or request employment service personnel to assist in screening workers on the premises.

Testing—Employment service proficiency, ap-

---

5. Jeff Schrader, "Sixty Million Dollars," *The Executive News,* Vol. 12, Elk Grove Association of Industry and Commerce, Elk Grove Village, Illinois.

titude, or achievement tests can be used as a selection device to screen prospective workers. The employment service aptitude tests are presently being revalidated to include minorities in the test samples.

Test Validation—This is part of a national program to revalidate employment service tests. Working with cooperating firms, test technicians analyze a selected occupation which includes minority workers, administer the aptitude test to the work group, and then validate the test results through performance evaluations.

Job Analysis and Job Evaluation—The techniques used are those developed by the U.S. Department of Labor. Applications of this technical service can include job restructuring, developing career ladders, and the design of on the job training.

Design of On the Job Training—Design and installation of OJT programs are usually provided through the local Work Incentive Program (WIN) or under the Comprehensive Employment and Training Act (CETA).

Interview Techniques and Advice on Records—The state employment offices are up to date on non-discriminatory practices in applicant selection and record keeping. Advice or information can be provided on request.

Seminars—Several SESAs conduct or participate in employer oriented seminars providing useful information on labor laws, EEO, recruitment selection techniques, and mandatory job listing.

LABOR MARKET INFORMATION

All of the SESAs responding to the survey provide labor force data which can be used in developing an affirmative action utilization analysis. Generally entitled "Manpower Information for Affirmative Action Plans," these data packs are developed in accordance with U.S. Labor Department guidelines and are consistent with the requirements of OFCC Revised Order No. 4. The data packs are usually available from the local employment service office or the administrative headquarters of each state agency.

The data details labor force participation of minorities and females. It is based on the 1970 census or projections from the 1970 census. The affirmative action data packs are generally available on the following geographical basis: statewide, standard metropolitan statistical area (SMSA), labor area, or county. A few states provide data on selected central cities within SMSAs. Detailed data on labor force participation of handicapped and veterans is not expected to become available until after the 1980 census.

WORKING WITH THE STATE EMPLOYMENT OFFICE

The state employment office is, no doubt, one of many sources to draw upon for employee recruitment. Here are several suggestions to help improve success in working with this resource.

● *Know who to deal with.* The Employment and Training Administration, U.S. Employment Service, and the Veterans' Employment Service are part of the U.S. Labor Department bureaucracy which provide direction and funding to the fifty-three SESAs. Usually, for recruitment, technical services, or labor market information, contacts should be with a local "Job Service" or "State Employment Service" offfice. They are listed under state government in your telephone directory.

● *Seek to establish accountability.* It is a frustrating experience to try to deal with nonentities in a government bureaucracy. The personnel manager will get better results by establishing a one-to-one relationship with a person who is responsive to individual needs. A number of state employment agencies are testing an "account executive" approach in which an employment service representative is responsible for serving several employer accounts. Find out whether the local employment service office can assign an account executive to the firm or make other similar arrangements. Also, one may find it worthwhile to invite employment service personnel to tour the facility to insure a better understanding of hiring needs.

● *Two way communication improves results.* Since time is valuable, be sure to provide adequate details on job opening requirements so that employment service interviewers can properly screen workers for you. This will help to minimize the referral of unqualified workers. When your job opening is filled, advise the employment service so that referrals may be shut off. These two tips will save a lot of your interviewing time.

● *Coping with job bank.* The advent of computer technology led to employment service job banks in most metropolitan areas. If you have experienced dissatisfaction with job bank, the best recourse is to establish a one-to-one relationship with an employment service office in the area to insure a greater accountability. Job bank provides a broad exposure of job openings to all Employment Service offices in the area. Therefore, it can be extremely useful for recruiting the highly skilled or professional worker and Affirmative Action target group applicants.

● *Return on the investment.* A large part of employment service funding comes from unemployment tax contributions. The personnel manager can improve the return on this investment by actively participating in efforts to improve the employment service system. All across the country, local employer committees are suggesting ways to improve the employment service. It's called the Job Service Improvement Program (JSIP) and it's a chance to speak out.

VARIOUS FUNCTIONS OF THE SESA

Technical Service	Percent of Agencies Providing Service
	0 10 20 30 40 50 60 70 80 90 100%
Labor Market Information	——— 100
Positive Recruiting	———————————————————————————— 65
Testing	——————————————————————— 55
Test Validation	———————————————————— 48
Job Analysis	——————————————————— 45
Interview Techniques	—————————————————— 42
Design on the Job Training	————————————— 35
Job Evaluation	————————— 27
Advice on Records	———————— 23
Seminars	—— 13

The United Nations has job-related language requirements for its translators like these in the French Section.

7

PERSONNEL SELECTION

Selection Process and Decisions

Initial Screening

Application Blank

Employment Testing

Interviewing

The Problem: Minority Candidates

Harry Lee, the personnel director of a two hundred employee firm, Decisions Unlimited, was uncertain about hiring an accounts manager. Lee and Accounting Department Manager Bob Roberts reviewed the three top candidates: the first was Mary Gronefeld, who had six years of excellent experience with a firm in a nearby city. She moved recently because her husband accepted a new position. Another candidate, Archie Vernon, was a young college graduate looking for his first permanent job. Vernon scored the highest on the company's validated written test. The third candidate, Paul Joseph, scored nearly as high on the test as Vernon (.5% difference) and had two years' experience with a local firm which employs about fifty workers. Joseph was a Vietnam veteran, which Lee and Roberts believed was an important factor.

Lee: "The problem is we have three great candidates!"

Roberts: "Yes, they are all good, and they interviewed well."

Lee: "But we only have one female who is not an hourly employee, and our affirmative action plan says we will hire more females."

Roberts: "Wait a minute! Joseph is a veteran; doesn't the government say something about that?"

Lee: "Yes, that's true. But Vernon scored the highest on the test, so I think we should hire him."

The personnel selection process begins when there are more qualified and available job applicants than there are positions open. It may be necessary to fill one particular position or several positions as they become open, or to continually fill positions through training programs so that people are ready to fill positions as they become vacant. In large organizations, which continuously recruit and select job applicants for future job openings, the time positions remain vacant is minimized. These firms, however, incur greater costs by supporting a larger staff than is necessary during some times of the year.

A BEST-GUESS
PROCESS

Personnel *selection* is the process of choosing qualified individuals who are available to fill positions in the organization. In the ideal personnel situation, selection involves choosing the best applicant out of many to fill a position. After the position opens, the personnel manager quickly reviews the available, qualified applicants and fills the position from that pool. The ideal situation, however, seldom occurs. The selection process involves a best-guess process of determining that an individual probably can do a job and will be successful on the job. There is no fail-safe method of determining the one, best person to fill any position. Many subjective factors are involved in the selection process because there is no perfect test or gauge of applicants to determine the best applicant for each job that becomes open. The selection process is, perhaps, at the heart of the organization's human resource program. If the selection process is well administered, the employee will be able to realize personal career goals while the organization benefits from a productive, satisfied employee.

A Personnel Responsibility

The selection process is usually centered in the personnel department although it involves many individuals from other departments. Particularly in larger organizations, centralizing the recruitment and selection process in the personnel department is both efficient and effective. Current employees, as well as job applicants, have one place to apply for jobs, transfers, or promotions, as well as to inquire about related personnel matters. In most situations the cost of recruiting and selecting employees is minimized because personnel specialists can perform these functions better than separate managers in different departments, and avoid a duplication of effort. The trained personnel specialist also can save money by ensuring that the organization's personnel selection practices comply with federal laws and restrictions. The personnel manager also can ensure that the selection process is objective and winnows out the best individuals possible. This minimizes the bias of individual department managers or employees who may wish to promote employees or hire applicants who are not necessarily the best qualified.

While the personnel department usually is responsible for the selection function, individual managers are involved in the interviewing process. Frequently, the applicant's second or third interview is with the department manager who has valuable insight about work methods and

FIGURE 7–1: *Performance Determinants*

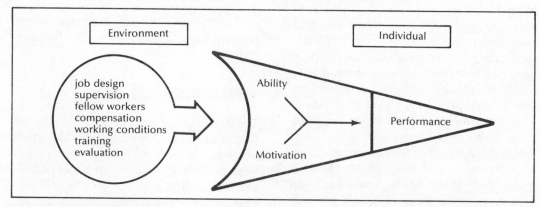

From *Performance in Organizations* by L. L. Cummings and Donald P. Schwab. Copyright © 1973 by Scott, Foresman and Company. Reprinted by permission.

departmental goals, and can evaluate the applicant's qualifications. The selection process also relies upon managers to assist in developing job specifications and writing job descriptions, which are critical in determining the needs for a particular position and the best qualified applicants.

EVALUATING ABILITY AND MOTIVATION

Maximizing employees' future performance is the objective of the selection process. As Figure 7–1 demonstrates, an employee's performance on the job depends on the employee's ability and motivation to perform the job. The entire selection process hinges on determining which applicants have the best ability and the greatest motivation to be successful employees.

Often failure on the job is not due to a lack of skill or ability to perform the job adequately, but to inappropriate personality traits or a lack of motivation. Skills and abilities can be developed in employees through training inside and outside the organization, but motivation cannot

be developed to the same extent. For example, 85 percent of the persons who failed to be successful sales representatives in one company did so from a lack of motivation rather than ability. The single most important indicator of how a job applicant will perform appears to be past performance. Therefore, during the selection process obtaining an accurate and verifiable record of the applicant's past job performance is critical. Unfortunately, this is very difficult to do.[1]

THE SELECTION PROCESS

As Figure 7–2 indicates the selection process pulls together organizational goals, job designs and performance appraisals of employees as well as the recruitment and selection function. The first basic element

1 Arthur Within, "Commonly Overlooked Dimensions of Employee Selection," *Personnel Journal* 59, no. 7 (July, 1980): 573–75.

FIGURE 7–2: *Basic Elements in Selection*

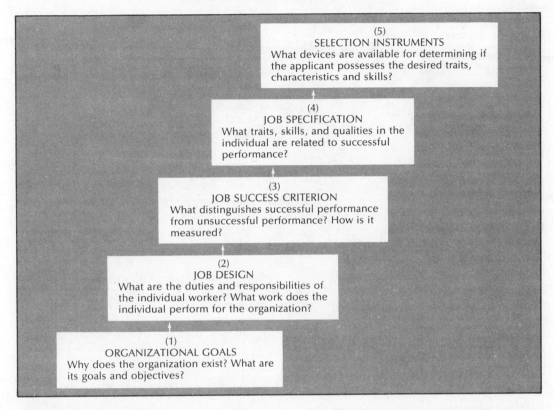

(5)
SELECTION INSTRUMENTS
What devices are available for determining if the applicant possesses the desired traits, characteristics and skills?

(4)
JOB SPECIFICATION
What traits, skills, and qualities in the individual are related to successful performance?

(3)
JOB SUCCESS CRITERION
What distinguishes successful performance from unsuccessful performance? How is it measured?

(2)
JOB DESIGN
What are the duties and responsibilities of the individual worker? What work does the individual perform for the organization?

(1)
ORGANIZATIONAL GOALS
Why does the organization exist? What are its goals and objectives?

SOURCE: Mitchell S. Novit, *Essentials of Personnel Management,* © 1979, p. 70. Reprinted by permission of Prentice-Hall, Inc., Englewood Cliffs, New Jersey.

in the selection process is the setting of organizational goals which must include the general hiring policy of the organization. Management can either employ the best people in the marketplace for particular jobs—often incurring high individual salaries and benefits—or pay the minimum wage allowed by law, and not be concerned with employee turnover or dissatisfaction about wages, benefits, and working conditions. Policymakers must determine how the employees fit into the overall framework of the organization and establish the relationship among the employees in the organization.

The second element is designing jobs by determining what duties and responsibilities each job will entail. How motivating or repetitious each job becomes greatly affects the performance of employees on that job. As indicated in Figure 7–1, the performance of employees will be affected by their ability and motivation. The job design will greatly affect both of these factors and, therefore, must be considered as an important element in the selection process.

The third element involves the measurement of job success. The discovery of which employees are successful will de-

FIGURE 7–3: *Selection Process Steps*

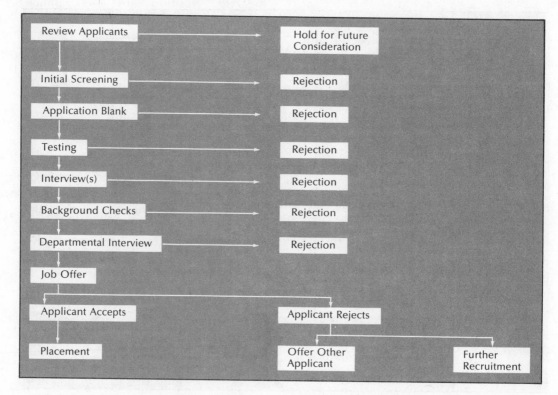

termine what kinds of employees to recruit and select in the future.

The fourth element, job specifications, comes from the job analysis which specifies what traits, skills, and background an individual must have to qualify for the job.

Finally, policymakers must determine which combination of interviews, tests, or other selection devices to use in the selection process. There is no magical combination of selection instruments which will minimize the cost of selection and facilitate choosing the best candidates available. While there are few new selection techniques in personnel today, there have been improvements in particular areas and restrictions due to federal guidelines

in other areas.[2] While the steps in the selection process outlined in Figure 7–3 may change from one organization to another, basically all of the steps are completed at one time or another. The sequence may vary within organizations according to the type of jobs being filled and the size of the organization. The process usually begins by reviewing current applications gathered through the organization's recruitment effort. The Equal Employment Opportunity Commission has warned that because minorities and females will not be represented well enough in a recruitment procedure which

2 Mitchell S. Novit, *Essentials of Personnel Management* (Englewood Cliffs, NJ: Prentice-Hall, 1979), pp. 70–74.

FIGURE 7–4: *Screening Interview Strategies*

Visual Screening:	Reject any totally unfit applicant—one who is under the influence of alcohol, unable to fill out an application, etc.
Knockout Questions:	Ask key questions which may indicate quickly if an applicant is unqualified, such as:
	What are your salary requirements?
	Can you work weekends or nights?
	Can you work shift hours?
	Do you have transportation to work?
	Can you stay out-of-town three nights per week?
	Do you have an accounting degree?
	Are you a registered nurse in this state?
	How fast can you type and take shorthand?
Brief Job Description:	Many applicants will not be interested once they learn the exact nature of the job, salary, or hours.

Adapted from Erwin S. Stanton, *Successful Personnel Recruiting and Selection: Within EEO/Affirmative Action Guidelines* (New York: AMACO, a division of American Management Associations, 1977), pp. 76–84.

relies strictly on word-of-mouth or walk-in applicants, these methods can be discriminatory practices.[3]

3 U.S. Equal Employment Opportunity Commission, *Affirmative Action and Equal Employment—A Guidebook for Employers*, Vol. 1 (Washington, D.C.: U.S. Government Printing Office, 1974), pp. 29–30.

Applicants who appear to be qualified for the position are then initially screened. This screening looks for the minimum requirements still available in the job market as determined by the job specifications. The third step is to have the applicants complete an application blank which standardizes information about all of the applicants to be considered. Any tests which are relevant to the job and have been validated by the organization are then administered to applicants. The next step is usually to interview applicants within the personnel department. Desirable applicants' background information is checked next, especially their references, and employment history. Finally, the few applicants remaining are interviewed by the departmental supervisor or department head. During this in-depth interview, job requirements are discussed so that the applicant as well as the supervisor will be able to judge each other's interest in the job. At this point a job offer can be made to the applicant determined to be the best qualified for the job. If that applicant rejects the offer, management can either contact other qualified applicants or begin the recruitment process all over if there are no other equally qualified applicants available. When the applicant accepts the offer, then the process of placing the applicant in the organization begins.

Initial Screening

Initial screening minimizes the time the personnel department must spend during the selection process by removing obviously unqualified or undesirable applicants. For most jobs many of the applicants do not deserve the serious attention and time of the personnel specialist, particularly if many applications are blind resumes or walk-ins. To maintain a favorable corporate image, every applicant must be given courteous treatment. Primarily, the *initial applicant screening* determines if the applicant possesses the critical job specifications and expedites the departure of the unqualified applicants to minimize the total cost of the selection process.[4]

In reviewing resumes or letters from applicants, the personnel officer must determine which applicants have the minimum qualifications indicated in the position opening or the job description. Qualified applicants are then queried about their interest in the position. If the initial screening can be done by direct contact with the applicant, then one or more of the techniques outlined in Figure 7–4 may be utilized.

Applicants who are rejected at this point in the selection process or at any other point must be included in an "applicant flow record." EEOC requires that companies with federal contracts record for each job applicant, the name, race, national origin, sex, reference source, dates of application, and position applied for. The applicant flow record should also indicate whether a job offer was made to the applicant and reason why an offer was not made or rejected. Applicant flow records provide data to be reported in quarterly reports and annual EEO-1 reports.[5]

Application Blank

An *application blank* is a formal record of

an individual's application for employment. This record is later utilized by the personnel department and may be reviewed by governmental agencies. The application blank provides pertinent information about the individual which is utilized in the job interview and in reference checks to determine the applicant's suitability for employment.

DISCRIMINATORY PRACTICES

In recent years the greatest changes in application blanks have come about after consideration of what questions should be eliminated from the application or very carefully worded. Primarily these questions regard:

Race, national origin, religion. Employers have been warned by EEOC and the courts that application forms which indicate race, national origin, religion, and sex often have been used to discriminate against minorities. Employers immediately eliminated this information from personnel records (including the application blank) only to find that to comply with EEO/AA requirements this information had to be gathered in the application process. The EEOC advised that this data should be kept separate from the individual personnel files. Such information can be coded, incorporated into payroll or other records, and kept separate from the individual's personnel file. Requesting this information on application blanks is not a violation of the Civil Rights Act per se, but such information recorded on application forms would be carefully reviewed should discrimination charges be filed.[6]

Age, date of birth. The Age Discrimination Employment Act prohibits discrimination

---

4 Erwin S. Stanton, *Successful Personnel Recruiting and Selection* (New York: AMACOM, 1977), pp. 73–79.
5 U.S. Equal Employment Opportunity Commission, *Affirmative Action*, pp. 29–30.

6 Ibid., pp. 40–60.

against applicants between the ages of 40 and 70. Therefore, asking the date of birth or age of an applicant is unlawful. However, applicants may be asked if they are of minimum age in order to comply with state and federal child work laws. The employer may also ask if the individual is between 40 and 70.

Marital status. Asking if applicants are married or have children may be discriminating. Because such questions can be used to discriminate against women, and rarely relate to job performance, they are violations of the Civil Rights Act of 1964.[7] While such information is needed for Social Security and tax records, it may be obtained after the applicant has been employed, but not during the selection process.

Education. The Supreme Court has prohibited establishing an education requirement as a condition of employment if such a requirement is not job related. The necessity of requiring a diploma should be determined through job analysis.[8]

Arrest Record. The courts have ruled that requesting arrest record information is an unlawful selection consideration unless it can be proven to be a business necessity. This is due to the fact that a greater proportion of minority group members are arrested than nonminority members. Therefore, making decisions regarding employment on the basis of arrest records would discriminate against minority members.[9] The federal court has also ruled that a felony or misdemeanor conviction should not be an absolute criterion for rejecting a job applicant. Instead, the

employer should consider the nature of the offense and its relationship to the position.[10]

Credit Rating. Any inquiry into an applicant's credit record is unlawful. Since on the average some minority applicants have poorer credit records than nonminority applicants, using credit records as a basis for employment would have an adverse impact on minority groups.[11]

Photograph. Since a photograph would identify an individual's sex, race, or national origin, it can be used to discriminate against minority applicants. The photograph does not provide any job-related information about the applicant. An employer may request a photograph of an employee for identification purposes after the employee is hired.

Height and weight requirements. Court decisions have determined that height and weight requirements discriminate against Hispanic or Asian Americans, and women because many in these minority groups are shorter and slimmer than nonminority individuals. Height and weight requirements should only be made if they are shown by the employer to be a business necessity or a bona fide occupational qualification.[12]

The local branch of the Equal Employment Opportunity Commission or the state civil rights commission will review application forms to be sure that any possible discriminatory practices are elimi-

7 Sprogis v. United Air Lines, 444 F. 2d 1194 (7th Cir. 1971).

8 Griggs v. Duke Power Co., 401 U.S. 424 (1971).

9 U.S. v. Bethlehem Steel Corp. 446 F. 2d 652 (2nd Cir. 1971).

10 Griggs, p. 431.

11 EEOC Decision 72-0427, (1971), *CCH Employment Practices Guide*, para. 6312 (New York: Commerce Clearing House, Inc., 1970); Parham v. S.W. Bell Telephone Co., 433 F. 2d 421 (8th Cir. 1970).

12 Castro v. Beecher, 459 F. 2d 725, C.A. 1, (1972); *CCH Employment Practices Guide*, para. 6231, 6286.

nated. While future court decisions may alter the items which can lawfully be included in application blanks, Figure 7–5 includes those questions which can be included in the application blank.

USES OF THE APPLICATION BLANK

The application blank is a permanent record of the applicant's qualifications for a job. In addition to providing information required for the selection process, the application supplies EEO/AA report input. Personnel specialists use the application to develop background checks and interview questions during the selection process. An important part of the selection process is verification of the applicant's past work history and references. Applicants and their previous employers sometimes disagree about the duties and

FIGURE 7–5: *Appropriate Application Blank Inquiries*

Applicant's name.

Applicant's address and telephone number.

If the applicant is a U.S. citizen.

If the applicant is of minimum working age.

If the applicant can speak or read and write foreign languages (if job-related).

Applicant's educational background (if job-related).

Applicant's work history including dates of employment, salary progression, job responsibility and duties, and reasons for leaving.

If applicant can meet special job requirements, such as evening work hours.

Applicant's military experience.

If a health problem will impair the applicant's job performance.

Applicant's arrest record (if job-related).

Applicant's willingness to travel.

Applicant's special skills or training.

responsibilities of previous jobs, length of employment, salary levels, and especially the reason for leaving prior employment. Applicants tend to overestimate the duration of prior employment as well as salary and importance of jobs performed.[13] In an effort to obtain accurate, complete information from the applicant, the personnel specialist starts with the application and follows through with background checks of the applicant, as well as later interviews. During the interview some applicants will give different accounts of prior experience as well as skills than they provided on their application blanks.

Application blanks can also be used as screening devices to generate "global assessments," wherein the personnel specialist reviews the total applications and determines the general desirability of each applicant. A very subjective technique, global assessment is often utilized when many applicants are being considered and those lacking an appropriate background or skills can be quickly screened out.

A more objective screening technique using application blanks is to have the personnel specialist rate each applicant on particular job-related areas such as the level of specific skills or experience in particular work areas or supervisory positions. This, of course, would change from job opening to job opening as different skills and background requirements become more relevant. Generally, if one particularly relevant job specification does not appear on application blanks, then these applicants can be screened out.

Perhaps the most valid and least subjec-

---

13 I. L. Goldstein, "The Application Blank: How Honest Are the Responses?" *Journal of Applied Psychology* 55 (1971): 491–92.

tive use of the application blank is the practice of using a *weighted application blank* on which responses have different weights on the application blank. This usually entails selecting application blanks of some of the most and least successful current employees. Then a distribution of these employees' responses in the different areas of the application blank is made. For example the difference between the percentages of the very best and the poorest employees who had three years or more of supervisory experience is determined. If the organization's best and worst employees do not differ on items, these items are not given weights. Where there are great differences, these particular items differentiate between the best and poorest applicants and this becomes weighted information on the application blank. While the application blank itself does not indicate how information is weighed, the personnel specialist weighs applicants' various responses.

In using weighted information determined from current employees, it is critical that the process be cross-validated. When used with application blanks, *cross-validation* is the degree of correlation between the scores of employees on weighted application blanks and the job performance level of the same employees. Cross-validation is critical because if weights are determined with particular employees chosen in a not entirely random fashion, certain biases may be included which would not be true of the typical applicants in the future. Therefore, cross-validation serves as a check by comparing results with a different set of employees' performance ratings and applications to make sure that the weights are valid.

The weighted application blank is a selection technique which incorporates the predictive validation process. The weighted application blank utilizes predictive validation because it correlates employees' applications with their performance ratings and then uses the items which differentiate between good and bad employees as a selection criteria for future job applicants. The weighted application blank technique has an advantage over most predictive validation techniques in that employers can develop it quickly and do not have to wait and hire all of the applicants to get their performance scores as is normally the case. In practice, weighted applications are used by very few employers due to the cost of development and the fact that they must be frequently updated to retain their validity. However, they may become more common in the future as federal guidelines restrict other selection devices.

Background Checks

In recent years thoroughly checking the backgrounds of perspective employees has become increasingly necessary. Such an investigation can be an energy-saving procedure as well as a cost efficient means of screening out undesirable applicants. Due to applicants' tendencies to misrepresent themselves on their applications or during interviews, *background checking* has become a more common practice in personnel. Between 7 and 10 percent of applicants do not have the experience and background they claim. More persons claim to have graduated from the Harvard School of Business than have ever been enrolled at the school! Thus, employers are turning to a confidential investigation of applicants' backgrounds before proceeding in the selection process.[14]

Primarily, there are three basic methods of checking references: The personnel specialist can personally visit previous employers or friends of the applicant. This method should be reserved for candidates being considered for high ranking positions because of the extra time and expense incurred. The most common reference checking technique is by mail, which has two distinct disadvantages: several days to weeks are required and it lacks the depth of information that a personal phone call can accomplish. In addition, most employers are increasingly wary of putting their perceptions about former employees in writing. The third method, the telephone call, is a time efficient, accurate means of getting complete information on applicants. Previous supervisors and employers are more likely to give complete information regarding a candidate's background over the phone. The personnel specialist can go into detail or ask particular questions concerning the applicant.[15]

Personal References

Many employers continue to request that applicants list the names, occupations, and addresses of three or more individuals who are not previous employers or relatives but who can attest to the applicants' suitability. In reality, of course, almost all applicants list individuals who will say something very positive about them and give good recommendations. Realizing

this, the personnel specialist does not use a good recommendation to determine the applicant's suitability for the position. A realistic use of personal recommendations includes:

- Verifying data received on the application blank or during the interview. Often personal recommendations can verify information on the application blank. For example, that individuals did attend certain schools, or do have experiences, or have lived at addresses for certain periods of time.

- Evaluating the quality of the personal recommendation. Applicants who give professional people or business executives as references, have a definite advantage over applicants who use their next-door neighbors, or former high school classmates as references.

- Determining the degree of knowledge the person has concerning the applicant. Surprisingly a personnel specialist may call a personal reference and find that the person has little or no knowledge of the applicant other than that the applicant lives down the street or went to the same high school. In some cases the references do not even give applicants good recommendations and simply say that they really don't know much about the persons. A lukewarm recommendation by a personal reference is certainly an indication of the applicant's suitability for a position.

Previous Employers

The most important background check involves the previous employer, co–

---

14 Jeremiah Bogert, "Learning the Applicant's Background Through Confidential Investigation," *Personnel Journal* 55 (June, 1976): 272–75.

15 Erwin S. Stanton, *Successful Personnel Recruiting*, pp. 90–92.

workers, and supervisor. Today, employers are concerned with the legal aspects of reference checking and personnel selection. Myths and half-truths abound concerning what information employers can release and should not release. In reality, there are few legal entanglements in reference checking practices; privacy laws restrict employers from releasing information only in certain areas. Employers can release accurate, verifiable information about previous employees in the following areas: dates of employment; job progression; job titles, duties and responsibilities; performance appraisals by employee's supervisors; or other objective measures of employee performance such as absenteeism, quantitative production, or sales.[16]

Employers should not release the following information without written consent: credit information, medical records, school records or other information, or results of polygraph or graphology tests.

Employers should never release false or unverified reference information, or information which is vague or misleading. For example, a past supervisor's feelings that the applicant did not get along with other employees due to personality conflicts, should not be included as reference information. Also, if information would have an adverse impact on a protected class of individuals, then it should not be given as reference information. For example, a supervisor might have commented that "She couldn't handle the job, it was too rough for a woman." This does not preclude or limit most background checking by employers. In fact, only rarely is a discrimination case based upon background information checks successful, unless the information released was completely false or vague and misleading.[17]

Employees' privacy in the job place promises to be a major employee relations issue during the next decade. How employees and employers feel about employees' rights to see their own personnel files and the right employers have to that information is a subject of discussion. A recent study of *Fortune* 1,000 companies' personnel executives, 77 members of Congress, and over 1,500 employees provided some interesting results. As Figure 7–6 indicates, a majority of employees, employers, and general public feel that asking questions of job applicants in at least ten areas is improper. Note that the employers felt much more strongly than either the employees or the public that the questions would be improper. The survey also showed that the public, employees, employers, and Congress strongly believed that the employees should be notified before previous employers release personal information. Only in the area of access to a supervisor's personal notes concerning employees did the employees and employers differ substantially concerning employees' access to their personnel records. Note that most employees did not believe their employers were engaged in improper collection and use of their personal data.[18]

Testing

Once the cornerstone of the personnel selection process, the testing of applicants has come under attack since the

---

16 Edward L. Levine, "Legal Aspects of Reference Checking for Personnel Selection," *The Personnel Administrator* (November, 1977): 14–17.

17 Ibid., pp. 15–77.
18 Allan Westin, "What Should Be Done About Employee Privacy?," *The Personnel Administrator* (March, 1980): 27–30.

FIGURE 7–6: *Sentry Insurance Survey on Employee Privacy*

Improper Questions to Ask Job Applicants	Public	Full-Time Employed	Employers
What kinds of friends the applicant has	87%	92%	97%
The type of neighborhood in which the applicant lives	84	86	96
Information about the applicant's spouse	77	78	85
Membership in political and community organizations	74	76	83
Whether the applicant owns or rents residence	70	73	81
Records of arrest without conviction	62	69	86
General credit record and ability to pay bills	54	58	65
The results of psychological tests	52	54	62
Race	52	57	74
Whether the applicant has ever received psychiatric or psychological counseling	50	54	62

Release of personal information	Public	Employees	Employers	Congress
Employees should have the right to look at and question the following information in their own files:				
● Promotability reports by supervisor	86%	88%	74%	65%
● Job performance reviews	86	88	95	65
● Supervisor's personal notes	64	65	46	30
Employers should be required to tell employees about any conditions at work affecting employee's health.	91	91	84	65
Laws, rather than employer discretion, should mandate that employees have access to their own personnel files.	65	70	33	44
Employers should inform employees before releasing personal information from files except when required by law.	83	85	84	94

SOURCE: Allan F. Westin, "What Should be Done About Employee Privacy?" Reprinted from the March, 1980 issue of *Personnel Administrator*, 30 Park Drive, Berea, Ohio 44017, $26 per year.

formation of the EEOC guidelines. The federal Equal Employment Opportunity Commission and the courts have alleged that most tests lack validity. Critics have contended that test specialists have manipulated different testing problems and test scores to apply to a single model of test validation. Tests have been given more than their weight in the selection process, sometimes the entire hiring deci-sion relies upon an individual's test score. While the validity of aptitude tests or other specialized intelligence tests can be determined, it is much more difficult to determine the validity for other types of employee tests.[19]

In the past part of the problem has been

19 L. Robert Ebel, "Comments on Some Problems of Employment Testing," *Personnel Psychology* 30 (1977): 55–63.

the use of general tests for purposes they were not developed for and the lack of specific validation by the organization utilizing them. The EEOC has emphasized that any test which adversely affects the employment status of groups protected by Title VII must be professionally validated within the organization utilizing it. In 1974 the EEOC emphasized that testing was a major area for review and action by employers. If employers believe tests are necessary in the employment process, they should validate them in accordance with EEOC guidelines. In the past, the use of intelligence, aptitude, and other tests having no proven relationship to successful job performance has had a major disproportionate effect in the rejection of minority job applicants. An EEOC alternative allows employers to compensate for adverse impact by methods which permit a reasonable proportion of minority candidates to pass selection tests. Test scores may be used as only one of several criteria for selection if the selection rate for minorities is 80 percent of the rate of other applicants. Employers have the option of substituting probationary periods for written tests as a means of evaluating the abilities of new employees.[20]

The most effective way to defend the use of selection testing may be to note its success. Ninety-five percent of employers who have tried applicant employment testing still use it. An industrial survey of over twenty five hundred companies conducted by Prentice-Hall revealed that almost 65 percent tested applicants. Over forty companies, including Xerox and IBM subsidiaries, produce tests for personnel selection which helps supply a $400 million annual market. Sears, Roebuck and Company, which has utilized testing since the early 1940s, gives over seven thousand tests annually because company executives believe that promotion and hiring decisions are too important to be made on such subjective bases as office politics, seniority, or even subjective supervisory evaluations.[21]

Employee personnel testing is generally far more objective than other selection procedures. Testing has often proved to be the most valid selection procedure utilized. An EEOC staff psychologist has noted the common misconception that the use of selection testing is the fastest way to incur trouble from the EEOC.[22]

GENERAL INTELLIGENCE TESTS

Decades ago, general *intelligence tests* were developed to predict the success of young children in schools. General intelligence test scores are measures of the ability to do well in a traditional school setting.[23] Testing the success of young school children in their academic careers is still what general intelligence test scores are best suited for and should be utilized for.

Research has shown a consistent relationship between the occupation/income level and general intelligence. Intelligence tests are useful to roughly categorize possible occupations for job applicants, as general intelligence minimums are required for each occupation. However, while intelligence and occupation are related, the results of intelligence tests do not predict potential success or failure within an occupation with a great deal of accuracy. Success within an occupation requires testing which is much

---

20 U.S. Equal Opportunity Commission, *Affirmative Action*, pp. 43–45.

21 Within, p. 588.
22 Ibid., p. 575.
23 Robert M. Guion, *Personnel Testing* (New York: McGraw-Hill, 1965), pp. 169–74.

more specific to the particular requirements of the occupation.[24] The person with higher general intelligence would however, have a greater range of occupations which could be successfully pursued.[25]

APTITUDE TESTS

Natural ability in a particular discipline, or ability to quickly learn or understand a particular area, reveals an aptitude for that area or discipline. *Aptitude tests* indicate the ability or fitness of an individual to engage successfully in any number of specialized activities.[26]

As the official U.S. Employment Services aptitude test, the General Aptitude Test Battery (GATB) is recognized as the basic denominator in estimating aptitude requirements. It is the aptitude test by which jobs are categorized in the *Dictionary of Occupational Titles* (DOT). Also, all state employment agencies use the GATB, which tests:[27]

General Intelligence

Verbal

Numerical

Spatial

Form Perception

Clerical Perception

Motor Coordination

Finger Dexterity

Manual Dexterity

Today a multifaceted set of aptitude

tests is given which tests applicants in each of the nine areas. Aptitude tests have

FIGURE 7–7: *Occupations Classified According to Highest Ability Scores*

Highest Ability	Occupation
General Intelligence	College Professors
	Dentists
	Engineers
	Lawyers
	Physicians
	Scientists
	Social Workers
Numerical Fluency	Accountants
	Office Managers
	Optometrists
	Painters
	Pharmacists
	Purchasing Agents
	Salesmen
	Treasurers
	Comptrollers
Visual Perception	Advertising Agents
	Architects
	Draftsmen
	Printing Craftsmen
	Radio, TV Repairmen
Mechanical	Airplane Pilots
	Carpenters
	Crane Operators
	Electricians
	Engine Mechanics
	Farmers
	Sheet Metal Workers
Psychomotor	Firemen
	Guards
	Machinists
	Miners, Drillers
	Plumbers
	Service and Recreation Managers

SOURCE: Robert L. Thorndike and Elizabeth P. Hagen, *Ten Thousand Careers*, pp. 32–34. (New York: John Wiley and Sons, Inc., 1959) Reprinted with permission.

24 Benjamin Schneider, *Staffing Organizations* (Pacific Palisades, CA: Goodyear Publishing, Co., 1976), pp. 79–83.

25 Schneider, pp. 80–83.

26 The Reader's Digest Association, *The Reader's Digest Great Encyclopedic Dictionary* (Pleasantville, NY: Funk and Wagnalls, 1968), p. 73.

27 Schneider, pp. 83–85.

potential validity; many have been proven to be valid predictors of employee performance. The actual validity of a particular test in a particular organization, however, must be established by that organization.

PERSONALITY AND INTEREST TESTS

In general, personality and interest tests seek to measure an individual's motivation in particular fields. *Personality tests*, such as the Bernreuter Personality Inventory, measure neurotic tendency, self-sufficiency, introversion and extraversion, sociability, and self-confidence. The Thematic Apperception Test (TAT) is a common projective personality test, one in which the subject is asked to interpret certain situations. TAT assesses the individual's need for achievement and has been successful in predicting individual motivation. Other personality tests such as the California Psychological Inventory (CPI) and the Thurstone Temperament Survey (TTS) have been developed to assess specific personality aspects. However, the validity of utilizing personality tests as useful indices of applicants' possible work motivation is highly questionable. Personality tests can be faked by individuals who give the answers they believe are expected. Generally, such tests simply do not accurately predict employee job performance, and thus, are not valid.

Interest tests generally are designed to measure individuals' activity preferences. For example, individuals are asked if they would rather watch a baseball game on television, read a novel, or attend a local little league game on a Saturday afternoon. Interest tests such as the Strong Vocational Interest Blank (SVIB) have been found to predict occupations people

will enter with reasonable accuracy. By matching the interests of individuals successful in different occupations, the SVIB indicates to applicants which fields most closely match their interests. SVIB has shown that within professions people's interests have been fairly stable. While interest tests are particularly useful for students considering many careers or employees deciding upon career changes, they are not particularly valid in selecting a particular employee for a job.

ACHIEVEMENT TESTS

Aptitude tests assess a person's capacity to learn, while *achievement tests* assess the degree to which a person has learned. Because achievement tests measure current behavior they may be the best predictor of future employee behavior. Therefore, personnel departments may use achievement tests to determine whether a person can do the job, and aptitude tests to measure whether or not someone can be trained to do the job. Through a job analysis for a specific occupation, a list of questions can be developed which will test an applicant's occupational experience. The U.S. Employment Service has developed a series of trade tests which measure an individual's knowledge of the behavior, tools, and equipment of a particular job. For example, electricians might be required to read wiring diagrams.[28] Because achievement tests can be validated, they are useful predictors of job performance where specific knowledge or experience is necessary to perform a skilled occupation.

WORK SAMPLES

One step beyond the achievement test

---

28 Ibid., pp. 168–70.

which measures knowledge of a particular job or occupation is the use of a *work sample* where the applicant performs part of the job as a test. Examples of work samples are typing tests for secretaries, assembly tests for production line workers, and trial balances computation tests for accountants. Work samples, obviously, are valid predictors of job performance since they measure job performance. However, work samples see limited use due to their specific nature; that is, they can only test an individual's ability on certain duties within the job setting. The other criteria are measured by other selection devices. Work sample tests are usually limited to jobs which are physical rather than mental in nature. In the future, more work sample tests for conceptual jobs can be expected.

When selecting a work sample test, the skills required by the test, ease of administration in scoring test results, and the abilities demonstrated on the test should be considered. For example, of the three major typing tests, the Typing Test for Business (TTB) has been found to be much easier to administer and score with higher demonstrated reliability, than the SRA Typing Skills Test or the National Business Entrance Test.[29]

POLYGRAPH TESTS

The *polygraph* is a device which measures the emotions of an individual by directly measuring galvanic skin response, blood pressure, and breathing rate. A sampling of 400 firms on *Fortune* Magazine's list of largest companies reveals that polygraph usage in corporations today falls into three common areas: (1) verification of employment application information; (2) periodic surveys to determine employee honesty and loyalty; and (3) investigation of a specific instance of theft within the company. About 20 percent of those companies that responded to the survey utilized the polygraph in some capacity; 50 percent of the commercial banks and retail companies utilized polygraph examinations. Transportation and industrial firms also indicated heavier usage of the polygraph examination.[30]

The polygraph has come under severe criticism; in fact, many states have passed laws to severely restrict or eliminate the use of a polygraph. The legal considerations involve an employee's self-incrimination and invasion of the right to privacy. However, even some critics feel that the polygraph examination should be available to the applicant or employee who chooses to use it to prove innocence of a specific theft or to speed up the selection process.[31] In some situations, employees request a polygraph test to prove their innocence if a theft or other incident has occurred which might adversely influence their later promotion within the company. If the guilty party was not found in such a situation, management would be hesitant to promote anyone within the department who could have been guilty.

The future of the polygraph test appears to be in the hands of the courts and Congress. If a critical court case determines that the polygraph is a valid and reliable instrument and that examinations can be

29 H. Birdie Holder, "A Critique of Three Current Typing Tests," *Personnel Journal* 58 (May, 1979): 291–94.

30 John A. Bolt and Peter B. Holden, "Polygraph Usage Among Major U.S. Corporations," *Personnel Journal* 57 (February, 1978): 80–86.

31 G. Philip Benson and S. Paul Kreis, "The Polygraph in Employment: Some Unresolved Issues," *Personnel Journal* 58 (September, 1979): 616–21.

FIGURE 7–8: *Personnel Directors' Reasons for Using or Not Using Polygraph Examinations*

Characteristic	Benefits as ranked by users	Objections as ranked by nonusers
Speed in obtaining results	1	5
Validity and reliability of tests	2	2
Cost, as compared to other methods	3	3
Availability of qualified operators	4	4
Moral or ethical considerations	5	1

SOURCE: Bolt and Holden, "Polygraph Usage Among Major U.S. Corporations," *Personnel Journal*, Vol. 57, (February, 1978), p. 85. Used by permission.

required of employees or job applicants, the use of polygraph examinations will probably increase dramatically in this country since they are inexpensive and effective. The American Polygraph Association has been striving to upgrade their profession by instituting state and muncipal licensing legislation for polygraph examiners. The American Polygraph Association has been supported by some lawyers, law enforcement officials, and other groups which realize that the polygraph examination benefits employees as well as employers.[32]

GRAPHOLOGY TESTS

A *graphology* test is administered by a trained graphologist who examines handwriting and determines the personality traits of the writer. However, like the administration of polygraph examinations, graphology is a fairly young field, without legal status or professional licensing procedures. Employers find it difficult to validate the results of graphology tests. As in the case of polygraph examinations, the future of graphology in the personnel area will most likely be determined by the courts and government.

Interviewing

According to a nationwide survey, interviewing is the most widely used selection method. Some companies have reacted to EEOC and court decisions regarding testing by using fewer tests and turning to the interview as the primary selection technique. Ironically, interviewing is just as vulnerable to EEOC guidelines as the written test. The interview, however, has not received as much criticism as the written test.[33]

Research has constantly shown that the selection interview is low in reliability and validity. Reliability is a particular concern with interviews because the interview technique does not have the consistency of form that the written test or the reference check may have. Thus, the interview is not as consistent or reliable a selection technique as the other methods discussed.[34]

Low reliability or consistency in the interview process comes from many factors. First, interviewers must constantly work to curtail personal biases. Even though interviewers recognize their personal biases, an individual's sex, race, religion, school, or hobbies may influence them. Biases can be positive as well as

32 Bolt and Holden, *Polygraph Usage*, p. 81.

33 Robert Gatewood and James Ledvinka, "Selection Interviewing and EEO: Mandate for Objectivity," *The Personnel Administrator* (May, 1976): 15–17.

34 Ray Forbes, "Improving the Reliability of the Selection Interview," *Personnel Management* (July, 1979): 36–37.

negative. The sex of the interviewer and/ or the interviewee affects the total evaluation of the interview situation. This even occurs with trained, experienced interviewers.[35]

Second, the fact that the interviewees constantly are changing and have different characteristics also affects interviewing. The content of interviews changes because no two interviewees have the same background and experience; different aspects of the individuals, their skills, and work histories must be discussed with each individual. Third, the setting of the interview may affect the outcome. If one interview takes place early in the morning when the interviewer is fresh and the next interview is conducted late in the afternoon when the interviewer is in a hurry to leave, the latter interviewee may receive a short shrift when the interviewees are compared. Another example, an applicant interviewed right after the most impressive applicant the interviewer has ever seen, is more likely to get a less positive interview evaluation than normal. On the other hand, an applicant following one of the worst applicants the interviewer has seen, may get higher scores than normal.

Fourth, if the company has established a maximum number of people to interview and a deadline for filling the position, additional pressure is placed on the interviewer. The last applicant to be interviewed may be offered the position if the interviewer is in a hurry to fill it. Thus the applicant may get a break and fill the position which otherwise would not have been offered.

Primarily, conducting good interviews

is a two-step process: The first step is to create a good interview setting before the applicant actually arrives for the interview, and the second step is to conduct a useful questioning period during the interview. Broken down, these steps involve:

Setting Prepare a setting which will put the applicant at ease and provide consistent surroundings for each interview. Allow between 30 to 60 minutes for an adequate interview.

Documentation Prepare a system of written records and formalized procedures for the interview. Determine how the interview will be documented at its conclusion to provide a formal record of the outcome.

Standardization Standardize the interview format. Determine a line of questioning that includes the applicant's prior work history, military history, skills, and educational background. This will provide a framework for consistency in the information-gathering process.

Scoring the Interview Determine how the interview will be scored. That is, how will the employee ultimately be evaluated as a result of the interview process. An employee may be scored in each different area relevant to the job description as well as the employee's response to questioning.

Reviewing the Job Description Specifications Review the job description and job specifications for that particular job before each interview. Since the interviewer may see applicants for different jobs, the particular, important aspects of each job must be fresh in the interviewer's mind.

Reviewing the Application Blank Review

---

35 Gerald Rose, "Sex Effects on Managerial Hiring Decisions," *Academy of Management Journal* 21 (1978): 104–12.

the application before the interview looking for possible problem areas which require additional information and areas of possible strengths and weaknesses which should be gone into in more detail during the interview.

Training the Interviewer Train the interviewer to recognize personal biases and other possible causes of lack of interview reliability.

Job-Related Questions Prepare a line of questioning which keeps the interview job-related and does not waste time by straying from the subject or delving into personal areas which could be seen as discriminatory.

Conducting an interview is an art as much as a science. Only through experience and training can an interviewer thoroughly question a job applicant and get maximum information in minimum time. Figure 7–9 contains some of the do's and don't's of effective job interviewing.

The end of the job interview is a critical period of time. At the end the applicant should be able to ask questions concerning the job, pay, or working conditions. The interviewer should ask when the applicant will be available to work and tell the applicant when the job will be filled. If more people will be interviewed or there will be a waiting period for a final decision to be made, the applicant should be given an estimate—such as ten days or two weeks—of when a decision should be reached. The applicant should also be told whether to call to find out the results of the job decision or to wait for notification. Interviewers should be positive toward all applicants, even those who may have to be ruled out, as applicants may be

FIGURE 7–9: *Effective Interview Questions*

DO	DON'T
Ask open questions: Why did you apply here? What specific skill do you have?	Ask all closed questions: Could you work here three to five years? Do you enjoy working with figures?
Ask job-related questions: Can you work the 3 to 11 shift? What COBOL experience do you have?	Ask personal questions: Does your husband work? Are your parents Spanish?
Ask reflective or "follow-up" questions: You said you didn't work the counter. Why? How could you accomplish that?	Ask broad or vague questions: Do you like people?
Open the interview by putting the applicant at ease—discuss an easy topic such as the last job or education.	Do the talking. Let the applicant talk as much as possible.
Look for areas the applicant is uneasy about and find out why.	Ask judgmental questions: Don't you like flextime? I think a good health insurance plan is critical, don't you?
Ask positive questions: Tell me your reason for leaving XYZ Company.	Be impatient, constantly hurry the applicant, or look at the clock.
Use summary statements to ensure your understanding: Then you did train employees in COBOL programming?	Ask more than one question at a time: Why did you choose accounting? What courses did you like, dislike?

available and suited for other positions at a later date.

While the interview concentrates on verbal cues, much nonverbal information is given by the candidate which influences the interviewer's perception. Interviewers allow firmness of handshake, physical appearance, and eye contact during the interview to affect their selection decisions. Body language is a *nonverbal cue* which can greatly influence the interviewer. Candidates who appear nervous or apprehensive do not make a positive impression. The lack of eye contact during the interview can also have a strong, negative impact on the selection decision if it is interpreted to indicate a person's lack of self-confidence or inability to communicate. Survey information indicates that some interviewers make a tentative decision about an applicant within a few minutes largely due to impressions based upon dress and appearance, eye contact, or other nonverbal cues. While these cues might be invalid, subjective impacts on the interview decision, they are, nevertheless, important.[36]

A board or panel interview could replace the traditional one-on-one interview technique. The panel interview would minimize individual bias since all panel members would be scoring the applicant. The final evaluation for each applicant would be an average of several individuals' evaluations, and, therefore, balance out one individual's bias. The panel technique would also force interviews to become more structured and to the point. The obvious disadvantage of the panel interview is the increased cost to the organization of having more than one interviewer, and increased discomfort for some interviewees.[37]

THE SELECTION
DECISION

Deciding which applicant should be offered the job position may be accomplished by one of two techniques: the personnel manager can use a *compensatory selection model* or a *multiple hurdles selection model*. The multiple hurdles selection process is outlined in Figure 7–3. In this process the applicant must pass each hurdle such as the initial screening, application blank, testing, interview, background checks, and finally the departmental interview to be selected for the job. Whenever management finds that its bottom line percentage of minority candidates is not high enough, it may consider the compensatory model. In the compensatory model, all applicants who pass the initial screening complete the application blank, and are tested; each applicant is interviewed before the final choice is made. The applicants are then compared on the basis of all of the selection information. Under the compensatory technique, an applicant may score low in one area but that score might offset a very high mark in another area. This is particularly beneficial to candidates who receive a low interview score because they are very nervous and lack self-confidence during the interview but perform very well on aptitude and background checks. The disadvantage of the compensatory model is its cost because a larger number of candidates must be processed through the complete selection

---

36 John Hatfield, "Nonverbal Cues in the Selection Interview," *The Personnel Administrator* (January, 1978): 30–33.

37 *Forbes*, pp. 36–37.

procedure before a final decision is made. Primarily due to the cost factor, the multiple hurdles technique, where a candidate might be rejected at each stage of the selection process, is more common.

When the selection decision results in an employee being hired who is successful on the job, then the cost of the selection decision is the normal cost of filling a vacant position. However, if an erroneous selection decision is made, than additional costs are incurred. Primarily, management can make two types of errors in the selection decision process: First, selecting someone for a position who fails on the job (false positive). Second, rejecting an applicant who could have been successful on the job (false negative). Expenses due to hiring the wrong employee primarily involve the cost of replacing that individual, termination costs, costs of undesirable job behavior, and costs incurred by a lack of morale or cooperation with other employees. These costs must be weighed against the cost of rejecting the individual who could have been successful on the job. Included in these costs are the opportunity costs of having a successful employee who could have added to the productivity of the organization, and the competitive disadvantage lost if the individual is hired by a competing firm. The cost of recruiting an additional applicant to replace the rejected individual also must be considered.[38]

---

38 Marvin D. Dunnette, *Personnel Selection and Placement* (Belmont, CA: Brooks–Cole Pub., 1966), pp. 173–75.

While it is difficult to attach dollar values to some of the above costs, the decision boils down to estimating the possible losses incurred due to hiring poor employees who should have been rejected, in comparison with the direct costs incurred of possibly rejecting employees who could have been successful and, therefore, incurring additional recruitment and selection costs.

In summary, whenever a job applicant is selected to fill a position, this is management's affirmation that the employee has the future ability and motivation to perform the job. Many times, personnel specialists and managers base their selection on the applicant's past work behavior, which is, they believe, the best indication of future work behavior. The job interview process is not always reliable; it can be affected by the interviewers' personal biases, a lack of standardized interview settings, as well as an unstructured interview format. Interview information should be documented and preserved for future needs. Federal legislation requires that all selection devices including written tests, interviews, and background checks must be validated and should be job–related. The Privacy Act and other legislation permits only accurate, verifiable information related to the employee's job performance to be released.

The Solution

Having three well-qualified candidates like Mary Gronefeld, Archie Vernon, and Paul Joseph is not an unusual situation. Managers become confused about what they should do in a hiring decision because of governmental intervention; any of the three candidates could be hired and the selection decision defended. Mary Gronefeld is a female, and the firm's affirmative action plan indicates an underutilization of females; thus more women should be hired if they are equally qualified. Is she equally qualified? Archie Vernon scored the highest on the test and could be hired for that reason. But Gronefeld passed the test and has six years' experience that Vernon does not have. Joseph did almost as well on the test and has related experience; he is eligible for consideration under the Vietnam Veterans Readjustment Act of 1974.

Note that Decisions Unlimited can defend its decision to hire any one of the three, because it has an affirmative action plan, a validated test, and is aware of federal selection laws.

KEY TERMS AND CONCEPTS

Selection	Interest Tests
Initial Applicant Screening	Achievement Tests
Application Blank	Work Samples
Weighted Application Blank	Polygraph
Background Check	Graphology
Intelligence Tests	Nonverbal Cues
Aptitude Tests	Compensatory Selection Model
Personality Tests	Multiple Hurdles Selection Model

FOR REVIEW

1. Why is the selection process usually centralized in the personnel department?

2. Why should an organization be cordial to those applicants it rejects?

3. Should the personnel office ask an applicant for date of birth, marital status, or a photograph?

4. How does the personnel specialist use the application blank?

5. What real uses are there for an applicant's personal references?

6. Which type of tests are the most useful in employee selection?

7. How is the polygraph used by firms?

8. Why should a firm use the multiple hurdles selection model? Compensatory model?

FOR DISCUSSION

1. What inappropriate personality traits would overshadow an employee's skills and abilities enough to cause the dismissal of the following persons: a food store checkout clerk, a research assistant, an elementary school teacher?

2. If you inherited a shoe factory which had a history of high turnover and low wages, would you attempt to attract only the best workers by raising salaries, or continue a minimum wage policy and disregard employees' dissatisfaction? What factors would influence your decision?

3. While interviewing two well-qualified applicants for an accounting manager's position, you notice that one applicant has had one job for seven years and the other has had five jobs in ten years, each change involved a salary increase. Would this information affect your decision?

4. Why should age and sex biases not color a personnel specialist's choice of persons to fill positions as car wash employees, tool makers, receptionists, or sanitation workers?

5. You work in a department store's personnel department. The owner requested that all of the store's employees take polygraph tests periodically, to minimize employee theft. Employees find this approach insulting and demand that you do something. What would you do?

═══ SUPPLEMENTARY READING ═══

Anderson, Howard J. *Primer of Equal Employment Opportunity*. Washington, DC: Bureau of National Affairs, Inc., 1970.

Dunnette, Marvin. *Personnel Selection and Placement*. Belmont, CA: Brooks–Cole Publishing Company, 1966.

———. "Aptitudes, Abilities, and Skills." In Dunnette, Marvin D., ed. *Handbook of Industrial and Organizational Psychology*. Chicago: Rand McNally, 1976.

Grimsley, Glen, and Jarrett, Hilton F. "The Relation of Past Managerial Achievement to Test Measures Obtained in the Employment Situation: Methodology and Results." *Personnel Psychology* 26 (Spring 1973): 31–48.

Pursell, Elliott D.; Campion, M. A.; and S. R. Gaylord. "Structured Interviewing: Avoiding Selection Problems." *Personnel Journal* 59 (November 1980): 907–12.

Sundberg, Norman D. *Assessment of Persons*. Englewood Cliffs, NJ: Prentice–Hall, 1977.

For Analysis: The New Personnel Director

John Spencer Jones has just been hired as the first full-time personnel director of Treasury Productions. Producing media events from concerts to commercials, Treasury has relied in the past upon its general manager to hire, supervise, and direct its ninety employees. The general manager, however, said he could "do it all when we had ten people" but not anymore.

The firm received a serious blow five weeks ago when it was ordered by a court to pay Sherry Seneca $10,000 in back pay and give her the position she was denied when one of the owners hired his son, rather than Seneca. The company's attorney, Pat Homes, said that they did not have a prayer because no records of the hiring decision had been kept. Two weeks later the EEOC notified the firm that a EEO-1 report had to be filed, within sixty days.

During his first day on the job, Jones has been told by the owners that they want a professional personnel office with "Job descriptions, EEO reports, and everything." Jones had just explained that to develop a professional personnel program, it takes time and he needs a secretary for more than five hours per week. The owners responded that if the firm loses another court case or is challenged by the EEOC, Jones will be fired.

Questions:

1.   What action should Jones take?

2.   Which areas (job descriptions, EEO reports, etc.) should be addressed first?

3.   Are the owners' demands reasonable?

SELECTED PROFESSIONAL READING

Personal Privacy and the Personnel Record

PHILIP G. BENSON

Recent years have seen increasing interest in protecting privacy in the United States. Much of this concern has probably resulted from the growth of computer technology, which now allows massive amounts of data to be amassed quickly and relatively economically. Because of this public concern, legislation has been drafted, and in some cases passed, to control the types of information which can be maintained about people, the range of uses for that information, and the extent to which that information can be disclosed to others.

THE PRIVACY ACT OF 1974

The Privacy Act of 1974 (Public Law 93-579)[1] was enacted to "provide certain safeguards for an

1. 5 U.S.C. 552a. For a review of the Privacy Act, see R. P. Bigelow, "The Privacy Act of 1974," *The Practical Lawyer*, Vol. 21 (1975): 15–24. Reviews which relate the act to other laws relevant to personnel administrators include M. Arnold and A. Kisseloff, "An Introduction to the Federal Privacy Act of 1974 and its Effect on the Freedom of Information Act." *New England Law Review*, Vol. 11 (1976); 463–496; R. R. Smith, "The Privacy Act's Impact on Federal Labor Relations," *Public Personnel Management*, Vol. 5 (1976); 33–40; K. A. Kovach, "A Retrospective Look at the Privacy and Freedom of Information Act," *Labor Law Journal*, Vol. 27 (1976); 548–564.

individual against an invasion of personal privacy." This law was passed December 31, 1974 and went into effect in September 1975. It represents the major federal legislation dealing with personal privacy and indicates the probable direction of future privacy legislation.

The Privacy Act of 1974 does not apply to private industry. Rather, it is limited to the federal government and specifically applies to all executive departments, the military, independent regulatory agencies, government corporations and government-controlled corporations such as the Federal Reserve Bank. In addition, any private business or state or local government which contracts with one of the agencies listed above is considered a part of that agency and is thus also covered during performance of that contract. The Privacy Act does not pertain to Congress, governments of territories or possessions, the District of Columbia or the federal courts.

The Privacy Act limits federal agencies which "maintain records" about individuals. Maintaining is given a broad definition and includes collecting, using and disseminating information. Records are *any* information or items about individuals, including (but not limited to) education, finances, medical history, criminal history and employment history. But, to be a record, this information must also include some identifying item such as a name, social security number, fingerprint, or photograph. Thus, information which cannot be identified as pertaining to a specific individual is appropriately not seen as a threat to privacy and is largely ignored by the Privacy Act.

A major purpose of the act is to control dissemination of information from one agency to another. A basic tenet of this approach is that information should be collected for a specified purpose and subsequently used for only that purpose. As such, records of one agency may not be disclosed to any other agency, unless done under the written request of the individual to whom the record pertains, with the written prior consent of the individual, or within certain exceptions (for example, under subpoena).

When a disclosure is made, it is necessary for the agency to record the date, nature and purpose of the disclosure, as well as the name and address of the person to whom the disclosure is made. This information must be retained for five years or the life of the system of records, whichever is longer. In addition, this information about disclosures must also be made available to the individual at his or her request.

Individuals must be allowed access to any personal records about them. Upon request, the individual (and any other person of his or her choice) must be allowed to have access to a record, to review its content, to copy any portion of it, and to request amendment of that record. In the case of a request for amendment of a record, an agency is required to do several things.

First, an agency must acknowledge receipt of a request within ten working days. Then it must make the requested correction or notify the individual that it refused, the reason why it refused, and the procedure by which the individual may review the refusal with the head of the agency (or a designated officer). The notification must also include the agency head's business address.

If after review the agency still refuses to amend the record, it must allow the individual to write a "concise" statement to be included as part of the record. This statement can outline the dispute and give the individual's position on the matter. It must be included in all further use or disclosure of the record, but is not retroactive.

Agencies can only maintain "necessary" information, as required by statute or executive order. This information, as far as possible, should be collected directly from the individual. At the time of collection, the agency must inform the individual of the purpose of the information, the uses to be made of it, and the effects of refusing to give all or part of the information.

In addition, agencies must establish rules of conduct for handling records, and those persons who have reason to use records must be informed of these rules. Agencies must also establish administrative, technical and physical safeguards for a system of records.

If an agency fails to comply with the Privacy Act and an individual is adversely affected, litigation is possible. Civil suit can be brought for actual damages or $1,000, whichever is more, plus reasonable costs and attorney fees. The court can also require that a record be amended.

In addition to civil action, certain activities are misdemeanors and punishable by fines of up to $5,000. Any officer or employee of an agency is subject to criminal prosecution for unlawful disclosure of a record, the illegal maintenance of a record system, or obtaining a record under false pretenses.

THE FUTURE OF PRIVACY LEGISLATION

The release of the Privacy Protection Study Commission's report would seem likely to generate a flurry of legislative activity. It is reasonable to expect that any legislation passed will follow the commission's recommendations in large part.[2]

Past attempts at regulating private industry's use of personal information have been patterned after the Privacy Act of 1974. In particular, H.R. 1984, introduced in 1975 by Representatives Koch and Goldwater, was designed to require very similar privacy protections in the private sector. However, the commission has recommended that the Privacy Act not be extended directly to private industry and has instead made a series of specific recommendations for each type of relationship an individual has with organizations (e.g., the employment relationship, the medical-care relationship, the insurance relationship, etc.).[3]

In general, the commission argues that

effective policy for protection of individual privacy requires concentration on three major objectives. First, it is necessary to minimize intrusiveness, i.e., to control the information maintained by organizations. This requires that individuals be informed of organizations' information needs and collection practices before entering into relationships with them, that certain information should not be collected at all, that limitations be placed on collection methods, and that where necessary, governmental mechanisms should be established to handle complaints and direct public policy.

The second major objective is to maximize fairness in record keeping, i.e., to minimize the occurrence of unfair decisions based on recorded information. A principle means of achieving this objective is to allow the individual to review and amend records, and to set up procedures to ensure the accuracy and timeliness of information about individuals.

The last major objective is to create legitimate, enforceable expectations of the confidentiality of records. This requires that an organization be limited to its discretion to disclose records voluntarily and that individuals be given a legal interest in any records about them.[4]

In recommending legislation to protect individual privacy, the commission also recognized and considered five legitimate competing interests. These were First Amendment interests and restrictions on the free flow of information, freedom of information interests (e.g., the Freedom of Information Act), the societal interest in law enforcement, an interest in cost of operation for organizations, and an interest in maintaining the current federal–state balance of power.

Against this general background for protection of personal privacy, the commission made thirty-four recommendations pertaining to employers. Relative to the types of recommendations made for other types of relationships,

---

2. Privacy Protection Study Commission, *Personal Privacy in an Information Society* (Washington, D.C.: U.S. Government Printing Office, 1977).

3. For example, see C. W. Pauly, "Let Industry Beware: A Survey of Privacy Legislation and Its Potential Impact on Business," *Tulsa Law Journal*, Vol. 11 (1975); 68–84.

---

4. Indeed, legislation to control the use of the polygraph has already been introduced.

the commission placed a large emphasis on the voluntary compliance of employers in adopting suggested privacy protections.

GENERAL RECOMMENDATIONS

The first two recommendations are general and give a good summary of an overall approach to individual privacy protection in employment. First, employers are requested to periodically and systematically review their personnel record keeping practices. This review should specifically consider:

- The number and types of records an organization maintains on employees, former employees and applicants
- The items in each record maintained
- The uses made of information in each type of record
- The uses of information within the organization
- The disclosures made to parties outside the organization and
- The extent to which individuals are aware and informed of the uses and disclosures of information in the records kept about them.

After the above review of an' organization's current practices, the commission recommends that policies be set forth. Specifically, the second recommendation is that employers articulate, communicate, and implement fair information policies by the following means:

- Limit the collection of information about individuals to that which is relevant to specific decisions
- Inform individuals of the uses to be made of such information
- Inform individuals as to the types of information being maintained about them
- Adopt reasonable procedures to ensure the accuracy, timeliness, and completeness of information about individuals

- Permit individuals to see, copy, correct, or amend records about themselves
- Limit the internal use of records
- Limit external disclosures of information, particularly those made without the individual's authorization and
- Provide for regular review of compliance with articulated fair information practice policies.

These two recommendations are in fact very broad. Indeed, an examination of the remaining recommendations shows that they are largely a further articulation of the first two, giving the commission's interpretation of their intent in the general recommendations.

Personnel and payroll records should be available internally only on a need-to-know basis. Security records should be maintained separately, and an individual should be notified if security information is transferred to his or her file. Medical records must be treated with extreme care in this regard; employers who provide voluntary health-care services should set up procedures which severely limit the use of this medical information in making employment decisions. In addition, insurance records (including both life or health insurance offered as a service and work-related insurance such as workers' compensation) should be available internally on a need-to–know basis.

EXPECTATION OF CONFIDENTIALITY

At present, the degree of confidentiality to be attached to employee records is purely at the discretion of the employer. Even so, the commission found that most employers are reasonably sensitive about this issue and refrain from freely disclosing information to third parties. Employers are requested to clearly inform employees and applicants of the types of disclosures they may make of information. In general, disclosures to outside entities should be prohibited, with certain specified exceptions (e.g., disclosures of directory information, disclosures for law enforcement purposes under subpoena or disclosures to fulfill collective bargaining agreements). Beyond such exceptions, disclosures should only be made with the explicit authorization of the individual.

Certain requirements of the Occupational Safety and Health Act (OSHA) lead to problems of confidentiality. Under OSHA, it is necessary for employers to provide medical surveillance of employees exposed to hazardous environments or substances. Thus, medical records disclosed from one employer to another in the interest of protecting workers may in fact enter into decisions regarding employability. For this reason, the commission recommends that Congress require the Department of Labor to review the extent of this problem and to examine the feasibility of restricting the use of OSHA-mandated information in employment decisions.[5]

Taken as a whole, such recommendations are requesting that employers voluntarily assume a tremendous administrative burden. A major concern of private industry, therefore, is complying with these recommendations and knowing why compliance is necessary.

THE ROLE OF PRIVATE INDUSTRY
The Privacy Protection Study Commission makes the strongest case for voluntary compliance by private industry. Because legislative compulsion to protect the privacy of employees would entail a wide variety of disadvantages for the employment relationship, the commission feels a voluntary approach should be tried first. This would allow employers to develop guidelines specific to their own situation, a much more flexible approach than legislation requiring specific practices. However, unless employers are willing to conscientiously approach this problem and develop

meaningful guidelines, the voluntary approach will not succeed. Thus, the commission implies that legislators or future commissions will need to review the response of private industry to the privacy issue, and unless substantial progress is shown, it will be necessary to resort to specific legal requirements.

It seems that these views are not an unrealistic threat of future legislation. Unless employers can show that advances have been made in the absence of legal requirements, it seems certain that some amount of legislation *will* be passed by Congress to require compliance. So, the question is not whether or not industry will operate within certain constraints regarding personal privacy, but rather whether industry will voluntarily take on this responsibility or be required to do so through legal mandates.

There are, in fairness, considerations against private industry's voluntary adoption of privacy guidelines, including the cost of administration for these programs. It has been estimated that an organization with 10,000 employees, using a computer to maintain data on routine payroll and benefit activities, would require an initial outlay of $142,000 to convert its system to handle typical privacy issues.[6] Thereafter, the annual privacy cost to maintain the system would be $40,000. Clearly, these are estimates which would vary considerably among organizations, but it is apparent that the cost of these procedures is substantial. Yet, to ignore the issue in the interest of saving expense may be more costly in the long run, as legally required protections are almost certain to entail additional administrative details, such as periodic reports to government agencies.

It is then likely, overall, the business community will be very receptive to voluntary measures to protect employees' privacy. The Privacy Protection Study Commission noted the concern of the business representatives with whom they dealt, and recent literature also

---

5. A related issue is the release of medical records to government agencies for research purposes. For example, see "Health Records Face a Privacy Challenge," *Business Week*, October 31, 1977, p. 38.

6. R. C. Goldstein and R. L. Nolan, "Personal Privacy versus the Corporate Computer," *Harvard Business Review*, Vol. 53, No. 2 (1975); 62–70.

indicates this interest.[7] In addition, one recent survey showed extreme concern for privacy by business leaders. In fact, 94 percent endorsed the notion that external disclosures of personnel files should only be made with the permis-

sion of the individual.[8] In general, it seems that the personnel departments of American businesses are already committed to the protection of employee privacy and that voluntary adoption of guidelines may prove sufficient.

7. See T. M. Jackson, "The Personnel File— What and Whose?" *The Personnel Administrator,* Vo. 22, No. 2 (1977); 41–42.

8. D. W. Ewing, "What Business Thinks about Employee Rights," *Harvard Business Review,* Vol. 55, No. 5 (1977); 81–94.

When appraisal is an ongoing process, there are no surprises during an employee's appraisal interview.

8

APPRAISAL OF HUMAN RESOURCES

Performance Appraisal

Appraisal Process

Appraisal Techniques

Appraisal Interview

Effective Appraisal Program

The Problem: Annual Performance Evaluation

When David Gaines knocked on his boss's office door, he was invited in and asked to take a seat. Gaines was a first-line foreman for the Southeastern Hat Company, a small manufacturer of knit caps and ear muffs located in Valdosta, Georgia. After graduating from the Georgia Institute of Technology with a major in industrial management, he came to Southeastern Hat a year ago. Gaines declined an offer of coffee from his boss, Production Manager Gary Roth, as he didn't want anything to upset an already queasy stomach. This was Gaines' first performance evaluation, and he was quite apprehensive about the interview. After taking a sip of coffee, Roth began:

"David, as you know, the purpose of our meeting this morning is to review your performance for the past year. We do this for all salaried employees annually with this rating form that personnel sends us. I know we're both pretty busy, so we may as well get going. This shouldn't take too long. I'll just go down this rating form and make some comments.

"First, your 'quantity of work' has been pretty good. You and your thirty-two workers have done an above-average job in getting the work out. Mostly your schedules are met with no delays. Also, I can't complain about the quality of your group's work. Except for that problem we had with the two knitting machines and their operators, I don't recall any real problems with quality.

"The next item is dependability. I gave you a high rating on this. I don't think you were ever late or absent. Also, your attitude is good. I think we have gotten along *pretty well and most of your workers speak fairly well of you.*

"There is, however, a problem with 'leadership ability.' I think you need to improve your supervisory style a good bit. I think you're too easy on your employees. When they get out of line, you need to crack the whip a little. I've noticed on several occasions you let some of the older guys run all over you. You need to work on that some, David. I see no problems with the other items—'Initiative,' 'Judgment,' and 'Loyalty.' Well, that's about it. I'm recommending that you receive the normal 5 percent salary increase which we more or less promised you when you took the job. And, don't forget to work on those areas I mentioned. Any comments, David?"

Gaines thought for a moment. He had a lot of questions but didn't know where to start. As he thought further, he wondered just what Gary Roth had said to him. Gaines shook his head negatively, "No sir, no questions."

Performance appraisal is a method of evaluating the behavior of employees in the workplace, normally including both the quantitative and qualitative aspects of job performance. Performance appraisal is one of the basic personnel functions; sometimes it is called performance review, employee appraisal, performance evaluation, employee evaluation, merit evaluation, or personnel rating. All of these terms refer to the same process.

Performance appraisal is an entirely different process from job evaluation. Performance appraisal refers to how well someone is doing an assigned job. Job evaluation determines how much a job is worth to the organization and, therefore, what range of pay should be assigned to the job. While a performance appraisal may show that someone is the best computer programmer the organization has ever had, the job evaluation is used to make sure that the programmer only receives the maximum pay a computer programmer's position is worth to the organization.

Even though they are the most integral part of the performance appraisal process, many supervisors complain that appraising their employees' behavior is the most difficult and unpleasant task they must perform. In fact, supervisors often find ways to avoid performance appraisals. Almost everyone agrees that it is important to know how well employees are doing their jobs. But, few people want to be involved in the actual analyzation of employees' performance or discussions of strengths and weaknesses with employees.

PERFORMANCE ═══ APPRAISAL ═══

Why then should management utilize *performance appraisals* if, indeed, they are such an unpleasant and often time-consuming process? There are several important objectives for a performance appraisal program which cannot be achieved by any other method. For the most part, the objectives of performance appraisal fall into two categories: evaluative and developmental.

Evaluative Objectives

Evaluative methods of performance appraisal determine how well the employee is doing the job for policymakers who use this information to decide on promotions. Evaluative performance appraisal methods are often fairly uniform, quick, and easy to perform. The evaluative technique compares all employees to each other or to some standard so that decisions can be made based upon their performance records.

The most common decisions based on evaluative objectives are compensation decisions, which include merit increases, employee bonuses, and other increases in pay. As far as employees are concerned, this is one of the primary objectives of performance appraisals. That is why the term *merit review,* or merit evaluation, can be found in organizations using the performance appraisal to determine pay increases. Performance appraisal nor-

mally has a two-step effect on employees' future pay with the organization. In the short run, it may determine merit increases for the following year; in the long run it may determine which employees receive higher paying jobs.

Staffing decisions are a second major evaluative objective of performance appraisal, as the managers and supervisors must make decisions concerning promotions, demotions, transfers, and layoffs. Past performance appraisals are normally one of the key factors in determining which employee is most deserving of a promotion or other desirable job change.

Performance appraisals can be used to evaluate the recruiting, selection, and placement system. The effectiveness of these functions can be partially measured by comparing employees' performance appraisals with their test scores as job applicants. As an example, management may find that applicants who scored approximately equally on selection tests show quite a difference in performance after one year on the job; thus, the tests may not accurately predict behavior. Such analyses not only validates selection techniques but also determines strengths and weaknesses of the selection process as well as the appraisal process.

Developmental Objectives

The second objective of performance appraisal is to develop employees' skills and motivation and to provide performance feedback. Because the employee has input in the appraisal, the process becomes more time consuming than when a supervisor simply fills out an appraisal form.

Performance feedback is a primary

developmental need as almost all employees want to know how their supervisors feel about their performances. They want to know whether the results are satisfactory, and if they were behaving as expected. People want to be reassured that they are on the right track.

Developmental performance appraisal also involves giving employees the direction for future performance. This feedback recognizes strengths and weaknesses in past performances and determines what direction employees should take to improve. Employees want to know specifically how they can improve in the future. Because performance appraisals are designed to cope with the problem of poor employee performance, appraisals should be designed to develop better employees.[1]

Appraisal results influence decisions concerning the training and development needs of employees. Below-average evaluations may signal areas of employee behavior that may be strengthened through on- and off-the-job training techniques. Of course, not all performance deficiencies may be overcome through training and development. Supervisors must differentiate performance problems resulting from a lack of a critical skill or ability compared to those caused by low morale or some form of job dissatisfaction.

▬ APPRAISAL PROCESS ▬

In creating and implementing an appraisal system, administrators must determine which process should be used; this deci-

---

[1]Guvenc Alpander, "Training First-Line Supervisors to Criticize Constructively," *Personnel Journal* (March 1980): 216–21.

sion is just as important as which appraisal method is chosen or the actual content of the appraisal. If employees believe the appraisal is being taken lightly, or if management is sloppy in its administration, then employees take the appraisal process less seriously than they should. Possible legal ramifications exist wherever management is not uniform in its performance appraisal procedures. Even if discriminatory performance appraisal practices by supervisors and managers do not lead to lawsuits, the loss of morale and employee productivity resulting from poorly administered performance appraisals can be critical to an organization's success. The appraisal process includes:

DETERMINING PERFORMANCE REQUIREMENTS First, administrators must determine what skills, outputs, and accomplishments will be evaluated during each performance appraisal. These may be derived from job descriptions or they may be a uniform set of employee requirements included in all performance appraisals. For example, managers may determine that requirements fall into broad categories, such as quality of work, cooperation with other employees, dependability, etc. Or, they may decide that specific requirements should be set for each employee or different job. The importance of this step is that the policymakers determine exactly what areas of performance are going to be reviewed and how these areas are related to the organization's goals.

CHOOSING AN APPROPRIATE PERFORMANCE APPRAISAL TECHNIQUE Several techniques may be used to appraise performance; no one method is best for all organizations. The method of performance appraisal should be carefully chosen because most often the method becomes the focal point of involvement between the supervisor and the employee. The manner in which a supervisor conducts the performance appraisal is greatly determined by the method. Within an organization, separate appraisal methods might be used for different groups, for example, production employees, sales employees, and administrative employees.

TRAINING THE SUPERVISORS A critical step in performance appraisal is training of supervisors so that they do not commit errors during performance appraisal. Such errors may result in charges of discrimination, loss of employee morale and productivity due to inept supervisors, or inaccurate performance appraisals which lead to poor compensation or staffing decisions.

DISCUSSING METHODS WITH EMPLOYEES Supervisors should discuss the method of performance appraisal used in the organization with employees. This discussion should specify which areas of performance are evaluated, how often, how the evaluation takes place, and its significance to the employee. The use of appraisals varies greatly—some organizations directly tie pay and promotion to performance appraisal; others only conduct appraisals in a perfunctory manner to meet some broad goals or policies. Understanding the significance of the performance appraisal, how it is conducted in the particular organization, and what consequence it may have, are germane to the employee's future in the organization.

APPRAISING ACCORDING TO REQUIREMENTS The actual performance appraisal should evaluate the employee's work according to predetermined work requirements. Comparison to specific requirements indicates what the employee has done well or not done well.

The supervisor's feelings about the employee should not affect the appraisal. Feelings cannot be evaluated; they are only mental constructs which are easily biased. However, by discussing the employee's behavior, which has been observed and documented, the supervisor focuses the appraisal on concrete, actual performance by the employee.

DISCUSSING APPRAISAL WITH EMPLOYEES In some organizations, appraisal discussions are omitted whenever specific evaluative appraisal objectives for merit raises or promotions have been met. The general trend, however, is to make sure that supervisors discuss the appraisal with their employees, allowing employees to discuss areas of agreement and disagreement. The supervisor should emphasize positive work performance, those areas in which the employee has met or exceeded expectations, as well as areas which need improving. Supervisors must not let the appraisal become a criticism session. In most cases, discussion of salary or promotion possibilities should not be mixed with the appraisal discussion. Mixing the two may divert the employee's attention from development of future performance goals or the review of the past performance.

DETERMINING FUTURE PERFORMANCE GOALS A critical aspect of performance appraisal is the use of goal setting.[2] How specifically or rigidly these goals are to be followed or pursued is determined by the method of performance appraisal. Even if they are only broadly discussed, setting goals for the employee's future appraisal period is critical because it gives the employee a specific direction to follow for continued

---

[2]Harold Koontz, "Making Managerial Appraisal Effective," *California Management Review* (Winter, 1972): 46–55.

or improved performance. Leaving the appraisal discussion, the employee feels comfortable knowing how past performance has been viewed and what needs to be accomplished to improve future performance.

Legal Considerations

The entire performance appraisal process, in recent years, has come under scrutiny by EEOC and federal courts, which have warned employers about the discriminatory effects of their performance appraisals. The burden of proving the validity of a performance appraisal instrument is clearly on the shoulders of the organization's administration. Thus, policymakers must be cognizant of recent EEOC and court decisions in this area.[3] Analysis of court decisions has revealed that performance appraisals are potentially illegal if:[4]

- The method has not been shown to be job-related.
- The content of the appraisal has not been developed through job analysis.
- The supervisor has not been able to consistently observe the performance of the employee; e.g., supervisor is usually in another building; supervisor was sick during the last several months.
- The evaluations use subjective or vague factors; e.g., personality, work attitude, interest.

- The biases of evaluators' have influenced appraisal; e.g., the evaluations show significant differences according to sex, age, race.
- The evaluations have not been given under standardized conditions; e.g., evaluating some employees quarterly, others annually; giving feedback to some employees but not to all.

Personnel managers can best avoid legal entanglements if their performance appraisal processes include:

- *Documentation of all performance appraisals.* Documentation ensures that the management can defend its appraisal and consequential outcomes such as decisions for promotion or pay based upon actual appraisals. Documentation should include written, dated, signed appraisals, and all performance records.
- *Standard appraisal process.* Standardization ensures that all employees are given equal and consistent treatment. This will avoid possible claims of discrimination based on unequal conditions.
- *Job relatedness.* Managers should be sure that the content and the focus of the performance appraisal process is on actual aspects of the job performed and not supervisor and co-worker biases or attitudes. The areas included in the process should be as specific to the job as possible.

Common Appraisal Problems

Appraisal process problems should be recognized and minimized by trained supervisors, who should not only become

[3]William H. Holly, Hubert Field, and Nona Barnett, "Analyzing Performance Appraisal Systems: An Empirical Study," *Personnel Journal* 55 (September, 1976): 457–59.
[4]Ibid., p. 463.

aware of problems but also learn how to avoid committing common appraisal errors. All methods of performance appraisal are subject to error, but management can minimize appraisal errors and problems through training.

SUPERVISORY BIAS

The most common error which exists in any appraisal method is conscious or unconscious supervisory *bias*. Such biases are not related to job performance and may stem from personal characteristics such as age, sex, or race, or organization-related characteristics such as the individual's seniority, membership on an organization's athletic team, or familiarity with top administrators. For example, a supervisor may give a high rating to the bowling team captain. Managers need to eliminate the biases that they may have for individual subordinates or set such biases aside during the appraisal process.

HALO EFFECT

When a supervisor lets one particular aspect of an employee's performance influence other aspects which are being evaluated, a *halo effect* has occurred. For example, the manager who knows a particular employee always arrives at work early and helps to open the business may let the halo caused by that employee's dependability influence other areas of the appraisal such as quality of work or job knowledge. Thus, even though the employee may be only mediocre in terms of quality or quantity of performance, the employee receives all high ratings for being dependable and arriving at work early.

Negative halos also exist. Resenting the fact that an employee shows no initiative in learning new aspects of the work within the department, a supervisor may give the employee low evaluations in all areas of performance appraisal even though the employee performs capably. Halo errors are minimized when the appraisal process is open to review by employees who will point out that they are not particularly weak in areas which they have been rated poorly. Employees with positive halos seldom point out, however, that they did not perform as well as their supervisors had indicated. Thus, positive halos are difficult to minimize.

CENTRAL TENDENCY

Supervisors may find it difficult and unpleasant to evaluate some employees higher or lower than others, even though their performances may reflect a real difference. A *central tendency* problem results when they evaluate everyone as average. Central tendency problems also occur when supervisors cannot objectively evaluate employees' performance due to a lack of familiarity with their work, a lack of supervisory ability, or fear that they will be reprimanded if they evaluate individuals too highly.

LENIENCY

Inexperienced or poor supervisors may decide the easiest way to appraise performance is to simply give everyone a high evaluation. The supervisor may believe that employees will feel that they have been accurately appraised, or that even if they know they have been inaccurately appraised, it will be to their benefit. Employees cannot complain about their appraisals if they all receive high appraisals. Thus, everyone is evaluated highly in almost all areas of performance. However, *leniency* seldom creates good feelings among all employees. The best performers in the department will complain about supervisors who give lenient appraisals because those who are giving 100 percent receive no more credit than fellow employees who are average or poor workers. Eventually this lack of accurate appraisal can lead to turnover among the best employees who go to other organizations which can accurately appraise their performance and give them their justified recognition. Thus, supervisors' intentions of creating good feelings by giving all employees high evaluations may result in losing the very best employees.

STRICTNESS

Sometimes supervisors consistently give low ratings even though some employees may have achieved an average or above–average performance level. This *strictness* problem is the opposite of the leniency problem. In practice, problems of strictness are not nearly as widespread as problems of leniency.

Supervisors are often guilty of rating strictness because they feel that not one of the subordinates is "living up to their standards of excellence." Unreasonable performance expectations that employees find impossible to achieve can be demoralizing. Failure to give recognition when it is due can quickly result in serious damage to supervisor-subordinate relationships.

RECENCY

When organizations use annual or semi-annual performance appraisals, there may be a tendency for supervisors to remember more about what their employees have done just prior to the appraisal than in prior months. It is human nature for supervisors to remember recent events more than events in the distant past.[5] Where severe *recency* problems occur in the appraisal process, managers may conduct more frequent monthly, or quarterly, appraisals. Or, they may require that supervisors keep a running log of employee behaviors to help them avoid the recency distortion.

Appraisal Techniques

The method of appraisal technique dictates the time and effort spent by supervisor and employee alike and determines which areas of performance are emphasized. Ideally, an appraisal method is objective, accurate, and easy to perform.

WORK STANDARDS

In the past, setting *work standards* and comparing employees to those standards was often thought to be the most ideal appraisal method. Work standards established the normal or average production output for employees on the job. Standards were set according to the production per hour or the time spent per unit produced. While this standard allowed firms to pay employees on a piece rate basis, setting the standard rate of output for employees was a difficult task. Time studies set output criteria for persons on particular jobs. Work sampling, a statistical technique for setting standards of production based on random sampling, can also be used to set work standards. When the average production of the work group is used as a standard in a group piecework plan, members of the group receive pay

[5]Paul Greenlaw and William Biggs, *Modern Personnel Management* (Philadelphia: W. B. Saunders, 1979), p. 187.

based on the average pay earned by the group.[6]

Few organizations today use direct production standards as a performance appraisal technique. In some cases, production standards are still used as part of the appraisal process, usually when employees are paid on a piece rate basis. Quantity of production is only a part of job performance; other aspects should be included in the appraisal process. Use of employees' piecework records as the sole performance appraisal creates problems when decisions on promotions and salary increases are made by comparing employees to each other. Further, in the last twenty years fewer and fewer jobs can be measured *solely* by production levels. One employee's output is at least partially dependent upon the performance of other employees. If the production line stops moving, or if other members of the team are not successful, individual production is severely hampered. Most jobs today do not entail tasks which simply produce a certain number of units per hour. Instead, they involve other duties and responsibilities which cannot be directly measured. Therefore, other methods of performance appraisal are much more common in today's organizations.

RATING SCALE

One type of performance appraisal method compares employees to some cognitive standard, which is not a measure of performance but rather a norm of what employees are expected to accomplish on a job, such as a "high level of cooperation" with fellow employees. The

ratings scale is one of the oldest and still the most commonly used performance appraisal method. As depicted in Figure 8–1 ratings scales itemize job attributes which describe the employee's performance. Each item is followed by a scale on which the supervisor rates the employee somewhere between poor and excellent. The ratings scale is, perhaps, one of the most popular performance appraisal techniques because supervisors find it fairly easy to complete, and the scale takes less time to learn and utilize than other performance appraisal techniques.

The rating scale achieves the evaluation goals of appraisal because it produces a numerical evaluation for each employee which is the total of the employee's ratings on each of the attributes. The total can be easily transferred to a scale of merit increases or used to compare employees for promotion decisions.

The rating scale in Figure 8–2 is a *nongraphic form* which often is more valid than the less-detailed *graphic form*. A nongraphic scale is usually more valid because it contains a brief description of each point on a scale, rather than simply low and high points of a scale. The supervisor can give a more accurate description of the employee's behavior on a particular attribute because a description clarifies each level of the rating scale. On the graphic scale, supervisors arbitrarily decide what various points represent about an attribute; for example, what is "below average" cooperation? Most rating scales used today are nongraphic because of their inherent ability to be more job related and specific to employee behavior.

In general, rating scales are quick, easy, and less difficult for supervisors to utilize than many other methods of performance appraisal. Also, decision makers find this

[6]Richard Henderson, *Compensation Management* (Reston, VA: The Reston Publishing Company, 1979), 237–39.

FIGURE 8–1: *Graphic Rating Scale*

Employee's Name _____ Date _____

Evaluator's Name _____ Period of Evaluation _____

Directions: Circle the point on each scale which best approximates the employee's performance.

	Poor	Below Average	Average	Above Average	Excellent
1. Job Knowledge	├	┼	┼	┼	┤
2. Quality of Work	├	┼	┼	┼	┤
3. Quantity of Work	├	┼	┼	┼	┤
4. Cooperation	├	┼	┼	┼	┤
5. Customer Courtesy	├	┼	┼	┼	┤
6. Company Loyalty	├	┼	┼	┼	┤
7. Ability to Learn	├	┼	┼	┼	┤
8. Dependability	├	┼	┼	┼	┤
9. Safety Habits	├	┼	┼	┼	┤
10. Ability to Follow Directions	├	┼	┼	┼	┤

method to be very satisfactory for most evaluative purposes because it provides a mathematical evaluation of the employee's performance which can be used to justify compensation or job changes, and to validate selection instruments. For example, if the rating scale contains twenty attributes with a five-point scale for each attribute, employees can receive 100 points if they perform perfectly. Any percentage of that total can be directly related to a merit increase or promotion probability.

Rating scales have distinct disadvantages: while using the scale, supervisors can easily make halo or central tendency errors. Since everyone can quickly be rated very high or very average on most items, supervisors who want to use central tendency or leniency in their appraisals can easily do so. Most rating scales have the disadvantage of not being related to a specific job. The attributes of the scale are so broad they may apply to all jobs in the organization and are not developed to specifically relate to any particular job. Rating scales also allow supervisory bias and the halo effect to enter the appraisal process.

FORCED CHOICE

In a *forced choice* performance appraisal, the supervisor must choose one statement (sometimes two) out of a possible

FIGURE 8–2: *Nongraphic Rating Form*

NAME: _____ FOR PERIOD ENDING: _____

DEPARTMENT: _____ JOB TITLE: _____

INSTRUCTIONS:
Listed below are a number of traits, abilities, and characteristics that are important for success. Place an "X" mark on each rating scale, over the descriptive phrase which most nearly describes the person being rated.

ACCURACY is the correctness of work duties performed.

Usually accurate; makes only average number of mistakes	Makes frequent errors	Requires absolute minimum of supervision; is almost always accurate	Requires little supervision; is exact and precise most of the time	Careless; makes recurrent errors

ALERTNESS is the ability to grasp instruction, to meet changing conditions and to solve novel or problem situations.

Requires more than average instructions and explanations	Slow to catch on	Exceptionally keen and alert	Grasps instructions with average ability	Usually quick to understand and learn

CREATIVITY is talent for having new ideas, for finding new and better ways of doing things and for being imaginative.

Continually seeks new and better ways of doing things; is extremely imaginative	Has average imagination; has reasonable number of new ideas	Frequently suggests new ways of doing things; is very imaginative	Rarely has a new idea; is unimaginative	Occasionally comes up with a new idea

FRIENDLINESS is the sociability and warmth which an individual imparts toward customers, other employees, the supervisor, and persons supervised.

Approachable; friendly once known by others	Extremely sociable; excellent at establishing good will	Very distant and aloof	Very sociable and outgoing	Warm; friendly; sociable

PERSONALITY is an individual's behavior characteristics or personal suitability for the job.

Very desirable personality for this job	Personality unsatisfactory for this job	Outstanding personality for this job	Personality satisfactory for this job	Personality questionable for this job

PERSONAL APPEARANCE is the personal impression an individual makes on others. (Consider cleanliness, grooming, neatness, and appropriateness of dress on the job.)

Very untidy; poor taste in dress	Generally neat and clean; satisfactory personal appearance	Unusually well groomed; very neat; excellent taste in dress	Sometimes untidy and careless about personal appearance	Careful about personal appearance; good taste in dress

PHYSICAL FITNESS is the ability to work consistently and with only moderate fatigue. (Consider physical alertness and energy.)

Energetic; seldom tires	Tires easily; is weak and frail	Excellent health; no fatigue	Meets physical and energy job requirements	Frequently tires and is slow

ATTENDANCE is faithfulness in coming to work daily and conforming to work hours.

Always regular and prompt; volunteers for overtime when needed	Often absent without good excuse and/or frequently reports for work late	Very prompt; regular in attendance	Lax in attendance and/or reporting for work on time	Usually present and on time

FIGURE 8–2: *Cont'd*

DEPENDABILITY is the ability to do required jobs well with a minimum of supervision.

Requires close supervision; is unreliable	Requires absolute minimum of supervision	Usually takes care of necessary tasks and completes with reasonable promptness	Requires little supervision; is reliable	Sometimes requires prompting

JOB KNOWLEDGE is the information concerning work duties which an individual should know for a satisfactory job performance

Lacks knowledge of some phases of work	Has complete mastery of all phases of job	Understands all phases of work	Poorly informed about work duties	Moderately informed; can answer most common questions

QUANTITY OF WORK is the amount of work an individual does in a work day.

Volume of work is satisfactory	Very industrious; does more than is required	Does just enough to get by	Superior work production recorded	Does not meet minimum requirements

STABILITY is the ability to withstand pressure and to remain calm in crisis situations.

Thrives under pressure; really enjoys solving crises	Goes "to pieces" under pressure; is "jumpy" and nervous	Tolerates most pressure; likes crises more than the average person	Has average tolerance for crises; usually remains calm	Occasionally "blows up" under pressure; is easily irritated

COURTESY is the polite attention an individual gives other people.

Always very polite and willing to help	Sometimes tactless	Inspiring to others in being courteous and very pleasant	Agreeable and pleasant	Blunt; discourteous; antagonistic

OVERALL EVALUATION in comparison with other employees with the same length of service on this job:

Definitely Unsatisfactory	Substandard but making progress	Doing an average job	Definitely above average	Outstanding

Signature of Supervisor	Date	Signature of Employee	Date

Signature of Reviewing Officer	Date	Signature of Personnel Officer	Date

Remarks:

three or four which best describe the employee's performance in a particular area. The supervisor may find that all of them describe the employee's performance; however, only the one or two which best describe the employee's behavior can be chosen. Unlike the rating scale form, the phrases top management considers positive or negative evaluations of performance are not obvious. Therefore, the supervisor does not know if an employee's appraisal is low, high, or average. Adopting the forced choice method will usually keep supervisors from making central tendency, leniency, halo, or other common errors of appraisal.

As illustrated in Figure 8–3 the forced choice method can utilize specific job behaviors, or broad descriptions which might apply to all employees throughout the organization. Like the rating scale, the forced choice technique results in a mathematical total for the evaluation and is fairly quick and easy for supervisors to complete.

The forced choice technique contains some serious disadvantages. Supervisors may try to guess which descriptions the personnel office weighted positively and which have negative weights. Thus, the supervisor may still utilize central tendency or other biases. Also, a good supervisor who wants to use performance appraisal as a developmental tool cannot use the forced choice method because no feedback is given to the employee. The supervisor completes the form which is sent to personnel or top administration for evaluation purposes; therefore, the forced choice method is difficult to use for developmental purposes.

RANKING

Ranking employees from the most effec-

FIGURE 8–3: *Sales Representative's Performance Report*

INSTRUCTIONS: For each set of phrases choose one statement. Circle the letter preceding the phrase which *best* describes the behavior of the employee.

1. a. Returns customers' calls quickly.
   b. Learns new products on schedule.
   c. Does not anger easily.
   d. Tires of same route.

2. a. Is accurate with figures.
   b. Cooperates with supervisor.
   c. Does not waste time on telephone.
   d. Keeps automobile clean.

3. a. Prefers to stay on own route.
   b. Is friends with local politicians.
   c. Usually exceeds sales goals.
   d. Doesn't complain.

4. a. Obeys orders without arguing.
   b. Is loyal to the company.
   c. Is intelligent.
   d. Requires minimum supervision.

5. a. Seldom critical of company rules.
   b. Stays within expense account.
   c. Socializes with other employees.
   d. Maintains good appearance.

6. a. Turns in reports on time.
   b. Obeys traffic laws.
   c. Requires little prompting.
   d. Receives high customer praise.

7. a. Respects opinions of other salespersons.
   b. Adds new customers to route.
   c. Liked by others.
   d. Follows OSHA regulations.

8. a. Active in civic affairs.
   b. Keeps route sheets current.
   c. Customers know by first name.
   d. Does not lose route customers.

9. a. Handles customer complaints well.
   b. Has friendly personality.
   c. Active in company sports.
   d. Willing to accept new customers.

10. a. Restores 1956 Chevrolets.
    b. Knows competitors' lines.
    c. Good communication skills.
    d. No serious traffic violations.

tive to the least effective is an appraisal method which utilizes instruments that compare employees to each other. Problems of central tendency and leniency are eliminated by forcing supervisors to evaluate employees over a predetermined range.

A common ranking method requires supervisors to rank their employees from the most effective to the least effective in total job performance. This first step results in as many different rankings as there are departments or areas within the organization. Some policymakers try to combine departmental rankings into a ranking for the total organization which is very difficult, if not impossible, because employees have not been compared to any common standard. Instead, employees have only been compared to each other. Assuming that an employee ranked second in one department is equal to one ranked second in another department is an unfair assumption on the part of the administration. Usually when rankings are used, comparisons among departments are not made. However, when a total organizational ranking is used, employees receiving high rankings receive the highest merit increases or promotion considerations.

The advantage of the ranking technique is that it is fast and easy to complete. A numerical evaluation given to the employees can be directly related to compensation changes or staffing considerations. In addition, the ranking technique completely avoids problems of central tendency or leniency.

There are, however, serious disadvantages to the ranking technique: Ranking is seldom developmental because employees do not receive feedback about performance strengths and weaknesses or any future direction. Forcing each manager to make a certain distribution of employees, the ranking technique assumes that each department has employees who can be distributed equally over a range from best to worst. This technique does not recognize that one department may have all excellent employees, while another has all poor employees. When the ranking technique is utilized, there is no common standard of performance to compare employees from various departments since employees in each department are only compared with each other. This makes it difficult to use ranking for purposes of comparing employees in different departments who might be considered for the same promotion or other staffing change.

FIGURE 8–4: *Ranking of Employees By Department*

Sales	*Office*	*Warehouse*	*Records*
1. Meehan	1. Vahaly	1. Wilbert	1. Black
2. Smith	2. Nelson	2. Brown	2. Alexander
3. Ryan	3. White	3. Henderson	3. Elbert
4. Lickteig	4. Jones	4. Ehrler	
	5. Sharbrough	5. Coe	
	6. Dean		
	7. Heavrin		
	8. Ward		

FORCED DISTRIBUTION

Forced distribution is another comparative method of performance appraisal. Similar to the ranking technique, forced distribution requires that supervisors spread their employee evaluations in a predescribed distribution. As Figure 8–5 illustrates, the supervisor places employees in classifications ranging from poor to excellent. Like ranking, forced distribution eliminates central tendency and leniency biases. However, forced distribution shares the same disadvantages of the ranking technique. The forced distribution method can be considered a specific case of ranking where employees are placed in certain ranked categories but not ranked within the categories. Often, administrators will use forced distribution evaluations to compare employees from different departments. However, this is only valid if there are an equal number of excellent, above average, etc., employees in each department. That assumption is very difficult to make.

PAIRED COMPARISON

Another comparative method of performance appraisal involves *paired comparison* where supervisors pair employees and choose one as superior in overall job performance. As illustrated in Figure 8–6, this method results in each employee being given a positive comparison total and a certain percentage of the total positive evaluation. This percentage of positive comparisons gives the paired comparison technique an advantage over the ranking and forced distribution methods. Paired comparison does not force distribution of employees in each department. For example, if a department has two outstanding employees and six average employees and paired comparison is correctly utilized, then those two employees will receive a much higher percentage of positive comparison than the other six. Or, if all employees have about the same performance except one poor performer, that employee may have a much lower total percentage of positive comparisons

FIGURE 8–5: *Forced Distribution of Employees*

Department _____ Supervisor _____

Date _____ Period of Evaluation _____

Directions: Begin with the excellent classification then proceed to the above average, etc. List the names of the employees who fall into the classification; the total number within each category may not exceed the percentage allowance for the classification.

Poor 10%	Below Average 20%	Average 40%	Above Average 20%	Excellent 10%
Ward	Lickteig	White	Meehan	Vahaly
Heavrin	Ehrler	Jones	Smith	Wilbert
	Coe	Ryan	Black	
	Elbert	Sharbrough	Nelson	
		Dean		
		Brown		
		Alexander		
		Henderson		

FIGURE 8–6: *Paired Comparison of Employees*

Instructions: Assign each employee's name a different capital letter on a separate sheet of paper. Example: A-Smith, B-Jones, C-Ryan, etc. Then, develop a chart such as the one below and for each plotted pair, write in the letter of the employee who, in your opinion, has done the superior job overall.

Example:

	A	B	C	D	E
A		A	A	A	A
B			C	D	E
C				C	E
D					E
E					

To Compute Employees' Positive Evaluations:

$$\frac{\text{Number of Positive Evaluations}}{\text{Total Number of Evaluations}} \times 100 = \text{Employee's \% Superior Evaluation}$$

Employee A	Employee B	Employee C	Employee D	Employee E
$\frac{4}{4} \times 100 = 100\%$	$\frac{0}{4} \times 100 = 0\%$	$\frac{2}{4} \times 100 = 50\%$	$\frac{1}{4} \times 100 = 25\%$	$\frac{3}{4} \times 100 = 75\%$

than the other employees in the department. Thus, the actual distribution of employees in the department is based on their performance; that distribution may be reflected in the percentage of positive comparisons if the supervisor was accurate in the comparison.

Like the ranking and forced distribution technique, paired comparison is quick if few employees are involved and fairly easy to use. In fact, supervisors may prefer paired comparison to ranking or forced distribution because they compare only two employees at a time rather than all employees to each other.

A particular problem associated with the paired comparison technique is the rapid increase in comparisons which must be made as the employees within a department increase. The number of comparisons required equals N(N–1)/2. Therefore, for 20 employees, 190 comparisons would be necessary [(20 × 19)/2 = 190]. Thus, this technique is time–consuming with large numbers of employees.

Another disadvantage of the paired comparison technique is that employees are simply compared to each other on total performance rather than specific job criteria. While the paired comparison technique does not completely eliminate the possibility of central tendency or leniency, those problems are minimized with this technique. The advantages of not forcing the employee evaluations into set distributions while minimizing problems of central tendency and leniency makes the paired comparison technique an attractive alternative to ranking and forced distribution.

CRITICAL INCIDENTS

Several performance appraisal techniques developed in recent years employ the use of *critical incidents* to make the appraisal process more job related than some of the techniques previously discussed. The critical incident methods of performance appraisal utilize specific examples of job behavior which have been collected from supervisors and/or employees. Normally, several employees and supervisors, compile a list of actual job experiences involving extraordinarily good or bad employee performances. Normal procedures, or average work performance, is not included. Outstandingly good or bad job performance separates the better employees from the average employees, and the poor employees from the average employees. Thus, the emphasis is on specific actions as critical examples of excellent or poor behavior. Once a list of critical incident appraisals is finalized, then a particular method of utilization may be chosen.[7]

ANNUAL REVIEW RECORD One method is for the supervisor to keep an ongoing record of employees' critical incidents during each period of appraisal. At the end of the performance appraisal period, the supervisor reviews each employee's record as a determination of the employee's behavior. The outstandingly good or bad examples represent the employee's performance for the period of time. Employees who have little or no record during the year are doing their jobs satisfactorily, not performing very much above or below job expectations. The advantage of the annual review record is that it is usually very job specific. Obviously, with specific dates and incidents included in the annual performance appraisal, the supervisor is less affected by bias.

The main disadvantage of using the annual review record is that most supervisors will not keep an accurate record. With other interests taking a much higher priority in their daily work, often maintaining records for employees is not given adequate time. Such incompleteness may be due to supervisory bias, other causes, or simply a lack of time and effort. If management can train supervisors to keep a complete, objective record of employees' critical incidents, the process can be used for developmental purposes as well as evaluative purposes.

Another disadvantage of the annual record is the lack of comparable data about employees as it would be very difficult to compare the performances of different employees using their annual review records of critical incidents.

CHECKLIST OF CRITICAL INCIDENTS Critical incidents may be used in the performance appraisal process by developing a checklist of critical behaviors related to an employee's performance. Such an appraisal form may have twenty or thirty critical items for one specific job. The supervisor simply checks if the employee has performed in a critical manner in any one of the incidents. Outstanding employees would receive many checks indicating that they performed in a good fashion during the appraisal period. Average employees would receive very few checks because only in a few cases do they perform outstandingly well.

The checklist method of critical incidents often involves weighting different

[7]Greenlaw and Biggs, *Modern Personnel Management,* p. 198.

items in the checklist to indicate that some are more important than others. Often, the weights are not given to the supervisors who complete the appraisal process. After the items checked on an employee's checklist are totaled, a numerical total evaluation for each employee can be made which will make the appraisal process evaluative. The checklist method of critical incidents is fairly fast and easy to use since it can produce a mathematical total for employees. While it is evaluative as well as developmental, the checklist is very time consuming and expensive to develop since checklists for each different job in the organization must be produced.

BEHAVIORALLY ANCHORED RATING SCALES (BARS) The most common use of critical incident performance appraisals is in combination with the rating scale method. Instead of using broad employee attributes, the points on the rating scale are critical incidents. Thus, the Behaviorally Anchored Rating Scale system is quick and easy to complete, as well as being evaluative because mathematical totals can be easily related to merit increases and promotion probability. BARS are also job related and more developmental than the typical rating scale because the items being evaluated are items which are critical to good performance. The BARS system has been favored by federal agencies and personnel researchers because it is job related. Like the other critical incident systems the primary disadvantage of the BARS system is the time and effort involved in adapting critical incidents to a rating scale format. A BARS system would require a separate rating scale for each different job involved in the organization. This does not mean a different rating scale for each employee since many employees might be performing the same job. An example of two BARS rating scales is given in Figure 8–7.

ESSAY METHOD

A performance appraisal primarily created for employee development is the written *essay method*. The supervisor writes an essay describing the employee's performance, specifying examples of strengths and weaknesses. Because the essay method forces the supervisor to discuss specific examples of performance, it can also minimize supervisory bias and halo effect. By asking supervisors to enumerate specific examples of employee behavior the essay technique also minimizes central tendency and leniency problems since no rating scale is being used.

The essay technique often includes some distinct disadvantages: the time the supervisors must spend writing separate essays about each employee can be formidable. Essays are not very useful for evaluative purposes; two hundred essays describing different employees' performance cannot be linked to merit increases and promotion probabilities because there is no common standard. The essay technique is best used in small organizations or small work units where the primary purpose is to develop the employees' skills and behavior.

MANAGEMENT BY OBJECTIVES

One of the most widely discussed performance appraisal methods is management by objectives (MBO). Some of the companies which implemented MBO reported excellent results, others disappointments, and many indecision. Generally, the MBO process is as follows:

- The subordinate and supervisor jointly determine goals to be accom-

FIGURE 8–7: *Examples of "BARS" for a Grocery Store Check out Clerk*

Behaviorally anchored rating scale for the performance dimension 1a: Organization of Checkstand	Behaviorally anchored rating scale for the performance dimension 1b: Knowledge and Judgment

Dimension 1a: Organization of Checkstand

Extremely good performance — 7

By knowing the price of items, this checker would be expected to look for mismarked and unmarked items.

Good performance — 6

You can expect this checker to be aware of items that constantly fluctuate in price.

You can expect this checker to know the various sizes of cans.

Slightly good performance — 5

When in doubt, this checker would ask the other clerk if the item is taxable.

This checker can be expected to verify with another checker a discrepancy between the shelf and the marked price before ringing up that item.

Neither poor nor good performance — 4

When operating the "Quick Check," this checker can be expected to check out a customer with 15 items.

Slightly poor performance — 3

You could expect this checker to ask the customer the price of an item that is unmarked

In the daily course of personal relationships, this checker may be expected to linger in long conversations with a customer or another checker.

Poor performance — 2

In order to take a break, this checker can be expected to block off the checkstand with people in line.

Extremely poor performance — 1

Dimension 1b: Knowledge and Judgment

Extremely good performance — 7

This checker would organize the order when checking it out by placing all soft goods like bread, cake, etc., to one side of counter; all meats, produce, frozen foods to the other side, thereby leaving the center of the counter for can foods, boxed goods, etc.

Good performance — 6

When checking, this checker would separate strawberries, bananas, cookies, cakes and breads, etc.

Slightly good performance — 5

You can expect this checker to grab more than one item at a time from the cart to the counter.

Neither poor nor good performance — 4

After bagging the order and customer is still writing a check, you can expect this checker to proceed to the next order if it is a small order.

Slightly poor performance — 3

This checker may be expected to put wet merchandise on the top of the counter.

This checker can be expected to lay milk and by-product cartons on their sides on the counter top.

Poor performance — 2

This checker can be expected to damage fragile merchandise like soft goods, eggs and light bulbs on the counter top.

Extremely poor performance — 1

NOTE: BARS go beyond the typical MBO action planning of identifying activities (means) to achieve goals (ends) and specifies within these activities the job-specific behaviors that are known to result in more or less effective performance (goal achievement).

SOURCE: Adapted from Lawrence Fogli, Charles L. Hulin and Milton R. Blood, "Development of First-Level Job Criteria," *Journal of Applied Psychology*, Vol. 55 (February 1971): 3–8. Copyright 1971 by The American Psychological Association. Reprinted by permission.

plished during the appraisal period, and what level of performance is necessary for the subordinate to satisfactorily achieve particular goals.

- During the appraisal period the supervisor and employee update and alter goals as necessary due to changes in the business or environment.

- Both supervisor and subordinate decide if goals were met by the employee and discuss if not, why not. Taken into consideration is the cause of deviation from expected performance such as a strike, market change, or labor dispute.

- New goals and performance objectives are determined by the supervisor and employee for the next period based on performance levels.

The advantages of the MBO method are many: Both the supervisor and employee participate in the appraisal process. The focus of the appraisal process is on specific goals and not broad objectives, such as dependability, or cooperation. What is most unique about the MBO procedure is that goals and objectives are determined before the appraisal period begins.[8] Previously-discussed methods of appraisal take place after the employees' performance has occurred. The MBO process gives employees direction before the appraisal period begins. Thus, the MBO process is developmental in defining the direction employees should take and the expected level of achievement. The goal–setting orientation of an MBO program is also fairly unique among performance

appraisal systems. The disadvantage of the MBO procedure is the time and effort that must be spent by both the supervisor and the subordinate in the appraisal process.

Numerous studies of organizations' experiences with MBO show that for an MBO program to be successful, several guidelines should be considered before the MBO process begins.[9] First, an independent review committee of management and employees should be set up as an appeals mechanism. Thus, if an employee feels that a supervisor is setting unrealistically high goals, or if a supervisor feels that employees are making excuses about goals not met, there is an independent body to which they can appeal for a decision. Objectives and goals should be mutually accepted by the employee and supervisor. Generally, four or five specific objectives, which are measurable in terms of dollars or units of time should be established. Whenever possible, objectives should be constructed with allowances for individual differences, but still be realistic and feasible.[10] If possible, there should be a target date for completion of each specific objective. Several target dates for different objectives can be established at the beginning of the appraisal process. Figure 8–8 is a good example of an MBO performance appraisal form because there is adequate room for position objectives and results. The employee and supervisor sign and date each objective as it is achieved as well as appraise the performance. In general, the MBO objectives should be spe-

[8]Dallas De Fee, "Management by Objectives: When and How Does It Work?," *Personnel Journal* (January, 1977): 37–39.

[9]Jack Bucalo, "Personnel Directors . . . What You Should Know Before Recommending MBO," *Personnel Journal* (April, 1977): 176–78.

[10]Richard Steers, "Achievement Needs and MBO Goal-Setting," *Personnel Journal* (January, 1978): 26–28.

FIGURE 8–8: *MBO Appraisal Form*

Managerial Job Objectives			

John Atkins   7/2   PLANT MANAGER

Prepared by the manager   Date   Manager's job title

F. W. Crawford   7/2   PRESIDENT

Reviewed by his supervisor   Date   Supervisor's job title

Statement of Objectives Col. 1	Pri- ority Col. 2	Date Col. 3	Outcomes or Results Col. 4
1. TO INCREASE DELIVERIES TO 98% OF ALL SCHEDULED DELIVERY DATES	A	6/31	
2. TO REDUCE WASTE AND SPOIL-AGE TO 3% OF ALL RAW MATERIALS USED.	A	6/31	
3. TO REDUCE LOST TIME DUE TO ACCIDENTS TO 100 MAN-DAYS/YEAR	B	2/1	
4. TO REDUCE OPERATING COST TO 10% BELOW BUDGET	A	1/15	
5. TO INSTALL A QUALITY CON-TROL RADIOISOTOPE SYSTEM AT A COST OF LESS THAN $53,000	A	3/15	
6. TO IMPROVE PRODUCTION SCHEDULING AND PREVENTA-TIVE MAINTENANCE SO AS TO INCREASE MACHINE UTILIZA-TION TIME TO 95% OF CAPACITY	B	10/1	
7. TO COMPLETE THE UCLA EXECU-TIVE PROGRAM THIS YEAR.	A	6/31	
8. TO TEACH A PRODUCTION MANAGEMENT COURSE IN UNI-VERSITY EXTENSION	B	6/31	

From MANAGING BY OBJECTIVES by Anthony P. Raia. Copyright © 1974 by Scott, Foresman and Company. Reprinted by permission.

cific, giving a time frame, a priority ranking, and a plan of action.[11]

[11]Mark McConkie, "A Clarification of the Goal Setting and Appraisal Processes in MBO," *Academy of Management Review* 4, no. 1 (1979): 29–40

Appraisal Schedule

How often to appraise employee performance is an important and difficult question. Probably the most common answer fixes a specific interval between appraisals, for example, one year or six months. The schedule provides consistency in the evaluation process as all employees are evaluated for the same period of time. A variable interval process can be utilized when a goal-setting approach establishes specific time periods to achieve certain goals. Thus, at the end of each time period, which will differ for various employees, an appraisal determines the achievement level for a particular goal. When goal achievement does not have to be tied to a specific time period, it can be linked with the company's standard appraisal period to maintain appraisal consistency.

At the end of a probationary period employees are informed if they have achieved a level of proficiency which would justify changing their status from probationary to permanent. This appraisal should be combined with an annual fixed interval method which includes all employees. The most important question, then, is how long a time to allow between appraisals. Twelve– or six-month periods are most commonly used, although monthly and quarterly reports ensure that recency in the appraisal process will not affect the accuracy of the employee's evaluation.

For performance appraisal to be of significant value, the appraisal process should be conducted at regular intervals such as quarterly or semiannually. This provides a series of appraisals which supply useful comparative information to managers.

Supervisors as Appraisers

The person in the best position to observe the employee's behavior and determine whether the employee has reached specified goals and objectives is the best person to conduct the appraisal. In a great majority of cases, the employee's direct supervisor or manager should conduct the appraisal. Generally, only that person has directly and constantly observed the employee's performance and knows what the level of performance should be. Supervisors would often prefer to avoid the appraisal process because uncomfortable face-to-face confrontations often result. Even so, policymakers should ensure appraisals are conducted in a professional manner because performance appraisals of subordinates are a legitimate and critical part of supervison. In fact, most managers believe that supervisors who cannot accurately and honestly appraise and discuss employee behavior cannot be effective supervisors.

In some situations, if an employee is working very closely with other employees in a noncompetitive, work group environment, then peers may be in the best position to evaluate a co-worker's performance. Subordinates can, in some situations, provide information that the organization could not get from the employee's supervisor due to a lack of direct contact between the supervisor and employee. These subordinates, however, often will not give objective, honest appraisals due to possible retaliation. For jobs where outside clientele are affected by the performance of an employee, evaluations by customers can add a dimension to the appraisal process. They can comment either orally or in writing about the employee's contact with them and the service provided. However, outside clientele cannot give a total performance appraisal because they only view a small portion of the employee's activity.

In most situations, an employee's direct supervisor should complete the performance appraisal. Only in situations where that person cannot give objective, complete appraisal due to lack of information or lack of constant direct observation should peers or outside individuals be included in the appraisal process. Supervisors must be aware that their performance in the appraisal process will affect how they are rated by their superiors.

APPRAISAL
INTERVIEW

One of the final—and most important—steps in the appraisal process is discussing appraisals with employees. Most administrators require that these interviews take place in order to provide performance feedback to employees. Thus, employees learn where they stand in the eyes of the organization and are coached and counseled about how performance may be improved.

Problems with the Appraisal Interview

Unfortunately, the appraisal interview is a very troublesome and difficult obligation for a great many managers, who devise ways to avoid the interview even though it may be required by company policy. In other cases, where the interview is glossed over or conducted in a mechanical fashion, its value is highly suspect.

PLAYING GOD

In a classic 1959 article, behavioral scientist Douglas McGregor pointed out that many managers who view the appraisal as playing God are uncomfortable in simultaneously playing helper and judge. According to McGregor,

The modern emphasis upon the manager as a leader who strives to help his subordinates achieve both their own and the company's objectives is hardly consistent with the judicial role demanded by most appraisal plans. If the manager must put on his judicial hat occasionally, he does it reluctantly and with understandable qualms. Under such conditions it is unlikely that the subordinate will be happier with the results than will be the boss. It will not be surprising, either, if he fails to recognize that he has been told where he stands.[12]

CONSTRUCTIVE CRITICISM

In appraisal interviews, supervisors must evaluate the performance of each employee. Many supervisors, however, have difficulty giving criticism constructively, and many employees have difficulty accepting criticism even though it may be given with sensitivity and diplomacy. One important study showed that defensiveness and poor performance can result from criticism given during the appraisal interview. About half the time employees become defensive when criticized; a majority of employees felt they performed more favorably than their supervisors' assessments indicated.[13]

PERSONALITY BIASES

During the appraisal interview, the focus should be on performance and achievement of the goals, objectives, duties, and responsibilities that comprise the employee's job. Some supervisors assume roles as amateur psychologists and attempt to bring about personality changes which may improve job performance. But such

---

[12]Douglas M. McGregor, "An Uneasy Look at Performance Appraisal," *Harvard Business Review* (May–June, 1957): 89–94.

[13]H. H. Meyer, et al., "Split Roles in Performance Appraisal," *Harvard Business Review* (January—February, 1965): 127.

an approach is unwise, according to Douglas McGregor. In citing the advantages of the objectives-oriented appraisal process whereby the supervisor and subordinate set performance targets, McGregor states:

Consider a subordinate who is hostile, short-tempered, uncooperative, insecure. The superior may not make any psychological diagnosis. The target setting approach naturally directs the subordinate's attention to ways and means of obtaining better interdepartmental collaboration, reducing complaints, winning the confidence of the men under him. Rather than facing the troublesome prospect of forcing his own psychological diagnosis on the subordinate, the superior can, for example, help the individual plan ways of getting "feedback" concerning his impact on his associates and subordinates as a basis for self-appraisal and self-improvement.[14]

SPECIFIC FEEDBACK

For the appraisal interview to be a truly developmental process, the employee must receive specific feedback on performance areas in need of improvement. All too often, supervisors cloak criticism in vague, subjective terms and phrases. Some examples:

Your communication skills need improving

Your absenteeism rate is too high

Your output has not been up to par lately

You need to dress a little more conservatively

Your quality of work could stand a little upgrading

---

[14]McGregor, "An Uneasy Look at Performance Appraisal," p. 91–94

Comments such as these provide little basis for positive behavior change; supervisors are responsible for making their expectations clear to employees. For example, rather than saying "Your absenteeism rate is too high," it would be much more constructive to state "You have accumulated six unexcused absences in the past three months and we expect no more than one unexcused absence per month. Can you suggest ways you may be able to achieve this standard in the future?"

Interview Format

The problems discussed above may be minimized by following a planned standardized approach to the appraisal interview. While the precise interview format will vary to some extent from employee to employee, these steps should be generally covered:

● Prepare for the interview. Preparation is a key factor in a successful appraisal interview. During preparation, the supervisor should gather and review all relevant performance records. These normally include all data regarding work output and quality, schedules made and missed, absenteeism and tardiness, and so on. For supervisors using an objective-oriented appraisal system, all performance goals should be reviewed to determine which were met and which were not. The supervisor must be able to support the appraisal with facts. The supervisor may then want to make note of the specific items to be discussed during the interview. Finally, preparation includes setting a date for the appraisal interview with the employee which gives the employee plenty of lead time to prepare for the interview and develop a list of items to discuss.

● State the purpose of the interview. The employee should be told if the interview will cover personnel compensation or internal staffing decisions (merit increase, promotion, transfer, etc.), employee development, or both. Some managers, however, avoid mixing compensation and internal staffing decisions with employee development issues in the same appraisal interview, contending that this practice is "mixing apples and oranges." For example, it may be very difficult to motivate an employee who has just been told she is not receiving a salary increase because of mediocre performance to undertake a program of development.

● Indicate specific areas of good performance and those that need improvement. Supervisors generally begin the discussion of performance by highlighting areas of good performance. Appreciation and recognition for good work is an important part of the appraisal interview. Areas of performance that are in need of improvement are discussed next. Again, supervisors must be as specific as possible about performance needing improvement and avoid straying onto personality issues. The focus must remain on job performance.

● Invite participation. After an employee's performance record is reviewed, the employee should be invited to comment. This enables the employee to "let off steam" and tell why certain performance problems exist. This is also an opportune time to clear up any

misunderstandings which may still exist about job expectations. Wherever supervisors have done a good job of communicating job goals, objectives, and standards, employees should not receive any surprises during the interview.

● Focus on development. The next step involves setting up the employee's development program. Employees are much more likely to be committed to developmental programs if they agree with the supervisor that the program is necessary to improve job skills and abilities. Employees who feel that performance problems exist, or that a program of development is unnecessary to promote career goals, will be minimally committed to development. Supervisors must clearly show their employees how development is related to job success.

In many cases, a developmental program involves various kinds of on- and off-the-job training, development programs, and exercises.

Throughout this chapter, we have emphasized that one of the primary purposes of the performance appraisal is to enhance employee development. Most managers and administrators agree that a well-planned and implemented appraisal system can contribute enormously to employees' growth and enhance skills. According to Norman R. F. Maier, the problem-solving interviewing technique lies at the core of the employee development process. To successfully conduct a problem–solving interview, a supervisor must assume a certain role and possess certain attitudes and skills. Figure 8–9 illustrates characteristics of the problem–solving method and compares it to two other popular (but often ineffective) appraisal interviewing techniques.

An Effective Appraisal Program

While there is no one best technique for appraisal, and some methods are clearly superior to others, the choice of the appropriate technique depends on the primary purposes of the program. Figure 8–10 evaluates the abilities of four popular appraisal techniques to satisfy different personnel management needs.

Overall, Figure 8–10 shows that objectives-oriented evaluation systems generally serve more purposes than other appraisal techniques. This is, no doubt, one important reason for the widespread growth and popularity of MBO during the past decade. The analysis also shows that the traditional trait rating receives low marks in all categories. Most personnel administrators and line managers agree that no significant purpose is served by using the trait rating approach. Unfortunately, organizations cling dearly to this method because it is quick, easy, and, therefore, relatively cheap. It is also tradition bound and change resistant. This is exemplified by a personnel manager for a medium-sized light fixture company who complained vehemently about his company's trait rating system, until he was asked why that particular technique was still used. He responded "We've always done it that way. Why rock the boat?"

DESIGN INPUT

In creating an appraisal system, or redesigning an existing program, the participation of line managers and employees is beneficial. Often, the employees who will use the system are able to make valuable suggestions and contributions to strengthen the program. Further, they may be able to see potential problems that are hidden from the personnel specialist.

Aside from gaining technical input, participation brings psychological benefits. Behavioral scientists have long recognized that those who participate in the development of a program are more likely to accept the program. Users of the new system must support it and be committed to its success; soliciting the advice and recommendations of managers and employees is likely to result in their endorsement.

TRAINED APPRAISERS

No one is born with the ability to accurately appraise others' performance and experience does not, of itself, prepare one to conduct performance appraisals. Rather, formal training is the most effective way to prepare managers and supervisors to conduct successful employee appraisals. Appraisal processes and techniques are often included in training programs for new supervisors. One-day training seminars sponsored by various personnel and management associations or schools of business are attended by large numbers of supervisors and middle managers. Topics normally included in appraisal training are:

- The purposes of performance appraisal
- How to avoid rater problems—halo, bias, central tendency, etc.
- How to conduct nondiscriminatory appraisals
- The ethics of appraisals
- How to conduct effective appraisal interviews

FIGURE 8–9: *Performance Appraisal Interview Techniques*

	Tell and Sell	Tell and Listen	Problem Solving
Objectives	Communicate evaluation	Communicate evaluation	Stimulate growth and development in employee
	Persuade employee to improve	Release defensive feelings	
Psychological Assumptions	Employee desires to correct weaknesses if known	People will change if defensive feelings are removed	Growth can occur without correcting faults
	Any person who desires to do so can improve		Discussing job problems leads to improved performance
	A superior is qualified to evaluate a subordinate		
Role of Interviewer	Judge	Judge	Helper
Attitude of Interviewer	People profit from criticism and appreciate help	One can respect the feelings of others if one understands them	Discussion develops new ideas and mutual interests
Skills of Interviewer	Sales ability	Listening and reflecting feelings	Listening and reflecting feelings
	Patience	Summarizing	Reflecting ideas
			Using exploratory questions
			Summarizing
Reactions of Employee	Suppresses defensive behavior	Expresses defensive behavior	Problem-solving behavior
	Attempts to cover hostility	Feels accepted	

FORMAL AND INFORMAL METHODS

Unfortunately, many supervisors think about the appraisal process only annually or semiannually—whenever the personnel department notifies them that an employee's anniversary date is approaching and the appraisal must be completed. Feeling greatly relieved upon completing the mandatory appraisal, some supervisors do not tackle the often-painful subject of performance until it is time to complete another appraisal form. While this mechanical approach toward perfor-

mance appraisal may facilitate decision making about pay increases, by and large it neglects the fact that performance feedback for developmental purposes is a continuous responsibility of supervision. Regular informal appraisal sessions let employees know how they are doing and how they can improve their performances. Then, too, good work should not go unnoticed, and frequent supervisory recognition is an important technique for sustaining high levels of employee motivation.

FIGURE 8–9: *Continued*

	Tell and Sell	Tell and Listen	Problem Solving
Employee's Motivation for Change	Use of positive or negative incentives or both Extrinsic: motivation is added to the job	Resistance to change reduced Positive incentive Extrinsic and some intrinsic motivation	Increased freedom Increased responsibility Intrinsic motivation interest is inherent in the task
Possible Gains	Success most probable when employee respects interviewer	Develops favorable attitude toward superior, which increases probability of success	Almost assured of improvement in some respect
Risks of Interviewer	Loss of loyalty Inhibition of independent judgment Creates face saving scenes	Need for change may not be developed	Employee may lack ideas Change may be other than what superior had in mind
Probable Results	Perpetuates existing practices and values	Permits interviewer to change views in light of employee's responses Some upward communication	Both learn, because experience and views are pooled Change is facilitated

SOURCE: Reprinted from Norman R. F. Maier, *The Appraisal Interview: Three Basic Approaches.* San Diego, CA: University Associates, 1976. Used with permission.

FIGURE 8–10: *Four Appraisal Approaches*

	Traditional Trait Rating	Single Global Rating	Behaviorally Anchored Ratings	Objectives Oriented Evaluation
Acceptance by superior and subordinate	Poor	Moderate	Good	Good
Source of counseling and development information	Poor	Poor	Moderate	Good
Explanation of salary and reward administration	Poor	Moderate to good	Good	Moderate
Improve motivation based upon goal setting	Poor	Poor	Poor	Good
Clarification of the nature of job	Poor	Poor	Moderate to Good	Good

SOURCE: Porter, Lawler, and Heckman, *Behavior in Organizations* (New York: McGraw Hill Book Company) p. 332.

PERIODIC PROGRAM EVALUATION

An organization's performance appraisal program is generally created and implemented to satisfy certain stated objectives. Detailed listings of the goals and purposes of an organization's appraisal program are found in the company's personnel policy manual. Many organizations fail to periodically assess if those objectives are being achieved. Often appraisal programs are set in motion and left to function—sometimes dismally—without a thorough examination. In extreme cases, ill–conceived and poorly implemented appraisal programs may contribute to negative feelings between employees and management, perceptions of unfairness, hindered career development, and discriminatory (and illegal) employment practices. The periodic evaluation of the organization's appraisal program indicates good management, and makes good sense.

How can an appraisal system be evaluated? One company with approximately twenty thousand employees followed these assessment procedures:

● Interviews. Key managers from various departments were interviewed. Discussions focused on strengths and weaknesses of the present system and recommendations for improving the system.

● Analysis of employees' records. A random sample of almost two hundred performance appraisal forms was selected to uncover possible discrimination. The forms were also examined to spot rater errors such as central tendency, leniency, and the halo effect.

● Analysis of the relationship between the ratees and their characteristics. Employee ratings were correlated with certain personal and work factors such as age, tenure, race, and whether or not appraisal results were discussed with the ratees.

● Analysis of appraisal systems in comparable settings. The organization's appraisal was compared to the systems used by thirty-nine similar organizations.

The evaluation pinpointed problem areas that were corrected through the design of a new appraisal system, which included:[15]

● Development of two separate appraisal forms for nonmanagers and one for managers and professional employees.

● Meeting the legal requirement of job-relatedness by having the rater weight various rating factors according to their relevance.

● Defining rating factors in behavioral terms to make the appraisal more objective.

● Design of a MBO system for managerial and professional employees under which employees and their supervisors jointly determined performance goals. Employee performance was appraised by examining the degree to which these goals were met.

In summary, supervisors who manage human resources should use performance appraisals developmentally to improve employees' skills and abilities. In

[15]William H. Holly, et al., "Analyzing Performance Appraisal Systems: An Empirical Study," *Personnel Journal* 55 (September 1976): 457–59.

addition to formal, scheduled appraisals, supervisors should give employees frequent, periodic feedback and counseling on how they are doing and what may be done to improve performance. New employees and existing employees who change job assignments should be counseled about specific job duties, responsibilities, goals, and objectives. Many potential problems surround the performance appraisal interview. Some supervisors who dislike playing God find it difficult to simultaneously act as judge and helper. Giving criticism in a constructive, sensitive manner is another problem.

Other rater problems which may hamper the effectiveness of the appraisal process are the halo effect, central tendency, leniency, strictness, and recency. To a large extent, these problems are characteristic of appraisal systems that require supervisors to evaluate employees by making subjective performance ratings. To minimize the problems related to the performance appraisal interview, personnel administrators should include interviewing skills training during developmental programs for supervisors—particularly during courses for new supervisors.

The Solution

Gary Roth made a number of serious errors during his appraisal interview with David Gaines. One of the most serious errors was Roth's inability to discuss performance in specific, concrete behavioral terms. Gaines was told several times he was doing well but only in vague, general phrases. The criticism levied by Roth was very subjective and nonspecific. Gaines was told that he had a "problem" with certain knitting machines and was also informed that he needed to "crack the whip a little bit" because he was "too easy" on his older employees. Roth committed a grave error by totally disregarding the developmental aspect of performance appraisal. He did not mention a program of development to overcome any shortcomings Gaines may have had.

Obviously, Roth needs training in conducting performance appraisals. Some of his errors could be reduced through coaching by a supervisor, or by training in a program designed to strengthen communication and counseling skills.

Further, an objectives-based system of performance appraisal may serve more purposes than the rating form presently being used by the Southeastern Hat Company. In the manufacturing area, detailed production, quality, and cost data are normally gathered daily or weekly and quantitative performance objectives may be written with little difficulty.

KEY TERMS AND CONCEPTS

Performance Appraisal	Nongraphic Rating Scale
Supervisory Bias	Forced Choice
Halo Effect	Ranking
Central Tendency	Forced Distribution
Leniency	Paired Comparisons
Strictness	Critical Incidents
Recency	Behaviorally Anchored Rating Scale (BARS)
Work Standards	Essay Method
Graphic Rating Scales	

FOR REVIEW

1. What are the major purposes of performance appraisal?
2. What are the steps in the performance appraisal process?
3. Describe the major techniques of performance appraisal.
4. What are the major problems that surround many performance appraisal programs?
5. Describe some of the performance appraisal practices in use by organizations today.
6. What are the conditions necessary for an effective performance appraisal program?

FOR DISCUSSION

1. Think of two professors you have had—one very good and one very poor. What specific behaviors distinguish the two instruc-

tors? If you were the instructors' dean who had to conduct performance appraisals for the instructors, what technique would you use to gather performance data?

2. Write five MBO objectives for an individual selling vacuum cleaners door-to-door. How would you weigh each objective in terms of overall performance of the salesperson?

3. A small number of organizations have subordinates rate the performance of their supervisor. What advantages do you see in doing this? What problems may occur?

4. Supervisors may ask employees to furnish a self-rating at the appraisal interview for discussion. What are the benefits and drawbacks of this procedure?

5. What technique or techniques would you use to appraise the performance of the following kinds of employees? Keypunch operator, first-line supervisor in a manufacturing plant, professor of management, airline pilot, office clerk in large government office, police officer

6. When the process of evaluating employees is viewed as purely perfunctory, supervisors show little or no interest in completing the forms and conducting the interview. In some cases, the appraisal interview is not conducted. Why do these problems exist? What can be done to reduce them?

7. As a personnel administrator who is developing a performance appraisal system for department store sales personnel, you have decided to implement the BARS technique. Write three behavioral statements that may illustrate good performance and three that describe poor or mediocre performance.

SUPPLEMENTARY READING

Carrell, M. R., and Elbert, N. F. "Some Personal and Organizational Determinants of Job Satisfaction of Postal Clerks." *Academy of Management Journal* 17 (June 1974): 368–73.

Cummings, L. L. and Schwab, D. P. *Performance in Organizations.* Glenview, IL: Scott, Foresman and Co., 1973.

DeFee, Dallas T. "Management by Objectives: When and How Does It Work?" *Personnel Journal* 56 (January 1977): 37–39, 42.

Drucker, Peter, F. *The Practice of Management.* New York: Harper and Row, 1954.

Dwyer, James C., and Dimitroff, Nick J. "The Bottoms Up/Tops Down Approach to Performance Appraisal." *Personnel Journal* 55 (July 1976): 349–53.

Fleishman, Edwin A. *Studies in Personnel and Industrial Psychology,* 2d ed. Homewood, IL: The Dorsey Press, Inc., 1967. Section 2.

Gellerman, Saul W. *Motivation and Productivity.* New York: American Management Association, 1963. Chapter 19.

Ivancevich, John M. "Changes in Performance in a Management by Objectives Program." *Administrative Science Quarterly* 19 (December 1974): 563–74.

Kearney, William J. "The Value of Behaviorally Based Performance Appraisals." *Business Horizons* 13 (June 1976): 75–83.

Kellogg, Marion S. *What to Do About Performance Appraisal.* 2d ed. New York: AMACOM, 1975.

Luthans, Fred, and Creitner, Robert. *Organizational Behavior Modification.* Glenview, IL: Scott, Foresman and Co., 1975.

Oberg, Winston. "Make Performance Appraisal Relevant." *Harvard Business Review* 50 (January–February 1972): 61–67.

Odiorne, George S. "How to Succeed in MBO Goal Setting." *Personnel Journal* 57 (August 1978): 427–29, 451.

Raia, Anthony P. *Managing by Objectives.* Glenview, IL: Scott, Foresman and Co., 1974.

Schwab, Donald P.; Heneman, Herbert G., III; and DeCotiis, Thomas A. "Behaviorally Anchored Rating Scales: A Review of the Literature." *Personnel Psychology* 28 (Winter 1975): 549–62.

For Analysis: Centralized Performance Appraisal

The performance appraisal policy of a private service organization is uniformly applied to the three hundred professional employees of twelve regional offices as well as the home office. The firm provides professional technical assistance to clients in a three-state region. In five years twelve regional offices were added to the home office.

Once a year all professional personnel are evaluated through the same rating scale. Top management has required separate evaluations from the department head, division chairman (the employee's immediate supervisor), co-workers, and each of over one hundred clients. The results from the clients are totaled to produce an average score for each rating scale item.

Each employee's appraisals are tabulated by a formula known only to the home office. The final evaluation is an overall rating of "excellent," "superior," "satisfactory," or "marginal," which is transmitted by letter to the department head of the local office. The department head informs employees of their overall evaluations and salaries for the following year as directly determined by the home office's formula.

At one regional office the professional staff, who are the organization's only contact with its clients, complained harshly about the three-year old appraisal process. They met with their department head, Steve Quigley, to discuss their concerns. Quigley only reinforced their complaints because he knew nothing more than the overall evaluation and salary figures he was given by the home office. Therefore, the professional staff pursued the issue with the home office. The reply from the home office was an immediate, large across-the-board pay raise for all employees.

The next year, evaluations were carried out just as they had been in prior years. The professional staff began to complain again, claiming that they received no useful feedback and saw no justification for their individual salary adjustments. In one case, Quigley was told by the home office to reevaluate an employee he had rated as marginal. The vice-president instructed Quigley that the company "had no marginal employees."

Questions:
1. Why would top management benefit from separate evaluations?

2. *If the organization has used the same appraisal process since it began, why are employees only now complaining?*

3. *How can the employees complain again when they received a large across-the-board pay increase?*

4. *Should the appraisal process be altered? If so, how? If not, why?*

SELECTED PROFESSIONAL READING

The "Refined" Performance Evaluation Monitoring System: Best of Both Worlds

MELVIN E. SCHICK

Every company has a performance evaluation monitoring system (PEMS) to measure individual job performance against company standards. It may not be recognized, formalized or documented, but the need to evaluate performance is present in all business environments. In smaller companies, the system may be totally informal and simply operate on the judgments and insights of the president or a manager. The limited number of employees in smaller companies provides the manager with the distinct advantage of first-hand observation of the performance of all key company employees. This omnipresent field of vision is a significant asset in evaluating and monitoring employee performance and is the single most important factor in sustaining a workable, informal evaluation system.

But as a company grows, top management loses its immediate contact with the broader-based middle managers and supervisors. More formalized performance evaluation systems are then necessary and may even become a crucial vehicle for advancement and salary increases. The U.S. Army, a classically large organization, relies almost entirely on a formalized system to differentiate individuals for promotion and assignments. Since these formalized systems are very important to the long-term well-being of an organization, one must question how good today's methods really are. Any organization that has released a "marginal performer" who subsequently rose to the top in a new environment should seriously question its internal performance evaluation system. In fact, it is very possible to conclude that many of today's methods still leave substantial room for improvement. Thus, refinement of the PEMS methodology toward a fully computerized approach would seem in order.

VAST DIVERGENCE

A recent article by Harry B. Anderson in *The Wall Street Journal* suggests the vast divergence of performance appraisal systems in use today: "Martin Marietta Corporation, for instance, requires supervisors in its Aero

Space Division to write broad essays describing an individual's strengths and weaknesses . . ."[1] A more common approach, however, is to qualify observations. This requires that the rater categorize areas of performance, behavior or personal characteristics into numerically related assessments. A good, average, poor or 1, 2, 3 system is widely-used technique for quantifying subjective judgments of individual performance. Not infrequently, the major thrust of controversy in a 1, 2, 3 system concerns the optimum numerical span of categories for use by the organization, i. e., should the company use 1 to 3, 1 to 5 or perhaps 1 to 100?

The more recent addition to the PEMS field centers around the MBO technique of supervision. This system offers distinct advantages in harmonizing corporate and individual goals and provides a meaningful feedback and evaluation system when goal and objective accomplishment are measurable. However . . . the major strength of MBO is also its chief weakness, since it focuses attention exclusively on the results of tasks which accomplish objectives.[2] Significant behavioral or personal qualifications can frequently be overlooked in an MBO system, particularly when they were not originally defined as an explicit objective. While such a system can be beneficial, there is still a need for a traditional, quantifiable PEMS.

TOWARD COMPUTERIZATION

Fortunately, with decreasing costs for computer storage devices and faster central processors, a totally computerized PEMS should now be possible. Along with a substantial commitment to mechanization, significant tangible benefits are probable. For example, a good system could well do the following:

1. Harry B. Anderson, "The Rating Game, Formal Job Appraisals Grow More Relevant But Get More Criticism," *The Wall Street Journal*, May 23, 1978.
2. Michael Beer and Robert A. Rich, "Employee Growth through Performance Management," *Harvard Business Review*, July 1976, pp. 55–66.

1. Be easy to use.
2. Provide quantified results.
3. Be totally objective in comparing relative performance.
4. Be inflation-proof.
5. Allow room for individual raters to use the evaluation form as a motivating vehicle, while still providing meaningful results.

Many systems today use the power of the computer to retain performance data and provide various reports. However, few, if any, have done much more than store data, report on historical data, and, at best, provide statistical calculations on individuals' performances relative to others in a similar work situation. In other words, these systems do not provide benefits beyond point two as listed above.

Before suggesting a method for capturing these remaining benefits, there is one additional significant problem with existing computerized PEMS which should be considered. Large organizations often use a large number of evaluations, often from different raters, to provide the necessary objectivity factor in the system. The logic flows something like this: Given a sufficiently large sample size of evaluations for an individual, the statistics of the sample will describe that individual fairly accurately. While this may be a correct statistical inference, it still leaves some rather pragmatic problems. Typically, the sample of evaluations will not be from randomly selected supervisors. Often one or two individuals contribute more evaluations about one individual than about many others, which will introduce their biases in the sample. Also, often the number of evaluations is too small to accurately judge an individual. This is particularly true in an employee's important first few years with an organization.

A PEMS methodology should be able to provide the total range of advantages possible through automation. Such a system would likely employ the following key reporting features:

1. Evaluation of a rated individual.
2. Comparison of rated individuals within a similar work situation.
3. Evaluation of a rated individual based on the statistical history of all prior evaluations of the rater.
4. Comparison of rated individuals within a similar work situation, based on the statistical history of all prior evaluations of the rater.

By making the rater responsible for the reasonableness of his or her own "rater average" relative to company standards, the PEMS moves toward the inflation-proof system, while providing flexibility in its actual application by specific supervisors.

REFINED VERSUS TRADITIONAL

Let's take a specific example and visualize some possible reports which will illustrate the differences between a refined and a traditional computerized performance evaluation monitoring system. While the specific use would likely be broken down into numerous rating categories, subgroups and items, these examples use only one composite score—an overall rating number on a 1 to 100 scale.

In our example (Figures 1 and 2), the company standard for average was predetermined to be 70 as a matter of policy. The traditional information in both the evaluative and comparative sense indicates that Mr. Public is an average performer. While a refined methodol-

FIGURE 1: *Traditional Performance Evaluation Monitoring System Information*

EVALUATION For: John Q. Public

Rating	Date	Rated By
70	12/11/78	Smith
75	9/30/78	Black
65	6/28/78	Fram
70	3/29/78	Abe
70	12/30/77	Rose

Composite Rating: 70

FIGURE 2: *Comparison* **For Individuals in Class A**

Composite Rating	Individual	Ranking
78	Prince, Judy	1
72	Jackson, Carl	2
70	Public, John Q.	3
69	Fisher, Linda	4
62	Elton, Tom	5

ogy would likely retain the traditional features, it would also incorporate additional data, as shown in Figure 3.

The example shows an inflation effect. Mr. Public is really a below-average performer when viewed from a perspective of all others rated by the same individuals and normalized to company standard. Without these refinements to traditional systems, results could potentially be misinterpreted by top management and thus result in less than optimal personnel decisions. To the rated individual, an evaluation could be misinterpreted as a better or worse evaluation than the rater intended. There are numerous statistical tools which could be employed to accurately quantify the process shown above. For example, it is possible to fit the historical rating data in each category, subgroup and item to theoretical distributions, such as a normal distribution, and then use standard deviation units to normalize the results.

Figure 3 suggests that a methodology could use weighting factors, if appropriate, in a specific organization. For instance, individual raters might be assigned unique weighting factors to add significance to their evaluations. Additionally, the number of prior ratings given by individuals could also be used to weight specific raters evaluations. These two alternatives or others could then aid in the overall development of a normalized rating.

Figures 3 and 4 use simple normalizing and weighting assumptions. A specific application of the techniques should be tailored to each company's specific needs. In Figures 3 and 4, the following simple rules were used:

FIGURE 3: *Additional, or Refined, Performance Evaluation Monitoring System Information*
Relative Evaluation For: John Q. Public

Rating	Date	Rated By	Weight of Rater	No. of Prior Ratings to Others	Rater's Average Rating	Simple Normalized Rating
70	12/11/78	Smith	1	0	0	N/A
75	9/30/78	Black	1	10	75	70
65	6/28/78	Fram	1	5	70	65
70	3/29/78	Abe	2	20	80	60
70	12/30/77	Rose	1	10	77	63

Weighted normalized rating: 62.38

Simple Normalized Rating = Rating + (Company Standard for Average − Rater's Average Rating)

Weighting factor = (Weight of rater—number of prior ratings to others)

Weighted normalized rating =
$$\frac{\Sigma(\text{weighting factor} * \text{Simple Normalized Rating})}{\Sigma \text{weighting factors}}$$

In summary, a refined computerized PEMS can now offer the following:

Ease of use by retaining quantifiable categories of performance evaluations.

FIGURE 4: *Relative Comparison*

Weighted Normalized Rating	Individual	Ranking
74.67	Prince, Judy	1
70.43	Jackson, Carl	2
69.21	Fisher, Linda	3
63.09	Elton, Tom	4
62.38	Public, John Q.	5

Quantifiable results based on summarized and stratified input data.

Total objectivity by comparing employee performances based on normalized assessments.

Inflation proofing by making raters aware that their individual rating records establish a pattern to be used in normalization. (Consistently high evaluations will not be advantageous to the rater or the rated.)

Room for individual flexibility in using evaluations as a motivational tool. Individuals can then establish their own norms, within limits of reason, without affecting the composite standard of performance.

New employee evaluations would also become more meaningful, given the weighting effect of employees' initial supervisors. Such an approach offers a wide range of advantages and could make use of proven statistical methods. Today's computer technologies should easily support these refinements, while still retaining the cost-effectiveness of traditional systems.

Models are used for on-the-job training at the Tennessee Valley Authority.

9

EMPLOYEE
TRAINING

Training Process and Evaluation

Off-the-Job Training

On-the-Job Training

Effective Training Techniques

The Problem: Georgia Trust Bank

John Merritt, the director of training for Georgia Trust Bank, had a particularly busy week. His office was in Georgia Trust's home office in Atlanta; nine training and clerical personnel work for Merritt. Georgia Trust employs nine hundred persons in forty-two offices throughout Georgia.

Early in the week, Merritt received a call from Marcia Moore, the head of Georgia Trust's computer services division:

"Good morning, John. As you probably know, we've bought a totally new computer hardware system from National Business Machines. The system should be up and running in about eight months. At the same time, we'll also be converting our programming language from FORTRAN to COBOL. Of course, this means our staff of about twenty programmers will need training in COBOL. Can you get with National's training people and design a program specifically for our operation? Please get back to me soon . . . our programmers simply must learn these skills by the time the new hardware is installed."

The next day Merritt received a memo from Tom Dewis, head of keypunch services for Georgia Trust. Part of Tom's memo read:

"John, I've got a real problem, and I need your help. I've got about sixty keypunch operators and because of the tight job market, I'm continually understaffed by at least 10 percent. This means we can't be too choosy and we've hired a number of marginal performers in the past several months. Quite honestly, they're causing me real problems. Can you put

together a training program to improve the keypunch skills of some of our low performers? The sooner the better."

And on Wednesday afternoon, Bill Blalock, Georgia Trust's vice-president for branch operations, phoned Merritt:

"John, recent court rulings about equal employment and affirmative action have some of our personnel interviewers totally confused. We've decentralized the hiring of most branch personnel, and many of our branch people are really puzzled about how recent legislation affects hiring practices. Could you put together a one-day seminar for our branch administrators on the current legislation and how it relates to employment practices? Could you have it ready in two or three weeks?"

Friday morning's mail brought the following letter from Gail Schoen, personnel vice-president:

"John, I've just received a report concerning the results of the exit interviews for the last six months. I was alarmed to find that a major reason for turnover was a lack of training for career advancement. Specifically, what are we doing in this area? Do you feel we need a more planned approach to employees' training so they become more upwardly mobile? Let me know your feelings on this in a day or two."

To round out the week, Merritt met with his staff of six training officers on Friday afternoon to discuss Georgia Trust's revised employee orientation program. Merritt delegated the task for expanding the training program to three assistants. Mary Gilbert, the team leader for the project, summarized changes in the program and asked for Merritt's approval:

"In sum, John, the new one-day orientation program blends topics covered in the previous program with the following new material: a brief history of the organization, job responsibilities, performance appraisal, promotional opportunities, and a new grievance procedure. I think the new program will be much more effective than our old program,

which was primarily a reading of our benefits package. If the new program has your okay, I think we will be ready to send the package to the personnel vice-president for final approval."

Today, policymakers are constantly looking for ways to make their organizations more effective. Managers of privately–owned enterprises strive to enhance their profits—and ultimately stockholders' returns—by increasing sales and/or reducing operating costs. Government administrators at local, state, and federal levels are coming under increasing pressure to provide more effective and efficient services to their citizenry. Leaders of voluntary organizations, too, such as the American Cancer Society, United Way, and the March of Dimes, must seek ways to grow and prosper as critical financial resources become more and more difficult to obtain. The need to achieve goals as effectively as possible is common to all organizations, public and private, large and small.

Our brief glimpse at the demands made on John Merritt provides a clue to how a strong training function enhances organizational effectiveness. Some managers mistakenly believe that training is a luxury. It is not. When performed effectively, training holds a critical place in the spectrum of organizational activities which foster greater human and organizational performance.

The major purposes of training may be broadly grouped into five general areas:

TO UPDATE EMPLOYEES' SKILLS AS TECHNOLOGY CHANGES Our hypothetical training director's responsibility to provide training for Georgia Trust's computer programmers reflects an important part of most training officials' jobs: ensuring that employees can effectively perform new technologies. Managers in all areas must be constantly aware of technological advances that will make their organizations function more effectively. Technological change, in turn, means that jobs often change, and that employee skills and abilities must be updated through training so that technological advancements are successfully integrated into the organization.

TO REDUCE THE LEARNING TIME FOR NEW EMPLOYEES TO BECOME JOB COMPETENT Frequently a new employee will not possess the skills and abilities required to be "job competent," that is, to be able to achieve expected output and quality standards. First, employee selection systems are not perfect. Even though the results of tests, interviews, and other data may indicate a high probability of job success by the job applicant, there will be times when the predictions prove invalid. No selection device is able to accurately predict employee success or failure all the time; training is often necessary to fill the gap between the new employee's predicted and actual performance. Second, managers knowingly hire employees who need training to perform at standard levels. When the number of job openings exceeds the number of applicants, management has little choice but to hire an applicant with few or no job skills and supply the required abilities through training. In addition, an organization's affirmative action program may mandate hiring minority employees who require training before being placed on a particular job. Third, many times management will hire employees who possess the aptitudes to learn a variety of low or semi-skilled jobs rather than employees skilled in one job area. Large manufacturing concerns hire large numbers of employees for a wide variety of routine jobs. For example, in hiring new employees for its manufacturing operation in Louisville, Kentucky, the General Electric Company uses an aptitude test that measures general manual dexterity and motor coordination skills. To learn a specific assembly job, new employees undergo company-provided training that may last from a few hours to several days.

TO HELP SOLVE OPERATIONAL PROBLEMS Managers report they must achieve their goals with both scarcities and abundances: a scarcity of financial and human technological resources and an abundance of financial, human, and technological problems. Perhaps, the two are closely intertwined. Managers are expected to reach—and often exceed—challenging goals in spite of interpersonal conflicts, vague policies and standards, scheduling delays, inventory shortages, high levels of absenteeism and turnover, marginal union-management relationships, and a restrictive legal environment. While organizational problems are attacked on many fronts, training is one important way to solve many of the dilemmas that managers must confront. Training courses dealing with personnel, marketing, accounting, finance, manufacturing, purchasing, information systems, and general management are given by training personnel, universities, and training consultants to assist employees in solving organizational problems and performing their jobs more effectively.

TO PREPARE EMPLOYEES FOR PROMOTION One important way to attract, retain, and motivate personnel is through a systematic program of career development. Developing employees' promotional capabilities is consistent with a personnel policy of promotion from within; training is a key ingredient in the career development system. Training enables an employee to acquire the skills needed for the next job up the organizational ladder, and eases the transition from the employee's present job to one involving greater responsibilities.

Organizations which fail to provide training for upward mobility may experience the same kind of problem faced by Gail Schoen, the fictitious personnel vice-president for Georgia Trust Bank. Frustrated by lack of opportunity for advancement, achievement-oriented employees often seek employment with organizations which provide training for career advancement. By continually developing and promoting its human resources through training, management can enjoy a qualified, motivated, and satisfied work force.

TO ORIENT NEW EMPLOYEES TO THE ORGANIZATION During the first few days on the job, new employees form their initial impressions of the organization and its management team. These impressions may range from very favorable to very unfavorable and may influence employees' overall job satisfaction and productivity. For this reason, many administrators make a concerted effort to properly orient new employees to the organization and the job. Orientation may be brief and

FIGURE 9–1: *Orientation Checklist for Personnel Representatives and Supervisory Personnel*

NAME OF EMPLOYEE _____ STARTING DATE _____

DEPARTMENT _____ LOCATION _____

ITEMS COVERED BY PERSONNEL RELATIONS DEPARTMENT OR BRANCH OFFICE ON FIRST DAY OF ORIENTATION: (45 minutes)

PART I—Organization and Personnel Policies & Procedures

- 1. XYZ Company Organization
- 2. Basic Insurance Benefits *(Paid in full by the company)*
  - A. Hospitalization
  - B. Short-Term Disability
  - C. Basic Life Insurance
  - D. Travel Accident
- 3. Optional Insurance Benefits *(Paid for by you and the company)*
  - A. Comprehensive Medical
  - B. Contributory Life Insurance
  - C. Long Term Disability
- 4. Vacations
- 5. Holidays
- 6. Probationary Period
- 7. Compensation
- 8. Job Evaluation
- 9. Medical Absence
- 10. Personal Status Change Notice
- 11. XYZ Company News
- 12. Tuition Refund Plan
- 13. Building Facilities
- 14. New Building
- 15. XYZ Company and You
- 16. Equal Opportunity Employment

* * * * * *

APPOINTMENT FOR SECOND MEETING: (45 minutes)

DATE _____ TIME _____

IMPORTANT: BE SURE TO BRING THIS FORM BACK WITH YOU, SIGNED BY YOUR MANAGER WHEN YOU COME TO YOUR SCHEDULED SECOND MEETING.

PART II—Personnel Policies and Procedures

- 1. Review & Questions on Part 1
- 2. Retirement Program
- 3. College Gift Matching Plan
- 4. Time Off the Job
- 5. Award for Recruiting
- 6. Credit Union
- 7. XYZ Company Investment Plan
- 8. U.S. Savings Bonds
- 9. Employee Activities
- 10. Suggestion System
- 11. Personnel Inventory

PERSONNEL RELATIONS STAFF REPRESENTATIVE _____

DATE _____

ITEMS TO BE DISCUSSED BY DEPARTMENT HEAD OR SUPERVISOR WITH NEW EMPLOYEE:

FIRST DAY OF EMPLOYMENT

- 1. Introduction to Co-workers
- 2. Information on Location of Facilities
  - A. Coat Room
  - B. Cafeteria
  - C. Wash Room
  - D. Bulletin Board
  - E. Coffee Service
  - F. Provision for Lunch

RULES AND POLICIES

- 3. Hours: starting, lunch, dismissal time, hours per week
- 4. Pay: when, where, and how paid—overtime policy (Explain deductions when 1st check is received.)
- 5. Holidays and Vacations in Detail
- 6. Probationary Period
- 7. Absences: Pay Policies—before and after 5 months. When and whom to phone. Visit to Medical Dept. or Doctor's note before return to work after absence of 3 or more days.
- 8. Organization of Department Corporation—Division—Department—Section
- 9. Rules on: Tardiness, Telephone Coverage, Behavior, etc.

DURING FIRST TWO WEEKS OF EMPLOYMENT

- 10. Accident: Reporting accident or injury on job
- 11. Employee's Discount on XYZ Company products
- 12. Salary Check—Explanation of Deductions
- 13. Salary Reviews
- 14. Employee Appraisal Plan
- 15. Suggestion System
- 16. Reporting Change in Address, Name, Phone, etc.
- 17. Invite Questions and Help on Problems

As indicated by check marks, all of the above items have been discussed with the employee.

The employee has been advised as to the time and extent of 1st vacation as shown by the Table on last page of this form.

Employee has been instructed to attend the second scheduled meeting and to bring this check list with him.

DEPARTMENT HEAD OR SUPERVISOR _____

DATE _____

FIGURE 9–2: *Management Principles Important to the Training Function*

Ensure clarification of line and staff authority and responsibility for training. Training personnel usually act in an advisory manner; line management has the ultimate authority to accept, reject, or revise the proposed training.

Communicate the benefits of training to top management. Training personnel must receive top management's support for the training function. By recognizing the importance of training in achieving organizational objectives, top managers are more likely to provide trainers with the necessary budget and other resources.

Recognize that on-the-job training is the most common form of training and give supervisors and other key trainers instruction in how to train. In addition, reward supervisors and on-the-job trainers who do a particularly effective job—through praise and recognition if nothing else.

Recognize that training often creates production problems for supervisors. Work closely with managers and be flexible in setting up training schedules.

Don't expect training to solve all organizational problems. Examine performance gaps carefully to be sure that training is the appropriate remedy.

Ensure that training performed off-site teaches methods, techniques and philosophies consistent with those of the trainee's organization.

Design the training evaluation system that everyone agrees on—both line and staff. Make your evaluation as objective as possible.

Audit your training function periodically. Large organizations should use an outside consultant who reports audit findings to top management.

informal, focusing only on traditional topics such as company benefits, holidays, vacations, and pay. Or, orientation may be a one- or two-day program involving a company tour, meetings with managers and personnel officials, and discussions of a variety of subjects including organizational objectives and philosophy, employee expectations, relevant legislation, and other topics important to employees and their jobs. As suggested in our opening scenario with Georgia Trust Bank, training officials must not only update the organization's *orientation program* as various aspects of the program change, but also expand the program to include topics that may help the employee adjust more easily, quickly, and effectively. Both line and staff managers play an important role in employee orientation and share the responsibilities illustrated in Figure 9–1. During the orientation process, personnel or industrial relations department representatives basically discuss company history, benefits, and personnel policies, while the employee's immediate supervisor will be involved with job-related factors such as job rules and regulations, safety procedures, introduction to co-workers, and performance standards.

The time and effort invested in a well-planned and implemented orientation program may reap many returns. Research shows that orientation programs can reduce employees' anxiety, save supervisors' and co-workers' time, develop positive attitudes toward the company, and create realistic job expectations.[1] In an often-cited research study conducted at Texas Instruments, Inc., one group of employees attended the company's traditional two-hour orientation program fo-

1. B. W. Marion and S. E. Trieb, "Job Orientation: A Factor in Employee Performance and Turnover," *Personnel Journal* (October 1969): 799–804.

FIGURE 9–3: *Training Process Model*

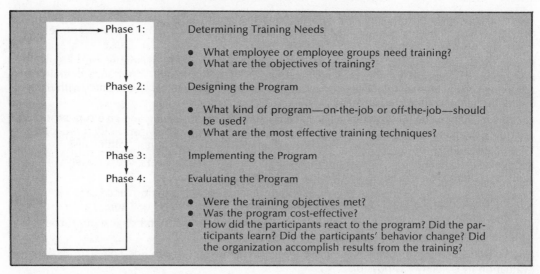

Phase 1: Determining Training Needs

- What employee or employee groups need training?
- What are the objectives of training?

Phase 2: Designing the Program

- What kind of program—on-the-job or off-the-job—should be used?
- What are the most effective training techniques?

Phase 3: Implementing the Program

Phase 4: Evaluating the Program

- Were the training objectives met?
- Was the program cost-effective?
- How did the participants react to the program? Did the participants learn? Did the participants' behavior change? Did the organization accomplish results from the training?

cusing on employee benefits and minimum levels of performance. An experimental group attended the conventional two-hour program and, in addition, a six-hour program devoted to social orientation that covered: a) the high probability that they would succeed on the job, b) how the company grapevine worked and what to expect from it, c) taking the initiative in requesting help from supervisors, and d) the behavioral patterns of individual supervisors. Compared to the control group, employees in the expanded one-day session required less training time and fewer training costs; their records indicated reduced absenteeism, tardiness, waste, and product rejects.[2]

Good training and good management go hand in hand. While the utilization of learning principles is vitally important to successful training, the need to apply the fundamentals of good management to the

training function cannot be overlooked. A good working knowledge of basic management and organizational principles—and an appreciation for the politics of organizational life—often help training administrators design programs that consistently achieve their objectives. Management basics that are important to the training process are summarized in Figure 9–2.

TRAINING PROCESS

Training is a systematic process by which employees learn skills, knowledge, abilities, or attitudes to further organizational and personal goals.[3] To many, the thought of training brings to mind a trainer, participants, and traditional techniques: a film being shown, workbooks

---

2. Earl R. Gomersall and M. Scott Myers, "Breakthrough in On-The-Job Training," *Harvard Business Review* (July–August 1966): 62–71.

3. In this chapter, the focus is upon the training of nonmanagement personnel. The development of managerial potential is discussed in the following chapter.

being completed, or a chalkboard, overhead projector, or flipchart-assisted lecture. To the army veteran, the thought of training may conjure up not-so-pleasant thoughts of basic training, replete with long hours of marching, physical training, and military science lectures. These examples illustrate the importance of the tangible part of training—the physical setting where training is actually conducted. The actual implementation of training is only a small part of the overall training function; successful training involves considerable effort both before and after the trainer and trainees are brought together. In other words, training is best thought of as a multi-part process that involves four distinct but highly interrelated phases. Key elements in the *training process model,* in addition to some important questions concerning each phase, are illustrated in Figure 9–3.

Training Needs

In many cases, the determination of training needs is a fairly straightforward process which may be conducted without an extensive analysis of the organization. For example, normally all new employees undergo orientation training. An impending technological change such as the introduction of new computer hardware or a new assembly process will automatically require the need for training work groups affected by the new work methods. On the other hand, determining training requirements to resolve employee skill deficiencies necessitates a much greater research effort by the training administrator. In this case, training needs are created when an employee's actual performance does not meet expected performance: a lathe operator who operates at 85 percent of the standard output, a secretary who types 20 words per minute below the expected rate, or a police officer who fails an annual physical exam. To detect training needs that result from performance problems, the trainer must systematically collect and analyze employee output, quality, and attitudinal data.

Donald Kirkpatrick suggests this information may be gathered in four ways:[4]

By observing employees

By discussing training needs with employees.

By discussing training needs with employees' supervisors

By examining employees' problems

Questionnaires may also be designed to gather training needs data; this technique enables training personnel to systematically survey large numbers of employees with a minimum expenditure of time and money. An example of the type of form that may be used for this purpose is illustrated in Figure 9–4. On this form, supervisors are asked to rank the skills necessary for a particular job in addition to the level of proficiency of the employee holding the job. An analysis of the questionnaire data would help the training director determine potential training groups and job skills training.

Following an assessment of training needs, a *training objective* is written reflecting what the participant should be able to do upon the completion of training. Training objectives indicate the kinds and levels of skills, abilities, knowledges,

4. Donald L. Kirkpatrick, "Determining Training Needs," *Training and Development Journal* (February 1977): 22–25.

FIGURE 9-4: *Training Needs Analysis Survey Form*

Position: Clerical

Employee _____ Department _____

Supervisor _____ Date _____

Instructions:

In column A, rate the skill necessary for the employee to successfully perform the job. Use the following ratings: 1—very important; 2—moderately important; 3—not important.

In column B, rate the need for training for each skill area which received a rating of 1 or 2 in column A. In assessing training needs, use the following ratings: 1—no training need; 2—moderate need for training; 3—immediate, critical training need.

Skill Area: Clerical	(A) How important is the skill?	(B) Employee's need for training
Ability to read and comprehend rough draft material		
Typing speed		
Typing accuracy		
Proofreading skills		
Ability to use office machinery		
Filing skills		
Ability to compose letters and memos		
Oral communications		
Ability to organize daily routine		
Human relations skills		

and attitudes the participant should possess after the program has been completed. Well-written objectives will benefit the training function in at least three important ways:

● Training objectives help determine which training methods and techniques are appropriate by focusing on the areas of employee performance that need to change.

● Training objectives clarify what is

expected of both the trainer and participants.

● Training objectives provide a basis for evaluating the program after its completion.

What are the qualities of good training objectives? A well-written training objective will state:

● terminal behavior, that is, what the learner will be able to do upon completion of training;

- the conditions under which terminal behavior is expected to occur; and
- the minimum level of achievement that will be accepted as evidence that the learner has learned.

These sample objectives are based on the preceeding criteria for good training objectives:

Condition	Terminal Behavior	Minimal Achievement
Given a standard key-punch operator's examination	to type	no fewer than ten cards per minute with an error rate no higher than 3 percent
Given a standard set of tools	to conduct	preventive maintenance on a lathe within thirty minutes according to company standard
Given a business letter containing grammatical errors	to locate	95 percent of all errors after studying the letter for no more than five minutes

Program Design

The focus of Phase 1 was on employee behavior: determining how—and to what degree—employees must change to enhance organizational and personal goals. Phase 2 decisions concern the kinds of training that will be most effective in changing behavior. A wide array of training technologies exist, and care must be taken to ensure training methods are effectively matched with training needs and objectives. Training personnel must avoid the temptation to select a program or technique simply because it is popular, entertaining, or in vogue. Unless a particular training method or technique is based on a valid need—as indicated through a well-planned needs assessment—the organization will bear few, if any, returns on its training dollars.

The great majority of training programs attended by employees of business, government, and not-for-profit organizations will fall into the broad categories of on-the-job and off-the-job training. Specific kinds of on- and off-the-job training will be briefly discussed, along with the advantages and disadvantages of both training methods.

ON-THE-JOB TRAINING

On-the-job training is job instruction given by an employee's supervisor or experienced employee. After being shown how to do the tasks and duties the employee works closely with the trainer until the job is performed at an expected level of performance. The Bureau of National Affairs reports that 90 percent or more of all forms of training is performed on the job.[5] On-the-job training may involve learning how to run a machine, to complete forms and paper work, to drive a vehicle, to conduct an interview, or to sell the company's product. Both new and existing employees at all job levels—unskilled, skilled, clerical, management, and staff—are often trained on the job. Some common on-the-job training methods include job rotation, enlarged job responsibilities, job instruction training, and apprentice training.

5. "On-The-Job Training," *Personnel Management: BNA Policy and Practices Series* (Washington, DC: Bureau of National Affairs, Inc., 1975), p. 205.

JOB ROTATION Also referred to as cross–training, *job rotation* involves placing an employee on different jobs for periods of time which may range from a few hours to several weeks. Skilled, unskilled, or clerical employees who undergo job rotation usually learn specific tasks such as how to run a machine or perform a routine assembly or clerical process. At this job level job rotation normally consumes a short period of time such as a few hours or, perhaps, one or two days. On the other hand, this form of training for staff positions may consume much larger time periods, as staff trainees often learn major functions and responsibilities during job rotation. For example, on-the-job training for a bank lending officer may consist of one or two months in each department, including loan operations and collections, bookkeeping, trust operations, data processing, and commercial lending.

ENLARGED JOB RESPONSIBILITIES Giving an employee added job duties, responsibilities, and assignments is another way to train an employee during the present job. Rather than simply giving an employee more of the same work to perform, this popular form of job training involves delegating more decision making to the employee through challenging job assignments and problem solving. Widely used in training managers, professional staff, and skilled clerical employees, the enlarged job responsibilities technique has seen limited use in the blue-collar manufacturing ranks.

JOB INSTRUCTION TRAINING (JIT) Faced with massive training needs during World War II, the federal government developed *Job Instruction Training* to enable supervisors to train their employees quickly and effectively. In essence, JIT is a series of steps for supervisors to follow when training their employees. Because of its simplicity and common sense approach, JIT remains a popular tool for many trainers today.[6] The steps in the JIT system are shown in Figure 9–5.

APPRENTICE TRAINING A combination of on– and off-the-job training, apprentice training is widely used in skilled occupations, such as barbering, carpentry, printing, welding, and plumbing.[7] Apprentice training involves a cooperative partnership among employees, the government, educational institutions (usually vocational or technical schools), and labor unions. The U.S. Department of Labor regulates apprentice training programs and determines the length of apprenticeships and minimum requirements for classroom instruction. Certain conditions of employment and training may also be negotiated with individual unions.

Upon acceptance into an apprenticeship program, apprentices receive on–the-job instruction from an experienced worker called a journeyman, at a wage rate considerably below that of the journeyman. Apprentices also receive formal classroom training during the day or evening and, occasionally, off-the–job instruction through an approved correspondence school. The length of apprenticeships will vary considerably depending on the skills and abilities required. Barbers and cosmeticians may complete their apprenticeship in two years; however, electricians tool and dye makers, or electrical workers may be

---

6. Methods for modernizing the JIT method are discussed in Fred Wickert, "The Famous JIT Card: A Basic Way to Improve It," *Training and Development Journal* (February 1974): 6–9.

7. For a detailed description of apprenticeship training, see U.S. Department of Labor, *Apprenticeship Training* (Washington, DC: U.S. Government Printing Office, 1969).

FIGURE 9-5: *Job Instruction Training (JIT) Methods*

Step 1: Preparation
After putting the learners at ease, find out what they know and do not know about their jobs. Motivate them to learn more about their jobs.

Step 2: Presentation
Convey knowledge and operating skills by telling, showing, and illustrating. Go slowly; be patient. Go over each point individually. Question learners' understanding and repeat if necessary.

Step 3: Performance Tryout
Ask learners to perform the job. Query apprentices about why, how, when, and where. Watch their performances closely. While correcting errors, repeat instructions as often as necessary.

Step 4: Follow-up
Allow learners to work independently, and check back frequently to make sure they can do their jobs correctly. Reduce direct supervision gradually as satisfactory performances are reached.

---

required to serve apprenticeships of four to five years.

ON-THE-JOB TRAINING: THE BALANCE SHEET
The widespread use of on-the-job training is, no doubt, due to the many benefits it offers. Some of the assets of this type of training include:

- The employee is doing the actual work, not hypothetical or simulated tasks.

- The employee receives instructions from an experienced employee or supervisor who has performed the task successfully.

- The training is performed in the actual work environment under normal working conditions and requires no special training facilities.

- The training is informal, relatively inexpensive, and easy to schedule.

- The training may build cooperative relationships between the employee and the trainer.

However, there are potential liabilities to on-the-job training:

- The trainer may not be motivated to train, or to accept the responsibility for training; thus, training may be haphazard.

- The trainer may perform the job well but lack the ability to train others how to do the job well.

- The trainer may not have the time to train and may omit important elements of the training process.

- While the employee is learning on the job, resources will be inefficiently utilized, performance (at least initially) will be low, and costly errors may be made.

OFF-THE-JOB TRAINING
Off-the-job training is any form of training performed away from the employee's work area. Two broad forms of off-the-job training programs exist: in-house programs are coordinated by the employee's organization and conducted within a company training facility. Off-site programs are held away from the organization and sponsored by a professional association, educational institution, or independent training firm.

A wide variety of training methods is employed to train employees off the job; these range from lecturing to using relatively new techniques involving expensive and sophisticated audiovisual techniques.

LECTURE While it remains the most popular technique for providing factual information to many people at the same time, the *lecture* involves one-way communication only. Students will testify that overuse of the lecture method can quickly result in boredom and frustration. Lectures are particularly effective when used sparingly and combined with other training techniques.

CONFERENCE/DISCUSSION Many training programs focus on organizational problems, innovative ideas, and new theories and principles. Discussing problems and critical issues permits a dialogue between the trainer and trainee, and among the trainees. This two-way communication process provides trainees with immediate feedback on their questions and ideas, and heightens motivation for the learner.

AUDIOVISUAL This method employs sight or sound to assist the trainer.[8] Contemporary training techniques such as videotape and closed circuit television are often used, in addition to traditional methods such as chalkboard, films, slides, and flipcharts. *Audiovisual* techniques work best when used with other training methods; the trainer must bear in mind that sophisticated equipment is no substitute for a well-planned training program.

VESTIBULE In a training area created to resemble the employee's actual work area, *vestibule* training is performed with the aid of an instructor who demonstrates on the same kinds of machines and uses processes the trainee will use on the job. Vestibule training has been successfully used for a variety of skilled positions, including retail sales personnel, bank tellers, machine operators, and aircraft pilots.

PROGRAMMED INSTRUCTION This method involves self-instruction without the presence or participation of the trainer.[9] In *programmed instruction*, the material to be learned is presented in text or machine form. Information is broken down and presented to the trainee in small, logical steps. After receiving a small segment of information, the trainee answers a question concerning the material by writing in the text or, if a machine is used, pushing a button on the machine. The trainee is immediately informed if the answer is correct. When the answer is correct, the trainer receives new information. An incorrect answer, however, usually results in the trainee being presented with remedial material.

Programmed instruction offers unique advantages not found in other training methods. Programmed instruction recognizes individual learning differences by allowing each of the trainees to learn at an individual pace. In addition, learning is enhanced through active trainee participation and immediate feedback on responses to questions. Finally, its highly individualized nature offers flexibility in scheduling training by eliminating the need to assemble large groups of trainees at the same time.

---

8. For details regarding the use of video tape in training, see Thomas F. Stroh, *The Uses of Video Tape in Training and Development,* AMA Research *Study 93* (New York: American Management Association, 1969).

9. Effective applications of PI are discussed in John Murphy and Irving Goldberg, "Strategies for Using Programmed Instruction," *Harvard Business Review* (May–June 1964): 115–32.

FIGURE 9-6: *Matching Off-The-Job Training Techniques and Training Situations*

Training Techniques	Training Situations
Lecture	Provides factual information to a large number of people at the same time.
Conference/Discussion	Enables trainees to discuss, question, and debate issues and problems.
Audiovisual	Provides factual material in an organized manner; presents theories and principles and/or organizational problems for discussion; analyzes the dynamics of interpersonal relationships.
Vestibule	Provides training for jobs in which the employee's work environment may be replicated in a classroom setting.
Programmed Instruction	Provides factual information that may be presented in a logical sequence to individual trainees.

A wide assortment of off-the-job training techniques is available, and training personnel often question the relative effectiveness of each. In reality, each technique is effective if properly matched with training objectives. Some of the needs that may be satisfied by specific training techniques are illustrated in Figure 9–6.

OFF-THE-JOB TRAINING: THE BALANCE SHEET Some of the assets of off-the-job training include:

- Cost-efficient training, because groups, rather than individuals, are usually trained.

- Trainers, usually full-time instructors or training personnel, are likely to be more competent trainers than on–the–job trainers, who normally spend only a fraction of their time training.

- More planning and organization often go into this type of training than into on-the-job training.

- Off-the-job training enables the trainee to learn in an environment free from the normal pressures and interruptions of the work place.

- Off-site courses and seminars enable small companies with limited resources to train employees without the formidable expenses of a large training staff and training facilities.

- Exposure to employees of other firms often enables participants to learn about new methods and techniques in addition to the material presented during the prepared program.

Although many benefits of this form of training exist, there are also potential liabilities:

- Employees attending off-the-job training are not performing their jobs. This is an added expense of training, although training benefits should exceed costs in the long run.

- Perhaps the biggest drawback of this type of training is the "transfer of learning" problem. Sometimes off–the-job training is theoretical and of limited practical value to the trainee—particularly when the training is conducted away from the organization. Because it is impossible for the trainer to customize a course for each participant, off-the-job programs normally contain limited applications for a trainee's specific problems and situations.

ON- OR OFF-THE-JOB TRAINING?

Suggesting that either on-the-job or off–the-job training programs will always be the most effective type of training to use is naive. Because each organization has its own unique set of assets and liabilities, the selection should be made after closely examining the organization's specific training environment.[10]

First, training needs and objectives must be considered. If the trainee's job contains relatively uncomplicated tasks and immediate production by the employee is an important objective, such as learning how to run a copy machine or selling encyclopedias door-to-door, then on–the-job training may be preferable. On the other hand, if employees need exposure to new concepts, tools, and techniques, this goal may be best achieved by off-the-job programs.

Second, training resources often play an important role in deciding between on–the-job and off-the-job programs. Managers of organizations which have few or no training resources—facilities, equipment, and qualified on-the-job trainers—often have little choice but to look to off-site programs for training employees.

Third, the money available for training obviously significantly constrains training activities; on-the-job training becomes increasingly attractive as training budgets shrink. Many administrators are simply unable to afford off-the-job training offered by professional associations and pri-

vate training groups, as the cost per participant of a three-day seminar, including travel, food and lodging, and seminar fee may run well over four figures. For the small, financially-strapped organization, on-the-job training and low cost off–the–job programs, such as university and government-sponsored courses are often the only economically feasible training alternatives.

To conclude, many personnel specialists combine both on- and off-the-job training programs to maintain a satisfied, productive work force. Each situation poses a unique challenge to trainers; blending theory and practice through a balance of on- and off-the-job training programs enables trainers to make maximum use of the many resources and technologies available.

Program Implementation

The next phase of training brings the trainer and trainees together so that training may be conducted. This phase also involves careful planning and consideration as the structure and environment of the program will also affect its overall success. To ensure that all necessary arrangements have been made for an off-the-job training program, some organizations use a checklist as an aid in planning the program. The form used by the university of Louisville's Center for Management Development is shown in Figure 9–7.

Training Evaluation

Training evaluation should determine whether trainees actually learned new skills, abilities, or attitudes as a result of the training program. In the eyes of the

---

10. The question of on-the-job training versus off-the-job training is dealt with in William McGehee and Paul Thayer, *Training in Business and Industry* (New York: John Wiley & Sons, 1961): 184–92.

FIGURE 9-7: *Training Checklist*

Seminar: _____ Date(s): _____

Speaker: _____ Time: _____

Speaker: _____ Facility: _____

No. of Participants: _____ Meeting Room: _____

Luncheon Room: _____

Date Ordered: _____

LUNCHEON MENU:

1st day: _____

2nd day: _____

3rd day: _____

COFFEE BREAK TIMES AND MENUS:

Registration: _____

Morning break: _____

Afternoon break: _____

AUDIOVISUAL AIDS FOR SPEAKERS: PHYSICAL SETUP:
_____ Flipchart and Markers   _____ Proper Posting in Lobby
_____ Overhead Projector   _____ Proper Storage for Equipment
_____ 35mm Projector   _____ Proper Lighting
_____ Screen   _____ No Phone Calls
                                                  _____ No Piped-in Music

DIAGRAM OF SEATING ARRANGEMENTS:

MATERIALS FOR PARTICIPANTS:
_____ Name Tags   _____ List of Participants
_____ Pens   _____ Handout Material
_____ Pencils   _____ Textbooks
_____ Notebooks   _____ Evaluation Forms
_____ Filler Paper   _____ Upcoming Seminar Brochures
_____ Legal Pads

ADVERTISEMENTS: CONCLUSION OF MEETING:
  Publications and Dates: Collect:
NEWS RELEASES: _____ Evaluation forms
  Publications and Dates: _____ Excess Materials
  Radio Stations and Dates: _____ Audiovisual Equipment

trainee, training has ended when the trainer and trainee go their separate ways. Upon returning to job duties and responsibilities the employee hopes to perform the job more effectively or, perhaps, to be better prepared for promotional opportunities. When direct involvement in the program has ended, as far as the employee is concerned, training is over! But even though the instruction has ended, the training process has not yet run its full cycle.

One very important question remains: Was the training effective? This often overlooked question involves the fourth and final phase of training—evaluation. Over $100 billion a year are spent nationwide on training activities, and the cost of training to large individual organizations can run into the millions of dollars. With training costs often consuming a sizeable portion of the personnel budget, any prudent manager should ask: Are we getting our money's worth? Any one of three different evaluation strategies may answer this question.

STRATEGY 1—WERE THE TRAINING OBJECTIVES MET?

Most trainers and personnel administrators would agree that training is successful if program objectives are met. Training program development—including the selection of trainers, program types, and training techniques—is largely planned to achieve training objectives. This achievement is the standard by which managers throughout an organization are appraised; the performance of training personnel, too, is often assessed by their track records in creating training that accomplishes its stated objectives.

With this strategy, some programs are much easier to evaluate than others. Gen-erally, if objectives are quantitative and measurable, evaluation will be relatively easy to perform. For example, the training objective "to punch 5,000 computer cards per day with an error rate no higher than 3 percent within one month upon completion of training" may be easily evaluated, as a keypunch operator's output and quality data are quantitative, measurable, and regularly gathered by the organization. On the other hand, the training objective "to increase recruiting skills for all college recruiters" presents problems, as recruiting skills are not easily quantifiable or measurable. In short, the easier it is to measure the human performance that training is designed to strengthen, the easier it is to determine whether or not training objectives were met.

STRATEGY 2—DO TRAINING BENEFITS EXCEED TRAINING COSTS?

Many personnel administrators find the strategy that involves computing the return on the training dollar particularly appealing. In this case, training is an investment that must generate a sufficient return to justify its existence. This approach involves comparing program costs to estimated dollars saved or profits increased through conducting a program.[11] Obviously, a program whose costs exceed benefits would be laid to rest in the training graveyard.

Computing the cost of training is normally a relatively simple matter, determined by adding direct training costs e.g., the fee of a training consultant, rental of equipment, materials, lost trainee productivity, and indirect costs e.g., a portion

11. For a detailed discussion of cost-benefit analysis of training evaluation, see T. Cullen, et al., "Cost Effectiveness: A Model for Assessing the Training Investment," *Training and Development Journal* (January 1978): 24–27.

FIGURE 9–8: *An Example of a Cost-Benefit Training Evaluation*

The following example of cost-benefit evaluation involves training 2,700 management personnel of a large corporation in speedreading techniques. It was estimated that each employee trained would save two hours per day after training, and that each hour would result in a savings of $10 per hour in salaries. Total first year savings were estimated at $8,910,000, resulting in a return of thirty-five times the original investment of $250,895.

Months	SCHEDULE OF SAVINGS AS PROGRAM DEVELOPS		
	Cumulative Number of Graduates	Reading hrs. saved Per month @ 2 hrs. per day	Cumulative Compensation Saved @ $10 per hr.
Jan.	270	11,880	$ 118,800
Feb.	540	23,760	237,600
Mar.	810	35,640	356,400
Apr.	1,080	47,520	475,200
May	1,350	59,400	594,000
Jun.	1,620	71,280	712,800
Jul.	1,890	83,160	831,600
Aug.	2,160	95,040	950,400
Sep.	2,430	106,920	1,069,200
Oct.	2,700	118,800	1,188,000
Nov.	2,700	118,800	1,188,000
Dec.	2,700	118,800	1,188,000
		TOTAL	$8,910,000

DIRECT COSTS OF THE ABC COURSE

Instructors' Training	No charge
Instructors' Travel .... (54 Trainers @ $150)	$ 8,100
Lodging .... (54 Trainers @ $20 per night for 2 nights)	2,160
Per Diem .... (54 Trainers @ $11 per day for 2 days)	1,188
Student Training .... (2700 Trainees @ $20)	54,000
Total Direct Cost	$ 65,448

INDIRECT COSTS OF THE ABC COURSE

Instructors' Training .... (54 Trainers @ $44.60 per day for 2 days)	$ 4,817
Classroom Trainer Cost .... (54 Trainers @ $5.75 per hour for 60 hours)	18,630
Student Training .... (2700 Trainees @ $10 per hour for 6 hours)	162,000
Total Indirect Cost	$185,447
TOTAL DIRECT AND INDIRECT COST	$250,895

SOURCE: Reproduced by special permission from the June 1975, *Training and Development Journal.* Copyright 1975 by the American Society for Training and Development, Inc.

of the personnel department overhead. Estimating the benefits of training is not quite as straightforward. To estimate benefits, the change in trainee performance must be translated into economic terms; performance criteria which are difficult to measure or gather are also difficult to define in dollars and cents. For example, a three-day in-house program entitled "Communication Skills for Personnel Interviewers" for twenty staff employees may be estimated to cost $2,750, including a consultant's fee, materials, rental of audiovisual equipment, lost productivity, and overhead. Yet, measuring the change in communication skills as a result of training and placing a dollar value on that change would involve extremely subjective and highly debatable estimates. As with the first evaluation strategy, this method of training evaluation gains appeal wherever performance criteria are measurable and translated into financial terms with little difficulty. An example of this evaluation method is shown in Figure 9–8.

STRATEGY 3—LEVELS OF EVALUATION
This strategy has four different levels of evaluation, and in fact, comprises four separate evaluation strategies. However, the designer of this system, D. L. Kirkpatrick, advocates applying each level of evaluation to a program.[12] He suggests measuring the participants' reaction, participants' learning, change in participants' behavior, and results of the program upon organizational effectiveness.
LEVEL 1—HOW DID PARTICIPANTS REACT TO THE PROGRAM? Throughout training, each

trainee formulates opinions and attitudes about the overall effectiveness of the program. Perhaps the trainee is favorably inclined toward the content of the program but feels that the trainer is too cold or too impersonal. Or, the trainee may like the instructor but feels the program is too long or, perhaps, too short. Probably some aspects of the program will be both liked and disliked by the participants. At this level of evaluation, the trainee normally completes a questionnaire regarding the adequacy of training facilities, the skill of the trainer, the quality of the program content, and relevancy of training techniques. After the questionnaires are tabulated and reviewed, the program quality is judged on the basis of the overall responses. This level of evaluation is, of course, highly subjective, and training administrators must ensure that the participants are not responding favorably simply because they enjoyed the program or instruction. Figure 9–9 is a questionnaire used for evaluating training programs offered through the University of Louisville's Center for Management Development.

LEVEL 2—WHAT DID THE PARTICIPANTS LEARN? Training is an educational experience. Without exception, each participant is expected to learn some skill, knowledge, or ability. This level of evaluation examines the extent of learning that took place as a result of training, and involves more effort and sophistication than simply measuring the participants' reaction to training.

Participant learning is often assessed by testing a trainee both before and after a program. For example, if a program is designed to teach BASIC (a popular computer language), the trainee would be expected to score significantly higher on

12. Donald L. Kirkpatrick, "Techniques for Evaluating Training Programs," Journal for the American Society of Training Directors 13, 14 (1969–70): 1–17.

FIGURE 9–9: *Seminar Evaluation Form*

Your candor and feedback will be of great value to our program planning.

	Very Little	Some	Quite A Bit	A Great Deal
1. To what extent did this seminar present material that met my needs?	1	2	3	4

Comments: _____

_____

2. To what extent were the handouts and reference materials appropriate for this program?	1	2	3	4

Comments: _____

_____

3. To what extent did the seminar leader:

a. present the material in an organized manner;	1	2	3	4
b. present important content;	1	2	3	4
c. solicit questions from the group;	1	2	3	4
d. make the seminar interesting;	1	2	3	4
e. provide a forum for group discussion?	1	2	3	4

Comments: _____

_____

_____

4. How can this seminar be improved? _____

_____

_____

5. In the future, I would like to see the Center for Management Development offer the following seminars and workshops:

_____

_____

_____

Signed (optional)

SOURCE: Center for Management Development, University of Louisville. Used with permission.

the test after completion of training than before training. This level of training evaluation is easily conducted if tests are readily available to measure learning; however, the absence of valid tests makes this level of evaluation difficult to administer. In addition, creating a test to accurately measure many human behavioral skills and abilities, such as communication skills, interpersonal relations, and leadership skills, is difficult.

LEVEL 3—HOW DID THE PARTICIPANT'S BEHAV-

IOR CHANGE? Not only are participants expected to learn a skill, knowledge, ability, or attitude through training, but trainers and managers expect learning to result in a positive change in job behavior. Learning time management techniques, for example, is purely an academic—and costly—exercise unless the participant's behavior changes on the job as learning is applied. The important question to ask concerning this level of evaluation is whether learning transferred from training to job.

LEVEL 4—WHAT RESULTS, IN TERMS OF ORGANIZATIONAL OBJECTIVES, WERE EFFECTED BY TRAINING? Ultimately, training is expected to result in a more effective organization. The fourth level of evaluation examines the impact of training upon organizational objectives regarding productivity, quality, and job satisfaction and decreased turnover, accidents, and grievances.

While training program evaluation is appealing in theoretical and practical terms, it is not always possible or relevant to do so. Where it is difficult to relate acquired skills directly to organizational objectives the training administrator must implement a less sophisticated evaluation strategy, such as the measurement of learning or behavior change that resulted from training.

Training effectiveness can be evaluated by the simple and uncomplicated process of measuring participants' reactions or by sophisticated, time-consuming strategies which compare training costs and benefits, and measure organizational results. Flexibility should be the key to evaluating training programs; training personnel should apply the most sophisticated strategy that is relevant and economically feasible. Combining the four levels of training evaluation with a cost-benefit strategy would certainly enable management to ascertain whether or not a program was contributing to the effectiveness of the organization, but this approach would involve considerable time and money. Minimally, measurable objectives should be written during the training needs assessment phase and evaluated after training has been completed. If the costs and benefits of training may be estimated with little difficulty, a cost/benefit analysis should be undertaken in addition to other strategies that may be implemented.

EFFECTIVE TRAINING

As we indicated earlier in this chapter, training is a form of education. Whether training takes place on- or off-the-job, employees are expected to learn and apply new skills and abilities to benefit both the organization and its employees. Because training and learning processes are closely interwoven, trainers can benefit from applying certain learning principles when designing and implementing training programs.[13] Since neglect or misapplication of learning principles could easily result in training that fails to achieve results, some principles of learning are summarized here:

Motivation

Sometimes the need for training is not clear to employees, who may consider training a waste of time and resist being

---

13. The relationship between training and learning principles is described in Craig E. Schneier, "Training and Development Programs: What Learning Theory and Research Have to Offer," *Personnel Journal* (April 1974): 288–300. See also Lee Hess and Len Sperry, "The Psychology of the Trainee as Learner," *Personnel Journal* (September 1973): 781.

taken away from their jobs. One effective way to motivate trainees is to show employees how training will help accomplish organizational and/or personal goals. These goals may include improved job performance, the assumption of greater responsibility, and increased opportunities for promotion. Trainers should not automatically assume all employees want to be trained, and training personnel must make prospective trainees aware of how they will benefit from training.

Participation

A second area of motivation concerns the trainees' active participation in the training process. While direct involvement is an integral part of on-the-job training, classroom training sometimes fails to include this important principle of learning. The lecture method is certainly a valuable training technique, but reliance on lecturing alone will result in training boredom and apathy—with little learning taking place. Active participation in the learning process through conferences, discussion, role-playing, and case studies, enables trainees to become directly involved in the act of learning.

Feedback

Many college students like to know at all times where they stand in their courses; professors sometimes joke that students often demand test results before the ink has dried. Feedback on progress in courses reduces anxiety and lets students know what they must do to improve.

In a similar vein, employees taking part in a training program want to know how they are doing and how their progress compares to training objectives. Giving the employee *training feedback* is usually an informal part of on-the-job training; close communication between the trainer and trainee facilitates the feedback process. Feedback in short courses and seminars is usually less frequent and normally centers around informal comments by the instructor, or the results of tests taken during the program.

Organization

Like a college classroom, organized training programs facilitate learning. Training must be presented so that segments of materials build on one another; gaps, contradictions, or ambiguities in the material must be avoided. For example, in organizing a course about the operation and maintenance of a large printing press, the safety precautions that must be taken when operating the machine would be presented first. Next, the major parts of the machine and the functions of each would be explained. Then a competent operator would be observed running the machine, followed by hands-on experience with several uncomplicated tasks, and later more difficult tasks. The final portion of training may involve preventive maintenance and minor repairs. In this example, each part of training flowed into another without inconsistencies or gaps in the training content.

Repetition

A wealth of behavioral research shows that frequent practice during training facilitates the learning process. Practice is important whether the skills being learned are technical (e.g., operating a lathe, computer, or typewriter) or behavioral (e.g., communication, or interpersonal skills). Integrating practice sessions into technical training is relatively easy, but practicing interpersonal skills presents challenges to the trainer. Frequently, role-playing techniques are used to practice behavioral and interpersonal skills.

Application

Time and time again graduates complain "the real world is different than school. I can't apply the theories I learned in class." Similarly, organizational training is useless unless learning can be applied on the job. This *transfer of learning* problem is particularly troublesome in off-the-job instruction where the training and the trainee's job environments may differ considerably. The problem is less severe for technical training (especially with the vestibule technique), as the technology used on the job should be identical to that used during training.

Minimizing transfer of learning prob-

FIGURE 9–10: *Extent to Which Training Techniques Utilize Certain Principles of Learning*

	Motivation: Active Participation of Learner	Reinforcement: Feedback of Knowledge of Results	Stimulus: Meaningful Organization of Materials	Responses: Practice and Repetition	Stimulus-Response Conditions Most Favorable for Transfer
On-the-Job Techniques					
Job-Instruction Training	Yes	Sometimes	Yes	Yes	Yes
Apprentice Training	Yes	Sometimes	?	Sometimes	Yes
Internships and Assistantships	Yes	Sometimes	?	Sometimes	Yes
Job Rotation	Yes	No	?	Sometimes	Yes
Junior Board	Yes	Sometimes	Sometimes	Sometimes	Yes
Coaching	Yes	Yes	Sometimes	Sometimes	Yes
Off-the-Job Techniques					
Vestibule	Yes	Sometimes	Yes	Yes	Sometimes
Lecture	No	No	Yes	No	No
Special Study	Yes	No	Yes	?	No
Films	No	No	Yes	No	No
Television	No	No	Yes	No	No
Conference or Discussion	Yes	Sometimes	Sometimes	Sometimes	No
Case Study	Yes	Sometimes	Sometimes	Sometimes	Sometimes
Role Playing	Yes	Sometimes	No	Sometimes	Sometimes
Simulation	Yes	Sometimes	Sometimes	Sometimes	Sometimes
Programmed Instruction	Yes	Yes	Yes	Yes	No
Laboratory Training	Yes	Yes	No	Yes	Sometimes
Programmed Group Exercises	Yes	Yes	Yes	Sometimes	Sometimes

From *Training in Industry: The Management of Learning*, by B. M. Bass and J. A. Vaughn. Copyright © 1966 by Wadsworth, Inc. Reprinted by permission of the publisher, Brooks/Cole Publishing Company, Monterey, California.

lems poses a real challenge to trainers. The trainer must study the job environment of prospective trainees and create settings that resemble each trainee's own job environment as much as possible. When constructing the training environment consideration must be given to both physical and human factors, such as the physical setting, the technology of the work, intergroup and interpersonal relationships, and supervisory behavioral styles.

Training Techniques

Some of the training techniques discussed earlier effectively utilize the principles of learning. Training administrators should attempt to match training techniques and learning principles when designing training programs. Figure 9-10, by Bernard Bass and James Vaughn, illustrates how important principles of learn

ing may be utilized by various on- and off-the-job training techniques.

TRAINING === RESPONSIBILITIES ===

Like many staff functions, training is a joint venture between line management and staff administrators. Effective training requires that line and staff are able to work closely together on all phases of the training process, and that both parties understand and recognize their intertwined scopes of their authority and responsibility. Trainers or line managers unwilling to approach the training process in a cooperative manner find that training does not facilitate goal achievement in their organizations. While the responsibility for various functions of training will differ from organization to organization, certain responsibilities are usually reserved for line managers and staff person-

FIGURE 9–11: *Line and Staff Responsibilities in a Training Process*

Training Phases	Training Personnel's Role	Line Management's Role
Phase 1—Analyzing needs and setting objectives	Conduct actual needs analysis; design tools that may be used to survey needs; determine personnel who need training; write training objectives.	Supply training personnel with necessary performance data; review and approve needs analysis and training objectives.
Phase 2—Designing the program	Determine the type of program and training techniques.	Review and approve training program and techniques.
Phase 3—Implementing the program	Conduct and/or coordinate training.	If applicable, perform on-the-job training (or supervise on-the-job training if conducted by a nonsupervisory employee)
Phase 4—Evaluating the program	Perform the evaluation; present findings to line management.	Supply trainer with necessary performance data; review evaluation results.

nel. Figure 9-11 illustrates some of the training activities and responsibilities normally carried out by line and staff.

Like most staff activities, the structure of the training function is determined largely by the number of employees the function must serve. Depending on the size of the organization, the training function may be undertaken by a single individual or divided among several training administrators.

Small Organizations

The personnel manager of the smaller organization is a jack-of-all-trades, performing a wide variety of personnel functions including recruiting, interviewing, selecting, counseling, wage and salary administration, maintaining labor relations, and training. Rather than assume a major role in conducting training, however, this personnel manager will normally coordinate instruction with other training resources, such as supervisors and other on-the-job trainers, training consultants, association groups, and local educational institutions. The personnel manager may work closely with line management to determine training needs and the most appropriate methods, to schedule training, and to evaluate the results.

Medium-Sized Organizations

As the organization grows, the job of training usually becomes too demanding for one individual on a part-time basis. In medium-sized organizations, a director of training or director of employee training and management development (who usually reports to the personnel manager) is given full responsibility for the training

function. Occasionally the training director may actually conduct training in addition to carrying out the other phases of the training process. Typically though, the training director will look toward internal and external resources for the lion's share of training programs.

Large Organizations

The demand for training in large organizations is so great that several full-time professionals coordinate and conduct training programs for management and nonmanagement personnel. Their responsibilities include the entire four-phase training process; most training is conducted in-house. In very large multi-division organizations, this type of structure may exist within each major plant or division, with overall organizational training goals and policies set at the corporate training department.

In summary, through training employees gain skills, abilities, knowledge, and attitudes that help them perform more effectively in their present and future jobs. As such, training may be considered an investment in human resources that will benefit the organization. To a large degree, the organization of training depends upon the size of the company. In small companies, the personnel manager often coordinates the training process, normally calling upon on-the-job trainers and external resources to conduct most training. In medium-sized organizations, a full-time training administrator may conduct some training, although frequently other internal and external resources will implement programs. In large organizations, several full-time professionals may administer training programs; where there are several large divisions or subsidiaries, major training policies are written at corporate headquarters and implemented in a consistent manner throughout the operating units. Regardless of the organization's size, training involves a close cooperation between line and staff personnel. Normally training personnel will design and conduct a training needs analysis, write training objectives, recommend employees for training, suggest program types and training techniques, conduct training, evaluate, and present the findings to line management. Line managers will supply trainers with employee performance information, review and approve the training needs analysis, training objectives, and training design, conduct on-the-job training, and review and approve the results of training evaluation.

The Solution:

A brief look at John Merritt's job at the Georgia Trust Bank illustrates the kinds of problems that many training administrators face today. Let's look a little more closely at John Merritt's week, his problems, and what might be done to effectively solve these problems.

1. *Training computer programmers. Merritt must now begin working closely with Marcia Moore, head of the computer services division, to determine specifically what skills and abilities the programmers currently possess and those which are necessary to successfully write the COBOL language. As our training process model indicates, it is critical to accurately assess needs before training begins. Not until this is accomplished can Merritt meet with National Business Machines to set up a program.*

2. *Training marginal keypunch operators. It might seem pretty obvious that Merritt's program for marginal performers would simply involve instruction on how to more effectively use the machines. But John must first consider if the marginal performers can improve their*

performance through training. Because selection decisions may have hastily been made, it is quite possible that employees who lack the basic aptitudes for keypunch work were hired. Should this be the case, training will not solve the performance problems. In addition, Tom Lewis, head of keypunch services, noted in his letter that some of the low performers were "causing me some real problems." Merritt must find out specifically what these problems are to help him determine what kind of training is necessary.

3. *Equal employment opportunity training.* In this particular training situation, Merritt must carefully assess training needs and determine the specific problems facing each branch bank. It is very likely that training needs may vary somewhat from branch to branch. In previous chapters, we have seen that EEO legislation affects a wide range of selection activities including recruiting, selection, testing, and interviewing. An in-depth needs analysis may show that a program must be tailor-made for each branch bank. Also, Merritt should not begin to tackle this training problem with the firm notion that the program may be solved in a one-day seminar. Possibly, the seriousness of the problem may require a lengthier off-the-job program, perhaps to be followed up with on-the-job training.

4. *Training for career advancement.* Many good employees quit because they feel the organization is not adequately preparing them for promotion. Trainers must be aware of this fact and design programs that not only help people perform their present jobs better but also help them acquire skills and abilities that will help them get promoted. To do this, trainers must work closely with managers to (1) determine which employees are

promotable, (2) determine what specific skills and abilities they will need to successfully perform their jobs when they get promoted, and (3) determine what kinds of programs (i.e., on-the-job, and/or off-the-job) will most effectively enable employees to acquire new skills and abilities. Trainers must also be familiar with the theories, principles, issues, and problems that center around the career development function.

5. Orientation program. Merritt has recognized that "standing" training programs such as orientation must continually be scrutinized to ensure that they have not become outdated and that the program includes all topics that are important to the new employee. Oftentimes, administrators look upon orientation as simply a time—consuming exercise which reaps few returns. But as we have suggested in this chapter, good orientation can help build employee morale, reduce employee anxiety, and save a great deal of the supervisor's time. Like any training program, trainers must diligently assess orientation needs, select and use effective training techniques for orientation, and periodically assess the effectiveness of their orientation programs.

KEY TERMS AND CONCEPTS

Employee Orientation Program
Training Process Model
Training Objectives
On-the-job Training
Job Rotation
Job Instruction Training (JIT)
Apprentice Training
Off-the-job Training
Lecture

Conference/Discussion
Audiovisual Methods
Vestibule
Programmed Instruction
Training Evaluation
Training Feedback
Transfer of Learning

FOR REVIEW

1. What is training?
2. What are the major purposes of training?
3. Of what value is a strong employee orientation program?
4. What are the phases involved in the training process model?
5. Describe the activities involved in each phase of the training process model.
6. Distinguish between on- and off-the-job training techniques and describe the advantages and disadvantages of each type.
7. Describe three strategies for evaluating training effectiveness.
8. Distinguish between line and staff responsibilities in regard to carrying out the training function.
9. Describe the principles of learning as they apply to the training function.
10. Describe the management principles that are important to the training function.

FOR DISCUSSION

1. Below are several training situations and potential training methods. How would you match them?

   A. Train 50 new employees to run a small printing press.

   B. Train 20 personnel administrators on the federal legislation as it applies to equal employment opportunity hiring, firing, promotions, and training.

   C. Train one new receptionist how to run a copy machine, automatic collating machine, and the proper techniques for handling incoming calls.

   D. Train six personnel interviewers on the techniques of employee interviewing.

   E. Outside university sponsored seminar.

   F. On-the-job instruction.

   G. Apprentice training.

   H. Vestibule training.

   I. Programmed instruction.

   J. Lecture, discussion.

2. Do you believe the principles of learning are effectively applied by professors in college and university classrooms? Which principles are most effectively applied? Least effectively?

3. "Training is not a luxury. It is a critical human resource process that has a major impact on organizational goals." Comment.

4. If you were a newly appointed training director for a manufacturing company with 750 employees, how would you communicate the importance of the training function to top management?

5. Some managers feel that the training function is more important in some organizations than others. For example, it could be argued that training is more important in a computer components manufacturing firm than for a corrugated box manufacturer employing approximately the same number of employees. Do you agree? Why, or why not?

6. Prepare an orientation program for pledges selected by a fraternity or a sorority. What should be covered?

7. Often, college and university faculty are evaluated by means of student opinion questionnaires upon completion of the course. What are the advantages and disadvantages of this type of evaluation procedure?

8. Think of a simple task that can be performed in the classroom such as building a paper airplane. Using the job instruction technique, list the steps involved and train a classmate to perform the task. Ask for feedback from the trainee concerning your effectiveness as a trainer. Switch roles with your classmate who becomes the trainer, as you become the trainee.

SUPPLEMENTARY READING

Bass, Bernard, and Vaughn, James. *Training in Industry: The Management of Learning.* Belmont, CA: Wadsworth Publishing Co., 1969.

Goldstein, Irvin. *Training: Program Development and Evaluation.* Monterey, CA: Brooks/Cole Publishing Co., 1974.

Hendricks, John. "Personnel Training." In Dunnette, Marvin, ed., *Handbook of Industrial and Organizational Psychology.* Chicago: Rand McNally & Co., 1976.

Mirsberger, Gerald. "The Four Crucial Phases of Evaluation." *Training,* August 1974, pp. 34–35.

Newell, Gale. "How to Plan a Training Program." *Personnel Journal,* May 1976, pp. 220–25.

Odiorne, George. *Training By Objectives.* New York: MacMillan Publishing Co., 1970.

Otto, Calvin, and Colaser, Rollin. *The Management of Training.* Reading, MA: Addison-Wesley Publishing Co., 1970.

Quick, Thomas. "Putting Responsibility for Training Where it Belongs." *Personnel,* March–April 1975, pp. 45–51.

Salinger, R. D. "Why Training Fails." *Training,* February 1975, pp. 28–33.

Schneier, Craig. "Training and Development Programs: What Learning Theory and Research Have to Offer." *Personnel Journal,* April 1974, pp. 288–300.

Skjervhiem, Terry. "Training: Evolution of a Profession." *The Personnel Administrator,* October 1977, pp. 13–17.

Stumm, D. A. "On-The-Job Training: Make Learning Theory Work for You." *Supervisory Management* 18 (January 12, 1973): 7.

Tracey, William. *Designing Training and Development Systems.* New York: American Management Association, 1971.

Traynor, W. J. "Evaluate Your Training and Development Manager." *The Personnel Administrator,* October 1977, p. 13+.

For Analysis: Mayflower Manufacturing Corporation

Jim Greely is personnel manager for the Mayflower Manufacturing Corporation, a small manufacturer of gas heating equipment and fireplace fixtures. Located in Jeffersonville, Indiana, Mayflower employs about one hundred fifty people. The industry is very competitive, and Mayflower management strives to keep costs at a minimum.

During the past several months, the firm lost three major customers because of defective products. Further investigation found that defects were running at 12 percent as compared to an overall plant standard of 6 percent. In discussions with Vice–President and General Manager Tim Metcalf, Greely decided that the problem was not in engineering, but in a lack of proper training in quality control for machine operators. Greely convinced Metcalf that a training program in quality control would reduce manufacturing defects to acceptable levels and received Metcalf's approval to design and implement a program for operators. As Metcalf was concerned that the course might cause production scheduling problems, Greely emphasized that the training program would consume no more than eight working hours and would be broken into four two-hour segments, with one segment held every week.

Greely began designing, the course; first he assessed training needs and created training objectives. Greely contacted James Farrell, an engineering professor from a nearby state university, about conducting the project. Highly regarded as an expert on quality control, Professor Farrell had written a widely-used text. Farrell gave Greely a brief outline of the course in which he included factors affecting product quality, production standards, inspection techniques, and safety procedures.

Next, Greely sent a memo to all first-line supervisors urging them to review their records, determine which employees had quality problems, and schedule these employees for the program. A copy of the professor's course outline was attached to the memo. As a final design step, Greely wrote the following training objective for the program, "to reduce the current levels of product defects to standard plant levels of 6 percent within a six-month period.

Farrell's training program consisted mainly of lectures, discussions, case studies, and an occasional film. In preparing for the course, the professor drew heavily from his text which was given to each participant, so that chapters could be assigned to prepare trainees for each session. Trainees spent a considerable portion of the training program discussing the questions and cases following the chapters in the text.

Because of a lack of space, the training sessions were held in the company's cafeteria. The training was scheduled to take place between breakfast and lunch, while cafeteria personnel were preparing the luncheon meal and washing breakfast dishes.

About fifty employees were expected to attend each session, but average attendance was closer to thirty. In checking, Greely heard many supervisors state, "If I let everybody go who's supposed to attend, I won't make my quota this week. Then I'll really be in hot water. Sorry, but production comes first." Greely also heard comments from some of the trainees that, "the employees who really need to be here are still back in the shop."

Greely decided that the best way to evaluate the course would be to determine if the training objective was met by closely observing the product defects after the training program. The resulting chart of monthly trends for total product defects before and after the program was not encouraging.

Upon reviewing the evaluation data, Greely was dismayed and frustrated that the program failed to achieve results. Six months after the program, defects were still running well above standard—almost as high as before the program was implemented. The pressure on Greely was really mounting— he was not looking forward to meeting with Metcalf to review the results of the training evaluation.

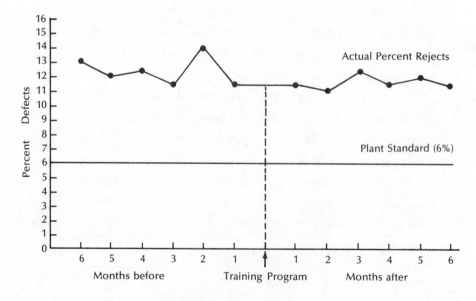

Questions:

1. *What are the flaws in the design of Greely's training program? What are the problems involved with each phase of the training process?*

2. *How would you assess training needs?*

3. *Would you write training objectives any differently?*

4. *Would you consider training methods and techniques other than those used by Farrell?*

5. *Would you make any changes in your training evaluation strategy?*

6. *Are problems in quality control always solvable by employee training? Discuss.*

═══ SELECTED PROFESSIONAL READING ═══

Changing Demands on the Training Professional

RONALD W. CLEMENT
JAMES W. WALKER
PATRICK R. PINTO

"How has your organization's training and development activity changed during the past five years?"

"In what way is your job changing?"

"What is the most important skill or knowledge requirement for success as a training and development professional?"

"What is the most important behavioral requirement?"

"What new requirements do you feel are emerging as important?"

These questions were asked of members of the American Society for Training and Development (ASTD) in a survey conducted in 1978. They were part of a study commissioned by ASTD's Professional Development Committee to determine the competencies required for effective performance in training and development. Other reports have presented the primary results of this study.[1] This article reports findings of the study relating to the five open-ended questions shown above.

Usable responses were received from 2,790 members of ASTD, 74 percent of whom were training and development practitioners. The balance of the respondents included academicians, personnel generalists, consultants, vendors, and others. This article focuses upon the content analysis of narrative comments provided by these respondents. Major categories were identified, and the frequency of responses in each was tabulated. The results provide a heuristic value in pointing out trends and development needs perceived by those in this changing profession.

ACTIVITIES HAVE CHANGED

First, most respondents indicated their organizations' training and development activities expanded in the past five years. Fifty-five percent of respondents offered remarks indicating expansion of their activity, e.g.:

"Expanded in terms of breadth and depth of services provided."

"More emphasis on long-range development, less on pure training."

"Expanded—we have developed a career–counseling service."

"Expansion of Organization Development, minority development and increased emphasis on upper-management development."

"We have expanded our function to include manpower planning and Organization Development."

Additionally, some members indicated that new facilities and expanded budgets had been obtained. "We have noted that industry is much more aware of the necessity for training. . . . We have a new 26,000 square-foot training institute in our operation to meet our needs," reported one respondent.

Many trainers said their organization's activities had become more professional over the years. This was meant to include the establishment of formal in-house capabilities, addition of more competent staff, better planning and organization of activities, and increased emphasis on the measurement of performance in the organization, e.g.:

"Training and development was ad hoc in the past; we now have skills training and are moving into management programs."

"We have well-trained staff rather than rejects from other functions."

The structure of training and development functions has also changed. Some organizations have become more decentralized, while others have become more centralized. Some larger organizations have established regional training and development functions, appar-

ently to accommodate expanded activities. In others, the more basic training is decentralized while the more advanced, specialized training is centralized. As respondents noted:

"We tend to centralize our subject-matter expertise."

"We have become the focal point for all training and development in the company, to prevent duplication of effort."

"Policy is made at corporate level and adjusted to suit local needs."

Thus there are dual tensions: toward decentralization to place training where the needs are, and toward centralization to provide consistency, specialization, and efficiency.

SHIFTING JOB EMPHASIS

Nearly one third of the respondents said they are spending more and more time on management activities such as planning, delegation and administration. Less time is spent in traditional training-related functions such as designing, conducting, and evaluating training programs. As one member noted, "I am becoming more an administrator of people rather than programs." "We have less emphasis on goal-setting and supervision." This pattern is probably related to the expansion of training and development activities, creating a need for more administrative activity. As this shift occurs, ". . . our jobs are requiring managerial abilities, not technical knowledge and skills; but we try to keep abreast of training developments without being swamped with details."

Many individuals reported they are spending more time on organization development activities, program development and evaluation activities, and internal consulting activities, e.g.:

"We will become less involved with specific programs and more concerned with broader organizational needs."

"More emphasis on team and inter-team workshops and follow-up."

"We're doing a better job in measuring the effectiveness of our contribution to the organization."

"More a designer/provider of training tools for others to use; devoting more time to development of audiovisuals and preparation of course materials for others."

"If the present trend continues, my job will be more consulting than training."

Expansion of training and development activities appears to be in the direction of these nontraditional activities. Increasingly, training professionals see themselves more in the role of helping others to design, conduct, and evaluate programs rather than as actual performers of training.

IMPORTANT SKILLS AND KNOWLEDGE

Human relations and communications skills were predominantly mentioned as being important for success as a training and development professional. Most respondents focus on the ability to relate, persuade or influence—typical "people skills" considered important, e.g.:

"People skills—must be able to relate and develop a mutual trust."

"Careful handling of managers and their prerogatives."

"Being able to manage interpersonal relationships."

"Ability to communicate on a one-to-one basis; communicate ideas to management."

"An ability to make good presentations to groups of people."

Thus, skills in dealing with individuals on a personal basis as well as more formal presentation and communications skills are seen as important.

Some respondents said that knowledge of the training and development field was the most important knowledge requirement, e.g.:

"Maintaining professional competency—constantly read and be aware of new innovations in the field."

"Know instructional technology (Mager, et al)."

Knowledge of new technology for training and development is considered important, but also knowledge of how adults learn. Typical responses were:

"Understanding the adult learner."

"A knowledge of the learning process itself."

Analytical skills were reported most important to 203 members, including skills in "analyzing performance deficiencies—finding real problems" and "diagnostic skills—to determine appropriate directions for training." Emphasis was on skills in front-end analysis, rather than in assessing training outcomes, e.g., ". . . how to evaluate a particular problem by compiling data to determine whether the problem may be solved through training, and if so, how?"

Management skills and knowledge of the organization were also rated as most important by some. Comments on management skills included:

"The ability to manage and organize people."

"A working knowledge of management skills—to manage performance, learning, people."

Knowledge of the organization helps build management skills and aids analysis of training needs, e.g., ". . . ability to identify corporate goals; anticipate training needs and not react to performance problems; must have a good overall knowledge of the company."[1]

IMPORTANT BEHAVIORAL REQUIREMENTS

The more specific question was also asked, "What is the most important behavioral requirement for success as a T&D professional?" Many said that the most important attribute is credibility for getting results accomplished. By this, they meant that clients must trust the professional's ability to develop

1. Patrick R. Pinto and James W. Walker, "What Do Training and Development Professionals Really Do?" *Training and Development Journal* (July 1978), 58–64. Also see the complete study report, *A Study of Professional Training and Development Roles and Competencies* (Madison: ASTD, 1978). Additional research based on the study is presented in Ronald W. Clement, Patrick R. Pinto, and James W. Walker, "Unethical and Improper Behavior by Training and Development Professionals," *Training and Development Journal* (December 1978), 10–12.

effective programs. Trainers must also be open and honest regarding problems that cannot be solved by training. Credibility also means that the professional should protect personal confidences which arise from having an open relationship with clients.

Credibility among middle-level managers is seen as the key to obtaining support from senior management, and thus obtaining needed resources. It was felt that credibility is preferred over "ability to sell management," e.g.:

"I find many training people intelligent but 'running scared' as if under the gun of a VP bent on cost reduction or some other evaluation. Thus they spend an excessive amount of time collecting statistics to prove the value of their work and themselves."

"There is the feeling that many individuals and organizations are becoming hucksters for training. Selling training for the sake of training—the fast sell. As in other professions, the problem of integrity looms large."

"I feel the trainers have brought this situation upon themselves since we have far too often complicated the training process and in many cases have made promises to management that are impossible to keep. I also feel we sell media to management and not the basic fact that people teach people. There is no magic."

"One of the areas important to our continued success is maintaining and building credibility in the eyes of top management. Too often our functions are buried under 'personnel' and therefore are not used fully."

Flexibility was also widely mentioned as an important behavioral quality, e.g.:

"Openmindedness when it comes to creating a program to fill a need. The need to get closer to the actual operations rather than apply a standard training program which may not be right for the situation. Too many training people have an attitude of aloofness and rigidity."

The respondents suggested that because "training involves different situations, differ-

ent personalities, different cultures, and because new developments are constantly changing the field," the professional must have the ability to "think fast on his or her feet and maintain a calm demeanor under pressure."

Empathy was considered important— ". . . caring a great deal about developing people to their fullest potential and communicating this caring quality." This involves a willingness to listen and to understand needs of clients or training participants:

"I have felt strongly that many professional trainers are too 'ivory towerish.' Those on my staff have advanced degrees, yet they work hard to not talk down to any training participant."

Creativity in developing programs was seen as important, as well. As more professionals spend more time in program development, emphasis is being given to "being creative in planning of training programs," and "creativity for developing ways to change the organization—inventiveness."

EMERGING FUTURE REQUIREMENTS

What new requirements are emerging as important for the training and development professional? Increased technical awareness and increased behavioral science knowledge were cited as the two most important emerging requirements.

"Increased technical awareness" means staying abreast of the rapid changes in training and development technology, particularly the advancements in computer technology and audiovisuals. The concern is not only to stay abreast of developments, but to resist "leaping forward to some new approaches as a panacea for our problems."

"Behavioral science knowledge" relates not only to professional competence in human relations, but also to the broader capacity to apply behavioral science research and training. The respondents would like to be able to teach the latest developments in behavioral science to participants in training (particularly supervisors and managers), and also to understand their applications.

More effective assessment of needs is continuing to be an important concern. "We need to look at jobs and at people, and to be more selective about applying training as a solution to problems." Emphasis on job-related objectives for training will require new and stronger tools in this area.

"Emphasis on criterion-based, performance-oriented instructional systems with attendant emphasis on job analysis and development of training objectives will include definitions of expectations of both the trainees and the trainers."

Knowledge of governmental regulations will become increasingly important, as well. Respondents were concerned with two broad categories of governmental regulations: those which affect personnel practices of T&D managers (e.g., tax legislation affecting educational aid), and those which affect the personnel practices of the organization as a whole (e.g., ERISA, OSHA, EEO). As professionals responsible for the education of managers, awareness of relevant governmental regulations is considered a responsibility in training and development.

CONCLUSION

This study of narrative comments by more than two thousand ASTD members indicates that the tasks and the associated competencies expected of the training and development professional are changing. Major trends identified in the responses are:

1. Expansion of the training and development activity in terms of programs provided and the clients served. Such services as career counseling and broader organizational development were noted.

2. An increasing proportion of time devoted to managerial and administrative activities, as opposed to more traditional training and

development activities. Included in this trend is increased attention to needs analysis and training evaluation.

3. Increasing importance placed on human relations and communications skills. These are necessary in the identification of training and development needs and maintaining good relations with client managers. As a result, the credibility of training and development professionals is also viewed as critically important to their success.

4. Increased awareness of new technology and increased knowledge in behavioral science are important to assure quality programs which achieve the desired results. Further, it will be increasingly necessary for the effective T&D professional to keep abreast of legal, technical, and research developments going on around them.

In summary, demands are being imposed on training and development professionals to manage their activities and their own personal development effectively, with emphasis on the consultative roles: needs analysis and diagnosis, determining appropriate training approaches, managing working relationships with managers and clients, and managing the training and development function itself.

These, we believe, are positive signs of a maturing profession—a dynamic profession where career-oriented individuals are aware of changes occurring in their management environment and are acting to influence the effects of these changes in a meaningful and practical way. As one respondent noted:

"The training and development practitioner has a very real opportunity. It is not an elusive dream, but it may very well slip away from us unless we begin to listen to what we are saying and how we are viewed by our clients. We are vulnerable in economic downturns and probably for good reasons. Measured against the contributions of other functions we probably deserve our 'first to go' status. Our success lies in a more critical challenge of our own tools and approaches."

Role playing can reveal which employees have management potential.

10

MANAGEMENT DEVELOPMENT

Managerial Skills

Management Development Programs

Women Managers

Successful Management Development

The Problem: Management Development at Cabinet Craft

Sam Rodriguez left the meeting with Rita Borden, personnel manager, in a state of mild euphoria. He had just been promoted to the newly-created position of director of management development for Cabinet Craft Manufacturing Company, a medium-sized manufacturer of quality kitchen cabinets in Perth Amboy, New Jersey. With a labor force of 1,620 employees, including 125 managerial and staff personnel, Borden felt Cabinet Craft's present size and optimistic plans for future growth justified the creation of a position to develop the company's existing and future managerial personnel. The president of Cabinet Craft agreed that such a position was necessary, and Borden had little trouble getting budget monies to pay the director's salary and operating expenses.

Before his promotion, Rodriguez was an assistant to John Stalworth, director of employee training. His duties centered around the coordination of skills training programs for the operative employee groups. He worked with trainers both inside and outside the company to strengthen the technical skills of the assembly line workers and machine operators. Stalworth had been offered the management development job, but declined for personal reasons.

A high achiever, Rodriguez began the job with eagerness and enthusiasm. In addition to joining the American Society for Training and Development, he spent a great deal of time reading about the various kinds of management development programs available. He also talked to several people responsible *for management development in local organizations to get a feel for "what works and what doesn't." He placed much faith in the opinions of other trainers as he felt he could profit considerably from their experience.*

Based on his discussions and readings, Rodriguez developed a list of courses he felt were necessary to improve the skills of Cabinet Craft's management team. Then Rodriguez compiled a management development plan for the coming year. The plan included eight courses, course outlines, external consultants as instructors, and the dates each course was to be held. Visiting each department head to draw up a list of course participants, he had hoped that twenty managers would attend each class.

After three days of discussions with department heads and other key management personnel, Rodriguez's initial zeal and enthusiasm swiftly eroded into discouragement and dejection. Only nineteen managers signed up to attend all the courses. He was given a variety of reasons for nonparticipation: "We don't need these courses." "I don't approve of the instructors you have selected." "We don't have time to attend." "The course is too long." And so on.

Depressed, Rodriguez set up a meeting with Stalworth and Borden to discuss his problems; he was also thinking about asking for his old job back.

What is the most critical element in an organization's success? There is little argument that the effectiveness of an organization hinges, to a large degree, upon the quality of its management team. The absence of high quality management guarantees, at best, mediocre organizational performance. At worst, the organization will not survive over the long run.

Management development is a systematic process by which individuals acquire the skills, knowledge, and abilities, to lead and manage organizations successfully. A well planned and implemented management development effort satisfies a number of organizational objectives:

- To ensure that managers at all organizational levels are able to perform their jobs effectively. In today's highly complex and rapidly changing organizations, very few individuals are able to successfully assume the job of management without adequate preparation. Through management development activities, managers acquire the tools and techniques to successfully achieve their goals and objectives.

- To avoid *managerial obsolescence*. In an organizational context, obsolescence may be defined as not keeping pace with new methods, processes, and techniques that enable employees to remain effective. Rapidly-changing technical, legal, and social environments have affected the way managers perform their jobs; management personnel who fail to adapt to these changes become obsolete and ineffective.[1] Management development reduces the threat of managerial obsolescence.

- To provide for managerial succession and prepare managers for promotion into upper managerial ranks. A manager's career may involve six or seven promotions within a single organization. A manufacturing vice-president, for example, may have come up through the ranks by holding positions as a first-line supervisor, superintendent, assistant plant manager,

plant manager, and assistant vice–president. Each new position requires a new set of skills and abilities; management development activities often are implemented to ease the transition into jobs involving greater responsibilities.

- To satisfy the personal growth needs of managers. Most managers are achievement oriented and need to face new challenges and opportunities on the job. Management development can play a dual role by providing activities that result in greater organizational effectiveness and lead to increased personal growth and job satisfaction.

As our definition suggests, management development is closely related to the training function described in the previous chapter. Both training and management development stress the processes by which employees acquire the skills and abilities that make them competent and prepare them for future responsibilities. Historically, the term *training* has been used to designate the acquisition of technically-oriented skills by unskilled, semiskilled, skilled, technical, and clerical workers. On the other hand, management development is normally associated with the methods and activities designed to enhance the skills of managers or future managers.

Aside from this difference, the terms *training* and *management development* may be contrasted in other ways. First, management development activities tend to focus on a broad range of skills, while training programs for nonmanagers center around a smaller number of technical skills. For example, a training program for printing press operators would be de-

---

1. See Elmer Burack and Gopal Pati, "Technology and Managerial Obsolescence," *MSU Business Topics* (Spring 1970): 49–56; and Herbert Kaufman, *Obsolescence and Professional Career Development* (New York, AMACON, 1974).

signed to enable operators to upgrade technical skills such as printing speed and accuracy. On the other hand, a development program for printing managers may focus on a wide variety of interpersonal and managerial decision-making skills such as leadership, communication, motivation, work scheduling, and quality control.

Second, management development is long range, while training is often oriented toward the short run. Developmental activities should take place continually throughout a manager's career and comprise an integral, ongoing part of the manager's job. In many organizations, a strong commitment to management development means a manager may spend many weeks each year in developmental programs and activities.

MANAGERIAL SKILLS

Managers' skills and abilities are quite distinct from those of nonmanagers. Underlying effectiveness at all levels of the managerial hierarchy are basic technical, conceptual, and human relations skills.[2] Figure 10-1 illustrates how the mix of these skills varies according to the level of the management job.

Technical skills, knowledge of equipment, work methods, and technologies are much more important for first level managers than middle and top managers. First level managers often conduct on-the-job training for employees and troubleshoot problems that center around the organization's technology. Too, some first-line managers are working supervi-

2. Robert L. Katz, "Skills of an Effective Administrator," *Harvard Business Review* (January–February 1955): 33–42.

sors and on occasion perform their subordinates' jobs in their absence.

Conceptual skill is the ability to view the organization as a whole; to recognize the interdependence of parts; and to coordinate and integrate a wide array of diverse organizational functions, activities, goals, and purposes. For example, the manager of a large manufacturing plant must integrate production, marketing, engineering, and financial functions and objectives so that departmental and organizational goals are achieved. The need for conceptual skills becomes increasingly critical as the individual progresses from first level management into top management ranks.

One popular definition of manager is "one who accomplishes his or her work through others." In this sense, every manager is a leader, and *human relations skills* are equally important for managers on all organizational levels. Some key human relations skills include the ability to create strong interpersonal relations and build cooperative, satisfying relationships among work group members.

MANAGEMENT DEVELOPMENT PROCESS

In some organizations, management development takes place on a very informal basis. Occasionally managers may attend a seminar; join a professional association; or subscribe to professional journals in order to keep abreast of new tools, methods, and techniques. At times the manager may be solely responsible for development, and the organization may play a passive role in creating developmental

FIGURE 10–1: *Management Levels and Skills*

<table>
<tr><td>TOP
MANAGEMENT</td><td rowspan="3">TECHNICAL
SKILLS</td><td rowspan="3">CONCEPTUAL
SKILLS</td><td rowspan="3">HUMAN-
RELATION
SKILLS</td></tr>
<tr><td>MIDDLE
MANAGEMENT</td></tr>
<tr><td>FIRST-LINE
MANAGEMENT</td></tr>
</table>

activities. Unfortunately, informal approaches to management development are seldom planned, coordinated, or evaluated on a systematic basis and, therefore, their overall effectiveness is open to question.

A formal, planned approach is more likely to result in successful and satisfying management development for the organization and the individual. The management development model, whose key elements closely parallel the training model discussed in the previous chapter, is illustrated in Figure 10–2.

The first phase of the model, the assessment of management development needs, involves both the examination of current performance criteria and the analysis of future managerial manpower needs. Based on the needs analysis, programs and activities are created which normally include both on- and off-the-job developmental techniques. Following the implementation of developmental programs, the overall effectiveness in bringing about changes in managerial behavior is evaluated. The development of managers is an ongoing process, and the feed-back loop from evaluation to needs assessment indicates the continuous nature of management development.

Needs Assessment

Organizations are rare, indeed, where each member of management is motivated, competent, and fully qualified. In the real world an organization's total management team will possess widely-varying skills, motives, and abilities. Some managers will consistently turn in a superlative effort, far surpassing organizational expectations. Others may fail miserably, indicating an obvious mismatch between the individual and the job. Another group of managers, perhaps the majority, will fall into "above-average," "average," or "marginal" categories. Persons in these categories are obvious candidates for management development as they have room for improvement. They may be new managers, promoted from nonmanagement ranks, strong in technical skills but lacking experience and expertise in interpersonal and conceptual skills such as leadership, communication, planning, or-

FIGURE 10–2: *Management Development Model*

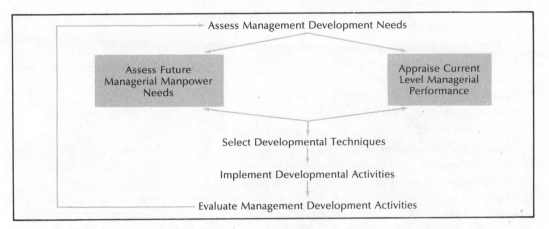

ganizing, and control. Many newly appointed first-line supervisors need a considerable amount of development early in their management careers. Other candidates for management development are obsolete managers who are out of touch with new managerial methods, tools, and techniques. Managers at any level and in any stages of their careers can fall victim to obsolescence, particularly in rapidly-changing environments. For example, managerial obsolescence is more likely to become a problem in highly dynamic industries, such as the computer or communications industries.

CURRENT NEEDS

Because current developmental needs are tied directly to prevailing levels of performance, a well planned and administered performance appraisal system is a key element in an organization's assessment efforts. Personnel administrators must ensure that the organization's performance appraisal system includes a description of developmental activities that may strengthen areas where performance

problems exist. Further, by relating needs assessment to performance appraisal, the link between management development and managerial effectiveness becomes more clear to the superior who conducts the appraisal. Figure 10–3 illustrates how needs assessment ties directly into the appraisal process.

LONG-RANGE NEEDS

Over a period of years, the composition of the management team will undergo many significant changes. A small number of managers may be fired; others will quit in order to seek better opportunities elsewhere. Some will remain in the same position, and a certain percentage will climb the organizational ladder to upper level management positions. For some, the ascent will be slow and arduous; for others, the climb will be swift and spectacular.

The likelihood of numerous management changes, particularly where objectives include rapid growth, creates career opportunities for the aspiring, motivated manager or the employee who strives to

FIGURE 10–3 *Assessing Management Development Needs Through Performance Appraisal*

THE KENTUCKY OIL COMPANY
ANNUAL PERFORMANCE REVIEW FOR THE PERIOD _____ to _____

EMPLOYEE: Herb Satterlee   SUPERVISOR: Ralph Pedigo

JOB TITLE: Superintendent, Foundry   DATE: January 14, _____

OBJECTIVES	RESULTS
1. Meet production quotas with 95% reliability	96.3% reliability
2. Reduce reject rate to 4% of all products manufactured	3.8% reject rate
3. Reduce waste and spoilage to 5% of materials used	4.3% waste and spoilage
4. Reduce unexcused absenteeism to 3% annually	5.2% unexcused absenteeism
5. Reduce employee turnover to 10% annually	19.5% annual turnover
6. Reduce grievances to 1 per 15 employees annually	3.7/15 employees

PRINCIPAL ACCOMPLISHMENTS

Herb has done an excellent job in increasing the foundry's productivity and reducing rejects, waste, and spoilage. His technical and problem-solving skills have been a great asset in accomplishing the objectives.

AREAS OF PERFORMANCE IN NEED OF IMPROVEMENT

Herb would benefit greatly from developing a more people-oriented leadership style. Also, Herb needs to sharpen his skills in employee motivation and corrective counseling procedures. With these improvements, there is a good chance that he will achieve his goals concerning absenteeism, turnover, and grievances.

SPECIFIC ACTIONS PLANNED TO IMPROVE PERFORMANCE

Herb and I have agreed that the following developmental activities will assist him to achieve personal and organizational goals:

1. Attend university-sponsored seminars on leadership, employee motivation, absenteeism control, and corrective counseling procedures.

2. Continual coaching on my behalf that focuses specifically on the reduction of employee-related problems.

3. Become a temporary member on the committee on employee absenteeism and turnover to learn more about these problems and how to control them.

Signature of Supervisor _____

Signature of Employee _____

Employee's Comments:

_____

_____

_____

join management ranks. While the processes of organizational growth and change create heavy demands for managerial expertise, efforts must be made to ensure that managers are adequately prepared to assume their new jobs and responsibilities. Few managers are able to tackle increasingly challenging positions without exposure to formal developmental activities.

Assessing long-range management development needs begins with a forecast of the demand for managers. The prediction in a medium-sized tractor company, for example, may be that the management team must increase by 10 percent per year for the next five years to satisfy optimistic plans for business expansion. To a significant degree, the company's continued growth hinges on its ability to ensure a continual supply of competent managerial power. Where will it get the managers it needs? Basically, two alternatives exist. First, the organization may hire most of the new managers from the outside; there are certain advantages to hiring from the outside. New managers may prevent stagnation by bringing fresh, innovative ideas to the company. In addition, recruitment from the outside lessens the need for a strong internal management development and operating expenses. Second, even though these advantages exist, the company will more than likely choose to develop existing personnel, and follow a policy of promotion from within. Research shows that most companies follow this practice.[3]

Assuming that the organization satisfies

most personnel demands from inside, policymakers must then judge the promotion potential of current managers. Strengths and weaknesses are closely examined to predict how the managers will perform if promoted. During this assessment, managers with considerable skills and experience may be considered promotable without additional development. A certain percentage of managers may have "peaked" in their present jobs and be deemed unpromotable. Others may be judged promotable but only after further preparation; an analysis is made of the specific skills and abilities they need to be successful after being promoted.

To assist in making these decisions, some organizations prepare a personnel planning tool called a *management* or *executive replacement chart*. Replacement charts indicate successors for each position in the management hierarchy and often combine current performance data with a judgment of promotion potential. Although the primary focus of a replacement chart is upon an organization's current structure, the performance and promotion data on the chart are valuable in determining promotions for a growing company. Figure 10–4 illustrates the information normally contained within a typical management replacement chart.

The assessment of management development needs—whether they be to improve current performance or prepare employees for promotion— should result in an individualized program for each employee. First, no two management jobs are exactly alike; nor is the performance of any two managers identical. One plant supervisor's developmental needs may focus on weaknesses in counseling employees, conducting performance ap-

3. Newman Peery and Y. K. Shetty, "An Empirical Study of Executive Transferability and Organizational Performance," *Proceedings*, Academy of Management, Kansas City, Missouri 1976.

FIGURE 10–4: *Management Replacement Chart*

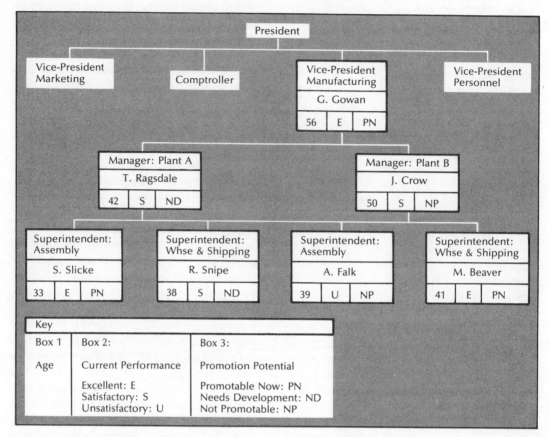

praisals, and leading committee meetings. Another supervisor may need development in quality control, preventive maintenance, or interviewing skills. Yet a third supervisor, who is performing excellently, may be considered strong promotion material and need development in various middle-management planning and control techniques.

Second, recent trends suggest that managers are participating in the design of developmental activities, resulting in individualized programs that satisfy both organizational and personal needs. A sales manager, for example, may desire to attend a continuing education seminar on "Reducing Executive Stress" or "Life Planning." While the immediate payoff to the organization may not be apparent in terms of increased sales and profits, the manager's boss may finance the seminar to acknowledge the individual's personal growth and development goals. Of course, even though there is no scientific proof, the argument can be easily made that personal growth in turn enhances the manager's overall worth to the organization. In sum, a tailor-made program is likely to be more effective in maximizing both current and future organizational and personal goals.

Developmental Techniques

The increased emphasis upon management development in recent years has lead to a proliferation of various management development methods and techniques; personnel administrators have a wide choice of developmental strategies. Like employee training activities, management development techniques may be grouped into two broad forms: development through work experience or through off-the-job techniques. In this chapter, we'll confine our discussion to the more popular methods that are usually reserved for improving the skills and abilities of employees who hold managerial positions.

ON-THE-JOB MANAGEMENT DEVELOPMENT TECHNIQUES

How does one learn the difficult and challenging task of management? What may organizations do to ensure that their managers possess a healthy and balanced mix of technical, conceptual, and human relations skills?

To turn young, inexperienced, but ambitious men or women into skilled and confident managers, most organizations put a great deal of time and trust into on-the-job development techniques. Through these methods, managers essentially learn by doing. On-the-job methods enable managers to actually practice critical management skills, make mistakes, and learn from their mistakes under the careful guidance of an experienced, competent mentor. Properly planned, coordinated, and implemented on-the-job de-

velopmental techniques can be powerful teaching devices; research findings suggest that most organizations make extensive use of these methods.[4]

COACHING As in the field of athletics, the organizational coach assumes the role of helper, teacher, and tutor. The coach—usually the new manager's boss—provides development by setting goals with the manager, providing assistance in reaching goals, and by giving timely and constructive performance feedback. The coach answers questions, lets the employee participate in making decisions, stimulates the employee's thinking, and helps out when problems occur. Trust, cooperation, and mutual respect are imperative for coaching to be effective. *Coaching* is usually done informally and, in practice, a thin line exists between coaching and effective leadership. Properly done, coaching can be an extremely effective way to develop employee confidence and build strong supervisory-subordinate relations.

Coaching, however, is not problem-free. According to Harry Levinson, coaching will fail unless there is a rapport conducive to learning between the manager and the supervisor. Levinson suggests that the coach must be willing to give sufficient time to the development process and allow the subordinate to assume some risks and make mistakes.[5]

Another potential problem is that coaching may simply perpetuate current management styles and techniques in need of change. In this situation, coach-

4. "On-The-Job Training," *Personnel Management: BNA Policy and Practice Series* (Washington, DC: Bureau of National Affairs, Inc. 1975).
5. Harry Levinson, "A Psychologist Looks at Executive Development," *Harvard Business Review* (November-December 1962): 69–75.

ing simply promotes managerial obsolescence and may do more harm than good.[6]

JOB ROTATION AND LATERAL PROMOTION *Job rotation* enables an employee to learn new skills and abilities by performing different jobs. A commonly-used teaching device at all organizational levels, job rotation for managers usually involves temporary assignments that may range from several months to one or more years in various departments, plants, and offices. Job rotation for management trainees usually involves several short-run assignments which teach a wide variety of skills and give them a greater understanding of how other work areas function. Management trainees are new, inexperienced managers such as recent college graduates or employees promoted from the blue-collar or clerical ranks into first level management.

Job rotation benefits management trainees in other ways: By being able to compare the rewards and satisfactions gained from working in different jobs and organizational environments, management trainees get a feel for the kind of positions they would like to fill on a permanent basis. As an example, following a few months in the assembly, warehouse, and shipping departments, a manufacturing management trainee may have a significant input into the decision which leads to a permanent job assignment.

For middle and upper level management, job rotation usually takes on a different meaning. At these levels, job rotation assignments normally involve *lateral promotions* which may last one or more years. In contrast to a vertical promotion,

where an employee takes over a supervisor's job, a lateral promotion involves a move to a different work environment and is designed to develop competence in general management decision-making skills. Much like the relatively short-run job rotation assignment, a lateral promotion allows the manager to be exposed to many organization operations, functions, methods, and management styles.[7]

While job rotation and lateral promotion developmental methods enable managers and management trainees to broaden organizational knowledge and hone decision-making skills, these methods are not without flaws. First, some organizations need managers with specialized skills in technical areas rather than general management skills. Second, for upper level managers job rotation and lateral promotion often involve an expensive and emotional move to a new geographical location. While companies may bear the moving costs, managers are forced to pull up stakes, leaving behind close social relationships and other community ties. More and more, managers are turning down promotions which involve relocating to a new city. While promotions were accepted with little question several years ago, a 1975 study showed that 42 percent of the companies sampled employed managers who refused transfers.[8] Finally, a job rotation or lateral promotion may force managers to take short-run views of their jobs. For

6. Chris Argyris, "Puzzle and Perplexity in Executive Development," *Personnel Journal* 39 (1969): 463–65 ff.

7. For a detailed discussion of the advantages and disadvantages of job rotation for managers, see Yoram Zeira, "Job Rotation for Management Development," *Personnel* (July–August 1974): 25–35.

8. See "Taking the Jolts Out Of Moving," *Nation's Business* (November 1975): 36–38; and "Moving On Loses Its Glamour for More Employees," *The Wall Street Journal* (August 3, 1976): 1.

example, a colonel assigned to battalion headquarters for a one-year tour of duty may focus on short-range programs with immediate payoffs and neglect planning and policy decisions which may not generate benefits for three or four years—long after the officer has been reassigned.

UNDERSTUDY ASSIGNMENTS Some organizations create understudy positions to ensure that qualified managers are always available to fill management vacancies. An understudy is an individual being groomed to take over the boss's job. Normally reserved for middle and top management positions, this form of development is used sparingly at the first level of management.

The effectiveness of this technique depends on the working relationship between the understudy and the boss and the amount of time the boss is willing to take to develop the understudy. Much like the effective coach, the boss should solicit ideas and suggestions from the understudy on major decisions, allow risk taking, give constructive performance feedback, and increasingly delegate authority. In essence, the supervisor also should possess the coaching skills discussed earlier.

COMMITTEE ASSIGNMENTS A great deal of a manager's time is spent on *committee assignments*. Permeating all levels of management, committees are formed to solve current problems, plan for the future, and discuss and act upon issues critical to the organization.

Serving on a committee and participating in decision making enables a manager to strengthen conceptual and human-relations skills. For example, a newly-appointed production foreman may be asked to formulate recommendations to solve a quality control problem. While working on this committee assignment, the foreman gains a greater understanding of the issues involved in quality control, meets and discusses the problem with personnel from other departments, and develops an appreciation for good working relationships among quality control inspectors, production managers, supervisors, and line employees.

OFF-THE-JOB TECHNIQUES

In most organizations, management development takes place both on and off the job. Off-the-job activities enable a manager to get away from the day-to-day pressures of the work environment and devote full attention to strengthening managerial skills and abilities. This method of development usually centers around formal courses conducted in-house or perhaps sponsored off-site by a university, consulting group or nonprofit association such as the American Management Association, American Society for Training and Development, or American Society for Personnel Administrators.[9]

The length and breadth of these courses vary considerably. A one or two-day seminar normally focuses on a specific management technique or problem such as "Time Management" or "Executive Speaking." One- or two-week courses may focus on a wide variety of managerial methods, techniques, and processes. For example, the American Management Association's popular five-day "Developing Supervisory Leadership Skills" course covers leadership, communications, discipline, employee

9. For a description of the soaring demand for off-the-job courses and seminars, see "More Executives Take Work-Related Courses To Keep Up, Advance," *The Wall Street Journal* (March 3, 1980): 1.

development, job satisfaction, and morale.

Some universities sponsor advanced management programs that closely resemble a highly concentrated MBA degree program. Perhaps the most popular course of this nature is Harvard Business School's Advanced Management Program. Other colleges and universities offering similar programs include the University of Chicago, UCLA, and Georgia State University.

In recent years, several large, progressive organizations have created in-house educational programs to satisfy their needs for skilled management talent. Many corporate programs, which closely resemble those sponsored by universities, offer managers and executives instruction in timely issues and topics involving management theory and practice. Some large companies that have established their own management development centers include IBM Corporation, General Motors Corporation, Exxon Company, and General Electric Company.

Perhaps, the organization with the greatest management development need is the nation's largest single employer—the United States government. With over five million civilian and military employees to manage, a development program is imperative for federal managers. The federal government offers extended management programs for managers in the civilian and military sectors; most of this training takes place at the U.S. Army War College and Federal Executive Institute, and some in smaller training facilities located throughout the world.

Managers who participate in off-the-job developmental programs will be exposed to a wide array of teaching techniques. Several of the methods, especially lec-

ture, conference/discussion, and audiovisual methods, are used extensively in the development of managerial personnel. The following techniques, however, are most effective in the development of managers:

CASE STUDIES A written description of an organizational problem, the *case study* was developed at Harvard Business School in the 1920s; it remains a popular teaching technique there and in many other universities today. Given information concerning the case, participants are required to identify and analyze specific problems, develop alternative courses of action, and recommend the best alternative. A case study may be tackled individually or in groups. In management development programs, participants commonly form teams to study cases, and present their recommendations to other teams for discussion and analysis. Cases may cover a wide variety of typical management topics including business policy, finance, marketing, and personnel. As an illustration, a case of this type may require recommendations about dealing with an employee who is continually late for work. Or the cases may be 20 pages long or more involving a complex set of organizational problems. For example, when considering expansion into international markets, a firm may face decisions involving the development of new marketing channels, new product development, financing arrangements, and personnel planning.

Primarily case studies strengthen problem-solving skills. Participants practice defining problems, generating solutions, and deciding upon optimal solutions. Working in a group gives team members greater insight into group dynamics and group decision-making processes. For maximum effectiveness, cases should be written to simulate the manager's real-life problems, situations, constraints, and working environment.

ROLE PLAYING Participants act out, or play the role, of individuals involved in an organizational problem during *role playing*. Usually, there are no scripts and participants have limited data on which to base their roles. For example, assume managers are receiving instruction in use of effective employee counseling. One member of a group may play the role of an employee who has had several incidents of tardiness and absenteeism. Another member plays the role of the employee's supervisor. With as much realism as possible, the two players act out their roles in front of the instructor and other participants. Discussion and a critique normally follow role playing, which lasts only a few minutes. Role playing may be videotaped and played back in segments for an in-depth analysis of the roles and how they were acted out.

Role playing usually focuses on interpersonal relationships; as such, the primary goal of role playing is to analyze interpersonal problems and develop human relations skills. Role playing is commonly used to develop skills in interviewing, job counseling, discipline, performance appraisal, sales, and other job duties and responsibilities that involve communication. For this technique to be successful, the instructor must ensure that the role playing situations are credible and that each role player performs realistically.[10]

MANAGEMENT GAMES Usually involving competing teams which make decisions concerning a hypothetical organization, *management games* are designed to replicate conditions faced by real life organizations. Teams make decisions concerning advertising, production, finance, and research; the winner is typically the team which achieves the highest net profit by the completion of the game. More complex games involve the use of electronic data processing equipment. In this case, teams input decisions into a specially–programmed computer and receive a printout detailing the overall impact of their decisions on the effectiveness of the enterprise.

A number of benefits may be derived from playing a management game: First, as a team member, the participant is able to study group dynamics—conflict reduction, communication patterns, and the development of interpersonal relationships. Second, the trial and error process of game playing enables participants to learn from mistakes without jeopardizing the effectiveness of a real organization. Third, participants can examine how various functional areas of an organization interrelate—for example, how advertising expenditures affect sales volume or how various levels of research affect long-range profits. Finally, participants report that games are fun and interesting. Team players eagerly await the computer printout which impersonally judges the strengths and weaknesses of their collective decision making, and the winning group takes great pride and satisfaction in victory.[11]

---

10. For applications, see J. Maxwell Towers, *Role Playing for Managers* (Oxford: Pergamon Press, 1974).

11. While interest in management games usually runs high, there is little empirical evidence supporting their effectiveness. See Janet Schriesheim and Chester Schriesheim, "The Effectiveness of Business Games in Management Training," *Training and Development Journal* (May 1974): 14–17.

IN-BASKET EXERCISE This technique is based on the assumption that the participant's boss was suddenly fired. Having been selected to take the job, the participant looks over the memos and letters that have accumulated in the former boss's in-basket from disgruntled customers, irate employees, threatening supervisors, and hostile union officials. Specific examples contained in the in-basket include:

● A letter from an equal employment opportunity representative who wants to talk about alleged discrimination in the work unit.

● A note from an employee who wants a six-week leave of absence to stay with her sick mother. Without her work, production goals probably won't be met.

● A note from a trusted and valuable employee who will quit if she doesn't get a 10 percent raise.

● A letter from the personnel director stating that he is having extreme difficulty finding qualified candidates for five vacant positions in the work unit.

The *in-basket* exercise forces the individual to make immediate decisions and determine priorities. The participant must quickly think through alternative courses of action, select the best solution, and determine how it should be implemented. After completing a series of in-basket exercises, participants discuss their decisions and receive feedback on their performances from the instructor.

SENSITIVITY TRAINING Through *sensitivity training* (also called T-group—"T" for training), individuals become more aware of their feelings and learn how their behavior affects the feelings, attitudes, and behaviors of others. The following scenario illustrates how some forms of sensitivity training take place.

Imagine that your boss has told you to attend a three-day sensitivity training session to improve your human relations skills. On the first day of training, you and fourteen other people you have never met before are seated around a large conference table. A man walks in the room, introduces himself as the group facilitator for the training session, sits down, and says nothing more. After several minutes of agonizing silence, people begin to wonder aloud what is going on. Why doesn't the trainer start a lecture or begin a group discussion about common organizational problems? A little while longer, someone says, "I don't know about you people, but I don't have time to waste sitting around here staring at the ceiling. I suggest we start doing something or get the hell out of here." Several people may nod their heads in agreement, and someone may suggest an agenda for the remainder of the day. Other participants who disagree with the agenda may offer alternative ways to spend the day. Polite disagreements lead to vociferous arguments. People talk openly about their dissatisfactions with the other participants. At some point before blood is shed, the facilitator may intervene and ask the group to analyze the events that have just taken place.

An open, honest, "no holds barred, tell it like it is" discussion of participants' conduct is an important part of the training experience. For the first time, many individuals learn how their behavior is perceived by others. For some participants, the experience is a tremendous emotional high; others leave the training session depressed and demoralized.

Sensitivity training has many opponents.[12] Critics argue—justifiably—that there is very little documentation that performance "back home in the organization" improves as a result of participation in sensitivity training. Others argue that openness, sensitivity, and trust are not always productive or appropriate behavior in some organizational situations. Further, some critics believe that innermost feelings and beliefs are highly personal and that sensitivity training is an invasion of personal privacy.

Does sensitivity training result in greater managerial effectiveness? Two research investigations have proven inconclusive.[13] According to the studies, sensitivity training can produce behavioral changes. For example, greater openness, trust, and respect for the feelings of others; but it has not been demonstrated that behavioral change has led to more effective job performance. Because its impact upon an organization's effectiveness is questionable, sensitivity training has lost much of the popularity it enjoyed during the 1960s.

MEMBERSHIP IN PROFESSIONAL ORGANIZA-TIONS One informal way to keep abreast of new theories, principles, methods, and techniques in a discipline is through membership in a *professional organization*. Regardless of the occupation or field of interest, there is probably a group which meets periodically to discuss important issues in their line of work. Hundreds of such associations exist, with memberships varying from a handful to several thousand.

How does membership in a professional organization help develop managerial skills and abilities? During monthly chapter meetings, and perhaps an annual convention at the regional or national level, members can socialize with their colleagues, exchange ideas, and discuss mutual problems. They listen to a variety of speakers and learn about advancements in their field. Many companies encourage their managers to join professional organizations and to attend meetings regularly by paying membership dues and travel expenses to annual meetings. As a final benefit, some larger professional organizations publish journals for their membership; examples include the American Society for Personnel Administration's monthly *The Personnel Administrator*, the Industrial Management Society's *Industrial Management*, and the American Management Association's *Management Review*, *Supervisory Management*, and *Personnel*. These journals feature articles written by both practitioners and academics about new ideas, trends, issues, and problems in a particular field of interest.

Implementation

Implementation of a manager's individual developmental plan will vary considerably from manager to manager, depending on

---

12. For detailed criticisms of this form of training, see John R. Kimberly and Warren R. Nielsen, "Organization Development and Change in Organization Performance," *Administrative Science Quarterly* (June, 1975): 191; and Martin Lakin, "Some Ethical Issues In Sensitivity Training," *American Psychologist* (October 1969): 923–28.

13. John P. Campbell and Marvin D. Dunnette, "Effectiveness of T-Group Experiences in Managerial Training and Development," *Psychological Bulletin* (August 1968): 73–104; and Robert J. House, "T-Group Education and Leadership Effectiveness: A Review of the Empiric Literature and a Critical Evaluation," *Personnel Psychology* (Spring 1967): 1–32.

the number and kind of skills that need improving and the particular stage of a manager's career. Classroom developmental activities, such as seminars and courses, usually last a day or two or several weeks at the most. Coaching, job rotation, lateral promotions, understudy, committee assignments, and professional memberships are ongoing in nature and may encompass many months, or perhaps, several years. Lateral promotions and transfers, for example, may consume a major portion of a manager's entire career. For these longer term developmental strategies, the distinction between management development and the manager's actual job duties and responsibilities is blurred. Similar to the employee training function, only off-the-job developmental activities afford the opportunity to clearly state that a manager is undergoing development.

In reality, development should be viewed as a permanent part of the manager's job rather than a knee-jerk reaction to the problems of aspiring young managers and obsolete executives. Effective personnel administrators work with line managers to create developmental plans that prevent significant managerial performance problems. Progressive organizations view management development as a continuous process, not simply a one-shot program or activity. Strong, competent managerial talent rarely results from a smattering of one- or two-day seminars every year or scattered, disjointed on-the-job development efforts.

Evaluation

Developmental activities are designed to strengthen a manager's abilities, skills, motivation, confidence, and overall job performance. In turn, the organization expects these activities to benefit not only the manager but the organization. By offering and supporting developmental activities, private organizations seek greater profits and returns for stockholders; governmental organizations expect better services for their citizenry. In this respect, management development may be viewed as an investment that will return dividends in the form of a stronger and healthier organization.[14]

Because an investment in management development can involve significant time and money, efforts should be made to determine whether or not certain expenditures are justified. Perhaps managerial skills could be obtained more efficiently in other ways—for example, through a strong policy of bringing in experienced managers from the outside. The skilled personnel administrator will make every effort to ensure development dollars are wisely spent.

Strategies for evaluating management development programs are basically the same as those evaluating employee training. One approach is to ensure that the written objectives of the management development program are being met. This can be accomplished by examining a manager's performance appraisals and by observing changes in the manager's behavior.

The second evaluative strategy, the cost-benefit analysis of developmental efforts, is feasible only if changes in managerial behavior may be translated into dollars and cents. Only developmental activities that generate benefits greater than costs would be maintained; unfortu-

---

14. Donald L. Kirkpatrick, "Techniques for Evaluating Training Programs," *Journal for the American Society of Training Directors"* 13, 14, (1969–70): 1–17.

nately, this type of evaluation is often difficult to implement. Assume, for example, that a supervisor improves written communication skills by participating in a two-day seminar sponsored by a local university business school. What is this experience worth in economic terms? How many dollars does a more clearly written memo or business letter save the company? Because assessments are clearly subjective, this form of evaluation is used quite sparingly in practice.

A third strategy focuses on measuring four levels of evaluation through the analysis of participant reaction, participant learning, changes in participant behavior, and changes in organizational effectiveness criteria. Evaluating management development by examining these four levels would certainly enable the personnel executive to make a valid judgment of the worth of the developmental activities. But such a strategy is too time consuming and costly for all management development activities. Research shows that most organizations measure participants' reactions but fail to assess changes in the manager's job behavior.[15]

FEMALE MANAGERS

Since the beginning of the industrial era, female employees have actively participated in all sectors of the economy. Traditionally, however, women have been almost exclusively restricted to low–paying, monotonous jobs involving little responsibility and few opportunities for advancement. Rarely did the female role within an organizational setting include

management; and when it did, her pay was lower. Even though equal employment opportunity and affirmative action programs have led to more women managers today, statistics indicate that women are still lower paid and greatly underutilized in management positions. As of May 1979 women made up 41.5 percent of the total labor force. However, only 24.3 percent of the approximately 10.3 million nonfarm managers and administrators were women.[16] Also, many women managers and administrators hold relatively low level positions. According to one estimate, women make up less than 6 percent of middle management and less than 1 percent of top management.[17] One need only peruse the photos of management and board members in corporate annual reports to see which sex dominates the top executive suites.

Barriers

The underrepresentation of women in managerial ranks is in part due to obstacles hindering their upward mobility. One set of barriers concerns the stereotypes of woman workers frequently encountered in the world of work. Generally, these stereotypes hold that "woman's place is in the home" and that women lack the mental and physical makeup to successfully perform a management job. Specific stereotypes about women include:[18]

15. Ralph Catalanello and Donald L. Kirkpatrick, "Evaluating Training Programs," *Training and Development Journal* 22, no. 5 (1968): 2–9.

16. Taken from U.S. Department of Labor Statistics Bulletin 2000, *Handbook of Labor Statistics 1978*, pp. 40–41; and U.S. Department of Labor Bureau of Labor Statistics, *Employment and Earnings* 26, no. 6 (June 1979): p. 20.

17. Gwenyth Cravens, "How Ma Bell is Training Women for Management," *New York Times Magazine* (May 29, 1977): 12.

18. Rosalind Loring and Theodora Wells, *Breakthrough: Women Into Management* (New York: Van Nostrand Reinbold Company, 1972).

- Women work merely to supplement the family income; they do not need equal pay or benefits because men support families.
- Women do not want to be managers because it would involve an extra workload which would interfere with family obligations.
- Women are unable to meet certain work demands for emotional toughness and stability because of their psychological makeup. They tend to take things personally, to respond to anger and frustration by crying, and to not be sufficiently hard-nosed to make unpleasant decisions.

An additional stereotype concerning women workers involves unreliability as indicated by women's higher absence rates. While it is true that the overall absence rates are higher for women than for men, the difference in absence behavior narrows considerably when such rates are compared for the managerial job category. For example, the annual inactivity rate (aggregate hours lost as a proportion of aggregate hours usually worked) for 1973 to 1976 for males was 3.0 compared to 4.3 for females. For the same period, however, absence rates for male and female managers were 1.7 and 2.3 respectively.[19] Clearly, differences in attendance patterns are nonsignificant when job factors are taken into consideration.

Another widespread barrier is the *old boy network* or informal advice and assistance that often facilitate upward mobility into management ranks. The fast tracks on which many male managers have swiftly traveled have been amply greased through membership in the old boy network. For example, at a Rotary Club luncheon, one member may ask another if he would be interested in a job opening. By belonging to this informal fraternity, the aspiring manager becomes privy to inside information: who to know, important positions coming up, job assignments that count, and other valued information that strengthens visibility and credibility. One particularly important aspect of the old boy network includes coming under the patronage of a sponsor or mentor who eases the path into upper management ranks. Because of the paucity of females in top executive ranks, few women are able to provide guidance and advice to women at lower management levels. Many women, however, are forming their own career related informal communication systems; through *networking*, women create and support information systems which someday may be analagous to the old boy network. Networking provides a means to disseminate and collect valued information on jobs available, jobs becoming available, and other information helpful to career-oriented females.

Developmental Activities

Each member of an organization must recognize the responsibility to eliminate inequities that may exist against female employees. Equal employment opportunity is not personnel's job; it is the responsibility of each individual regardless of position or level. Management development personnel, however, are in a unique position to push for bona fide equal employment opportunities for employees of both sexes. Some of the ways management development administrators

---

19. Janice N. Hedges, "Absence From Work—Measuring the Hours Lost," *Monthly Labor Review* (October 1977): 21.

can facilitate the movement of women into management ranks include:

- Ensure that performance appraisal data used for management development decisions are free of bias against women. For example, if a female's performance appraisal includes statements such as "not fit for promotion into management" or "performing unacceptable work as a manager—recommend demotion to a nonsupervisory role," be sure that the reasons for these assessments are valid.

- Include a presentation about prejudice and discrimination in all developmental programs for new managers and supervisors. Programs should include discussions of relevant EEO guidelines, what discrimination is and how to avoid it, and how to conduct fair and impartial performance appraisals.

- Implement special programs that deal solely with discrimination and equal employment opportunity. Many organizations regularly offer programs such as "Positive Approaches to EEO and Affirmative Action," "What First-Line Supervisors Must Know About EEO," and "Developing Minority and Female Employees."

- Create programs especially for aspiring women managers. Individuals who have studied the problems of female managers suggest that women would greatly benefit from developmental activities that focus on their particular problems and needs. Some of these needs are included in these statements:[20]

20. J. Stephen Heinen, D. McGlauchlin, C. Legeros, and J. Freeman, "Developing the Woman Manager," *Personnel Journal* (May 1975): 238.

Women need to increase their self-esteem as managers. Effective leaders are often defined in terms of typically masculine traits such as aggressive, independent, and achievement–oriented. However, women are more "properly" defined as people-oriented and dependent upon others. Thus, achievement-oriented women who aspire to leadership positions face potential problems with role conflict because they may be perceived as unfeminine. Developmental activities must bolster women's self-concepts and minimize the doubts and fears that some women may have about succeeding in a male-dominated world.

Women need to learn new behaviors for managing interpersonal conflict. Women managers can expect negative attitudes about their ability to manage effectively. Therefore, women managers must develop skills to deal with these negative attitudes and understand that attitudinal change is often a slow, arduous process. Further, research suggests that females tend to avoid conflict or to prefer to smooth things over, rather than to openly confront problems. Reducing conflict is a key managerial task, and women managers must develop skills to handle personal conflict in constructive ways.

Women need to develop leadership in team building skills. Women working with men in a group often play a subordinate role. Culture has long dictated that men assume dominant roles in male-female dealings. In effect, this minimizes the opportunity for the female group member to develop and utilize team building skills. Developmental activities should focus on skills that enable women managers to become effective group leaders.

Women need help with career planning. Even though the obstacles that block women's movement into management ranks are slowly eroding today, many women receive little guidance about career opportunities or informal advice on how to climb the organizational ladder. Women must learn how to analyze their own behavior, to assess their strengths and weaknesses, and to set realistic goals. Organizations must assist career planning by providing realistic feedback about opportunities and potential career paths for women managers.

Training for women only is desirable initially. Developmental programs for beginning women managers should be conducted solely for women. Because women managers have unique problems, a women-only group would enable participants to openly and honestly share their problems, fears, experiences, and perceptions. Development must take place in a climate that encourages openness and candor; women may feel defensive, threatened, or reluctant to assume a leadership role with men participants.

MANAGEMENT DEVELOPMENT PROBLEMS

Unfortunately, many problems and mistakes can lead to an unsuccessful management development; some of these problems are caused by placing unqualified individuals in charge of management development. These persons may lack the technical or "how-to" skills to perform the management development function, such as how to assess developmental needs, how to match needs with techniques, or how to evaluate management development activities. Further, trainers may be deficient in conceptual skills, failing to understand how management development must be coordinated with other organizational activities and functions. Finally, interpersonal problems, particularly between line managers and the management development staff, may result in less than optimal management development. For example, line staff may have strong differences of opinion over the content of a course, or they may disagree over how the authority and responsibility for management development should be divided. One list of the ten most serious mistakes in management development is given in Figure 10–5.

SUCCESSFUL PROGRAMS

Modern facilities, expensive equipment, abundant staff administrators, and an ample training budget will not guarantee the success of management development efforts. The true value of management development lies in the results achieved through developmental activities. These results include a steady stream of competent, motivated managers able to meet current and future organizational goals. To achieve these results, a number of conditions must be satisfied:

Performance Appraisal

The developmental needs of current managers are most effectively pinpointed

FIGURE 10–5: *Ten Serious Mistakes in Management Development*

1. Fixing the primary responsibility for development on the staff. Executives must recognize that the responsibility to develop human resources belongs, ultimately, to each line manager. The staff should assist line managers in achieving this goal.

2. Lack of instruction in training for trainers. Line managers must possess the specific skills and abilities that are necessary to develop their subordinates. The management development staff should see that managers are trained in these skills.

3. Hasty or shallow needs analysis. Programs must be built upon the particular developmental needs of each individual. Further, programs must focus only on those needs which may be met through developmental activities—and not, for example, needs that can be most effectively met through policy revisions or reorganizations.

4. Substituting training for selection. Developmental processes cannot take the place of good selection techniques. A skill or ability cannot be developed where basic aptitudes are nonexistent.

5. Limiting the planning of development activities to courses. The greatest opportunities for learning exist through work experiences. While seminars and courses are important, on–the–job development through techniques such as job rotation, committee assignments, and coaching are superior mechanisms for fostering personal growth.

6. Over concern with personality. Attempts to modify an individual's basic personality through training and development are not only of questionable effectiveness, but also raise many moral and ethical issues. Programs that include a self-examination and critique of one's own behavioral patterns are certainly important, but efforts to restructure one's personality are not within the domain of management development.

7. Lumping together training and development needs. Each individual manager has a unique set of developmental needs. While some of a manager's needs may be the same as others, no two developmental programs will be identical.

8. Preoccupation with mechanics. Management development activities sometimes center around a trainer's favorite training techniques—such as videotape or role playing—rather than the real needs of the participants. Developmental methods should be selected after specific needs have been defined and the program objectives have been set.

9. On again, off again crash programs. To achieve consistent results, management development must be applied in a regular, uninterrupted manner. Subordinates cannot be expected to maintain an interest in development unless they perceive it as an important, ongoing part of running the organization.

10. Lack of provision for practical application of the training. Individuals must be able to effectively utilize their newly learned skills and abilities back on the job. Relating management development to the learner's working environment is a key consideration in writing developmental objectives and planning developmental activities.

SOURCE: J. W. Taylor, "Ten Serious Mistakes in Management-Training Development," *Personnel Journal*, May 1974, pp. 357–62. Reprinted with permission of *Personnel Journal*, Costa Mesa, CA © May 1974

through objective, results-oriented appraisal techniques. A vague, subjective appraisal system, such as a graphic rating scale, will offer little help in uncovering specific deficiencies in managerial skills and abilities. Objectives-oriented systems, such as management by objectives, remove many of the obstacles in conducting a thorough, valid needs assessment program.

Long-range Planning

Management development activities must also be based on future needs for managers and on the skills and abilities required to fulfill job responsibilities. For example, potential changes in government legislation, technology, and other internal or external organization variables must be analyzed and incorporated into developmental activities today to prevent managerial obsolescence in the future. Ideally, administrators responsible for planning management development will also play an active role in the organization's long-range planning function.

Top Management Support

An organization's management development effort must receive a strong endorsement from top management. Without this support, management development programs may be viewed as a form of entertainment or a second rate, marginally-effective organizational activity. Support also means a sufficient budget to carry out a full program of developmental activities. The tendency to slash management development activities during hard times must be avoided.

Management development personnel, however, should not expect an automatic stamp of approval by top management. This backing must be earned by demonstrating in dollars and cents terms, if possible, how management development is contributing to the goals of the organization. Because of the importance of the bottom line, demonstrating the cost–effectiveness of management development activities may well be the most productive way to garner the backing of top management. Unfortunately, this form of evaluation is also the most difficult.

Shared Responsibility

Successful management development involves a cooperative effort: the company, the managers, and their bosses share in the responsibility for development. Companies have a responsibility to provide a supportive environment and resources for development, such as company-paid courses, seminars, and tuition assistance. Supervisors should encourage managers to take advantage of developmental resources the company provides and furnish performance feedback. Supervisors can also create meaningful on-the-job developmental activities, such as job rotation and the assignment of special projects. And finally, development will not take place unless managers are self-motivated. Managers cannot be forced or pressured to undergo development, but must recognize the link between management development and the achievement of organizational and personal goals.

Environment for Change

During development, managers are often exposed to new, innovative methods which may involve different techniques of employee motivation or new ways to approach the managerial decision-making process. For development to be fully realized, managers must be able to apply new skills and abilities within the work environment. Naturally, this environment must be receptive to new ideas and techniques, allowing managers to depart from old, well-established, ineffective ways of doing things. The transfer of learning problem becomes significant when managers attempt to apply new techniques in rigid, uncompromising environments.

One classic transfer of learning problem involved a well-cited human relations training program for supervisors. Testing before and after the program revealed that supervisors did, in fact, undergo a positive attitude change about people-oriented leadership. Supervisors' on-the-job behavior changed, however, only when their human relations-oriented behavior was supported by their bosses.[21]

In the end, environment has a significant effect on performance; management development cannot be effective if it conflicts with existing norms, values, beliefs, and customs. In assessing needs and creating developmental activities, management development must pay close attention to environmental considerations and ensure that what is learned can be transformed into on-the-job behavior.

Professional Staff

During the past two decades management development program design and implementation have been revolutionized. There are new technologies for needs assessment and program evaluation; the management development arena has experienced a virtual explosion of new developmental techniques and devices. Further, management development has expanded to include managers from all organization levels. Thus, developmental professionals must be able to design programs to strengthen a variety of managerial skills and abilities.

Management development has also broadened in other ways; today, the management development staff often directly implements developmental activities. In this case, management development pro-

fessionals must not only possess strong conceptual skills—such as the ability to plan and coordinate management development—but also must be technically competent to conduct developmental activities and exercises. Training professionals must be familiar with the wide assemblage of developmental activities and be able to select activities to satisfy wide-ranging management development needs.

In short, management development personnel must be talented, competent professionals. First and foremost, they must be experts in management development; in addition they must know and understand the intricacies and complexities of management and recognize effective management behavior at all levels. These professionals must also understand how the organization's culture affects managerial decisions and be able to design programs that complement the organization's culture, rather than clash head-on with informal norms, values, and customs.

How does an organization create a professional management development staff? To a significant degree, by recruiting and hiring individuals with a proper blend of education and job experience. A formal education in personnel, human resources, industrial psychology, or a related field, combined with a successful track record in carrying out management development efforts, would provide a sound professional base. Naturally, the staff must experience continual development themselves to avoid obsolescence within their own ranks; they must keep abreast of advancements in developmental technologies, methods, and processes. Membership in professional associations such as the American Society for

---

21. Edwin A. Fleishman, "Leadership Climate, Human Relations Training, and Supervisory Behavior," in Edwin A. Fleishman, ed. *Studies in Personnel and Industrial Psychology* (Homewood, IL: The Dorsey Press, Inc., 1967), pp. 250–63.

Training and Development, and the American Society for Personnel Administration will help achieve this goal. Also, short courses and seminars such as "Train the Trainer," or "Skills and Techniques for the Management Development Specialist" are particularly important for employees new to management development. Meaningful on-the-job experiences for the management development staff may include coaching, committee assignments, and job rotation.

In summary, effective management development activities result in a continual supply of competent, satisfied managerial personnel. Underlying successful management development are sound performance appraisal and work force planning techniques which assess current and future development needs. Also important is the support of top management which must be earned by showing how management development contributes to organizational effectiveness. All management jobs require technical, conceptual, and human relations skills, although the mix will vary considerably according to management level. Training and development administrators should understand how the skills and abilities of effective management behavior vary among first–line, middle, and top management levels. Individual developmental programs should be created for each manager based on current strengths and weaknesses, career potential, and personal goals and needs. Line and staff personnel and the manager must understand that they all share the responsibility for development. The environment the manager works in should be receptive to change and open to new ideas, methods, and techniques. Finally, the management development staff must undergo continual development to avoid stagnation and obsolescence.

The Solution

Rodriguez's dilemma with his new management development job can be traced to four sources. First, he perceived management development as a number of courses rather than a system that includes several integrated activities. Second, Rodriguez overlooked the need to conduct a systematic needs assessment. Clearly, the creation of management development courses was based solely on his idea of what was necessary. He should have worked more closely with managers to systematically collect performance data that reflect current management development needs, in addition to information concerning future managerial needs. Third, Rodriguez failed to gather important inputs from line managers concerning scheduling and the time available for developmental activities. Fourth, he also fell into the all too common what-works-for-the-manufacturing-company-down-the-street-will-work-for-us trap. Each management team has its own unique set of strengths and weaknesses, and the selection of developmental courses and activities must be geared to meet the special needs of each individual organization.

To improve his chances for successful management development, Rodriguez must take a systematic approach toward management development becoming familiar with the various phases of the management development model. Further, he must recognize that management development is a two-way partnership between line managers and the management development staff and that plans for management development must be made with cooperation and participation between both parties.

━━━━━ KEY TERMS AND CONCEPTS ━━━━━

Managerial Obsolescence	Case Study
Management Development	Role Playing
Conceptual Skill	Management Games
Human Relations Skills	In-basket Exercises
Executive Replacement Chart	Sensitivity Training
Coaching	Professional Organizations
Job Rotation	Old Boy Network
Lateral Promotion	Networking
Committee Assignments	Technical Skill

━━━━━ FOR REVIEW ━━━━━

1. What is management development and what are its major purposes?

2. Discuss how both current and long-range management development needs may be assessed.

3. Describe the major parts of the management development model.

4. Describe the various kinds of on- and off-the-job management development techniques.

5. Explain the importance of creating an individual developmental plan for each manager.

6. Describe an effective strategy for evaluating a management development effort.

7. Describe the problems of career development for women and explain how management development activities facilitate the upward mobility of females in management ranks.

8. Enumerate some of the key mistakes in carrying out the management development function.

9. List the major considerations for conducting successful management development.

═══ FOR DISCUSSION ═══

1. It is often said that management development should take place throughout a manager's career—not just in the initial stages. Do you agree? Explain the meaning behind this statement.

2. Write a brief job description for a position titled director of management development. List some of the major duties and responsibilities of the position.

3. In line with question two, write a brief job specification for the director of management development. What skills and abilities should the director have? What formal education and job experience would you expect the director to possess?

4. Management development involves a partnership between line management and staff administration. How does the role of the director of management development differ from the role of the line manager in carrying out management development?

5. In practice, it is often very difficult to conduct an accurate assessment of management development needs. Why is this so?

6. Assume you are the head of a personnel department in a large hospital that employs about one hundred twenty-five first level, middle, and top managers. At present, management development takes place on a very informal basis and you feel the hospital needs to formalize the developmental function by creating the

position of director of management development. What arguments would you use to get the position approved?

7. Your boss calls you, as the head of your organization's management development, into his office and says: "You have requested a $250,000 management development budget for the coming fiscal year. Can you prove we are getting our money's worth?" What would you tell your boss?

8. One occasionally hears the old adage, "You can't make a silk purse out of a sow's ear." Do you see any relationship between this old cliche and the management development function?

SUPPLEMENTARY READING

Bowers, Charles P., Jr. "Let's Put Realism into Management Development." *Harvard Business Review*, July-August 1973, pp. 80–87.

Connellan, Thomas K. "Management Development As A Critical Investment." *Human Resource Management*, Summer 1972, pp. 1–14.

Cone, Paul B. and McKinley, Richard N. "Management Development Can Be More Effective." *California Management Review*, Spring 1972, pp. 13–19.

Crane, Donald P. "A Dynamic System for Management Development." *Personnel Journal*, September 1972, pp. 667–74.

Gordon, Francine E., and Stroeber, Myra H. *Bringing Women Into Management*. New York: McGraw-Hill Book Company, 1977.

Hass, Frederick C. *Executive Obsolescence. AMA Research Study 90.* New York: American Management Association, Inc., 1968.

Hennig, Margaret, and Jordon, Anne. *The Managerial Woman*. Garden City, NY: Anchor Press/Doubleday, 1977.

Hodge, B. J.; Anthony, William P.; and Swindle, Orson. "Management Development: 12 Months Later." *The Personnel Administrator*, September 1976, pp. 49–55.

Huse, Edgar F. "Putting In A Management Development Program That Works." *California Management Review* IX: 73–80.

Kirkpatrick, Donald T. *A Practical Guide for Supervisory Training and Development*. Reading, MA: Addison-Wesley Publishing Company, 1971.

McLarney, William J., and Berliner, Wilham M. *Management Training*, 5th ed. Homewood, IL: Richard D. Irwin, 1970.

Pearse, Robert F. *Manager to Manager: What Managers Think About Management Development*. New York: American Management Association, 1974.

Tasca, Anthony J. "Management Development: A Need or a Luxury?" *Training and Development Journal*, March 1975, pp. 16–22.

Taylor, B. and Lippitt, G. L., eds. *Management Development and Training Handbook*. New York: McGraw-Hill Book Company, 1975.

Welch, Mary Scott. *Networking: The Great Way for Women to Get Ahead*. New York: Harcourt Brace Jovanovich, Inc. 1980.

Wessman, Fred. "Determining Training Needs of Managers." *Personnel Journal*, February 1975, pp. 109–25.

For Analysis: Cincinnati Trust Bank

With over nine hundred employees and assets of over $2 billion, Cincinnati Trust Bank (CTB) is the city's largest bank in terms of human and financial resources. Offering a wide range of banking services, CTB has twenty-seven branches located throughout the city. Its growth and profit figures are impressive, and the bank's outlook appears bright.

For over two decades, the bank has operated a formal training department for clerical and operative personnel. New tellers, clerks, receptionists, and other kinds of lower level administrative personnel usually spend their first one or two weeks of employment in the bank's training department at the home office downtown. After being permanently assigned to a branch or home office department, employees usually receive on-the-job training from their supervisors.

About a year ago, the vice-president for personnel sensed a need for a more formal development of managerial personnel and created the position of manager, supervisory and executive development. Before the creation of the position, management development consisted primarily of informal on-the-job coaching and job rotation. Occasionally, managers would attend seminars or short courses if they desired and budget monies were available.

Keith McCloud was hired to fill the manager's job. McCloud had an MBA with a personnel concentration and five years' experience as a training and development manager with a medium-sized bank in Indianapolis, Indiana. He was charged with the overall responsibility of assessing management development needs at all levels of the management hierarchy and implementing, coordinating, and evaluating developmental efforts.

McCloud's first assignment was to create a comprehensive developmental program for the bank's entire first level of supervision. Some of these supervisors were the head teller, accounting supervisor, operations officer, and keypunch supervisor. McCloud began by conducting an assessment of developmental needs. Because the bank did not have a formal personnel planning function, he was unable to get a firm fix on the future need for managers or who the managers might be. In turning his attention to the assessment of current supervisory development needs, McCloud ran into another problem. The bank's performance appraisal system centered around the use of a general, trait-oriented appraisal system. The appraisals were virtually worthless in determining developmental needs. McCloud then determined he had to rely on other techniques to assess needs; he interviewed supervisors and their bosses. He implemented a morale survey for all nonsupervisory employees to get a feel for supervisory-related problems they experienced. Based on his interviews and the morale survey, McCloud uncovered these problem areas experienced by large numbers of supervisors:

- *a lack of knowledge about the budgeting process—how to create a budget and use it to control financial resources*
- *inability to hold effective performance appraisal interviews*
- *inability to delegate authority effectively*

- *lack of knowledge about different techniques to motivate employees*
- *inability to manage time and plan effectively on a day-to-day basis*
- *lack of skills in selecting new employees*
- *inability to manage meetings effectively*
- *lack of understanding about how a supervisor's leadership style affects employee productivity and morale*
- *inability to define clear expectations for subordinates*
- *lack of understanding concerning the role of the supervisor*
- *inability to write clear and concise letters and memos*
- *employee dissatisfaction with pay, health benefits, and the bank cafeteria*

Questions:

1. *Of the problems uncovered by Keith McCloud, which may be classified as technical skills? Conceptual skills? Human relations skills?*

2. *Which problems are solvable through management development activities and which are not?*

3. *Which problems should be dealt with during on-the-job developmental activities? Off-the-job activities? Both on- and off-the-job activities?*

4. *In addition to the list of problems McCloud developed, what other problems must he deal with and how can they be remedied?*

This wet limestone scrubber model at the Tennessee Valley Authority's engineering lab at Norris, Tennessee, requires teamwork.

11

ORGANIZATIONAL DEVELOPMENT

Organizational Problems

Values, Processes, and Technologies

Sensitivity Training

Grid® Organizational Development

Evaluating Planned Change

The Problem: Southwester Plastics

John Redmer is president of Southwester Plastics, Inc., a medium-sized manufacturer of plastic fittings in Dallas, Texas. Southwester Plastics serves a large midwestern market for plastic fittings and—until recently—has had a healthy record in both sales and profits.

Redmer was visibly upset when he walked into the executive committee meeting. The frown he wore remained unchanged throughout his opening remarks to the assembled department heads: "Ladies and gentlemen, I have just spent the last two hours poring over our earnings figures for the past quarter. And I'll tell you—they stink!

"Profits are down 27 percent, sales are down 16 percent, and earnings per share dropped 12 percent from $3.10 to $2.73. I don't think the cause of these dismal figures is a mystery to anyone. Six months ago, we lost the Cardinal Extrusion account—our biggest customer—because we missed several critical shipping dates. And Midwest Piping—another major customer—is now giving us token business compared to what we used to get. They, too, have complained about our unreliability. And these are just some of our more recent headaches. You all know that we have been plagued with high absenteeism and turnover for many months, and it's getting worse."

Redmer looked around at his management team. Heads were bowed. Several executives fidgeted nervously and squirmed in their chairs. Redmer spoke again. "We're going to get at the cause of these problems and we're not leaving today until we come up with some sound recommendations that will *improve our situation. Now let's talk specifics. Why the hell can't we meet our shipment dates? Fern, let's start with you."*

John Fern has been marketing manager at Southwester Plastics for about twelve years. "John, I hope this doesn't sound like I'm passing the buck, but marketing obviously has no control over production scheduling. When the product comes off the line, we get it to the customer as rapidly as possible. We lost Cardinal Extrusion because we simply couldn't get the products manufactured quickly enough."

Frank Cusick, manufacturing manager, cut in sharply. "Now just a minute, John. You know we couldn't meet our production quotas in time because of material shortages and excessive employee absenteeism. We have no control over the materials problem and personnel was no help in getting us temporary replacements for all the absent workers."

Joan Pierce, personnel manager, interrupted Cusick. "Frank, I thought I explained to you there was no budget money to hire temporary help."

Cusick continued, "Yes, I realize that, but it seems to me you could have gotten with the budget people and worked something out. Sometimes I think you people in personnel couldn't care less about some of the employee problems we have in the plant. . . ."

Redmer temporarily excused himself, went to his desk, and called his wife. "Doris, I'm going to be late tonight . . . Yes, I know, but . . . well, we'll just have to cancel our dinner plans with the McCabes. We've got some real problems here and I can't leave until they're resolved."

To the business novice, organizations may represent collections of carefree, satisfied employees who happily and eagerly go about their daily tasks and duties. Customers are frequently greeted with cheer and enthusiasm by employees in banks, retail stores, fast–food restaurants, and many other types of establishments. After touring large factories, visitors sometimes report that employees sing and whistle while they work and occasionally join in laughter with co-workers and supervisors over a practical joke. College seniors tell of job interviews at corporate headquarters where executives talk a great deal about teamwork and describe their management cadre as "one big happy family." On the surface, organizations appear to function like a real-life Camelot where employees live out their careers in harmony, compatibility, and esprit de corps.

Unfortunately, such is rarely—if ever—the case. In large and small organizations, whether public or private, distrust, strife, conflict, dissension, and job dissatisfaction often typify the human relationships and employee attitudes from the factory floor to the executive suite. Some unfortunate results of these problems are illustrated in the following scenarios:

- Senior executives in the marketing department of Acme International intensely disagree with research and development managers over the design of a major new product. They stop communicating with each other, and the project loses valuable time getting off the ground. When the product is finally ready to ship to wholesalers, the competition has captured a sizable share of the market with a similar product.

- In a large southern bank, college educated management trainees are initially assigned to job rotation among six or seven departments for several weeks at a time. But instead of the challenging and interesting work assignments promised during the job interviews, the trainees are given thankless, boring tasks that contribute little to their development. As a result, many quit after two or three months; the bank loses valuable talent, and suffers extraordinarily high turnover costs.

- In a medium-sized manufacturing company, reports and memos from the first level of management to middle management reflect a deceivingly optimistic picture. Actual productivity figures are padded and severe quality control problems are glossed over. First-line supervisors are afraid to tell the full truth in their communications, fearing that heads would roll if their superiors knew the real situation. The communication problem continues until a surprise productivity audit takes place, and heads really *do* roll.

- Rumors of mass layoffs at a Virginia tobacco manufacturer are rampant. Nobody knows what top management's plans really are—there is no official word from the executive suite. Employee morale sags to new lows, and many workers look around for new jobs. Absenteeism skyrockets.

- In the business school of a large urban university, the faculty is deeply divided concerning the school's future. One large group of young turks urges the dean to place increasingly greater emphasis on scholarly research and recruit only faculty with strong research credentials. An old guard group decries what they perceive as a lack of concern over teaching excellence and pressures the dean to make promotion and tenure decisions primarily on the basis of classroom skills and teaching expertise. The dean wavers, and turmoil within the faculty increases. Because of the internal strife, two professors retire early and four others leave to take jobs in more collaborative environments.

ORGANIZATIONAL PROBLEMS

To a large extent, the problems at Southwester Plastics and the companies described in these scenarios stem from the increasing complexity of many organizations. Environmental turbulence is often used to define the conditions that envelop organizations today; the environmental stability enjoyed years ago shows little sign of returning to contemporary industrialized society. The specific forces that have led to dangerous levels of organizational turmoil are:[1]

Growth and Size

Significant gains in growth and size have created a mix of complex and sophisticated technologies, specializations, and highly diverse personnel. As organizations grow, problems of coordination among different departments, organizational levels, and technologies can become immense. Effective managers coor-

dinate human and material resources to achieve common goals and purposes.

Increased Diversity

As organizations grow, they often become diversified by adding unique, highly specialized roles and tasks. New groups working on research and development, corporate planning, management development, product planning, and equal employment may be required to effectively and legally manufacture and market the company's product. Specialized roles and functions may also result in conflicts over how companies should be organized and managed. For example, marketing and accounting executives may have different pricing strategies for a new product. Organizational mechanisms must keep these conflicts at creative and manageable levels.

Internal Change

Growth, size, and diversity have caused managers to change from traditional management techniques to practices more suited for today's dynamic organization environments. Increasingly, effective management behavior is characterized by delegation, participation, collaboration, and teamwork. Further, managers must strive to dovetail their leadership styles with the needs of the new breed of employees whose attitudes and values are markedly different from those of employees decades ago. Today, many employees are rejecting authoritarian leadership styles and demanding greater voices in matters that affect their work.

Rapid internal changes may also place stress and strain on an organization's health. These pressures include increased

---

1. John Swanda, *Organizational Behavior* (Sherman Oaks, CA: Alred Publishing Co., 1979), p. 462.

demands from minority groups and widespread obsolescence among managerial and nonmanagerial ranks. To remain effective, an organization must possess mechanisms to manage change rather than succumb to change.

External Change

Pressures from economic, political, sociocultural, and technological forces in the external environment continue to mount. Often-cited examples include double digit inflation, increased government legislation, unrestrained domestic and foreign competition, rapid technological advancements, and a rapidly changing work force.

Problems of unplanned, unregulated change beset enterprises in all areas of the economy—the corporation, university, government agency, military command, and nonprofit association. Unchecked, these problems may result in high labor and administrative costs, marginal employee productivity, poor product quality, mediocre profits, and sluggish growth. In severe situations, the organization may fail, succumb to bankruptcy, or fall prey to a healthier, more powerful organization. In more hopeful cases, the organization may continue as a marginal, struggling competitor given little due by its stronger, more potent rivals.

Faced with a number of critical problems, what action should be taken to improve an organization's outlook for the future? Management could do nothing, and hope that the problems are only temporary and will somehow magically disappear. This option is rarely successful. Another option is to call in a management consulting team which studies the organization's problems and reports what man-

agement must do to overcome them. A third option is for the organization to beef up its management development efforts and hope that management's exposure to some of the activities discussed in the previous chapter will result in a more effective organization. Four, the organization's administration may consider organizational development.

ORGANIZATIONAL DEVELOPMENT

Organizational development (OD) is a long-range effort to improve an organization's problem-solving and renewal processes. This is done through more effective and collaborative management of organizational culture, emphasizing formal work teams, assisted by a change agent, or catalyst, and utilizing applied behavioral science theory and technology, including action research.[2] A discussion of the key phrases in this definition may highlight the nature and characteristics of organizational development.

Organizational development is a long-range effort. Organizational development does not offer shortcuts or quick remedies to improve organization effectiveness. Organizational development processes and activities may extend over several months or even years. Because these activities are often designed to change the entire organization or a major organizational subsystem, a great deal of time is involved in planning, implementing, and perhaps, altering the organizational development program. Some theorists add an air of perpetuity to organiza-

---

2. Wendell L. French, and Cecil H. Bell, Jr., *Organization Development* (Englewood Cliffs, NJ: Prentice-Hall, Inc., 1973), p. 15.

tional development by describing the change effort as "an ongoing process." This perception stems primarily from the belief that complex organizations naturally and continually give rise to significant problems which demand effective problem-solving mechanisms.

to improve an organization's problem solving and renewal processes. Primarily, organizational development emphasizes creating effective mechanisms to deal with real-life organizational problems. After problems are confronted and properly defined, they are resolved in a manner that taps the ingenuity, creativity, and resourcefulness of the organization's total human resource group—not simply a few key managers and staff administrators.

Organization renewal processes focus on mechanisms for maintaining organizational vitality. As theorist Gordon Lippitt puts it, renewal is "the process of initiating, creating, and confronting needed changes so as to make it possible for organizations to become or remain viable, to adapt to new conditions, to learn from experiences."[3]

through a more effective and collaborative management of organization culture. Like societies, organizations have cultures which describe the prevailing attitudes, beliefs, norms, and values of human groups. Much of an organizational development effort focuses on changing the *organization's culture* as proponents believe that employees' attitudes and values play a major role in effectively dealing with problems. An organization where strife, conflict, fear, and distrust separate department heads, for example, would be unable to effectively tackle problems

which demand cooperation and teamwork.

One way to illustrate the organization's culture is to contrast its informal aspects—its hidden cultural variables—with the formal components of the enterprise such as goals, technology, and structure. In a sense, the organization's formal systems represent only the tip of the *organizational iceberg* as shown in Figure 11–1. Organizational development proponents claim that effective problem-solving efforts must focus on the formal and informal elements of the organization. Further, advocates suggest that traditional problem-solving techniques result in only mediocre success because they place primary emphasis on changing the formal aspects of the organization, neglecting the organization's powerful, hidden culture.

emphasizing formal work teams. Within the organizational development philosophy, the *work team* is considered the most critical unit in the organization's total human resource system. And many high-ranking practitioners agree. During the presidencies of Gerald Ford and Jimmy Carter top officials were dismissed for not being team players. Ford Motor Company Chairman Henry Ford II cited teamwork as a critical factor in deciding when to leave the company. He stated: "The supremely important issue is that the company have in place management that can run the company efficiently and as a team. And now we have that team."[4]

Work units may be permanent—such as a manager and subordinates—or tem-

---

3. Gordon L. Lippitt, *Organization Renewal* (New York: Appleton-Century-Crofts, 1969), p. 1.

4. Leonard M. Apcar, "Caldwell Succeeds Ford As the Chairman of Ford Motors; Peterson is New President," *The Wall Street Journal*, March 14, 1980, p. 4.

FIGURE 11–1: *Organizational Iceberg*

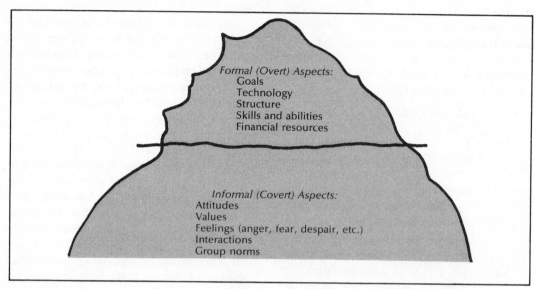

SOURCE: Wendell L. French, Cecil H. Bell, Jr., *Organization Development: Behavioral Science Interventions for Organization Improvement*, 2nd. ed., © 1978, p. 16. Reprinted by permission of Prentice-Hall, Inc., Englewood Cliffs, NJ.

porary—such as ad hoc committees, special project teams, and task forces. Other human resource units—such as the individual employee, the department or division, and the organization as a whole—also receive attention during organizational development processes, but the work team is normally recognized as the backbone of the organization and the target of most organizational development strategies.

assisted by a change agent, or catalyst. Individuals who plan an organizational development effort and carry out these activities must understand how human systems function within an organization. *Change agents* must know a great deal about human motivation, group dynamics, and what makes a job satisfying, fulfilling, and rewarding. Too, these planners must understand the formal aspects of the organization—particularly how its

goals, structure, and technology affect human and group behavior. Further, they must be unbiased in their attitudes toward various groups and individuals, avoiding opinions such as "the really important people in the organization are the high level staff experts" or "it looks to me like management is always giving the workers the shaft." To a degree, the success of an organizational development effort depends upon the skills, abilities, and attitudes of the individuals who plan and implement the program.

Because an organization rarely contains the talent necessary to implement a major organizational development effort—at least in the program's initial stages—most organizations employ an outside group experienced in all aspects. These consultants are called change agents or catalysts because their goal is to assist the client organization in making very definite changes in how people and groups relate and how jobs are designed and performed. Note that the role of the change agent is not to come in and fix the organization as is typical with conventional management consultants; rather, the change agent is a facilitator working with management to bring about needed changes.

utilizing applied behavioral science theory and technology. Beginning with the classic Hawthorne Studies in the 1920s, the behavioral sciences—notably psychology, social psychology, and sociology—have had a significant impact on management theory and practice. Managers and administrators have increased their effectiveness by studying well-defined and researched theories about human motivation and group behavior in college courses, seminars, books, and journal articles.

Organizational development is based on behavioral science theory and research; through organizational development exercises and techniques, change agents directly apply this knowledge to individuals and groups within the organization. The primary emphasis is upon strengthening behavioral rather than technical skills; minor attention is given to improving employees' competence in functional disciplines, such as marketing, finance, accounting, or personnel.

including action research. Throughout an organizational development effort, data about the company are systematically collected, analyzed, and acted upon. These data reflect current problems—primarily those dealing with the organization's culture. Through action research, data are collected, problems identified, and changes planned and implemented, enabling the organization to function more effectively. As a final step, data are collected again to assess the impact of those changes. In theory, this series of events becomes a natural, permanent part of the organization's problem-solving processes. The term action research underscores the fact that data are collected about real problems in real organizations, and those problems are acted upon.

Objectives

While specific content and OD methods will vary from program to program, their results are fairly typical, regardless of the size or type of organization, or the particular change agent implementing the program. With the broad, general goal of increased organizational effectiveness, specific objectives of organizational development include:

- Increasing the level of trust and support among organizational members.

- Increasing confrontation of organizational problems, both within groups and among groups, in contrast to "sweeping problems under the rug."

- Creating an environment in which assigned authority is augmented by authority based on knowledge and skill.

- Increasing open communications laterally, vertically, and diagonally.

- Increasing the level of personal enthusiasm and satisfaction in the organization.

- Finding synergistic solutions to problems with greater frequency. (Synergistic solutions are creative solutions in which the cooperative result is greater than the sum of individual efforts; all parties gain more through cooperation than through conflict.)

FIGURE 11–2: *An Integrative OD Model*

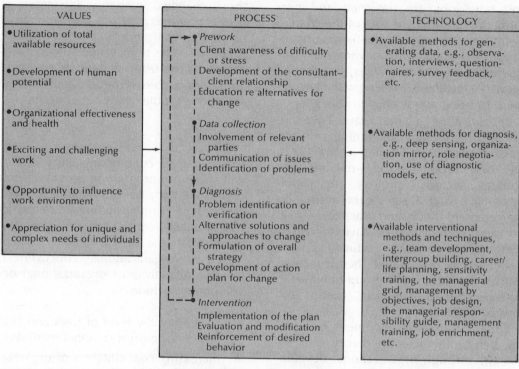

VALUES	PROCESS	TECHNOLOGY
• Utilization of total available resources	*Prework* Client awareness of difficulty or stress Development of the consultant–client relationship Education re alternatives for change	• Available methods for generating data, e.g., observation, interviews, questionnaires, survey feedback, etc.
• Development of human potential		
• Organizational effectiveness and health	*Data collection* Involvement of relevant parties Communication of issues Identification of problems	• Available methods for diagnosis, e.g., deep sensing, organization mirror, role negotiation, use of diagnostic models, etc.
• Exciting and challenging work		
• Opportunity to influence work environment	*Diagnosis* Problem identification or verification Alternative solutions and approaches to change Formulation of overall strategy Development of action plan for change	• Available interventional methods and techniques, e.g., team development, intergroup building, career/life planning, sensitivity training, the managerial grid, management by objectives, job design, the managerial responsibility guide, management training, job enrichment, etc.
• Appreciation for unique and complex needs of individuals		
	Intervention Implementation of the plan Evaluation and modification Reinforcement of desired behavior	

SOURCE: From *Conceptual Foundations of Organization Development* by Newton Marguiles and Anthony P. Raia. © 1978 McGraw-Hill Book Co. Used with permission of McGraw-Hill Book Co.

• Increasing the level of individual and group responsibility in planning and implementation.[5]

Despite an abundance of articles, monographs, books, college courses, and seminars devoted to organizational development, there still appears to be some confusion. Perhaps, organizational development is best described as a unique, integrative approach to organizational problem solving and change which combines an explicit set of values, processes,

_____
5. Wendell French, "Organization Development: Objectives, Assumptions, Strategies," *California Management Review* 12, no. 2 (1969): 23.

and technologies. Figure 11–2 illustrates the integrative nature of these major components.

Values

While specific change technologies vary from organization to organization, the values of organizational development's philosophy do not. As Figure 11–2 illustrates, organizational development is heavily laden with humanistic or people-oriented values which reflect a set of norms and beliefs about how organizations should be designed and managed.

Organizational development values clearly mirror the ideals of the behavioral scientists who developed it in the late 1950s and early 1960s. The principals in the movement—Douglas McGregor, Herbert Shepard, and Robert Blake—have devoted their careers to examining and writing about how individuals can maximize their potentials within organizations, integrating personal needs with those of the organizations. Each of these humanists strongly believed that working in an organization need not be boring, frustrating, stressful, or dissatisfying. Instead, they held that individuals on all levels of the enterprise can grow, develop, and enjoy satisfying, rewarding careers if the proper organizational culture and problem-solving techniques exist.

Because the implementation of organizational development will likely result in pronounced changes in an organization's culture, executives must be fully aware of how these changes will affect the way the organization functions. For organizational development to be successful, most key members of the organization must want to change and embrace the values that underlie the philosophy. Wherever some managers hold values that clash with organizational development, particularly in top management ranks, attempts to implement it will likely result in failure. Thus, initial discussions between the change agent and client should focus on whether organizational development is a potentially beneficial strategy for that particular organization. Early on, key organizational decision makers must answer these questions: Is organizational development right for us? Are the forces that will resist stronger than organizational development itself? And, what are the major roadblocks to the adoption of organizational development values and what are the chances for eliminating them?

Processes and Technologies

To bring about greater organizational effectiveness through planned changes in an organization's culture, management becomes involved in steps or procedures referred to as organizational development processes. As Figure 11–2 illustrates, the four processes include prework, data collection, diagnosis, and intervention. Each process is important and cannot be neglected. While in theory these steps appear distinct, in practice they overlap and are not easily separated from one another.

A technology is simply a way of achieving a purpose or goal. Organizational development technologies include the specific methods and techniques that are used to implement this change process. Some of these technologies are familiar by now—for example, job enrichment and management by objectives. Other technologies, such as process consultation and team building, are unique, innovative methods that were spawned during the organizational development movement. Too, new technologies are still emerging as organizational development continues to become more refined and sophisticated. A more detailed discussion of each process and some of the technologies may clarify the interrelationships between values, processes, and technologies.

PREWORK

Prework involves activities marking the beginning of a program. After the client has become aware of one or more serious organizational problems which may be rectified through OD, a change agent is contacted. Then the client and change agent begin their relationship through a mutual education process. The change agent explores in detail the organization's existing culture, major problems, key work units and individuals, and traditional problem-solving methods. The client, in turn, becomes familiar with norms, values, and techniques and learns a great deal about the change agent's specific approach to organizational development. Mutually, the client and change agent determine if this process will be a workable problem-solving strategy for the client. Should they agree that it is, a game plan is developed for implementing the program.

DATA COLLECTION

Prework sets the stage for collecting a great deal of data about the organization's problems and existing culture. *Data collection* is the beginning of the action research process where management, staff, and employee perceptions are typically gathered about:

- The quality of supervision; the likes and dislikes about the prevailing styles of leadership.

- The quality of inter– and intragroup relationships—trust, openness, honesty, etc.

- The degree of satisfaction experienced by employees due to their jobs, co-workers, supervisors, and the organization.

- The major roadblocks to high levels of organizational effectiveness, job performance, and job satisfaction.

Some of the more common technologies used during data collection include interviews and surveys. The change agent generally interviews key members of all major functions such as manufacturing, marketing, research and development, finance, and personnel. In smaller organizations, interviews may take place with individuals at all levels of the organization. Within a program, surveys are normally used to systematically gather information from all organizational levels— management, staff, and operative personnel. A survey that may be used to collect data from large groups of employees is shown in Figure 11–3.

DIAGNOSIS

Following the data gathering stage, the change agent and key members of the organization jointly *diagnose* the data to identify specific organizational problems and develop potential solutions. During this stage, conferences are held during which the results of interviews and surveys are fed back to managers and administrators for discussion. The change agent encourages the client group to actively participate in explaining and interpreting the data. By taking an active role in diagnosis, key managers and administrators are more likely to understand the organization's existing culture, and its deficiencies, and give their full commitment to a planned change effort.

INTERVENTION

In the context of organizational development, the term *intervention* is used to describe a specific technology for bringing about planned organizational change. The particular interventions management selects from the wide variety of interventions is, by and large, decided by: one, organizational needs as defined by the problems uncovered during the diagnosis stage; and two, the preferences the change agent or client organization may

FIGURE 11–3: *Profile of Organizational Characteristics*

	Organizational variables	System 1	System 2	System 3	System 4	Item no.
Leadership	How much confidence and trust is shown in subordinates?	Virtually none	Some	Substantial amount	A great deal	1
	How free do they feel to talk to superiors about job?	Not very free	Somewhat free	Quite free	Very free	2
	How often are subordinate's ideas sought and used constructively?	Seldom	Sometimes	Often	Very frequently	3
Motivation	Is predominant use made of 1 fear, 2 threats, 3 punishment, 4 rewards, 5 involvement?	1, 2, 3 occasionally 4	4, some 3	4, some 3 and 5	5, 4, based on group-set goals	4
	Where is responsibility felt for achieving organization's goals?	Mostly at top	Top and middle	Fairly general	At all levels	5
	How much cooperative teamwork exists?	Very little	Relatively little	Moderate amount	Great deal	6
Communication	What is the usual direction of information flow?	Downward	Mostly downward	Down and up	Down, up, and sideways	7
	How is downward communication accepted?	With suspicion	Possibly with suspicion	With caution	With a receptive mind	8
	How accurate is upward communication?	Usually inaccurate	Often inaccurate	Often accurate	Almost always accurate	9
	How well do superiors know problems faced by subordinates?	Not very well	Rather well	Quite well	Very well	10
Decisions	At what level are decisions made?	Mostly at top	Policy at top, some delegation	Broad policy at top, more delegation	Throughout but well integrated	11
	Are subordinates involved in decisions related to their work?	Almost never	Occasionally consulted	Generally consulted	Fully involved	12
	What does decision-making process contribute to motivation?	Not very much	Relatively little	Some contribution	Substantial contribution	13
Goals	How are organizational goals established?	Orders issued	Orders, some comments invited	After discussion, by orders	By group action (except in crisis)	14
	How much covert resistance to goals is present?	Strong resistance	Moderate resistance	Some resistance at times	Little or none	15
Control	How concentrated are review and control functions?	Very highly at top	Quite highly at top	Moderate delegation to lower levels	Widely shared	16
	Is there an informal organization resisting the formal one?	Yes	Usually	Sometimes	No—Same goals as formal	17
	What are cost, productivity, and other control data used for?	Policing, punishment	Reward, punishment	Reward some self-guidance	Self-guidance, problem-solving	18

SOURCE: From *New Ways of Managing Conflict* by R. Likert and J. G. Likert. © 1976 by McGraw-Hill Book Company. Used with permission of McGraw-Hill Book Company.

FIGURE 11–4: *Organizational Development Interventions*

Individuals	Work Teams	Intergroup Relationships	Total Organizations
Sensitivity Training: Stranger Groups	Sensitivity Training: Family Groups	Intergroup Team Building	Survey Feedback
Training and Development	Team Building	Third Party Peacemaking	Managerial Grid
Life and Career Planning Activities	Process Consultation		Management by Objectives
Job Enrichment			Technostructural Activities

have for certain kinds of interventions.[6] Typically organizations experience many different kinds of problems and normally conduct multiple interventions during the course of a program.

One useful classification for interventions is by the target group that participates in a particular intervention. Using this typology, an intervention may improve the effectiveness of the individual, the work team, intergroup relationships, or the total organization. Some of the more popular interventions for these target groups are illustrated in Figure 11–4. Often, a particular intervention is used to increase the skills of several target groups. For example, survey feedback may strengthen work team skills and intergroup relations, in addition to strengthening the total organization. Figure 11–4 is a general guide in matching target groups and interventions

SENSITIVITY TRAINING: STRANGER GROUPS In the previous chapter, we saw that sensitivity training is a well-known management development technique for improving the

interpersonal skills of managerial personnel. Sensitivity training was once considered the cornerstone of the movement. Although its use has diminished considerably today, sensitivity training is still looked upon by many behavioral scientists as an effective way to strengthen human relations skills.

While sensitivity training is always conducted in a group setting, the composition of groups may vary considerably. If a manager or administrator does not know any other group participants, the group is referred to as a *stranger group*. All participants are, in fact, strangers—until the training gets under way. In this type of group, the objective is to improve individual interpersonal skills that could be applied on the job within other respective organizations. Other types of sensitivity groups focus on group effectiveness and will be discussed later in this section.

TRAINING AND DEVELOPMENT Traditional training and development activities are also important individually-oriented organizational development interventions. These activities are primarily designed to (1) upgrade knowledge, (2) change outmoded beliefs and attitudes, and (3) increase skill levels. One or more of the many varieties of on- and off-the-job training and development activities may be

---

6. Of course, the primary criterion for selecting interventions should be the organization's needs. In practice, however, the client's or change agent's likes or dislikes toward certain interventions play an important part in determining which techniques are selected.

included as organizational development interventions.

LIFE AND CAREER PLANNING These activities focus on life and career objectives, helping individuals exert greater control over their lives. During these activities, participants normally (1) assess their lives and careers to date, highlighting both very satisfying and dissatisfying events, (2) create life and career goals for the future, (3) create a plan for achieving these goals. Normally, these activities are completed individually and then discussed in small groups. Life and career planning techniques are particularly useful for individuals considering career changes or experiencing great stress or pressure in their jobs.

JOB ENRICHMENT Discussed in detail in Chapter 4, job enrichment may be implemented as a separate job redesign strategy or may be one of several interventions used during an organizational development effort. In the latter case, the change agent and client see job enrichment as a technique that will help fulfill the program's goals and objectives.

SENSITIVITY TRAINING FAMILY GROUPS Sensitivity training which involves a manager and subordinates is known as a *family group.* This form of sensitivity training is designed to improve intragroup trust, communication, participation, empathy, and other human relations skills among work team members. The goals, methods, and processes of family groups are very similar to those of stranger groups. Family groups may include an emphasis on task-oriented issues (such as how to approach the group decision–making process or how to delegate authority throughout the group), but the primary purpose of the training is to strengthen the team members' working culture.

TEAM BUILDING *Team building* exercises are among the most important and widely-used organizational development interventions. Participants in team building exercises may include family groups or special groups such as committees, task forces, or project teams.

Specific issues that may be dealt with during team building include:

- Task-oriented issues: decision making and problem solving, clarifying roles, responsibilities, and goals.
- Process-oriented issues: interpersonal communication between the boss and subordinates and among work team members, intergroup conflict, delegation of authority, allocation of responsibilities, and power equalization.

While team building meetings may be conducted in a variety of ways, a change agent usually interviews team members before the meeting to collect data on issues to be discussed during the meeting. For example, the change agent may ask what the major problems are and what could be done to make the group function more effectively. With the change agent acting as a facilitator during the meeting, issues are confronted and analyzed, solutions to problems are generated, and a plan of action for remedying problems is developed.

PROCESS CONSULTATION During *process consultation*, the change agent usually observes the work team's problem–solving techniques, communication and interaction patterns, and methods for assigning work and delegating authority; the agent then gives the team alternative ways to achieve work team goals.

Throughout process consultation, the change agent plays the role of resource person rather than an expert who "tells the group how to behave properly." As one OD theorist described it,

> The job of the process consultant is to help the organization to solve its own problems by making it aware of organizational processes, of the consequences of these processes, and of the mechanisms by which they can be changed. The ultimate concern of the process consultant is the organization's capacity to do for itself what he has done for it. Where the standard consultant is more concerned about passing on his knowledge, the process consultant is concerned about passing on his skills and values.[7]

INTERGROUP TEAM BUILDING Organizations—like wars—are often characterized by enemies, battle lines, strategies to divide and conquer, minor skirmishes, and major battles. The manufacturing department, for example, may wage continuing hostilities with the personnel department because of major disagreements over hiring and selection procedures, assessment of training and development needs, wage and salary levels, or implementation of the company's affirmative action program. These conflicts normally result in poor communication, competition rather than cooperation, decreased interaction, and each group feeling that it is always right and the other group is always wrong. The purpose of intergroup team building activities is to change this combative environment into collaborative, cooperative working relationships between groups. Specific goals of intergroup team building include improved communications and interactions,

cooperation, and an awareness that maximum group effectiveness results from working together.

During intergroup team building, each group typically meets individually and creates a list of feelings and beliefs about the other group. The manufacturing staff, for example, may feel that the personnel department "exerts too much authority," "doesn't appreciate our problems," and "wants change for the sake of change." On the other hand, personnel may view manufacturing as "concerned only with the status quo," "not wanting to implement new and useful personnel techniques," and "not understanding how personnel operates or caring to." Assisted by a change agent, groups meet and share their lists. Through discussion of what they have learned about one another, the departments confront areas of disagreement and conflict, gaining a greater understanding of how conflict is created and why it should be minimized. After deciding which issues to resolve and ways to resolve these issues, the groups develop a plan of action to improve relationships between groups.

THIRD PARTY PEACEMAKING During peacemaking, the third party—normally a change agent—is the mediator between two conflicting groups. In addition to being completely familiar with the functions of each group, and the conflicts between the groups, the change agent must diagnose the sources of conflict. Issues are normally resolved during a meeting involving the third party peacemaker and key members of the conflicting parties. Normally, the change agent prepares an agenda, referees the meeting, and moves the groups toward a resolution of problems.

SURVEY FEEDBACK Organizational develop-

---

7. E. H. Schein, *Process Consultation* (Reading, MA: Addison-Wesley Publishing Co., 1969), p. 135.

ment efforts that include employee surveys during the data collection process often later involve an important and useful activity known as *survey feedback*. While there are many variations to this popular technique, survey feedback commonly includes:

Step 1: Key organizational members and the change agent plan the survey.

Step 2: Surveys are implemented and data collected from most or all of the organization.

Step 3: Beginning at the top of the hierarchy, data are fed down to each supervisor and each subordinate.

Step 4: With the assistance of a change agent, supervisors and subordinates discuss and interpret the results, pinpoint problem areas, and make plans for change.

The survey feedback process is much different than traditional employee survey techniques. Figure 11–5 compares the organizational development survey feedback approach to conventional survey methods.

GRID® ORGANIZATIONAL DEVELOPMENT Organizational development interventions including most or all departments and key staff members are usually referred to as total organization interventions. Of these

FIGURE 11–5: *Survey Feedback Processes*

	Traditional Approach	Survey Feedback Research Approach
Data collection from:	Rank and file, and maybe supervisor	Everyone in the system or subsystem
Data reported to:	Top management, department heads, and perhaps to employees through newspaper	Everyone who participated
Implications of data are worked on by:	Top management (maybe)	Everyone in work teams, with workshops starting at the top (all superiors with their subordinates)
Third-party intervention strategy:	Design and administration of questionnaire, development of a report	Obtaining concurrence on total strategy, design and administration of questionnaire, design of workshops, appropriate interventions in workshops
Action planning done by:	Top management only	Teams at all levels
Probable extent of change and improvement:	Low	High

SOURCE: J.M. Ivancevich, A.D. Szilagyi, Jr., and M.J. Wallace, Jr., *Organization Behavior and Human Performance* (Santa Monica, California: Goodyear Publishing Company, Inc., 1977), p. 521. Used with permission of Goodyear Publishing Company.

techniques, Grid remains one of the most popular and widely used. Developed by behavioral scientists Robert Blake and Jane Mouton, Grid training involves a six-phase program whereby key organization members develop and implement an ideal corporate model. The general nature and purposes of Grid OD training may be understood by examining the main elements of each Grid phase.

Phase One: the Managerial Grid. In this phase, individual managerial styles, are assessed. The *managerial grid,* illustrated in Figure 11–6, depicts participants' leadership orientations along two dimensions: concern for people and concern for production. The *9, 9 management* style (optimal concern for people and pro-

duction) is normally thought of as the best leadership style, and participants are encouraged to close the gap between their actual leadership styles and the 9, 9 style.

Phase Two: Teamwork Development. During phase two, emphasis is placed upon perfecting the work teams' interpersonal and task–oriented skills. Activities in this phase closely parallel the team building interventions discussed earlier.

Phase Three: Intergroup Development. In phase three, pairs of groups which interact frequently define ideal intergroup relationships. Typically, this ideal state includes high degrees of collaboration, cooperation, communication, and trust. Specific plans are developed that will

FIGURE 11–6: *The Managerial Grid®*

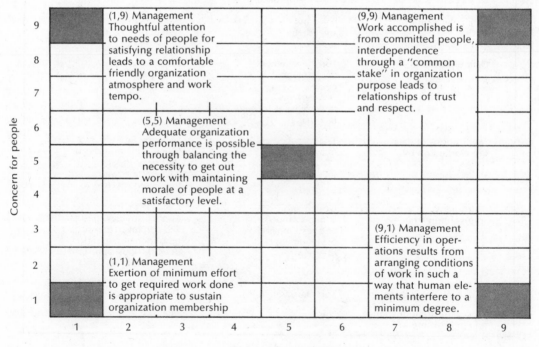

Concern for production

SOURCE: *The New Managerial Grid,* by Robert R. Blake and Jane Srygley Mouton. Houston: Gulf Publishing Company, Copyright © 1978, p. 11. Reproduced by permission.

enable groups to move toward this ideal model.

Phase Four: Developing an Ideal Corporate Model. In phase four top management defines the ideal corporate model—the state at which a corporation is operating at peak performance. During this phase, a great deal of time is spent on strategic planning and goal-setting activities. The changes the organization's culture must make to realize the ideal corporate model are emphasized.

Phase Five: Implementing the Ideal Strategic Model. During phase five, management implements the model developed in phase four. Often, the organization must undergo significant structural changes, such as the development of new product lines or profit centers. Implementing the model is facilitated by special planning teams which study the ideal model and recommend how organizational change can most effectively be made.

Phase Six: Systematic Critique. After phase five has been operating for a sufficient time, the Grid program's overall effectiveness to date is closely analyzed. The overall implementation of the ideal corporate model is assessed to identify those aspects of the model that have been successfully implemented and those that have met with problems. Where barriers exist, methods for overcoming those barriers are developed.

MANAGEMENT BY OBJECTIVES (MBO) In Chapter 8, MBO was presented as a potentially effective way to create objective, measurable performance standards for an organization's human resource group, and to compare actual performance against stated objectives. In reality, MBO is much more than a performance appraisal system. Management by objectives is a planning and control system, an employee

motivation system, a technique to clarify roles and responsibilities, and a reward system, in addition to a mechanism for appraising employee performance. Perhaps MBO is best described as a philosophy of management whereby management's total thinking is focused on the achievement of measurable and relevant organizational objectives. As such, MBO and organizational development can be highly compatible with one another:

It's entirely possible to start with OD and end up with MBO or start with goal-setting and end up with team-building. Some companies start with team-building to get people to work together, and follow this with a development of mission statements. There's no reason you can't do that. If the management team is working together, there's no point in spending time in team building. If they have good teams but don't know where they are going, then it makes sense to start off setting goals.

If, however, people are not working together, an MBO system won't do anything but change the topic over which they're going to fight. In this case, team building should precede, or at least parallel, the goal-setting process. But regardless of the situation, MBO and OD are perfectly consistent with one another.[8]

TECHNOSTRUCTURAL ACTIVITIES These activities may take one of two broad forms: changes in the organization's structure, and innovations in the organization's technologies. Structural changes may involve reorganization from a centralized to a decentralized corporate form, or streamlining the organization by eliminating needless functions and operations. Technical changes focus on improving nonhuman resources so that the organiza-

8. Frank E. Kuzmits, "An Interview With George Odiorne," *Supervisory Management* (August 1978): 16.

FIGURE 11–7: *The Impact of OD on Outcome and Process Variables*

	Outcome Variables			Process Variables	
Variable Level	Number of Studies	Average Change Rate	Number of Studies	Average Change Rate
Group	8 (12)a	63%	11 (69)a	49%
Organization	12 (31)	47	27 (96)	36
Individual	14 (40)	42	10 (21)	62
Leader	3 (3)	—	20 (36)	45
Total	22 (86)	51%	35 (222)	46%

aFigures in parentheses represent the total number of variables measured in each class.

SOURCE: Jerry I. Porras and P.O. Berg, "The Impact of Organization Development," *Academy of Management Review*, April 1978, pp. 254–256. Used with permission.

tion may function more effectively. Common examples include advanced computer technologies and automated assembly techniques.

Evaluating the OD Effort

In general, the researcher may draw from three broad strategies to evaluate any form of planned social change: the preexperimental design, the true experimental design, and the quasi-experimental design.[9]

A popular form of the *preexperimental design* includes the one group, pretest-posttest. Applying this design to an organizational development effort, one or more organizational effectiveness criteria—for example profits, absenteeism, turnover, or an index of job satisfaction—would be measured before the program began and after it had a chance to "take hold." The length of time is arbitrary. Organizational development is a long-

9. Donald T. Campbell, and Julian C. Stanley, *Experimental and Quasi-Experimental Designs for Research* (Chicago: Rand McNally Publishing Co., 1963).

term process, and decisions concerning when to take the second measurement must take this into account. The major problem with this evaluative strategy is inability to control extraneous factors that may have influenced the changes observed during the measurement process. Harsh weather conditions, for example, may have led to increased absenteeism. On the other hand, a tighter sick leave policy, unrelated to the organizational development program, may have decreased absenteeism. Because the preexperimental design contains problems which may significantly lessen its validity, the overall worth of this evaluative approach is minimal.

A *true experimental design* incorporates a control group—as a check on extraneous factors not related to the change effort. In theory, individuals are randomly assigned to experimental and control groups to ensure that any changes observed in the experimental group are due to the treatment (for example, a team building exercise) and not to any unique characteristic of the individuals. In the most common form of pretest-posttest control group design, important productivity criteria of both the experimental and control groups are measured before and after a change effort.

Quasi-experimental designs are, in terms of rigor, somewhere between the preexperimental and the true experimental design. A widely-used design of this type includes the nonequivalent control group design. In this case, the experimental and control groups receive before and after measurements, but individuals are not randomly assigned to these groups. For example, assume organizational development is being implemented in a large bank with several branches of similar size and operation. If OD is implemented in two or three branches as a pilot study, those branches not participating could be used as control groups and would be considered nonequivalent control groups.

Research Results

A major review of organizational development evaluative research by Jerry Porras and Per Olaf Berg included thirty-five studies completed between 1959 and 1975.[10] Of those studies, none used a true experimental design, eight used a preexperimental design, and twenty-seven used a quasi-experimental design. Based on the type of evaluative designs used for these studies, Porras and Berg note that "the data . . . do not support one common myth about OD research, i.e., that very little research has been done that deserves the designation of scientific . . . [relatively strong] designs account for approximately

50 percent of all the OD empirical research reported here."[11] Thus, the research indicates that many organizations have applied sound evaluative strategies to their programs. Because approximately half of the studies did not employ rigorous evaluation strategies, the need for improvement in evaluative research designs certainly exists.

Porras and Berg also examined the impact of organizational development upon organizational outcome and process variables.[12] Outcome variables include end result performance criteria such as profits, productivity, sales, costs, absenteeism, turnover, and job satisfaction. Process variables refer to an organization's cultural variables such as openness, influence, trust, support, participation, and intimacy. Porras and Berg measured the effect of organizational development upon outcome and process variables at four different organizational levels: group, organizational, individual, and leader.

IMPACT ON OUTCOME VARIABLES

The effects of organizational development upon outcome and process variables are illustrated in Figure 11–7. Overall, the results indicate that outcome variables changed in a positive direction 51 percent of the time compared to 31 percent of the time for satisfaction measures. Further, organizational development has its greatest impact on changing outcomes at the group level. Given that many interventions are directed toward improving group effectiveness, these results are not surprising.

10. Jerry I. Porras, and Per O. Berg, "Evaluation Methodology in Organization Development: An Analysis and Critique," *The Journal of Applied Behavior Science* 14, no. 2 (1978): 151–73.

11. Ibid., p. 157.
12. Jerry I. Porras, and Per O. Berg, "The Impact of Organization Development," *Academy of Management Review* 3, (1978): 254–56.

IMPACT ON PROCESS VARIABLES

The average rate of change for process variables for all levels was 46 percent, a figure slightly lower than the average rate of change recorded for outcome variables. Interestingly, the greatest impact on process variables occurred at the individual level where positive changes were recorded 62 percent of the time. Some of the changes recorded in individual process variables included self-awareness, understanding, openness, and self-actualization or self-development. These data suggest that organizational development has its greatest impact on changing individual attitudes and values.

What do these results suggest about the process's effectiveness? The research review indicates that organizational development has the potential to produce a very definite impact upon outcome and process variables. Through the program, the organization may effectively reach end result goals and may improve the climate in which people and groups work and interact. Further, the results lay to rest at least two common myths: The first myth is that the major impact is upon processes and not outcomes. The data suggest that organizational development affects outcome and process variables about equally for all organizational levels. The second myth is that organizational development has the greatest impact on organizational and group process variables. The study shows, however, that the average rate of change in individual process variables far exceeds the rate of change for organizational process variables.

Practices

In about two decades, organizational development has risen from a relatively obscure training specialty to a full-fledged academic discipline accompanied by an abundance of books, articles, short courses, and seminars. Several colleges and universities, including Harvard University, MIT, New York University, The Ohio State University, and Case Western Reserve University have established major fields of study in organizational development. The American Society for Training and the American Management Associations created special divisions in 1968 and 1971, respectively. The volume of organizational development literature and educational offerings has multiplied geometrically, and the process appears firmly ingrained within personnel and human resource management.

In addition to a few key articles and books extolling its virtues and benefits, early academic interest has led to the creation of organizational development programs in organizations of all sizes representing manufacturing, public utilities, insurance, banking, construction, health services, and others. Of course, no two programs are identical, but research suggests that many programs have several common elements:[13]

- Organization size—total employees and gross sales—strongly influence the decision to implement organiza-

13. See W. J. Hensler, "Patterns of OD in Practice," *Business Horizons* 18 (February 1975): 77–84; William F. Glueck, *Organization Planning and Development* (New York: American Management Association, 1971); Thomas H. Patten, et al., *Characteristics and Professional Concerns of Organization Development Practitioners* (Madison, WI: American Society for Training and Development, 1973); and Harold M. Rush, *Organization Development: A Reconnaissance* (New York: The Conference Board, 1973).

tional development, which is found in larger firms more frequently than smaller firms.

- By and large, organizational development staff members are involved in studies and projects that focus on the organization's culture. They assist in making positive changes in interpersonal and intergroup relationships, work climates, communication patterns, and leadership styles. Attitude surveys are used extensively to measure organization climate. To a lesser extent, activities are directed toward changes in the organization's formal structure.

- The majority of organizational development programs involve participative methods to identify and solve problems.

- In-house organizational development departments are typically small—less than a dozen professionals—and the department head normally reports to top management.

- Some of the most popular interventions include team building, MBO, process consultation, and survey feedback. The improvement of individual effectiveness, in addition to group effectiveness, is a prime goal of many organizational development programs.

- Program evaluation is seen as a problem area by many organizations. Most enterprises measure the impact of organizational development, but rely heavily on subjective methods such as staff observations or verbal evaluations by the participants. Only a few organizations employ objective means to measure the process's effectiveness.

THE PERSONNEL ROLE

Personnel administrators often receive key assignments during organizational development programs. Because their basic roles are to recruit, maintain, and strengthen the skills of the organization's human resource group, they possess the knowledge and abilities to implement and sustain an organizational development effort. Frequently, personnel administrators participate in making significant decisions related to the process, such as the diagnosis of critical organizational problems and the selection and timing of interventions.

As the program matures, the personnel specialist may assume some of the duties and responsibilities initially performed by the change agent. In this capacity, the personnel administrator is referred to as an *internal change agent* or internal consultant. This person may gather data, diagnose data, select interventions, and facilitate implementation of interventions, such as job enrichment or team building exercises. According to one research review, careful selection of internal change agents is an important characteristic of successful programs.[14] The study showed that change agents in these programs were not only skilled at identifying problems and their causes but also skilled in selecting and planning interventions relevant to the program's goals. Seldom does the external change agent completely sever ties with the organization, but visits become fewer and fewer as the organization's staff becomes increasingly skilled in carrying out organizational development activities.

14. Jerome L. Franklin, "Characteristics of Successful and Unsuccessful Organization Development," *The Journal of Applied Behavioral Science* 12 (1976): 488.

SIMILARITIES WITH EMPLOYEE TRAINING
AND MANAGEMENT DEVELOPMENT

In the previous two chapters, we discussed the purposes, processes, and techniques of employee training and management development. We emphasized the importance of strong employee training and management development functions, and suggested that these strategies are key factors in maintaining organizational effectiveness. And in this chapter, we have introduced yet another change strategy for enhancing the strength and competence of the organization's human resources. Perhaps at this point the student may wonder: How does OD differ from training and develop-

ment? What are the similarities and differences between these approaches?

To begin, training, development, and organizational development all share a broad, similar end: increased organizational effectiveness. Through a satisfied, motivated, and competent human resource group, favorable outcomes are expected in employee productivity, profits, organizational and personal growth, and other kinds of end result or outcome variables. But the means by which these approaches seek to satisfy the sought after ends will vary considerably. Perhaps a primary difference is that both training and development focus on changing the individual, whereas organizational devel-

FIGURE 11–8: *Comparison of traditional training and the organization change process*

Dimension	Traditional training	Organization change process
Unit of focus	The individual	Interpersonal relationships—teams, work units, intergroup relations, superior-subordinate relations
Content of training	Technical and administrative skills	Interpersonal and group membership skills—communication, problem solving, conflict management, helping
Target subjects	Primarily first-line employees and supervisors; managers trained outside organization	All levels; usually initial intervention with upper management in-house
Conception of learning process	Cognitive and rational	Cognitive, rational, emotional-motivational
Teaching style	Subject matter and teacher centered	Participant, immediate experience, problem solving, and subject matter centered
Learning goals	Rationality and efficiency	Awareness, adaptation, and change
View of organization	Discrete functional skill units	Social system

SOURCE: William B. Eddy, "From Training to Organization Change," *Personnel Administration*, January-February 1971, pp. 37–43. Reprinted by permission of the International Personnel Management Association, Washington, DC 20006

opment activities are geared toward altering the organization's culture. Some specific differences between organizational development and employee training and management development are illustrated in Figure 11–8.

While training, management development, and organizational development are somewhat distinct and unique approaches to change, they are, in fact, complementary strategies, often operating concurrently within an organization. Many behavioral scientists and personnel specialists consider training and development to be important process interventions. Rarely is a full scale OD effort void of employee training and management development activities.

In summary, organizational development is a mechanism to bring about planned change by improving the organization's cultural variables such as trust, participation, collaboration, support, openness, communication, satisfaction, and teamwork. Organizational development philosophy draws heavily on the behavioral sciences and normally includes an external change agent who assists in implementation. Values engendered by organizational development are decidedly humanistic and people oriented. In addition to indicating that organizational development has the potential to strengthen an organization's effectiveness, research has found that these elements are common to most existing organizational development programs: The process takes place primarily in large organizations, focuses on changing cultural variables, involves participative methods, and employs a small staff of in-house professionals. Often, it has methodological problems with evaluation, and includes team building, MBO, third-party consultation, and survey feedback as intervention technologies. Personnel specialists often play major roles in the planning and implementation of organizational development. As internal change agents, they may collect and diagnose data, select process interventions, and act as facilitators during exercises. The role of the internal change agent often expands as the program matures and in-house personnel become more skilled and experienced in organizational development.

The Solution

President John Redmer is experiencing some problems at Southwester Plastics that may be remedied through an organizational development effort. A great deal of intergroup conflict and distrust among management and staff exists at Southwester Plastics, and there is some evidence that these culturally-oriented problems have led to the firm's inability to meet production and shipping schedules.

Based on the limited data we have about Southwester Plastics, some form of intergroup team building exercises might be useful in creating a more collaborative working environment. Information gathered during the data collection stage may pinpoint other problem areas that need to be attacked, such as employee absenteeism and turnover. However, organizational development cannot guarantee success, and it is somewhat speculative to predict the extent to which team building or other forms of interventions would rectify Southwester Plastics' current problems.

KEY TERMS AND CONCEPTS

Environmental Turbulence
Organizational Development (OD)
Organizational Culture
Work Team
Organization Iceberg
Change Agent
Action Research
Prework
Data Collection
Diagnosis
Intervention
Stranger Groups

Family Groups
Team Building
Process Consultation
Third Party Peacemaking
Survey Feedback
Managerial Grid
9, 9 Management
Preexperimental Design
True Experimental Design
Quasi-experimental Design
Internal Change Agent

FOR REVIEW

1. What environmental factors have forced decision makers to seek innovative, nontraditional problem-solving methods?

2. What are the major characteristics of organizational development?

3. List the objectives that characterize organizational development programs.

4. What are the values upheld by the organizational development philosophy?

5. Describe the four organizational development processes and the technologies that are used in implementing them.

6. Describe the practices and characteristics of organizational development programs currently in existence.

7. How may the personnel administrator and other internal change agents assist in the implementation of organizational development?

8. In what ways are organizational development and the training and development function similar? Dissimilar?

FOR DISCUSSION

1. Think of various organizations you have worked for; describe two contrasting cultures—one favorable and one unfavorable. What effect did these cultures have on your output and job satisfaction?

2. Refer to question 1 and the organization with an unfavorable climate. What specific aspects of the climate do you feel need changing? How would you collect data to pinpoint the severity and location of problem areas? What specific organizational development interventions might reduce these problems?

3. Some managers hold values that are contrary to those of organizational development. Why is this so? How difficult is it to change a manager's values and attitudes about how organizations should be managed?

4. Assume a large organization has a widespread problem with employee absenteeism and turnover. Compare the organizational development approach to solving these problems to the methods that might be used by a conventional management consultant.

5. Do you think organizational development would be an effective problem-solving mechanism in a military command unit? Why or why not?

6. Assume that an organizational development program was implemented in a large automobile factory to improve employee productivity. After a three-year period, statistics show that productivity increased 12 percent. How can one be sure the increase in productivity was due to organizational development and not other extraneous variables? What might some of those extraneous variables be?

7. What are your own feelings about organizational development? Do you view it as a potentially beneficial method for increasing organization effectiveness? Why or why not? If you were the pres-

ident of a company with problems in its organizational culture, would you implement organizational development or some other change strategy?

SUPPLEMENTARY READINGS

Applebaum, S. "Contemporary Personnel Administrators: Agents of Change?" *Personnel Journal,* November, 1974, pp. 835–37.

———. "Management Development and OD—Getting It Together." *Personnel Management,* August, 1975, pp. 33–35.

Baumgartel, Howard. "Using Employee Questionnaire Results for Improving Organizations: The Survey 'Feedback' Experiment." *Kansas Business Review,* March-April 1967, pp. 149–55.

Blake, R., and Mouton, J. *Building a Dynamic Corporation Through Grid® Organization Development.* Reading, MA: Addison-Wesley, 1969.

Burke, W. *Current Issues and Strategies in Organization Development.* New York: Human Sciences Press, 1977.

Dowling, W. "At General Motors: Systems 4 Builds Performance and Profits." *Organization Dynamics,* Winter 1978, pp. 23–28.

Howe, R., et al. "Introducing Innovation Through Organization Development." *Management Review,* February 1978, pp. 52–56.

Huse, E., and Beer, M. "Eclectic Approach to Organization Development." *Harvard Business Review,* September-October 1971, pp. 103–12.

Kahn, R. "Organization Development: Some Problems and Proposals." *Journal of Applied Behavioral Sciences,* October-December, 1974, pp. 486–500.

Kuzmits, F. "Considering An Organization Development Program?" *The Personnel Administrator,* October 1977, pp. 29–32.

Marguiles, N., and Raia, A. *Conceptual Foundations of Organization Development.* New York: McGraw-Hill Book Company, 1978.

Miner, J. "The OD-Management Development Conflict." *Business Horizons,* December 1973, pp. 31–36.

Selfridge, R., and Sokolik, S. "A Comprehensive View of Organization Development." *MSU Business Topics,* Winter 1975, pp. 46–61.

For Analysis: Chicago Mercantile Company

Roscoe Levitan slowly rose from his leather swivel chair and paced a few feet to a floor-to-ceiling office window. Looking out over the water churning near the shores of Lake Michigan and then at the Chicago skyline did little to reduce the pressure he felt. The Chicago Mercantile Company, which occupied the fifty-third floor of the Sears Tower, was in deep trouble; as chief executive officer, Levitan was principally responsible for saving it.

The Chicago Mercantile Company was one of the nation's oldest manufacturers of men's wearing apparel. Headquartered in Chicago with eight plants throughout the southeast, the company once enjoyed a national reputation for healthy sales and profits. But those were only memories. Chicago Mercantile was on the brink of bankruptcy.

Lured away from a vice-presidency at a major competitor eight months ago for a six-figure salary, Levitan was ordered by Chicago Mercantile's executive committee to "turn the company around within five years." If he succeeded, he would receive a generous bonus, and a great deal of personal satisfaction. If he failed, he would be fired.

As he watched a sailboat slice three-foot waves about a mile offshore, Levitan reflected on some of the company's major problems: eroding sales, high losses for the past two years, significant gains by competition, and an agitated and restless labor force. Once peaceful relations with the Amalgamated Clothing and Textile Workers Union slowly eroded into three lengthy strikes in five years which dealt significant blows to the company.

When he took command several months ago, Levitan was well aware of some of the company's problems. He contracted with two consulting groups to conduct independent studies; one was Arthur D. Small, Inc. (ADS), a highly respected, Boston—based management consulting firm. The ADS team was told by Levitan to "study the company's problems and make recommendations to solve them." A team of three ADS consultants spent six weeks with Chicago Mercantile and submitted a 195-page report to Levitan.

The second consulting group was Behavioral Science Associates, Inc. (BSA), a recognized leader in organizational development with a reputation for achieving impressive results through its processes. Four BSA associates spent four weeks in Chicago and at various plants interviewing key executives and administrators. An employee survey was also conducted by BSA and completed by the entire employee group.

Levitan watched the sailboat for another minute or so wishing he could trade places with the vessel's skipper. Today, he might even settle for third mate. During this afternoon's executive committee meeting a major decision must be made about which consultants' findings to accept. Levitan's recommendations on what course to follow would no doubt be approved by the rest of the committee. But even two hours before the meeting, he still was undecided about which recommendations to implement—if any at all.

Levitan returned to his desk to review the findings and recommendations by ADS and BSA. First, he studied the ADS report. Some of the highlights included:

Marketing Considerations

- Existing product lines are too conservative for today's market and reflect an overly conservative image. Products must focus on the affluent, 25 to 35 age group and be designed to fit their needs.
- A new advertising approach should be created and

implemented, focusing on the young-to-middle-age purchaser.

- *Channels of distribution need to be revamped. More retail outlets in large suburban shopping centers need to be included in the dealer network.*

- *Retail stores owned and operated by the company are too stuffy. Younger sales personnel need to be hired and trained and store layouts need to be modernized.*

Manufacturing Considerations

- *Three fifty-year-old manufacturing plants are hopelessly outdated and should be permanently closed. Manufacturing technologies in the remaining plants need considerable updating. Personnel who are laid off as a result of plant closings should be given priority on jobs which become available in other plants.*

Management Effectiveness

- *Management obsolescence is a critical problem. Four top managers should be fired and seven should be demoted. Vacancies should be filled from outside as new blood is sorely needed.*

- *Strong management development programs must be implemented at the middle and first-line levels with heavy emphasis on planning and control techniques. Human relations training for first-line supervisors is also important and should improve labor-management relations. The company should make greater use of the many top quality management development seminars that are frequently held throughout the Chicago area.*

Labor-Management Relations

- *To improve labor-management relations and reduce the*

threat of strikes, employee wage and benefit packages should be closely reviewed to ensure that all forms of employee compensation are fair and adequate. Employee relations will also improve with more people-oriented leadership styles by supervisors.

Levitan pushed aside the ADS report and reached for BSA's analysis. Their recommendations were of a much different nature; some of the BSA findings and recommendations are described:

In essence, Chicago Mercantile's financial problems are primarily a result of the company's inability to keep up with the rapid changes that have taken place in the internal and external environment. The company's bureaucratic management structure and style have stifled the creativity and initiative of its employee group and have resulted in problem-solving mechanisms which are no longer effective.

The data generated from interviews and the company survey suggest the following problems:

- *High levels of both inter and intragroup conflict, which is suppressed rather than dealt with openly.*

- *Communication between management levels is distorted and untimely.*

- *Many key managers and administrators are unsure of their goals, objectives, and responsibilities.*

- *Line managers are highly suspicious of staff administrators, and vice-versa. A high level of distrust permeates the entire organization structure.*

- *Short-range and long-range organizational goals have not been clearly defined.*

- *Effective problem-solving mechanisms are nonexistent. Major issues are not confronted or "owned up to" by anyone.*

- *Employee morale is low primarily as a result of inattention to the human needs of employees.*

- *Many operative jobs in manufacturing and clerical areas are viewed as boring and unchallenging. Based on these problem areas, BSA feels a systematic organizational development effort would have a significant, positive impact on organizational effectiveness, and that organizational development techniques such as intra and intergroup team building, MBO, and job enrichment would enable the corporation to become profitable again.*

Questions

1. *What should Levitan do? Adopt ADS's recommendations? Or BSA's?*

2. *Should Levitan suggest an organizational development program, how do you think the executive committee will react?*

3. *What are the advantages and disadvantages of implementing an organizational development program at Chicago Mercantile?*

4. *Assuming Levitan decides to conduct organizational development, which problems outlined by BSA should receive top priority? Why?*

SELECTED PROFESSIONAL READING

Merging Personnel and OD:
A Not-So-Odd Couple

ROBERT M. FRAME AND FRED LUTHANS

The old days when a personnel administrator simply hired, trained, insured, protected, and pensioned employees are long gone. These traditional functions are only part of what is expected of personnel managers today. Increased federal, state, and local government regulation; well-organized and often militant labor activity; local community pressures; and especially changing social values have led to a new ball game for personnel administration in the 1970s and beyond. Today, the personnel manager is expected to assist top management in dealing with these external pressures and the accompanying complex human resource management problems.

In essence, top management is beginning to look at the personnel professional as the interpreter and advocate of contemporary society. Ideally, personnel managers need to recognize what is happening in the external environment, analyze and interpret it, and transmit an accurate picture to those in charge. Although they are not necessarily expected to approve of what is going on outside their organizations, they are expected to recommend and implement a realistic response.

Many of today's personnel managers are reluctant and/or unsure of what this new role is all about. Historically, they have quietly waited to be consulted on the problems associated with the classic personnel functions. Frequently they were reactors to, rather than anticipators of, personnel problems. Rarely were personnel managers requested to tell top management what was wrong and equally rarely did they take it upon themselves to do so.

An even stronger departure from tradition is the need for greater flexibility in personnel programs and practices. In the past, too many personnel departments established tightly controlled programs that inevitably became sources of inflexible bureaucratic rules and regulations. Such an approach often led critics to label personnel managers as "monitors of conformity," "master architects of dehumanizing systems," or "chief instructors in the science of worker seduction."

EMERGENCE OF ORGANIZATION DEVELOPMENT

During the past decade, interest has developed in human-centered approaches to managing large industrial, educational, social, and governmental organizations. Management theorists and practitioners, sensitive to the pressures from rapidly changing technological and social environments, have been willing to experiment with new and different organizational forms and strategies. During this period, a number of organizations have contributed to an evolving field of knowledge labeled "organization development" or simply OD. Rooted in applied behavioral science technology and aimed at improving organizational effectiveness, it involves efforts such as:

● Clarifying roles and reducing overlapping responsibilities that reduce effectiveness.

● Increasing the sense of ownership of organization objectives throughout the workforce.

● Identifying objectives with sufficient clarity that they become useful in measuring progress toward goals.

- Ensuring that those with relevant information can make it available to those who make decisions.

- Creating organizational climates that facilitate problem solving rather than cover-up.

- Developing reward systems that recognize achievement of both organizational and individual goals.

- Working with trust issues that hinder organization effectiveness.

OD's methodology is consultative, working directly with the people affected by an organizational improvement effort. OD practitioners tend to be process-oriented as opposed to content-oriented. Their focus is on total system change.

The OD process involves a reorientation of management thinking and behavior. It employs the scientific method (with its underlying values of open investigation of and experimentation with individual and work group behaviors) for the solution of organizational problems.

OD advocates assume employees have the capability to grow through learning how to improve their own work climate, work processes, and the resulting outputs. They also assume that conflicts among the needs of individuals, groups, and organizations are inevitable but advocate openly confronting these conflicts using problem-solving strategies and techniques. The goal of OD is to optimize the use of organizational resources in solving work problems to the optimal use of human potential.

In other words, the focus of OD is on the difference between what organizational participants are and what they are capable of becoming. Individual and organizational change strategies and techniques used in OD are directed toward narrowing this gap.

SOME COMMON MISCONCEPTIONS ABOUT OD

A major problem currently facing OD is that it is sometimes identified as being a separate value system imposed upon the organization. Negative reactions to such a perceived imposition are predictable: It is often labeled as "goody-goody," "hand holding," "soft," or "permissive." But the truth is that OD is a relatively hard-nosed, practical form of management; it asks more of organizational members than perhaps any other form.

Another misconception is that the OD approach typically seeks group consensus in decision making and therefore management authority is undermined. While OD methods frequently lead to general consensus, management seldom loses significant power or authority. The OD reasoning is that the higher the mutual trust and openness in most groups, the more freedom a manager has to act without fear of being misunderstood and to handle urgent demands in a unilateral manner should it be necessary.

A related misunderstanding is to define OD in terms of its methodology and techniques (confrontation, feedback, self-analysis, intergroup conflict confrontation and resolution, team building, and so forth) instead of concentrating on OD in terms of its *objectives*, the specific results that are to be accomplished in the organization. OD, however, is much broader than any one of the techniques it employs.

THE CASE FOR MERGER

The established legitimacy of the traditional personnel function and the potential contributions from OD technology make integrating the two seem very desirable for more effective human resource management. To survive in the long run, OD must be associated with the mainstream of available staff resources; it must not simply become some new fad doomed to extinction because of lack of identification within the organization. OD also needs to be linked to key power sources within the existing hierarchy.

Indeed, power and authority issues provide especially important reasons for a personnel/OD merger. The new role of the personnel manager calls for expert power and the demonstrated ability to help solve broad organizational problems rather than power based on bureaucratic authority. Integration can contribute to the desired power-authority relationship between personnel and the rest of the organization by moving it toward the consultant-client relationship found in OD. Such an approach will modify the personnel manager's role to "pure staff" and help alleviate the encroachment on line authority inherent in the "behavioral cop" role often attributed to this function. At the same time, personnel managers will get needed relief from being held responsible for behavioral problems over which they have little control or authority.

The external pressures on today's organization for which personnel managers are charged with coping and solving can be adapted to the OD process. The growing concern for social responsibility provides one example. Traditionally, management is charged with and committed to taking care of the organization's interests. Outside of personnel managers, few, if any, managers are in charge of or committed to representing employees or society's interests. To meet the challenge of social responsibility, credible internal OD-type personnel managers are needed who can learn about the needs and aspirations of people within the organization so that genuine contacts with people and institutions outside the organization can be established.

A personnel manager armed with skills in the OD process can serve as a buffer between dissident outside groups and/or internal departments and promote an environment in which conflict can be healthy. Rather than discouraging organizational philosophical differences and rewarding conformity, the personnel/OD professional can help anticipate the consequences of conflict and suggest ways to intervene in order to resolve it. Whereas traditional methods of resolving conflict (withdrawal, compromise, or coercion) often led to unresolved conflict, win-lose results, or half-way measures, the new OD approach of confrontation has demonstrated considerable success. If the reward system for superior-subordinate confrontation can broaden the use of the OD process as a problem solving technique, healthy conflict can be viewed as acceptable in forward-thinking organizations.

An open, dynamic organizational climate where healthy conflict is accepted and conformity is not rewarded can move the organization toward more effective goal attainment. Personnel/OD professionals can provide the needed processes for employees to release their hostility and create a realistic climate in which confrontation is accepted as an organizational norm. OD can help personnel effect this climate in a manner contributive to organizational effectiveness—whether through process consultation such as team building, structural intervention such as job redesign, or positive reinforcement strategy such as organization behavior modification.

POTENTIAL PROBLEMS

A merger between personnel and OD certainly would not be problem-free. In making the transition from a reactive-passive to a proactive-consultative position, personnel will encounter many doubters and obstacles. For example, Art Baars and Hoyt Hayes of Western Illinois University recently conducted a survey on the merger of OD and personnel. The survey respondents who were critics of the merger accused personnel of having too little involvement in the realities of line management. They suggested that personnel's focus was realistically one of shuffling paper dealing with people and not dealing in the actual work context. The survey also reflected a number of other more specific potential problems with the merger:

● Future OD specialists will need considerably more skill in systems dynamics, political theory, and long-range planning and forecasting than is evidenced today. A thorough integration with personnel may result in OD's failure to develop in this desired direction because personnel's orientation tends to be short range.

- At present, labor relations and dealing with unions is viewed in a negative, adversary light, and most OD practitioners don't want to see their process oriented this way.

- Related role confusion will place a strain on the credibility of both the personnel and OD functions.

- Personnel must always deal within the framework of reality. OD, on the other hand, usually tries to be on the boundary of what might be. There is only so much time and energy for both, and many OD people believe they may be spread too thin.

- Personnel activities tend to respond to immediate needs. OD activities, on the other hand, attempt to be aimed at improving future functions of the organization.

- By being associated with personnel, OD may be seen narrowly as a "people" or human relations activity rather than as a more preferred total systems process.

- Personnel functions tend to strive for stability, smoothness, and conflict reduction, while OD often has the opposite ends. Only if the OD process initiates needed change in the personnel function itself and then integrates, disseminates, and desystematizes these changes can the two functions work compatibly.

- Personnel is too tied into the hierarchical power structure. OD attempts to be broader based and cannot be viewed as a narrow management tool.

- Finally, anyone held responsible for policy application may encounter difficulty in being seen as a neutral helper. Policies are often an important target for change, and the same staff function cannot simultaneously be the defender and the attacker of policies.

In addition to the problems suggested in the survey, there are other potential problems. One is the area of trust. For a number of reasons (for example, the image as the controller of career destinies and/or real or imagined betrayal of shared confidences), personnel managers are not always highly trusted. Consequently, some employees may fear that in an open climate of communication created during an OD intervention, certain things may find their way into personnel files or the ears of top management. This fear will undermine the personnel professional's acceptability as an OD practitioner.

Another problem is that the less-than–positive image of the personnel function in many organizations has made it difficult for many OD practitioners to accept integration with enthusiasm. They believe that personnel has generally been insensitive to the external changes in society. They also believe that today's employees clearly desire challenging growth at work.

Personnel professionals, to the contrary, have tended to perpetuate highly structured, specialized work and organizations characterized by tall hierarchies, status differentials, and strict chains of command. They have supported practices that emphasize money, working conditions, and job security and have continued to support career planning paths and design reward systems based on competition and upward striving.

BALANCING THE POSITIVE AND THE NEGATIVE

Despite these problems, the positive seems to outweigh the negative aspects of a personnel/OD merger. With the changing role of personnel in today's organization, the OD approach seems very compatible and can make a significant contribution.

For example, in the staffing area commitment to the idea that personnel ought to be concerned about the total human resources of an organization is widely evident. This means that personnel need not be simply a service group responding solely to requests; instead, it may proactively seek opportunities to be heavily involved in areas such as organizational and manpower planning, initial selection, promotion decisions, new organization start-up, job design, career planning, and appropriate behavior change.

In the performance appraisal area, personnel can, through training, facilitate a higher level of open and supportive dialogue between the boss and subordinate and help create a climate for more subordinate participation.

In the compensation area, the major challenge is the design of a total system of rewards optimizing the attainment of organizational goals. Obviously, current practices that increase the contributions of subordinates but do not proportionately increase their rewards are hypocritical and dysfunctional. Personnel can help this problem by emphasizing incentive programs and appraisal and reward systems that are based on results.

In the area of organizational justice, a personnel/OD merger can help promote an atmosphere of inquiry and honest constructive dissent in which integrity and authenticity in human relationships are emphasized and procedures of appeal and a wide spectrum of opinions about effective managerial behavior are protected.

Another key component of balancing the positive and negative aspects of the personnel/OD merger involves change. Most current organizational structures do not permit adjustment to the rapid and overwhelming changes that intensify human resistance. But armed with OD technology, the personnel professional can affect an organization's receptiveness to new ideas and change.

For example, OD can help personnel with creating and implementing techniques such as flexible working hours, early retirement, second careers, or life-planning opportunities. Personnel with help from OD can conduct employee surveys and other approaches such as following up on problems identified via various upward communications programs involving employees. Equal employment oppor-tunity programs can also get help from an OD perspective for positive organizational change. An enlightened approach to affirmative action starts with the development of an organizational climate that is supportive and encouraging for minorities and women. Such a climate can be created through a combined personnel/OD effort.

ACCOMPLISHING THE MERGER

In the merger of personnel and organization development a synergistic effect can be gained from the functional legitimacy of an established approach and the growing potential of a successful developmental process. The OD practitioner brings to the merger the potential for demonstrating a proactive mode of consulting not enjoyed by the historically passive and reactive personnel unit. Thus the merger between the two may result in a more energetic, responsive, and potentially effective human resource management function from which everybody gains: the OD practitioner in legitimacy and new vehicles for intervention; the personnel professional in improved contributions and credibility; and, of greatest importance, the organization in effectiveness through improved staff services to line management.

To bring about a successful merger, three broadly based elements seem necessary:

Understanding. A clear philosophical framework for the services offered by the two functions must be established. This should include an understanding of behavioral science theories and research, articulated by both top management and the chief personnel officer so that the actions of this newly merged function have a central purpose and do not simply become a source of more fads and gimmicks.

Capability. Personnel professionals must develop credible skills in OD technology, and OD practitioners must acquire and reflect an appreciation for basic personnel subsystems and functions.

Commitment. Both personnel and OD units must build an alliance of mutual support and work to achieve organizational goals via synergized integration of skills, credibility, and programs.

Without understanding and capability as defined above, little commitment will evolve. The two functions will continue to simply cohabit under the same roof, each growing in separate and often parallel directions with little linkage or mutual support.

A successful merger between personnel and OD should give attention to the following strategies for gaining appropriate influence and support:

- The resultant personnel/OD function should work with the forces within the organization that are supportive of change and improvement rather than against those that are defensive and resistant. This requires good diagnostic work—for example, not doing anything across the board without efforts to gather data reflecting disparities between performance and potential.

- The new personnel/OD function should work with the relatively healthy parts of the organization first rather than with the lost causes. The strategy here would be to become identified with winners instead of with losers.

- The merged function should establish direct communication with multiple levels within the organization. For the new process to be viable, it must be tied into the mainstream of activity and have access to power. This means working with individuals and groups that have as much freedom and discretion in managing their operations as possible and actively involving management levels in development programs where effective control resides. The only way the OD-oriented personnel manager can influence is through expertise. Direct contact and discussion with powerful clients and legitimate information sources are vital. Reliance upon intermediaries or a bureaucratic chain of command hampers this effectiveness.

- The new function should selectively advertise what it is doing, particularly where there are successes to report on the basis of diagnosis and evaluation. This can be accomplished by holding seminars for client systems. With key-project clients participating, joint presentations describing successful change projects can be made.

- Another strategy is to link together people in groups who are working to improve organizational processes so that their activities reinforce and complement one another. For example, link training (especially in areas such as leadership and effective group processes) to follow-up activities in the actual work situation. Training can be built into some on-the-job change activity that will reinforce the training and in turn reinforce the use of the organizational process in actual practice.

- Experiential, action-oriented training programs to develop confidence and credibility in the newly created personnel/OD function should be used. These educational situations provide the client some low-risk opportunities to evaluate the new techniques. Also, the use of diagnostic studies can be used to begin dialog with new clients.

- Finally, to maintain a successful effort in the long run, the personnel/OD approach must be able to show contributions to overall organizational effectiveness and goal attainment.

Discovering, measuring, and closing the discrepancies between actual and potential effectiveness of human resources is what a personnel/OD merger can hopefully accomplish. A merger will not only mutually benefit personnel and OD but, most importantly, meet the challenge of more effective human resource management now and in the future.

Employees expect their career development ladder to include congratulatory scenes like this.

12

INTERNAL STAFFING AND CAREER MANAGEMENT

Promotion, Demotion, Layoff

Closed and Open Promotion Systems

Internal Staffing Policies

Personal Career Planning

Career Management Benefits

The Problem: Citizens Savings and Loan

Janice Pauling has been the personnel manager for Citizens Savings and Loan, a large Houston-based financial institution, for about two years. She came to Citizens directly from the highly-respected MBA program at Stanford University in Palo Alto, California, where she concentrated her studies in personnel-industrial relations.

    Pauling has achieved quite a bit in her two years at Citizens. She implemented a job analysis program, upgraded salaries to be more competitive, created and implemented an affirmative action program, and began a formal management development function. But she has experienced little success in reducing one of Citizens most pressing personnel problems: exorbitant turnover in middle management. Statistics showed that about two of every three professionals on Citizens midmanagement and staff levels left for jobs elsewhere.

    To get a better feel for the causes that underlie the problem, she recently decided to implement a formal exit interview program. The following comments of employees who quit recently were characteristic of many employees who had left the company:

Charlotte Golden: "My experiences during the training program were excellent. I received high quality training and learned a great deal about the company. But after my second promotion, it became clear to me that my next promotion was light-years away. The management level above me was riddled with deadwood, and there was no doubt in my mind they were firmly entrenched in their

*positions. I wouldn't get promoted again unless someone
retired or dropped dead."*

*Richard Bernson: "I was ready to be promoted but there was
no place to go. The only way I could get promoted was
within my own chain of command, where job vacancies
were few and far between. I'm sure there were more
challenging jobs elsewhere in the company, but I had no
idea where. Besides, my boss made it clear to me he didn't
want me to leave the department. He told me, 'Dick,
you're one of my best employees. I don't want to lose you.
Stick with me, I'll take care of you.' That was four years
ago, and I was still doing the same job."*

*Lyle Quigley: "In getting promoted here, your annual
performance appraisals mean practically nothing. Everybody
gets high ratings. It boils down to who you know, what
clubs you belong to, and whether or not you occasionally
play golf with the big wigs. I just got fed up."*

*Jerry Myers: "When I was recruited, I was told that I would
get promoted as fast as my abilities would allow. But that's
all baloney. What really counts is seniority. Keep your nose
clean, hang around long enough, and you'll eventually get
what you want. But I can't wait."*

*Janice Pauling sat in her office with stacks of notes
taken during the exit interviews. Absently gazing out the
window she wondered what to do next.*

The typical organization chart, with neatly drawn boxes labeled and connected by horizontal and vertical lines, often fails to convey the great degree of personnel movement which takes place in enterprises today. People are shifted up, down, across, and out in organizations of all kinds and sizes. These internal staffing decisions which concern promotions, demotions, transfers, and layoffs, represent an important area of personnel policy and human resource management. Effective *internal staffing* plans, policies, and procedures will ensure the achievement of both organizational and personal goals. On the other hand, mismanagement of internal staffing may result in a great deal of personal job dissatisfaction and reduced organization effectiveness. In the first part of this chapter, we will study internal staffing decisions and the issues connected with them.

The second part of this chapter deals with another important area concerning internal staffing—career management. In recent years, many personnel professionals have designed programs and procedures that enable employees to progress upward in a planned, systematic fashion. Successful career management leads to an improved quality of working life through effective personnel development and maximum utilization of employees' skills. In our discussion, we will focus on the elements of a career management model and current career management programs and practices.

■ INTERNAL STAFFING ■

Several important factors bring about a need for internal staffing decisions. These include:

Creation Of New Jobs. Business or government expansion generally results in new positions being filled by promoting existing employees. Increases in new positions are particularly commonplace for companies within growth industries, such as minicomputers, energy, and home entertainment.

Reorganization. A major restructuring of the organization may result in various types of personnel actions. As an example, while Jimmy Carter was the governor

of Georgia from 1970 to 1974, the state government reorganization plan included centralization of many staff services, such as the motor pool, computer services, purchasing, and employee training and development. The reorganization brought about many employee transfers, promotions, and some demotions.

General Business and Economic Trends. One unfortunate consequence of major economic downturns is that a significant number of workers will temporarily or permanently lose their jobs. Companies that manufacture durable goods, such as automobiles and home appliances, are particularly vulnerable to fluctuations in the business cycle. On the other hand, companies that produce services and nondurable items are sometimes said to be recession proof and may enjoy a stable or growing labor force through both good and bad economic times.

Individual companies, which experience major declines in demand for their products or services, are often forced to make significant cuts in their labor forces. A striking example of this dilemma is the American automobile industry. As the price of gasoline began to skyrocket in the mid 1970s, consumers purchased fuel-efficient foreign imports, drastically reducing the demand for larger, less fuel-efficient American cars. In the late 1970s and into the 1980s, the impact on employment levels at major auto manufacturers reached the white-collar suites as well as the factory floor. As shown in Figure 12–1, cutbacks for both blue-collar and salaried personnel were commonplace in 1980 at the Big Three.

Quits, Terminations and Retirements. Voluntary and involuntary turnover and retirement create vacancies which may be filled by promoting or transferring exist-

FIGURE 12–1: *Auto Sales Slump Hits Blue- and White-Collar Levels*

"A salaried position with one of America's big automobile companies has usually been a ticket to the good life.

"White-collar employees—from secretaries to senior executives—have parlayed the auto firms' above-average pay scales and generous benefits into the comfortable lives traditionally associated with hard work and upward mobility. And above all, they have enjoyed a sense of security, unlike their blue-collar brethren, who are also well-compensated for building the nation's cars but for whom the threat of periodic layoffs is ever present.

"But suddenly all this is changing. The auto industry has tumbled into one of its steepest declines ever and may be a long time coming out. Red ink is showing up on ledgers. Some 200,000 production workers are already jobless and now, in a desperate bid to slash overhead costs, the Big Three are laying off or retiring unprecedented numbers of their quarter–million white-collar workers from top to bottom.

"In just the last three weeks, auto makers have announced new white-collar cutbacks. By summer, some 40,000 salaried jobs will have been eliminated. That dwarfs the cutbacks of the 1974–75 auto slump, which at that time were considered staggering."[1]

Reprinted by permission of *The Wall Street Journal.* © Dow Jones & Company, Inc. 1980. All Rights Reserved.

ing personnel. Employee reductions that result from resignation, retirement, and death are collectively referred to as attrition. In a period of austerity, however, vacancies caused by attrition may go unfilled in order to reduce labor costs. One example of this so-called "freeze on hiring" was Kentucky Governor John Y. Brown, Jr.'s decision in 1980 to reduce the state labor force by 1,800 permanent full–

1. "White-Collar Workers Are Singing the Blues in the Auto Industry," *The Wall Street Journal* (May 9, 1980): 1.

time employees—about 5 percent—until the state financial situation improved. Brown told state employees that the 5 percent reduction in personnel would be achieved through normal resignations and retirement. However, significant morale problems occurred when Kentucky Personnel Commissioner Dick Robinson "repeatedly warned that some layoffs of merit system employees would be forthcoming to meet Brown's ordered 5 percent personnel reduction."[2]

The internal staffing decisions which result from the preceding factors include promotions, demotions, transfers, and layoffs.

Promotion

A *promotion* involves the reassignment of an employee to a higher level job. When promoted, employees generally face increasing demands in terms of skills, abilities, and responsibilities. In turn, employees generally receive an increase in pay, and sometimes benefits, greater authority, and greater status. Promotions serve many purposes and provide benefits to organizations and employees. First, promotions enable organizations to utilize employee skills and abilities to the greatest extent possible. An effective promotional system permits an organization to match its continuous need for competent personnel with the employees' desires to apply the skills they have developed. Second, promotions are often given to reward employees for excellent performance. Employees who value promotions are motivated to high levels of performance if they feel that effective job per-

2. "129 Will Be Laid Off in Human Resources," *The Louisville Courier-Journal* (April 25, 1980): B–6.

formance leads to promotion.[3] Third, research by behavioral scientist Frederick Herzberg suggests that opportunities for advancement and high levels of job satisfaction are significantly correlated.[4] In sum, an effective employee promotion system can result in greater organizational efficiency and high levels of employee morale.

RECRUITING FOR PROMOTION

Two general approaches, or methods, may be used to recruit employees for promotion. The most common approach is a *closed promotion system,* which places the responsibility for identifying promotable employees with the supervisor or manager of the job to be filled. In addition to reviewing the past performance and potential of all subordinates, the supervisor may inquire in other departments and work groups about employees who may be qualified for the job. With the closed promotion system, however, many employees who may be qualified and interested in a promotion are often overlooked. For example, the vice-president of a large bank with an opening for a commercial loan officer in its home office, may be unaware of qualified or interested employees throughout the banking system. In this case, the job may be filled by an employee known by the executive but less qualified than other employees. Or

the job may be filled by someone from the outside, a practice which conflicts with the company's policy of promotion from within. An internal staffing approach that overcomes these problems is known as an *open promotion system,* more popularly known as job posting. With job posting, job vacancies are publicized on bulletin boards and internal communication systems so that all interested employees may apply. Job posting strengthens employee participation and equal opportunity but also increases administrative expenses and takes more time. A recent survey by the Bureau of National Affairs showed that job posting systems are used mostly at the clerical and blue-collar levels in government and unionized companies. Open and closed systems were used about equally for professional and technical employees, and closed systems were used almost exclusively for managerial personnel.[5]

PROMOTION CRITERIA

For many employees, a promotion is a highly sought organizational prize. Getting ahead or climbing the ladder have long been an integral part of the American dream. Generous amounts of status, prestige, and ego satisfaction, in addition to attractive financial rewards, are heaped upon those who are able to ride the fast tracks to organizational stardom. However, frustration, stress, and even severe depression may occur when personal goals of upward mobility are unheeded by the organization—particularly when an employee feels passed over for a deserved promotion. Because organi-

---

3. This thesis is supported by the expectancy theory of job motivation, which suggests that employees will be motivated to perform well if (1) they value a certain outcome, and (2) expect that high performance will lead to the outcome. See J. Richard Hackman and Lyman W. Porter, "Expectancy Theory Predictions of Work Effectiveness," *Organizational Behavior and Human Performance* (November 1968): 417–26.

4. See Frederick Herzberg, et al. *The Motivation to Work* (New York: John Wiley and Sons, 1959), pp. 59–83.

5. *Employee Promotion and Transfer Policies,* Personnel Policies Forum Survey No. 120 (Washington, DC: Bureau of National Affairs, Inc., 1978).

zational effectiveness and personal job satisfaction are influenced by the way promotions are made, it is important for organizations to gather sound, reliable data for making promotional decisions. Some of the criteria that organizations examine in deciding which candidate to promote are:

SENIORITY Many organizations place significant weight upon an employee's seniority when making a promotion decision. Seniority refers to an employee's length of service and constitutes an important part of the American work culture. For generations, the senior employee has expected—and often received—a greater share of organizational rewards than a junior employee. Benefits such as vacation time and sick leave are often distributed on the basis of seniority.

Students of management feel seniority should be given very little or no weight in promotional decisions. They suggest that seniority goes against the grain of private enterprise by rewarding length of service rather than performance. But this attitude overlooks sound arguments for using seniority as a criterion for promoting employees. First, seniority may be considered a legitimate way to make promotions because it avoids problems of bias and partiality by management which gives favored employees the first promotions. Second, seniority is a time saving, easy, and painless way to make a promotion decision. Third, there is usually some correlation between seniority and performance. Up to a point, employees usually become more competent at their jobs as they gain experience. And fourth, seniority rewards the loyal employee who has, perhaps, labored for many years to produce the organization's products and services.

As a promotion criterion, seniority is generally given considerable weight in unionized companies. Striving to treat their membership fairly and impartially, unions have found these goals are best achieved by allocating organizational rewards on the basis of seniority. Labor–management agreements commonly specify that promotions involving union members are to be made on the basis of seniority whenever an employee is qualified for the job. Also, many labor contract provisions require that vacant jobs be publicized via job posting techniques.

While seniority may have its merits as a promotion criterion, it also poses some problems. Employees may lose motivation if their high performance does not count in getting a promotion. Also, achievement and career-oriented employees may become impatient waiting for a promotion and seek employment in organizations that base promotions on performance. Perhaps, the strongest argument against using seniority as a criterion is that the senior employee may not be qualified for the job. Length of service may have little bearing on the levels and kinds of skills and abilities required to assume a new position.

PERFORMANCE AND PROMOTABILITY Because of the drawbacks in using seniority as a promotion criterion, many organizations place importance on performance and promotability when moving employees into jobs of greater responsibility. This approach is widespread for management and professional level jobs. In this case, seniority is given very little or no weight; however, seniority may be a factor if everything else is equal. The candidates' prior performance appraisal reviews, training and development history, formal education, special awards, and other performance data are often combined with an informal judgment of the employee's chances for success in a higher level job. Using this approach, the chances that the organization will make an effective promotion decision are relatively good when the candidate's present job and higher job level require similar skills and abilities. For example, promoting:

- a receptionist to secretary
- a police sergeant to police captain
- an associate professor to full professor
- a bookkeeper to accounting assistant
- a foreman to superintendent
- a regional plant manager to district plant manager

In the examples cited above, both the present job and promotion would require similar employee skills and abilities; thus past work performance could be a fairly good indicator of future success. But past performance is not always a valid indicator of future performance, particularly when the employee is promoted into a job which requires skills and abilities considerably different than those used in the previous job. A common situation involves the promotion of an operative employee to supervisor, such as progression from assembly line worker to first—line supervisor. Supervisory skills are almost totally different than those required for successful assembly line work; many organizations have made grave personnel errors by promoting an employee into supervisory ranks solely because of technical expertise. As one recently—promoted employee put it:

I really looked forward to my promotion from printing press operator to print shop manager. The job was given to me because I was the best operator in the shop. I got a big pay increase and my own office. My family and friends really bragged about me. But it didn't take long to realize that I didn't like supervision. I don't feel I'm one of the gang anymore and I find it difficult to give orders to men I used to joke and drink beer with. I really wish I could have my old job back but don't have the guts to admit I can't hack it as a supervisor.[6]

The problems inherent in the print shop employee's promotion are very common in organizations of all kinds today. Employees are often promoted because of past and present talents which may bear little resemblance to the skills and abilities needed in the employee's new job. Promotion into sales management is an often-cited example. The top salesperson, demonstrating a unique ability to sell effectively, may be promoted to the vacant sales manager's job. Top management may believe that a good salesperson is also a good manager. But the sales manager often becomes frustrated by having to work with subordinates rather than with customers; motivating employees to sell is much different and much more difficult than persuading customers to buy. Management and nonmanagement jobs involve different skills, and many employee-job mismatches have resulted from promotions which have ignored this fact.

Many examples in the sports world illustrate that success or mediocrity in one job does not automatically spell success or mediocrity in another. Bill Russell, Yogi Berra, and Bart Starr performed brilliantly as professional athletes, but enjoyed much less success as coaches. Both John Wooden and Adolph Rupp had lackluster

---

6. Personal conversation with author.

FIGURE 12–2: *Job Pressures Bring Swift Resignation*

William E. McAnulty Jr. checked into Louisville's St. Anthony Hospital for stomach tests the day after he pulled the biggest surprise in Governor John Y. Brown Jr.'s young administration. The 32-year-old former Jefferson District judge resigned as state justice secretary only seven working days after he began his new job full time.

In a printed statement released through Jefferson District Court yesterday, McAnulty cited family reasons and said there were no secrets behind his decision: "There is only the very immediate fact that I am unwilling to make the sacrifices that are necessary to be fully effective." But in an interview at the hospital last night, McAnulty cited the pressures of his cabinet job. He also wanted to regain his place on the bench.

In the interview, McAnulty said that managing a department with three thousand employees demanded long hours and the pressures had affected his health. He talked about several aspects of the justice department job that made him feel uncomfortable.

One discovery, he said, was that *the skills of a judge were not immediately transferable to a position requiring a manager. "The management aspects of it were not only totally foreign to me, but uncomfortable." He said he felt qualified to make decisions "about people's liberty and life with sensitivity and fairness,"* but that he didn't believe he could develop the same level of skills as a manager. (author's italics)

Several sources in Frankfort, Kentucky, said McAnulty had been overwhelmed by the problems facing the agency.

Starting on February 6, he immediately plunged into various administrative problems, including legislation for the General Assembly, personnel cuts ordered by Brown, budget preparation, and a prisoners' rights suit facing the corrections department.

"The sheer volume of decision making" was overwhelming. Making judicial decisions, he said, is different from carrying out a government program.

McAnulty was appointed January 15, the birthday of Martin Luther King, Jr. He said he was bothered by how frequently people referred to the fact that he was the first black to fill a cabinet-level post in Kentucky government.

"It's not easy to be Jackie Robinson," he said.

As a representative of the black community, McAnulty said he was expected to be a liaison with state government about black issues. He also was expected to help see to it that a fair share of state business was given to minorities. McAnulty said he didn't like being forced "to deal with people in a black/white capacity, when I have never in my life done that."

Condensed from "Job Pressures Hurt His Health, McAnulty Says from Hospital," *The Louisville Courier-Journal,* February 16, 1980, p. A-1. Used with permission.

---

college basketball careers, but their achievements as basketball coaches are legendary. Fran Tarkenton, O.J. Simpson, Alex Karras, and Bruce Jenner have all carried their successes from the athletic world into the field of entertainment.

By working different jobs, people learn the depth and breadth of their skills and abilities. Some discover they possess multiple talents and the aptitudes to perform several different jobs effectively; others find that their abilities and aptitudes are more limited. Occupational enlightenment can lead to either joy or pain. A detailed description of how a promotion unpredictably led to grief is given in Figure 12–2.

ASSESSMENT CENTER To improve the chances for making successful promotional decisions—particularly from non-management to management—many organizations are using *assessment centers.* Job candidates are brought to assessment centers for evaluation of their promotability, as measured by a series of individual and group exercises. These exercises focus on the kinds of skills and abilities that are required to effectively perform higher level jobs which the candidates seek.

The purpose and nature of the assessment center are more readily grasped by examining a center currently in operation. For this purpose, we will review the details of American Telephone and Telegraph's (AT&T) assessment center program, one of the largest and most sophisticated in practice today.[7] AT&T has over fifty assessment centers across the United States. Each is in a conference room or seminar area, away from the work site.

In general, the primary purpose of the assessment center is to improve an organization's selection of managerial talent, particularly for the first level of management. A secondary purpose is to increase the pool of employees from which managers may be selected. An AT&T employee may ask to attend an assessment center, or, a supervisor may feel an employee is supervisory material and suggest the employee attend. In either case, the final decision whether or not to participate is the employee's.

Roughly a dozen participants undergo tests and exercises specifically designed to determine their potentials as successful managers. Some common exercises during the two and one-half day program include:

An in-depth interview concerning career goals, plans, etc.

A general mental ability test.

A reasoning ability test.

A knowledge of current affairs test.

A series of In-Basket Exercises.

A business game involving the start-up and operation of a toy company.

Two role-playing situations.

Throughout the session, six assessors and a director are observing, taking notes, and evaluating each participant. They are experienced, successful line managers who volunteered to be trained as assessors. The job of assessor is a temporary assignment, which usually lasts about six months.

After the sessions are over, the participants return to work. Using pooled judgments, the assessors place each participant into one of the following managerial potential categories: more than acceptable, acceptable, less than acceptable, and unacceptable. These ratings then become important criteria for selecting managers in the future. The assessment center rating is not the sole criterion for making a promotion decision. Traditional promotion criteria—such as past performance and supervisory recommendations—are also used.

AT&T participants may request full reports concerning their performances at the assessment center. About 85 percent of the participants request this information. Receiving a rating of "less than acceptable" or "unacceptable" is not the kiss of death for participants. These employees may still get promoted into management—with the help of a persuasive supervisor.

AT&T figured the cost of each assessment center participant is about $400, but that was in 1967. No doubt, costs are considerably higher now. The important question, however, is whether or not the benefits exceed the costs, and AT&T feels without a doubt that they do. Begin-

---

7. This discussion taken from Walter S. Wikstrom, "Assessing Managerial Talent," *The Conference Board Record* (March, 1967): pp. 39–44.

ning in the late sixties, AT&T conducted a number of sound, sophisticated studies concerning the effectiveness of their program. The results clearly show that the assessment center is a more effective selection method than traditional practices such as past performance reviews, interviews, and recommendations.

While assessment center techniques and practices will vary somewhat from company to company, AT&T's methods are fairly typical. Other firms using assessment centers include Standard Oil of New Jersey, IBM, General Electric Company, Sears, Roebuck and Company, and the Brown and Williamson Tobacco Company. Because of the large costs involved, only large firms have thus far been able to afford permanent assessment center operations. Generally, smaller organizations do not have enough promotions to justify the expense of assessment centers.

In general, research concerning assessment center validity is favorable. Studies show that the assessment center approach improves the odds that an effective promotion decision will be made.[8] In comparing the assessment center method to traditional selection techniques, one researcher stated that "comparison with the literature on traditional methods for predicting managerial success reveals that the average validity of the assessment center is about as high as the maximum validity attained by use of these traditional methods."[9]

UNOFFICIAL CRITERIA Many semesters ago, after a personnel management lecture about internal staffing, a student came up

8. S. D. Norton, "The Empirical and Content Validity of Assessment Centers vs Traditional Methods for Predicting Managerial Success," *Academy of Management Review* 2 (1977): 442–53.
9. Ibid., pp. 442–43.

to me and said, "Professor, what you say about making effective promotional decisions is all well and good. But it's all theory. Where I work, promotions depend on who you know, not what you do."

Of course, I had heard this old personnel proverb many times before and, perhaps, have even muttered it myself during some of my various work experiences. I confessed to the student that we should have spent more time discussing the stark realities that often affect the promotion decision-making process. All too often, a wide gulf exists between theory and practice when an employee is tapped for promotion. Rational criteria, such as seniority, performance and promotability, and assessment center ratings may be cast by the wayside in lieu of political factors. While little research exists in this important area of personnel management, the following unofficial criteria may influence, or even dominate, a promotion decision:

Personal Characteristics Title VII of the Civil Rights Act of 1964 and the Age Discrimination Act of 1967 prohibit discrimination in all terms and conditions of employment on the basis of age, race, color, religion, sex, or national origin. Of course, all internal staffing decisions fall under the domain of these acts just as external recruiting, selection, and placement practices do. While most all organizations profess to abide by the EEO laws and include an "Equal Opportunity Employer" line at the bottom of their help wanted advertisements, not all organizations practice what they preach. Certain personal characteristics of the candidate may either help or hinder progression into the upper levels of the organization; being black, female, Jewish, or of the wrong national origin may create an artificial and unspoken barrier to advancement. Such practices are not only immoral and unethical, but clearly illegal. These prejudices cause a sizeable pool of valuable human talent to be overlooked and wasted.

Nepotism Being of a certain bloodline sometimes helps hasten one's progression into a higher level job. *Nepotism,* from the Italian *nepotismo* ("favoring of nephews") refers to showing favoritism or patronage to relatives. Nepotism is often criticized because family members get desirable jobs and promotions primarily by virtue of their lineage.[10]

Nepotism is legal unless it adversely impacts against protected classes of employees. Nonetheless, widespread nepotism results in the promotion of employees who are not qualified for jobs.

Social Factors Membership in a certain club or political party, graduation from the right university, and participation in the right sport (traditionally golf, perhaps now racquetball) are strong factors for getting promoted in some organizations, particularly at the upper management and staff levels. One classic account of the importance of these factors in promotional decisions is given by sociologist Melville Dalton. During the 1950s, Dalton conducted in-house research on managerial practices at several large companies. Dalton's question, "What are the things that enable men to rise in the plant here?" drew this response from a 53-year-old foreman:

> I'm surprised that anybody who's been around here as long as you have would ask that question. You know as well as I do that getting in and running around with certain crowds is the way to get up. Nearly all the big

boys are in the yacht club, and damn near all of 'em are Masons. You can't get a good job without being a Mason. Hell, these guys all play poker together. Their wives run around together, and they all have their families out to the yacht club hob-nobbing together. That's no mystery. Everybody knows it. It's the friendships and connections you make running around in these crowds that makes or breaks you in the plant.[11]

Mutual Friendships In organizations of all forms and sizes, strong informal bonds are created between employees who share mutual interests, ideals, values, beliefs, and attitudes. In turn, such informal bonds between decision makers and promotional candidates may be a significant factor in deciding who gets promoted and who doesn't. Particularly at the top organizational levels, executives prefer to work with people whose feelings and perceptions mirror their own. In a sense, this personal chemistry may be just as important as ability in getting ahead.

Demotion

Many people join organizations with the hope of periodically progressing upward through promotions. Others seek just a job and desire to stay put at the jobs for which they are hired. Very few people begin working with the expectation that they will be party to one potential consequence of organizational life: the demotion.

A *demotion* involves the reassignment of an employee to a lower status job, with less pay, involving fewer skills and responsibilities. Demotions may take place for reasons beyond the control of the employees. Major organizational

---

10. This point may be debated. It can be argued—and often is—that the family member is the most qualified person for the job.

11. Melville Dalton, *Men Who Manage*, (New York: John Wiley & Sons, Inc., 1959), p. 154.

changes such as reorganizations, company mergers, or business contractions may result in an overall shrinkage in jobs, forcing some employees to accept lower positions. In these cases, blue- and white-collar employees may be demoted. Further, the common union practice of bumping normally results in the employee with the least seniority being demoted to a lower paying job. In these cases, the stigma attached to the demotion may be minor. While employees will no doubt suffer anxiety and frustration over being demoted, they may rationalize the situation by claiming to be "simply in the wrong place at the wrong time; it could have happened to anybody."

In other situations, employees may be demoted for inability to perform their jobs according to acceptable standards. In these cases, demoted employees' frustration, resentment, anger, and fear can run at high levels for a considerable length of time. When demotion is viewed as a devaluation of the employee, the psychological damage can be significant.

Many managers and personnel administrators agree that demotion is not an effective way to handle disciplinary problems. Demotion will not improve the behavior of an employee who has a long record of poor work habits such as chronic absenteeism, insubordination, or drinking on the job. Rather, these problems are most likely to be remedied by supervisory counseling and the corrective approach to employee discipline.

Because of the problems demoted employees may suffer, some organizations avoid making demotions by letting employees remain in their positions. While employees may view this approach as an attractive solution, organizational effectiveness suffers. In other situations, employees may be the recipients of a rather common aberration of personnel management: the promotion–demotion. Here, employees are kicked upstairs to higher paying and high status jobs which typically involve little authority or responsibility. Demotion-promotion is a common way of dealing with a loyal long-term employee who has become obsolete or untrainable in the job. A more meaningful and equitable approach would be to keep the employee in the present job but reassign a portion of the authority and responsibilities to another individual or individuals.

Transfer

A *transfer* involves an employee's reassignment to a job with similar pay, status, duties, and responsibilities. Whereas a promotion involves upward movement, a transfer entails horizontal movement from one job to another.

Transfers take place for several reasons. First, because personnel placement practices are not perfect, an employee/job mismatch may result. A transfer moves the employee to a more suitable job. Second, an employee may become dissatisfied with the job for one or a variety of reasons: serious conflicts with co-workers or a supervisor that appear unresolvable; or a dead-end job from which a transfer would facilitate career advancement goals. Third, organizations sometimes initiate transfers to further the development of the employee, especially at management and staff levels. Even though the transfer involves a job with the same or similar title, working in an environment with new co-workers, unique problems, and a different organizational atmosphere is usually a broadening experience which strengthens the employee's skills and abilities. Lastly, organizational needs may require that employees be transferred. Voluntary or involuntary turnover, promotions, demotions, and terminations may result in job vacancies that may be filled through transfers.

Layoff

In good economic times, business and government expand, hiring is on the upswing, sales are up, jobs are plentiful, and unemployment drops. But economic downturns create economic woes; the personnel action that hits workers the hardest is the *layoff*.

A layoff separates surplus employees from the payroll. If the need for human resources increases after a layoff, some or all of the employees who have been laid off may be recalled. If the demand for the organization's products or services does not increase, however, the layoff becomes permanent and employees are formally separated from the firm.

Normally, layoffs involve hourly, blue–collar workers in the manufacturing and production centers of the organization. In unionized organizations, layoff and recall procedures are spelled out in great detail in the labor-management agreement. Typically, the contract spells out how layoff is defined, the maximum period in which laid-off employees may be recalled, and the rights and privileges that employees hold while laid off. Naturally, seniority plays a major role in determining the order of layoffs. As an illustration, the labor-management contract between Joseph E. Seagrams & Sons, Inc., and the Distillery, Rectifying, Wine, and Allied Workers' International Union of America for August 1, 1975, through July 31, 1978, included the following layoff and recall provisions:

ARTICLE XII: Seniority, Promotions, Layoff, and Recall

1. The employee's length of service for the purpose of determining seniority rights shall be deemed to have commenced on the first day of employment with the Employer. In all cases of promotion, recall, increase or decrease of the number of employees, seniority rights of employees shall govern. The principle of seniority shall govern in all cases, including the filling of vacancies occurring in shifts or new positions created. If vacancies occur in a higher rated position, seniority including the ability to perform the work shall be the controlling factor in the selection of employees to fill such vacancies.

Generally, union contracts mandate *bumping* privileges enabling an employee to bump, or displace, a shorter service employee. Under most union agreements, an employee may bump a less–senior employee whether a layoff is imminent or not. Because widespread bumping practices reduce the efficiency of the company's operation, management usually restricts bumping provisions. For example, the contract will state that only employees qualified to hold the new job may bump other employees.

While production employees are usually among the first to be laid off, managers, staff administrators, and other skilled employees are not immune to layoffs. Usually, a layoff at these levels is an admission that an organization is in very serious trouble. Administrators generally strive to avoid laying off management and staff employees because the firm has spent a great deal of time and money recruiting these employees and developing their skills and abilities. Faced with the realities of survival, they may have little choice. Because managers and staff administrators are not union employees, no formal, written agreement covers the terms and conditions of their layoff. Usually, employee performance plays a major role in deciding which upper level employees to lay off; other criteria such as seniority, age, family obligation, and political considerations may also be given weight.

INTERNAL STAFFING
═══ POLICIES ═══

Sound internal staffing policies and practices will more than likely resolve many problems for the organization. Whenever employees feel their skills are being disregarded or underutilized, dissatisfaction and turnover are likely to occur. Further, if employees feel that they are being treated unfairly or discriminated against in promotion, transfer, or layoff decisions, dissatisfaction may again lead to turnover. Employees frequently file complaints with the Equal Employment Opportunity Commission about discriminatory promotion practices. Also, management may lay off employees with little concern for the workers' interests creating considerable ill will with labor and the community. Each of these potential problems reflects a lack of concern for human resources and reduces the organization's overall effectiveness. Therefore, administrators must create and implement meaningful internal staffing practices that are fair and equitable and make the greatest use of employees' skills and abilities. Important areas for policy considerations are:

Promote or Hire

All in all, the most prudent approach to filling job vacancies is to follow a policy of *promotion from within* but maintain enough flexibility to go outside when personnel within the organization are not qualified. Supporting a policy of promotion from within, administrators need tools to accurately predict the promotability of employees, particularly when decisions concern the promotion of personnel to management positions. In these situations, an assessment center should prove valuable.

Performance Appraisal

The quality of internal staffing decisions is based on the quality of information used to make those decisions. Managers who consider past performance in making demotion, transfer, and layoff decisions for nonunion employees must ensure their performance appraisal systems generate accurate, valid data that reflect a true picture of the candidates' past and present achievements. Unfortunately, some firms are bound to vague, subjective, and biased rating systems which provide little meaningful performance information. Often, these systems permit politics to become a major factor in internal staffing decisions. Results-oriented appraisal systems, such as management by objectives, and behavioral systems, such as BARS, eliminate much of the subjectivity and bias of rating scales and result in higher quality internal staffing decisions. Personnel policies and practices must create and implement information systems that provide accurate measures of employees' performance.

Assistance For Laid Off Employees

Economic misfortunes may cause a firm to lay off masses of workers; the continued existence of the firm may depend on it. Layoffs can be professionally managed to reduce the economic strains that laid off workers and the community face when large numbers of jobs are temporarily or permanently eliminated. Providing assistance to employees during layoffs reflects a genuine concern for the organization's human element and is an act of social responsibility to the community inevitably affected by the layoff. Assistance to laid off employees includes:

SEVERANCE PAY

A lump sum payment to employees who are permanently laid off. A Conference Board study of 1,600 companies showed that 56 percent had *severance pay* for upper level employees and 35 percent planned to give lower-level personnel severance pay.[12] Usually, payments are not made if the employee was discharged for just cause.

SUPPLEMENTAL UNEMPLOYMENT BENEFITS (SUB)

The state unemployment compensation programs pay unemployed workers a certain percentage of their regular wages for a limited time. Benefits depend on the employee's length of service; senior employees may receive up to 95 percent of their take-home pay from unemployment payments and *supplemental unemployment benefits (SUB)*. Like severance pay, SUB are provided only when an employee is laid off and not discharged for just cause or on strike.

OUTPLACEMENT ASSISTANCE

Many firms help laid off employees find employment with other organizations. For lower level employees, assistance may involve channeling surplus employees to local firms which may be hiring new workers. For managers and staff professionals, *outplacement assistance* may include resume preparation and job counseling. Some firms employ outplacement consultants to assist laid off or fired executives find new jobs. These consultants help individuals gain self-confidence, sharpen interviewing skills, develop contacts, and negotiate salaries and other forms of remuneration. Generally, the company which laid off or discharged the employees pays the consultant's fee, which may amount to as much as 15 percent of an executive's annual salary.

Plant Closing Notification

Many labor advocates are strongly endorsing legislation that would require companies to give advance notice to their workers and communities before closing plants.[13] Such legislation is common in several European countries. While about 10 percent of the labor management agreements contain provisions for advance notice, in many cases little or no notice is given. Of course, the biggest advantage to receiving notice of an imminent layoff is being able to prepare for the layoff. A lengthy notice period would give workers a chance to find new jobs. But many managers see numerous problems in giving advance notice; they claim advance notice of a plant closing down may hurt their credit ratings and reduce

12. Mitchell Meyer and Harland Fox, *Profile of Employee Benefits,* Report No. 645 (New York: The Conference Board, 1974), pp. 78–80.

13. This discussion taken from Robert B. McKersie, "Advanced Notice," *The Wall Street Journal* (February 25, 1980): 24.

new customer orders. They also worry about employee morale, motivation, and increased absenteeism as workers look for new jobs.

How much advance notice should a company give? One professor of industrial relations suggests learning from West Germany's experiences:

> Of all the European countries, Germany appears to have the greatest success in achieving the growth and increasing the productivity that go with change, while also avoiding the political and social disruption that have occurred in France and Great Britain. German legislation requires that a firm give notice "in good time," which has usually been interpreted to be about three months."[14]

Equal Employment Opportunity

Personnel policies should dictate that internal staffing decisions are made without regard for race, color, religion, national origin, sex, or age unless situations involve BFOQ's. Any personnel procedure or practice which adversely impacts upon protected classes of employees is illegal and may result in a complaint being filed against the organization.

Methods and practices for making promotions should conform to EEOC guidelines which require that objective job descriptions be used and that promotion procedures be valid and in writing. An affirmative action program may require management to post promotional opportunities, to use skills inventories when recruiting promotion candidates, to develop and implement formal employee appraisal systems, and to establish career counseling programs.

---

14. Ibid.

Including seniority as a factor in promotion decisions is not generally favored by women and minorities, as these groups have made major gains in employment only recently and have less seniority. As indicated earlier, most labor-management agreements give employees with seniority the first chance at vacant jobs. Generally, the courts have upheld the use of seniority as a criterion for layoff decisions involving unionized employees. Research shows that a majority of firms use seniority to determine the order of layoffs. Yet, wherever seniority systems appear to be designed to keep minorities in low paying and low status jobs, they have been dismantled by the courts. One often cited example: in 1969 the Crown Zellerbach Company was ordered by the U.S. Court of Appeals to revise its seniority system because labor-management provisions only enabled employees to progress within certain job lines. The effect of this provision was to keep blacks out of departments with high paying jobs. Crown Zellerbach was ordered to revise its job line system of promotion and adopt a plantwide seniority system.

Human Resources Planning

Decisions which involve internal staffing must consider both short-run and long–run work force goals. Short-run decisions involving promotions, demotions, transfers, and layoffs are made with little thought about their impact on the organization's long-run human resource goals and objectives. Economic factors, in particular, introduce considerable risk in strategic human resource planning; personnel administrators should be prepared to alter goals and strategies as the need arises.

Generally, internal staffing decisions are made by line managers. The promotion, demotion, or transfer of employees is decided by the immediate supervisor and/or the supervisor-to-be. Decisions concerning the kinds and numbers of production employees to lay off are normally made by manufacturing management and other upper level executives.

On the other hand, the personnel department creates policies which spawn effective internal staffing decisions. Personnel administrators contribute to organizational goals and the satisfaction of employee groups by recommending and implementing policies and programs which make maximum utilization of employees' skills. Internal staffing policies that conform to the letter and spirit of equal employment laws will also result in a greater fulfillment of the organization's social responsibility goals.

CAREER
MANAGEMENT

People have varying expectations about the rewards, fulfillments, and satisfactions they seek from their jobs. To some, work is purely a necessary evil, a painful mechanism for earning enough money to support one's self or family. These employees do not expect to be fulfilled in their work: they may, in fact, feel that working and enjoyment are totally incompatible. Other labor force participants not only seek good salaries and benefits, but also desire to satisfy certain human needs. They want to work with agreeable and friendly co-workers, and to receive ego satisfaction from performing their jobs, rather than from middle or upper level management or staff positions. These

workers feel that management positions may involve stress, too much responsibility, pressure, long hours, and weekends at the office. A good family life with the time to pursue hobbies and other interests may be perceived as being just as important—or more important—than a high status job.

For other persons, work is the most significant part of their lives. Totally committed to their jobs, they receive a great deal of personal pride and satisfaction from their work. Many such individuals consider themselves on the fast track to the highest rungs of the organizational ladder. A vice-presidency or presidency is the pot of gold at the end of the rainbow, and large groups of overachievers are more than willing to invest long hours, weekends, and holidays in order to pursue their dreams. To these employees, the job comes first and everything else— family, hobbies, social obligations, and other interests—comes second.

On a continuum of organizational involvement, work may be viewed as "just a job" on one end and a career on the other. Historically, managers have not tried to clarify this distinction for their employees. Management has long felt that employees should take personal responsibility for defining their employment goals and aspirations. Managers have assumed that those possessing extraordinary human talent and ambition would rise to the top, much like cream in a bottle of milk. Employees with lesser skills and more modest achievement drives would, mostly through personal choice, remain in lower status jobs. In the end, people would naturally find the jobs for which their skills and abilities were best suited. Generally management was interested but passive, making promotion and transfer decisions when necessary, and leaving long-term occupational plans and strategies up to the individual.

Contemporary personnel professionals, however, are playing an increasingly active role in designing and implementing programs that not only help employees focus on career choices and objectives but also assist individuals in achieving the objectives they create. Brought on by a greater concern for the quality of working life, federal equal employment opportunity guidelines, and a need to effectively utilize the organization's human resource group, these programs draw upon traditional personnel tools and techniques designed specifically for the development of career paths. In general, all of these programs and techniques fall under the general heading of career management. Important terms and concepts in career management are:

- A *career* is a sequence of jobs held during a person's work life.

- *Career management* is the process of designing and implementing goals, plans, and strategies that enable administrators to satisfy work force needs and allow individuals to achieve their career objectives. Career management involves the integration of three distinct yet highly interrelated career management functions: individual career planning, organizational career planning, and career development.

- *Individual career planning* is the process whereby each employee personally plans career goals and objectives.

- *Organizational career planning* centers around management's career plans for employees.

- *Career development* involves the implementation and coordination of policies and programs that meet organizational

human resource needs and satisfy individual career goals and objectives.

Career Management Success

Three key factors determine the success of an organization's career management efforts: First, decision makers must recognize that career management must be formal and planned and that haphazard or ill-conceived attempts to manage careers will fail. Line managers and personnel administrators who share the responsibility for effective career management must work together to ensure that line and staff efforts are coordinated. Second, top management must back career management if it is to be an effective, viable organization function. Such support comes from an organization climate which encourages promotion from within, the development of employees' skills, and sound, objective performance and promotability criteria for promotion decisions. Third, managers and administrators must not omit or neglect any of career management's many programs and processes. While the career management process will vary to some extent within organizations, certain key elements are central to every program. Figure 12–3 illustrates the major components of the career management model and how they interrelate.

Organizational Career Planning

An important part of the human resource planning process involves the forecast of both long- and short-term human resource demands. During this process, decision makers predict the major changes the organization is likely to face (growth, decline, reorganization, new technologies) and assess their impact on

FIGURE 12–3: *The Career Management Model*

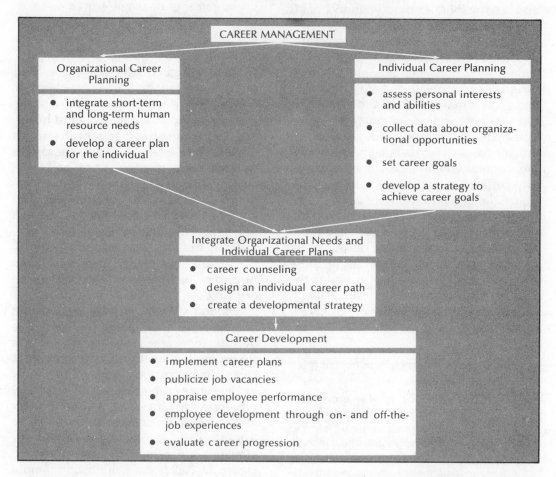

the organization's labor force. Specific emphasis is placed upon predicting changes in the numbers of employees and the kinds of employees. Long-range plans, of course, must be flexible and adjust to contingencies such as rapid, unpredicted organization growth or decline. Short-term plans of one or two years' duration must be consistent with long-term organizational plans for the next five, ten, or more years.

Some organizations develop individual career plans for managers or staff. The executive development chart—a human resource planning tool discussed in Chapter 10—is sometimes used as an aid in career planning. Organizational decision makers develop individual plans based on future organizational needs, the employee's performance and promotability, and equal employment opportunity considerations.

Individual Career Planning

In recent years, increasing numbers of

individuals have plotted their own career goals and created strategies to achieve them. Their actions are consistent with— and may actually result from—new attitudes and values which stress that individuals should take greater responsibility for the events that shape their lives. Books and seminars assist individuals in creating and molding personal, social, family, and work goals.

In addition, many progressive organizations offer counseling about career opportunities for employees who desire to discuss career advancement with qualified professionals. Usually, career counseling is voluntary and available to all employees. Typically, career counselors are in the personnel or human resources department; in smaller firms, a personnel administrator may conduct career counseling and other personnel functions.

Whether employees conduct career planning with the aid of printed material, a short course or seminar, or through formal career counseling, the first step is the assessment of personal interests, aims, skills, and abilities. Employees find out as much as possible about themselves— ambitions, needs, values, strengths, and limitations. The second step is the collection of information about existing and future organizational opportunities. Career counselors are generally prepared to offer this kind of information. In addition, the organization's informal grapevine often contains valuable data about upward progression—for example, what important jobs are likely to open up, who the good managers are, and which departments or work projects have the highest status. Many practicing managers and administrators have testified to the value of this informal network. Unfortunately, many old boy networks have long been closed to women and minorities. Centralizing the career counseling function in a personnel or human resources department will reduce the inequities of informal networks and promote greater career opportunities for all employees.

Based upon their self-assessments and organizational opportunities, employees set career goals. Of course, employees must set realistic goals that have a high probability of being achieved. Not everyone who aspires to a top level position in an organization or dreams of a six-figure salary can achieve such goals. Frustrations and disappointments can be kept to a minimum, however, if realism and practicality are part of the career goal setting process. Career goals will vary considerably, but three are common:[15]

- To supervise or manage a certain number of people by a certain age. For example, an employee may desire to manage ten personnel administrators by age 30 or to manage a manufacturing plant with 1,000 employees by age 40.

- To receive a specified salary within a certain number of years. A young business school graduate may wish to receive a salary of $25,000 five years after graduation and, perhaps, a 10 percent salary increase annually thereafter. Other personnel may create salary targets based on labor statistics, desiring to be in the top half of all wage and salary earners by age 25, the top fourth by age 35, and the top 10 percent by age 50.

- To achieve a title by a certain date. By age 45 or 50 many high-achieving middle managers may want to be presidents or chief executives. Often, employees create stair step title/age goals: district sales manager by 30, regional sales manager by 36, or group vice-president by 45.

15. "Plotting A Route to the Top," *Business Week* (October 12, 1974): 128.

The final step in the individual career planning process is the development of a strategy to achieve career goals. Strategic decisions are often informal, rarely put in writing, and subject to considerable adjustment as an employee progresses through a career. The realities of organizational life demand flexible planning; uncertainty and risk underscore any form of long-range planning. Usually, strategies combine work experience and formal education. Work experience strategies may involve line management experience in manufacturing or sales or staff work in finance, personnel, or research and development. Naturally, previous education and expertise strongly influence the work experiences employees seek. Formal long-term education strategies often include earning an advanced degree such as an MBA or Master's degree in health care, management science, or industrial psychology. The MBA remains—as it has since the 1960s—*the* ticket to many lucrative and desirable management and professional jobs. Short-term educational strategies may include participation in short courses or seminars. Frequently, employers will reimburse some or all of the tuition and other expenses, particularly if the employee's work is related to the additional education.

Organizational and Individual Career Plans

To be effective, career management efforts must strike a workable balance between the organization's human resource needs and employees' career goals. In reality, this balance is difficult to achieve. The dynamic nature of organizational life and powerful informal forces make it extremely difficult, if not impossible, for each individual to carry out career plans within specific time constraints. Business contraction, deadwood, and company politics are some of the roadblocks that have created detours in the career paths of employees. Unpredictable delays in career progression will inevitably result in disappointment, frustration, and turnover as employees join organizations that promise to fulfill career objectives.

To a considerable extent, employee frustration and turnover caused by career stagnation can be minimized through practical career counseling which integrates organizational needs and individual career goals. With the aid of professional career counselors, employees can realistically appraise career goals and the organization's predicted human resource needs. In some cases, overly optimistic personal career goals may have to be trimmed back. In other cases, the counselor may suggest opportunities and, perhaps, alternative career paths to accelerate an employee's career aims. Regardless of the plan finally agreed upon, however, it must be evaluated and updated when organizational or personal factors necessitate changes.

Many organizations find the career ladder or career path manual useful in matching organizational needs and personal career goals. In addition to illustrating normal progression to successively higher jobs, the manual may incorporate other important career information such as whether a natural progression through work experience or formal training and development activities are required for promotions. Many *career paths* also chart potential interdepartmental transfers or promotions to new jobs that may better suit an employee's career needs. As an example, the city of Atlanta created an extensive career path manual for its employees in 1978. The manual shows job progression within each department and across various departmental lines. Figure 12–4 illustrates the career paths contained within the personal and real property appraisal job series.

In matching organizational and personal career needs, a mutually-agreed upon developmental plan for each employee should be created. Normally, this plan meshes personal developmental plans and strategies with input from the organization. Career counselors and superiors may alter personal strategies based on the employee's career path and, perhaps, recommend additional on- or off-the-job experiences to facilitate the employee's career progression.

Career Development

During the career development phase, the strategies for achieving career goals are implemented. Career development is a long-term process spanning an employee's entire working career. By linking together several key ingredients of the career development process, progression along the career path is made relatively smooth and unobstructed. While minor (and occasionally major) adjustments in career paths are expected, effective career development enables career progression to proceed with greater regularity and predictability. The primary elements in the career development process include the publication of job vacancies, employee performance appraisal, employee development, and the evaluation of career progression.

JOB VACANCIES

Publicizing job vacancies is an excellent way to disseminate career information and notify employees who may be qualified for a vacant job. Bulletin boards and internal company news bulletins are normally used for this purpose. Job announcements generally include the job title, a brief description of duties, necessary qualifications, starting salary, and location of the job.

APPRAISAL DATA

Sound, objective employee performance appraisal data are particularly valuable for career development. Performance feedback by an employee's supervisor will include an analysis of strengths, weaknesses, and shortcomings so that any problems may be overcome. Continued inattention or disregard of performance shortfalls will limit career progression. Thus, supervisors have the important responsibility of collecting performance data and honestly telling employees whether performance is satisfactory in light of career goals. Further, personnel administrators play an important role in this process by designing and implementing valid, objective performance appraisal systems.

TRAINING AND DEVELOPMENT EXPERIENCES

Perhaps the most meaningful aspect of career development is the accumulation of work experiences and off-the-job developmental activities that broaden employees' skills and abilities. Effective development enables the employee to assume increasingly challenging job responsibilities and to successfully perform at higher job levels. Many training and development activities—for example, job rotation, coaching, committee assignments, and both short and long-term off–

FIGURE 12–4: *City of Atlanta Career Ladder, Personal and Real Property Appraisal Job Series*

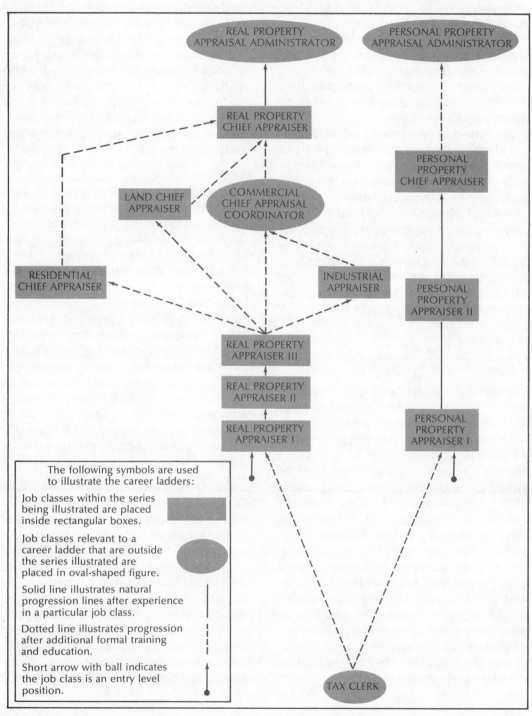

the-job educational strategies—are core components of career development for many organizations. Any serious attempt at career development must emphasize a well-planned and coordinated employee development function.

CAREER PROGRESSION EVALUATION

As the final phase of the career development process, evaluation of the employee's progress toward career goals takes place annually or biannually, possibly during an annual performance review session. During the evaluation phase, employees review career progress with supervisors and, perhaps, career counselors. Particular emphasis is placed upon whether or not career goals and timetables have been reached; if progress has been less than expected, reasons for this are explored and discussed. Shortfalls in career progression may be remedied through additional work experiences and off-the-job development. Where the initial career aims and paths were unrealistic, a major downscaling of the employee's career goals may be required. Good counseling skills are particularly important for supervisors or counselors who deal with disappointed, frustrated employees facing career failure.

Program Benefits

Organizations take different approaches to managing employees' careers. Some organizations are passive, allowing individuals to assume complete or near–complete control over their own work destinies. Others provide moderate guidance, through counseling services which may offer some ideas and suggestions about career choices or training and development activities that may be help-

ful in pursuing a particular career path. More progressive organizations have formal, planned, systematic approaches to career management; they are most likely to enjoy the benefits that enhance organizational effectiveness and employee satisfaction.

REDUCED PERSONNEL TURNOVER

A frequently cited reason for management and professional staff turnover is, "there was no future for me at that company. Promotional opportunities were few and far between." Effective career management eliminates many of the career blockages that force employees to seek greener working pastures in other organizations.

COMPETITION FOR EMPLOYEES

An organization's career management policies and programs have become important considerations for job seekers today. Many college graduates desire to work for an organization that supports and assists career endeavors in addition to offering a meaningful entry position and good starting salary with a strong benefits package.

HEIGHTENED MOTIVATION

One important product of the career management process is the development of an individual career path for each employee. Because progression along the career path is directly related to job performance, an employee is likely to perform at peak levels so that career goals are accomplished according to the employee's time frame.

PERSONAL CAREER CONTROL

Employees desire more control over their careers. They want to make meaningful input into decisions concerning their work life and prefer to actively formulate career alternatives and design career paths.

EQUAL EMPLOYMENT OPPORTUNITY CONCERNS

The letter and spirit of federal equal employment guidelines demand fair and equitable recruiting, selection, and placement policies, and elimination of discriminatory practices concerning promotions and career mobility. Many affirmative action programs contain formal provisions to enhance the career mobility of women and minorities, including the development of career paths and the design of formal training and development activities. Further, several court actions have forced organizations to strengthen their equal employment opportunity career advancement policies and procedures by removing the barriers to the career progression of minorities.

In summary, organizational growth, major reorganizations, changes in business and economic conditions, terminations, resignations, and retirements cause significant internal staff changes. Personnel administrators should monitor these changes closely to ensure planned, orderly internal staffing decisions and to integrate short- and long-term human resource needs. Criteria for making promotion decisions should be consistent with the nature of the work force and organizational goals. Among organized employees, seniority is a prime factor in making promotions; performance and promotability are important factors in promoting nonunion employees. An open promotional system offers greater utilization of employees' skills and abilities than a closed system. Normally, the advantages of promoting from within far outweigh those of filling vacancies from the outside. Some companies promoting from within use assessment centers to identify potential managers among nonmanagerial personnel. Closely related to internal staffing is career management, which involves the integration of organizational human resource needs and individual employees' career goals. Effective career management is a formal and planned process which coordinates many separate yet interrelated personnel techniques. These include posting job vacancies, performance appraisals, and training and development activities. Periodically the extent to which career management efforts actually benefit the organization, and individual employees, should be assessed. These benefits may include the reduction of employee turnover, the attraction of high quality job candidates, increased employee motivation, greater personal control for employees over their careers, and equal opportunities for all employees.

The Solution

To bring about a reduction in Citizens Savings and Loan's alarming turnover rate, Janice Pauling must create and implement personnel policies which will advance an equitable promotional system. Realistically, there may be little she can do about the deadwood strewn throughout the hierarchy; an open promotional system will ensure that all qualified and interested personnel are aware of job vacancies. In addition, Pauling needs to study how promotion decisions are made, and minimize company politics in deciding who gets promoted. The implementation of new, objective performance appraisal systems, such as MBO, may be necessary to ensure that promotions are based on performance and promotability. Accurate reading of employees' performances, coupled with a strong policy statement about promotion based on performance and promotability, will significantly curtail the use of seniority as a promotion criterion.

KEY TERMS AND CONCEPTS

Internal Staffing	Promote from Within
Promotion	Severance Pay
Closed Promotion System	Supplemental Unemployment Benefits
Open Promotion System	Outplacement Assistance
Assessment Center	Career
Nepotism	Career Management
Demotion	Individual and Organizational Career
Bumping	Planning
Transfer	Career Development
Layoff	Career Path

FOR REVIEW

1. What are the benefits of an effective system for making promotion decisions? What criteria may be used for making promotion decisions?

2. What are the major factors that cause employee demotions, transfers, and layoffs?

3. What are some important personnel policies and practices that have an impact on internal staffing decisions?

4. What are the major components of the career management model and how does the model work?

5. What benefits may be gained from a career management program?

FOR DISCUSSION

1. In many organizations, new employees are placed on probation for a three- or six-month period. New employees who do not work out may be terminated without the right to appeal the firing during probation. Do you feel a similar probationary period should be in effect for employees who receive promotions? Can you think of any arguments for and against this proposal?

2. Seniority is a common criterion for deciding which blue-collar workers to lay off. Should seniority be the major factor in deciding upon white-collar layoffs? Defend your reasoning.

3. Most organizations use closed promotion systems when selecting candidates for promotion, although this approach minimizes the pool of candidates. Why do organizations continue to use the closed promotion system?

4. An often cited advantage of using seniority as a criterion for making promotions is that it eliminates supervisory bias that may accompany a supervisor's promotion recommendations. Are there any ways to reduce the possibility of supervisory bias while using performance criteria in making promotion decisions?

5. Personnel literature generally holds the assessment center concept in high regard. Can you think of reasons why an organization would not adopt the assessment center approach in gathering promotion data?

6. Usually, there is a tremendous stigma attached to an employee's admission that "I received a promotion and I am failing on my

new job. I would like a job with less authority and fewer responsibilities." How can this stigma be eliminated?

7. If an employee receives a promotion and fails, is it the organization's or the employee's fault?

8. Would you favor U.S. legislation modeled on European laws requiring that advanced notice be given to employees before plant closings? Why or why not? If you support such legislation, how much advanced notice should be given?

9. Assuming you were employed full-time, what would you perceive as some of your immediate supervisor's responsibilities in the career management process?

10. How would you evaluate your college or university's efforts at preparing you for a career in the world of work? Cite your school's strong and weak areas.

SUPPLEMENTARY READING

Alfred, T. M. "Checkers or Choice in Manpower Management." *Harvard Business Review,* January–February 1967, pp. 157–69.

Burack, E. A. "Why All the Confusion About Career Planning." *Human Resource Management* 16: 21–23.

Dahl, D. R., and Pinto, P. R. "Job Posting: An Industrial Survey," *Personnel Journal* 56 (1977): 40–42.

Dalton, Melville. *Men Who Manage.* New York: John Wiley & Sons, Inc., 1959.

Hall, D. T. *Careers in Organizations.* Pacific Palisades, Calif: Goodyear Publishing Co., 1976.

Hall, F. S. "Gaining EEO Compliance with a Stable Workforce." *Personnel Journal* 56 (1977): 454–57.

Hersler, W. J. "Promotion: What Does It Take To Get Ahead?" *Business Horizons,* April 1978, pp. 57–63.

Kraut, Allen. "New Frontiers for Assessment Centers." *Personnel,* July–August 1976, pp. 30–38.

Moses, J. L., and Byham, W. C., eds., *Applying the Assessment Center Method.* Elmsford, NY: Permagon Press, 1977.

Sheehy, Gail. *Passages.* New York: E. P. Dutton & Co., 1974.

Yoder, D., and Heneman, H. G., Jr., eds.*Staffing Policies and Strategies.* Washington, DC: Bureau of National Affairs, Inc., 1974.

For Analysis: Assessment Center at Piedmont Insurance

The Piedmont Insurance Company personnel committee entered the executive conference room, took their seats, drank coffee from styrofoam cups, and chatted amiably among themselves. Each of the organization's six major departments was represented, typically by the department head. They were waiting for Jerry Smyth, head of Piedmont's personnel department and chairman of the personnel committee. The committee members had only a vague notion of what the meeting was all about; the memo calling the session spoke sparingly of "problems with promotion decisions" and a need to develop "a system for making more effective promotion decisions."

The Piedmont Insurance Company is a medium-sized, rapidly growing insurance company based in Indianapolis, Indiana. Piedmont Insurance is one of eighteen insurance companies owned by Tidewater, Inc., a large insurance holding company. Offering a variety of personal home and life insurance coverage, Piedmont has recently captured a sizeable niche in the group insurance market. Piedmont's labor force totals about forty five hundred employees, including about six hundred line managers and staff administrators.

Smyth, about five minutes late, hurriedly took his chair at the end of the conference table. After uttering a brief apology for his tardiness, he got to the point: "This afternoon, we need to discuss a serious personnel problem that we've had in this organization for some time. As I'm sure you are all aware, we have recurring performance problems at the first level of management. Deadlines are frequently missed and quality control is almost nonexistent. Turnover among the clerical staff and sales personnel is about twice what it should be. And our annual employee attitude surveys show that our

supervisors are in dire need of both work-oriented and people—
oriented skills. We have much job dissatisfaction at the clerical
and salesperson level, and all fingers point to supervision.
Besides, the productivity audit conducted last year by our
management consultants, Van Auken & Associates, confirmed
that our first level of supervision was one of the organization's
weakest links. To make a long story short, we need to consider
alternative ways to strengthen our first-line supervision."

Kathy Morris, claims manager: "But Jerry, each new manager
is required to attend a forty-hour supervisory training
program offered by your department. Isn't the program
having any impact?"

Smyth: "Well, we haven't been satisfied with the results of our
evaluation studies. Currently we're looking at ways to
improve our management training."

Allen Morris, manager of personal lines: "Jerry, you don't turn
someone into a supervisor in one week. What else are we
doing to develop the skills of our new managers?"

Smyth: "Several things. First, we generally pay for an
employee to attend a seminar as long as it's related to the
job. Second, we reimburse employees for expenses they
receive in getting a college degree. And as you know, we
also encourage all middle managers to work closely with
their supervisors to develop skills through on-the-job
coaching."

Lynn Snead, manager of group insurance: "Besides taking a
closer look at our training and development programs, what
else can we do to improve our supervision?"

Smyth: "I think we need to make some significant changes in
the way we make promotion decisions, particularly when
promoting a nonmanagement employee into the first level of
management. We're presently promoting about seventy-five
employees a year into supervision. Historically, we've

promoted someone because of a high degree of technical skills. But technical skills only play a minor role in supervision. And I'm afraid we've tried to make supervisors out of a good number of people who simply don't have the aptitudes to be successful managers. And we're probably overlooking a lot of employees who have the basic qualities that it takes for successful supervision."

Snead: "And how do we deal with these problems?"

Smyth: "A couple of months ago I sent to each of you a memo and several current journal articles that described the assessment center concept. I think this is the real key to long-run improvements at our lower management levels. I've been toying with the idea of going ahead with the project for some time and decided to make a formal request to top management. I'm going to propose that we begin an assessment center for selecting first level managers and I want to discuss with you several different strategies for getting the program into action.

"One approach is to put our own assessment staff together under my direction. We could study other programs, select our own tests and exercises, train our own assessors, and periodically conduct our own exercises, say every three months or so. Another alternative is to hire an outside consulting firm to come in and do the assessments. And a third approach is to persuade the corporate personnel office at Tidewater to put together a program that could be used by each company. The economies of scale of this approach would be tremendous; with the great number of promotions that are made annually in the Tidewater system, a full-time professional staff would easily keep busy the year around."

Snead: "Hold on, Jerry. We all realize that a lot of successes have been recorded for the assessment center concept, but it's not a perfect system. It won't guarantee success. Besides, it's pretty costly. How will we know we're getting our money's worth? To improve the quality of our supervision, maybe we should consider some other alternatives to the assessment center. We could beef up our supervisory training. Or, we could make our promotion decisions much more carefully than we do now, perhaps by a formal committee. And to get more candidates, we could use the job posting technique for the first level of supervision. That way all interested personnel would be welcome to apply.

"But if we do finally decide to go with the assessment center, let me strongly encourage that we start slowly at first with a pilot program in one department. That way we can iron out the bugs in the system before we go any further with it."

Questions

1. Evaluate the following alternatives for improving Piedmont's first level of supervision:

   More supervisory training for new supervisors

   Promotion decisions made by a promotion committee

   Implementation of an assessment center

2. If you recommend an assessment center for Piedmont, who should conduct it—Piedmont's Personnel Department, Tidewater Corporate Personnel Office, or an outside consulting group? Should the program begin on a pilot study basis?

3. Are the training and the assessment center approaches mutually exclusive strategies for improving the quality of supervision? Discuss.

Lewis Hine photographed this young worker in a southern textile mill in 1910, twenty-eight years before the Fair Labor Standards Act was enacted.

13

COMPENSATION

Compensation System Objectives

Job Evaluation Methods

Designing a Compensation System

Federal Compensation Guidelines

The Problem: Perceived Pay Inequity

Andy Stark is quite upset. At lunch today he learned that another employee, Helen Pontiac, is being paid just one step below him, only $.70 an hour less. Andy has had his semiskilled job with the Chambers Sandal Company for three years and only three months ago was given a merit increase from step 3 to step 4 within his pay grade. Until today Andy was satisfied with his pay. He knows two people on his street who have similar jobs with other manufacturing firms, and they both make less than he does.

But Stark has felt for the last couple of years that his firm was giving in to the federal government by hiring and promoting females and blacks over more qualified white males. This situation with Helen Pontiac convinced him he was right; after all, the company always says that it rewards loyalty, and here it hires someone in just one step below him! During the afternoon Stark notices that Pontiac is very good at her job; in fact, Stark wasn't that good for almost a year.

By the end of the day Stark is at a decision point; he can either go in and ask the supervisor if it's true, or forget about it. There is a company rule which says employees should not discuss pay, so Stark decided to forget it but keep it in the back of his mind.

FIGURE 13–1: *The Total Compensation System*

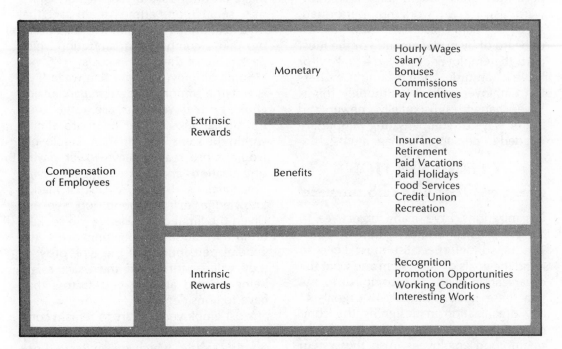

One of the traditional personnel functions is determining employees' compensation. In today's organization, with a variety of costly employee benefit programs, wage incentive programs, and structured pay scales, the compensation task is even more difficult and challenging for a personnel specialist. Employees' compensation affects their productivity and their tendency to stay with the organization or seek employment elsewhere. While managers and researchers do not agree about the degree to which compensation affects productivity, compensation is of great importance. Employees' need for income and their desire to be fairly treated by the organization make developing the compensation program all the more important for the personnel department. Unfortunately, there is no exact, objective method of determining compensation for any one job or employee. Compensating employees for what they give the organization is to some extent as much an art as a science.

The term *compensation* is often used interchangeably with the wage and salary administration; however, the term *compensation* actually is a broader concept. Compensation refers not only to the monetary or *extrinsic rewards* but also the benefits or *intrinsic rewards* an organization gives, such as recognition, chance for promotion, and more challenging job opportunities. The term *wage and salary administration* usually refers strictly to the monetary rewards given to employees.

The compensation of people at work has become one of the most demanding problems facing management in this decade. In previous years, payment for work performed was simple and straightforward. Paying for work not performed, such as paid vacations, was simply unheard of by management. For the most part, the employer displayed a "take it or leave it" attitude when making pay offers for employees. Today although things have changed substantially, newer and better ways of compensating people are needed in personnel management.[1]

COMPENSATION OBJECTIVES

Organizations have many objectives in designing their compensation systems. The personnel specialist must keep in mind the goals of the system and what the organization needs to accomplish to obtain these goals. Primarily, the goals of any organization in designing the compensation system should be to attract and retain good employees. Also the system should motivate employees and comply with all legal requirements.

Attracting Employees

While most job applicants are not aware of the exact wages offered by different organizations for similar jobs within the local labor market, they do compare job offers and pay scales. Job applicants who receive more than one offer will naturally compare monetary offers. Since it is easier to compare dollars, job applicants often will put more weight on the salaries being offered than on the other compensation factors, such as benefits and intrin-

sic rewards. While one organization may make an offer $500 a year higher, which may seem more attractive, in fact that organization may provide less take-home pay than a competing organization which pays more of the benefit costs.

Some employers argue that wage level is not the important determinant of job choice; if that were the case, wage levels for similar jobs would be more similar within the same labor market. Employees would more readily leave lower paying organizations and seek out higher paying organizations. Indeed, a lack of market knowledge exists among job seekers. Given the limited knowledge job seekers often have about various employers, the general perceptions of the type of work they will perform and the exact salary being offered are the best factors they have to consider.[2]

Most employers will try to remain competitive within the local labor market by offering salaries which are similar to those offered by competing employers. Usually this means determining what the going rate is for jobs within the local labor market. This entails using *wage surveys* which estimate average salaries for entry level positions. The employer has two alternatives: The first is for the organization to conduct a wage survey and determine the going rate for jobs in the local labor market; the second is to use published market data.

Conducting a wage survey is a difficult, expensive process for an individual organization. The personnel specialist must determine which employers have roughly comparable positions within the local

1. R. C. Pilenzo, "Compensation: The State of the Art," *The Personnel Administrator* (September, 1977): 11.

2. L. Dyer, D. P. Schwab, and J. A. Fossum, "Impacts of Pay on Employee Behaviors and Attitudes: An Update," *The Personnel Administrator* (January, 1978): 51–53.

FIGURE 13–2: *Objectives of the Compensation System*

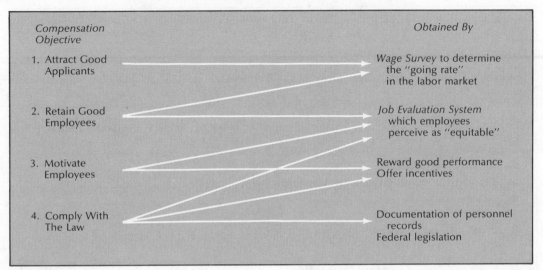

labor market. Job titles are no longer an acceptable means of proving comparability of positions. By comparing brief job descriptions, the specialist must determine if the job is similar to other organizations' positions on a particular wage level.

A further requirement for conducting wage surveys is determining which information about each job is necessary. The wages being paid for each job type included in the survey must be precisely defined. If possible, survey information should include hiring salary ranges, incentives, normal wage changes such as cost of living increases, and specific wage policies and practices within each organization in the survey. Information about seniority provisions, paid vacations, sick leave, and the number of paid holidays per year is helpful. Also, any additional pay, such as a uniform allowance or bonus plans, should be reported. Lastly, a wage survey should include questions concerning unusual working conditions such as high levels of noise or fumes.[3]

In recent years more organizations have turned to published wage survey information for a variety of reasons. First, published information can be obtained quickly, at low cost, and with little effort by the organization. Second, conducting wage surveys has become a science in recent years; few organizations have personnel capable of undertaking such a task. Third, using an organization's wage survey may cause problems in court cases. Opposing lawyers will try to prove that the survey caused the organization to perpetuate past discriminatory practices which occurred in the surveyed organizations, and therefore led to misleading wage information in other organizations. The abundance of market data in most large communities has made more effective wage and salary administration possible in most geographic areas; sufficient market data are available to accurately price anywhere from 5 to 50 percent of

3. David W. Belcher, *Wage and Salary Administration* (Englewood Cliffs, NJ: Prentice–Hall, Inc., 1962), pp. 106–13.

FIGURE 13–3: *Wage and Salary Survey Data Sheet*

Name of participating company_____ Code_____

Address_____ Business_____

Survey No._____ Data furnished by_____ Title_____ Date_____

	SHOP	OFFICE	SALARY	INCENTIVE
1. Number of employees in your company.......	____	____	____	____
2. Minimum hiring rates........................	____	____	____	____
3. Do you use training rates for new employees?	____	____	____	____
4. Number of hours worked. Per week	____	____	____	____
Per year	____	____	____	____
5. What method of progression do you use				
Within the range	____	____	____	____
Automatic Increase	____	____	____	____
Merit Increase	____	____	____	____
Part Automatic—Part Merit	____	____	____	____
6. Are you granting rest periods				
With pay	____	____	____	____
Without pay	____	____	____	____
7. Do employees working on holidays receive				
Straight hourly rate	____	____	____	____
Time and one-half	____	____	____	____
Double time	____	____	____	____
Other compensation	____	____	____	____
8. What is the average percentage of base rate paid as supplemental wages?......................	____%	____%	____%	____%
9. In percent of base rates how much do you pay for a 40-hour workweek?				
Afternoon shift	___%	___%	___%	___%
Night shift	___%	___%	___%	___%
Saturday	___%	___%	___%	___%
Sunday	___%	___%	___%	___%
Holiday	___%	___%	___%	___%
10. Do you supply work clothes and laundry?.....	____	____	____	____
11. Do you use a single rate (SR) SR	____	____	____	____
or a rate range (RR) for each job? RR	____	____	____	____

12. If you use an incentive plan, briefly explain the incentive method used _____
_____
_____

| 13. What are the average incentive earnings per hour as a percentage of base rate?......................... | ___% | ___% | ___% | ___% |

SOURCE: Zollitsch, Herbert G. and Adolph Langsner, *Wage and Salary Administration*, (Cincinnati: South-Western Publishing Co., 1970), pp. 337–38. Used by Permission.

WAGE AND SALARY SURVEY DATA SHEET (continued)

	Shop	Office	Salary	Incentive

14. Do you pay supplemental wages (Fringe Benefits)?
Annual Bonus____   Attendance Bonus____   Christmas Bonus____   Profit Sharing____
Stock Purchase Plan____   Seniority Bonus____   Vacation with Pay____   Paid Holiday____
Other Payments _____

	Shop	Office	Salary	Incentive

15. Are you guaranteeing an annual wage?

Yes   ____   ____   ____   _____
No   ____   ____   ____   _____

If "yes," please explain amount and number of weeks per year, etc. _____
_____
_____

16. Which of the following holidays do you grant with pay?

	Jan. 1	Feb. 12	Feb. 22	May 30	July 4	Labor Day	Thanksgiving	Dec. 25
Shop	____	____	____	____	____	____	____	____
Office	____	____	____	____	____	____	____	____
Salary	____	____	____	____	____	____	____	____
Incentive	____	____	____	____	____	____	____	____

	Shop	Office	Salary	Incentive

17. Are vacations granted with pay

After 1 year employment	____ wks.	____ wks.	____ wks.	____ wks.
" 2 " "	____ "	____ "	____ "	____ "
" 3 " "	____ "	____ "	____ "	____ "
" 4 " "	____ "	____ "	____ "	____ "
" 5 " "	____ "	____ "	____ "	____ "

18. If you have employee benefit plans, excluding social security and workmen's compensation, who contributes—

	Company only	Employee only	Both Company	Both Employee
Accident Insurance	_____	_____	____%	____%
Life Insurance	_____	_____	____%	____%
Hospitalization Insurance	_____	_____	____%	____%
Pension	_____	_____	____%	____%
Savings	_____	_____	____%	____%
	_____	_____	____%	____%

	Shop	Office	Salary	Incentive

19. If sick leave is granted with pay, how is it paid?

Full Pay   ____   ____   ____   _____
% of Base Rate ___% ___% ___% _____%

20. Attached are condensed descriptions of key jobs designated by our job numbers as indicated below. These jobs will also be used in repetitive surveys. Please fill in correct current data.

Job Code No.	Job Code No.	Job Code No.	Job Code No.
_____	_____	_____	_____
_____	_____	_____	_____
_____	_____	_____	_____
_____	_____	_____	_____

comparable positions in many organizations. The relative availability of market data today has changed the basic approach to salary classification work. Employers can receive wage survey information from their local chambers of commerce, unions, trade services, and the U.S. Department of Labor.

Retaining Good Employees

After the organization has attracted and has hired new employees, the compensation system should not hinder efforts to retain productive employees. While many factors may cause employees to leave an organization, inadequate compensation is the most frequent cause of turnover. Fortunately, turnover can be minimized within an organization. To retain good employees, the personnel manager must make sure that there is compensation equity within the organization.

If employees perceive that they are being treated inequitably by the organization, tension results. The perception of inequity causes an unpleasant emotional state which may cause employees to reduce their future efforts, change their perceptions regarding rewards for their work efforts, or as often is the case, leave the organization.[4] Research has found that employee perceptions of equitable treatment were affected when an organization altered its pay system to increase the pay of about 50 percent of its employees. However, the same employees reported diminished inequity perceptions nine months after a change in pay systems. This suggests that such perceived inequity is short-term in nature; however, additional perceptions of unfair treatment may cause employees to leave the organization.[5]

Employee job satisfaction is often considered to be a strong determinant of turnover. However, employee perceptions of inequitable treatment have been found to be even stronger predictors of absence and job turnover than job satisfaction. If employees perceive that they will be more fairly or equitably treated by another organization, the probability of their leaving increases.[6]

To provide for equity between jobs, administrators usually produce a systematic relationship among the pay scales for various jobs within an organization. This process is usually called job evaluation.

Job evaluation is the systematic determination of the relative worth of jobs within the organization, which results in a pay system within the organization. Primarily, jobs are compared upon the traditional basis of skills required to complete the job, effort required to perform the job, responsibility of the job holder, and working conditions of the job. The primary purpose of job evaluation is to develop a system of compensation which employees will perceive to be equitable. Thus, job evaluation strives to obtain internal consistency between jobs while wage surveys help the organization to maintain external consistency with other organizations in the local labor market.

4. J. S. Adams, "Inequity in Social Exchange," in L. Berkowitz, ed., *Advances in Experimental Social Psychology*, Vol. 2 (New York: Academic Press, 1965), pp. 422–36.

5. Michael R. Carrell, "A Longitudinal Field Assessment of Employee Perceptions of Equitable Treatment," *Organizational Behavior and Human Performance* 21 (1978): 108–18.

6. John E. Dittrich and M. R. Carrell, "Organizational Equity Perceptions, Employee Job Satisfaction, and Departmental Absence and Turnover Rates," *Organizational Behavior and Human Performance* 24 (1979): 29–40.

FIGURE 13–4: *Motivation and Performance Model*

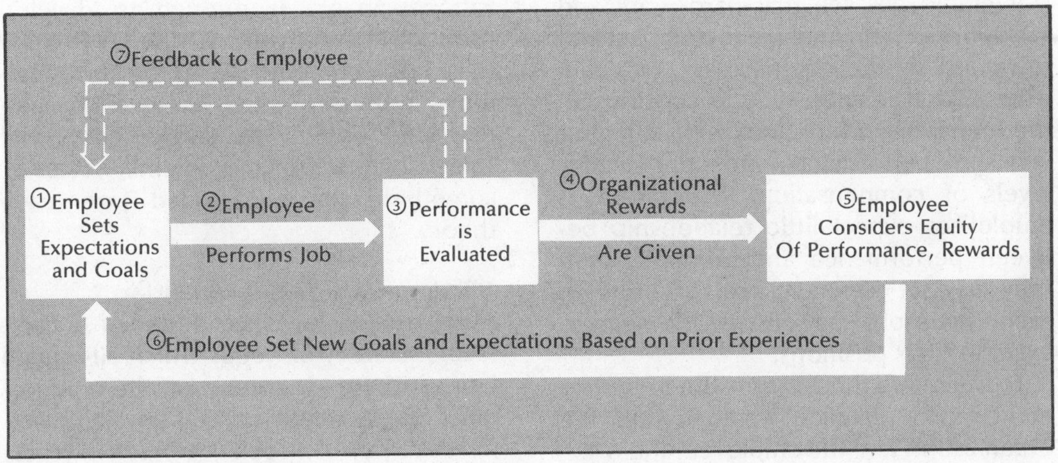

While no compensation program will keep all employees satisfied all the time, if management is able to minimize turnover and lost production due to perceptions of inequitable compensation, then its goal of retaining good employees has been achieved. Not only must an organization have a very fair and equitable system, this system must be explained to its employees. Administrators must tell employees the various wage rates paid to different positions and how those wage levels are determined. Many managers involve employees in job classifications and compensation matters. The most equitable and fair compensation system is useless unless employees perceive it to be equitable.

Motivation

Employees expect that their performances will correlate with the rewards received from the organization. Generally, that perceived relationship takes the form exhibited in Figure 13–4. Employees set expectations about rewards and compensation to be received if certain levels of performance are achieved. These expectations determine goals or levels of performance for the future. During the second step in the model, employees achieving the desired level of performance expect a certain level of compensation. At some point management evaluates and rewards the employee's performance. Examples of such rewards include merit increases, promotions, and intrinsic rewards such as recognition and increased status. In the fifth step of the model, employees consider the relationship between the performance they have given their organization, the rewards related to that performance, and the fairness of that relationship. The final step of the process involves employees setting new goals and expectations based upon prior experiences within the organization.

If employees see that hard work and superior performance are recognized and rewarded by the organization, they will expect such relationships to continue in the future. Therefore, they will set higher levels of performance expecting higher levels of compensation. Of course, if employees expect little relationship between performance and rewards, then they may set minimum goals in order to retain their jobs, but not see the need to excel in their positions.

To safeguard this relationship of performance and motivation, which benefits the organization and the employee, the organization must provide:

Accurate Evaluation:

Management must develop a system of accurate performance appraisal in order to identify those employees who are outstanding performers, minimum achievers, and poor performers. While developing an accurate performance appraisal is not easy, it is a critical link between employee performance and motivation.

Performance Rewards:

Management should identify which *organizational rewards* relate to performance levels and tell employees that pay, increased benefits, change in hours or working conditions, or recognition will be directly related to high performance.

Supervisors' Feedback:

Supervisors must give complete and accurate feedback to employees when appraising their performances. Employees must be told what they are doing well, and which performance areas need improvement.

Many managers have theories regarding the motivation of employees' performance; some believe that only one motivational theory is enough to develop productive employees. Others may claim that no technique works because employees are born either achievers or loafers. Undoubtedly no single theory will solve all motivational problems; however, something can be learned from each theory.

MASLOW'S HIERARCHY OF NEEDS

Abraham Maslow has identified a five–level *hierarchy of needs* which all human beings share. In order of their importance, these needs are: (1) physiological; (2) security; (3) social; (4) self-esteem; and (5) self-actualization.[7]

Physiological needs, according to Maslow, are the primary needs for food, shelter, and clothing. These needs can be directly satisfied by compensation; employees who are adequately paid can provide for their basic needs. Once the physiological needs have been satisfied, the safety or security need becomes a motivational factor. Many employees' most important security need is, of course, job security. Other security factors include increases in salary and fringe benefits.

On the next level is the social need. At this level, employees desire social relationships inside and outside the organization. Peer group acceptance within the work force is often an important psychological need for employees. Once employees have friendships within the organization and feel a part of the peer group, the need for esteem or status takes precedence. Organizational factors such as job title, status items within the organization

---

7. A. H. Maslow, "A Theory of Human Motivation," *Psychological Review* (1943): 370–96.

such as parking spaces or office size, and level of responsibility become important to the employee at this level.

Finally, the highest need is self-actualization. At this level employees seek a fulfilling, useful life in the organization and in society. Employees will seek challenging and creative jobs to realize self-actualization. Maslow contends that individuals will climb the ladder of need fulfillment until they have become self-actualized. If any need is not fulfilled, the individual will continually strive to fill that need which becomes a motivational factor. At any level, needs may be fulfilled outside the organization as well as within the organization.

Perhaps the most valuable aspect of Maslow's theory is its emphasis on employees' individual needs. The implication is that managers must accurately assess individuals' needs and link those needs to the organization's compensation methods.

GOAL SETTING

Research has shown that job performance can be increased when individuals are given specific goals rather than simply being evaluated on performance. If individuals are given specific goals which they perceive to be difficult but reasonable, they will be more successful in attaining these goals.[8] *Goal setting*, of course, is an integral part of management by objectives.

REINFORCEMENT

The concept of reinforcement is central to most motivation techniques. The principle theory behind reinforcement is that behaviors rewarded by the organization are repeated by the employee more often than unrewarded or punished behaviors. The *law of effect* states that behavior which leads to a pleasant response will be repeated, whereas behavior which results in unpleasant experiences tends not to be repeated.[9] Reinforcement is at the heart of the merit pay increases which will be discussed later in this chapter. In order for reinforcement to continue to affect future employees' behavior, a manager must make certain that rewards are meaningful and desired by each employee. As Maslow pointed out, employee needs are different; therefore, the manager must tailor the reward, whether it be recognition, pay, or changing job requirements, to fit the employee. In addition the manager must be sure that employees realize that rewards are contingent upon correct behavior.

Legal Considerations

A fourth major objective of the compensation system is to comply with federal legislation. Government has affected compensation by legislating pay levels and nondiscriminatory pay practices. As an employer in competition with private employers, the government also affects pay systems. At any time, government can increase its control over compensation by freezing wages; this occurred during the Korean War and from 1971 through 1974. A governmental wage freeze requires that federal regulatory bodies review wage increases. Wage guidelines are not strict wage controls but simply requests to employers to voluntarily comply with wage increase maximums.

8. E. A. Locke, "Toward A Theory of Task Motivation and Incentives," *Organizational Behavior and Human Performance* 3 (1968): 157–80.

9. E. L. Thorndike, *Animal Intelligence* (New York: The Macmillan Co., 1911), p. 1–56.

FIGURE 13–5: *U.S. Minimum Wage Changes Under the Fair Labor Standard Act as Amended*

	Per Hour
1938	$ .25
1945	.40
1950	.75
1956	1.00
1962	1.15
1967	1.40
1974	2.00
1978	2.65
1979	2.90
1980	3.10
1981	3.35

FAIR LABOR STANDARDS ACT

The major compensation legislation regulating employers is the *Fair Labor Standards Act of 1938.* This act has been amended by Congress several times to provide higher minimum wage levels. The provisions of this law include the following:

MINIMUM WAGES Under the Fair Labor Standards Act employers must pay an employee at least a minimum wage per hour. The minimum wage per hour in 1938 was $.25; in 1981, $3.35 as set by the 1978 revision. Exempted from the act are small businesses whose gross sales do not exceed $362,500 (1981 ceiling). Also exempted are organizations which operate within one state. However, several states have minimum wage laws, which parallel the federal minimum wage provisions; some have lower minimum wages.

OVERTIME COMPENSATION The Fair Labor Standards Act stipulates that hourly employees must receive overtime pay of one and one-half times normal rate when they work over forty hours per week. Employees paid on an hourly basis receive an hourly wage and are *nonexempt* within the overtime provision of the act. Employees paid on a salaried basis are *exempt* from the overtime provision of the Fair Labor Standards Act. Exempt employees normally occupy professional, technical, managerial, and supervisory positions; they are entitled to minimum pay under the Fair Labor Standards Act.

Some organizations have tried to lower their overtime costs by classifying more employees as exempt. In effect, this possibly illegal act reduces total payroll costs as exemplified in Figure 13–6. The restaurant, tourist, and medical industries are exempt from the overtime provision, as are agricultural workers. When calculating overtime, a workweek is 168 consecutive hours or seven consecutive days, not necessarily a calendar week. Special provisions allow hospitals to utilize a fourteen-day period instead of a seven–day period.

CHILD LABOR The act prohibits hiring individuals between the ages of 16 and 18 for hazardous jobs, or employing individuals under 16 in interstate commerce except in nonhazardous work for a parent or guardian. The act also requires individuals under 18 to obtain temporary work permits to be given to their employers.

THE DAVIS-BACON ACT

The *Davis-Bacon Act* of 1931 regulates employers who hold federal government contracts of $2,000 or more, for federal construction projects. It provides that employees working on these projects must be paid the prevailing wage rate. In most urban areas the union wage is the prevailing wage for that particular geographic area. If the local union wage for plumbers is $10 per hour, then any plumbers hired to work on federal construction projects in the area must be paid $10 per hour. The reasoning behind the Davis-Bacon Act is that often governments will award contracts to the firm submitting the lowest bid, for certain construction

FIGURE 13–6: *Fair Labor Standards Act Minimum Wage and Overtime Examples*

Example I:	Nonexempt Employee Receives $6.00/hr. and works 48 hours in one week.

Normal pay =   40 hrs. × $6.00/hr. = $240.00
Overtime pay =   8 hrs. × $9.00/hr. = $ 72.00
　　　　　　(1½ rate)　　　　　　$312.00 Total Pay

Example II:	Exempt Employee Receives $280.00/week salary but works 50 hours in one week lowering the company's labor cost.

Normal Hourly Rate = $280 ÷ 40 hrs. = $7.00/hr.
  (40 hrs.)
Hourly Rate = $280 ÷ 50 hrs. = $5.60/hr.
  (50 hrs.)

Example III:	Exempt Employee Receives $160.00/week salary but works 53 hours in one week.

Normal Hourly Rate = $160.00 ÷ 40 = $4.00/hr.
  (40 hrs.)
Hourly Rate = $160.00 ÷ 53 = $3.02/hr.*
  (53 hrs.)

*Illegal under FLSA of 1938; total minimum wage for 53 hrs. = 40 hrs. × $3.35 + 13 hrs. × $5.025 = $199.33.

specifications. By requiring all employers in construction projects to pay the prevailing wage, the Davis-Bacon Act puts bidders on an equal basis, and ensures that craft workers will not be underpaid.

WALSH-HEALEY ACT

A forerunner to the Fair Labor Standards Act, the *Walsh-Healey* Act passed in 1936 contains many similar provisions. The Walsh-Healey Act requires employers to pay overtime for any hours worked over eight per day at a rate of one and one-half times the normal hourly rate. In some situations, as exemplified in Figure 13–7, this will result in the employee receiving greater compensation for the same total hours worked.

FEDERAL WAGE GARNISHMENT ACT

In 1970 Congress passed the Federal Wage Garnishment Act to limit the amount individuals can have garnisheed from their paychecks. Employees who do not pay outstanding debts are often taken to court by collection agencies or companies. The court may order their employers to deduct from employees' paychecks a certain amount of money which is forwarded to the courts and then to the debtor. Under this 1970 act, the maximum *garnishment* of an employee's paycheck is 25 percent of take-home pay or thirty times the minimum wage per hour, whichever is smaller. The act also prohibits employers from firing employees who have had their pay garnisheed.

JOB EVALUATION

Job evaluation is a process of systematically analyzing jobs to determine the relative worth of jobs within the organization. This analysis is the basis of a job hierarchy and pay ranges. The result is a pay system with the pay rate for each job commensurate with its status within the hierarchy of jobs.[10] Job evaluation should not be confused with performance evaluation, the

---

10. Belcher, *Wage and Salary*, pp. 176–77.

FIGURE 13–7: *Walsh-Healey Overtime Example*

Example I: Nonexempt Employee Receives $6.00/hr. and works 45 hours in one week.

Hours—Monday thru Wednesday = 11 hrs./day
Thursday and Friday   = 7 hrs./day

Pay Under FLSA

Normal Pay =
  40 hrs. × $6.00/hr = $240.
Overtime Pay =
  5 hrs. × $9.00/hr =   45.
      Total Pay $285.

Pay Under Walsh-Healey Act

Normal Pay =
  38 hrs. × $6.00/hr = $228.
Overtime Pay =
  9 hrs. × $9.00/hr =   81.
      Total Pay $309.

Difference = $309.00/week − $285.00/week = $24.00/week.

Example II: Nonexempt Employee Receives $6.00/hr. and works 40 hours in one week.

Hours = Monday, Tuesday, Wednesday, Friday = 10 hrs./day

Pay Under FLSA

Normal Pay =
  40 hrs. × $6.00/hr = $240.
      Total Pay

Pay Under Walsh-Healey Act

Normal Pay =
  32 hrs. × $6.00/hr = $192.
  8 hrs. × $9.00/hr =   72.
      Total Pay $264.

Difference = $264.00/week − $240.00/week = $24.00/week.

process of determining how well employees are accomplishing their jobs. Job evaluation does not review the employees within a position but reviews the worth of the position to the organization. Thus, employees in positions that are less important to the organization are paid less than employees in more important positions. For example, a systems analyst would not receive a higher salary than the director of data processing.

Through job evaluation, management can recruit productive employees to fill positions and maintain internal perceptions of pay equity by paying each position fairly in comparison with all other positions within the organization. Job evaluations may also be used to involve employees in the evaluation process. By understanding how the organization's compensation system is established and maintained, employees can ensure that the system is accurate and complete. Also, employee involvement will help communicate to other employees that the system is fair and equitable.

Job Evaluation Committee

The process of job evaluation is expensive and not completely objective. Primarily a problem-solving, subjective judgmental process, job evaluation requires the best input from individuals within the organization. Because it is impossible for one individual to have adequate knowledge of all the jobs in the organization, a job evaluation committee is necessary. The expertise and varying backgrounds of different committee members contribute to the accuracy of the evaluation process. In toto, the members of the committee should have adequate knowledge of all work areas within the organization and a basic familiarity with the jobs within each department. Members should be trained in the basic concept of job evaluation and

FIGURE 13–8: *Ranking Method of Job Evaluation*

Dept.	Rank	Job	Total Company Rankings	
			Rank	Job
Sales	1.	Sales Manager	1.	General Manager
	2.	Route Foreman	2.	Asst. General Manager
	3.	Route Sales Worker	3.	Production Foreman
	4.	Trainee	4.	Sales Manager
			5.	Route Foreman
Office	1.	General Manager	6.	Machinist
	2.	Asst. General Manager	7.	Lathe Operator
	3.	Accounting Clerk	8.	Route Sales Worker
	4.	Clerk Typist	9.	Assembler
	5.	File Clerk	10.	Drill Press Operator
			11.	Accounting Clerk
Shop	1.	Production Foreman	12.	Laborer
	2.	Machinist	13.	Clerk Typist
	3.	Lathe Operator	14.	File Clerk
	4.	Assembler	15.	Trainee
	5.	Drill Press Operator	16.	Janitor
	6.	Laborer		
	7.	Janitor		

specifically in the method chosen by the organization to develop job evaluation.[11] Organizations often maintain a permanent job evaluation committee.

Once established, the job evaluation system should be flexible and reviewed periodically. The job evaluation committee can provide this review since those individuals are most familiar with the compensation system. For example, when supervisors ask that a job be reclassified, the committee would be able to make the determination faster and easier than an inexperienced committee made up of new individuals.

Outside Assistance

The first decision the job evaluation committee makes is whether the organization should produce a job evaluation system or hire outside consultants. Outside con-

sultants offer experience and expertise in the area because they are employed by many firms to produce similar systems year after year. Often faster and more objective than internal employees, outside consultants need substantial internal input to analyze jobs and make difficult comparison decisions. Many decisions critical to the job evaluation process can only be made by individuals familiar with the organization and its basic jobs. While over 70 percent of the organizations in this country are estimated to utilize job evaluation, less than 20 percent bought packaged evaluation plans from a consultant or other source.[12]

A more viable alternative is hiring an evaluation consultant to set up the evaluation process and train the job evaluation committee. Once trained, the members do the decision making; the consultant

11. Richard Henderson, *Compensation Management* (Reston, VA: The Reston Publishing Co., 1979), pp. 231–33.

12. *Job Evaluation Policies and Procedures*, Personnel Policies Forum Survey No. 113 (Washington, DC: Bureau of National Affairs, Inc., 1976), pp. 1–8.

can be brought in at the end of the process to make necessary adjustments.

Methods of Job Evaluation

Primarily there are four methods of job evaluation: ranking, classification, point, and factor comparison. While several derivations of these methods and other techniques combine some aspects, these four methods include the framework of most job evaluation systems. These methods and all of their derivations can be characterized as either quantitative (point method and factor comparison) or nonquantitative (ranking and classification).

RANKING METHOD

The oldest method of evaluating jobs is the *ranking method* which requires the job evaluation committee to rank all of the jobs in the organization according to their relative worth in comparison to each other. Ranking the jobs within their departments, as in Figure 13–8, may be the easiest way to begin. The committee must come to a consensus regarding the ranking of the jobs within a department. The actual final ranking may be made by having each committee member rank the jobs within the department and then compute the average ranking for each job to determine the final rankings.

After the jobs are ranked within the department, then the job evaluation committee has one of two choices: First, it can develop separate compensation systems for each department; therefore, in Figure 13–8, three compensation systems would be developed. As a second alternative, the committee may choose to produce a total ranking as is the case in Figure 13–8. To determine this total ranking, the committee compares the top ranked jobs in each department. Thus, the production foreman would be compared to the general manager and the sales manager and the job considered most important to the company would be ranked first. The process continues until all jobs in the company have been ranked by the committee. The ranking method requires that committee members objectively compare different jobs.

After the rankings have been completed, pay scales must be assigned to the ranked jobs. The first step in this process is to ensure external equity by comparing *benchmark jobs* with jobs of other organizations within the local labor market.

A benchmark job contains standardized characteristics that can be easily identified in jobs of a similar nature within other organizations. If, for example, the committee identified the sales manager, lathe operator, drill press operator, and clerk typist positions as benchmark jobs, they could identify the average wage paid for similar jobs in the local market, and set pay scales for these jobs first. Once these pay scales were set, then the pay scales for jobs between benchmark jobs must be set according to their ranking; jobs ranked higher than the sales manager job obviously would be given a higher pay, whereas jobs ranked lower would be given lower pay, which would still be higher than the next ranked benchmark job.

Job evaluation determines the worth of each job in the organization, not each individual employee. In the example in Figure 13–9, while there are sixteen jobs ranked, there may be forty or more employees in this particular organization because several employees hold the same job.

FIGURE 13–9: *Compensable Job Factors*

Skill

Accuracy of calculations	Knowledge of equipment and tools
Accuracy of measurement	Knowledge of materials
Accuracy of reading	Knowledge of methods
Accuracy of selection	Knowledge of other operations
Adaptability	Leadership
Adjustability	Length of schooling
Analysis	Management ability
Analytical ability	Manual dexterity
Aptitude	Manual skill
Artistic ability	Math skill
Attention to orders	Mechanical ability
Complexity	Mental capability
Cooperation	Mentality
Creativity	Motor accuracy
Decision	Originality
Details	Personal requirements
Education	Physical skill
Foresight	Precision
Ingenuity	Previous training
Initiative	Resourcefulness
Inventiveness	Tact and diplomacy
Job knowledge	Training time
Job skill	Versatility
Judgment	

Effort

Alertness	Mental stability
Application	Monotony of work
Concentration	Muscular coordination
Endurance	Physical effort
Exertion	Physical pace or energy
Fatigue	Quickness of comprehension
Honesty of effort	Strength
Memory	Visual effort
Mental effort	

Responsibility

Avoidance of shutdowns	Material
Company policy	Money
Confidential data	Production levels
Cost of errors	Property
Effect on subsequent operations	Quality
Equipment	Safety of others
Good will	Reports and records
Inventory	Supervision of others
Maintenance of pace	

Working Conditions

Accident hazard	Eyestrain
Clothing spoilage	Fumes
Current expense	Health hazard
Danger	Nervous strain
Discomfort	Noise level
Environmental deterrents	Surroundings

Speed and ease of completion are the main advantages of the ranking method of job evaluation. Another advantage of the ranking technique is that since it can be done in-house fairly easily, it is less expensive than some other techniques of job evaluation. The ranking technique also is easy to explain to members of the job evaluation committee since the concept of ranking is familiar to most individuals.

The ranking technique contains serious disadvantages. Due to its very nature, the ranking technique is limited to smaller organizations where individuals are very familiar with various jobs and can have the complete knowledge of the jobs required to make an accurate comparison of jobs. Another serious disadvantage is the assumption of equal intervals between the rankings. For example, in Figure 13–9, the assistant general manager is ranked one notch lower than the general manager and only one notch higher than the accounting clerk; however, the assistant manager's job is worth more than the one notch indicates. This magnitude of difference is shown in Figure 13–9 when the assistant general manager is ranked second in the total rankings and the accounting clerk is ranked eleventh. However, the same problem exists in the total company rankings; the difference between positions is not always equal to one interval.

The problem of unequal intervals becomes acute after the benchmark pay scales are determined from wage surveys, and the positions between benchmarks are assigned pay scales either more or less than the benchmark positions. Hopefully, most companies that use the ranking technique will realize that the intervals are not equal and objectively try to create rea-sonable differences between the ranked positions in pay scales.

Another major disadvantage of the ranking technique is the fact that the method is a *global appraisal* of the worth of the jobs. Instead of evaluating the various factors of each job, the ranking technique simply evaluates the job in its entirety and thus makes a global appraisal in comparing it to another job. While all job evaluation techniques are subjective, a global appraisal and job evaluation are more subjective than more discerning techniques.

Another serious problem of the ranking method is the difficulty of defending it to employees. When employees ask why their jobs are not as highly paid as others', the personnel officer or supervisor who responds that these jobs were ranked two notches lower than other positions does not completely satisfy the employees. Hopefully the ranking method will be utilized only by small organizations which can satisfactorily compare all the jobs and make accurate comparison decisions.

CLASSIFICATION METHOD

The job classification method, also called the grade description method, enables an organization to analyze its jobs and place them in broad class descriptions or grades. Classes are often defined similarly to those used by the U.S. Civil Service Commission and found in the *Dictionary of Occupational Titles*. The *classification method* can be accomplished in the following steps:

STEP 1: REVIEW ALL JOBS AND CREATE CATEGORIES. The job evaluation committee first reviews the job descriptions and determines the duties and responsibilities of various jobs. The usual breakdown of job categories would be: supervisory or technical, factory or production, clerical, and sales.

STEP 2: DETERMINE THE GRADES OR CLASSES FOR EACH CATEGORY. The larger the organization and the more jobs within each category, the more grades within each particular job category. The well-known, commonly used Westinghouse Plan uses the following broad definitions for grades within each category:[13]

Grade 1. Unskilled: The positions of this group, usually clerical in nature, require accuracy and dependability but no extended training. Office worker, records clerk, and file clerk are examples.

Grade 2. Skilled: The positions of this group, mostly clerical in nature, require training of either physical or mental abilities. The group includes such positions as stenographer, production clerk, detail draftsperson, and bookkeepers. The nonclerical positions for this group would include laboratory assistants, plant operators, and draftspersons.

Grade 3. Interpretative: The highest positions in this group would include chief clerk, office manager, and other positions which are mostly supervisory in nature. First-line supervisors would be the highest supervisory positions within this group.

Grade 4. Creative: This group includes positions of a creative character such as engineer, salesperson, staff supervisor, designers, attorneys, and other technical and professional positions.

Grade 5. Executive: Most positions at this level are executive in nature and

include department managers, sales manager, superintendent, foreperson, and assistant general managers. Generally this is a function of departmental management.

Grade 6. Administrative: The positions of this group involve responsibilities of a large, overall character of mixed, functional divisions. District sales manager, chief engineer, director of research, purchasing director, and treasurer, would be examples of positions at this level.

Grade 7. Policy: This level includes those positions held by the senior policy officers of the organization.

If the job evaluation committee decided to use Westinghouse's seven grades for each of the four different classes of jobs, then there would be a total of twenty–eight possible job descriptions.

STEP 3. WRITE GRADE DESCRIPTIONS. If there are twenty-eight different combinations to be utilized, then twenty-eight broad definitions must be written. Writing a broad description which can be general enough to include the variety of jobs which fall into that description, yet be specific enough that employees will recognize their jobs being described is difficult. If they are too broad in nature, then individuals do not recognize their jobs being that described and feel that the system is unfair or vague. If descriptions are too specific, it will be difficult to assign a number of jobs to a few grades. The definitions for each grade within each broad category should include such items as the type of work being accomplished, the degree of supervision required, the complexity of duties and decisions involved in accomplishing the job, education and experience necessary for performing the

---

13. *Industrial Relations Manual* (Columbus, OH: Westinghouse Electric Corporation, 1940) p. 4.

job, level of effort and responsibility demanded by the job, and contact with others.

STEP 4. ASSIGN JOBS TO A GRADE. After reviewing job descriptions of the various jobs and preparing the grade definitions, the committee can assign each job in the organization to a particular grade. Each job has peculiar duties or responsibilities which differentiate it from other jobs in the organization. However, using a classification system divides jobs within an organization into a hierarchy of grades so that employees performing jobs of a similar worth to the organization will receive similar pay. Again, the job evaluation committee members must have some knowledge of jobs to be able to objectively assign jobs to the grades.

STEP 5. ASSIGN PAY RANGES TO GRADES. As in the ranking method, the evaluation committee should first compare its benchmark jobs to benchmark jobs of other organizations to be sure that the pay ranges assigned to each grade will keep the organization competitive in the local labor market. Then the committee determines pay ranges from starting pay levels to maximum pay levels for each pay grade. Usually the total range is broken into levels within the pay grade so that as employees receive merit increases and acquire seniority they move to a higher pay level.

The primary advantage to the classification or grade description method is that it has been in use by federal, state, and local civil service bodies for many years. For this reason employees in other organizations may accept it. This is also a good system for a very large organization with many offices located in several geographic regions in the country. By being broad in nature the grade description system allows all plants and offices to be included in the same compensation plan. Cost of living adjustments can be made for different locations and still utilize the same classification plan. Of course, this is helpful in union negotiations and for employees transferring from one area to another within the organization.

Because the descriptions are broad and not specific to the jobs assigned to them, the system can last for many years without being changed substantially, which saves the company money and time in keeping the system functional. As jobs change slightly from one year to the next, their grade classifications will not be affected; more detailed systems, like those which follow in this chapter, require constant updating.

The major disadvantage to the system is that the descriptions are so broad that they do not relate specifically to jobs that are assigned to them. This can lead to abuse of the system by a job classification committee or a supervisor. It also causes many employees to question if there are specific reasons for their jobs being classified in a certain grade. Employees may not recognize how grade descriptions apply to their particular jobs. Often, after reading the grade descriptions employees feel that their jobs are more similar to a higher grade than the assigned grade. Some employees simply do not accept the system as a valid and objective means of job classification.

POINT SYSTEM

One of the most popular, basic systems of job evaluation today is the *point system,* which divides jobs into specific factors which the job evaluation committee believes are critical and valued by the organization. Rather than globally reviewing jobs, the point system breaks jobs down into their components, reviews each of the components, and compares the jobs by those components. There are countless variations of the point system; all are basically mathematical and compare jobs on factors chosen by the job evaluation committee. Because the point system specifically compares jobs according to their content and because it is quantitative, the point system is generally accepted by federal agencies and the courts. Most point systems follow these steps:

STEP 1. SELECT COMPENSABLE JOB FACTORS. The evaluation committee identifies factors which describe the fundamental elements of the jobs, and aspects which differentiate them. The committee considers if one job requires more mental effort or more monetary responsibility than another job. Since the passage of the Equal Pay Act of 1963, many point systems utilize job factor categories indicating skill, effort, responsibility, and working conditions. While a limitless number of factors can be chosen, the more factors chosen the more expensive the job evaluation

process becomes. Therefore, the evaluation committee generally chooses between eight and sixteen factors in the point system.

The committee should determine which factors make some jobs more valuable than others and which factors are common to all jobs in the organization. After the factors have been determined, they should be clearly defined so that others know exactly what each factor entails. In Figure 13–10 Allis-Chalmers Manufacturing Company has determined ten compensable factors.

STEP 2. DIVIDE FACTORS INTO DEGREES. Once the factors have been chosen, the next step is to divide each factor into different degrees signifying the extent to which that factor exists in a particular job. Each degree must then be defined so that the evaluation committee agrees upon its specification. Usually between three and seven *degrees of factors* will be utilized for each factor.

STEP 3. ASSIGN POINTS TO DEGREES. The assignment of points to each degree within factors provides a system of

FIGURE 13–10: *Point Plan of Job Evaluation for Nonexempt Salaried Positions of the Allis-Chalmers Manufacturing Company*

FACTORS	Points for Degrees					
	1	2	3	4	5	6
Skill						
1. Knowledge	7	17	30	47	70	100
2. Training and experience						
3. Complexity of duties	9	20	36	56	84	120
4. Contacts with others	7	17	30	47	70	100
Responsibility						
5. Responsibility for trust imposed	6	14	26	40	60	—
6. Monetary responsibility	9	20	36	56	84	120
7. Performance	4	10	18	28	42	60
Effort						
8. Mental or visual	4	8	15	24	35	—
9. Physical	0	4	9	16	25	—
Job Conditions						
10. Work conditions	0	6	14	25	40	—

FIGURE 13–10: **continued**

SELECTED FACTORS

1. Knowledge
Education provides the basic prerequisite knowledge that is essential to satisfactorily perform the job. This knowledge may have been acquired through formal schooling such as grammar school, high school, college, university, night school, correspondence courses, company education program, or through equivalent experience in allied fields. Analyze the requirements of the job and not the formal education of individuals performing it.

POINTS

1st Degree
Requires ability to read, write, and follow simple written or oral instructions, use simple arithmetic involving counting, adding, subtracting, multiplying, and dividing whole numbers, etc.   7

2nd Degree
Requires ability to perform work requiring advanced arithmetic involving adding, subtracting, dividing, and multiplying of decimals and fractions; maintain or prepare routine correspondence, records, and reports. May require knowledge of typing or elementary knowledge of shorthand, bookkeeping, etc.   17

3rd Degree
Requires specialized knowledge in a particular field such as advanced stenographic, secretarial or business training, elementary accounting or general knowledge of shop practice and manufacturing methods, blueprint reading, shop specifications, basic principles of production control, welding, chemistry, electricity, etc.   30

4th Degree
Requires ability to understand and perform work requiring general engineering principles, commercial theory, principles of advanced drafting; knowledge and application of general accounting fundamentals. Originate and compile statistics and interpretive reports; prepare correspondence of a difficult or technical nature. Requires a broad knowledge of complicated shop procedures and processes, purchasing, accounting, general sales work, foreign trade, labor laws, time study, etc.   47

5th Degree
Requires ability to understand and perform work of a specialized or technical nature. Examples are work involving use of all types of drawings or specifications in which application requires theory or analysis of design or principles involved; use of advanced formulas for determining relationships; apply highly specialized technical theory in determining causes of and correcting design or operating difficulties; knowledge of theory and practices in accounting and finance, business administration, chemistry, physics, journalism, and related technical or specialized fields.   70

6th Degree
Requires knowledge in a highly advanced and specialized field in order to understand and perform work requiring creative endeavor.   100

2. Training and Experience
Experience is the length of time usually required by an individual with the specified knowledge to acquire the skill necessary to satisfactorily perform the duties of the job. Where previous experience is necessary, time spent in related work or in lesser positions, either within the company or with other organizations, shall be considered as contributing to the total experience required to effectively perform the job. This consideration will be based on continuous progress by an individual and will not include time spent on jobs due to lack of promotional opportunities.

FIGURE 13–10: **continued**

	POINTS
1. Up to and including 3 months	9
2. Over 3 months, up to and including 6 months	19
3. Over 6 months, up to and including 9 months	28
4. Over 9 months, up to and including 12 months	35
5. Over 1 year, up to and including 2 years	62
6. Over 2 years, up to and including 3 years	82
7. Over 3 years, up to and including 4 years	97
8. Over 4 years, up to and including 5 years	108
9. Over 5 years, up to and including 7 years	123
10. Over 7 years, up to and including 10 years	134
11. Over 10 years	140

3. Complexity of Duties

This factor appraises the complexity of job duties, such as the amount of judgment required in the making of decisions; analyzing problems and situations; planning of procedures and determining methods of action; and the extent to which initiative and ingenuity are required to successfully complete the job.

POINTS

1st Degree

Work is routine consisting of simple repetitive operations, such as filing, sorting, duplicating, copy typing, etc., performed under immediate supervision or where little choice exists as to method of performance.   9

2nd Degree

Perform work from detailed instructions or where variation in procedures is limited. Work is semirepetitive requiring minor decisions and some judgment in analysis of data or situations from which an answer can readily be obtained.   20

3rd Degree

Perform work where procedures are of a varied or diversified nature within a well-defined field under direct supervision. Requires initiative and independent judgment to analyze data or situations and determine solutions to problems within the limits of standard practice.   36

4th Degree

Plan and perform complex work where only general policies or procedures are available in an established field requiring their application to cases not previously covered. Job duties involve working independently toward general results, devising new methods, and modifying or adapting standard procedures to meet new conditions. Requires analytical ability, initiative, and exercise of judgment to obtain solutions to problems and make decisions based on precedent and company policy.   56

5th Degree

Plan and perform highly complex or technical work where no procedures or standard methods are available. Duties require a high degree of originality, initiative, and independent action to deal with complex factors difficult to evaluate or the making of decisions based on conclusions for which there is little precedent.   84

6th Degree

Final analysis and judgment in planning and coordinating the work of a large group or department. Requires initiative and aggressiveness; original and creative planning and formulation of policy.   120

4. Contacts with Others

Contacts with others is the extent to which the job requires cooperation and tact in

FIGURE 13–10: **continued**

meeting, dealing with, or influencing people, whether by telephone, correspondence, or personal contact. Consider the frequency and importance of contacts, the tact required to maintain harmony and efficiency within the company and good will of the general public.

POINTS

1st Degree
Contacts usually limited to persons in the same section or department.   7

2nd Degree
Contacts with persons outside the department or occasionally outside the company, furnishing or obtaining routine information only.   17

3rd Degree
Regular contacts with other departments or other companies, furnishing or obtaining information or reports, under conditions requiring the use of tact to obtain cooperation and maintain good will.   30

4th Degree
Contacts with other departments or other companies, involving carrying out company policy and programs and influencing of others, where improper handling will affect operating results; or involving dealing with persons of substantially higher rank on matters requiring explanation, discussion, and obtaining approvals.   47

5th Degree
Contacts inside or outside the company requiring a high degree of tact, judgment, and the ability to deal with and influence persons in all types of positions.   70

6th Degree
Contacts with persons inside or outside the company on matters of company policy, difficult adjustments, or the settling of controversial matters, where adverse conditions make it essential that the highest caliber of diplomacy and tact be used to obtain favorable decisions or maintain good will.   100

SOURCE: *Compensation Management* by Richard I. Henderson, 1979. Reprinted with permission of Reston Publishing Company, Inc., a Prentice-Hall Company, 11480 Sunset Hills Road, Reston, Virginia.

weighting the factors within the point system. Therefore, more important factors will be given larger point totals than lesser factors. For example, in the Allis-Chalmers point plan, the degrees in the factor "monetary responsibility" comprise a larger point total than the performance factor.

There are various nonstatistical and statistical approaches to assigning weights or points to each degree. The evaluation committee should consider three or four different systems and choose the one which best reflects the weights of the different degrees according to how important the factors are to the organization.

STEP 4. RATE JOBS ON EACH FACTOR. The evaluation committee begins with the first factor and evaluates each job on that factor. For each job the degree which best defines the level of that factor required for the job is determined. All of the jobs are rated on one factor before the committee moves on to the second factor. The reason for this is to maximize the objectivity of the decision process. Any biases a committee member may have concerning a particular job will be minimized if that job is not evaluated in total but is compared against other jobs as each factor is reviewed.

STEP 5. TOTAL POINTS FOR EACH JOB. Once all the jobs have been assigned degrees and point totals on each factor, the committee can total the points for each job. After being divided into clerical, production, and administrative areas, jobs within each area are listed with point totals. Through routine checks the committee makes sure that no obvious discrepancies exist. For example, a supervisory position should have a greater point total than the position supervised. Administrators may divide jobs into different functional areas (such as sales, production, professional) at this point in order to develop separate pay systems for each area to ensure external equity as well as internal equity.

STEP 6. IDENTIFY BENCHMARK JOBS. Benchmark jobs should be compared to the other jobs in the organization to ensure that the point totals appear to be in line. After a system of tying in point totals to a pay structure is developed, these benchmark jobs will be compared to jobs of other organizations within the labor market to ensure external equity.

The most important advantages of the point system are that it is detailed and specific. Jobs are not globally assessed as they were in the nonquantitative systems; they are compared on specific factors important to the organization. This makes the point system—and other quantitative systems in general—more valid because management cannot manipulate the system or allow intentional bias by a supervisor to enter into the job evaluation process. In most cases, employees accept the point system because of its mathematical nature and complex, sophisticated methodology. Personnel specialists can explain to employees how the job was evaluated, what degree was allocated in the various factors and, therefore, how the total points were derived and pay scale determined. Another important advantage is that the system is easy to keep current and

accurate as jobs change. If a job is given increased duties in a specific area, the supervisor or employee can request that the job be reclassified. Reclassification is quite simple under the point system since the specific factors affected by the change in the job can be reevaluated and possibly given a higher degree. Thus the total points allotted to the job change, and in some cases, the job's pay grade must be changed. The point system's mathematical comparison of jobs makes it easy to assign monetary values to different jobs which have quantitative differences. Therefore, differences in point totals between jobs can be easily converted to differences in pay scales.

The obvious disadvantages of the point system are that it is much more time consuming and costly to develop than the ranking or classification systems. The point system also requires a great deal of interaction and decision making by the job analyst and job evaluation committee. If the organization contains several hundred different jobs and several compensable job factors are chosen, then thousands of decisions regarding degrees and factors must be made by the committee.

The advantages of the point system—particularly acceptance by employees and governmental agencies—have made it more attractive than other systems in recent years. Most likely the point system will continue to gain popularity until a more sophisticated and valid version of a quantitative system is developed.

FACTOR COMPARISON METHOD

Developed in the 1920s by Eugene Benge, the *factor comparison method* combines the ranking and point systems. This method develops a wage scale for each factor in an evaluation process. The total wage rates for benchmark jobs are then compared to the local area wage survey to ensure external consistency. Benge's method may utilize the following procedure:

STEP 1. SELECT BENCHMARK JOBS. Benchmark jobs comparable to other jobs in similar organizations within the local labor market are chosen. These jobs should be clearly defined in the minds of evaluation committee members, and represent a cross section of jobs in all departments of the organization.

STEP 2. CHOOSE COMPENSABLE FACTORS. As in the point system, primary compensable factors of various jobs in the organization are chosen. Between four and seven factors are selected. Commonly five factors are used representing the component areas of skill, effort, responsibility, working conditions, and physical requirements.

STEP 3. RANK ALL JOBS ON EACH FACTOR. The evaluation committee then ranks all of the benchmark jobs, one factor at a time. Comparing one factor at a time minimizes subjectivity or bias for the jobs.

STEP 4. ALLOCATE WAGES TO FACTORS. Using current wage scales and wage surveys of the local labor market area, each factor for each job is allocated a certain wage rate either on a per hour, per month, or annual salary basis. The factors can be weighted by giving one factor more total dollars than another factor.

STEP 5. DETERMINE FINAL RANKING. Benchmark jobs may now be ranked according to their total wage allocation and compared to the external market to ensure that the organization is competitive. After this is done, other jobs can be added to the rankings and given a wage rate by judging the difference between each job and the nearest benchmark job. This is a

very difficult and subjective process for the evaluation committee.

The end product of a factor comparison method is shown in Figure 13–11. The Olympia Machine Tool and Die Shop developed the wage scale for five compensable factors: skill, mental demands, physical demands, responsibility, and working conditions. Ten benchmark jobs were selected for the job evaluation process. A job evaluation committee ranked the jobs, reviewed market surveys, ranked the benchmark jobs one factor at a time, totaled the rankings, and assigned wage levels. The committee did not utilize mathematical averages for rankings and wage scales but discussed differences where they occurred and developed satisfactory compromise levels. These scales for the benchmark jobs can now be used to evaluate all other jobs within the organization. The committee members will analyze each of the other jobs, determining which benchmark job it most closely resembles, assign the corresponding monetary value, and finally total up the wage rate assigned to the job.[14]

Like the point system, the factor comparison system has the advantage of evaluating jobs on a component basis rather than in their entirety. Also like the point system, the method compares jobs one factor at a time, minimizing problems of bias or committee subjectivity. The factor comparison system is usually easier to develop than the point method because it involves fewer factors. Also, the factor comparison system is tied to the external market because wage surveys are used to determine rates for each factor consistent with other organizations.

14. Henderson, *Compensation Management*, pp. 491–95.

FIGURE 13–11: *Factor Comparison Method, Olympia Machine Tool and Die Shop*

CENTS PER HOUR PER FACTOR	MENTAL REQUIREMENTS	SKILL REQUIREMENTS	PHYSICAL REQUIREMENTS	RESPONSIBILITY	WORKING CONDITIONS
3.30	Electronic Tech.	Tool Maker, Machinist			
3.15	Tool Maker, Electrician				
3.00	Machinist	Electronic Tech.			
2.85	Inspector	Electrician		Inspector, Electronic Tech., Tool Maker	
2.70			Laborer	Electrician	
2.55		Engine Lathe Oper.	Assembler, Fork Lift Oper.	Machinist	
2.40		Turret Lathe Oper.			
2.25	Engine Lathe Oper.		Turret Lathe Oper., Electrician	Engine Lathe Oper.	Laborer, Fork Lift Oper., Floor Sweeper
2.10		Inspector	Machinist, Floor Sweeper	Fork Lift Operator	Assembler
1.95	Turret Lathe Oper.		Toolmaker, Engine Lathe Oper.	Turret Lathe Oper.	Machinist, Turret Lathe Oper., Tool Maker, Engine Lathe Oper.
1.80	Assembler, Fork Lift Oper.	Assembler, Fork Lift Oper.			Electrician
1.65			Inspector	Assembler	Inspector
1.50			Electronic Tech.		Electronic Tech.
1.35			Electronic Tech.		
1.20	Laborer, Floor Sweeper	Laborer		Laborer	
1.05		Floor Sweeper		Floor Sweeper	

SOURCE: *Compensation Management* by Richard I. Henderson, 1979. Reprinted with permission of Reston Publishing Company, Inc. a Prentice-Hall Company, 11480 Sunset Hills Road, Reston, Virginia.

449

The factor comparison method has the disadvantage of being limited primarily to manufacturing organizations employing hourly workers. Other types of organizations would lack external market information to help them tie wage rates to some meaningful source; without such input, setting wage rates for individual factors of jobs would be difficult. Therefore, the factor comparison system is used almost solely by manufacturing organizations.

The factor comparison system is also more difficult to explain to employees who are less likely to accept something they do not understand. Another disadvantage is that the factor comparison system uses monetary comparisons of factors in contrast to the point system which uses abstract quantitative differences or points. Thus, the point system can be more easily adapted to cost of living changes or merit increases whereas the factor comparison system cannot change as jobs change or as the industry changes.

OTHER METHODS

Countless varieties of each method of job evaluation have been developed by individuals and groups. Some of the methods have become widely utilized by particular industries and trades. Obviously, there is a distinct advantage in utilizing a method which has been applied to other organizations; comparative information from other organizations is invaluable and saves a great deal of time and effort for the job evaluation committee. Two of the most widely used systems for factory jobs were developed by the National Electrical Manufacturers Association and the National Metal Trade Association which is known today as the American Association of Industrial Management. These systems utilize factors, subfactors, and degrees of factors as standards similar to the point and factor comparison methods.

One of the most popular methods used today is the Hay Guide Chart-Profile method. The Hay method uses three compensable factors: (1) know-how which encompasses the variety of tasks performed, depth of job or the complexity of tasks performed, and human relations skills; (2) problem-solving which includes the degree of supervision received and the new situations that require creative thinking; and (3) accountability which refers to freedom to act on the job, as delineated by policy and supervisors, and the job holder's ability to make work decisions. In the second area of accountability, the levels of impact are considered: the first is remote; the second level, contributory; the third level, shared; and the fourth level, primary. The third area of accountability is magnitude, that is, how the job affects the organization.

The U.S. Office of Personnel Management recently developed a point factor method called the Factor Evaluation System (FES). Like most point factor systems, job evaluators must compare the content of each job with compensable factors written in general terms which apply to all of the jobs of the organization. FES's written benchmarks relate to specific job content and describe an actual job situation which typically represents jobs within an occupation.[15]

DESIGNING THE PAY ═══ SYSTEM ═══

When job evaluation is completed, administrators must determine a final pay

---

15. Ibid., pp. 203–205.

FIGURE 13–12: *Selected Hourly Pay Grades and Steps*

Pay Grade	Step 1	Step 2	Step 3	Step 4	Step 5	Step 6	Step 7
1	$ 3.35	$ 3.49	$ 3.62	$ 3.77	$ 3.91	$ 4.05	$ 4.18
2	3.85	4.01	4.17	4.33	4.49	4.65	4.81
3	4.42	4.59	4.75	4.92	5.09	5.26	5.52
4	5.08	5.29	5.50	5.71	5.93	6.14	6.35
5	5.84	6.08	6.32	6.57	6.81	7.06	7.30
6	6.71	6.98	7.27	7.55	7.82	8.10	8.38
7	7.71	8.03	8.35	8.67	8.99	9.31	9.63
8	8.86	9.22	9.60	9.96	10.33	10.71	11.07
9	10.18	10.60	11.03	11.45	11.87	12.30	12.72

FIGURE 13–13: *Scatter Diagram*

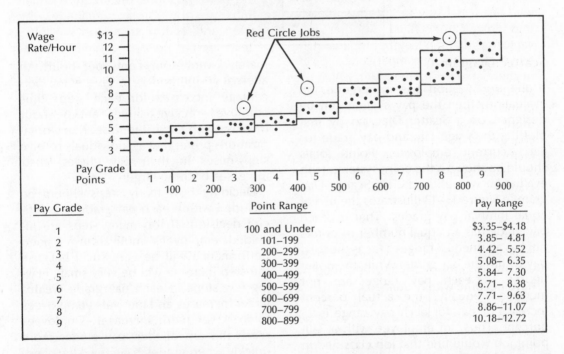

Pay Grade	Point Range	Pay Range
1	100 and Under	$3.35–$4.18
2	101–199	3.85– 4.81
3	200–299	4.42– 5.52
4	300–399	5.08– 6.35
5	400–499	5.84– 7.30
6	500–599	6.71– 8.38
7	600–699	7.71– 9.63
8	700–799	8.86–11.07
9	800–899	10.18–12.72

system to apply to jobs within the organization. Their decisions involve establishing minimum and maximum pay levels for each pay grade and determining how individuals will advance in pay grades. An organizationwide standardized pay system must be promulgated and documented in order to maintain internal as well as external *pay equity*. Also, management will be able to document and defend its pay system in court. Administrators have found it advantageous to develop pay grades and steps, or levels, which specify the annual amount paid salaried employees in a particular pay grade and step and to use a monthly or hourly basis for other jobs as depicted in Figure 13–12.

FIGURE 13–14: *Pay Grade 5 with Internal Steps*

Pay Grade 5		
Step 7	$7.30	TOP LEVEL STEPS
Step 6	7.06	
Step 5	6.81	
Step 4	6.57	MID POINT
Step 3	6.32	ENTRY LEVEL STEPS
Step 2	6.08	
Step 1	5.84	

Scatter Diagram

If the organization has undergone job evaluation, then the pay system can be designed on a Scatter Diagram by first plotting the wage rate and pay grade for each current employee. Point totals should be shown if the point system of job evaluation was utilized. The Scatter Diagram in Figure 13–13 illustrates the use of equal interval pay grades. That is, each pay grade has an equal number of points but has an unequal range as far as the total pay within the pay grade. While the dollar figures in each pay range are not increased equally, the actual percent increase of pay for each pay range is 25 percent. Thus, an employee with a 340-point job would find that job classified in pay grade four with a minimum pay of $5.08 and a maximum pay of $6.35 per hour.

NUMBER OF STEPS

In developing a compensation system the number of steps within each pay grade must be decided. Figure 13–14 illustrates how pay grade five could be divided into seven equal step increases of approxi-

mately twenty-four cents per hour. An alternative method is to give equal percentage increases for each step; thus employees receive a larger cents per hour increase with each step raise. Many organizations prefer that as individuals receive step raises in their pay grades, their increases become larger.

Deciding how many *steps* should be included within each *pay grade* is a difficult decision. If too many steps are included, employees' motivation for good performance will be very small because the step increase will be very small. Having few steps in each pay grade creates larger increases and motivates employees to work for merit increases. Employees reach the top of their pay grades more quickly when grades have few steps and, therefore, have no opportunity for advancement within the jobs they currently hold. Once individuals have reached the top of their pay grades, the practice is usually to keep them at that highest step, to transfer them to jobs in a higher pay grade, or promote them. Organizations with relatively few opportunities for promotion, or turnover so low that many individuals stay within one pay grade for several years, find it wise to have many steps and, perhaps, even wider-ranging pay grades.

Figure 13–14 illustrates the practice of using two or more entry level salaries for jobs within a particular pay grade. The reason for this is that while managers wish to be consistent and pay similar jobs similar wages, allowances must be made for individual differences in job candidates who are hired. Candidates with more experience and skills can be hired in a higher step; a recruit who has just finished school and has no experience would logically be hired at step one. In most situations this would not violate federal laws because consistency within the pay system could be proved since similar wages were paid for similar work, making allowances for individual differences.

RED CIRCLED EMPLOYEES

Another decision to be made by the evaluation committee is illustrated in Figure 13–13. Three individuals within the pay grade system have been *red circled*. A red circle indicates that this individual is currently being paid more than the maximum of that pay grade. Through seniority or for some other reason the individual is currently being paid more than the organization planned to pay any employee to perform jobs of that pay grade. Red circled individuals remain at the same pay level until either being promoted to a higher pay grade or cost of living adjustments increase to catch up to the pay they are currently receiving. Management may not decrease pay due to the red circles since the Equal Pay Act of 1963 protects individuals from having their pay lowered through the job evaluation process.

In Figure 13–13 one person in pay grade four and two in pay grade one are currently being paid less than the minimum of the pay grade. Those individuals normally have their pay increased to the minimum of their pay grade. When the compensation system is finalized, no individual will receive less pay than the minimum of the job grade; any individual currently receiving more than the maximum will be red circled until sometime in the future.

OVERLAP OF GRADES

The organization must also decide whether to overlap pay grades so that the maximum of one pay grade is higher than the minimum of the next higher pay grade. The compensation system in Figure 13–13 allows pay grades to overlap. One advantage is that employees can be transferred or promoted from one job to the next without necessarily being given pay increases. For example, an employee paid $6.90 per hour in pay grade five could be promoted to a job with a larger point total in pay grade six without an increase in pay.

Management has the option of not paying individuals higher salaries immediately but offering them higher salaries if they prove themselves and receive merit increases, thus moving up in the pay grade. Another advantage of overlapping pay grades is that this gives grades a greater range with more steps of a meaningful size. Thus, employees are rewarded with merit and seniority increases while they stay in the same job and pay grade.

One disadvantage of overlapping pay grades is that a promotion may not bring a pay increase and could even bring a cut in pay. Also, overlapping grades makes it possible for an individual in a higher pay grade to supervise employees in a lower pay grade who receive higher paychecks than the supervisor. For example, when a new supervisor is promoted to a department in which an employee is at the highest step of the next lower pay grade, the employee will receive higher pay than the supervisor. In manufacturing and construction organizations this is not unusual.

Pay Increases

Primarily two types of increases are made: across the board, where everyone in the organization receives an equal pay increase, and merit or seniority increases given to selected individuals.

ACROSS THE BOARD

These increase the employee's income due to the cost of living allowances or in order to make the organization's pay system compatible with the local labor market. An across the board cost of living adjustment (COLA) can be an equal percentage or equal dollars. Managers often prefer to give equal percentage increases because COLAs are related to the cost of living which is measured in percentages. Hearing that the cost of living has gone up a certain percentage, employees realize that their buying power has decreased. Therefore, they hope to receive a cost of living allowance at least equal to the increase in their cost of living.

Unfortunately, using equal percentages can be deceiving since employees must use increased wages and not percentages to purchase goods and services. Using cost of living figures can also be misleading because any individual's actual increase in cost of living depends upon spending habits, the age of major assets such as automobile and home, and other

factors. The national increase in the cost of living may have little bearing on individual employees' actual bills.

Management prefers to give across the board cost of living increases in equal percentages. Equal percentage increases mean that employees in higher pay grades will receive greater actual dollar increases than employees in lower pay grades. An across the board percentage increase simply changes the dollar amounts for each grade and step in the compensation system but would not move any employee or job within the system. Therefore, if a 7 percent cost of living pay increase were given to the pay grades and steps in Figure 13–12, all of the amounts would change but pay grades and steps would not. In Figure 13–13, the pay grade configuration would become more sloped as the higher pay grades experienced greater dollar increases than the lower pay grades.

If an equal dollar across the board increase is given as a cost of living allowance, the amounts in Figure 13–12 would increase by an equal dollar figure. In Figure 13–13 the scale on the left side would slide down because individuals in lower pay grades get a larger percentage increase than the individuals in higher pay grades. Individuals in higher pay grades argue that this is unfair because they cannot keep up with the cost of living since their increase is not as great as those in lower pay grades. In summary, equal dollar across the board cost of living adjustments decrease the differentials in pay between jobs and pay grades.

Equal dollar and equal percentage increases have advantages and disadvantages. In previous years percentage increases and COLAs have been more common. However, due to the effects equal percentage COLAs and rising inflation have upon employees in low pay grades, some administrators have reconsidered in recent years; they are giving greater percentage increases to lower pay grades or equal dollar increases to the entire labor force.

MERIT INCREASES

As a reward for good performance determined through performance evaluation or some other appraisal technique, an organization often awards *merit pay increases* to employees. Merit raises are designed to increase employees' motivation and strengthen the relation between employees' performances and the rewards the organization gives them.

When employees receive merit increases, they do not change pay grades since they are in a pay grade due to the point total of their jobs or their classifications. However, employees who receive merit increases move up one or more steps within their pay grades. Administrators may give two step increases to the top 5 percent of their employees and one step increases to the next highest 20 percent of their employees. The amount of increase would depend, of course, upon the pay grade and step of each employee. Employees find this system is fair since everyone gets an equal step increase even though the amount changes according to the job classification. How large the increases are in actual dollars and cents, of course, depends upon the number of steps within each pay grade.

Some organizations will give seniority increases to employees who have successfully performed their jobs for a certain length of time. These increases move employees up one or more steps within their pay grades. If the organization in Figure 13–12 gave merit increases, the num-

bers in the figure would stay the same but employees would move up one step within their pay grades. Figure 13–13 also would not be changed due to employees receiving a merit or seniority increase.

Compensation Issues

Several important issues are facing personnel managers in the 1980s in the area of compensation. Faced with inflation constantly decreasing their disposable income, employees have to pay higher Social Security and income taxes. Employers, however, are in no position to simply give away dollars to help employees; instead, employers must be innovative in their approach to compensation problems.

WAGE COMPRESSION

Wage compression refers to decreasing the differentials between higher and lower pay grades. Faced with high turnover in low paying jobs and employees who cannot live within their means, employers have had to give greater increases to lower paying positions than higher paying positions. In recent years pay differences between top and middle level jobs and middle and lower level jobs have decreased. With the graduated income tax scale, salary differences after taxes will become even more compressed in the future.

Compression, however, takes a number of forms. A manager may find the salary difference after taxes between his salary and those who report to him is insignificant. Another similar form of compression occurs when a recent college graduate with no experience finds little difference between her pay and that of a qualified, successful graduate with ten years of experience.

When the results of compression are fully perceived, employees complain of pay inequity. Naturally, this results in a loss of morale and a tendency to work less effectively. Unfortunately, qualified successful employees turn down promotions because the incremental increases in pay are not worth the extra responsibility or risk.[16]

COLA OR MERIT INCREASES?

Employers have been faced with the dilemma of using increased revenues to grant cost of living adjustments to all employees or to increase job performance by giving merit raises. During highly inflationary periods employers have stressed COLAs rather than merit increases; however, there seems to be no slowing of inflation and employers are beginning to change their thinking. Usually there is not enough in the company budget for increases that match cost of living increases as well as sizeable merit increases to motivate the employees.

A 1977 survey revealed that employers were beginning to increase merit raises and stop automatic across the board cost of living increases for all employees. Continental Can, a large container producer, has abandoned their merit pay system based on a "write-up from the manager stating why the increase was justified" and instituted special qualitative and quantitative performance criteria for merit increases. Marginal workers no longer will receive merit increases while outstanding workers may earn as much as a 12 percent increase. At International Multi Foods Corporation employees and managers mutually set goals which determine merit pay increases. Pitney-Bowes, Inc., a business equipment producer, allows a few employees each year to become eligible for a lump sum merit increase of up to 15 percent of their base pay. The one time extra incentive allows the company to give large motivational paid bonuses without being burdened with a permanently higher salary commitment. Company management reasons that yesterday's outstanding performance should not have to be paid for on a continuing basis into the future.[17]

Employers will continue to struggle with the problem of choosing between adequate COLA increases or merit increases in the years to come. Since most corporate profits are not keeping up with inflation, there will not be room in company budgets to provide both types of increases to the employees. One result may be fewer employees on the payroll to make available more dollars for larger merit increases which would motivate other workers to pick up the slack caused by lost positions.

PAY SECRECY

One compensation issue which has been debated in recent years is whether to have an open system—that is, one in which employees know the pay grade each job is classified in and the pay ranges for those grades. In a closed system employees are told that pay is a personal matter and they are not to discuss other employees' pay levels.

Many organizations still have a closed system of compensation. In some cases,

16. Robert Gibson and Paul Dorf, "Compensation: New and Better Tools," *The Personnel Administrator* (May, 1978): 29–30.

17. James C. Hyatt, "More Firms Link Pay to Job Performance as Inflation Wanes," *The Wall Street Journal* (May 7, 1977): 1.

written policies demand that employees not discuss pay with each other. This obviously minimizes possible morale problems due to employees' feelings of pay inequity. Even if a pay system is equitable, employees may perceive it to be unfair if they are not informed about the system or do not fully understand it.

Companies with open systems have found, however, that problems of perceived inequity can be minimized by explaining to employees how the system was developed and what pay levels are given to various jobs in the organization. Under the open system while employees do not know what other employees are making, they do know the pay ranges for all jobs in the organization. Obviously, the open pay system gives employees a basis for accurate comparisons between jobs; if the pay system is equitable, they will generally perceive that it is. Supervisors will sometimes prefer the open system because employees realize that they cannot demand pay changes which are not within the system provided by the organization.

INCENTIVE PAY SYSTEMS

Incentive pay systems are compensation techniques which directly relate all or part of an individual's pay to the quantity or quality of work performed. In situations involving work groups, the same principle is applied and each individual receives a share. Most incentive systems pay for performance; employees are directly paid a set rate per unit produced. This rate may apply to all units produced or only to those produced above a certain minimum or standard. Some incentive systems increase employees' compensation according to costs of operation.

The individual incentive plan in which an employee is paid a certain amount per unit produced is called piecework; possibly it is the oldest type of plan. Most piecework systems pay the employee a base rate per hours worked and a piece rate for each unit produced above the standard. Another common individual incentive system involves paying commissions to sales representatives, who receive a percentage of gross sales and expense money.

Group incentive pay schemes vary substantially in nature; profit sharing plans are one form. Employees, however, may not relate their efforts to the company's profits, especially in large organizations; thus the motivational effect is lost. Stock purchase plans are another type of group incentive; most give employees the opportunity to purchase company stock at a discounted rate. Administrators hope to increase employees' loyalty and interest due to their private investment; however, such plans usually only interest employees during highly successful years. Suggestion systems are another form of incentive plan. In most systems the employee who drops an idea into the suggestion box might receive a bonus or a percentage of one year's savings to the company if the idea is adopted. Incentive systems may also allow a group of employees to benefit from savings in operating costs due to their suggestions; see the article about the Scanlon Concept at end of this chapter.

While incentive pay systems are quite common and well established, they have never become as popular as compensation plans which pay employees according to time worked. The following problems associated with incentive systems may account for their lack of popularity: First, while increasing motivation by directly linking pay to productivity sounds good, it is often difficult to implement. The greatest problem is creating an accurate quantifiable measure of employee performance; the job must have a quantifiable output. Most jobs today simply do not produce one or two easily-measured products which become an acceptable and accurate measure of an employee's performance. Jobs which require more mental than physical effort generally do not adapt to incentive systems. A second type of problem is created by systems which offer employees additional pay for each unit beyond the standard or expected production rate. The obvious problem here is determining the performance standard; many union grievances have been filed over standards perceived to be arbitrary or unfairly high. A third problem with incentive systems is the interdependence of work activities. Most jobs today are at least partially interrelated; employees depend upon others for data, equipment, cooperation, etc. A sales representative, for example, may lose a big sale and commission due to late delivery by the warehouse. A fourth problem encountered when utilizing incentive systems is that of total compensation determination. Since some employees ul-

timately determine their total pay for any period of time, a highly successful TV sales executive may have an annual income greater than the company president. Another example is the production worker whose monthly paycheck is only one-third of last month's due to a shortage of parts.

In summary, a firm's pay system should be competitive with outside organizations and internally equitable to minimize labor and legal problems. Competitive compensation systems attract, retain, and motivate employees; employers who have a fair, objective system need not pay the highest wages in the community. Employees expect to be paid according to the difficulty and importance of their jobs. A fair and acceptable pay system can be established and maintained by using job evaluations in which each job's worth to the organization is established through comparison of specific factors. Before a method of job evaluation is chosen, the size, complexity, and history of the organization should be considered. All compensation programs must comply with federal legislation which has established minimum pay levels and nondiscriminatory pay practices and requires that jobs be classified as exempt or non-exempt.

The Solution

Andy Stark should have talked to his supervisor about Helen Pontiac. If he had, the supervisor would have told him that Pontiac had four years' experience with another firm, which is why she knows the job so well. The supervisor also could have told Stark that company policy is to hire experienced people like Pontiac at a higher step within the pay grade than someone with no experience, like Stark was three years ago. Stark would have realized that his loyalty did pay off—he is making more than someone who has more experience.

Chambers Sandal Company could actually have a fair pay system, but it is not communicating that to employees by suggesting that employees should not discuss pay.

KEY TERMS AND CONCEPTS

Extrinsic Rewards
Intrinsic Rewards
Compensation
Wage Survey
Job Evaluation
Organizational Rewards
Hierarchy of Needs
Goal Setting
Law of Effect
Fair Labor Standards Act of 1938
Exempt
Nonexempt
Davis-Bacon Act
Walsh-Healey Act

Garnishment
Ranking Method of Job Evaluation
Benchmark Job
Global Appraisal
Classification Method of Job Evaluation
Point Method of Job Evaluation
Compensable Factors
Degrees of Factors
Red Circle Job
Pay Grades and Steps
Pay Equity
COLA
Merit Pay Increases
Factor Comparison Method of Job Evaluation

FOR REVIEW

1. Outline at least four reasons why an organization needs a compensation system.

2. What steps should a personnel specialist take to maximize employee performance motivated by the organization?

3. What is the difference between employee evaluation and job evaluation?

4. When are employees' wages garnisheed?

5. In job evaluation why should a committee be utilized instead of one person?

6. What are the comparative advantages of each of the four job evaluation methods?

7. Should pay grades be allowed to overlap?

FOR DISCUSSION

1. If you were working on an assembly line would you prefer receiving cost of living raises or merit increases? Why? If you were a supervisor, would your decision be the same? If you were the owner of a manufacturing plant?

2. You are the newly-established personnel department for a small company. The owner, who began the firm fifty years ago, refuses to allow employees to discuss their wages—and for good reason. The owner's relatives receive 10 percent more than other employees. Various employees have asked you why salaries have been kept secret, and you say . . .

3. Should federal and state governments be able to legislate minimum wages rather than adopting a laissez-faire attitude which would allow employers operating on a slim profit margin to pay only what they could afford?

4. What arguments would you offer to support the repeal of the Davis-Bacon Act?

5. Which method of job evaluation would you prefer if you were implementing one? What factors would influence your decision?

SUPPLEMENTARY READING

Berg, J. Gary. *Managing Compensation: Developing and Administering the Total Compensation Program.* New York: AMACOM, 1976.

Carrell, M. R., and Dittrich, J. E. "Employee Perceptions of Fair Treatment." *Personnel Journal* 55 (October 1976): 523–24.

Fleuter, Douglas L. "A Different Approach to Merit Increases." *Personnel Journal* 58 (April 1979): 225–26, 262.

Moore, Russell F., ed. *Compensating Executive Worth.* New York: American Management Association, 1968.

Schuster, Jay R., and Collette, Jerome A. "Pay Secrecy: Who is For and Against It." *Academy of Management Journal* 16 (March 1973): 35–41.

Towle, Patrick M. "Calculating Sick Leave and Vacation with an Hourly Accrual System." *Personnel Journal* 58 (May 1979): 303–305.

Yount, H. Hoover. "Pay Guideline Maximization Approach to Salary Administration." *The Personnel Administrator* 24 (June 1979): 69–72.

Zollitsch, Herbert G., and Langsner, Adolph. *Wage and Salary Administration.* 2nd Ed. Cincinnati: South-Western Publishing Co., 1970.

For Analysis: Job Evaluation

The Metropolitan Office Machines Company is located in a large northeastern city with a population of about three million. A three-employee operation in 1956, the firm has over two hundred employees today. The work force includes industrial sales representatives, buyers, office personnel, and warehouse operators/drivers. Profits have been very good, and the firm recently moved into its new custom-designed facility. Generally, the employees have been very loyal to the firm and appear to be happy in their work. Since the late 1950s Metropolitan has had a generous profit sharing plan. Turnover has averaged less than 1 percent for the last ten years and absenteeism has never been a problem.

At a recent board of directors meeting some concern was expressed over the company's lack of a modern job evaluation system tied into various pay grades and levels. Several board members mentioned that other organizations caught napping in this area had become involved in costly litigation as a result. In recent years the few employee complaints concerning pay had been dealt with by the grievance committee without much difficulty. The personnel director, an employee with twenty-two years in the company, challenged the need for a new system of job evaluation at the board meeting. His method of job rankings had worked well for over twenty years and been accepted by the employees. Once a year a wage survey was conducted before COLAs are determined to keep Metropolitan's pay structure higher than the competition's.

The board members were not convinced; they held on to the issue with beagle-like tenacity. A few discussed the fact that the company offered almost no fringe benefits except a generous annual profit sharing plan. Employees pay their entire premiums in the group health insurance plan and group life insurance plan. Although no pension plan is provided, employees could have a portion of their monthly pay directly deposited in Individual Retirement Accounts at local banks.

The board of directors could not reach a consensus. One member expressed concern that the company would be sued by someone claiming discrimination, "because today everyone wants something for nothing." Other members were concerned that the firm pay and benefits plans be kept up to date.

Questions:

1. What benefit costs does the firm have? Should more benefits be offered?

2. Should a "modern" job evaluation system be adopted?

SELECTED PROFESSIONAL READING

Five Years with a Scanlon Plan

ROBERT J. SCHULHOF

The trend continues—inflation and taxes keep reducing effective buying power; COLA increases labor costs without making workers happy; fringe benefits increase; the minimum wage escalates, pushing the bottom toward the top—all decreasing the incentive proportion of the paycheck. Productivity increases are a thing of the past. Workers are down on the system. Management has little good to say about the workers.

Surely any cure for this dilemma would be welcome. One suggested cure for the ills of the labor/management standoff has been "The Scanlon Concept," first advocated in the 1930s by a labor official in the steel industry. Basically, the Scanlon Concept provides a monthly cash bonus based upon improved productivity for everyone in the plant proportionate to salary. The proponents of the Scanlon Concept argue that by paying for increased productivity, productivity will increase—meaning more pay for the workers, greater profits for the stockholders and fewer price increases for the customers.

Companies have reported immediate productivity increases on the order of 20 percent. But what are the long-term effects? This article deals with one company's experience with such a productivity bonus program over a five–year period, through good times and bad, to answer the question, "What are the long-term effects of the world's only free lunch?"

The company under study is Rocky Mountain Data Systems (RMDS), a specialty service company providing diagnostic information to the dental profession based upon computerized analysis of X-rays. The company is rather small ($1 million sales and thirty employees), so that some judgment will have to be exer-

cised in applying the information to a larger situation.

To explain the rationale behind Productivity Sharing, the company's version of the Scanlon Concept, it is necessary to understand how and why it started. As usual with a state of the art pioneering project, RMDS's growth the first five years was steady, but profit was nil. Each new worker had to be taught a new skill—reading and recording data from X-rays using computer equipment. It takes a year to develop a really good technician and adding the usual 20 percent turnover to a 20 percent growth rate meant constant training and thus, inefficiency.

I thought our workers were fairly productive. We had a merit review system which rewarded each worker according to his or her own total production and the quality of work. Every six months, the work was reviewed and the employee received a raise proportionate to quantity and quality. Certainly we were doing all we could to provide incentive.

The end of 1973 had seen a break-even year. Although we were pleased with this, inflation was rampant. Our average production salary was $145 a week plus benefits; but if each employee were to keep up with the cost of living, salaries would have to be raised 10 percent. There was just no way to do it. Since the company was breaking even, the workers were getting every dollar we could afford to pay them. As president, I had not had a raise in four years.

So we had to do something new. *We accepted the objective to pay everyone working for us as much as we could, consistent with the individual's contribution and the company's ability to pay.*

Reprinted from the (June 1979) issue of *Personnel Administrator,* 30 Park Avenue, Berea, Ohio 44017, $26 per year.

After much experimentation, we hit on the following formula:

1. We took a base year which we considered to be adequate in terms of profits—not so high that it was achieved under fortuitous circumstances, but not so low that we could not exist if we could not better it. For us, that amounted to the twelve months, July, 1973 to July, 1974. At that time, we were basically scraping by with a 5 percent return on invested capital.

2. We calculated two figures: The total gross receipts, and the total salary figures.

3. We divided our gross sales or receipts by the salaries paid in the past year. This gives the productivity base.

4. Each month, we divide the sales by the salaries paid to calculate the productivity ratio for the month. If the month's productivity ratio is greater than the productivity base, we pay a bonus* that month to each employee equal to one-half of the increase; therefore, sharing the productivity gain between management and labor.

For example, in the base year 1973–74, salaries paid equaled 45 percent of the gross; therefore, the productivity base is 2.2. If, in a given month, the productivity ratio is 2.6, which is a 20 percent increase over the base, we would give each one of our employees a separate check at the end of the month for 10 percent of their salary, which is equal to one–half the productivity increase. The productivity bonus has the following advantages over other methods of incentive:

1. *We can afford to pay it.* The people make more as we make more.

2. *It is paid monthly.* The reward is not far away, maximizing motivation. In addition, it has an advantage over straight salary in that the workers cannot rest on their lau-

rels. They must perform each month to get their money.

3. *It is easy to calculate.* We do not need to do a complete accounting in order to pay it. All we need to know are gross receipts and gross salaries.

4. *It is an incentive geared to the success of the whole team,* not just one individual trying to look like a hero. It develops a positive attitude toward the company.

5. *It solves the problem of employees who have reached the maximum in their category.* They have new hope to make more.

In addition, we offered a quarterly cash bonus equal to 10 percent of the profits. This was done so that profits "became a dollar you put in your pocket." The profit-sharing bonus had the (one) disadvantage of requiring an extensive calculation.

We are willing to show our official profit statement to any of our employees as a matter of record. We continued our merit review program as before, to reward individual performance and to make sure that the salary system pays the best employees the most money. The merit review system ranks our employees and gives them their proportionate share of the wealth. The productivity bonus determines how much wealth there is to share.

What was the result of all this? The immediate result was, of course, an enthusiastic reaction. Everyone seemed to respond well to the goal that we shall all try to get rich together. After all, if we didn't want to become wealthier, why were we working?

This new system was started in August, which is usually a fairly good month, but not a peak. We noticed immediately that the cases began going out faster. People were not only working harder, but smarter; since it was their business, they wanted to make their customers happy. Even though business hadn't increased, backlog decreased and service and quality improved. In addition, discussions changed from, "Why haven't you repainted the bathrooms?" to "Is there money in the

---

*Our policy is that the employee must have at least six months' service to be eligible for the bonus.

budget to repaint the bathrooms, or should we wait? We certainly don't want to cut into the profits."

The result was a real cash bonus the first month of about twenty real dollars per employee. This really excited them and was likely a key element in the success of the program. We hadn't set the goal too high and had shown them we were serious about paying them real money. That lump sum of $20 meant a lot more than a raise of $5 a week which would have been dribbled away.

In succeeding months, some strange things happened. The marginal workers who were previously "ripping off the company" were now "ripping off the workers." A few found the environment unfriendly, subsequently quitting, as it was no longer socially acceptable not to work to capacity.

Who were these people replaced by? Well, as each vacancy occurred, there was a discussion as to whether or not the gap could be filled by current employees. The employees were allowed to decide whether they could find a way to take over the heavier load and thereby increase productivity (and their take–home pay), or whether they needed help. In every case, they elected to bear the burden.

After the marginal employees left, another phenomenon ensued. The real performers, who had been holding back, became more highly motivated than ever! Under the previous policy, they apparently had held the attitude, "If they don't care, why should I?" We find that equality is a myth. In our work, people are very unequal and a key to our success has been to have the most unequal people we can find.

LONG TERM EFFECTS

After five years, what have we learned about the long term? The positive things include:

1. *Profits.* Profits have been up for the last five years. Pretax net is now 11 percent on sales, 22 percent on assets.

2. *Employee compensation.* Those employees who are still with us have seen their total pay go from an average of $7,540 per year to $14,500 per year—an increase of 14 percent per year compounded.

3. *Customer satisfaction.* Sales have increased at the rate of 16 percent per year, with no price increases. New products have been added, but old products have held their price.

4. *The peakout phenomenon.* A major problem we had previously was employees advancing to the maximum salary for their particular job. Here we had a choice. We could either not increase the individual's salary once that person reaches the maximum assigned value of a particular job category or we could ignore maximums and continue to increase wages. In one case, we got a decrease in motivation and productivity, since nothing to look forward to is not very motivating. In the other case, the company in fact paid more than the individual was really worth. Neither answer was beneficial to the company. Under productivity sharing and profit bonuses, there is no maximum for anyone. Everyone, by continuing to work harder and finding more efficient, more profitable ways of doing things, can continue to have a future and see their earnings increase, even if their nominal base salary is fixed at the maximum for their category.

5. *Empire building.* In our company we had previously experienced the middle–management phenomenon of empire building. The tendency was to reward middle-management according to the amount of money they spend—not according to the profit they make. Generally speaking, the larger portion of the budget a department can command, the more people working for it, the more the manager justifies his salary. This is actually opposite to the company's benefit.

Under productivity sharing, we find middle-managers making more money by finding ways to have their departments do the same amount of work with less people, not more.

6. *The "It's not my department" syndrome.* There is nothing more frustrating than calling a service agency and being transferred from one place to another, because no one really cares. Under productivity and profit sharing, the employees have had the feeling that it was their company, not someone else's company. Therefore, everyone tends to take the same interest the proprietor would and customer service is not handled with a careless attitude.

7. *Labor versus management.* Generally, the classic picture is that management makes money by getting labor to do as much as possible and paying as little as possible. Labor, on the other hand, finding itself stifled, usually reacts just by doing less work. It is like a football team where the line and the backfield are on opposite sides.

   Under productivity and profit sharing, the benefits are all coming out of the same pot. A fair way has been decided to divide up the pie and as the pie grows everyone is going to profit proportionately. Therefore, everyone is working in the same direction and the distinction between labor and management has more to do with degree rather than kind.

8. *Acceptance of new methods.* Generally speaking, new methods do not provide any benefit for the worker. If they involve a productivity increase, they require learning (a new sense of frustration for the worker), the possibility that his job will be phased out and little else. Therefore, all change is met with firm resistance.

   Under productivity sharing, a new change is sold on the basis of how it will increase productivity and profits and, therefore, what it means to take-home compensation. Acceptance of change is never easy, but at least we now have a method for selling it. Leadership becomes just a matter of getting people to understand what we want done and how it will benefit them if they do it.

9. *Turnover.* Turnover has dropped over 70 percent, down to around 5 percent. This has been the main contributor to profits, since our previous problem was constant training.

10. *Good times.* The world still has not found a way to curing the business cycle. There are always periods of boom when production approaches capacity. In those times, employers steal from one another by paying ever-increasing wages as an enticement to switch companies. Under productivity sharing, we tend to lose fewer workers to the competition, since bonuses usually will bring compensation to more than what the fellow down the street is paying. Salaries are usually set in accordance with a conservative projection of business. Therefore, during periods of boom, bonuses (since they are not a long-term commitment) tend to be considerably higher than standard wages. You tend to lose fewer people to your competitors.

11. *Bad times.* When the bad times come, those people who were hired in at high rates because of good times are the first to be laid off. Paying excessive wages in good times tends to bring a problem, since quite often the older employees feel themselves at a great disadvantage compared to the new employees and morale goes down. Our experience during the repression of 1974 was, first of all, a decline in bonuses, thereby protecting profits—but also jobs. It is much better for the group for everyone's take-home to decline 5 or 10 percent, rather than lay off 5 or 10 percent of our good workers who we will need back some day. When the bonuses decline, it is much less pain-

ful than an actual salary cut, since base salaries are by definition set close to the going rate and bonuses are merely that additional premium earned for increased productivity over our competitors.

The positive side of a recession is that it is an opportunity to rid yourselves of truly marginal workers. In our previous history, this caused a problem, since when an individual was laid off the other people would complain that they now had to bear a heavier burden. Under productivity sharing, the layoff involves an increase in bonus for the people remaining . . . who are therefore more highly motivated to "pick up the ball" and keep things moving.

12. *Will the workers really invest in the future?* Yes, but not for too long. Early in 1977 we decided productivity and profits could be greatly improved by totally new methods. This possibility was greeted with enthusiasm for a while. However, productivity did not increase during the changeover period, which meant no increase in earnings during 1977, or a loss of 8 percent due to inflation, since we did not have COLA.

In 1978, we reaped the benefits of the investment. This was a good thing, because our people were well aware that their take-home earnings had lagged. They were willing to postpone the payoff, but *not forever.* If we would have seen no progress for a second year, we would have had the same morale problem as any other company that did not raise wages during an inflationary period. Management is still under constant pressure to produce and to keep pay going up.

13. *Price pull rather than cost push.* Compensation should still go up with inflation, but in a price pull fashion rather than cost push. Our goal as management is to maximize profits. Therefore, if inflation makes our product look cheap and profit would be maximized by raising prices,

then we would do it . . . and we probably will, next year. This will increase the productivity ratio and therefore increase compensation. It is similar to a cost of living increase; the wages could be raised because we could safely raise prices. That is far different than having to raise the prices because you had to raise wages— and risking the ruin of the company.

THE NEGATIVES

1. *If you think just because you're paying more money than the fellow down the block that everybody's happy—you're wrong.* People will tend to forget the total amount of money they've earned in bonuses and to remember only what their base salary is when comparing themselves with their friends and neighbors. Therefore, it is important to continue a barrage of information showing what the average bonus has meant for the last year and showing what that means in terms of average salary per week. Otherwise, they may forget how good they have it.

Secondly, *increased money doesn't solve all your problems.* We have had a tendency, because of the good wages we were paying, to be a little lax on the other aspects of management. However, it doesn't work. A good communication program is still essential to keeping employee morale and motivation up. The increased compensation and participation in profits does not solve your problems. All it does is open the door so that people are willing to listen to solutions, because they believe the employer really intends to behave in a way that is in their benefit.

2. *Fight to hire.* In most situations, before productivity sharing, it was management's job to keep employment down. Middle-management would constantly try to justify hiring more people, while top management would put them in the hot seat to provide justification. Now we have an opposite fight which is just as fierce, but possibly a little more healthy. If we feel a

person is required in a department, management generally has to fight to get someone hired. We have shown a general tendency, if anything, to be understaffed rather than overstaffed. In some situations, this might be just as costly as the reverse mistake, so it is necessary to exercise caution.

3. *Even though you are giving productivity and incentive bonuses, it is still necessary to upgrade the base salary structure to keep up with inflation.* Otherwise, you may find that you cannot hire new people in. The promise of a bonus in the future, since it can't be guaranteed, is a relatively poor negotiating position. Therefore, base salaries must continue to be competitive with the outside. In addition, if incentive variable compensation becomes more than about 20 to 30 percent of total compensation, and there is very little risk that it is going to go to zero in the near future, the employees would probably appreciate being able to bank on a higher fixed salary and forego a smaller percentage of bonus. Whereas people do like to gamble and one of the beautiful aspects of productivity sharing is the sky is the limit, 20 percent is probably an optimum proportion of incentive compensation for most people.

4. *It costs a lot.* When you begin productivity sharing, you are paying a bonus that doesn't cost you anything until performance is improved. However, after several years when you look and see that bonus payments are equal to profits and you could have twice as much profit if you cancelled the bonus payments, management begins to question the program. The fact is, we do find ourselves at times paying more than what the same person might be making in a different company. It is, therefore, necessary to always remember that, although you are paying more, by definition you are getting more, because the employees are more productive. We are still paying less per unit than formerly.

5. *Group size.* The closer the reward is to an action, the greater the incentive to perform the positive action. If your productivity bonus is spread over a company of one hundred people, then the action of one person or a small group of people has relatively little affect on the bonus. For instance, suppose a particular secretarial pool with five people in it has one of the members terminate. The choice then becomes, "should we each work 25 percent harder and pick up the slack, or should we hire a new person?" The one person out of the total one hundred in the company is only a 1 percent productivity increase. Therefore, their 25 percent effort goes poorly rewarded and the effort may not be made. For this reason, we have found it advisable to attempt to control our productivity bonus according to the individual performance of departments or approximately twenty people. The overall profit sharing bonus can be for the whole company, but it does provide the greatest incentive if you can make the reward as close as possible to the effort for the productivity bonus.

6. *Pay something fast.* One of our affiliate companies tried a similar system which failed, whereas ours succeeded. One of the major differences was that they had set their goal so high that the bonus during the first few months was negligible. In our situation, we started the bonus in such a way that it would pay off immediately. I cannot overemphasize the importance of an immediate payoff, since otherwise people will not think you are serious about wanting to pay them more money. Actions speak louder than words. Only when they see actual money will they feel secure that management is interested in their welfare—not just paying for miracles.

Since wages continue to go up 7 percent a year, you might use this fact and gear your productivity bonus so that for sure it pays off equivalent to a cost of living increase. The cost of living increase would be something you gave for nothing, whereas the productivity bonus (even though it would be the same amount) would stimulate increased activity. I am reminded of a famous statement made by statesman Dean Acheson, in which he defined statesmanship as "The art of yielding gracefully that which you no longer have the power to withhold."

7. *Changing the formula.* It is quite often difficult to arrive at a formula which will hold now and forever. An important concept is that both management and labor should be confident in the fact that management is implementing this bonus system as an attempt to pay fairly for effort. It may be necessary to adjust the bonus system in the future as product mixes change, or situations change. For instance, many of our productivity improvements involve expenditures for new capital equipment. Therefore, it was necessary to incorporate some factor for the cost of the capital equipment into the bonus system.

Another problem is "value added." Some products may be made totally from the ground up; others may be just adding a small increment of value to an expensive raw material. You may find that your product mix is indeed changing, and that materials cost becomes a greater or lesser portion of what is produced. It might be, therefore, important to define your bonus in terms of value added rather than productivity as was stated previously. The important thing is that management attempts to keep things fair.

I have seen another bonus system fail where management paid bonuses for increased production over the previous year. Therefore, in order to get the same bonus you did last year, it is necessary to do even better than last year. This is a very frustrating situation, which will cause more antagonism than it does good.

Sharing the wealth in order to create more has become the management philosophy and style of our company. It has been so successful that we added an additional 10 percent to our profit sharing bonus this year. It is not the unique solution to all problems. However, we have found that all problems become more amenable to solution when everyone is benefiting by having the problems solved.

Retirement is more than sittin' and rockin' for this New Orleans member of the Retired Senior Volunteer Program at Charity Hospital.

14

EMPLOYEES' BENEFITS

Increased Benefit Costs

Financing Retirement Income

Pay for Time Off

Employee Services

Total Benefit Planning

The Problem: Funeral Leave Policy

Earl Alexander was informed one Sunday evening that his wife's Aunt Bertha had died a few hours earlier. Alexander's wife, Bess, was shocked and depressed because she had lived with her aunt since her parents died when she was three. Aunt Bertha had raised Bess as her own child until she was 23 when she married Alexander.

Alexander immediately realized that he must take care of the funeral arrangements as well as comfort his wife. An hour after receiving the news, Alexander telephoned Bruce Wayne, his supervisor, explained the situation, and asked to take the company's three-day funeral leave. Wayne said he thought it would be all right and to "take good care of Bess." An employee of the company for twenty years, Alexander had not taken funeral leave previously. He was aware that the personnel director made the final decision in such matters.

Upon returning to work on Thursday, Alexander was asked to report to the personnel department, where he was told that the funeral leave Wayne requested for him had been rejected and that he would be docked three days' pay. The personnel director Leon Hardin was apologetic but the company funeral leave policy in the employees' handbook clearly stated: "Paid funeral leave may be granted by the personnel director for a period not to exceed three days. Eligible employees include those who suffer the death of a parent, spouse, child, brother or sister, or parent of spouse."

Already emotionally drained, Alexander became upset and went home without speaking to anyone.

The policy of awarding employee benefits in addition to monetary compensation increased dramatically in this country during World War II. As governmental wage controls were imposed, employees and unions looked to benefits as a means of increasing the quality of work life. For many years benefits were called "fringe benefits"; this is no longer the case. Today between 25 and 40 percent of an organization's total payroll costs may be made up of employees' benefits. When one-third to one-half of an organization's total labor costs are awarded to one area, it can no longer be called fringe.

As part of the compensation package, benefits are not typically aimed at the same objectives as the monetary portion of the package discussed in the previous chapter. Monetary compensation attracts, retains, and motivates employees, while few organizations award benefits because of employees' performance. Instead, critical benefits such as paid vacations and pension plans are tied to seniority or other factors. Benefits have not become a motivational tool because few employees realize the cost of benefits or appreciate many organizational benefits until later years.

Benefit costs of vacation time, paid holidays, sick leave, insurance, and pension plans have grown almost twice as fast as wages since 1967. From 1969 to 1979, benefit costs jumped 171 percent while wages and salaries grew 107 percent. During this time the average weekly cost of benefits per employee increased from $39 to $107.[1] The United States Chamber of Commerce has noted that benefit costs vary widely among industries. The petroleum, public utility, and chemical industries pay the highest benefits for their employees. The lowest benefits are paid by the textile and apparel industries, department stores, and hospitals. Two benefit areas which have rapidly increased in recent years are medical insurance and wages paid for time not worked. For example, coffee breaks, rest periods, wash up time, and any other time on the job paid for but not worked averages over seventeen minutes a day, an increase from thirteen minutes a day only ten years ago, and an increase from less than one minute a day forty years ago.[2]

As Figure 14–1 indicates, the greatest cost increases were in workers' compensation, thrift plans, and paid sick leave, as well as employee education expenses. Christmas and other special bonuses have noticeably declined as other types of benefits increased. The same is true of discounts on goods and services purchased from the company.

BENEFIT INCREASES

While the increases in benefits may differ from one industry to another, the rapid increase experienced by U.S. companies in the last three decades can be generally attributed to four causes:[3]

1. Federal wage ceilings during World War II and again in the 1970s caused unions and employees to look to benefits as a means of compensation and, in some cases, a way to avoid government regulation.

2. Companies use benefits to gain employee compliance and loyalty. When

---

1. Fred Lindsey, "Employee Benefits Hit New Highs," *Nation's Business* (October, 1980): 82–84.

2. Ibid., p. 84.

3. Richard I. Henderson, *Compensation Management*, (Reston, VA: Reston Publishing Co., 1979), pp. 321–22.

FIGURE 14–1: *Average Weekly Employees' Benefits*

	1969	1979	Percent Change
Old-Age, Survivors, Disability and Health Insurance (FICA taxes)	$6.44	$16.87	+162%
Insurance (life, hospital, surgical, medical, etc.)	5.00	16.56	+231
Pensions (nongovernment)	5.88	15.87	+170
Paid vacations	6.17	13.63	+121
Paid rest periods, coffee breaks, lunch periods, etc.	4.12	10.37	+152
Paid holidays	3.85	9.27	+141
Workers' compensation	1.29	4.90	+280
Unemployment compensation taxes	1.10	4.40	+300
Profit-sharing payments	1.63	4.15	+155
Paid sick leave	1.25	3.60	+188
Christmas or other special bonuses, suggestion awards, etc.	0.67	1.23	+84
Salary continuation or long-term disability	N.A.	0.88	N.A.
Thrift plans	0.23	0.83	+261
Dental insurance	N.A.	0.77	N.A.
Employee education expenditures	0.12	0.48	+300
Employee meals furnished free	0.29	0.44	+52
Discounts on goods and services purchased from company by employee	0.17	0.27	+59
Other employee benefits	1.25	2.40	+92
Total employee benefits	$39.46	$106.92	+171
Average weekly earnings	$141.44	$292.13	+107

N.A.   Data not available.

employees have accumulated several years' seniority, they often find that taking a higher paying job with a different organization would be a great loss because their benefits are based upon company seniority.

3. Most employees' wages satisfy their basic needs; therefore, they have become interested in bargaining for more and greater benefits, especially in the area of health care cost and pay for time not worked.

4. Inflation and rising wage levels have created interest in using benefits as tax shelters. Since employers can consider benefit costs a tax deductible expense of doing business, employees have found that it is cheaper for employers to provide many benefits than for them to purchase identical benefits. Thus, the employer's tax burden is reduced and employees' disposable income increases because they do not need to purchase benefits with after-tax dollars.

The First National Bank of Chicago's Vice President for Personnel, Richard Shultz, believes that the government has only begun to intervene in employee benefits. Government influence on employee benefits through regulations concerning employment opportunities, safety, health care, and retirement in recent years, as well as unemployment compensation and workers' compensation, points the way to even greater governmental influence in the future. The government appears to be

Weekly Employee Benefits Costs by Industry in 1979

	Per Employee per Week
All industries	$106.92
Manufacturing:	
Petroleum industry	175.48
Chemicals and allied industries	135.79
Transportation equipment	128.17
Primary metal industries	126.44
Machinery (excluding electrical)	113.83
Electrical machinery, equipment and supplies	106.81
Fabricated metal products (excluding machinery and transportation equipment)	102.38
Instruments and miscellaneous products	101.00
Stone, clay and glass products	100.94
Food, beverages and tobacco	99.87
Printing and publishing	98.35
Pulp, paper, lumber and furniture	97.35
Rubber, leather and plastic products	88.67
Textile products and apparel	59.58
Nonmanufacturing:	
Public utilities	143.58
Miscellaneous nonmanufacturing industries (research, engineering, education, government agencies, mining, construction, etc.)	111.06
Banks, finance and trust companies	101.48
Insurance companies	101.31
Wholesale and retail trade	74.17
Hospitals	64.60
Department stores	58.35

SOURCE: "Employee Benefits Hit New Highs," by Fred D. Lindsey, *Nation's Business*, (October, 1980), pp. 82–84. Used by Permission.

actively transferring the cost of welfare or social programs to private industries in the form of required employee benefits. To stem the tide of rising employee benefit costs, Shultz believes that organizations must change their traditional methods and approaches to employee benefits.[4]

Employers' concern about their benefit packages as a part of total compensation is reflected in the number of ads which appear in journals directed at practicing personnel specialists. Many employers find that their employees do not under-

stand company benefits, nor do they appreciate them; thus employers need experts to communicate benefit information. Another part of the solution, as perceived by personnel administrators, is the rapidly expanding field of benefit consultants, who can train personnel specialists in complex benefit areas such as financing of retirement or executive compensation.

═ TYPES OF BENEFITS ═

The various employee benefits offered by employers can be divided into retirement benefits, insurance benefits, paid time

4. Richard Schulz, "Benefit Trends," *The Personnel Administrator* (September, 1977): 19–20, 35.

off, and employee services. Each of these areas has a different challenge for the personnel profession today and in the future. Skyrocketing costs of insurance and retirement benefits have forced employers to reexamine their usefulness and to evaluate whether benefits provided by the government should also be provided by the employer. At the same time, employees are demanding more days away from the work place with pay. Finally, employee services, which includes benefits ranging from tuition reimbursement to out placement counseling, have increased rapidly in recent years.

Retirement Benefits

Individuals have two primary sources of retirement income: from government sources—primarily Social Security, Medicare, and Medicaid—and from private pension plans provided by employers. Employees should gauge whether the retirement income they will receive from these two sources will enable them to live comfortably during retirement. If not, then they should accrue additional retirement savings through private investment and savings plans. Traditionally, employees do not carefully analyze their employers' pension plans or government Social Security provisions until they are close to retirement age. Too late they realize that they do not have adequate income to maintain their lifestyles in retirement.

PENSION PLANS

Employer-provided pension plans are designed to supplement the employee's Social Security benefits. For employers, pension benefits combined with Social Security costs represent the single most costly employee benefit. If an employer's

Figure 14-2

Earn a Professional Designation in Employee Benefits

through the Certified Employee Benefit Specialist program

CEBS

CEBS is a ten-course national examination program co-sponsored by the International Foundation of Employee Benefit Plans and the Wharton School of the University of Pennsylvania.

Employee benefits subjects covered in the program—

- Law
- Pension Plans
- Social Security
- Management Principles
- Group Benefits
- Accounting
- Asset Management
- Labor Relations
- Economics
- Benefits Administration

- CEBS courses are applicable for reaccreditation units under standards of the Personnel Accreditation Institute.
- See the CEBS exhibit at the ASPA 32nd Annual Conference, June 17-20, Salt Lake City.

For information, mail the coupon to:
International Foundation of
Employee Benefit Plans
P. O. Box 69
Brookfield, WI 53005
Or telephone: (414) 786-6700

Please send me the CEBS Catalog of Information.

Name ____________
Company ____________
Address ____________
City/State/Zip ____________

PA-680

Used by permission of the International Foundation of Employee Benefit Plans.

pension plan qualifies under the Internal Revenue Code, the employer may deduct pension costs as a business expense and also must meet the standards set by the Employee Retirement Income Security Act of 1974 (ERISA). The nature of a pension plan, or how good a pension plan is for employees, is determined by how the plan addresses several basic pension issues:

SUPPLEMENTAL PLANS Pension plans often are tied to Social Security benefits. A *supplemental pension plan* provides retirees with a certain amount of pension dollars to be added to Social Security benefits. The intention is for a guaranteed level of retirement benefits created by a pension augmenting Social Security benefits. Therefore, as Social Security benefits increase each year, the amount employers must pay in pension benefits decreases. In recent years, since Social Security benefits have risen rapidly, flat rate pension plans are becoming more common. The flat rate pension guarantees employees a certain pension income based upon years of service and the level of pay. This amount is determined and paid by previous employers regardless of any other income employees may receive in retirement. The flat rate system is usually requested by unions.

FINANCING Pension benefits received by employees are financed primarily through two plans: Under a *contributory plan* the employee and employer share the cost of pension benefits. The percentage contributed by the employer changes according to the type of contributory plan. A *noncontributory pension plan* is financed entirely by the employer. Employees and union representatives make strong arguments for noncontributory plans. Their argument is that because employers incur lower absenteeism and turnover costs with loyal employees who stay with the company due to the pension plan, the employer should pay the pension costs. Also, employers can charge their contributions to pension plans to the cost of doing business; therefore, they do not pay the tax rate on pension costs that employees must pay. Employers, however, argue for a contributory plan because they feel that employees will value their pension plans more when they contribute something. Small employers believe that they cannot afford to provide pension plans when they must contribute to Social Security.

FUNDED PLANS Pension plans which accrue money in special accounts for future payments to former employees are termed funded plans. *Nonfunded retirement plans* exist on a pay-as-you-go basis. The *Social Security System* of the United States is a nonfunded plan. This comes as a shock to many employees who feel that they have an account with the system in which their Social Security dollars are drawing interest. This is not the case.

RETIREMENT AGE The age at which employees can begin collecting pension benefits is an important aspect of the pension plan. Many plans stipulate a minimum age must be reached before collecting pension benefits; in most cases it is 65, although in recent years this has been reduced to 60 or even 55. Some companies offer supplemental retirements to employees who retire before they can collect Social Security to encourage them to retire early. Supplemental retirement pensions are given to those employees until they reach the minimum age to receive full Social Security benefits. Other pension systems do not set a retirement age but require specific years of service;

FIGURE 14–3: *Determining Retirement Benefits*

EXAMPLE I:
Base pay = Average pay for last three years worked.
25 years service × $18,000 base pay × 2.0% = $9,000/year or $750/month

EXAMPLE II:
Base pay = Average pay for total years worked.
25 years service × $8,000 base pay × 2.0% = $4,000/year or $333/month

EXAMPLE III:
Base pay = Average pay for total years worked.
35 years service × $6,000 base pay × 2.0% = $3,600/year or $300/month

---

for example, "twenty and out" or "thirty and out." The advantage of pensions specifying a service requirement is that employees may collect one employer's pension while working for another employer, and building up a second retirement income. For example, an employee who begins working for an employer at age 20 is eligible to collect retirement benefits and begin working a second career with a different employer at age 40. At age 65, this employee receives two full pensions, often in addition to the Social Security.

BENEFIT FORMULA Every pension plan is based on a formula which determines the benefits employees will receive upon retirement. The size of benefits received by employees is usually determined by multiplying the average earning figure by the years of service by a stipulated benefit percentage such as 2 or 3 percent. Today, more systems use an average of the last three or five years of the employee's career as the average pay figure because inflation substantially lowers the average pay figure and, therefore, retirement benefits. As the years of service increase, the benefit amount increases to a maximum plateau of 30 or 35 years of service.

VESTING Vesting refers to employees' rights to receive retirement benefits should they leave the organization before normal retirement age.

Figure 14–3 illustrates how various average pay figures affect the determination of an individual's retirement benefits. In the first example, the employee's base pay is the average pay for the last three years worked. This amounts to $18,000, not an unusually high salary in today's inflationary times. An employee with 25 years' service and a 2 percent rate is eligible for $9,000 a year in retirement benefits or $750 per month.

If, however, the average pay for total years worked is used, as in the second example, the retirement benefit is substantially changed. Due to inflation the employee's average pay for a total of 25 years is only $8,000 and therefore, with the same percentage and service figures, the retirement benefit is only $4,000 per year or $333 per month. If that same employee had worked the previous 35 years the average pay is even lower due to inflation.

EMPLOYEE RETIREMENT INCOME SECURITY ACT OF 1974

Prior to 1974 private pension systems were criticized because in too many cases they were not providing employees with sufficient funds to live comfortably in retire-

FIGURE 14–4: *Employment Retirement Income Security Act of 1974 (ERISA)*

MINIMUM VESTING STANDARDS
[§1042]

Act. Sec. 203. (a) Each pension plan shall provide that an employee's right to his normal retirement benefit is nonforfeitable upon the attainment of normal retirement age and in addition shall satisfy the requirements of paragraphs (1) and (2) of this subsection.

(1) A plan satisfies the requirements of this paragraph if an employee's rights in his accrued benefit derived from his own contributions are nonforfeitable.

(2) A plan satisfies the requirements of this paragraph if it satisfies the requirements of subparagraph (A), (B), or (C).

(A) A plan satisfies the requirements of this subparagraph if an employee who has at least *10 years of service* has a nonforfeitable *right to 100 percent* of his accrued benefit derived from employer contributions.

(B) A plan satisfies the requirements of this subparagraph if an employee who has completed at least 5 years of service has a nonforfeitable right to a percentage of his accrued benefit derived from employer contributions which percentage is not less than the percentage determined under the following table:

Years of service:	Nonforfeitable percentage	Years of service:	Nonforfeitable percentage
5	25	10	50
6	30	11	60
7	35	12	70
8	40	13	80
9	45	14	90
		15 or more	100

(C) (i) A plan satisfies the requirements of this subparagraph if a participant who is not separated from the service, who has completed at least 5 years of service, and with respect to whom the sum of his age and years of service equals or exceeds 45, has a nonforfeitable right to a percentage of his accrued benefit derived from employer contributions determined under the following table:

If years of service equal or exceed	and sum of age and service equals or exceeds	then the nonforfeitable percentage is
5	45	50
6	47	60
7	49	70
8	51	80
9	53	90
10	55	100

(ii) Notwithstanding clause (i), a plan shall not be treated as satisfying the requirements of this subparagraph unless any participant who has completed at least 10 years of service has a nonforfeitable right to not less than 50 percent of his accrued benefit derived from employer contributions and to not less than an additional 10 percent for each additional year of service thereafter.

ment. In addition, many systems were cheating employees out of pension dollars to which they were entitled. Finally, some mismanaged pension systems did not increase the value of their benefit portfolios. In response to these complaints, in 1974 Congress approved the Pension Reform Act. Officially designated the *Employee Retirement Income Security Act (ERISA)*, or Public Law 93–406, Congress accomplished the most complete overhaul of pension and benefit rules in United States' history. The reform act affects virtually every pension and benefit plan. Responsibility for administering the complex, new employee benefit program is shared by the U.S. Treasury Department and the U.S. Department of Labor.[5] In addition to placing strict requirements on private pension plans, the act protects the vested rights of employees, limits the participation standards which employers can impose upon employees, and requires the employer to file certain documents with the Secretary of Labor.

Before the Pension Reform Act employees' rights to their employers' contributions varied greatly. Section 203 of the act, shown in Figure 14–4, provides that employers may choose among three methods of determining the vested rights of employees to the employers' pension plan contributions. For example, under Section 203 an employee with seven years' service who retired at age 43, would have no vested rights to the employer's contributions under alternative A. Under alternative B, the employee would have the right to 35 percent of the employer's contributions, and under alternative C, the employee would have a right to 70 percent of the employer's contributions. The

5. *Pension Reform Act of 1974*, (New York: Commerce Clearing House, Inc., 1974), p. 2.

employer chooses the vesting method of greatest benefit to the employees and the organization. Note that Part 1 of Section 203 guarantees the employees' rights to 100 percent of their own contributions to a pension plan.

Section 202 of the Pension Reform Act limited the minimum participation standards that employers may require of employees participating in a retirement plan. Previously, an employer could set any age or service minimum for employees to be eligible for the retirement system. Section 202, however, provides that the employer may only require the employee to be 25 years of age or to have completed one year of service. Each year employers are required to file reports of their pension plans for the U.S. Secretary of Labor's approval. When a new plan is developed, a plan description must be submitted to the U.S. Secretary of Labor within 120 days after it is effective. Updated descriptions of existing plans must be submitted every five years. The act also requires that copies of the plan description be given to employees with a description of their benefits. The Secretary of Labor can reject any plan that does not meet the act's standards. The administrator of any benefit plan is required to furnish a copy of employees' accrued benefits to any employee who requests it. Thus, employees contemplating retirement may find out exactly what their benefits will be upon retirement.

Another major provision of the act was the creation of the *Pension Benefit Guaranty Corporation* (PBGC). Established within the Department of Labor, the PBGC's purpose is to encourage employers to continue voluntary pension plans and to continue payment of pension benefits to former employees. The PBGC per-

FIGURE 14–5: *Schedule of Social Security Taxes*

Years	Employer and Employee Tax Rate	Self-Employed Tax Rate	Maximum Earnings Taxed Annually	Employee Maximum Annual Tax
1937–1949	1.0%	*	$ 3,000	$ 30
1950	1.5	*	3,000	45
1951–1953	1.5	2.25%	3,600	54
1954	2.0	3.0	3,600	72
1955–1956	2.0	3.0	4,200	84
1957–1958	2.25	3.375	4,200	94.50
1959	2.5	3.75	4,800	120
1960–1961	3.0	4.5	4,800	144
1962	3.125	4.7	4,800	150
1963–1965	4.625	5.4	4,800	174
1966	4.2	6.15	6,600	277.20
1967	4.4	6.4	6,600	290.40
1968	4.4	6.4	7,800	343.20
1969–70	4.8	6.9	7,800	374.40
1971	5.2	7.5	7,800	405.60
1972	5.2	7.5	9,000	468
1973	5.85	8.0	10,800	631.80
1974	5.85	7.9	13,200	772.20
1975	5.85	7.9	14,100	824.85
1976	5.85	7.9	15,300	895.05
1977	5.85	7.9	16,500	965.25
1978	6.05	8.1	17,700	1,070.85
1979	6.13	8.10	22,900	1,403.77
1980	6.13	8.10	25,900	1,587.67
1981	6.65	9.30**	29,700	1,975.05
1982–1984	6.70	9.35	To be determined	
1985	7.05	9.90	To be determined	
1986–1989	7.15	10.00	To be determined	
1990 and after	7.65	10.75	To be determined	

*Self-employed persons were not covered until 1951.

**The sharp tax rate increase for the self-employed in 1981 reflects a change for Old Age, Survivors, and Disability insurance back to the original basis of 1½ times the employee rate (which was abandoned in 1973).

SOURCE: Dale Detlefs, *1981 Guide to Social Security*, (Louisville, KY: Meidinger and Associates, 1981), p. 7.

mits tax-free transfer of vested pension benefits in a voluntary portability program. Portability is the right of an employee to transfer pension benefits accrued from one employer to a new employer. Under this program, employees may place their benefits in the PBGC which serves as a clearinghouse for employee benefits. If the former employer releases an employee's vested rights, the rights may be transferred to the employee's new employer without paying income taxes. Previously, the income an employee collected as vested rights upon leaving an employer was subject to normal income taxes that year. Currently, an employee may choose to leave the funds in the PBGC until retirement.[6]

SOCIAL SECURITY

In 1935 Congress established the Social Security System within the United States to provide supplemental income to individuals during retirement. The basic concept of Social Security is that employers and employees will pay taxes into a system which pays out benefits to currently retired individuals. Those who pay into the system subsequently become eligible and their benefits will be paid by future generations of employees.

The Social Security taxes an individual pays depend upon the tax rate set by Congress; the earnings that individual receives are subject to Social Security taxation, up to a maximum taxable amount. This amount can be determined by referring to Figure 14–5. If, for example, in 1981 an individual earned $20,000 in taxable income, then the total Social Security tax for the year would be $1,330. If another employee earned $40,000 during the year, that employee would pay the maximum of $1,975.05 in Social Security taxes. The employee and the employer pay Federal Insurance Contributions Act (FICA) or Social Security taxes; every dollar an employee contributes to the Social Security system is matched by the employer. Note that while employers pay half the cost of the system, the employees receive all of the benefits.[7]

If an employee works for two or more employers, then each employer must withhold Social Security taxes up to the maximum taxable amount shown in Figure 14–5. However, if the total withheld by the two employers exceeds the maximum amount, the employee may file for an income tax refund of the excess amount withheld.

In addition to retirement benefits, Social Security has provided disability, survivors, and Medicare benefits. Figure 14–6 enumerates the various recipients of Social Security benefits in 1981. Approximately 80 percent of the total Social Security tax in 1981 went toward the old age, survivors, and disability tax; the remainder to the Medicare tax.[8] Alarmed by this high percentage, government officials have tried to decrease the scope of the Social Security System to ensure that the original purpose of the system—retirement benefits—would be fulfilled.

In recent years the Social Security System has also been criticized because the fund has been running short of dollars to pay out benefits even though Congress has consistently increased Social Security taxes. From 1965 through 1979 the Consumer Price Index (CPI) increased 120 percent while Social Security benefits increased by more than 160 percent. One effect of this disproportionate increase has been that some workers who have retired fare better than working employees.[9]

SOCIAL SECURITY REVISION OF 1975 The increased cost of benefits trend is likely to continue in future years due to a revision of Social Security benefits passed by Con-

---

6. Henderson, *Compensation Management,* pp. 331–32.

7. Dale Detlefs, *1981 Guide to Social Security,* (Louisville, KY: Meidinger and Associates, 1981), pp. 6–10.

8. Ibid.

9. Thomas C. Sassman, "Postretirement Increase Plans: Why You Need Them and How to Pick the Right One," *Personnel Journal* (April, 1980): 285–87.

FIGURE 14–6: *Social Security Benefits—1981*

WHEN THIS HAPPENS:	BENEFITS WILL BE PAID TO:			
	YOU	YOUR SPOUSE	YOUR CHILD	YOUR PARENTS
You RETIRE	Age 62 and over	● Any age, if caring for your child under age 18; or ● Age 62 and over	Under age 18, or 22 if a student	—
You Become DISABLED	Any age	● Any age, if caring for your child under age 18; or ● Age 62 and over	Under age 18 or 22 if a student	—
You DIE	—	● Any age, if caring for your child under age 18; or ● Age 60 and over	Under age 18, or 22 if a student	Age 62 and over if dependent upon you

Monthly Benefits At Retirement (Age 65)

YOUR PRESENT AGE	WHO RECEIVES BENEFITS	YOUR PRESENT ANNUAL EARNINGS					
		$10,000–14,000	$14,000–18,000	$18,000–22,000	$22,000–26,000	$26,000–30,000	$30,000 & UP
65	You	482	598	644	666	676	676
	Spouse; each child	241	299	322	333	338	338
64	You	440	532	592	610	610	610
	Spouse; each child	220	266	296	305	305	305
63	You	420	516	566	582	590	592
	Spouse; each child	210	258	283	291	295	296
62	You	396	488	538	552	562	564
	Spouse;each child	198	244	269	276	281	282
61	You	398	490	540	556	566	570
	Spouse; each child	199	245	270	278	283	285
56–60	You	402	496	544	564	580	584
	Spouse; each child	201	248	272	282	290	292
51–55	You	408	504	550	576	596	604
	Spouse; each child	204	252	275	288	298	302
46–50	You	416	514	560	592	618	628
	Spouse; each child	208	257	280	296	309	314
41–45	You	424	524	572	610	642	656
	Spouse; each child	212	262	286	305	321	328
36–40	You	430	532	580	626	666	682
	Spouse; each child	215	266	290	313	333	341
31–35	You	438	536	586	636	682	702
	Spouse; each child	219	268	293	318	341	351
Under 31	You	442	540	588	640	688	710
	Spouse; each child	221	270	294	320	344	355

SOURCE: Dale Detlefs, *1981 Guide to Social Security*, (Louisville, KY: Meidinger and Associates, 1981), pp. 5 and 10.

gress in 1975. This act provides that Social Security benefits will increase by the CPI percentage of increase each year that the CPI increases by 3 percent or more. Since it is unlikely that the CPI will not increase by at least 3 percent each year, Social Security taxes will be increased each year until Congress rescinds the 1975 revision.

Some economists question whether the cost of living for retired individuals increases equally with the CPI, particularly since a large percentage of the CPI is made up of mortgage rates and interest rates on durable goods. Frequently retirees have low interest mortgages on their homes, set between 3 and 6 percent decades ago. Retirees deciding to sell their homes are eligible to receive up to $100,000 in capital gains, tax free—a special benefit for the elderly.[10]

Congress originally passed the Social Security Revision to tie benefit increases directly to the Consumer Price Index; thus, Congress would not face this difficult political vote each year. Since the revision was approved, economists have questioned where those benefit dollars will come from.

Another problem within the Social Security System is its lack of total coverage. At present only 90 percent of all employees in this country contribute to the Social Security program. The majority of the 10 percent who do not pay into the Social Security System are federal, state, local government, and nonprofit association employees. The Social Security System does not include all employees at this time because government employees have effectively lobbied Congress to remain out of the Social Security System.

Originally, governmental employees were excluded because their retirement system, the Civil Service Retirement Program, was designed to attract individuals to traditionally lower paying government jobs. Today that argument no longer is valid since most federal and state governmental jobs pay as well as those in the private sector and the Civil Service Retirement Program is much more lucrative than Social Security. Proponents of universal coverage note that it is only fair that all employees pay into the Social Security System. The additional revenues generated would allow substantially lower FICA payroll taxes upon the 90 percent who now pay into the system.[11]

Inflation and the nation's birthrate have hampered the Social Security System. Since the 1975 revision of the system, the inflation rate in the United States has advanced in an unprecedented fashion, forcing increases in the benefits awarded to individuals unforeseen during the passage of the revision. The leveling off of the national birthrate in recent years has also added to the problem. Combined with the younger average age of retired individuals, the lower birthrate means that fewer working individuals provide benefit dollars to a greater number of retired individuals receiving Social Security. This trend is likely to continue and greatly increase as employees born during the baby boom retire in another 30 to 35 years.

Finally, another problem is that too many individuals today feel that Social Security should provide full retirement benefits, something Social Security was never designed to do.

---

10. Jerry Flint, "The Old Folks," *Forbes* (February 18, 1980): 51–53.

11. Richard Schulz, "Universal Social Security Coverage," *The Personnel Administrator* (May, 1979): 21–23.

Pay for Time Off

Employees today expect to be paid for holidays, vacations, and miscellaneous days they do not work, even though employers' policies vary greatly.

VACATIONS

Employers have long believed that vacations increase the employees' productivity upon returning to the job. Employees who take strenuous vacations may not receive physical rest from the job but usually receive a mental break from the workplace. Today virtually all organizations have a schedule of paid vacations based upon years of service with the organization. A typical system is:

Service	Vacation Days
1 year	1 week
3– 5 years	2 weeks
5–10 years	3 weeks
11–15 years	4 weeks
16–20 years	5 weeks
Over 20 years	6 weeks

Employers often require employees to stagger their vacation dates throughout the warmer months to provide the organization with a steady flow of goods or services. Manufacturing and production industries may shut down during the summer, requiring all employees to take their vacations during the shutdown while the company retools or makes necessary repairs within the plant. The steel industry utilizes an unusual form of paid vacation termed a sabbatical. Sabbatical vacations are given to employees every five years to provide them with thirteen weeks of continuous paid vacation. Employees may not take second jobs during their thirteen-week vacations, but must rest. A sabbatical vacation gives employees in particularly unhealthful and tedious work environments time away for a complete rest.

HOLIDAYS

Following World War II, unions and employees increased demands for paid holidays; previously, many holidays were unpaid. The average number of paid holidays in 1950 was three; thirty years later employees in most organizations receive eight holidays. Employees required to work on normal holidays are often given double or triple pay. In the chemical, hotel, and restaurant industries which operate every day, employees are given double pay for working holidays and another day off during the following week. Normally, when a holiday falls during an employee's paid vacation, the employee is scheduled for one extra day's vacation.

In recent years, Monday holidays have been observed by many organizations as well as the government. This practice of not giving employees the actual holiday off but taking it on the nearest Monday was designed to give employees more three-day weekends during the year. Increasing absenteeism on Fridays and Tuesdays has been minimized by organizations which require that employees work "the last scheduled working day before the holiday and the first scheduled working day after the holiday to receive pay for the holiday." Of course, this may be waived for employees with certified illnesses or deaths in the family.

DISMISSAL PAY

Dismissal pay, commonly called *severance pay,* is usually awarded to employees in manufacturing or unionized industries. Dismissal pay includes payments to workers who lose their jobs due to technological change, plant closings, plant mergers, or disability. Employees who quit their jobs, or refuse to take other jobs within the company, are not covered. Nor does severance pay cover employees who are terminated for unsatisfactory performance. The amount of dismissal pay employees receive is determined by their years of service and past average salary.

REPORTING PAY

In manufacturing and construction industries *reporting pay* is the minimum pay guaranteed employees who report for work even though work is not available. If employees have not been instructed by the company not to report for work within a minimum number of hours before they were due to report, they are guaranteed four hours of pay, even if work is not available.

CALL-IN PAY

A supplemental pay given to employees called back to work before they were scheduled to report is termed call-in pay. Thus, employees who do not take their complete rest between scheduled workdays receive a lump sum bonus for being called-in before their next normal reporting time.

ON-CALL PAY

Commonly used in hospitals and airlines, on-call pay is given to workers available to be called-in to work if needed. *On-call* pay is usually paid on a daily basis. Thus, when on-call employees who normally work five eight-hour days are called in before the next scheduled working day, they might receive overtime payment, on-call pay, and call-in pay for working an extra shift.

PERSONAL ABSENCES

Employees may receive full pay for a number of personal absences: summons by federal, state, or local courts to serve as jurors or witnesses, for example. Employees are not counted absent and are paid during the period covered by the summons. However, some employers require that employees reimburse them for any pay received from court.

When a death occurs in the immediate family (spouse, child, parent, sister, brother, or in-laws), employees are eligible to receive from three to five days of funeral leave. Usually employees are not considered absent during the leave nor do they lose any pay during funeral leave.

MILITARY LEAVE

Military leave is provided for members of United States Armed Forces Reserve Units. While most employers do not charge leave time against employees' vacation time, they do not pay employees for *military leave*. Some employers, however, give employees full pay during military leave.

PERSONAL LEAVE

A new concept in personal absence is the awarding of personal days. For these personal leave days, employees need not specify why they missed work. They may take off a certain number of days per year to take care of personal business which requires missing work.

SICK LEAVE

Sick leave is accrued by employees at a specific rate; for example, one day per month from the first day of employment.

FIGURE 14–7: *Unemployment Insurance Program, 1975*

State	Average insured unemployment rate	Minimum employment requirement (weeks)	Average potential duration (weeks)
Alabama	6.8%	20	23.4
Alaska	6.1	11	27.7
Arizona	7.4	20	24.2
Arkansas	8.7	15	22.0
California	7.2	10	23.7
Colorado	3.6	18	21.4
Connecticut	8.6	20	25.9
Delaware	6.4	19	25.0
Dist. of Columbia	4.6	20	30.6
Florida	6.0	20	20.6
Georgia	6.3	19	19.7
Hawaii	5.7	14	26.0
Idaho	6.0	16	19.3
Illinois	6.4	11	24.9
Indiana	5.8	16	20.8
Iowa	4.0	11	25.3
Kansas	3.6	16	22.4
Kentucky	6.7	18	23.2
Louisiana	4.6	18	24.7
Maine	8.9	10	19.8
Maryland	5.9	20	26.0
Massachusetts	9.2	10	26.5
Michigan	10.9	14	23.2
Minnesota	5.5	18	23.4
Mississippi	5.7	18	23.2
Missouri	6.4	20	22.0
Montana	6.4	20	22.5
Nebraska	4.2	11	22.3
Nevada	6.6	17	22.3
New Hampshire	7.5	11	26.0
New Jersey	8.6	20	24.2
New Mexico	5.9	16	29.1
New York	7.8	20	26.0
North Carolina	7.4	20	23.8
North Dakota	3.6	20	23.4
Ohio	6.1	20	25.7
Oklahoma	4.4	20	21.2
Oregon	8.9	18	25.6
Pennsylvania	8.4	19	30.0
Puerto Rico	16.7	18	20.0
Rhode Island	11.2	20	21.6
South Carolina	8.2	20	22.8
South Dakota	3.4	19	21.5
Tennessee	7.2	18	23.9
Texas	2.3	20	21.4
Utah	5.4	19	24.4
Vermont	8.8	20	26.0
Virginia	3.7	19	23.1
Washington	9.4	16	24.9
West Virginia	5.6	10	26.0
Wisconsin	7.0	17	26.0
Wyoming	2.2	20	20.4

Source: Saul J. Blaustein and Paul J. Kozlowski, *Interstate Differences in Unemployment Insurance Benefit Costs: A Cross Section Study*, (Kalamazoo, Michigan: The W. E. Upjohn Institute), 1978, pp. 37, 42, 43.

Many employers allow unused sick leave to be accumulated without any maximum. While a doctor's certification is not necessary for normal short-term illnesses, extended sick leave requires medical evidence. Sick leave pay provides income during personal or family illness. Normally sick leave should only be taken for illness; however, often sick leave is used for personal reasons other than illness.

Unemployment Insurance

Federal and state *unemployment insurance* programs have been in operation since 1938. The maximum length of unemployment benefits of sixteen weeks has been increased to twenty-six weeks and temporarily to thirty-nine weeks in recent years. During the 1975 business recession, Congress enacted temporary legislation extending the maximum benefit coverage from thirty-nine to sixty-five weeks. The government realizes that the unemployment program helps maintain the economy and also helps workers rejoin the work force.[12]

Some employers offer supplementary unemployment benefits for employees who are laid off. Begun by the auto workers in the 1950s, supplementary unemployment benefits (SUB) have supplemented unemployment income received from the state. Normally, employees must have completed one to five years of service to be eligible for a SUB benefit; in addition, employees must have registered with the state and be willing to accept other work. Usually, employees who are out of work due to strikes, disciplinary procedures, or acts of God are not paid SUB benefits.

States normally provide unemployment insurance by imposing unemployment payroll taxes upon employers. State unemployment tax rates vary according to the unemployment levels within the state and other factors. States with high unemployment tax rates have a disadvantage when trying to attract new industry; high unemployment tax structures may be considered as an unfavorable business climate. Therefore, while attractive to employees, overly generous unemployment provisions may create fewer job opportunities within a state. The factors that account for interstate differences in the cost of unemployment compensation are:[13]

ECONOMIC:

Increases in unemployment, such as those which accompany recessions, raise state unemployment insurance costs. Thus, states which experience high unemployment rates would tend to experience high unemployment insurance costs.

STATUTORY:

State unemployment insurance laws affecting benefit costs differ. A generous compensation for loss of weekly wages produces higher benefit costs for the state's employers. Differences in eligibility requirements and benefit lengths also contribute to differences in benefit costs. Each state requires claimants to have had a minimum amount of employment or earnings during a base period, usually one year prior to the filing of the claim, to qualify for benefits. State formulas for cal-

12. Evan Clague and Leo Kramer, *Manpower Policies and Programs: A Review 1935–75*, (Kalamazoo, MI: W. E. Upjohn, 1976), pp. 82–83.

13. Saul Blaustein and Paul Kozlowski, *Interstate Differences in Unemployment Insurance Benefit Costs: A Cross Section Study*, (Kalamazoo, MI: W. E. Upjohn Institute, 1978), pp. 1–11.

culating benefits usually specify minimum and maximum levels of unemployment benefit compensation.

ADMINISTRATIVE:

The size of staff and the skill of the administrative personnel within state unemployment insurance departments affect the efficiency of the operation. The degree to which state departments ensure that laid off employees' application forms are honest and accurate appears to vary greatly.

A statistical study of the factors which cause higher unemployment insurance tax rates in some states indicates that the unemployment rate is by far the most important determinant of the employer's unemployment taxes. For example, if Rhode Island's 11.2 percent unemployment rate replaced Texas' 2.3 percent rate, but Rhode Island's statutory and administrative variables remained unchanged, Rhode Island's unemployment insurance costs would be reduced 73 percent. Thus, employers cannot realistically expect states to reduce their cost of unemployment insurance taxes by changing statutory provisions. Only techniques which would lower the unemployment rate within the state would effectively lower an employer's tax.[14]

Insurance

Most companies today provide employees with life and medical insurance plans and pay part of the plans' costs. Employees' health insurance packages normally cover group life, accident and illness, hospitalization, and accidental death or dismemberment. The life insurance program is usually part of a group plan which permits the business and employee to benefit

from lower rates based on the total value of the group policy. A good rule of thumb in determining the coverage needed for each employee is to provide twice the employees' annual salary in life insurance. Most companies provide a base life insurance policy and allow employees to provide additional coverage at their expense. In addition to life insurance benefits, a fixed lump sum benefit is usually paid when accidental death or dismemberment occurs. Most employers provide some type of hospitalization plan which pays fixed cash benefits for hospital room and board as well as other routine hospital charges. In addition, some employees receive vision and dental care benefits with the employer paying at least part of the costs.[15]

Many employers feel that health insurance costs are out of control. Today, the biggest supplier to General Motors is not U.S. Steel, it is Blue Cross/Blue Shield. Health care costs to employers increased 70 percent from 1966 to 1976, a larger increase than any other cost. The health care industry has become a supplier that determines its own supply of doctors, prescribes its own demand for services, and controls its own price levels. Close to 40 percent of the nation's total health care costs are provided through health insurance programs paid for by employers.[16] Many companies today are beginning to deliver health care to employees in-house. Employers have found less reliance on outside insurance and governmental agencies and more reliance on internal company health programs can

---

14. Ibid., pp. 30–37.

15. Henderson, *Compensation Management,* pp. 323–25.

16. K. Per Larson, "How Companies Can Rein In Their Health Care Costs," *The Personnel Administrator* (November, 1979): 29–33.

minimize their health care insurance costs.

▄ EMPLOYEE SERVICES ▄

Employee services include a variety of employee benefits. Organizations vary greatly in the services they offer and the service costs they pay. *Employee services* have been developed to increase employee loyalty to organizations and decrease absenteeism and turnover.

Credit Unions

Company credit unions are a long-established employee service provided by many organizations. After becoming members by purchasing shares of stock for a small fee, employees may deposit savings in the credit union to accrue interest at rates higher than those provided by local financial institutions. Employees may apply for loans from their credit union at lower rates than those charged by many financial institutions. Normally administered by a separate board of directors, the credit union is an entity independent from the organization.

Individual Retirement Accounts

The individual retirement account is a relatively new employee service which was developed with the Pension Reform Act. Individual retirement accounts (IRA) allow employees of organizations that do not have pension benefits to contribute to a personal retirement account and, therefore, participate in the tax advantages of deferred income. In the future more and more companies will probably offer to set up IRAs for employees as an alternative to

pension or profit sharing plans. Small companies may find it especially advantageous to place part of employees' wages in individual retirement accounts which benefit the company as a taxable deduction and also provide employees with some retirement income.[17]

Food Services

Most companies provide some type of food facility to minimize the time taken for breaks and lunch periods. The food services vary according to the size of the company and the nature of the work. While some organizations may only provide vending machines and a few tables, others provide complete cafeteria services underwritten by the company which provide employees with an inexpensive lunch or supper break.

To minimize the time employees spend on coffee breaks, companies have experimented by placing coffee and soft drink stands in each department, or providing mobile coffee stands to bring doughnuts and coffee to individual employees. These alternatives minimize the time employees spend away from their work sites to take coffee break.

Education Expenses

Many organizations offer employees partial or total tuition reimbursement. A highly sought benefit, employees often use this chance to increase their educations to prepare themselves for promotion opportunities. Generally, the portion of tuition organizations reimburse depends upon the grades received in classes taken. For example, the organization may

---

17. Schulz, "Benefit Trends," pp. 18–19.

pay 100 percent of the tuition costs for an A, 50 percent for a B, and 25 percent for a C. Employers may also require that employees take career-related courses to receive tuition reimbursement.

Outplacement

Outplacement removes marginally productive employees with a minimum of disruption to employee morale and productivity. A good *outplacement* program is helpful to employees in obtaining new jobs and even more so to the organization because it minimizes employee relation problems and possibly reduces total separation costs, such as unemployment benefits.[18] The personnel department can assist outgoing employees with resumé preparation, develop their interviewing techniques, and provide them with job sources. The outplacement counselor can be particularly useful in developing a positive attitude within an employee leaving the organization. Once potential employers have been contacted, the outplacement counselor can help the employee in salary negotiations by providing wage survey data and other information. The company may choose to hire an outside outplacement firm in order that employees become more relaxed with the process.[19]

Profit Sharing

In addition to their regular salaries, many employees are given a percentage of com-

18. Carl Driessnack, "Outplacement: A Benefit for Both Employee and Company," *The Personnel Administrator* (January, 1978): 24–26.

19. John Erdlen, "Guidelines for Retaining an Outplacement Consultant," *The Personnel Administrator* (January, 1978): 27–29.

pany profits. *Profit sharing* has become very popular in recent years as managers realize that this employee service directly relates the organization's goals with employee goals. Individual company profit sharing plans must be approved by the U.S. Internal Revenue Service. Smaller organizations find profit sharing plans particularly useful because employees can directly relate their work to the success of the organization. Such a relationship may be damaged as organizations become very large and employees become lost in the organization. One potential problem with profit sharing is that changes in the economy may decrease the company's profitability; therefore, employees may increase their productivity, and yet receive less in profit sharing.

Recreational Facilities

One employee service which has been reevaluated in recent years is company–owned recreational facilities. Company picnics and athletic teams provided employees with opportunities to satisfy their social needs in past decades. Increased community–sponsored recreation has made employers question whether employees really want recreational facilities, since a small percentage of employees utilize them.

Work Environment

In recent years employers have found that many employees especially appreciate the attention given to improving the work environment. Employees have suggested changes in the work place to reduce noise levels, to create a more pleasant atmosphere by adding large windows overlooking the surrounding area, or to incorporate shower and sauna facilities. Allowing employees to determine their own office decors and eliminating the need to punch time clocks are other employee services which have increased the pleasantness of work environments.[20]

Workers' Compensation

States have enacted workers' compensation laws to protect workers and their families in case of accidental injury, occupational diseases, or death on the job. Under most state laws, the employer's negligence or fault in causing the injury is not an issue. Instead, states provide employees with assured payment for medical expenses and lost income. Most *workers' compensation* systems are funded by employers paying money into a state fund; an industrial commission decides when employees are entitled to compensation due to injury on the job. Some states allow employers to purchase workers' compensation insurance from private insurance companies. Most state laws limit the damages employees can recover. Often, employees are able to recover the total medical expenses and up to two-thirds of income lost due to time off the job or disability.[21]

TOTAL BENEFIT
PLANNING

With benefit costs increasing up to 40 percent of total payroll costs, employers today are reevaluating their total benefit packages. Many benefit packages today have little effect on employee motivation and performance. Since many of the costly and expensive benefits are tied to seniority, such as vacation and retirement income, employers seldom link benefits to level of performance. Some personnel specialists believe that most employees do not truly understand the nature of their benefit packages, nor do they appreciate the total cost of providing them with benefits. When given the choice between additional benefits or disposable income, overwhelmingly, employees tend to choose additional disposable income. The organization may find it less expensive to offer employees fewer benefits and more wages in order to help employees keep pace with inflation and also lower the benefit program cost.

Companies can best utilize their benefit dollars by assessing employees' needs and determining which benefits are truly demanded. Through meetings with employee representatives and union leaders, employers may find that the employees do not truly desire some costly benefits and have a greater need for benefits that may be less expensive. The company's total benefit package should be reviewed as a whole and not as separate components. The company's total compensation and benefits should meet employee needs in the four areas depicted in Figure 14–8.[22]

Cafeteria Approach

The cafeteria approach to benefit compensation allows employees to determine

---

20. Richard Woodman and John Sherwood, "A Comprehensive Look at Job Design," *Personnel Journal* (August, 1977): 284–87.

21. Michael P. Littea and James E. Inman, *The Legal Environment of Business: Text, Cases and Readings,* (Columbus, OH: Grid Publishing, Inc., 1980), pp. 464–65.

22. Richard J. Farrell, "Compensation and Benefits," *Personnel Journal,* (November, 1976): 557–59.

FIGURE 14–8: *Employee Compensation Needs*

	Basic Living Wage	Protect Against Loss	Meet Major Expenses	Improve Standard of Living
Salary	X			
Wages	X			
Commissions	X			
Life Insurance		X	X	
Survivor Benefits		X	X	
Accidental Death		X	X	
Social Security		X	X	
Salary Continuance		X	X	
Sick Pay		X	X	
Long Term Disability		X	X	
Medical Insurance		X	X	
Workmen's Compensation		X	X	
Unemployment Benefits		X	X	
Severance Pay		X	X	
Pensions, Profit Sharing		X	X	
Credit Union			X	
Tuition Refund Program			X	
Scholarship Program			X	
Low Interest Company Loans			X	
Automobile Lease Plan			X	
Relocation Expense Plan			X	
Equity Advance Plan			X	
Bonuses			X	X
Financial Counseling		X	X	X
Perquisites		X	X	X
Capital Accrual:				
Stock Options			X	X
Stock Purchase Plans			X	X
Thrift Incentive Plans			X	X
Savings Plans			X	X
Deferred Compensation			X	X

SOURCE: Richard Farrell, "Compensation and Benefits," *Personnel Journal*, (November, 1976), p. 558. Reprinted with permission *Personnel Journal*, Costa Mesa, CA Copyright 1976.

some of the benefits to be included in their compensation packages. Employees pick and choose from a menu of benefit items. The obvious advantage of the cafeteria approach is that all employees do not have the same needs and desires to be satisfied by their employers' benefits. Younger employees with families, for example, may prefer to have complete hospitalization, dental, and vision care with minimal retirement benefits. Older workers who can meet most normal expenses are more concerned with retirement income which will allow them to meet the normal cost of living expenses in later years.

In a true *cafeteria approach,* employees might choose to expend a certain number of company dollars on increased vacation pay, extra life insurance, or to provide day-care facilities for employees' children. In order to satisfy all employees' needs, the personnel specialist must incorporate a variety of benefits into the menu. Figure 14–9 includes some of the benefits that can be included in a cafeteria

FIGURE 14–9: *Employee Benefits Questionnaire*

1. In the space provided in front of the benefits listed below indicate how important each benefit is to you and your family. Indicate this by placing "1" for the most important, and "2" for the next most important, etc. Therefore, if Life Insurance is the most important benefit to you and your family, place a "1" in front of it.

IMPORTANCE		IMPROVEMENT
(5)	Dental Insurance	(18)
(6)	Disability (Pay while Sick)	(19)
(7)	Educational Assistance . . .	(20)
(8)	Holidays	(21)
(9)	Life Insurance	(22)
(10)	Medical Insurance	(23)
(11)	Retirement Annuity Plan .	(24)
(12)	Savings Plan	(25)
(13)	Vacations	(26)
(14–15)		(27–28)
(16–17)		(29–30)

Now, go back and in the space provided after each benefit, indicate the priority for improvement. For example, if the Savings Plan is the benefit you would most like to see improved, give it a "1", the next a priority "2", etc. Use the blank lines to add any benefits not listed.

2. Would you be willing to contribute a portion of earnings for new or improved benefits beyond the level already provided by the Company?

(31) □ Yes   □ No

If yes, please indicate below in which area(s)

(32) □ Dental Insurance   (36) □ Retirement Annuity
(33) □ Disability Benefits   Plan
(34) □ Life Insurance   (37) □ Savings Plan
(35) □ Medical Insurance

3. As you know, in the past the Company has made certain employee benefit improvements each year, in addition to wage and salary adjustments. Which of the following statements reflects your view:

(38) □ a. Place more emphasis on improving wages and salaries and less on employee benefits.

    □ b. The current mix of benefit improvements and wage and salary adjustments is about right.

    □ c. Place more emphasis on improving employee benefits and less on wages and salaries.

In order that we may effectively analyze the replies, please check the appropriate boxes.

AGE:
(39) □ under 26   □ 26–35   □ 36–45
    □ 46–55   □ 56 & over

SEX:
(40) □ Male   □ Female

MARITAL STATUS:
(41) □ Single   □ Married   □ Other

YEARS OF SERVICE:
(42) □ under 1 year   □ 1–4 years   □ 5–9 years   □ 10–14 years
    □ 15–24 years   □ 25 & over

PAY GROUP:
(43) □ Hourly   □ Weekly   □ Foremen
    □ Monthly

DIVISION:
  □ Agricultural   □ Central Research   □ Chemicals
  □ Corporate HQ   □ Cosmetics   □ Instrumentation
  □ Metals   □ Minerals   □ Pharmaceuticals
  □ Toiletries

LOCATION:
(Field Sales employees should check "FIELD" rather than the name of their distribution centers.)
  □ Atlanta   □ Boston   □ Chicago
  □ Dallas   □ Field   □ Green Bay
  □ Houston   □ Los Angeles   □ Manitowoc
  □ Milwaukee   □ Newark
  □ New York   □ St. Louis

FOR OFFICE USE ONLY Division (44–45)   Location (46–47)

WE'D LIKE TO KNOW . . . If you would like to take this opportunity to explain further any of your answers or comment on any other matter, please use the back of this form.

PLEASE RETURN THIS QUESTIONNAIRE IN THE ENCLOSED PREPAID ENVELOPE

(Compliments: Pfizer, Inc.)

SOURCE: David Thompson, "Introducing Cafeteria Compensation in Your Company," *Personnel Journal*, (March, 1977), pp. 128–129. Reprinted with permission *Personnel Journal*, Costa Mesa, CA Copyright 1977.

---

approach.[23] Such a program would be offered by a large company where many employees are involved and, therefore, benefits such as a day-care center are practical. Many companies have already made advances in cafeteria compensation by offering alternatives limited to a few benefits. Employees' appreciation of the cafeteria approach will be maximized when organizations limit the percentage of salaries which can be expended on employee benefits.[24]

Employers experimenting with the cafe-

23. David Thompson, "Introducing Cafeteria Compensation in Your Company," *Personnel Journal* (March, 1977): 124–25.

24. Schulz, "Benefit Trends," p. 20.

teria approach have reported serious problems which possibly have retarded its popularity. A major problem is the lack of employees' appreciation and interest in the program. When asked to make their choices, employees may respond that they are not capable of choosing between benefit plans because they cannot predict which benefits will be more beneficial to them in the long run. They may even criticize management for not making the decision in the best interest of employees and accepting the consequences. Employers have complained that the paper work and time spent in designing and implementing cafeteria compensation is tremendous; quite possibly, greater than the benefits derived from such an approach.

Several organizations have caused companies to reexamine the usefulness of cafeteria compensation. The Internal Revenue Service has not always favorably reviewed compensation plans which involve cafeteria planning. Insurance companies have balked at cafeteria compensation because often only poor risk employees choose to participate in the company's group plan. Private insurance companies need total employee involvement to predict the level of claims that must be paid. Therefore, some companies experimenting with the cafeteria approach have found their costs of benefit planning skyrocketing, while disinterested or even hostile employees, insurance companies, and the government booby-trap successful completion of the program.

Companies which have experienced success with the cafeteria approach have begun by "dreaming big, but starting small." A small start in cafeteria planning can be successful if top management is aggressive in adopting the plan and involving employees.[25] The steps in adapting a cafeteria approach are:

1. Review employees' total compensation/benefits needs and obtain the top management support for the program.

2. Develop a timetable for implementation within the benefits section of the personnel department.

3. Survey employees to determine what their needs and desires are in the benefits area. Figure 14–9 is an example of a benefits questionnaire which has been utilized in a successful cafeteria approach program.

4. Start by selecting two to four benefit items from which employees can choose.

5. Allow employees to allocate small dollar amounts to various benefits initially.

6. Review the plan with the IRS and appropriate state agencies.

7. Design a data processing system which will minimize additional paper work and the cost of implementing the program.

8. Communicate to employees the program's "core coverage" which guarantees certain benefits such as life insurance and hospitalization that all employees will need.

9. Discuss the program with insurance companies and other outside agencies.

10. Implement the program through employee selection.

25. Thompson, "Introducing Cafeteria Compensation," pp. 126–28.

FIGURE 14–10: *A Sample Employee Earnings and Benefits Letter*

COMPANY NAME
ADDRESS
DATE

Employee's Name
Address

Dear _____ :

Enclosed are your W-2 forms showing the amount of taxable income that you received from _____ during 1980. Listed below in Section A are your gross wages and a cost breakdown of various fringe benefit programs that you enjoy. In addition to the money you received as wages, the company paid benefits for you which are not included in your W-2 statement. These are fringe benefits that are sometimes overlooked. In an easy-to-read form, here's what _____ paid to you in 1980.

Section A—Paid to You in Your W-2 Earnings

Cost-of-Living Allowance _____
Shift Premium _____
Suggestion Award(s) _____
Service Award(s) _____
Vacation Pay _____
Holiday Pay _____
Funeral Pay _____
Jury-Duty Pay _____
Military Pay _____
Accident & Sickness Benefits _____
Regular Earnings _____
Overtime Earnings _____
Allowances _____
    GROSS WAGES _____

Section B—Paid for You and Not Included in Your W-2 Earnings:

Company Contribution to Stock Purchase & Savings
   Plan _____
Company Contribution to Pension Plan _____
Company Cost of Your Hospitalization Payments _____
Company Cost of Your Life & Accidental Death
   Insurance _____
Company Cost for Social Security Tax on Your Wages _____
Company Cost of the Premium for Your Workers
   Compensation _____
Company Cost for the Tax on Your Wages for
   Unemployment Compensation _____
Company Cost for Tuition Refund _____
Company Cost for Safety Glasses _____
    TOTAL COST OF BENEFITS NOT INCLUDED
    IN W-2 EARNINGS _____
    TOTAL _____ PAID
    FOR YOUR SERVICES IN 1980 _____

You have earned the amount on the bottom line, but we want to give you a clearer idea of the total cost of your services to the company, and the protection and benefits that are being purchased for you and your family.

                          Personnel Manager

SOURCE: Jeffrey Claypool and Joseph Congemi, *Personnel Journal*, (July, 1980), p. 564. Reprinted with permission *Personnel Journal* Costa Mesa, CA Copyright, 1980.

PUBLICIZING
═══ BENEFITS ═══

As employers reexamine benefit programs and question if they are cost–effective, they could ask if part of the problem is a lack of communication with employees concerning the benefit programs. Without such communication, some employees simply cannot visualize the entire benefit program and its value to them. Since employers must report their pension program to employees under the Employment Retirement Income Security Act of 1974 (ERISA), the entire benefit program should be communicated.[26]

Studies have demonstrated that employees who give little thought to their benefits may not be able to recall 15 percent of the benefits they receive. Employers might be able to increase the productivity and the advantages of good employee benefits by making employees aware of what the company does for them that does not appear on their paycheck. One method of providing employees with this information is the *Employee Earnings and Benefits Letter* shown in Figure 14–10. This letter keeps employees informed and aware of what the company does in terms of benefits. Section A of the letter lists an employee's gross wages and breaks out the various costs of benefits included therein. Section B includes benefits which do not appear on an employee's W-2 earnings statement and, therefore, are not known to employees. Any benefit that does not show up on an employee's paycheck should be included in Section B to make the employee aware of benefit costs. Considering companies' investments in providing benefits to employees, it is unusual that more companies do not do a better job of making employees aware of the costs of the benefits. Only when a company translates benefits to dollar values can employees appreciate the magnitude of what their company does for them.[27]

In summary, good competitive salaries have always attracted and motivated employees more than an excellent benefits package because often employees do not know the value of their benefits, nor do they see them tied to performance. Therefore, employees should receive benefit cost enumerations and be able to choose between various benefits or higher pay. Cafeteria benefit planning should be carefully considered by employers and, like all benefit plans, be communicated to employees.

The U.S. Social Security System has become very expensive for both employees and employers and faces an uncertain future. While never intended to provide total retirement security, many people now expect Social Security to provide all of their retirement needs. In addition to retirement pensions, most benefit packages include paid vacations and holidays, unemployment insurance, medical and life insurance, and workers' compensation. Some employers also provide credit unions, food services, tuition reimbursement, out-placement, profit sharing, recreational facilities, and a very pleasant work environment.

26. Robert Krogman, "What Employees Need to Know About Benefit Plans," *The Personnel Administrator* (May 1980): 45–46.

27. Jeffrey Claypool and Joseph Cangeni, "The Annual Employee Earnings and Benefits Letter," *Personnel Journal* (July, 1980): 563–65.

The Solution

Earl Alexander's emotional upheaval caused by the death of a loved one coupled with Bruce Wayne's desire to give Alexander a comforting answer created this problem. Because he was upset and it was Sunday, Alexander did not think about checking his employees' handbook. Instead, he called his supervisor, Wayne—a normal reaction to the situation. While Wayne only said he thought it would be all right, he should have known the policy or checked the handbook before replying. Given the nature of the situation, Personnel Director Hardin could have discussed the matter with Wayne before reaching a decision. The fact that the aunt had raised Bess Alexander since age three could have changed the decision. If not, as his supervisor, Wayne should have been the one to tell Alexander.

What should be done now? Alexander should call Wayne and explain why he walked out. Wayne should discuss the matter with the personnel director. Management and personnel should decide if the policy is flexible enough to include Alexander's situation.

KEY TERMS AND CONCEPTS

ERISA
CEBS
Supplemental Retirement Plan
Noncontributory Retirement Plan
Nonfunded Retirement Plan
Retirement Benefit Formula
Vesting
PBGC
Social Security System
Paid Time Off Work
Dismissal Pay

Reporting Pay
On-Call Pay
Unemployment Insurance
Supplementary Unemployment Benefits (SUB)
Individual Retirement Accounts (IRA)
Outplacement
Profit Sharing
Workers' Compensation
Cafeteria Planning
Employee Earnings and Benefits Letter

FOR REVIEW

1. How can employee benefits attract, retain, and motivate employees?

2. About how much of the total personnel cost is included in benefits?

3. What factors are important in determining the size of an employee's retirement benefit?

4. Under each of the three ERISA vesting standards, what would be the unforfeitable vesting percentage of an employee who retired with eight years service at age 42?

5. Why do some states require employees to pay more unemployment insurance taxes?

FOR DISCUSSION

1. If you were establishing your own business, which benefits would you be required to pay and which would you choose to offer?

2. Cite examples to prove that the cost of living for retired individuals increases as much as or less than the Consumer Price Index increases. Therefore, should Social Security increase as the Consumer Price Index rises?

3. In view of the fact that there are fewer persons working to provide benefits for the Social Security System, would you agree that all state, federal, and local government employees and nonprofit association employees should enter the Social Security System?

4. Do you believe that the government will transfer support of welfare or social programs to private industries in the form of required benefits? If so, how soon? If not, what steps can business and industry take to block government intervention?

5. Periodically, pension fund frauds involving the loss of retirement funds for thousands of employees are reported. How can persons and companies which have contributed to the pension fund safeguard their contribution to the future?

SUPPLEMENTARY READING

Carrell, M. R., and Vahaly, J. "The Link Between Employee Morale and Office Location." *Personnel Journal* 57 (June 1979): 360–62.

Deric, Arthur J., ed., *The Total Approach to Employee Benefits*. New York: American Management Association, 1967.

Henderson, Richard. *Compensation Management: Rewarding Performances in the Modern Organization.* Reston, VA: Reston Publishing Co., Inc., 1976.

Koehn, Hank. "Work, Aging and Retirement." *Personnel Journal* 58 (May 1980): 359–62.

Patten, Thomas H. *Pay: Employee Compensation and Incentive Plans.* New York: Free Press, 1977.

For Analysis: Cafeteria Planning

A few months back Dick Roberts, personnel manager of Bel Air Insurance Company, returned to Passaic, New Jersey, from a two-day professional conference in Cleveland. Usually Roberts was not particularly impressed with seminars and workshops, but this time he was very excited about one session. During "Cafeteria Benefit Planning" the vice-president of human resources of a large manufacturing company explained that his company had instigated cafeteria planning six months earlier. Not only had they saved over one-fourth of a million dollars in benefits costs, but their employees were most satisfied.

Five months after returning from the conference Dick had a cafeteria plan operating at Bel Air. President Patrick Hunt had been very supportive of Roberts, citing that possible savings could curb rising personnel costs. Bel Air employees were given a wider range of benefit alternatives than is usually the case because the home office allowed great flexibility in the company's group life, major medical, auto, and home insurance plans.

Three months after Bel Air began its cafeteria plan a tragic accident occurred. The wife of Roberts' best friend who was an employee of the EDP section, Cathy Nomad, was struck by a taxi. After five months in the hospital, she died.

Grief stricken, Nomad came into Roberts' office on his first day back at work. "Dick, I'll have to file for bankruptcy. I've lost Cathy, and the medical bills have taken all the money the kids and I had. I didn't put any hospitalization or major medical insurance in my plan; none of us had ever been sick."

Questions:

1. *Should the firm assist Nomad? How?*

2. *Was Bel Air partly responsible for Nomad's lack of insurance?*

3. *How can Roberts keep this situation from recurring? Should he?*

SELECTED PROFESSIONAL READING

Some Practical Implications of the Pregnancy Discrimination Act

PAUL S. GREENLAW AND DIANA FODERARO

During recent years, a number of organizations have provided temporary pregnancy disability benefits to female employees, as well as temporary disability benefits due to sickness or accident to all employees. Temporary disability benefits for "normal" pregnancies have assumed two forms: either paid sick leave or, much more commonly, disability insurance providing benefits while disabled equal either to a flat benefit, or to a certain percentage of the employee's normal pay (sometimes up to a specified limit) up to a defined number of weeks. Typically, organizations have provided temporary disability income to their members up to 26 weeks for all illnesses, but, if any at all, only six weeks for normal pregnancies.

The passage of Title VII of the Civil Rights Act in 1964, as amended, prohibited employers from discriminating on the basis of race, religion, color, national origin or sex, and established the Equal Employment Opportunity Commission (EEOC) to interpret and enforce this title. The question soon arose as to whether the shorter duration of normal pregnancy and related disability benefits, as opposed to the longer periods for accidents and illness in general, constituted discrimination based upon sex as proscribed by Title VII. Apparently, Congress had not thoroughly considered this question when it passed the Civil

*Condensed from *Personnel Journal*, October, 1979, pp. 677–681, 708. Reprinted by permission, *Personnel Journal*, Costa Mesa, CA. Copyright 1979.

Rights Act, and statements of some EEOC officials, as compared with official EEOC guidelines on the issue, seemed to be contradictory.[1] Numerous lower courts interpreted the shorter pregnancy disability durations as constituting sex discrimination both on legal Title VII grounds and, for the states, on grounds of violating the equal protection clause of the Fourteenth Amendment. By the end of 1976, however, the Supreme Court had reversed these lower-court decisions on both Fourteenth Amendment and Title VII grounds. In the latter case, the Court invited Congress to develop legislation showing clear intent that lesser pregnancy disability benefits do indeed constitute sex discrimination as prohibited by the Civil Rights Act. The culmination of all of these events was the enactment into law on October 31, 1978 of the Pregnancy Discrimination Act (PDA), technically an amendment to Title VII of the Civil Rights Act of 1964 as amended.[2] This short one and one-third page statutory law has generated considerable confusion and compliance problems, as well as "freeze" and "escape" clauses. Here we will attempt to clarify simply one aspect of PDA—the normal pregnancy disability issue.

THE PREGNANCY DISCRIMINATION ACT EXAMINED

Part One: The first part of PDA adds a new subsection (k) to Section 701 of the Civil Rights Act. This section clarifies that prohibitions against sex discrimination specifically include, "but are not limited to," discrimination in employment based on "pregnancy, childbirth, or related medical conditions." Further, fringe benefit programs (including not only sick leave and disability benefits, but also health and medical insurance, etc.) were required to treat women affected by the above stated conditions the same as "other persons not so affected but similar in their ability or inability to work."

Two important aspects of this section deserve special attention. First, PDA did not require employers to offer any new benefits if they did not already have them as of the date of the enactment of the law—October 31, 1978. Second, this first part went above and beyond the Gilbert invitation by including not only disability benefits, but other fringe benefits such as health and medical insurance as well. Further, the language, "women affected by pregnancy, childbirth, and related medical conditions," was also intended to include abortions. The only limitation on abortion benefits specified by PDA was that employers were not required "to pay for health insurance benefits for abortion, except where the life of the mother would be endangered if the fetus were carried to term or except where medical complications have arisen from an abortion."[3] It restricted in no way, however, the payment of disability benefits or sick leave resulting from abortion. The abortion language was apparently introduced to protect employers' First Amendment freedom-of-religion rights by not requiring them to "subsidize" abortion health insurance costs: "Congress shall make no law respecting an establishment of religion, or prohibiting the free exercise thereof."[4] Ironically enough, the only challenge to PDA that we are aware of as of this writing has been a constitutional one, brought forward by two Catholic groups attempting to restrain the payment of abortion benefits on the same First Amendment grounds with which Congress

---

1. This was the interpretation given by the majority of the United States Supreme Court in the important Gilbert case, which will be discussed later.

2. Public Law 95-955, 92 Stat. 2076–77. The "as amended" refers to the 1972 amendments to the Civil Rights Act—the Equal Employment Opportunity Act. We will drop the phrase "as amended" in the remainder of this article for the sake of brevity.

3. PDA, 92 Stat. 2076. PDA also provided "that nothing herein shall preclude an employer from providing abortion benefits or otherwise affect bargaining agreements in regard to abortion."

4. For some of the key statements made in Congress on the abortion issue, see 123 *Congressional Record*—Senate, S15052–53, September 16, 1977; and 124 *Congressional Record*—Senate, S18978, October 13, 1978.

attempted to cope through the act's abortion language.[5]

Section Two: Section Two of PDA provided employers who already had disparate pregnancy benefits a "grace period" of 180 days after the enactment of PDA in which to comply—i.e., by April 29, 1979. The shortness of this grace period created certain problems which are important in understanding the full context of PDA as of October, 1979:

1. Very little time was available to insurance companies to develop the new higher actuarial rates mandated by PDA.

2. Employers in complying with PDA had little time in which to decide to stay with their current insurance carrier with its higher rates, change to another carrier, or make the decision to self-insure to effect compliance.

3. The EEOC had little time in which to promulgate regulations based on the new law, answer questions on the law, and finalize its regulations based on the input of outsiders. More specifically, the EEOC's new regulations were not promulgated until the March 9, 1979, issue of the *Federal Register*, nor finalized until they were published in the April 20, 1979, *Federal Register*.[6] (The latter, it should be noted, changed only one word from the former and appeared only nine days prior to the end of the compliance grace period on April 29, 1979.)

Section Three: Section Three of PDA may someday be popularly called the "freeze and escape" clause in the Civil Rights Act of 1964. Employers having benefits plans in existence prior to PDA's enactment, and who were required to change their pregnancy benefits to comply with the Act, were prohibited from reducing "the benefits or compensation provided any employee on the date of enactment of this Act" until "the expiration of a period of one year from the date of enactment of this Act or, if there is an applicable collective bargaining agreement in effect on the date of enactment of this Act, until the termination of that agreement." Thus, we have two freeze periods, in which no organization may escape the cost impact of the Act by reducing other compensation or benefits. The "one year after" is the important date referred to earlier—October 31, 1979.

The above mandate, however, appears ambiguous upon closer examination. Which comes first for firms with collective-bargaining agreements: October 31, 1979, or the expiration of a contract in effect on October 31, 1978? From a purely legalistic interpretation of the "or" phrase, one might well conclude that "either/or" implies "whichever comes first." In an internal EEOC document dated February 15, 1979, distributed to its district offices for purposes of their clarification of the Act, this issue was not addressed.[7] In the March 9, 1979, *Federal Register*, however, the EEOC inserted the phrase, "whichever comes later." From a legal point of view, Congressional intent seems to warrant their interpretation.[8] Further, from a practical point of view, a "whichever comes first" interpretation would have meant the following: (1) firms with collective-bargaining agreements falling due immediately after the enactment of PDA would be exempt from the "freeze," and (2) the EEOC would not have had time to develop any promulgations—its responsibility under the Civil

---

5. The challenge was raised by the National Conference of Catholic Bishops and the U.S. Catholic Conference on the Behalf of all Persons Similarly Situated, District Court, D.C., Civil Action No. 79-1606, June 21, 1979. These groups asked for a temporary restraining order on abortion benefits. Our latest information indicates that the hearing on this challenge was scheduled, then postponed and then rescheduled, but yet unheard.

6. 44 *Federal Register*, 13278–13281, March 9, 1979; and 44 *Federal Register*, 23804–23809, April 20, 1979.

7. Internal EEOC document distributed to district offices, entitled "EEOC Directives Transmittal, No. 320," February 15, 1979.

8. For example, see Senator Williams' statement in 123 *Congressional Record*—Senate, S14990, September 15, 1977.

Rights Act. Thus, as of October, 1979, a firm is "frozen" as described above until either October 31 of this year, or until later if its contract expires after this date. Consequently, it is legally possible for a three-year collective–bargaining freeze to exist until November 1, 1981, assuming such a contract was finalized one day after the enactment of the law.

Equally questionable are the "escape" aspects of PDA. There are basically three "escapes" from the mandated nondiscriminatory provisions of the Act. First is that after either of the two freeze periods, companies may reduce any or all compensation or benefits as long as such reductions are not discriminatory as defined by Title VII. Second, Section Three provides that benefits may be reduced for "reasons unrelated to compliance of this Act." To our knowledge, this somewhat ambiguous escape clause has not been used, at least not to any appreciable extent. Inclusion of the second escape clause in the Act appears reasonable, since some firms may have to reduce salaries in order to survive under adverse economic conditions, as has happened countless times prior to the conception of PDA. The third and final escape, and perhaps possibly the least recognized one, is the fact that nothing in the Act prevents employers from refraining (either during or after the two freeze periods) from increasing other benefits, or compensation, either previously planned or unplanned. For example, suppose a nonunion firm were seriously considering the addition of a dental insurance program to its benefits package during October, 1978, to take effect on January 1, 1979. If such a firm had been aware of the forthcoming enactment of PDA and had had little knowledge as to how much the Act would increase its premium rates, then it might well have scrapped the proposed new dental plan in order to keep benefit costs in line. We are unaware of any such occurrences, primarily because we doubt that any firms would have publicized any such cancellations.

AFTER OCTOBER 31, 1979

There are a number of strategies that a firm can legally choose to follow after either of the two freeze periods. Again, the first period is in the very near future—October 31, 1979. If forced earlier by the enactment of PDA to increase its pregnancy disability benefits to 26 weeks, for example, in order to render such benefits equal to its other sickness and accident disability benefits, a company may simply choose to maintain these legally mandated increases. Or, after the freeze period is over, an organization may choose to reduce all disability benefits to six weeks (a common pregnancy disability benefit duration prior to October 31, 1978). This would be perfectly legal, since all disabilities for all employees, regardless of race, color, religion, national origin or sex, would then be the same, and no discrimination as defined by Title VII would exist. Or, a firm might choose to eliminate all disability benefits in order to reduce costs in an inflationary economy. This step could not be considered discriminatory either, since all employees would be treated the same. Or, perhaps at the extreme, a firm might choose to get completely out of the medical benefits area and cancel its basic health insurance, major medical insurance, and dental insurance. Such a strategy might be chosen not only for cost-reduction purposes, but also to avoid the possibility of further compliance problems should the Congress and President put into law new regulatory provisions of a type not yet conceived in the medical area. This extreme strategy might, of course, be considered socially unacceptable, but nonetheless would still be nondiscriminatory under Title VII. All of the escapes mentioned above can also be used by organizations for forms of pregnancy benefits other than disability, as long as they are nondiscriminatory—e.g., health insurance.

We emphasize that in the above paragraph, we were simply suggesting what legally can be done after October 31 or the collective–bargaining "freeze." We were not recommending either what ethically should be done or practically can be done, say, in light of a firm's relationships with its unions and/or employees, or in light of top management's definition of what constitutes its social responsibilities. A firm with no disability benefits may wish to provide, for example, twenty-six weeks of disability insurance to all employees after October 31, 1979. Although they may become very important, the above considerations raise issues considerably more complex than can be covered in this article.

A MISCARRIAGE OF JUSTICE?

At this point, we believe a sufficient number of issues have been raised that the reader might question the desirability of the enactment of PDA. In this section, we will address more specifically the question of PDA's possible "miscarriage of justice" from the point of view of both employers and employees of both sexes.

Employers: There is little doubt that the enactment of PDA increased the cost of doing business for those employers who were compelled to comply with the Act. Some opponents of PDA have made high estimates of these costs. There seems little doubt, however, that in passing the Act, Congress believed that these costs could be borne without an undue burden to organizations.

A simple legally mandated increase in costs per se, however, in our opinion cannot be considered as a miscarriage of justice. The problem arises from the fact that some employers were required to incur higher costs than others by PDA and that in many cases these employers were or may have been those with the greatest sense of social responsibility and genuine interest in the welfare of their employees. In fact, PDA increased costs the greatest for firms employing the greatest number of women of child-bearing age. Certain industries, such as retailing and banking, were particularly susceptible to PDA-related costs because of their traditionally high percentage of women workers. Further, we are especially concerned about the following classes of employers:

1. Some employers with a traditionally low percentage of women employees have initiated vigorous affirmative action programs aimed at hiring and promoting to higher levels and higher-paid positions more and more women employees. In doing so, they have been acting in the context of the underlying and broad spirit and intent of eliminating discrimination based on sex since the effective date of the Civil Rights Act (July 2, 1965). In effect, PDA has penalized these employers for their prior affirmative action with respect to sex discrimination, since the resulting increase in female employees is associated with higher pregnancy disability costs.

2. Since PDA did not require employers who had no disability benefits at all as of October 31, 1978 to establish any such benefits, were not those employers most concerned with the greatest costs? Perhaps the word "most" is too strong, however, because, as indicated previously, a majority of employers with "liberal" disability benefits provided for a duration of only six weeks for pregnancy, as compared with twenty-six weeks for all sicknesses and injuries. Nonetheless, such employers did provide six weeks for pregnancy, while others who provided zero weeks of benefits for all disabilities were not affected by PDA's pregnancy disability provisions.

3. More liberal employers who had noncontributory disability benefit plans (as contrasted with those whose less liberal plans required employees to contribute to help bear the costs of the benefits) were also more adversely affected by PDA in terms of increased costs.

This latter point naturally leads us to our other "miscarriage" question—PDA's effect on employees.

Employees: In those plans which were funded solely by employee, rather than employer, contributions, most employees probably had to bear the full costs of PDA, whether or not they believed that pregnancy was really a disability. This fact stems most directly from one phrase of Section Three of PDA: "Provided that where the costs of such benefits on the date of enactment of this Act are apportioned between employers and employees, the payments or contributions required to comply with this Act may be made between employers and employees in the same proportion."[9] We do not have data on the number or percentage of purely contributory plans, but it is interesting to note that the very first plan involving the question of pregnancy disability to reach the scrutiny of the Supreme Court—the California plan in Geduldig—was funded "entirely from contributions deducted from the wages of participating employees, (and) participation in the plan is mandatory unless the employees are protected by a voluntary private plan approved by the State."[10]

Second, women may have been more adversely affected economically than men as a result of PDA. As pointed out by Senator Hatch on September 16, 1977, PDA:

> could discourage the adoption of new disability or medical insurance plans in companies employing a larger than average num-

ber of females. Certainly that would be true in those companies that do not have the plans now. So what is being argued here is something to the great disability and detriment of really most females in our society.[11]

Further, introducing a "family unit" concept into the PDA issue, females could be adversely affected if firms should adopt one strategy suggested in the previous section of this article: reducing all disability benefits to, e.g., six weeks after the expiration of either of the freeze periods. For example, suppose a woman has a normal pregnancy and gets six weeks of benefits, and her higher-paid husband receives benefits for only six weeks when he is disabled for a longer period due to an automobile accident. In such a case, the family unit would have to pay a much higher price for nondiscrimination than might have been the case prior to PDA. This assumes that the wife was then "discriminatorily" permitted only six weeks for pregnancy, and the husband for up to a full twenty-six weeks for his "accident."

---

9. PDA, 92 Stat. 2076.
10. Geduldig, 94 S. Ct. 2485 at 2487.

11. 123 *Congressional Record*—Senate, S15046, September 16, 1977.

Health hazards are not hard to spot at the Ontario-Hamilton steel mills.

15

EMPLOYEES' HEALTH AND SAFETY

OSHA Records and Requirements

Health and Safety Programs

Health Maintenance Organizations

Health Care Costs

Alcoholic Employees

The Problem: Unsafe Office Conditions

Joyce Ladd is an accounts clerk for a large pharmacy supply company. About eight months ago Ladd received a painful shock when she tried to open a file cabinet. After investigating, the maintenance engineer concluded that the cabinet had rubbed against an old extension cord baring the wire. Joyce forgot about the incident until a fire broke out in the storage room three months later. Again, faulty wiring was the cause. Since the company's office building is over sixty years old, Ladd and several of her colleagues asked Rudolph Black, the department head, if a safety inspection could be made. Black assured them that while the office space was cramped and filled with papers and files, there was a sprinkler system.

About one month later in the company's cafeteria Terry Walls, another clerk, saw the safety poster which urged employees to write the state safety and health office if an unsafe working condition existed. The state would then provide a courtesy inspection with no possibility of penalty. Walls wrote an anonymous letter stating the safety concerns of many of the employees. Two weeks later a state safety official inspected the office. The company was given a list of thirty-six safety violations, including inadequate wiring and a faulty sprinkler system. No fines were assessed and the inspector gave the company president several suggestions about how the violations might be corrected.

That afternoon Black called Ladd into his office and asked for her resignation. He indicated that he was "just following orders" and that she was seen as a troublemaker.

The U.S. Bureau of Labor Statistics reported that about one in every eleven workers experienced a job related injury or illness in 1978, which translates into 9.4 injuries or illnesses per one hundred full-time workers. In firms with eleven or more employees, work related deaths in 1978 were reported to be 4,590. Thirty-six percent of the work related deaths resulted from motor vehicle or airplane accidents. Approximately 5.66 million job-related injuries occurred in 1978. Injuries which caused lost work time were estimated to be 2.4 million with an average of sixteen days lost per work related injury. Approximately sixty-two days of lost work per one hundred full-time workers were reported in 1978.[1]

Many union leaders and activist groups have criticized the federal government for inaction in the area of employee health and safety. They have been concerned about *safety hazards*—those aspects of the work place which can cause burns, electrical shock, cuts, broken bones, loss of limbs or eyesight, or other impairment of the employee's physical well-being—and *health hazards*, which impair an employee's general physical, mental, or emotional well-being. Usually including toxic chemicals, dust, noise, or other physical or biological agents, health hazards cause sickness or illness which may take a long period of time to appear. While states had different safety and health laws, the federal government did not establish regulations to protect employees until 1970. The need for employee safety was first recognized during the Civil War when industries began to manufacture war materials at a fast pace. Rapid industrial expansion forced employers to disregard employee safety in an effort to maintain high output and low cost. In 1869 the first safety law, the Coal Mine Safety Law, was passed. In 1908 the federal government realized the need for workers' compensation for federal employees. The National Safety Council was formed in 1926 to compile injury and accident statistics involving the work place. Industrial and nonagricultural jobs increased rapidly from the 1920s through the 1960s; the U.S. Department of Labor estimated in 1969 that out of every four workers, one would receive an injury or illness before retirement.

The U.S. Public Health Service has estimated that 390,000 new cases of occupational disease appear annually. As many as 100,000 deaths occur each year as a direct or indirect result of occupational disease. Heart disease, a leading cause of death, could quite possibly be related to hazardous working environments. Cancer is the second leading cause of death in the United States; research in the United Kingdom indicates that more than 80 percent of cancer could be environmentally caused, although how much is due to occupational hazards is not known. Occupational illnesses are concentrated in mining, construction, transportation, and heavy manufacturing; most injuries also occur in these industries.[2]

The U.S. Department of Labor, Bureau of Labor Statistics defines *occupational injuries* on OSHA Form 200 as:

Any injury such as a cut, fracture, sprain, amputation, etc. which results from a work accident or from an exposure involving a sin-

1. American Society for Personnel Administration, *Occupational Safety and Health Review* (December, 1979), p. 4.

2. Nicholas A. Ashford, "The Nature and Dimension of Occupational Health and Safety Problems," *The Personnel Administrator* (August, 1977): 46–48.

gle accident in the work environment. Note: Conditions resulting from animal bites, such as insect or snake bites, or from a one-time exposure to chemicals are considered to be injuries. And *occupational illness* as any abnormal condition or disorder other than one resulting from an occupational injury, caused by an exposure to environmental factors associated with a person's employment. It includes acute and chronic illnesses or diseases which may be caused by inhalation, absorption, congestion, or direct contact.

The following categories of occupational illnesses and disorders are utilized to classify recordable illnesses:

Code

7a. Occupational Skin Diseases or Disorders
Examples: Contact dermatitis, eczema, or rash caused by primary irritants and sensitizers or poisonous plants; oil acne; chrome ulcers; chemical burns or inflammations; etc.

7b. Dust Diseases of the Lungs (Pneumoconioses)
Examples: Silicosis, asbestosis, coal worker's pneumoconiosis, byssinosis, siderosis, and other pneumoconioses.

7c. Respiratory Conditions Due to Toxic Agents
Examples: Pneumonitis, pharyngitis, rhinitis or acute congestion due to chemicals, dusts, gases, or fumes; farmer's lung; etc.

7d. Poisoning (Systemic Effect of Toxic Materials)
Examples: Poisoning by lead, mercury, cadmium, arsenic, or other metals, poisoning by carbon monoxide, hydrogen sulfide, or other gases; poisoning by benzol, carbon tetrachloride, or other organic solvents; poisoning by insecticide sprays such as parathion, lead arsenate; poisoning by other chemicals such as formaldehyde, plastics, and resins; etc.

7e. Disorders Due to Physical Agents (Other than Toxic Materials)
Examples: Heatstroke, sunstroke, heat exhaustion, and other effects of environmental heat; freezing, frostbite, and effects of exposure to low temperatures; caisson disease; effects of ionizing radiation (isotopes, X-rays, radium); effects of nonionizing radiation (welding flash, ultraviolet rays, microwaves, sunburn); etc.

7f. Disorders Associated with Repeated Trauma
Examples: Noise-induced hearing loss; synovitis, tenosynovitis, and bursitis; Raynaud's phenomena; and other conditions due to repeated motion, vibration, or pressure.

7g. All Other Occupational Illnesses
Examples: Anthrax, brucellosis, infectious hepatitis, malignant and benign tumors, food poisoning, histoplasmosis, coccidioidomycosis, etc.

OCCUPATIONAL SAFETY AND HEALTH ADMINISTRATION (OSHA)

In 1970 Congress passed the Williams-Steiger Occupational Safety and Health Act (Public Law 91-596). The Williams-Steiger Act culminates over one hundred years of effort by employee groups, unions, and the National Safety Council, to provide safety in the work place. The act established the *Occupational Safety and Health Administration*, commonly referred to as OSHA, within the U.S. Department of Labor, and the *National Institute for Occupational Safety and Health* (NIOSH) within the U.S. Department of Health, Education, and Welfare. NIOSH conducts research and gathers

FIGURE 15–1: *Injury and Illness Incidence Rates by Industry in the United States, 1975*

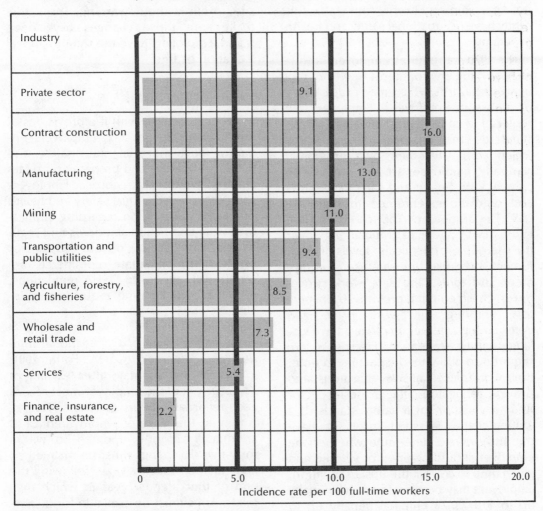

SOURCE: *Chartbook on Occupational Injuries and Illnesses in 1975,* U.S. Department of Labor, Bureau of Labor Statistics, 1977, p. 2.

data and statistics relating to the occupational safety and health of employees; it helps determine standards for safety within the work place by working closely with OSHA.

The Williams-Steiger Act is somewhat unique because it not only provides federal occupational safety standards through OSHA, but also allows states to

administer their own occupational safety and health programs. This rather unique state program provision is a compromise between those states which see employee safety as a national concern and those individuals who believe that the federal government is infringing on states' rights by creating red tape and determining regulations which may be unnecessary due to the diversity of industry across the country. Approximately twenty-four states currently have occupational safety and health programs.

The 1970 act requires employers to furnish working environments free from recognized hazards which may cause injury or illness to employees. Employers are required to comply with safety and health standards created by the act or by states which administer their own programs. Naturally, employees are also required to comply with health and safety standards and regulations. Enforced through the U.S. Department of Labor and/or state labor OSHA agencies, regulations cover the use of toxic chemicals; levels of dust, fumes, and noise; the safe use of equipment and tools, and safe work procedures. Enforcement is provided by inspectors entering the work place and determining whether employers have violated safety standards. Employers are required to allow the inspectors to enter their work places, answer questions, and provide requested data. If the inspector finds a violation of a safety standard, a written citation is issued; inspectors have the authority to determine whether the employer should be fined or warned and given time to correct the unsafe situation. Employers may be assessed a civil penalty up to $10,000, a criminal penalty up to $20,000, and/or a maximum of one year in prison. In most states, however, inspectors try to work with employers to correct the unsafe conditions rather than utilizing penalties. Inspectors may find as many as thirty or forty violations within a work site which has not previously been checked. Thus, the inspector could issue several thousand dollars in fines or instruct the employer to make alterations in order that the standards be met within a reasonable amount of time. Returning to the work site, often without warning, inspectors make sure those changes have been made. Employers have the right to appeal a citation or fine.

OSHA Requirements

In order to comply with the provisions of the Williams-Steiger Act, employers primarily must meet all state safety and health standards; and prepare and retain certain types of records. Employers should contact the local safety and health office for information regarding applicable safety and health standards and regulations. Almost all private businesses involved in interstate commerce are required to adhere to OSHA regulations. OSHA record keeping requirements include:

Log and Summary of Occupational Injuries and Illnesses (OSHA Form 200): Within six working days after learning of its occurrence, the employer must record each recordable injury or illness. The log is kept at the place of employment or at another location if updated to within forty-five days. Logs must be maintained and retained for five years following the end of the calendar year to which they relate. Logs must be available for inspection. A copy of the totals and information for the year must be posted at each establishment in the place or places where notices to employees are customarily posted. This copy must be posted no later than February 1 and must remain in place until March 1.

Supplementary Record of Occupational Injuries and Illnesses (OSHA Form 101): The employer must complete this form or an approved substitute state form for each injury or illness within six working days after notification of the incident. The supplementary record is the detailed report of each injury or illness which is recorded on OSHA Form 200. The supplementary record must be maintained by the employer for five years following the year in which it occurs.

Annual Occupational Injuries and Illnesses Survey (OSHA Form 200-5): Upon request the employer must provide the U.S. Department of Labor a completed survey of a year's injuries and illnesses. The report is mandatory and must be returned to the Bureau of Labor Statistics. The survey only requests information contained in OSHA Form 200, which the employer keeps. The data is used to compile occupational statistics.

The record keeping provisions of OSHA have sometimes been criticized by employers as more red tape provided by the government. In reality, the record keeping requirements are rather simple and straightforward.

OSHA Records

Elwood College, a small private four-year higher education institution, experienced five injuries or illnesses during 1980. The required OSHA records for Elwood College are presented in Figures 15–2, and 15–3. A brief description of each of the injuries or illnesses is provided:

January 7, 1980: Bill Hailey, a maintenance engineer within the security division, suffered a severe back strain while moving desks within the classroom building. An attending physician advised Hailey to stay home for five working days following the accident. After returning to work, Hailey was not allowed to perform many of his normal,

routine functions which required lifting or bending his back or arms. After two weeks at Hailey's request he was transferred to desk security which would require far less physical effort.

February 8, 1980: Ophelia Richards, an administrative assistant in the central office, dropped her IBM Selectric typewriter while moving it from one desk to another. The typewriter landed partially on the desk and partially on Richards' left hand causing multiple fractures. Metropolitan Emergency Medical Service took Richards to the hospital to repair her hand. Richards was kept in the hospital for two days for observance and then released but not allowed to use her left hand for typing or other office purposes for almost six weeks following the accident.

June 6, 1980: Ned Oaks, an assistant professor at the college, went to the health clinic with severe dizziness and headaches. Oaks had been exposed to toxic fluid writers used in place of chalk since new writing surfaces had been installed in the classrooms. After weeks of hospital tests, it was determined that Oaks should be kept in a carefully maintained environment for at least a year to restore his health. Further tests a year later determined that Oaks should live in a southern, dry climate to help speed his recovery. Thus, Oaks secured a teaching position at an Arizona university.

September 1, 1980: Joan Goldsmith, a clerk in the central office, received second degree burns on her right arm and hand while trying to put out a fire in her trash can. When Goldsmith accidently dropped a lit cigarette into her trash can filled with paper and other flammable materials it instantly caught fire. As a result of the injury, Goldsmith missed four days of work; after returning to her job she could not use her right hand completely for over three weeks.

November 7, 1980: Sandy Landon, an accountant in the payroll office, experienced a severe skin rash on her arms and hands. Landon developed the rash on both arms and hands while changing the copying machine. A clinic physician concluded that the rash was due to a reaction to the cleaning fluid. Landon was able to return to work the next day.

Injury and Illness Rates

OSHA statistics help employers determine how safe their work place is in comparison to others of similar size within

FIGURE 15–2: *OSHA Form 200*

Bureau of Labor Statistics Log and Summary of Occupational Injuries and Illnesses					
NOTE:	This form is required by Public Law 91-596 and must be kept in the establishment for 5 years. Failure to maintain and post can result in the issuance of citations and assessment of penalties. *(See posting requirements on the other side of form.)*		RECORDABLE CASES: You are required to record information about every occupational **death**; every nonfatal occupational **illness**; and those nonfatal occupational **injuries** which involve one or more of the following: loss of consciousness, restriction of work or motion, transfer to another job, or medical treatment (other than first aid). *(See definitions on the other side of form.)*		
Case or File Number	Date of Injury or Onset of Illness	Employee's Name	Occupation	Department	Description of Injury or Illness
Enter a nonduplicating number which will facilitate comparisons with supplementary records.	Enter Mo./day.	Enter first name or initial, middle initial, last name.	Enter regular job title, not activity employee was performing when injured or at onset of illness. In the absence of a formal title, enter a brief description of the employee's duties.	Enter department in which the employee is regularly employed or a description of normal workplace to which employee is assigned, even though temporarily working in another department at the time of injury or illness.	Enter a brief description of the injury or illness and indicate the part or parts of body affected. Typical entries for this column might be: Amputation of 1st joint right forefinger; Strain of lower back; Contact dermatitis on both hands; Electrocution--body.
(A)	(B)	(C)	(D)	(E)	(F)
					PREVIOUS PAGE TOTALS ➔
1	1-7-80	Bill Hailey	Maintenance Engineer	Security	Back strain
2	2-8-80	Mary Richards	Administrative Assistant	Office	Multiple fracture of left hand
3	6-9-80	Ned Oaks	Professor	Faculty	Systemic poisoning
4	9-1-80	Joan Goldsmith	Clerk	Office	Second degree burns on right arm and hand
5	11-7-80	Sandy Landon	Accountant	Payroll	Skin rash on arms and hands
					TOTALS (Instructions on other side of form.) ➔

OSHA No. 200

their industry. By compiling injury and illness rates reported by organizations across the United States, OSHA establishes average incident rates for different industries and various sized businesses throughout the United States. Some industries have higher average rates of injuries and illnesses than others due to

FIGURE 15–2: **continued**

U.S. Department of Labor

Elwood College — Company Name — For Calendar Year 19 80 — Page ___ of ___ — Form Approved O.M.B. No. 44R 1453

Establishment Name
Academia City, U. S. A.
Establishment Address

Extent of and Outcome of INJURY | **Type, Extent of, and Outcome of ILLNESS**

Fatalities	Nonfatal Injuries					Type of Illness							Fatalities	Nonfatal Illnesses				
Injury Related	Injuries With Lost Workdays				Injuries Without Lost Workdays	CHECK Only One Column for Each Illness (See other side of form for terminations or permanent transfers.)							Illness Related	Illnesses With Lost Workdays				Illnesses Without Lost Workdays
Enter DATE of death. Mo./day/yr.	Enter a CHECK if injury involves days away from work, or days of restricted work activity, or both.	Enter a CHECK if injury involves days away from work.	Enter number of DAYS away from work.	Enter number of DAYS of restricted work activity.	Enter a CHECK if no entry was made in columns 1 or 2 but the injury is recordable as defined above.	Occupational skin diseases or disorders	Dust diseases of the lungs	Respiratory conditions due to toxic agents	Poisoning (systemic effects of toxic materials)	Disorders due to physical agents	Disorders associated with repeated trauma	All other occupational illnesses	Enter DATE of death. Mo./day/yr.	Enter a CHECK if illness involves days away from work, or days of restricted work activity, or both.	Enter a CHECK if illness involves days away from work.	Enter number of DAYS away from work.	Enter number of DAYS of restricted work activity.	Enter a CHECK if no entry was made in columns 8 or 9.
(1)	(2)	(3)	(4)	(5)	(6)	(a)	(b)	(c)	(d)	(e)	(f)	(g)	(8)	(9)	(10)	(11)	(12)	(13)
	✓	✓	5	14														
	✓	✓	2	42														
	✓								✓					✓	✓	240	0	
	✓	✓	4	21														
						✓												✓
0	4	3	11	77	0	1	0	0	1	0	0	0	0	1	1	240	0	1

Certification of Annual Summary Totals By John A. Friend — Title Personnel Director — Date 1-27-81

OSHA No. 200 — **POST ONLY THIS PORTION OF THE LAST PAGE NO LATER THAN FEBRUARY 1.**

the nature of the work. In order that employers, employees, and other interested parties can determine the relative safety of employees in a particular work environment, they must be able to compare that organization's incident rate with similar organizations. Figure 15–5 illustrates how easily employers can determine an incident rate for their own organizations. The data necessary to determine the rate is compiled on OSHA Form 200.[3]

Assuming 150 employees working fifty forty-hour weeks, the incident rate for hypothetical Elwood College would be computed using the information in Figure 15–5: The formula is: $4 \times 200,000 \div 300,000 = 2.66$. Comparing this to the mean incident rate for colleges and universities of the size of Elwood in Figure 15–6 reveals that Elwood is experiencing just about an average incident rate.

OSHA Penalties

In recent years employers in various industries have begun to realize that OSHA means business. As an example, in 1979 Texaco, Inc. agreed to pay a record OSHA penalty. Texaco, OSHA, and the Chemical and Atomic Workers Union agreed on a payment of $169,400 as penalty for OSHA citations issued at Texaco's Port Arthur, Texas, refinery. The largest safety penalty agreed to, OSHA had originally recommended penalties totaling $394,000. The citations included six willful, ninety-nine serious, and seven repeated serious violations. A Texaco official stated that payment of the fine was not admission of negligence or a violation of the law in regard to a March 1978 fire in which eight workers died.[4]

In some instances OSHA has recommended criminal prosecution. OSHA law provides that employers who willfully violate standards can be fined not more than $10,000 or be imprisoned for not more than six months if that violation caused an employee's death. In two cases involving workers' deaths, for example, OSHA has recommended criminal prosecution. One case involved an explosion at a chemical plant owned by Rollins Environmental Services Corporation in Bridgeport, New Jersey, on December 8, 1977. That explosion killed six workers and resulted in serious injuries to others. The second case involved an employee who was crushed by an electrical tractor in the Lake County, Indiana, Number 2 Tin Mill of Youngstown Sheet and Tube Company. Dr. Eula Bingham, who headed OSHA at the time, noted that she was making the announcement of criminal prosecution in the two cases to demonstrate to employers that OSHA will closely examine employees' deaths to determine if the deaths resulted from employers' willful disregard of job safety and health rules.[5]

OSHA Problems

OSHA has received numerous criticisms since its inception in 1971. Employers cite the high expenses of meeting regulations and possible lack of actual benefits to

3. *An OSHA Guide to Evaluating Your Firm's Injury and Illness Experience, 1974,* U.S. Department of Labor, Bureau of Labor Statistics, Report 478. (Washington DC: U.S. Government Printing Office, 1976): 1–8.

4. American Society for Personnel Administration, *Occupational Safety and Health Review* (March, 1979): 7.

5. American Society for Personnel Administration, *Occupational Safety and Health Review* (June, 1979): 6.

FIGURE 15-3: *OSHA Form 101*

OSHA No. 101
Case or File No. ----------

Form approved
OMB No. 44R 1453

Supplementary Record of Occupational Injuries and Illnesses

EMPLOYER

1. Name --
2. Mail address --
   (No. and street)   (City or town)   (State)
3. Location, if different from mail address --

INJURED OR ILL EMPLOYEE

4. Name -- Social Security No. ----------------
   (First name)   (Middle name)   (Last name)
5. Home address --
   (No. and street)   (City or town)   (State)
6. Age ------------   7. Sex: Male----------- Female----------- (Check one)
8. Occupation --
   (Enter regular job title, *not* the specific activity he was performing at time of injury.)
9. Department --
   (Enter name of department or division in which the injured person is regularly employed, even
   though he may have been temporarily working in another department at the time of injury.)

THE ACCIDENT OR EXPOSURE TO OCCUPATIONAL ILLNESS

10. Place of accident or exposure --
    (No. and street)   (City or town)   (State)
    If accident or exposure occurred on employer's premises, give address of plant or establishment in which
    it occurred. Do not indicate department or division within the plant or establishment. If accident oc-
    curred outside employer's premises at an identifiable address, give that address. If it occurred on a pub-
    lic highway or at any other place which cannot be identified by number and street, please provide place
    references locating the place of injury as accurately as possible.
11. Was place of accident or exposure on employer's premises? -------------- (Yes or No)
12. What was the employee doing when injured? --
    (Be specific. If he was using tools or equipment or handling material,
    ----
    name them and tell what he was doing with them.)
    ----
13. How did the accident occur? ---
    (Describe fully the events which resulted in the injury or occupational illness. Tell what
    happened and how it happened. Name any objects or substances involved and tell how they were involved. Give
    full details on all factors which led or contributed to the accident. Use separate sheet for additional space.)

OCCUPATIONAL INJURY OR OCCUPATIONAL ILLNESS

14. Describe the injury or illness in detail and indicate the part of body affected. -----------------
    (e.g.: amputation of right index finger
    ----
    at second joint; fracture of ribs; lead poisoning; dermatitis of left hand, etc.)
15. Name the object or substance which directly injured the employee. (For example, the machine or thing
    he struck against or which struck him; the vapor or poison he inhaled or swallowed; the chemical or ra-
    diation which irritated his skin; or in cases of strains, hernias, etc., the thing he was lifting, pulling, etc.)

    ----
16. Date of injury or initial diagnosis of occupational illness ------------------------------------
    (Date)
17. Did employee die? ------------ (Yes or No)

OTHER

18. Name and address of physician ---
19. If hospitalized, name and address of hospital --

    Date of report ---------------- Prepared by --
    Official position ------------------------------

employees. Additional red tape and paperwork have been criticized as being unnecessary and unwieldy. One of the most severe criticisms came from a two-year congressional study of federal regulatory agencies released in 1979. The study concluded that OSHA "has been, at best, a disappointment" and suggested legislation requiring economic impact statements from OSHA in order to determine if OSHA regulations are desirable when costs are considered. The authors of the report, from the John F. Kennedy School of Government at Harvard University, noted that OSHA's impact on injuries has been minimal. The two-year study's major criticism noted that while human life and health are priceless entities which should not be traded off against dollars, economic comparisons, distasteful as they are, are inevitable.[6]

OSHA has tried to streamline its rules and regulations. On October 24, 1978,

6. American Society for Personnel Administration, *Occupational Safety and Health Review* (March, 1979): 4.

FIGURE 15–4: *Sample OSHA Safety and Health Regulations*

§1926.300 General requirements

(a) *Condition of tools.* All hand and power tools and similar equipment, whether furnished by the employer or the employee, shall be maintained in a safe condition.

(b) *Guarding.* (1) When power operated tools are designed to accommodate guards, they shall be equipped with such guards when in use.

(2) Belts, gears, shafts, pulleys, sprockets, spindles, drums, fly wheels, chains, or other reciprocating, rotating or moving parts of equipment shall be guarded if such parts are exposed to contact by employees or otherwise create a hazard. Guarding shall meet the requirements as set forth in American National Standards Institute, B15.1-1953 (R1958), Safety Code for Mechanical Power-Transmission Apparatus.

§1926.301 Hand tools.

(a) Employers shall not issue or permit the use of unsafe hand tools.

(b) Wrenches, including adjustable, pipe, end, and socket wrenches shall not be used when jaws are sprung to the point that slippage occurs.

(c) Impact tools, such as drift pins, wedges, and chisels, shall be kept free of mushroomed heads.

(d) The wooden handles of tools shall be kept free of splinters or cracks and shall be kept tight in the tool.

SOURCE: Occupational Safety and Health Standards for the Construction Industry, *Federal Register,* June 24, 1974 (Vol. 39), p. 22799

"nuisance or nitpicking standards" including 607 general industry standards, 321 special standards, and about 10 percent of the word volume of its rules, were deleted by OSHA. A "verticalization" project also consolidated construction rules within industry standards. As an example, the electrical code rules shrank from 300,000 to 30,000 words.[7]

HEALTH MAINTENANCE ORGANIZATIONS

Due to years of frustration with typical health insurance plans offered to employers and employees, in 1973 Congress passed the Health Maintenance Organization Act. The act sets standards for private

7. American Society for Personnel Administration, *Occupational Safety and Health Review* (December, 1978): p. 3.

individuals to qualify for federal financial assistance in the creation of a *Health Maintenance Organization* (HMO). The federal government provides financial assistance to establish an HMO as a means of providing employees with the alternative to other health care delivery systems. Once HMOs are established, they should become self-sufficient through income received from employees and employers they serve. Generally, HMOs provide employees with more comprehensive care, particularly preventive medicine which includes normal visits to a physician. This care is not included in most private health care plans. Secondly, HMOs are designed to provide total health care maintenance to the employee and family at a lower annual cost. At first private insurance companies such as Blue Cross, Blue Shield, and Delta Dental were not affected by HMOs. However, HMOs are

FIGURE 15–5: *Occupational Injuries and Illnesses Computation*

To compute an incidence rate the data required is:

A = Number of injuries and illnesses occurring during a calendar year. (Obtained from OSHA Form No. 100 or OSHA Form No. 102)

B = Number of hours worked by all employees during the year.

$$\text{Incidence Rate} = \frac{\text{Number of Injuries and Illnesses} \times 200{,}000}{\text{Employee Hours Worked}}$$

$$= \frac{A \times 200{,}000}{B}$$

Incidence Rate = Number of Injuries and Illnesses per 100 employees working 40 hours per week for 50 weeks per year.

SOURCE: *An OSHA Guide to Evaluating Your Firm's Injury and Illness Experience,* 1974, U.S. Department of Labor, 1976, Report 478, pp. 2 and 3.

steadily increasing and have made significant impact in the employee health care field.

According to the 1973 act, employers with twenty-five or more employees who currently offer a medical benefit plan must offer the HMO option to employees if a federally approved HMO exists in the local area. Primarily a prepaid group health insurance plan, HMO provides for the family's total health care. An HMO is a local hospital and clinic to which employees may take their families for routine check-ups, shots, and treatment for injuries or illnesses. Employers and employees see some advantages in choosing an HMO:

Fixed Costs

An HMO provides a specified list of health services for a specified maximum annual cost; therefore, unexpected health costs to the employees are minimized. The services are generally more comprehensive than those offered by private health insurance plans.

Minimum Administration Costs

The employers' formerly cumbersome and expensive claim review process is replaced by a monthly check sent to the HMO. No other financial transactions or vouchers are necessary.

Standard of Quality

HMO facilities and personnel are selected according to federal training and experience requirements.

Cost Savings

One goal of the HMO act is to minimize the cost of hospital care, the most expensive part of any health care program. HMO physicians have a financial stake in preventing unnecessary hospitalization costs, because every dollar spent on health care means a corresponding cost to them. One major American industry with 5 percent of its employees enrolled in HMOs is estimated to save about $2 million per year in health care costs.[8]

Less Production Loss

Since HMOs are open on evenings and

8. Herbert Notkin and Leland Meader, "Health Care Cost Containment," *The Personnel Administrator* (March, 1979): 58–59.

FIGURE 15–6: *Occupational Injury and Illness Incidence Rates for the Service Industries, By Employment Size and Quartile Distribution, United States, 1974*

Industry and employment-size		Incidence rates per 100 full-time workers			
		Column A	Column B	Column C	Column D
		Average incidence rates for all the establishments (mean)	One quarter of the establishments had a rate lower than: (1st quartile)	One-half of the establishments had a rate lower than: (median)	One quarter of the establishments had a rate greater than: (3d quartile)
Business Services	Duplicating, mailing, stenographic:				
	All sizes	4.7	0.0	0.0	0.0
	1 to 19	2.3	0.0	0.0	0.0
	20 to 49	4.2	0.0	0.0	6.5
	50 to 99	6.5	0.0	3.6	10.6
	100 to 249	9.1	2.5	7.9	13.5
	250 to 499	7.8	*	*	*
	Services to buildings:				
	All sizes	7.6	0.0	0.0	4.5
	1 to 19	5.5	0.0	0.0	0.0
	20 to 49	6.1	0.0	0.0	9.4
	50 to 99	7.3	0.0	3.3	9.3
	100 to 249	8.3	1.3	6.1	9.9
	250 to 499	9.4	3.4	7.2	12.6
	500 to 999	8.6	3.8	7.6	12.0
	1,000 to 2,499	9.6	*	*	*
	Miscellaneous business services:				
	All sizes	5.4	0.0	0.0	0.0
	1 to 19	3.8	0.0	0.0	0.0
	20 to 49	3.9	0.0	0.0	2.9
	50 to 99	4.8	0.0	0.2	6.5
	100 to 249	6.1	0.0	3.1	7.9
	250 to 499	8.7	1.8	4.6	11.4
	500 to 999	7.4	2.5	4.8	9.4
	1,000 to 2,499	3.1	1.7	3.5	6.0
	2,500 and over	4.3	*	*	*
Educational services	Colleges and universities:				
	All sizes	5.2	0.9	3.5	7.3
	100 to 249	2.9	*	*	*
	250 to 499	4.5	1.7	3.7	6.6
	500 to 999	4.8	1.9	3.7	6.4
	1,000 to 2,499	11.0	3.9	13.0	17.3
	2,500 and over	3.2	1.8	3.2	4.6

weekends, employees are absent less frequently. Also, since HMOs strive to prevent disability and serious illnesses employees will incur fewer disability days.

Unique Services

Many HMOs provide a wider range of health services than other health care sys-

FIGURE 15–7: *HMO Services*

BENEFITS and SERVICES		HCL MEMBERS pay a set monthly premium. Most health care services are provided at no extra charge. The following is a general description of HCL coverage. Complete details are contained in the contract. Its terms prevail.
SILVER SERVICE CARE	**Silver Service Care Benefits**	**Cost To You**
HEALTH CENTER SERVICES At the Family Health Centers, 4545 Bishop Lane and 1809 Standard Avenue, or outside office upon referral by HCL physician.	• All visits to HCL Physicians	NO CHARGE
	• Consultation, Diagnosis, and Treatment by Specialists	NO CHARGE
	• Health Screens, Routine Exams	NO CHARGE
	• Injections, Allergy Tests and Shots	NO CHARGE
	• X-ray, Laboratory, and other Diagnostic Services	NO CHARGE
	• Eye Screening	NO CHARGE
HOSPITAL SERVICES At the participating Louisville area hospitals chosen by your HCL physician.	• Room and Board — Unlimited Days in semi-private room	$175 service charge per admission
	• Physician's, Specialist's, and Surgeon's Services	NO CHARGE
	• Anesthesia, Use of Operating and Recovery Rooms	NO CHARGE
	• Drugs and Medications, Injections, Dressings, Casts and Miscellaneous Supplies	NO CHARGE
	• General Nursing Care	NO CHARGE
	• Laboratory, X-ray and Diagnostic Services	NO CHARGE
	• Intensive, Coronary and Intermediate Care Units	NO CHARGE
	• Use of Emergency Room and Emergency Services	$25 service charge per true medical emergency encounter
Maternity Care	• Full care for mother before, during and after confinement.	$175.00 service charge per admission
SPECIAL SERVICES At the HealthCare of Louisville Health Centers, participating hospitals, or outside office upon referral by HCL physicians.	• Emergency Care-World Wide	NO CHARGE
	• Medically Necessary Ambulance Service	Up to $25 charge maximum
	• Diagnosis and Acute Treatment for Abuse of Alcohol or Drugs	NO CHARGE
	• Home Health Services by Visiting Nurses	NO CHARGE

	• Care for Mental and Nervous Disorders
	  • 20 visits per year
	  • 30 days inpatient care
		$10 per visit
		$175.00 service charge per admission

	• Dental Care-Fluoride Application and Teeth Cleaning for Children under 12	NO CHARGE
	• Outpatient Surgery	NO CHARGE
	• Vision Care	Low fee for service
	• Hearing Care	Low fee for service

ADVANTAGES OF HCL MEMBERSHIP	EXCLUSIONS AND LIMITATIONS	
• NO CO-PAY OFFICE VISITS • NO CLAIM FORMS • HCL SERVICES ARE PREPAID • EMERGENCY CARE-WORLD WIDE • PREDICTABLE MEDICAL EXPENSE	• Any service not performed, or authorized by an HCL Physician • Cosmetic surgery • Use of personal convenience items in hospital such as television	• Dental care or oral appliances • Braces, wheelchairs, etc. except when approved by HCL • Crutches • Conditions covered by workers' compensation

HCLBP REV 5-27-80

SOURCE: *Silver Care Plan*, Health Care of Louisville, Inc., 1980.

tems. HMOs may include a human relations department which provides health counseling services regarding smoking withdrawal, weight reduction, abortion, and sterilization. Also, this department provides education about diet, diabetes, and hypertension.[9] See Figure 15–7.

HMOs are not without their disadvantages: the major problem in employee acceptance of HMOs is the limited choice of physicians. HMOs require that employees and their families choose HMO physicians, not physicians within the local area. Many people who feel more comfortable with physicians they have known for years are relatively unwilling to change. Cost is another factor. Many times the monthly HMO premium is more expensive than a private health insurance plan. While the annual HMO cost of health care to the employee might be less because it provides total health care, some employees think only of the higher monthly premium and are discouraged.

Some critics of HMOs allege that they are health clinics which do not provide the quality of health care that employees would receive elsewhere. The lack of HMO facilities has limited employee enrollment. Since HMOs are a relatively new concept in most cities there are far fewer HMOs than physician's offices and hospitals. Therefore, HMOs are less convenient as they may not be located within an employee's neighborhood.

HEALTH AND SAFETY
═══ PROGRAM ═══

Today more and more companies are developing health and safety programs. A Louis Harris poll estimated that six out of ten companies with a safety and health program did not have programs prior to the 1970 OSHA law. Without a doubt, compliance with OSHA standards has been a major consideration in companies' desires to develop health programs.[10] The health program is directed by a manager, who coordinates cost containment measures and health improvement activities. A *health program manager* can benefit the organization and its employees in many ways:[11]

Benefits Redesigned

To maximize employee health care benefits and minimize costs, benefits can be redesigned to increase outpatient care, stress preventive care, and provide second opinions on surgery and preadmission testing.

In-house Programs

Employees and the company benefit from in-house drug and alcohol counseling, physical fitness programs, and counseling for emotionally ill employees.

Employee Education

Training supervisors and employees to detect the early warning signs of physical and mental problems.

Improved Carrier Services

By dealing directly with insurance carriers

9. Robert Gumbiner, "Selection of a Health Maintenance Organization," *Personnel Journal* (August, 1978): 444–45.

10. Robert McClay, "Professionalizing the Safety Function," *Personnel Journal* (February, 1977): 72–77.

11. K. Per Larson, "How Companies Can Rein in Their Health Care Costs," *The Personnel Administrator* (November, 1979): 29–33.

managers can provide more information, increase services, and lower costs by speeding up needed treatment and cost reimbursement to employees.

Studies have shown that if the health program receives top management interest and involvement, costs are reduced significantly and health care services are increased.[12] Organizations with more than one thousand employees have found the cost of self-insurance is cheaper than purchasing insurance from outside companies. This program eliminates the need for insurance middle men and costly claims processing. Typically employers only begin to realize such economies when they develop their own health and safety programs.[13]

Alcoholic Employees

One of society's most persistent and devastating ills, alcoholism often leads to severe marital problems, family abuse, estrangement between parents and children, the loss of close friends and acquaintances, emotional illness, and in general, a disenfranchisement by society. Statistics show that alcohol and other mood-altering substances increase violent crimes and traffic accidents that result in death. The societal burdens of alcoholism have long been of major concern to professionals in social work, medicine, and psychiatry.

In recent years, alcoholism received a great deal of attention from both management academics and personnel practitioners. Much of this interest has been created by the publication of data which show that (1) an alarming percentage of

American workers are classified as alcoholics, and (2) the alcoholic worker has many more work related problems than a nonalcoholic worker. How many workers are alcoholics? While the exact numbers are impossible to pin down, most informed sources, including the *National Council on Alcoholism (NCA)*, estimate about 10% of the labor force. Alcoholics are in business, government, the professions, sciences, voluntary agencies, and academia on all organizational levels. The National Institute on Alcohol Abuse and Alcoholism (NIAAA) estimates that 25 percent of alcoholic employees are white–collar, clerical employees; 30 percent are blue-collar workers; and 45 percent are managers and professionals.[14]

While some alcoholic employees perform their work satisfactorily and meet job expectations, a great many cannot. The NCA reports that alcoholic employees are absent an average of two to four times more often; that on-the-job accidents are two to four times more frequent for alcoholic employees.[15] In addition to these costly problems, alcoholic employees may create other work related difficulties:

- The alcoholic's negligence may cause accidents and injuries to other employees.

- The alcoholic may disregard job details, use poor judgment, and make bad decisions.

- The alcoholic may perform unevenly in terms of quantity and quality.

---

12. Robert McClay, p. 77.
13. K. Per Larson, pp. 30–32.

14. Christine A. Filipowicz, "The Troubled Employee: Whose Responsibility?" *The Personnel Administrator* (June 1979): 18.
15. Frank E. Kuzmits and Henry E. Hammons, II, "Rehabilitating the Troubled Employee," *Personnel Journal* (April 1979): 239.

• The alcoholic may minimize contact with co-workers and supervisors and exhibit antisocial behavior.

The alcoholic employee's performance, including above-average absenteeism, injuries, accidents, and subpar levels of productivity and quality, all represent very real costs to the organization. For large organizations, the costs can be staggering. The U.S. Postal Service estimates its losses in productivity from alcoholism at $186 million annually. United California Bank—California's fourth largest bank—estimates losing $1 million a year to alcoholism among its ten thousand employees.[16] Nationwide, $25 billion are lost annually due to alcoholics' absenteeism, accidents, sick leave, decreased productivity, and poor work quality. A full-scale attack on alcoholism can be justified not only for social and moral reasons but for economic considerations as well.

What causes alcoholism? There is little agreement about the specific causes of alcoholism. Predicting precisely who will or will not become an alcoholic is impossible. Alcoholism does not discriminate against any particular social or economic class; this disease is as likely to victimize the middle manager as it is the assembly line worker.

Nonetheless, researchers have isolated a mix of circumstances that greatly influence problem drinkers. The NCA suggests that the *problem drinker* is one who:

experiences intense relief and relaxation from alcohol;

has difficulty in dealing with and overcoming depression, anxiety, and frustration; and

is a member of a culture in which there is pressure to drink and culturally induced guilt and confusion regarding appropriate drinking behavior.

According to the NCA, when these persons encounter problems with their families, spouses, jobs, loneliness, old age, etc., their probability of becoming problem drinkers increases significantly.

Researchers also recognize the possibility that certain work conditions may lead to alcoholism. In a HEW report entitled *Work In America*, the author stated that:

> Nonsupportive jobs in which the worker gets little feedback on his performance appear to cause the kind of anxiety that may lead to or aggravate alcoholism. Work addiction, occupational obsolescence, role stress, and unstructured environments (for certain personality types) appear to be other important risk factors for both alcoholism and drug addiction.[17]

The HEW report's suggestion that organizations do have some control over whether an employee becomes a problem drinker is important. Decision makers are faced with a difficult choice involving moral and economic considerations. They may create an environment that produces satisfying human experiences and strengthens mental and physical health. Or, they may create an environment that leads to frustration, anxiety, and stress; one that compels a certain type of employee to seek relief through alcohol or, perhaps, other addictive chemicals. Faced with these alternatives, managers have a twofold responsibility: to create programs for employees suffering from alcoholism, and to create a work climate that minimizes the conditions and

---

16. Ibid.

17. Filipowicz, "The Troubled Employee," pp. 18–19.

FIGURE 15–8: *Alcoholics Anonymous's Checklist for Alcoholism*

One device used in some companies to help the alcoholic to appreciate the seriousness of his problem is to ask him to answer 20 questions relating to his drinking pattern. This test has been used, occasionally with modifications, in a number of industrial alcoholism programs.

The test:

		YES	NO
1.	Have you lost time from work due to drinking?	( )	( )
2.	Has drinking made your home-life unhappy?	( )	( )
3.	Do you drink because you are shy with people?	( )	( )
4.	Has drinking affected your reputation?	( )	( )
5.	Have you gotten into financial difficulties because of your drinking?	( )	( )
6.	Do you turn to lower companions and an inferior environment when drinking?	( )	( )
7.	Does your drinking make you careless of your family's welfare?	( )	( )
8.	Has your drinking decreased your ambition?	( )	( )
9.	Do you want a drink "the morning after"?	( )	( )
10.	Does your drinking cause you to have difficulty sleeping?	( )	( )
11.	Has your efficiency decreased since drinking?	( )	( )
12.	Has drinking ever jeopardized your job or business?	( )	( )
13.	Do you drink to escape from worries or troubles?	( )	( )
14.	Do you drink alone?	( )	( )
15.	Have you ever had a complete loss of memory as a result of drinking?	( )	( )
16.	Has your physician ever treated you for drinking?	( )	( )
17.	Do you drink to build up self-confidence?	( )	( )
18.	Have you ever been in an institution or hospital on account of drinking?	( )	( )
19.	Have you ever felt remorse after drinking?	( )	( )
20.	Do you crave a drink at a definite time daily?	( )	( )

When he takes the test, the employee is reminded that only he can determine whether or not he is an alcoholic. However, if the employee answers *yes* to as few as three questions, he can be reasonably certain that alcohol has become, or is becoming, a problem for him.

SOURCE: Alcoholics Anonymous, *A. A. and the Alcoholic Employee*, (New York: Alcoholics Anonymous World Services, Inc., 1962), pp. 12–13.

circumstances that pressure an employee to seek relief in excessive drink.

Unlike job attitudes or opinions, alcoholism cannot be measured through traditional personnel tools such as surveys or questionnaires. Because many alcoholics are unwilling to admit they have the problem, a general purpose questionnaire—even though anonymous—would not generate much useful data on alcoholism within the organization. Second, alcoholism can only be defined in the most general terms. For instance, the *American Heritage Dictionary* defines alcoholism as "a chronic pathological condition chiefly of the nervous and gastroenteric systems, caused by habitual excessive alcoholic consumption." In conducting research, it may be difficult to distinguish between heavy or excessive drinking, and the various stages of alcoholism. Third, employees may perceive alcoholism as a sensitive, personal issue. Many employees would no doubt feel that the collection of information about alcohol abuse is an invasion of their privacy.

Even though alcoholism may be difficult to measure quantitatively, persons may determine if they have the symptoms of the problem. Both the NCA and Alcoholics Anonymous (AA) have developed checklists to help individuals decide if they may need help in combating alcohol. Although a checklist is not useful for research purposes, it may be part of an organization's alcoholism education program given to employees who inquire about the organization's rehabilitation services. The Alcoholics Anonymous checklist is reproduced in Figure 15–8.

Because alcoholism is difficult to measure within an organizational setting, research will be limited. For example, it may be impossible to accurately analyze which employees have the highest rates of alcoholism, or what work conditions and environmental settings tend to aggravate the problem.

A researcher may be able to evaluate the organization's rehabilitation efforts with known alcoholic employees and determine how these employees behave differently. By analyzing the work histories of alcoholic employees, it should also be possible to discover how their absenteeism, accidents, injuries, productivity, and work quality differ from organization-wide norms. This information will help

call management's attention to the seriousness of the problem.

REDUCING ALCOHOLISM

Because employee alcoholism may stem from both personal and work factors, the most effective strategy for combating alcoholism is to minimize the potential of alcoholism by keeping stress and anxiety at the lowest possible levels. Secondly, rehabilitation programs for employees currently suffering from alcoholism should be implemented.

The first of these strategies may be the most difficult for the personnel administrator to implement and control. Challenge, stress, and conflict seem to be inevitable in the jobs of many modern managers and administrators. Further, the personnel administrator has only moderate control over the work climate and goal-setting process for employees outside of the personnel department. Nonetheless, the personnel staff can educate top and middle managers about the potentially harmful effects of excessive job stress and anxiety. Through training and development activities, the personnel staff can make executives aware that the way people are managed and how their jobs are designed may significantly affect their mental and physical health.

The second strategy to fight alcoholism—the implementation of rehabilitation policies and programs—has rapidly become an important personnel responsibility in many larger organizations today. While these programs have different titles, the most popular term is employee assistance program. A 1978 NIAAA report states that these programs rose from about fifty in 1950 to nearly twenty-four hundred in 1977, with about two thousand in the private sector and four hundred in

FIGURE 15–9: *Kemper's Policies on Employee Alcoholism*

Alcoholism Policy. In accordance with our general personnel policies, whose underlying concept is regard for the employee as an individual as well as a worker:

1. We believe alcoholism, or problem drinking, is an illness and should be treated as such.
2. We believe the majority of employees who develop alcoholism can be helped to recover and the company should offer appropriate assistance.
3. We believe the decision to seek diagnosis and accept treatment for any suspected illness is the responsibility of the employee. However, continued refusal of an employee to seek treatment when it appears that substandard performance may be caused by any illness is not tolerated. We believe that alcoholism should not be made an exception to this commonly accepted principle.
4. We believe that it is in the best interest of employees and the company that alcoholism be diagnosed and treated at the earliest possible stage.
5. We believe that the company's concern for individual drinking practices begins only when they result in unsatisfactory job performance.
6. We believe that confidential handling of the diagnosis and treatment of alcoholism is essential.

The objective of this policy is to retain employees who may develop alcoholism by helping them to arrest its further advance before the condition renders them unemployable.

Supervisory Practices. Supervisors are instructed that they should *not* attempt to identify alcoholic employees. Further, supervisors should not discuss "drinking problems" with their employees, except where drinking on the job or an intoxicated employee is observed (the diagnosis of alcoholism is the job of trained professionals). Rather, the supervisor's responsibility is to closely and accurately monitor employee *performance and work habits* and confront the employee whose performance problems persist with the warning that continued poor performance will lead to disciplinary action. . . .

Treatment facilities. Kemper, as do most companies which conduct employee assistance programs, uses a variety of alcoholism treatment sources. These include both private alcoholism consulting and treatment firms and not-for-profit organizations such as AA and Al-Anon, which provides support and assistance to the family members of an alcoholic.

SOURCE: *Management Guide on Alcoholism* (Long Grove, IL: Kemper Insurance Companies, undated), pp. 6–11. Used with permission.

the public sector.[18] As management and labor continue to accept employee rehabilitation efforts, such programs will, no doubt, continue to expand during the 1980s.

While the details may vary, most employee assistance programs contain the following elements:

---

18. This report is entitled "Summary of 3rd Report on Alcohol and Health" and is available from the National Clearinghouse for Alcohol Information, Department AH3, NCALI, Box 2345, Rockville, MD 20852.

Top level policy and procedural guidelines which define employee alcoholism as an illness and spell out the details for guiding the employee to treatment.

Training for supervisors regarding the employee assistance program focusing on the progressive nature of alcoholism and motivating employees to seek help.

The creation of channels to guide alcoholic employees to treatment and rehabilitation.

Kemper Insurance Companies, one of the first organizations to implement a formal employee assistance program, has outlined its approach toward employee rehabilitation in a pamphlet entitled *Management Guide on Alcoholism.*[19] Kemper's program is highlighted in Figure 15-9.

Do employee assistance programs work? The answer is a qualified *yes.* The majority of alcoholic employees fully recover as a result of rehabilitation efforts. The NCA reports that business and industry success rates range from 65 to 80 percent and that Air Force and Navy success rates are 70 to 80 percent. A NIAAA research study reported that "72 percent of executives of *Fortune* 500 companies with occupational programs believe their firms have saved money as a result of these programs, and most of the executives are convinced of the effectiveness of the program."[20]

One of the most widely reported company success stories involves Oldsmobile Motor Division's employee assistance program.[21] Oldsmobile's Employee Alcoholism Recovery Program involves a cooperative effort between General Motors and the United Auto Workers. The mechanics of the program are similar to the procedures outlined in Figure 15-10. A 1973 evaluation study showed that 117 program participants significantly reduced their absenteeism, accidents, grievances, and disciplinary actions during the year following their participation in the program. Preprogram costs due to lost wages were estimated at $84,616; lost wages were estimated at $43,336 after their involvement in the program. Oldsmobile reported that economic benefits of the program far exceeded the costs involved and termed the program both profitable and worthwhile.

In summary, most employers have assumed the responsibility to safeguard the health of their employees by providing safe, healthful working conditions, health insurance, and medical assistance for alcoholics. OSHA regulations require that employers keep injury and illness records. Administrators can monitor the safety of their workplaces by comparing their occupational injury and illness incident rates to similar employers in OSHA reports. The second aspect of an employee health program is health insurance. Under the Health Maintenance Organization Act of 1973, organizations with twenty-five or more employees must give them the alternative of joining a local HMO rather than signing up for health insurance. Many companies maintain in-house health and safety programs as an alternative to purchasing insurance from outside companies because such programs cost less and provide more health and safety benefits. Forward looking companies also offer assistance to alcoholic employees because they are physically ill and can be rehabilitated.

19. The Kemper Insurance Companies publish a number of excellent guidebooks on alcoholism and drug abuse. For information on obtaining these guides, write Public Relations, Kemper Insurance Companies, Long Grove, IL 60049.

20. NCALI, "Summary of 3rd Report on Alcohol and Health," p. 6.

21. Alander Ross and Thomas Campbell, "An Evaluation Study of an Alcohol and Drug Recovery Program - A Case Study of the Oldsmobile Experience," *Human Resource Management* (Spring 1975): 14-18.

The Solution

Unfortunately, some of the company's employees have more interest in safety than top management. A safety program can minimize costly repairs, inventory and equipment loss, and employees' injuries and illnesses. This case demonstrates why federal and state laws often require posting notices for employees. Most likely the management of this company would not have made such information available to its employees.

Joyce Ladd has a more immediate problem. She needs to carefully consider her options. First, she can resign. Since some of the top managers may always view her as a troublemaker, her future with the company does not look bright. Second, she can request that the state inspector confirm she was not the employee who wrote to the state. This may partially clear her, but some will accuse her of signing another name or asking another employee to send the letter. Third, she can refuse to resign and threaten legal action if she is fired or discriminated against in any manner. Most employee safety laws prohibit retaliation against employees who reveal safety or health violations.

KEY TERMS AND CONCEPTS

Safety Hazards
Health Hazards
Occupational Illness
Occupational Injury
OSHA
HMO
Problem Drinkers
Health Program Manager
NCA

Incidence Rate of Occupational
   Injuries and Illnesses
Log and Summary of Occupational
   Injuries and Illnesses
Supplementary Record of Occupational
   Injuries and Illnesses
NIOSH
Kemper *Management Guide on Alcoholism*

FOR REVIEW

1. What actions should an employer take to comply with OSHA?
2. What have been some of the problems employers have had with OSHA?
3. Why must employers be interested in HMOs?
4. Why are there not more HMOs?
5. When is the problem drinker "cured"?
6. What are typical work related dilemmas the alcoholic must face?

FOR DISCUSSION

1. Today an increasing number of employees are turning to a variety of mood altering substances to help them through each day. In most instances, union workers can be dismissed for drinking or taking drugs on the job. If your nonunion company has a pleasant nonstressful environment, would it be justified in dismissing alcoholic employees or potheads, rather than wasting money on rehabilitation?
2. If OSHA took over the administration of the Indianapolis 500, what changes would take place?
3. Why are so many employees suffering from occupational illnesses which have become traditional in certain industries for many years?
4. Government officials frequently waver in their enforcement of OSHA. What influences have caused government officials to relax safety rules at times and to create more stringent regulations at others?
5. If supervisors warn their employees about the possible health hazards connected with their jobs and supply safety equipment to the employees, is the company responsible if employees do not use the safety equipment?

SUPPLEMENTARY READING

Ashford, Nicholas A. *Crises in the Workplace: Occupational Disease and Injury, A Report to the Ford Foundation.* Cambridge, MA: MIT Press, 1976.

Blake, Roland P. *Industrial Safety.* Englewood Cliffs, NJ: Prentice-Hall, Inc., 1963.

Carvey, Davis W., and Nibler, Roger G. "Biorhythmic Cycles and Incidence of Industrial Accidents." *Personnel Psychology* 30 (Autumn 1977): 447–54.

Corn, Morton. "An Inside View of OSHA Compliance." *The Personnel Administrator* 24 (November 1979): 39–42.

Foulkes, Fred K. "Learning to Live with OSHA." *Harvard Business Review* 51 (November-December 1973): 57–67.

Gardner, James. "Employee Safety." In Famularo, Joseph J., ed., *Handbook of Modern Personnel Administration.* New York: McGraw-Hill, 1972, Chapter 48.

Stead, W. E., and Stead, J. G. "Cancer in the Workplace: A Neglected Problem." *Personnel Journal* 58 (October 1980): 847–49.

For Analysis: Family Health Insurance

Laura Gains is a confused employee. Washington Electric Company, her employer, is offering a local HMO as an alternative to the company's health insurance plan. Gains attended the employees' meeting where an HMO official explained the medical services and costs. The official outlined many services such as dental checkups and flu shots which would be provided at little cost. Gains knows she spends over $200 a year in these areas alone. The HMO is located about two miles from Gains' home and is always open——something Gains thinks would add to her usage of the services. The company will provide the same dollars for HMO as it currently does for the employees' health insurance plan. Gains, however, is bothered by the lack of choice of physicians and dentists, although she is not really attached to the ones she is going to now. During this month Gains must decide whether to change to the HMO for at least a year or else wait until next year during the sign-up period.

A widow, Gains is the sole support of her three daughters, Shari, age 9; Mary, age 7; and Tracy, age 4. In the past her annual medical expenses often exceeded $3,000. While the company's health insurance plan does not cover most of her medical expenses, the HMO would cover most of her expenses; however, it would cost Gains $60 per month more in premiums. Gains' salary is about $35,000 per year. She prepares her own tax forms and always itemizes deductions.

Questions:

1. How should Gains compare the plans? What quantitative criteria should be considered?

2. Exactly what is the purpose of family health care insurance?

3. What additional information would help Gains?

The Industrial Workers of the World meet at their union hall in Arlington, Washington, in 1917.

16

LABOR UNIONS

Major Events in the Labor Movement

Labor-management Legislation

Union Structure and Management

Organizing Drive

Preventive Labor Relations

The Problem: Riverside Packing Company

Phillip Burns, personnel manager for Riverside Packing, stormed unannounced into President Art Floran's office. Floran looked up at his shaking, agitated personnel manager.

Floran: "What's the matter, Phil? You look like you've just seen a ghost."

Burns: "Worse than that, Art. I just got a letter from the Meatcutters' Union telling us they intend to begin an organizing drive here next week. Boy, that's just what we need around here——a union!"

Floran: "Are you sure its legit, Phil? You know, we've heard that union stuff from the blue collars for a long time now. Could be they're just bluffing. Let me see that letter. . . . Hmm. Could be trouble. We've been nonunion for sixty years and we are not changing now——not while I'm running this show. What's their problem, anyway?"

Burns: "Same old stuff, Art. Wages, benefits, safety, unfair treatment from supervisors, job security, and so on. They claim we're not competitive on salary and benefits and say they're tired of getting raw deals from supervisors. I have to admit that we've been dragging our feet on wages and benefits. But that can be blamed on decisions by the finance committee, not me. As far as supervision goes . . . well . . . maybe we don't have the world's greatest supervisors. I know they have a tendency to play favorites and can really make it tough on employees they don't like. Art, we may have to give in to a few concessions if we want to keep the Meatcutters out of here."

Floran: "You're probably right, Phil, but we won't give 'em

*much. Throw 'em a few bones to keep them quiet for a
while. Promise a 6 percent pay increase if they stop this
union nonsense. And tell them you'll review the benefits
package and beef it up a little. Let them know that one
good turn deserves another, and we'll wash their backs if
they'll wash ours. And I'll have a general meeting next
week with the whole bunch. I'll let them know a union will
do them absolutely no good whatsoever and that they'll be
cutting their own throats if they vote the Meatcutters in.
We've got to take the gloves off, Phil, and show them
who's boss around here."*

Two medium-sized distilleries are about three miles apart in Bardstown, Kentucky. Uncle John's Company employs 920 persons; the Jim Shaft Company 1,100 employees. Uncle John's is unionized, Shaft is not. In Uncle John's Company, the majority of the work conditions are largely defined by a legal contract signed by management and the Distillery, Wine, and Allied Workers' International Union. The three-year contract specifies how much workers will be paid; the number of holidays they will take; how much sick leave they receive; how promotions, transfers, layoffs, and discharges will be made; the maximum speed of the assembly line (in no event shall bottling line speeds exceed 300 quarts per minute and 320 pints per minute) and the length of workers' rest periods and numerous other details of working conditions.

Of course, the workers in the Jim Shaft Company also get paid; take vacations and sick leave; get promoted, transferred, laid off, and discharged; work on an assembly line that runs at a certain speed; and take rest periods. At Shaft Company, however, the rights and conditions of employment were defined solely by management without the involvement of a labor union. Management may change the conditions of employment unilaterally: raising or lowering wages, promoting or transferring whomever it wishes, altering assembly line speed, or change vacation policies.

Which company is most profitable? Best managed? Has the best products? Which company has the happiest and most satisfied employees? While there are many who would debate these questions, the truth is that *we don't know.* Profitability, the quality of management, products and services, and employee welfare cannot be accurately judged on a union or nonunion basis. In addition to union status, many forces and influences affect the extent to which personal and organizational goals are met. But one fact cannot be disputed: the presence of the union has significant implications on organization structure and management. For lower level employees, personnel procedures and policies are largely shaped by the written agreement between management and the union. The personnel administrator's job in a unionized firm will be markedly different from a nonunion counterpart.

Our brief introductory story about the two distilleries provides some clues about why the study of unions is important for any student of personnel management. Initially, the terms *union* and *collective bargaining* should be defined. A labor or trade union is an organization of workers formed to further the social and economic interests of its members. Collective bargaining is negotiation in good faith between the employer and union with respect to wages, benefits, other terms and conditions of employment, which results in a written contract which details the agreement they reach.

IMPACT ON MANAGEMENT

Unions hold an extraordinary source of power and influence over managerial practices, worker behavior, and the basic conditions of employment. Unionization results in a significant erosion of managerial decision-making authority to control employees. This reduction is particularly evident for first level supervisors who interact with employees on a day-to-day basis. Many important personnel decisions must conform to the letter of the labor-management contract. To illustrate a common example, a supervisor desiring to promote a high-performing employee to a more challenging job may find the contract specifies that seniority is the major criterion for making promotion decisions. As a result, a less qualified employee may be promoted to a higher paying job.

The struggle for authority is intensified because managers are ultimately responsible for the success or failure of the organization—not the union. For this reason, many managers testify the union forces them to violate the basic organizational principle which states that "authority should be commensurate with responsibility."[1] Because they are ultimately accountable, managers believe that they should retain the power and authority to make the major decisions that affect employee welfare and the success of the organization.

The labor contract between management and the union typically covers two or three years. Locked into many terms and conditions of employment for a long time, management and the union are unable to bargain for desired changes until the existing contract is about to expire. While provisions exist for negotiating changes in certain items while the contract is in force, the union would strongly resist management's attempt to take something away from the workers. For example, management may feel that the existing sick leave provision is too liberal and causing high absenteeism. The union, however, would surely oppose any attempt to alter the contract and cut back the sick days that workers could take.

History has recorded many lengthy, bitter conflicts between labor and management. Labor riots have resulted in the death of many hundreds of workers and injury for thousands more. The factories

1. See Harold Koontz, Cyril O'Donnel, and Heinz Weihrich, *Management* (New York: McGraw-Hill Book Co., 1980), p. 482.

and plants silenced by strikes have caused much financial suffering by management and labor alike. Since the first labor strike almost two hundred years ago, work stoppages have cost public and private organizations untold millions of dollars and have resulted in the loss of wages for great masses of workers in a wide variety of industries.

Even though a union has not struck an employer, the delicate and cautious relationships of many labor-management alliances produce daily stress and strain for both workers and lower-level supervisors. Constant agitation between labor and management often leads to a working climate that fosters high turnover and absenteeism, and low employee morale and productivity. This is not to suggest that cooperative, conflict-free labor–management partnerships are absent from industrial society. Many organizations have enjoyed strike free, harmonious labor-management relations for decades. But the possibility of labor–management conflict should be of major concern to future managers and personnel administrators who will bear an important responsibility for creating and maintaining peace between labor and management.

UNION HISTORY

The history of the labor movement is rich with tales of gallantry, risk, daring, success, despair, and failure. The movement has been peaceful and violent, law-abiding and lawless, spectacular and mundane. Many of the memoirs of the men who founded and strengthened the labor sector are profiles of ability, courage, power, and sometimes ruthlessness.

Some view the labor movement as a series of stories about great men who possessed uncanny skills to motivate and organize great masses of workers. Others see it as an inevitable outgrowth of corporate leadership's inability to create fair, safe, and rewarding environments for workers. The movement may also be studied from a political perspective. Doomsayers suggest that unions smack of communism and that sustained union growth will signal an end to the capitalistic system. Indeed, eleven unions were expelled from the Congress of Industrial Organization in 1949 and 1950 for following the program of the Communist party.[2] A complex and important part of American history, the labor movement has resulted from an array of social, political, and economic forces; individual leadership and organization skills; and an unpredictable chain of circumstances and events.

Early Unions

The labor union is not a new phenomenon on the American business scene. One of the first unions—the Federal Society of Journeymen Cordwainers (shoemakers)—was organized in Philadelphia in 1794. Boston carpenters organized in 1793 and New York printers in 1794. Early unions were comprised of craftsmen—workers who performed a single skill or occupation—such as shoemakers, tailors, and weavers.

The growth and development of the American economy fostered the emergence of craft unions. As new communities sprang up and markets developed, capitalists enlarged their operations and

---

2. Marten Estey, *The Unions* (New York: Harcourt, Brace & World, Inc., 1967), p. 28.

sought competitive edges by, among other tactics, lowering labor costs. By organizing, craftsmen bonded together and agreed that none would work for less than a specified wage. Many craft unions also sought a closed shop agreement, whereby only union members would be hired.

Early craft unions bore little resemblance to today's sophisticated, business–like unions. Typically, early unions would strike for "all or nothing"—the spirit of negotiation and compromise did not develop until the late 1800s; yet, craft unions were surprisingly successful. Strikes were generally brief and relatively peaceful, and many managers preferred to relent to union demands rather than suffer economic misfortune and lose their competitive edge in the marketplace.

Craft unions' successes were closely tied to the ebb and flow of the economy; a recession or depression spelled doom for many organized labor groups. Many of the gains in union membership during the early 1800s were wiped out during a major depression in 1819, and many—if not most—of the unions formed during a major expansionary period in the mid 1830s disappeared during the panic of 1837.

National Unions

In pre-Civil War years, unions were independently organized and managed. While their aims were similar—for example, job security, more pay, and improved working conditions—each operated as an autonomous unit. They were not affiliated with a labor federation (a league or association of several unions) such as the AFL–CIO today.

National Labor Union (NLU)

In 1866 the National Labor Union was organized to serve the common interest of laborers in different trades and occupations. Formed by Iron Molders Union President William Sylvis, the NLU represented the first serious attempt to bring all craft and reform unions into a single national organization. Because the NLU put long-term political goals (woman suffrage and abolition of the convict labor system) ahead of short-term wage-and–hour objectives, the union passed from the scene in 1872.

Knights of Labor

A second national, the Noble and Holy Order of the *Knights of Labor,* met with greater success. Led by Uriah Stevens, in 1869 nine Philadelphia garment makers formed the Knights as a secret society, which emerged as a national federation in 1878. The Knights' broad goal was "to initiate good men of all callings" and organize both craftsmen and unskilled workers. The Knights were not totally void of discrimination in their organizing efforts—they wanted "no drones, no lawyers, no bankers, no doctors, no professional politicians."[3] They also excluded prostitutes and representatives from the alcoholic beverage and tobacco industries!

The Knights enjoyed a steady growth amid general economic prosperity and aggressive membership drives. Participation grew from about nine thousand in 1878 to over seventy thousand in 1884. A dramatic and successful strike against

3. Arthur Sloan and Fred Whitney, *Labor Relations* (Englewood Cliffs, NJ: Prentice-Hall, Inc., 1972) p. 56.

business titan Jay Gould's Wabash Railroad in 1885 brought over six hundred thousand members to the Knights in a single year. The Knights' public status and prestige rose as spectacularly as its membership; the country watched David bring Goliath to his knees.

The Knights' meteoric rise reached its apex in 1886 and things went rapidly downhill. In 1890 membership shrank to two hundred twenty thousand and by 1900 the Knights were virtually extinct. Why the sudden plunge? Two prime factors led to the Knights' demise: First, the Haymarket Riot in which several people were killed and scores were injured resulted in strong national antilabor sentiment. Although the Knights were not directly involved, they suffered greatly from negative attitudes toward organized labor that resulted from the riot. Perhaps the greatest blow to the Knights came from within; Knights' leadership sought utopian, social goals—the establishment of consumer cooperatives, temperance, and land reform. The rank and file, however, sought more practical objectives—higher wages, better working conditions, and shorter hours. Such major philosophical differences, in addition to other internal conflicts, brought considerable disorganization and ultimately extinction to the Knights in the 1890s.

American Federation of Labor (AFL)

The fall of the Knights of Labor coincided with the rise of a national labor organization that still survives today: the American Federation of Labor. The AFL began as a federation of craft unions comprised of skilled workers only. The creation and subsequent success of the AFL was due, in part, to the craft unions' dissatisfaction with the Knights' failure to give proper attention to their special needs. Too, the craft union members were adverse to the Knights' attempt to organize anybody and everybody and mix skilled and unskilled workers under one roof. The AFL's founder and skilled leader, Samuel Gompers, was the former leader of the Cigar Makers Union; he saw to it that the AFL was built around the particular needs, practices, philosophies, and goals of craft unions.

The AFL is generally credited with introducing the concept of business unionism to union management and leadership. This term conveys that the union is more concerned with bread and butter issues than broad social goals and that it is business-like in its operations and dealings—much like unions today. Underscoring the AFL's business unionism approach were two basic policies:

1. National unions belonging to the AFL were granted "trade autonomy"—each union was given the ultimate authority to make decisions for themselves. This decentralization of authority particularly affected collective bargaining functions.

2. Each union was given "exclusive jurisdiction" over that particular craft or trade. If, for example, a tailor's union became part of the AFL, it was given the sole right to do "tailor's work" and was thus protected from competition from other AFL unions. Each union had, in effect, its own monopoly.

Under Gomper's able leadership, the AFL doubled from 140,000 members in 1886 to 280,000 by the turn of the century. Perhaps more noteworthy than impressive membership gains was the fact that the economic depression between 1893 and 1896 had only a minor impact on union membership. One of Gomper's goals was to strengthen the staying-power of the union during adverse economic times. A chief means for providing stability to the local union was to ensure that sufficient monies were available to fund authorized strikes at the local level.

The AFL's dramatic growth continued through the early years of the twentieth century. By 1904, the AFL had 120 affiliated unions—about 85 percent of all national unions in the United States. After 1904, membership gains were less dramatic but the union continued to grow, suffering only temporary setbacks during severe economic declines. At the time of the merger with the CIO in 1955, membership totalled 10.5 million.

Industrial Workers of the World (IWW)

While the AFL was primarily concerned with craft unionism, the IWW was moderately successful in organizing unskilled workers around the turn of the century. Founded by socialist union leaders Eugene Debs and "Big Bill" Haywood in 1905, the IWW was an odd collection of miners, loggers, barbers, socialists, and AFL dissidents, among others.

Primary among IWW goals was abolishment of the wage system. According to IWW leadership, the wage system, whereby workers received daily wages, represented a form of slavery in which workers were forced to sell themselves to capitalists. The capitalist, in turn, sold labor's product for a profit, and kept the profit. The IWW sought a return to earlier craft-type payment systems whereby workers received a price for the product they produced, not for the time they labored at a task. The IWW's communist leanings were evident in its proposed destruction of the free enterprise system, advocation of a genuine labor party, and proposed militant action against recalcitrant employers.[4]

The IWW scored significant victories in organizing western miners and lumber employees and East Coast textile workers. As many as seventy thousand workers claimed IWW membership by 1912. But the beginning of World War I marked the swift downfall of the IWW. The union so bitterly opposed the U.S.'s entrance into the war that they declined to fight because they believed only capitalists would benefit from the war effort. Thus, IWW lost all public support. When the federal government began convicting IWW leaders for sedition, the IWW faded into obscurity.

Congress of Industrial Organizations (CIO)

Beginning with the AFL in 1886, the craft union prevailed as the principal union model for a half-century. In 1935, however, the craft union's dominance of organized labor was challenged by the emergence of the *Congress of Industrial Organizations*. The CIO was briefly called the Committee for Industrial Organizations in its beginning.

A colorful, pugnacious event during the 1935 AFL convention launched the beginning of the CIO. When a delegate raised a question about industrial unionism, 6 foot, 220 pound "Big Bill" Hutcheson, president of the Carpenters' Union and

---

4. Ibid., p. 65.

staunch supporter of the craft union forces, raised a point of order, stating that the issue of industrial unionism had already been settled. John L. Lewis, president of the United Mine Workers and leader of the proindustrial camp within the AFL, strongly dissented, stating "this thing of raising points of order all the time on minor delegates is rather small potatoes." To which Hutcheson replied, "I was raised on small potatoes, that's why I'm so small." As Lewis retorted, "Well, then, it's about time you were mashed," he swung at Hutcheson and the two grappled on the floor.[5] In November of 1935 Lewis and seven industrial union presidents split from the AFL to form the CIO.

The CIO union model was markedly different from the AFL craft model. Whereas craft unions were organized into skilled occupations, the CIO represented industrial unionism whereby membership was based upon employment in a particular industry such as automobile, steel, or clothing.

A half-dozen years after its creation, the CIO scored spectacular successes by organizing the largest firms in the auto and steel industries. The United Auto Workers (UAW) switched its affiliation from the AFL to the CIO in 1936. A year later, major organizing campaigns were successful in the electrical, radio, clothing, textile, rubber, meat packing, and petroleum industries.

Under the organizing genius of John L. Lewis, the CIO continued to grow, reaching a peak of almost 5 million members in 1953. The CIO's rapid growth was due to several factors: Lewis's entrepreneurial skills, heightened economic activity due

5. Estey, *The Unions*, p. 28.

to World War II and the Korean War, the country's shift from an agricultural to a manufacturing economy, and the passage of the prolabor Wagner Act.

AFL-CIO Merger

After a twenty-year separation, the AFL and CIO united in December of 1955 into a single federation called the American Federation of Labor and Congress of Industrial Organizations (AFL-CIO). The union claimed a total membership of 16.1 million workers: 10.9 million members from 108 AFL unions and 5.2 million members from 30 CIO unions.

Why did the AFL and CIO merge? The following reasons are often cited for the reconciliation:

The passage of the promanagement Taft–Hartley Act in 1947 signaled a beginning of antilabor sentiments and the potential for further antilabor legislation. Combined forces were believed to be more effective in curtailing such legislation than a divided attack.

The merger brought a halt to the problem of raiding in which one union pirated members from the other. The signing of a no-raiding agreement in 1953 signaled the first step toward a merger.

Housecleaning by each union created new mutual respect. The CIO rid itself of eleven communist front unions in 1949 and 1950 and the AFL expelled the racket–ridden International Longshoremen's Union in 1953.

A change in top leadership in the AFL and CIO led to amiable relations between the unions. When the presidents of both unions died in 1952, George Meany and Walter Reuther assumed the presidencies of the AFL and CIO, respectively. Almost immediately Meany and Reuther embarked on a series of negotiations to bring the unions together.

Meany became president of the merged federation and reiterated labor's commitment to their traditional goals: greater job security, improved economic rewards, and increased employee benefits through aggressive collective bargaining. In terms of membership, however, the AFL-CIO did not become a more powerful force. While many labor observers believed the new federation would grow by leaps and bounds, membership has actually changed little throughout its history. The federation counted 16.1 million members in 1955; in 1977 the figure rose only slightly to 16.6 million.

Several factors are responsible for the federation's membership trend. For one, 1.5 million workers were lost when the Teamsters Union was expelled in 1957 for failure to oust president Jimmy Hoffa. Hoffa and many other union figures were castigated by Senator John McClellan's Select Committee on Improper Activities in the Labor or Management Field and proved to be a great embarrassment to

FIGURE 16–1: *Union Membership in the Nonagricultural Labor Force*[1]

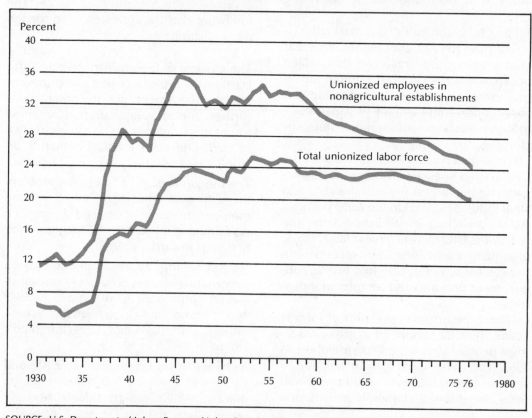

SOURCE: U.S. Department of Labor, Bureau of Labor Statistics, *Directory of National Unions and Employee Associations, 1977*, Bulletin No. 2044 (Washington, D.C.: Government Printing Office, 1979), p. 63.

the AFL-CIO. Two, the UAW, suffering serious conflicts with the federation leadership, refused to pay dues in 1968 and was expelled. The UAW's departure shrank the AFL-CIO's membership roles by 1.4 million. (In 1981 the UAW voted to rejoin the AFL-CIO.) A third critical factor dealt with the changing makeup of American industry. The economy was no longer ruled by heavy industry. Unskilled and semiskilled workers were declining as a percentage of the total labor force, while significant increases were being recorded by professional, technical, and administrative personnel.

Contemporary Trends

The overall trend in union membership, illustrated in Figure 16–1, reflects a current dilemma for union leaders today: a gradual decline in union membership as a percentage of the total labor force. Although the organized workers increased from 14.2 million in 1950 to 21 million in 1976, the percentage of union members has dropped from 22.3 percent of the labor force in 1950 to 20.1 percent in 1976. These stagnating membership figures have, to some extent, been caused by a shift from an industrial to a service oriented economy. Not all unions have suffered a membership slump; public sector and professional employee groups have seen significant gains in union membership in recent years.

PUBLIC SECTOR

While the organization of public employees is not new, recent presidential orders and legislative acts have enabled public sector unions to enjoy significant gains in the last two decades. John F. Kennedy's Executive Order 10988, "Employee Man-

agement Cooperation in the United States," required federal agencies to recognize unions that represented a majority of employees as determined by a vote. Executive Order 10988 was later amended and strengthened by Richard M. Nixon's Executive Order 11491. Nixon's action created a federal labor relations council to administer the order and to improve methods for conducting collective bargaining. As a result of these acts and state legislation, total union membership in federal, state, and local governments has increased from 915,000 in 1956 to over 5.3 million by 1974.

Organized public employees are concentrated in a few key unions. The American Federation of Government Employees (AFGE) reported 260,000 members in 1977. The American Federation of State, County, and Municipal Employees (AFSCME) is one of the AFL-CIO's fastest growing unions and counted 957,000 members in 1976. The American Federation of Teachers (AFT) increased its membership roles from 125,000 in 1966 to 446,000 in 1976.

WHITE-COLLAR GROUPS

Until recent times, the labor movement has been, by and large, a blue-collar phenomenon. White-collar workers and professionals shunned the prospect of organizing, feeling that union membership was beneath their status and dignity. They believed that gains in salaries and other areas of employment could be best achieved through their professional associations and lobbying efforts. This philosophy changed considerably in the past twenty years as white-collar and professional groups watched their salaries and benefits stagnate, while handsome gains were achieved by trade unions. In current times, doctors, professors, engineers, nurses, and professional athletes are taking part in collective bargaining.

UNION GOALS

The goals of unions have not changed significantly in almost two hundred years. In a broad sense, the primary goal of any union is to promote the interests of its membership. Through collective bargaining and lobbying for labor legislation, union leaders advance their members' standard of living and improve many conditions that surround their work.

The second broad goal that has long been an important part of the labor movement is the advancement of social goals as a whole. The pursuit of social aims has been a controversial part of the union philosophy, particularly among the rank and file who generally have preferred that union monies and energies be devoted exclusively to advancing their own welfare. In recent years, armed with the increasing support of their constituency, many unions have strongly supported critically needed changes in the way society functions; the betterment of society constitutes an important part of organized labor's philosophy today.

Union Security

Union security, or the ability to grow and prosper in either good or poor economic times, is organized labor's foremost goal. With the exception of the closed shop, labor legislation has fostered the following union security provisions that organized labor may collectively bargain for:

1. *The Union Shop.* All new employees must join the union within a specified time—usually thirty days. About twenty states have passed right-to-work laws which prohibit the union shop.

2. *Agency Shop.* Nonunion employees must pay union dues, but are not required to join the union.

3. *Maintenance-of-membership Shop.* Employees are not required to join the union. However, employees who do join must remain in the union until the contract expires or until a designated "escape" period occurs.

4. *Closed Shop.* In a closed shop, the new employee must be a union member at the time of hiring. While a closed shop is illegal, the closed shop exists in practice, particularly in the construction and printing industries. The practice is promoted through customer hiring, through the union's own placement services, and management's desire to avoid the trouble that may accompany the hiring of nonunion employees. In contrast to the closed shop is the *open shop* where employees are free to decide whether or not to join the union.

5. *Sole Bargaining Unit.* The union represents and bargains for all employees in a bargaining unit whether they are union members or not.

Job Security

Job security constitutes one of the union's primary goals. Without jobs, union goals of higher wages and greater benefits are meaningless. Unions promote job security primarily through restricting the labor supply, controlling output, and make-work projects. Aggressive attempts to restrict the labor supply to existing union members is particularly common in the building trades. One strategy involves limiting the enrollment in union–sponsored apprentice training programs. A second is to influence city codes so that only licensed craftsmen are permitted to perform certain types of work.

Control Worker Output

Union leaders have long feared that technological advancements and certain management practices would displace unskilled and semiskilled employees. At the turn of the century, union leaders strongly resisted Frederick Taylor's principles of scientific management whereby time and motion studies scientifically determined a fair day's work and replaced haphazard, rule of thumb job design methods.[6] They felt that mass implementation of Taylor's methods would result in widespread unemployment and reduce union membership. While scientific management failed to become the nemesis of organized labor, management attempts to mechanize or utilize other efficiency techniques are viewed with a jaundiced eye by organized labor today. In manufacturing situations, union members on job standards committees may apply pressure to create loose job standards; unions may also resist technological advancements such as mechanized high speed assembly lines or industrial robots.

Make-Work Activities

While it is illegal to require employers to pay for services not rendered (this is termed *featherbedding*), unions legally

6. See Koontz, *Management,* pp. 39–43.

FIGURE 16–2: *Make-Work Activities*

- Electrical workers performing unnecessary rewiring on apparatus purchased from another manufacturer
- Painters requiring paint brushes to be limited in width and rollers banned unless there is premium pay
- Compositors performing unnecessary resetting of advertisements run in another paper
- Plasterers requiring three coats of plaster when the building code requires only two
- Operating engineers employed to merely push buttons or turn switches
- More brakemen riding trains in some states (the number written into law) than in others
- Unnecessary stagehands in theaters
- Dock workers refusing to use pallets that would increase loading and unloading efficiency
- Meatcutters refusing to handle precut and prepackaged meats
- Union electricians required to replace light bulbs
- Airline employees who can unload baggage, and some who can unload cargo, but not both
- Thirteen separate crafts required to install bathrooms in a hotel or apartment house in New York City

SOURCE: Wendell L. French, *The Personnel Management Process* (Boston, MA: Houghton Mifflin Company, 1978), p. 478. French's sources are listed on page 478 of this book.

bargain for work rules or conditions that are actually unnecessary to produce a product or service. Examples of make–work activities are given in Figure 16–2.

Many union officials have no desire to engage in the make-work activities, preferring to cooperate with management on productivity and efficiency issues. In these cases, union leaders recognize that increased organizational productivity and worker output, in the long run, benefit both the employer and employee group. Many labor leaders have voiced strong support for technological changes designed to improve the nation's standard of living, to help industries deal more effectively with foreign competition, and to strengthen job security. Yet, some local union officials still oppose technological change for fear of worker displacement. In the future, labor and management must work more closely to determine how technological change may be implemented with minimal impact on employees.

Improved Compensation

Economic issues have been a central concern to unions since the beginning of organized labor. Particularly in the industrial sector, demands for higher wages are almost certain to be presented during labor-management contract negotiations. Following World War II, primarily because of government-imposed wage controls, unions struck for, and received, liberal benefits packages, including insurance, pensions, and paid holidays and vacations.

A relatively new type of wage system that several unions have successfully bargained for is the cost of living adjustment (COLA). In COLA plans, cost of living increases are normally tied to Bureau of Labor Statistics indices. Unions representing auto workers, steel workers, and U.S. Postal Service employees have successfully negotiated COLA plans; cost of living increases have also been applied to pension plans. Some workers, such as certain postal employees, enjoy retirement incomes much larger than their working incomes.

Working Conditions

Improvements in working conditions have been important union concerns in recent years. Unions have successfully bargained for better safety equipment; shorter workweeks; less mandatory overtime; and longer breaks, lunch periods, and cleanup time.

Fairness and Justice

Underscoring union philosophy is the fair and equal treatment of all employees. Without the protection of organized labor, union leaders claim that management will show favoritism by providing or withholding privileges and benefits to certain workers. Unions minimize the potential for favoritism and unequal treatment by insisting that major personnel decisions such as in-grade wage increases, job promotions, transfers, layoffs, and other job actions, be made according to seniority. While the seniority criterion can be criticized because the most effective employee may not receive a promotion or may be the first to be laid off, it does constitute an impartial and objective way to make important personnel decisions.

Social Action

Today many unions are advocating goals that affect society as a whole. These goals are not achieved through the normal collective bargaining process, but by lobbying for federal and state legislation and government-sponsored programs and policies. As the major voice for the labor

FIGURE 16–3: *AFL-CIO Social, Political, And Economic Goals*

AN ECONOMY THAT WORKS . . . BY
- increasing employment opportunities
- reducing inflation
- rebuilding the nation's cities
- providing adequate housing
- alleviating hardships caused by unemployment
- achieving energy independence
- encouraging competition
- strengthening the U.S. trade position
- assuring social justice
- strengthening rural areas

PROTECTING THOSE WHO WORK . . . BY
- strengthening the unemployment insurance program
- improving workers' compensation
- improving pension protection
- making the workplace safer
- strengthening fair labor standards
- improving labor laws
- protecting worker privacy
- protecting workers from sudden plant closings
- protecting federal workers
- protecting state and local government employees
- improving immigration laws

CIVIL RIGHTS . . . THROUGH
- strong enforcement of equal employment laws
- ratification of the Equal Rights Amendment
- eliminating discrimination against the handicapped
- strengthening fair housing laws

MAKING SOCIAL PROGRAMS WORK . . . BY
- improving Social Security programs
- improving health programs
- reforming the welfare system
- improving social services
- educating the young and old
- feeding the hungry

A GOVERNMENT THAT WORKS . . . BY
- making the representative processes more representative
- insuring the proper funding of government
- improving the regulatory process
- protecting consumers
- improving communications and promoting the arts
- improving the state and local governments
- improving the Postal Service

WORKING FOR PEACE AND FREEDOM . . . THROUGH
- the promotion and protection of human rights
- defense and disarmament
- coordinated defense policies with Western Europe
- trade limits with the USSR
- closer economic ties with Asian countries
- protecting U.S. and allied interests in the Persian Gulf
- closer political and economic ties with Latin American countries
- pressuring for social justice in South Africa
- encouraging a peaceful solution in the Middle East
- playing a more active role in international institutions such as the United Nations
- the use of foreign aid to advance world peace, stability, and humanitarianism

SOURCE: *The AFL-CIO Platform Proposals Presented to the Democratic and Republican National Conventions 1980* (Washington, D.C.: AFL-CIO, undated).

sector, the AFL-CIO takes a firm stand on social, political, and economic goals. These goals and AFL-CIO strategies for accomplishing them are outlined in Figure 16–3.

LABOR MANAGEMENT ▬▬ LEGISLATION ▬▬

Beginning in the early 1930s, labor–management relations have been heavily regulated by federal and state labor legislation. Prior to this period, lawmakers took a laissez-faire attitude toward unions and management and relied primarily on common law to govern labor-management relations. Common law, a product of the English legal system, is the system of law based on court decisions. In contrast, *statute law* is the system of laws established by legislative acts. Migration from the farm to the factory during the early 1900s created an urban, industrialized society; Congress reacted to public opinion and the special needs of labor and management by enacting formal written statutes. Important labor-management statutes are briefly described:[7]

Railway Labor Act (1926)

The *Railway Labor Act* in 1926 gave railroad workers the right to organize and bargain collectively and prohibited interference by employers.

Norris-LaGuardia Act (1932)

Throughout organized labor's early history, union power was often undercut by

---

7. For a detailed treatment of labor legislation, see Bruce Feldacker, *Labor Guide to Labor Law* (Reston, VA: Reston Publishing Co., 1980).

injunctions, which are court orders requiring performance or restraint of a particular act. Management frequently obtained a temporary or permanent injunction prohibiting a strike or picketing. However, the *Norris-LaGuardia Act* expressly forbid the federal courts to issue injunctions in labor disputes, except when in strict conformity of the act. The act also forbade employers from enforcing the yellow dog contract which stipulated—as a condition of employment—that an employee was not a union member and would not join a union. (Labor believed only a "yellow dog" would accept a job under such terms.)

National Labor Relations Act (1935)

The National Labor Relations Act—more popularly known as the *Wagner Act* because it was sponsored by New York's Senator Robert Wagner—is often called the Magna Charta of organized labor. In essence, the act protects a worker's right to join a union without the employer's interference. Bringing broad powers and sweeping reform to the labor movement, the act encouraged the movement's spectacular growth between 1935 and the early 1950s. Key provisions of the act include:

● The employer may not interfere with, restrain, or coerce employees in the exercise of their right to join unions and bargain collectively through representatives of their own choosing.

● The employer may not dominate or interfere with the formation or administration of labor unions.

● The employer may not discriminate against the employee in any condition of employment for taking part in legal union activities.

- The employer may not fire or discriminate against the employee for charging an unfair labor practice against the company.

- The employer may not refuse to bargain collectively with employee representatives in good faith.

NATIONAL LABOR RELATIONS BOARD
(NLRB)

The NLRB was created to administer and enforce the Wagner Act. The *National Labor Relations Board* is an independent agency of the federal government; members are presidential appointees. The first of NLRB's two primary roles is to prevent or correct any of the unfair labor practices described above. If the board finds an employer guilty of a violation and the employer fails to alter certain practices, the board will seek legal action through the U.S. Court of Appeals. Employers may appeal the decisions of the board. A second function of the board is to conduct secret ballot certification elections to determine whether employees will be represented by a union.

Labor Management Relations Act (1947)

While the Wagner Act may be appropriately called prolabor, the Labor-Management Relations Act—more commonly known as the *Taft-Hartley Act*—is decidedly promanagement and sought to create a balance of power between unions and employers. During the decade following the passage of the Wagner Act in 1935, a feeling developed that unions had

grown too big and too influential, that their escalating power had to be brought under control. Sponsored by Senator Robert Taft and Representative Frederick Hartley, the act actually amends the Wagner Act. Highlights of the Taft-Hartley Act include:

- The union may not coerce or restrain employees from exercising their bargaining rights. For example, the union may not make false statements to employees during organizing drives.

- The union may not cause an employer to discriminate against an employee in order to encourage or discourage union membership.

- The union may not refuse to bargain in good faith with the employer.

- The union may not engage in featherbedding whereby employers are required to pay employees for services not performed. As indicated earlier, the U.S. Supreme Court has decided that it is lawful to require employers to pay for certain services that are believed to be unnecessary.

Labor-Management Reporting and Disclosure Act (1959)

During the 1950s, unionism's reputation was tarnished considerably when a series of exposés uncovered corruption and racketeering in unions, particularly in the Teamsters Union. During 1952 and 1953, the State of New York found widespread racketeering on the New York City waterfront involving the Longshoremen's Union. The investigation, which uncovered gross mismanagement of the union pension fund, was a principal factor underlying the passage of the Welfare and Pension Plans Disclosure Act of 1958.

The most publicized account of union corruption was the investigation held by the McClellan Committee. The committee held "270 days of hearings, heard 1,526 witnesses, and produced volumes of testimony, over half of which were devoted to evidence of various types of racketeering and corruption in the Teamsters Union."[8] The committee hearings ultimately led to the Teamsters' and the Laundry and Bakery and Confectionery Workers' expulsion from the AFL-CIO. The committee hearings influenced the passage of the Labor-Management Reporting and Disclosure Act of 1959, more commonly known as the *Landrum-Griffin Act*. Key provisions of the act are:

- Creation of a Bill of Rights for union members. The bill provided equal rights for union members to attend, participate, and vote in meetings; the right to meet and express any views or opinions about union business and candidates; protection from unreasonably high dues, fees, and assessments, the right to testify against and sue the union for violation of their rights; and the right to inspect copies of collective bargaining agreements.

- Reporting Requirements. The act requires unions to submit an annual financial report covering assets, liabilities, income, expenses, etc. to the Secretary of Labor who must approve the report.

- Election Safeguards. The act set forth the ground rules for proper union conduct during elections. For exam-

---

8. Estey, *The Unions*, p. 112.

ple, ballots must be secret and every member in good standing must be allowed a vote.

- Restrictions on Officers. The act disallows convicted felons from holding union office for five years after conviction. The act also requires union officials to be bonded.

UNION STRUCTURE AND MANAGEMENT

In 1977 there were 175 national and international unions in America. *National unions* have collective bargaining agreements with different employers in two or more states; international unions are headquartered in the United States but have members in Canada. The three largest national unions were the teamsters (1,889,000 members); the auto workers (1,358,000 members); and the steelworkers (1,300,000 members) in 1980.

Unique Features of Unions

A union is a private, nonprofit organization whose primary purpose is to advance the interests of its members. In many respects, a union closely resembles the business firm or public enterprise that employs its members. Union leaders must plan and organize activities, staff certain union positions, create a budget and manage by it, influence and motivate other union officials and the union rank-and-file membership, see that union goals are met, and be sure that union policies, procedures, and rules are followed. Particularly, they must be able to influence and persuade management representatives when a new union contract is being negotiated. The union's structure contains basic elements common to all organization structures: Union goals must be created, jobs must be defined, leaders must be given responsibilities and authority to meet them, departments must be formed, and spans of control must be determined.

There exist many real differences in the operations and functions of a union and a private enterprise or public agency. The main differences include:[9]

Power Structure: In the business firm leaders are appointed; authority and power flow from the top to the bottom. Union officials are elected by the rank and file or by convention delegates; power flows (at least theoretically) from the bottom to the top of the pyramid.

Ultimate Authority: The ultimate authority in business and government organizations is held by the top management group. They decide the direction the organization will take and determine how to solve critical problems. However, the rank and file possess ultimate authority in the union, as collective bargaining agreements normally must be ratified (approved by a vote) by the membership. Ratification is not always a rubber stamp procedure. Union members frequently send their leaders back to the bargaining table for better economic rewards and working conditions.

Managerial Selection: In industry or government, an individual may become a manager with no managerial experience. For example, a recent college graduate may take a job as a production supervisor or office manager. Many corporate executives find little difficulty in job-hopping

from one industry to another. Almost without exception, union leaders work their way up through the ranks. Typically they begin as rank and file members. Moving as a leader from one union to another is rare. Also the rank and file feel more comfortable with leaders who have put considerable time in their union.

Salaries: Hundred-thousand-dollar-a-year-plus salaries for top corporate leaders hardly raise an eyebrow today. In fact, twenty-five executives each received a total compensation of over $1 million in 1979.[10] Seven-figure salaries—or anything close—are nonexistent for top level union leaders. Data filed with the U.S. Department of Labor for 1979 showed the highest paid union official was Teamsters Union President Frank E. Fitzsimmons with a salary of $156,250. However, only eleven top union leaders made over $100,000 in 1979. Lane Kirkland, president of the AFL-CIO, took home $97,940 including salary and expenses.[11]

Tenure: At the top of the corporate structure, executives rarely remain in the same position for ten or more years. A certain amount of value is placed on fresh leadership and an orderly system for transferring power to new groups of leaders. Historically, top union leaders have enjoyed tenures of considerable length. For example, John L. Lewis was president of the United Mine Workers for thirty-nine years; Dan Tobin lead the Teamsters through its early history for forty-five years. There are few roadblocks to long tenure, as length of service tends to perpetuate itself. The power and charisma of

---

9. Ibid., pp. 46–55.

10. "Stocks Sweeten Pay at the Top," *Business Week* (May 12, 1980): 56.

11. "The Inflationary Push on Pay for Union Brass," *Business Week* (May 12, 1980): 86.

a top union leader often prove to be formidable barriers to the up-and-coming union official.

LOCAL UNIONS

Most local unions are affiliated with national or international unions. *Local unions* receive their charters from the national union which may disband or suspend the local. Less than 2 percent of all local unions are completely independent; generally they serve a single employer or small geographical territory.

Local union leaders are elected by their members, usually for a one-year term. While local union leadership will vary by size and union, a typical management structure consists of a president, vice–president, secretary, and treasurer. In very large locals union officials work full–time for the local union. More often, however, the officials work full-time and conduct union affairs on their own time and on time allowed by a company during working hours.

Perhaps, the local union's most critical function is to collectively bargain with employers. The contract is most frequently negotiated by either the president or business agent, sometimes by representatives from the national union. A business agent is an elected, full-time, salaried official who represents a large local union. The agent may also be heavily involved in handling employee grievances or leading union members during a strike.

Another important local union member is the shop steward, sometimes referred to as a committeeman or grievance person. As the last term suggests, the steward acts as the union representative in processing grievances against management. Responsible for completely understand-ing the labor-management agreement, the shop steward supports the union employee when a grievance is justified. Grievance handling will be discussed in more detail in the following chapter.

NATIONAL AND INTERNATIONAL UNIONS

Like a corporate headquarters with plants and offices scattered throughout the United States, national or international unions direct and support local unions. This is achieved by creating major policies and maintaining key functions and programs. Some of these key policymaking areas, programs, and activities include:

- Creating uniform contract provisions about wages or seniority in locals in a given area or industry
- Assisting the local union in contract negotiations
- Training local union officials in union management and administration
- Creating and administering strike funds to support local union members on strike
- Providing data collection services for cost of living data, wage data, etc.
- Increasing union membership by organizing nonunion employees

National or international unions often employ elected officials and staff specialists appointed by top union leaders. Economists, lawyers, and public relations specialists provide valuable services in promoting the union effort.

INDEPENDENT UNIONS

Most national or international unions are affiliated with the AFL-CIO. Sixty-three of one hundred and seventy five national or international unions, with a combined membership of about 4.5 million, chose

FIGURE 16–4: *Organization Structure of the AFL-CIO*

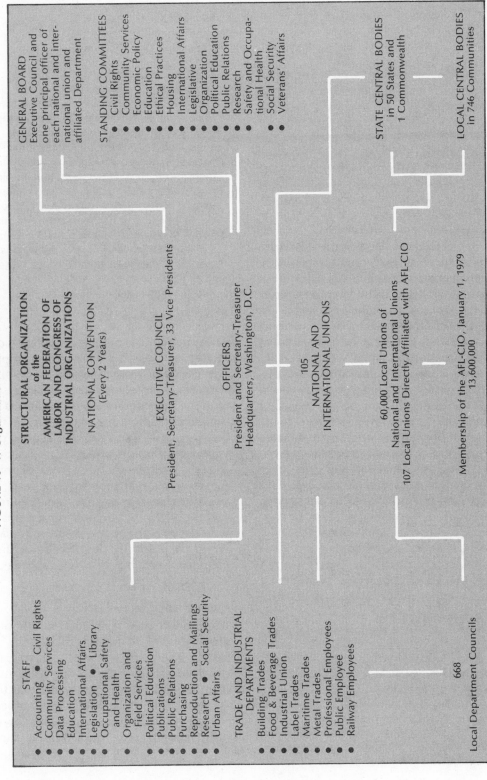

SOURCE: *This Is the AFL-CIO* (Washington, D.C.: AFL-CIO, 1979)

to remain independent in 1977. Some had decided to remain autonomous and never joined the AFL or CIO. Others, like the Teamsters, were expelled from the AFL for corruption; eleven unions, including the Longshoremen's Union, were expelled from the CIO in the late 1940s and early 1950s. None of the unions expelled years ago has since sought AFL-CIO affiliation.

THE AFL-CIO

The AFL-CIO is the heart of the American labor sector. A single federation of autonomous labor unions, the AFL-CIO influences the activities of its member unions and the labor movement as a whole. In 1979, one hundred and five of the nation's one hundred and seventy five national and international unions were AFL-CIO affiliates; this includes about three–fourths of all organized employees in America. The structure of the AFL-CIO organization is illustrated in Figure 16–4.

The national and international affiliates operate autonomously, retaining decentralized decision-making authority over their own matters and affairs. AFL-CIO officials are not authorized to call strikes, influence the negotiating process, or control the behavior of affiliate leaders. Why then have most unions joined the AFL–CIO? According to labor expert Marten Estey, the AFL-CIO provides its members with a number of specialized services:

> The plain fact is that the AFL-CIO is not directly involved in the fundamental union function of collective bargaining. For all practical purposes that function is reserved for the national unions and, to a lesser extent, for the locals.
>
> The primary role of the federation, instead, may be described as broadly political. The AFL-CIO is to organized labor roughly what the United States Chamber of Commerce is to business; it is engaged in lobbying, public

relations, research, and education to present labor's views on countless problems—not only on wages, hours, and working conditions, but also on topics ranging from public housing to foreign policy.

In addition, the federation performs various necessary functions within the labor movement. It charters new international unions, tries to minimize friction between affiliated unions and settle the disputes which occasionally break out between them, maintains a staff of organizers, and provides research and legal assistance primarily for unions too small to afford their own research staffs.[12]

The Organizing Drive

The impetus to organize craftspersons, factory workers, or white-collar employees may come from two sources. One, the workers themselves may be dissatisfied with their pay and/or work conditions and initiate contact with a union. This is typically the case. Two, workers may be contacted by a union organizer, a full-time, salaried staff member of a national union. As this individual's job title suggests, the organizer increases union membership and strength by organizing groups of workers who are not presently unionized. From this point on, the drive to organize includes a number of predictable events outlined in Figure 16–5.

LABOR'S STRATEGY

The union's goal is to successfully organize workers, bringing them into the union. Their strategy for achieving this goal is to convince the workers that union membership will bring them benefits they do not presently enjoy. Union officials will suggest that union representation will result in higher pay; more benefits; better

---

12. Estey, *The Unions*, pp. 36–37.

FIGURE 16–5: *The Organizing Process*

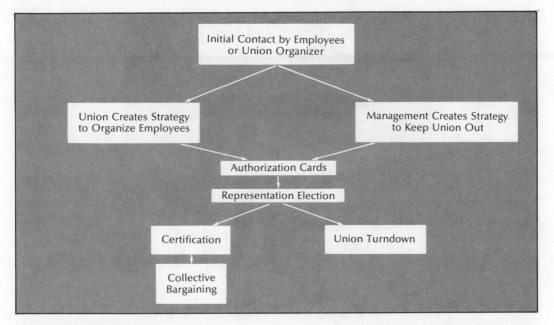

working conditions; and greater fairness and equality in promotions, job transfers, and layoffs. Speaking proudly of the benefits and work improvements they have achieved for other workers, officials often cite impressive and convincing statistics about wage gains achieved through collective bargaining.

To tell the union side of the story, labor advocates hold formal meetings at the local union hall and encourage supporters to informally spread the word about the advantages of unionizing the employees' place of work. Prounion handbills and flyers are often passed to workers as they leave work or go to lunch. One such handbill is illustrated in Figure 16–6.

MANAGEMENT'S STRATEGY

Management's goal is simply to keep the union out of the work place. Their strategy is to convince the workers that unionization will do them more harm than good. Management will assure the workers that their present pay and benefits are competitive and may show data to prove it. Emphasizing their philosophy of fair dealings with all employees, they may discuss the union's involvement in violent or corrupt activities if such has been the case. Talking dollars and cents, management will enumerate the costs of union membership which include initiation fees, dues, and other assessments; they will add that wages will be lost should a strike occur. Management may also talk about the loss of freedom and a potential erosion in labor-management relations that unionization might bring.

ILLEGAL ACTIVITIES

Throughout the organizing drive, emotions often run at high levels on both sides; union and management supporters often make passionate and dramatic arguments to further their causes. To ensure

FIGURE 16–6: *Union Handbill*

that both labor and management play fair during the organizing drive, labor legislation has spelled out in detail illegal campaign tactics.[13]

DURING THE ORGANIZING CAMPAIGN, UNION REPRESENTATIVES OR PROLABOR EMPLOYEES CANNOT:

Solicit employees where they are working unless employees are normally allowed to converse while they work. Oral solicitation is acceptable during breaks and lunch.

13. Feldacker, *Labor Guide to Labor Law*, Ch 3.

Distribute union literature in work areas; nonwork areas typically include lunch rooms and break areas.

Offer an employee free union membership before the election unless free membership is granted to everyone who joins the union up to the time the first contract is negotiated.

Offer excessive attendance prizes to employees who attend a campaign rally. Payment of a sum of money to each participant is an obvious infraction of the rule.

Make substantial statements of misrepresentation. While both management and labor are allowed a generous amount of

FIGURE 16–7: *Union Authorization Card*

```
    University of Louisville
American Association of University Professors


I, _____, hereby
designate the University of Louisville Chapter of the
American Association of University Professors to
represent my professional and economic interests
in collective bargaining.

Date:
_____  _____
                           Signature

             _____
                           Department
```

puffing (promises and propaganda), the Hollywood Ceramics rule forces the election to be set aside if either side makes a "substantial misrepresentation on a material fact made at a time when the other party has inadequate time to respond and correct the misrepresentation."[14]

DURING THE ORGANIZING CAMPAIGN, EMPLOYER REPRESENTATIVES CANNOT:

Discipline or threaten employees who engage in lawful solicitation or distribution of union material.

Prohibit existing employees from legal solicitation and distribution activities at work. Management can, if it desires, prohibit outside union organizers from entering the premises. The only exception to this rule is the rare case when employees are normally inaccessible—such as maritime workers on a ship.

Engage in antiunion rhetoric before a mass audience twenty-four hours before an election. However, the twenty-four hour rule does not forbid talks to individuals or small groups.

Speak to employees in areas of management authority such as the bosses' offices or management conference rooms. Such a setting is thought by the NLRB to be overly intimidating.

Tell employees that absolutely no good will come if the union gets in. Called the futility doctrine, this prohibits the employer from making statements suggesting it is futile for the employees to unionize.

Appeal to racial prejudice by pitting black or white workers against one another by suggesting that a certain race would benefit from unionization.

Promise certain benefits if the union loses. Further, a raise in pay or an increase in benefits cannot be given during the campaign unless the increase was planned before the election. Similarly, existing benefits or a planned increase in benefits cannot be rescinded because of the union campaign.

---

14. Ibid., p. 79.

Keep track of employees' union activities or give the impression that prounion employees are under surveillance.

AUTHORIZATION CARDS

Before an election is called, the union must prove that a sizeable number of employees favor union representation by getting at least 30 percent of the employees to sign authorization cards. Shown in Figure 16–7, the card states that the employee designates the union as bargaining agent. If more than 50 percent of the employees sign authorization cards, the union may formally request the employer to recognize it as the employees' bargaining agent. Even though a majority of the employees may have signed authorization cards, the employer still generally refuses to recognize the union. The union must then formally petition the NLRB to hold an election.

REPRESENTATION ELECTION

The NLRB oversees the *representation election* to ensure that at least 30 percent of the authorization cards have been signed and that no illegal campaign activities have taken place. At this time, the NLRB investigator also decides what the *bargaining unit* will be. The bargaining unit is the group of employees the union will represent and bargain for if the election favors the union. While the NLRB considers several factors in deciding the makeup of the bargaining unit, a key factor regarding this matter is the community of interest principle. This principle states that the more employees have in common, the more likely the board is to find that they constitute a valid bargaining unit. Specific factors examined by the board include: similarity of work performed; geographical proximity of workers; job integration; similarity of working conditions, prevailing wage rates, and benefits; and whether employees work under a common management group. If the union wins the election, all employees within the bargaining unit—both union and nonunion employees—will be represented by the union. Management may not treat the union employee any differently than the nonunion employee.

CERTIFICATION

The union becomes the official bargaining agent for the employees if it receives over 50 percent of the votes cast in a secret election. If the union does not receive at least 50 percent of the votes cast, it may not petition the NLRB for another representation election for at least a year.

Basically, the same process is used to vote an existing union out. If over 50 percent of the votes are cast against the union, the union no longer represents the employee group and is said to be decertified. A year must pass before the union can petition for another election.

BENEFITS OF UNIONIZATION

The decision to develop preventive labor relations should not be made on ideological or emotional grounds, but approached rationally and objectively as an important business decision. After considering both sides, the employer may believe that the union would enhance the effectiveness and profitability of the enterprise, and welcome an organizing drive. Potential benefits of unionization include:[15]

- Employee recruiting and selection are enhanced by using the union hiring hall. The union sends the employer

15. This section is drawn from John G. Kilgour, "Before the Union Knocks," *Personnel Journal* (April 1978) 186+.

only prescreened, qualified employees.

- Being organized by a union with which the employer has had good working relationships is preferable to being organized by a less acceptable union.
- By organizing all companies in an industry or area, the union forces all companies to pay union scale, which minimizes price competition for employees.

Preventive Labor Relations

A recent upsurge of activity has focused upon the strategies that businesses may implement to maintain nonunion status; these strategies are termed *preventive labor relations*. During the past few years books, journal articles, seminars, and labor consultants have offered an increasing number of methods and techniques for keeping an organization union-free. The growth in preventive labor relations is, no doubt, due to the desire to keep labor costs low in the face of double digit inflation. Many firms now aggressively pursuing a union-free status are experiencing considerable success.

DETERING THE ORGANIZING DRIVE

After weighing the advantages and disadvantages of unionization, if the company decides to remain nonunion, management will attempt to prevent the organizing drive rather than trying to win the representation election once a drive has gotten under way. One reason for this is that winning a representation election is expensive. A 1975 study of 146 NLRB representation elections found the employer paying between $100 and $125 per hourly employee.[16] Second, research shows that both union and employer campaigns are largely ineffective in changing employees' attitudes, as most will vote as they had planned before the actual campaign got under way. Thus, if management expects to change employees' attitudes toward the union, positive steps must be taken well in advance of the union organization drive.

In general, the most effective way for a firm to practice preventive labor relations is to give the employees the benefits of unionization without the union. Simply put, if an employer provides the kind of work environment that employees want, they will not seek out a union. Administrators who value their human resources and conduct an effective program of personnel management are much less likely to face an organization drive than those who view the work force as simply another factor of production. What conditions deter union drives? The list is generally comprised of those factors that employees have sought since the early stages of the labor movement: a system for resolving employees' complaints, safe working conditions, good wages and benefits, job security, fair and equitable personnel policies, people-oriented supervisors, channels of communication with management, a voice in the decisions that affect their work, and a feeling that management is concerned about their welfare. Inattention to most or all of these job conditions will more than likely find a union organizer at management's doorstep.

In summary, labor movement highlights include formation of the Knights of Labor, the AFL, and the CIO; the enactment of important labor legislation between 1930

---

16. Ibid., p. 18.

and 1960; and the merger of the AFL and the CIO. Union goals have not changed dramatically since their beginning; they include union security, job security, improved wages and benefits, favorable working conditions, and the fair and just treatment for their members. The heart of the union structure is the local union, although the national union provides important guidance as well as assistance during the collective bargaining process. Most national unions are affiliated with the AFL-CIO, which provides many support services. Because the work force has changed significantly in the past two decades as public service, white–collar, and professional groups increased, labor leaders face the challenge of organizing these workers. Unions have a major impact on the management of organizations because a great number of personnel decisions must be shared with the union, and a labor-management contract limits management's flexibility. The relations between organized labor and man-

agement are strictly governed by statute law.

Managers and personnel administrators who work in unionized organizations must be intimately familiar with labor legislation. When an organizing drive takes place within the company, labor law will also be important to managers. During the organizing process, the union attempts to convince workers that they will be better off by organizing, and management explains the advantages of nonunion status. Management's decision to remain nonunion should be made from a cost-benefit perspective: If the costs of remaining nonunion exceed the benefits, the union should be accepted. Firms desiring to stay nonunion, however, should practice preventive labor relations by providing workers with good wages and benefits, fair and equitable working conditions, secure jobs, supervisors who practice good human relations, and other job elements that represent sound personnel practices and procedures.

The Solution

Riverside Packing could be in serious trouble with the National Labor Relations Board. Under labor law, raising wages for the express purpose of keeping a union out is clearly illegal. Further, to tell the employees that the union "will do them no good whatsoever" is a clear-cut violation of the futility doctrine.

The reasons hourly employees want a union at Riverside Packing are not difficult to see. Even the personnel manager admits that the company's financial package is below *competitive levels and that the supervisors are guilty of poor human relations practices. Riverside Packing may be a prime example of a firm where only unionization will ensure that employees are adequately rewarded and treated fairly. If management wants to remain nonunion, the organization must provide employees with the economic rewards and working conditions for which unions have successfully bargained.*

KEY TERMS AND CONCEPTS

Labor or Craft Union
Knights of Labor
AFL-CIO
Union Shop
Agency Shop
Maintenance-of-Membership Shop
Closed Shop
Open Shop
Featherbedding
Railway Labor Act

Norris-LaGuardia Act
Wagner Act
Taft-Hartley Act
National Labor Relations Board
Landrum-Griffin Act
National Union
Local Union
Representation Election
Bargaining Unit
Preventive Labor Relations

FOR REVIEW

1. How do unions affect management decisions?
2. What major events took place during the history of the labor movement?
3. How has union membership changed in recent years?
4. What are the goals of the unions?
5. What are the major labor laws and what are their key provisions?
6. What are the functions and duties of the national and local union? What is the AFL-CIO and what are its functions?
7. What are the primary events in a union organizing campaign?

FOR DISCUSSION

1. Assume you are a recent graduate applying for a job as foreman trainee. During a series of interviews, the plant manager says "tell me your philosophy toward unions. We are nonunion and I would specifically like to know how you would feel about this company becoming unionized." How would you respond?

2. Would you prefer to manage union or nonunion workers? Why?

3. Why has the labor sector failed to significantly increase its membership in the past two decades? What do you believe must be done to increase union membership?

4. Comment on the following statement: "We live in an age of professional management. The average worker has a safe job, fair wages, good benefits, and competent supervision. Therefore, unions have outlived their purpose."

5. Many organizing campaigns are taking place at colleges and universities to bring their faculties into a union. Do you think that professors should organize? Why or why not?

6. One of the most controversial parts of the Taft-Hartley Act is Section 14B which enables individual states to ban union and agency shops. Since the passage of the act, the labor sector has lobbied long and hard to repeal Section 14B. On the other hand, many employers feel a federal right to work law should be passed banning union and agency shops throughout the country. Do you believe society would benefit most from a repeal of Section 14B, or the passage of a federal right to work law? Discuss.

7. How will the composition of the labor force change in the next twenty years? Do you believe the labor sector will be a stronger or weaker force in 2000 than it is today?

SUPPLEMENTARY READINGS

Chamot, Dennis. "Professional Employees Turn to Unions." *Harvard Business Review* 54 (May-June 1976): 119–26.

Fulmer, William E. "When Employees Want to Oust Their Union." *Harvard Business Review* 55 (September-October 1977): 22+.

Hagburg, Eugene C., and Levine, Marvin J. *Labor Relations: An Integrated Perspective.* St. Paul, MN: West Publishing Co., 1978.

McIssac, George S. "What's Coming in Labor Relations." *Harvard Business Review* 55 (September-October 1977): 22+.

Mussberg, Walter S. "On the Line: As Union Man at Ford, Charlie Bragg Deals in Problems, Gripes." *The Wall Street Journal*, July 26, 1973, p. 1.

National Industrial Conference Board. "White Collar Unionization." *Studies in Personnel Policy* 227 (1970).

"No Welcome Mat For Unions in the Sunbelt." *Business Week*, May 17, 1976, pp. 108–11.

Raskin, A. H. "The Labor Movement Must Start Moving." *Harvard Business Review* 48 (January-February, 1970): 110+.

Ross, Irvin. "How to Tell When the Unions Will Be Tough." *Fortune*, July 1975, pp. 100–104ff.

Stagner, Ross, and Rosen, Hjalmar. *Psychology of Union-Management Relations*. Belmont, CA: Wadsworth Publishing Co., 1965.

U.S. Department of Labor. *Brief History of the American Labor Movement*. Washington, DC: U.S. Government Printing Office, 1976.

For Analysis: A Union Time Study on Company Premises?[1]

Fafnir Bearing Company is a manufacturer and marketer of ball bearings and other related products. Since 1944 this New Britain, Connecticut, company has engaged in collective bargaining with the UAW.

The agreement in force in 1963 contained an incentive wage clause. According to the agreement, the company could establish the number of pieces that would be produced by an average employee with normal incentive. Employees who exceeded this rate were entitled to piecework compensation proportionately in excess of their regular hourly rate.

The company's industrial engineers, or ratesetters, were responsible for establishing the standard rates. Their procedures followed the generally accepted elemental time study method, described in production management or industrial management literature:

[1] Taken from S. H. Schoen and R. L. Hilgert, Cases in Collective Bargaining and Industrial Relations *(Homewood, Ill.: Richard R. Irwin, Inc., 1969). All names have been disguised.*

The ratesetter must observe the employee performing work tasks. As a preliminary step, the ratesetter writes up the conditions and circumstances under which the time study will be conducted. These include the layout of the place where the work is done; heat, if a factor; lighting; and all other components affecting the completion of the job. After this, the ratesetter reduces the job into individual work content elements, or cyclic elements. Noncyclic elements are taken into consideration, although they do not enter into every single cycle. Some noncyclic elements, for example, may involve occasional travel away from the work area to obtain a quantity of stock to work on, or visits to the washroom. Cyclic and the noncyclic elements combine to make a cycle which results in the production of one unit or a single piece.

The ratesetter then times an operator performing the particular cycle involved, using a stopwatch. The number of cycles which are observed varies. During this observation, the ratesetter decides if the operator is performing at a normal pace, below normal, or above normal. The ratesetter than normalizes the performance by applying a rating, or leveling, factor if the operator was performing above or below normal. By applying this normalizing factor to the operator's average time in a cycle, the ratesetter will arrive at the normal time for a cycle. After ascertaining normal time, the ratesetter makes allowances for personal fatigue and delay involving keeping time records, rest periods, or work area cleanup. Thereupon the total elapsed time per piece is computed. The standard is the number of pieces which should be produced in an hour at a normal pace; it is calculated by dividing the number of minutes in an hour by the total elapsed time per piece. If, for example, the total elapsed time per piece is 36 seconds (or 0.6 of a minute) then standard is 60 divided by 0.6, or 100 pieces an hour.

Since the company and union realized that even the best of time study procedures contain subjective judgment, the contract provided a four-step grievance procedure, the last step of which was arbitration. Disputes were submitted to a permanent arbitrator who was an industrial engineer. After conducting a time study of the job in question, the permanent arbitrator would rule accordingly.

On various dates prior to February 7, 1963, the union submitted four grievances to the company on certain piecework rates involving jobs within the bargaining unit. The union contended that these rates had not been properly established by the company under the governing provisions of the contract. These grievances were processed through the first two steps of the grievance procedure, but the company did not agree to the union's position. On February 7, 1963, the company's top officials met with top representatives of Local 133, including UAW International Union representatives, as required by Step 3 of the grievance procedure.

At this meeting, the union representatives requested and received all the time study data used by the company in establishing the piecework rates of the jobs involved in the grievances. Kermit Mead, a representative and director of the time study and industrial engineering department of the international union, analyzed the data and asked company officials several questions. These questions were answered fully. On behalf of Local 133, Mead then requested permission to make his own time study of the operations involved in the four grievances. Mead told the company officials that unless he made his own time studies, he would not be able to advise the union if the rates set for the disputed operations conformed with the provisions of the collective bargaining agreement. Mead stated that merely studying the data supplied by the company was not sufficient to form an opinion respecting the correctness of the rates, because there was no way for him to assess the validity of the time allotted by company's industrial engineers to the many subjective variables in each operation. Mead cited several subjective factors within the grievances which he wished to evaluate personally. Among these were the methods company ratesetters used to determine their leveling factors and allowance times for personal fatigue and delays, and to measure allowances for heat and stock loading conditions.

Company officials denied Mead's request, stating that such a union study was unnecessary, since the company had furnished the union with sufficient information to determine whether the grievances should be taken to arbitration; that the contract failed to grant the union the right to conduct an independent time study; and that the permanent arbitrator would conduct his own time study to determine whether the particular piecework price had been set according to the pertinent criteria established by the contract. The company also stated that the union should submit the four grievances to arbitration, if it was still dissatisfied with the results of the company time studies.

On February 11, 1963, the union filed an unfair labor practice charge against the company with the NLRB. The union charged that the company had violated Section 8 (a) (1) and (5) of the Labor-Management Relations Act in refusing to allow the union to conduct time studies on the disputed jobs. Section 8 (a) (5) makes it an unfair labor practice for an employer "to refuse to bargain collectively with the representatives of his employees, subject to the provisions of Section 9 (a)." The union contended that in refusing to allow the time studies the company was, in effect, refusing to bargain in good faith. This contention was based on the argument that the data provided by the company was inadequate for the union's purposes.

The union argued that Section 8 (a) (5) of the act obligates an employer to furnish upon request all information required by the bargaining representative. This obligation extends to information which the union may require in order to police and administer existing agreements. The time studies requested by the union were requests for information which were relevant and necessary for the union to fulfill its function as the bargaining representative. The union felt that compliance with the good faith bargaining provisions of the act required the company to cooperate with them by making plant facilities available for the union's time studies, because these studies were necessary for the union to properly make judgments as the bargaining representative of the employees.

The company contended that it did not violate Section 8 (a) (5) of the act, and that its actions in this case were proper. The company claimed that it was justified in denying the union's request for its own time studies, for the aforementioned reasons. The company noted that for some years, grievances of this type had been processed without independent time studies being made at any stage prior to submission of the grievances to the permanent arbitrator. In determining whether a grievance had merit, the arbitrator invariably made his own time study. The lack of a prearbitration time study was not a handicap to the union in the past, causing the union either to fail to process meritorious grievances or to process an excessive number of nonmeritorious grievances.

The testimony of Mead, the union's industrial engineer, did not establish that the information available from other sources (such as the company's time study data, and discussion with employees, stewards, and committee persons) was insufficient to determine if the grievance should be taken to arbitration. This was the only purpose for which the union time study was desired. Since the union did not prove either the necessity of access nor the unavailability of adequate alternative sources of information, there was no support for the union's charge that the company did not bargain in good faith by denying the union access to company premises to conduct its own time study. The union complaint should be dismissed.

Questions

1. Does Section 8 (a) (5) of LMRA require an employer to permit a union to conduct an independent time study on company premises? Is this question relevant to other conditions involved in a case situation? Does it appear that the Fafnir Company was attempting to impose arbitrary standards upon employees represented by the union?

2. Evaluate the union's argument that it needed its own time study in order to properly act as bargaining representative for the employees. Evaluate the company's argument that the grievance-arbitration procedure fulfilled its obligation to bargain over the issue of time standards.

3. Is the fact that the union had not requested its own time studies in the past germane to the case? What is at stake in terms of the relationships between parties?

4. Evaluate the precedent implications of this case to both management and union interests.

UAW Local 400 picketed the Ford Motor Company plant at Highland Park, Michigan, in 1961.

17

COLLECTIVE BARGAINING
AND
GRIEVANCE HANDLING

Bargaining Structures

Bargaining Impasse Resolution

Public Sector Bargaining

Arbitration of Grievances

Grievance Reduction Strategies

The Problem: Grievances at Midwest Steel

Jack Grayson, personnel manager for Midwest Steel Company, took the elevator to President Charles Abner's fourth floor office. Abner asked him to come up and discuss a "critical personnel problem." They met in the conference room that adjoined Abner's office.

Midwest Steel is a medium-size steel fabricator located in East Chicago, Indiana. The firm employs about thirty-two hundred hourly employees and 475 managerial, staff, and clerical personnel. Hourly employees were represented by the United Steel Workers union. Throughout the firm's forty—eight year history, labor relations have generally been good; however, a strike three years ago was the beginning of a downturn in union relations.

Abner: "Jack, I was just looking over the labor report I received from you a few days ago. I was a bit shocked to learn that we had 590 employee grievances filed against the company last year; that represents an 11 percent increase over the previous year. The controller also tells me that we spent over $100,000 on fees and expenses for grievance cases that went to arbitration. It appears to me that this grievance situation has become very serious. Jack, what's causing the problem and what are we doing about it?"

Grayson: "Chuck, we've been having real problems with the USW ever since they had a change in local leadership a few years ago. We're managing the same way we've always managed. Oh sure, we've got our share of dictators in the ranks of supervision. And working in this industry isn't all *peaches and cream—a steel mill is a steel mill. It will always be hot, dirty, noisy, and even a bit dangerous. But the union has nitpicked everything. We're getting a lot of grievances over issues we never did before—particularly in the area of supervisory practices and safety issues. Chuck, I really don't see that there's much we can do except wait for the union to improve its attitude."*

One of the union's key functions is to collectively bargain a labor agreement with the employer. The terms and conditions specified in the contract define the economic rewards and work environments for each union member. To many—if not most union members—a union's effectiveness is directly tied to its success in achieving their work-related wants and needs. While the methods and techniques of collective bargaining have changed throughout labor's history, it remains the cornerstone of union activity and represents the sine qua non of organized labor.

Through collective bargaining, individual workers participate in the decisions that affect their work. Thus, collective bargaining may be viewed as a form of participative management whereby the employees, through their union representatives, have a major say over their work environments. Collective bargaining is one of the earliest infusions of democratic principles into the industrial world.

Collective bargaining has two broad and highly related processes: The first involves activities associated with the creation of the labor-management contract. In essence, these are the rules of the game. But rules need interpretation and enforcement; therefore, the collective bargaining process includes a judicial mechanism for handling violations of the agreement. Referred to as grievance handling these steps are an important part of most labor-management contracts today.

BARGAINING STRUCTURES

Unions and employers may conduct contract negotiations within two basic structures: single employer bargaining and multiple employer bargaining.[1]

SINGLE EMPLOYER BARGAINING Most labor agreements involve a single employer and single union. Should a single employer have several geographically-dispersed plants, the union commonly represents employees at all plants with one master agreement. Certain issues—usually a small number—are left to local negotiation. For example, a basic agreement between the UAW and General Motors

---

1. Dale S. Beach, *Personnel* (New York: Macmillan Publishing Co., Inc., 1980), pp. 107–109.

covers employees at all GM plants, and each plant negotiates a supplemental agreement with the local union.

A large single employer with diverse activities and manufacturing processes may negotiate contracts with more than one union. For example, in Louisville, Kentucky, the *Courier-Journal* and *Louisville Times* publishers had contracts with six unions in 1979: the Electrical Workers, Graphic Arts, Mailers, Machinists, Printing & Graphic Communications, and Typographical workers. The structures for *single employer bargaining* are shown in Figure 17–1.

MULTIPLE EMPLOYER BARGAINING In *multiple employer bargaining,* two or more em-

ployers join together to bargain with one or more unions. Two types of multiple employer bargaining are common today: One involves contract negotiations between an association of two or more employers and a union council representing a group of craft or industrial unions. This bargaining arrangement is common in the construction industry where all unionized contractors in a given geographical area will bargain with a variety of craft unions through their building trades council. A second type centers around industry-wide bargaining whereby several companies in a given industry bargain through their employers' association with a union. To illustrate, an agreement dated June, 1980, was reached between the International Woodworkers of America and the Western States Wood Products Employers' Association which represented Crown Zellerbach Corporation, Georgia-Pacific Corporation, and the Weyerhaeuser Company among others. Multiple employer bargaining structures are illustrated in Figure 17–2.

Both the union and employer cite advantages to multiple employer bargaining. Bargaining with an employers' association is less costly for unions than bargaining individually with several employers. Further, the union favors the creation of uniform wages and work conditions among unionized firms within a particular industry.

A common wage and benefits package is also advantageous to the employers because it eliminates intercompany wage competition and the threat of employees leaving to work for competitors because of noncompetitive wages or benefits. Multiple employer bargaining has also enabled employers to increase bargaining strength and has, perhaps, enabled them

FIGURE 17–1: *Single Employer Bargaining Structures*

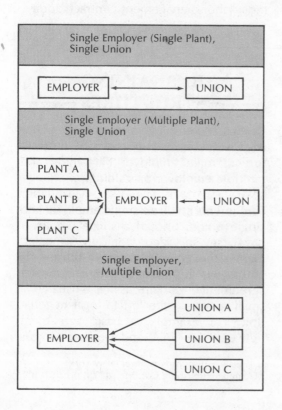

FIGURE 17–2: *Multiple Employer Bargaining Structures*

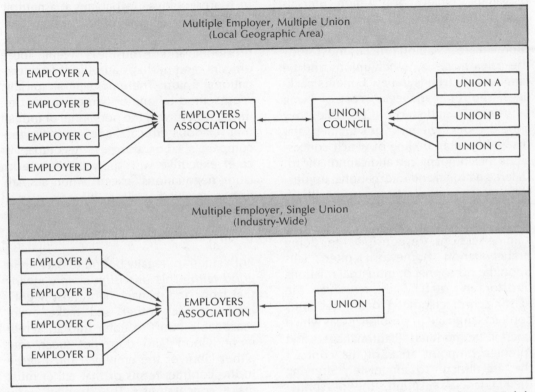

to achieve agreements more attractive than those which would be negotiated individually.

On the negative side, multiple employer bargaining may have drawbacks for the individual employer. For one, by negotiating through an association, the employer will lose some control over internal affairs. Two, the weaker employers in the association will most likely lose power and prestige normally reserved for the stronger association members.

COLLECTIVE
═══ BARGAINING ═══

According to a labor statute, an employer must recognize and bargain with a union which has been certified by the NLRB following a representation election. An employer is also required to bargain with an existing union for a new or modified agreement in order to replace a labor contract about to expire. Both parties are required, by law, to bargain in good faith, but neither party is compelled to agree or to necessarily conclude the negotiation with a contract. In either case, the collective bargaining process follows three distinct phases: prenegotiation, negotiation, and the labor-management agreement.

Prenegotiation

Labor and management representatives are involved in a great deal of preparation long before they actually sit down at the bargaining table. Local union officials meet with the rank and file to learn what they consider major contract issues and problem areas. Union officials must study the gains made by other unions and be familiar with trends in new benefits packages, shorter workweeks, cost of living adjustments, and so on. If possible, they should know the employer's financial status and have an inkling of which concessions the company can and cannot afford. In large national and international unions, full-time staff researchers assist in these preparations.

The employer also prepares for the bargaining sessions. Responsibility for doing prenegotiation homework often falls upon the personnel or industrial relations director and staff. They scrutinize the existing contract looking for any nebulous contract language or problem areas which need to be modified. Plant managers and foremen pinpoint areas of the contract that are difficult to administer. Studying their financial position, the personnel staff examines prevailing wage rates and benefits packages to determine what wage/benefits increases can be afforded, if any at all. A union may be forced to concede certain economic gains if the employer is in serious financial trouble. For example, the United Auto Workers had little choice but to accept a weakened agreement with the Chrysler Corporation in late 1979. The federal government made the UAW agree to certain economic concessions as one condition for guaranteeing a multimillion dollar loan package for the financially-troubled automaker.

Negotiation

To begin the actual negotiation process, both management and labor send a team of representatives to bargain at a neutral site—usually a hotel suite. Labor representatives may include the local union president and/or business agent, local officers, and perhaps an official from the national union. The employer is typically represented by one or two top manufacturing executives, the personnel or industrial relations director, and, perhaps, the company's labor attorney. A company's chief executive will rarely participate in labor negotiations, except when a small firm is involved.

Good Faith Concept

Both sides are legally bound to bargain in *good faith*. This provision simply means that labor and management must negotiate with each other and make every reasonable effort to enter into an agreement. Good faith does not mean that either labor or the employer must agree to the contract terms or that either must make concessions.[2] The stronger party may use its power to obtain a favorable agreement as long as representatives intend to reach an agreement.[3]

Bargaining Stages

The actual bargaining process follows a fairly predictable chain of events. Typically, union demands are followed by management's counterdemands. Initial demands on both sides are often puffed up; union and management proposals

2. A listing of practices which violate the good faith provision are included in Gary Dessler, *Personnel Management* (Reston, VA: Reston Publishing Co., 1978), p. 458.
3. Bruce S. Feldacker, *Labor Guide to Labor Law* (Reston, VA: Reston Publishing Co., 1980), p. 120.

include items that they are willing to discard or swap for something more important. A fair amount of haggling and horse-trading typifies most bargaining sessions. Lasting anywhere from a few weeks to several months, throughout the bargaining sessions the two parties often meet in joint subcommittees to work on problems while the negotiations continue on other issues. Finally, after both sides have arrived at an informal agreement, they take the agreement back to their representatives for final and formal approval. For the employer, top management—often the board of directors—must approve the contract; for labor, the rank and file will normally ratify the contract by a majority vote. In actuality, under labor law, union representatives may be given the authority to enter into a contract without ratification. Most unions, however, choose to allow their members to vote on the agreement. Failure to ratify the contract sends union representatives back to the bargaining table to negotiate a revised agreement. Most contracts are ratified on the first vote.

Labor-Management Agreement

The agreement becomes official once approved, ratified, and signed by labor and management representatives. Once signed, labor and management meet with their respective members to go over the details of the contract. Union members and officials and members of management all receive copies of the agreement. Supervisors and union stewards who have the day-to-day responsibility for administering the contract should be intimately familiar with the agreement so they may avoid any activity or decision that violates the agreement.

BARGAINING CATEGORIES

The NLRB identifies three broad categories of bargaining subjects: mandatory, permissive, and unlawful.[4] Typical mandatory subjects include provisions concerning wages, benefits, seniority, job assignments, promotions, and layoffs. The parties must negotiate mandatory items if either party requests to do so.

Permissive or voluntary subjects include those that are not directly related to wages, benefits, or conditions of work. If one party desires to bargain a permissive subject, the other party may agree or refuse to do so. For example, the union may wish to bargain for an increase in the size of the bargaining unit, but the employer could refuse to negotiate this permissive subject if it so desires. Neither side can refuse to sign a contract because the other refuses to bargain a permissive subject.

The inclusion of illegal subjects renders an agreement invalid and unenforceable. An example of a illegal item would be a provision that permits discrimination on the basis of religion, sex, or national origin. Any subject that violates any federal, state, or local law is, of course, an unlawful bargaining item.

STANDARD FORMAT

Labor contracts may vary considerably in length and content matter. Some agreements contain ten or fifteen pages; others, over two hundred pages. Of course, the more mandatory and permissive subjects that are negotiated, the lengthier the contract. The order of topics may also vary somewhat, but the following list is fairly representative of most agreements today.

---

4. Ibid., p. 124.

1. Union Recognition and Scope of Bargaining Unit. This section reflects the employer's recognition of the union as the sole bargaining agency for its employees and defines specifically which employees are included within the bargaining unit.

2. Management Rights. This section reflects the union's recognition of the employer's sole and exclusive right to determine the way in which the business shall be managed. Management rights include determining production methods, which products and services to produce, and how products and services should be marketed.

3. Union Security. This section defines the type of union security (union shop, maintenance of membership shop, etc.).

4. Strikes and Lockouts. This section outlines the approach each side will take toward strikes and lockouts. (A lockout is management's refusal to allow employees to work.) Typically, this section includes a statement which may read "there will be no strikes or lockouts during the term of this agreement" (although a strike may be permitted over certain specific items detailed in the agreement).

5. Job Rights and Seniority. This section defines how transfers, promotions, layoffs, and recalls are to be made. Generally, the contract will stipulate that these decisions be made primarily on the basis of seniority.

6. Wages. This section outlines the wage structures and related provisions such as wage adjustments, wage incentives, shift differentials, and bonuses.

7. Benefits and Time Off. This section lists the employee benefits such as hospitalization, pensions, holidays, vacations, sick leave, and rest periods.

8. Safety and Health. This section normally includes statements which underscore both the union and employer's desire to maintain safe and healthy working conditions. Many contracts include provisions for the creation of a labor-management safety committee and the administration of a health and safety program.

9. Discipline, Suspension, and Discharge. This section outlines the procedures an employer must follow to discipline, suspend, or discharge an employee. Many contracts include provisions for progressive disciplinary systems whereby additional infractions of a work policy, standards, rules, or regulations results in increasingly serious disciplinary action leading to discharge. Many progressive disciplinary systems include four steps: oral warning, written warning, suspension, and discharge. Some contracts include a very detailed list of violations and resulting penalties. For example, taking drugs on the job results in immediate dismissal, horseplay results in a verbal warning, and so on.

10. Grievance Handling and Arbitration. This section normally details (1) the steps an employee follows to lodge a formal grievance against the employer and (2) the procedure for bringing in an outside arbitrator if

the union and employer are unable to settle the grievance.

Bargaining Impasse

Historically, collective bargaining has proven to be a very effective method for settling differences between labor and management. Most negotiations end in a signed contract that is agreeable—although not necessarily favorable—to both sides. Management and labor generally recognize that continuous, dispute–free operations are important to preserve harmonious labor relations and maximize the goals of the worker and employer alike.

Serious conflicts do sometimes occur, however, during the course of negotiations. Labor and management may simply be unable to reach accord over certain issues dealing with wages or other contract provisions. When negotiations break down, or when the existing contract expires and the union and employer have been unable to reach an agreement, a *bargaining impasse* results. Should this occur, there are three options: One, the parties may ask for assistance in settling the dispute from an impartial third party called a mediator. Two, the union may exert a show of force so their demands will be accepted. Three, the employer may also show force through one of several pressure techniques. Let us first explore common union strategies for ending the bargaining impasse on their terms.

UNION POWER TACTICS

A union's primary power tactics include calling a strike, setting up a picket line, or imposing a boycott.

STRIKE Officially termed a work stoppage,

the strike, or the refusal of union members to work, is recognized as a basic union right. Strike tactics and procedures, however, are subject to considerable regulation by a variety of labor statutes. Various types of strikes include:[5]

- *Economic Strike:* A strike over an economic issue such as wages, benefits, or working conditions. The employer is free to maintain operations and hire permanent replacements for economic strikers. An employee who is not replaced is entitled to reemployment when the strike is over.

- *Unfair Labor Practice Strike:* A strike over an unfair labor practice by the employer; for example, discrimination against union members because of union activity. An unfair labor practice striker cannot be permanently replaced.

- *Sympathy Strike:* A strike in which other unions agree to a work stoppage, not because of actions by their own employer, but to support other union members striking other firms. A common example of the sympathy strike is truck drivers who refuse to cross a picket line and make deliveries to an employer whose employees are on strike. Legally, the sympathy striker is in violation of the no-strike clause in the agreement, unless the contract specifically permits this form of strike activity.

- *Wildcat Strike:* An unauthorized work stoppage. The wildcat strike is an unlawful activity if the contract contains a no strike clause; therefore wildcat strikers are not sanctioned by union leadership. If a wildcat strike

5. Ibid., Chapter 6.

does start, the union must disavow the strike, or risk being charged with violation of the contract and federal law. The employer may generally take disciplinary action, including suspension and discharge, against wildcat strikers.

Other forms of union pressure include a sit down strike (which is illegal) where employees strike but remain at their jobs and refuse to work; a sick out where employees call in sick en masse; and a slowdown where workers remain at work but cut back their output significantly. Unions, however, usually disapprove of individual worker pressures and support a work stoppage only if it has been formally approved by union leadership. For example, the national union must usually approve a strike by a local affiliate, even after a majority of the local members have approved it.

While an extended strike may deal a serious blow to a single company, union, or small geographical area, the time lost to strikes actually constitutes a relatively small percentage of the total working time for the nation as a whole. In 1977, only .17 percent of the total working time was lost to work stoppages involving only 2.04 million workers—about 2.4 percent of the total employed. Unions strike for a variety of reasons, but the majority of work stoppages are caused by disputes about general wages and plant administration (discipline, output standards, rules and regulations, and health and safety). Major work stoppage issues for 1977 are shown in Figure 17–3.

PICKETING The *picket,* a line of strikers who patrol the employer's place of business, can be a powerful union pressure tactic. Newspaper photographs of forlorn picketers warming their cold hands over oil drums filled with flaming scraps of wood court the public's sympathy. Picketing can keep a plant or building site closed down during a strike. While any violence like physically attacking non–striking employees during picketing is unlawful, many workers are reluctant to cross a picket line. Applicants who cross the picket line to apply for the jobs of striking workers often confront the jeers and taunts of the picketers. Such strikebreakers, or scabs are held in great contempt by union members. The courts allow picketing at the primary employer's place of business, or *primary situs picketing.* However, the Supreme Court has ruled that *common situs picketing* is illegal. At a common site, employees of several employers work side by side. At a construction site, for example, plumbers, carpenters, masons, electricians, and other skilled workers are represented by different unions and work for different subcontractors. Therefore, one striking union generally cannot picket the entire project; the courts have ruled that each employer at a common situs is a separate employer.

BOYCOTT A boycott is the refusal to purchase one employer's goods or services. An important distinction must be made between primary and secondary boycotts. A *primary boycott* involves only those parties directly involved in a dispute, such as a large appliance manufacturer and the electrical workers' union. In a primary boycott, the union compels members to avoid patronizing an employer, even going as far as to levy fines against those that do. Primary boycotts are generally legal. A *secondary* boycott involves a third party not directly involved in a dispute, such as an electricians' union persuading retailers

FIGURE 17–3: *Work Stoppages by Major Issue, 1977*

Major issues	Stoppages		Workers		Days idle	
	Number	Percent	Number*	Percent	Number*	Percent
All stoppages .	5,506	100.0	2,040.1	100.0	34,821.8	100.0
General wage changes......	3,135	56.9	899.5	44.1	21,694.8	60.6
Supplementary benefits......	78	1.4	22.8	1.1	453.5	1.3
Wage adjustments	141	2.6	65.3	3.2	1,625.3	4.5
Hours of work..	15	.3	2.8	.1	84.8	.2
Other contractual matters ..	276	5.0	71.4	3.5	1,350.7	3.8
Union organization and security	252	4.6	41.2	2.0	955.0	2.7
Job security	211	3.8	99.8	4.9	1,708.9	4.8
Plant administration	1,002	18.2	696.8	34.2	7,249.2	20.2
Other working conditions ...	137	2.5	62.7	3.1	338.8	.9
Interunion or interunion matters.........	246	4.5	77.1	3.8	335.4	.9
Not reported ...	13	.2	.5	−0.05	25.4	.1

*Thousands

SOURCE: Adapted from U.S. Department of Labor, *Analysis of Work Stoppages,* Bureau of Labor Statistics, Bulletin 2032, 1979, p. 18.

not to buy the manufacturer's products. A secondary boycott is an attempt to increase the power and strength of the union so that the employer is more likely to give in to union demands. Under the Taft-Hartley Act, secondary boycotts are illegal, except in the construction and clothing industries.

Boycott efforts by picket lines at grocery stores urge consumers to avoid buying a particular product, such as grapes or lettuce. Is this an illegal secondary boycott? No, as the Supreme Court has ruled that the use of pickets to discourage the pur-

chase of a specific product is not a secondary boycott.

EMPLOYER POWER TACTICS

Employers have a number of methods designed to end a bargaining impasse on terms favorable to management. These include the lockout of employees, hiring nonunion employees during a strike, and contracting out work.

LOCKOUT The first tactic, a lockout, is the refusal to allow employees to work until an agreement is signed. Because an employer must normally halt operations with this tactic, the lockout sees only limited use.

In addition, most contracts contain a no lockout clause prohibiting the lockout while a contract is in force. The courts allow the use of this strategy only if the following conditions are met:[6]

1. The contract must have expired.
2. A bargaining impasse must have been reached.
3. A legitimate economic or bargaining interest must be served.
4. Employees may not be permanently discharged or replaced. Replacement is apparently only permissible in multi-employer units.
5. No subjective intent to discourage or interfere with union members' rights to engage in concerted activity may be undertaken.

NONUNION WORKERS Should a union strike, the employer may still attempt to maintain operations. One way this may be done is for supervisors and other nonunion employees to perform the duties of strikers. This strategy may be successful where operations are highly automated and/or routine, and little training is required to perform the strikers' jobs. During a strike between American Telephone and Telegraph and the Communications Workers Of America Union, for example, many supervisors and administrators took over striking operators' jobs.

REPLACEMENT EMPLOYEES A second anti–strike tactic is to hire replacement employees for strikers. According to labor statutes, an employer may hire permanent replacements for economic strikers, but

only temporary replacements for unfair labor practice strikers. This strategy is not without problems. First, many workers will be extremely hesitant to cross picket lines and to be ridiculed as scabs. Second, in the case of an unfair labor practice dispute, realizing proffered jobs are only temporary, workers may hesitate to accept short-term employment. Third, this practice is almost sure to seriously damage labor-management relations and lower workers' morale once the strike has ended.

CONTRACT OUT Another technique for maintaining business is to contract out, or arrange for another company to handle the employer's business during a strike. This may be a useful strategy for firms in very competitive fields or those who fear a strike would damage customer relations. For example, a janitorial service that cleans office buildings may contract out their work until the strike is over. If the subcontractor is unionized, however, employees may legally refuse to perform work for the struck firm. Courts have ruled that this action does not constitute a secondary boycott.

RESOLVING THE BARGAINING IMPASSE

When a bargaining impasse occurs and negotiations stall, labor and management may implement certain techniques to ward off an impending strike or lockout. These techniques, which keep both parties communicating, negotiating, and examining each other's issues and positions, may lead to an eventual resolution of their differences. Each of these methods, mediation, fact-finding, and interest arbitration, requires the involvement of a third party.

MEDIATION The *mediation* process, in which a neutral third party attempts to

---

6. John A. Fossum, *Labor Relations* (Dallas: Business Publications, Inc., 1979), p. 291.

bring the union and employer into agreement, follows no particular format. Mediation may, in fact, take place before an impasse occurs. In this case, labor and management practice preventive mediation, requesting that a mediator participate in the negotiations during the early stages. The presence of a mediator during the collective bargaining process is often instrumental in keeping both parties working toward an agreement without an impasse. In other situations, an impasse may have been reached and a mediator may be called in after negotiations have completely broken off.

The primary role of a mediator is to lead the parties to agreement by acting as a go-between for the union and the employer. The mediator does not have the authority to impose a decision. After feeling out the parties, the mediator determines which demands are actually firm and which may still be negotiated. The mediator must have the confidence of both sides and be perceived as an individual who is truly unbiased and impartial.

After an initial joint session with all three parties, labor and management teams are often assembled in separate meeting rooms with the mediator presenting proposals and counterproposals to each side. While the mediator avoids injecting public opinion or personal feelings into the proceedings, it may become necessary to criticize an extreme demand or unworkable solution presented by either side. Fundamentals that underscore the mediation process and illustrate effective mediator behavior are shown in Figure 17–4.

Mediators are full-time employees of the Federal Mediation and Conciliation Service (FMCS), which was created by the Taft-Hartley Act to help solve labor dis-

FIGURE 17–4: *Elements of the Mediation Process*

1. Conveying understanding and appreciation of the problems confronting both parties.
2. Conveying to the parties a feeling that the mediator understands their problems.
3. Getting the parties to realize that all of their positions are not valid.
4. Suggesting alternative approaches that may facilitate agreement.
5. Maintaining neutrality.
6. Maintaining confidentiality of information disclosed by the parties.

SOURCE: Adapted from Walter A. Maggiolo, *Techniques of Mediation in Labor Disputes* (Dobbs Ferry, NY: Oceana Publications, 1971) pp. 12 ff.

putes. Before becoming mediators, most have had experience in labor relations. After formal training in Washington, mediators are assigned to a regional office to work with experienced mediators.

FACT-FINDING Compared to the mediation process, *fact-finding* is rarely used in the private sector. This public sector process is commonly used to settle disputes involving police officers, teachers, and public health employees. The fact-finding board, composed of three neutral individuals, holds a hearing where each side presents its views regarding the disputed issues. After studying each party's position and arguments, the board issues nonbinding recommendations to the parties.

The Taft-Hartley Act enables the president of the United States to postpone a strike or lockout that may imperil the nation. The procedures for settling these kinds of labor disputes include:

1. The president appoints a board of inquiry to study the issues. If the dispute will lead to a national emer-

gency, the president will order the attorney general to petition a district court to prohibit the strike or lockout.

2. If the court agrees that the dispute is of national significance, it will issue an injunction prohibiting the strike or lockout.

3. If agreement is not reached within sixty days, the board reports to the president the positions of labor and management and the employer's "final offer."

4. Over the next fifteen days, the NLRB secretly ballots the employees to determine whether a majority is willing to accept management's final offer.

5. The injunction is removed after the results are certified, or if a settlement is reached. If a settlement is not reached, the president submits a full report to Congress with the ballot results and his recommendations.

INTEREST ARBITRATION *Interest arbitration* occurs when an arbitrator is called to solve a dispute involving issues in a future contract. Like fact-finding, interest arbitration has seen relatively little use in the private sector. But unlike mediation and fact-finding, the arbitrator not only studies the dispute, but determines and dictates the terms of agreement as well.

Interest arbitration received considerable publicity in labor circles when the United Steelworkers Union and an employers' association of ten steel companies agreed to submit unresolved issues to an interest arbitration panel in order to avoid a strike or lockout. Although differences were resolved and the panel was not called, the inclusion of the interest arbitration provision in the negotiation agreement (formally termed an Experimental Negotiating Agreement) may have speeded the parties toward agreement.[7] Each side, no doubt, preferred to avoid the potential danger of having the arbitrator rule in favor of the other party.

PUBLIC SECTOR COLLECTIVE BARGAINING

By and large, the collective bargaining process for public sector employees on federal and local levels is closely patterned after private sector bargaining processes. This is primarily due to the fact that unionization of government employees did not reach widespread proportions until the 1960s, well after the establishment of collective bargaining procedures in the private sector. Some important distinctions for public sector collective bargaining are worthy of mention.

Right to Organize

While the Wagner Act provides the basic right to organize for private sector employees, federal employees were granted the right to join or refrain from joining unions by President John F. Kennedy's Executive Order 10988. Later, President Richard M. Nixon's Executive Order 11491 superseded E.O. 10988, and listed public sector unfair labor practices similar to those contained within the Taft-Hartley Act.

State laws regarding collective bargaining for public employees vary widely. About half of the states have enacted leg-

7. Ibid., p. 276.

islation which provides collective bargaining for state employees. Some states allow all public employees to organize; others prohibit certain classes of employees from organizing. For example, Georgia's state law forbids police officers from joining unions. The collective bargaining rights of public employees in some states remain neglected or uncertain. In Mississippi and Nevada, for example, no guidelines, statutes, or court decisions exist to clarify the rights of state and local government employees to join unions.[8]

Any member of management, including the first level foreman, is not protected by labor law in the private sector. However, some lower level administrators may join a union and bargain collectively with representatives of the government. As an example, U.S. postal supervisors have their own union, the National Association of Postal Supervisors.

Ban on Strikes

With rare exception, public sector employees are forbidden to strike; the Taft–Hartley Act prohibits strikes against any U.S. government agency. State legislation also prohibits strikes, but some states allow a limited number of exceptions. For example, firefighters may strike in New Hampshire "except where public health or safety is endangered."[9]

Of course, employees at all levels of government have struck in spite of no strike legislation. A nationwide strike by over 200,000 postal workers in 1970 over wage issues remains one of the country's greatest mass strikes, and the first major strike against the federal government. Most public sector strikes, however, take place at local and state levels typically involving teachers, firefighters, police, and sanitation workers. In 1975, no strikes took place at the federal level, 32 at the state level, 44 at the county level, and 252 at the city level. In every year except 1975, school employees have struck for more days than any other public sector employee group.[10]

A greater use of fact-finding and interest arbitration is found in the public sector as compared to the private sector. Because public employees are generally denied the right to strike, these mechanisms act as substitutes for the strike and enable the union to maintain a balance of power should an impasse result. Impasse procedures vary widely from state to state and differ for various bargaining units. Frequently, binding arbitration is applied to groups responsible for public safety such as police officers and firefighters.

▪ GRIEVANCE HANDLING ▪

Our discussion thus far has focused on the creation of a labor–management agreement and the methods for solving impasses that may result. Fortunately, many agreements are created without any serious stalemate. Even though problems may occur during the bargaining stage, an agreement will be signed at some point, except in the rare situations where a strike forces a company out of business or where a company destroys a union. The signing of the contract spells a new relationship between management and labor, as the agreement often reflects significant changes in wages, benefits, work regula-

8. Arthur A. Sloane and Fred Whitney, *Labor Relations* (Englewood Cliffs, NJ: Prentice-Hall, Inc., 1972), p. 522.

9. Fossum, *Labor Relations*, p. 386.

10. Ibid., pp. 389–90.

tions, and other conditions of employment. In effect, the agreement constitutes a new set of game rules, which legally bind management and labor to abide by new rules. Implementation and enforcement of the agreement, referred to as contract administration, represents a critical responsibility for the personnel or industrial relations director.

Unfortunately, regardless of how clearly and objectively a contract is written, disputes will generally arise during its enforcement. Only rarely does any agreement run its term completely void of any conflict. For this reason, most contracts contain a quasi-judicial process to internally solve disputes. If management finds an employee has violated work rules or some aspect of the contract, it will discipline the employee. An employee may be disciplined for any one of many causes: excessive absenteeism, fighting, drinking on the job, verbal abuse, deliberate work slowdown, or disregard for the safety of others. As mentioned earlier, most disciplinary systems are progressive and contain several separate disciplinary steps,

beginning with an oral warning and ending in discharge.

Many labor-management disputes also arise because the union feels the employer has violated some term or provision of the agreement. For example, employees may feel they were passed over for promotions, or unfairly disciplined. If employees and union representatives agree that the violation is serious enough, they will file a *grievance* or a formal complaint against the employer. This sets in motion a formal process designed to settle the differences between the two parties, known as *grievance handling*.

The process for handling grievances varies from agreement to agreement, but most involve four steps:

Step 1

In the initial step, the employee generally discusses the grievance with the shop steward. Experienced in grievance matters and familiar with contract terms and provisions, the steward probably has a good idea of how the contract language

FIGURE 17–5: *Grievance Form*

B. C. Cowen Plumbing Company
7th Street Shop

Grievant N. Collier   Union Local #6, Allied Plumbers

Job Classification Plumber

Grievance No. 14-38F   Date 5/6/81

Statement of Grievance: *I was unfairly discharged because of a minor altercation with the owner, Bruce Cowen. It was his fault and he started the argument. When I returned to the shop at the end of the day, he started ranting and raving at me in front of everybody just because I accidentally overcharged a customer. He was shaking his finger right in my face and I simply pushed it away. Then there was some shoving and I was fired. I have worked here for over four years and have always done a good job. I feel I should have my job back with full pay from the date I was fired.*

Signature of grievant *(N. Collier)*

Union representative *(K. MacLeod)*

Employer representative *(F. Kozmetsky)*

should be interpreted. In effect, the shop steward screens complaints and often persuades employees to drop those which are insignificant or trivial. However, the steward will encourage an employee to pursue a bona fide grievance, assist in the preparation of the grievance, and write it on a special form, like Figure 17–5. The written grievance is delivered to the supervisor, and a meeting of the three parties is held. In discussing the grievance, all of the parties make an honest attempt to settle the matter at that point. Research shows that most grievances are settled at the first step. If the grievance cannot be resolved at this stage, the employee may appeal the decision at step 2 of the process.

Step 2

The format for Step 2 is basically the same as Step 1: both sides meet to discuss the grievance, with labor representing the employee. Higher level union and management officials are involved at this step, however; the union representative may be the steward or business agent; the management representative is often the plant superintendent. If the employee and union representatives are not satisfied with management's results, they may appeal to the next step.

Step 3

At this step, the employee is often represented by a plantwide union grievance committee. The plant manager and industrial relations director often represent management. Again, management hears the employee's case and the union's arguments, and issues their ruling on the matter. If the employee and union are still unsatisfied with the results, they may appeal to a fourth and final step: arbitration.

Step 4

Arbitration is a quasi-judicial process in which the parties agree to submit an unresolved dispute to a neutral third party for binding settlement.[11] During the arbitration process, the arbitrator studies the evidence, listens to the arguments on both sides, and renders a decision. The arbitrator's decision, an *award* to one of the sides, is *binding* in that it must be accepted by both sides and cannot be appealed further. Just how does arbitration work? Some often-asked questions about arbitration are discussed below.

IS ARBITRATION INCLUDED IN MOST AGREEMENTS? Yes. About 95 percent of all contracts provide for binding arbitration if the parties are unable to settle the grievance internally.[12] Either side may request arbitration as a final step to resolving a grievance.

HOW ARE ARBITRATORS SELECTED? Labor and management may agree on the selection of an impartial arbitrator. However, if they cannot, the contract often stipulates that they request a panel or list of seven arbitrators from the FMCS. Arbitrators, are also supplied by the *American Arbitration Association* (AAA), which, like the FMCS, acts as a clearinghouse between the arbitrators and disputing parties. The AAA also sends a panel of names, normally five or seven. By a process of elimination, in turn, each side strikes through a name on the list until an arbitrator is left.

---

11. Ibid., p. 351.
12. W. J. Usery, Jr., "Some Attempts to Reduce Arbitration Costs and Delays," *Monthly Labor Review* (November 1972): 3.

WHO ARE ARBITRATORS? Arbitrators are private consultants, not employees of the FMCS or AAA. There are no special qualifications necessary to be an arbitrator; some are full-time arbitrators (many lawyers specialize in arbitration). Others are part-time arbitrators and full-time college professors who teach law, management, personnel-industrial relations, or economics.

HOW MUCH ARE ARBITRATORS PAID? Who pays their fees? As privately employed professionals, arbitrators set their own fees. The better known, more experienced arbitrators command higher fees than those just breaking into the business. Fees generally range from $250 to $400 per diem. The arbitrator's fee is generally jointly paid by the union and employer.

WHAT ARE THE MAJOR ISSUES THAT GO TO ARBITRATION? A great variety of contract issues are arbitrated every year, but most focus upon a few general areas. Of the 5,243 issues heard by FMCS arbitrators in 1975, 1,812 (34.6%) dealt with discharge and disciplinary issues; 229 (4.4%) with economic issues—wages and other forms of pay; and 691 (13.2%) centered around seniority issues—for example, promotions, bumping, layoff, and recall.[13]

WHAT ROLE DOES THE ARBITRATOR PLAY? Often thought of as a judge hearing a case between two disputing parties, the arbitrator's primary responsibility is to make a fair, impartial, and just decision based on the labor agreement. The arbitrator is free to study the awards of other arbitrators but not bound to the decisions handed down by other arbitrators. Generally, the arbitrator cannot modify the agreement in any way, even when certain language is unclear or the terms of the contract conflict with federal or state legislation.

Nonunion Organizations

Most formal grievance handling procedures are found in unionized companies; relatively few nonunion companies provide mechanisms for processing grievances on par with unionized firms. A 1977 survey of 1,958 *Harvard Business Review* readers showed that only 14 percent worked in companies which had a management grievance committee.[14] Another study found twenty-two of thirty-four nonunion companies had some type of formal grievance procedure.[15] These results are somewhat surprising, as an organizational climate of fairness and justice is dependent, in part, upon a formal channel for handling employee dissatisfaction.

Nonunion organizations that have formal grievance procedures generally pattern them after labor-management contract provisions. An example of a grievance procedure for two affiliated large nonunion hospitals is shown in Figure 17–6.

Reducing Employee Grievances

The best interests of management and labor demand that frivolous grievances be kept at the lowest level while giving serious attention to legitimate problems. Management should regularly monitor

---

13. U.S. Mediation and Conciliation Service, *Twenty-Eighth Annual Report* (Washington, D.C.: U.S. Government Printing Office, 1976) pp. 52–53.

14. David W. Ewing, "What Business Thinks About Employee Rights," *Harvard Business Review* 55, no. 5 (September-October 1977): 81–94.

15. Maurice S. Trotta, *Arbitration of Labor–Management Disputes* (New York: American Management Association, 1974), p. 218.

FIGURE 17–6: *A Formal Grievance Procedure in A Nonunion Organization*

In order to protect the individual rights of the employee, the hospitals have established and maintain a grievance procedure, whereby an employee may present what he/she considers to be a personal injustice regarding his/her employment relationship. Such a grievance must be filed by the employee within five days from the time the situation occurred that may have caused the grievance. Also the following steps should be taken in pursuing the grievance:

(1) The aggrieved employee should first let his/her supervisor know of the complaint. If the employee does not receive a satisfactory reply within two working days, he/she should proceed to Step 2.

(2) At this step, the department head is notified of the complaint in writing by the employee. If the employee wishes assistance in writing the grievance, he/she may request assistance from the personnel department. If a satisfactory reply to the grievance is not received in three working days, then the employee should proceed to Step 3.

(3) At this stage, the director of personnel services or his/her designate is informed of the grievance by the employee. After a review of the facts, the personnel director or his/her designate and the employee may reach a satisfactory solution to the grievance. However, if this does not occur, then the fourth step should be taken.

(4) A peer review committee composed of three impartial employees will be established to review the grievance and establish the facts of the complaint. The members of this committee are subject to the approval of the aggrieved employee. The director of personnel services or his/her designate will serve as a resource person for the committee. However, the peer review committee, alone, makes the recommendation of how the complaint is to be resolved. Within five working days of the hearing, the employee will receive the committee's written recommendation.

(5) Finally, if the employee and/or the department head is not satisfied with the committee's recommendations, then the last step in the appeal process is administration where the final determination is made.

In no way, either directly or indirectly, is the employee to consider his/her job in jeopardy as a result of participating in this procedure.

SOURCE: *Norton-Children's Hospitals Employee Handbook* (Louisville, Kentucky: Norton-Children's Hospitals, Inc., Undated), pp. 17–18.

the volume of grievances and take positive steps to reduce them should they reach excessive levels. While some grievances may be written for trivial reasons or simply to display union power, the grievance may be a true representation of some area of mismanagement or poor supervisory practice. Excessive grievances may result, for example, from inadequate employee training, faulty promotion procedures, discriminatory practices, or overbearing or antagonistic supervision. Thus, excessive grievances often indicate a real need to improve the organization. Concerned about the satisfaction, welfare, and morale of its membership, the union, too, should take excessive grievances seriously and work with management to keep grievances at a minimum.

A second reason to keep grievances at the lowest level possible is that they take a great deal of time and money to handle. The meetings and conferences within the grievance handling process take the employee and management representatives away from their jobs, decreasing productivity. Cases which end up in arbitration require that professional fees be paid to arbitrators; some of the largest industrial firms and labor groups easily spend many thousands of dollars a year on arbitration fees and expenses.

As in many areas of personnel management, maintaining minimum levels of grievances is a responsibility of line managers and staff administrators. The personnel or industrial relations staff should devise programs and procedures to keep employee discontent and grievances at a low level. While there is no one surefire program or technique that will guarantee a grievance-free operation, several methods and practices have been recognized as valuable ways to keep grievances at minimum levels.

ANTI-GRIEVANCE CLIMATE

An organization that strives to create and maintain a healthy, high-morale working climate is much more likely to enjoy a low grievance rate than one which shows little concern for the work conditions of the employee. What are some of the key ingredients in the antigrievance vaccine? The first element is a clearly written, easily understood labor contract, one which has been thoroughly studied by the first level supervisors who are primarily responsible for its day-to-day administration. Management and labor get off on the right foot toward peaceful coexistence by creating an agreement that does not contain ambiguous or vague terms and provisions.

A second element is the need for fair and just dealings with all employees. Fairness in promotions, transfers, layoffs, merit increases, disciplinary action, and other work conditions is critical to keep labor-management conflict at low levels.

Lastly, management and the union should cooperate in achieving peaceful and harmonious labor relations. While unavoidable problems are sure to occur throughout the lifetime of a contract, a spirit of problem solving—rather than a "what I win, you lose" atmosphere—will enhance the effectiveness of the union and the employer. Such cooperation can extend to joint labor-management training resulting in significantly fewer grievances. A large organization that handled up to 3,000 grievances annually sponsored a special program on grievance handling attended by first-line supervisors and shop stewards. During the next eight years, grievances per 100 employees dropped from 17 to 7.[16]

PEOPLE-ORIENTED SUPERVISORS

The attitudes and behavioral patterns of supervisors may have a very pronounced effect on the grievances written. By controlling many of the day-to-day work activities of the employee, the supervisor may become a powerful source of job satisfaction or dissatisfaction.

In a classic study at the International Harvester Company, researchers found a strong relationship between supervisory behavior and the number of grievances filed.[17] Supervisors characterized as considerate (exhibits trust, respect, and warmth toward employees) had significantly fewer grievances filed by their employees than did supervisors who scored high in structure (plans, organizes, assigns duties, shows a great concern for production).

Research findings indicate that management training programs should develop employee-oriented behaviors in addition

16. C. Pettefer, "Effective Grievance Administration," *California Management Review*, 12, no. 1 (Winter 1970): 18.

17. E. A. Fleishman and E. F. Harris, "Patterns of Leadership Behavior Related to Employee Grievances and Turnover," *Personnel Psychology* (Spring 1962): 47–48.

to traditional management skills such as planning, organizing, and controlling. Further, people-oriented skills and aptitudes should be considered when selecting new supervisors. The assessment center concept discussed in Chapter 12 is a valuable technique for determining the extent to which a management candidate may possess people skills in addition to technical and conceptual skills.

OPEN DOOR POLICY

Many times, a grievance may be avoided if an employee is able to discuss a problem with a manager who is willing to make a genuine effort to correct the situation. An open door policy dictates that managers at all levels of the hierarchy have their doors open and are willing to discuss employees' problems. Unfortunately, many open door policies are ineffective because supervisors really don't have the time to listen to the multitude of problems voiced by employees. For an open door policy to be effective, managers must be sincere in acting upon and correcting the problems that employees present.

EXIT INTERVIEW

The primary purpose of the exit interview is to determine the reasons why employees resign. While an employee may be basically content with a job but quit for a better deal elsewhere, job dissatisfaction is a significant factor in an employee's decision to leave. During the exit interview, an interviewer should attempt to determine the real reason for the resignation, even though an employee may be reluctant to discuss the reasons. One technique to minimize an employee's fear of a poor reference is to mail an exit questionnaire to each former employee sev-

eral weeks or months after their departure. By then, the employee is probably employed and will no longer worry about an unsatisfactory reference. Information gathered during exit interviews should be analyzed periodically to pinpoint problem areas such as harsh working conditions, hostile supervisors, or unsafe or unhealthy working environments.

OMBUDSMAN

Within the company setting, an ombudsman is an individual who investigates employee problems and makes recommendations to solve them. Ombudsmen are found in greater numbers in government and other nonprofit organizations than in private industry, although Xerox Corporation and General Electric Company report success with this technique.[18] While the procedure varies considerably, the ombudsman often acts as a complaint center for employees who have special problems which are difficult to deal with through normal channels. After studying and investigating a problem, the ombudsman makes a recommendation to solve the conflict. If the conflict remains unsolved, a recommendation may be carried to a top manager; in some cases, to the president.

ATTITUDE SURVEYS

One quick, relatively inexpensive way to gather data concerning the opinions, attitudes, and job discontent for large groups of employees is to formally survey them through questionnaires. Commercial questionnaires cover many job-related areas. Most general attitude surveys will focus on common topics: satisfaction or dissatisfaction toward (1) the work itself,

18. See "How the Xerox Ombudsman Helps Xerox," *Business Week* (May 12, 1973): 188–190.

(2) pay and benefits, (3) supervision, (4) co-workers, and (5) the organization as a whole. Many organizations implement an attitude survey periodically—often annually—in order to spot problems.[19] Typically, the personnel department will prepare and administer the survey, analyze the results, and, with line management, formulate a set of recommendations. In addition to warding off potential grievance issues, survey results may also be used to assess training needs, appraise management performance, and evaluate the effectiveness of an organizational change program such as job enrichment or organization development.

In summary, single and multiple employer bargaining structures are common today. Multiple employer structures are generally less costly for both parties; the union and the employer enjoy certain advantages from a uniform, industrywide wage structure. Before the actual negotiations begin labor and management do a great deal of prenegotiation homework. The union surveys members' needs and general trends in collective bargaining. Management determines if increased labor costs will affect profitability and which terms and provisions it can afford. The actual negotiation process typically involves a great deal of give and take on both sides before an agreement is reached. If they fail, the resulting bargaining impasse may cause a strike or lockout. During a strike or lockout, an employer may attempt to maintain operations by using nonunion staff, hiring strikebreakers, or contracting out. Fact-finding and interest arbitration are often used to resolve the bargaining impasse in the public sector; mediation is a much more popular technique in the private sector. As full-time employees of the FMCS, mediators do not have the authority to dictate the terms of settlement to the disputing parties. Public sector collective bargaining generally parallels the private sector process. But while federal employees have been given the right to organize by presidential executive order, state laws regarding unionization vary widely. Grievance handling is a critical part of the day-to-day administration of the labor agreement. Most procedures involve a four step procedure in which arbitration is a final step. The arbitrator's authority to decide the outcome of the case must be accepted by both parties. A high grievance rate should receive management's full attention because grievances may represent problem areas; in addition, the process is time consuming and costly. Grievances may be kept at minimum levels by creating a healthy working climate, dealing fairly with employees, hiring people-oriented supervisors, and establishing good two-way communication between labor and management.

---

19. M. R. Carrell, "How to Measure Job Satisfaction," *Training* (November 1976): 25-27.

The Solution

If Midwest Steel Company's president is serious about reducing employee grievances, management will have to do much more than "wait for the union to change its attitude." Grievances will be reduced when the firm takes positive action to find out the cause of so many grievances. Techniques that may be used include employee surveys, exit interviews, and interviews by the personnel staff. Based on the results of this data collection process, the firm may make changes in supervisory practices and/or implement personnel programs that are designed to improve the quality of work life. In cases such as this one the reduction of grievances also requires changes by management—not just the union.

KEY TERMS AND CONCEPTS

Single Employer, Multiple Employer Bargaining
Good Faith Bargaining
Bargaining Impasse
Economic Strike
Unfair Labor Practice Strike
Sympathy Strike
Wildcat Strike
Picket
Primary Situs Picketing

Common Situs Picketing
Primary Boycott
Secondary Boycott
Lockout
Mediation
Fact-Finding
Grievance
Grievance Handling
Interest Arbitration
Arbitration

FOR REVIEW

1. What are the various forms of bargaining structures?
2. What activities take place during the prenegotiation and negotiation phases of collective bargaining?
3. What pressure tactics may the union and employer use during a bargaining impasse? What techniques may be used to bring an end to a bargaining impasse?

4. How does the grievance procedure work and what is the role of arbitration in resolving grievances?

5. What strategies are available to management to keep grievances at a minimum level?

FOR DISCUSSION

1. The ABC Manufacturing Company has twelve work units on the factory floor. The grievances filed by employees in three work units are over four times higher than the other nine departments. Why might this be so? What should management do?

2. The strike has long been a controversial part of the collective bargaining process. Proponents claim the threat of strike provides a critical balance of power between the union and employer. Critics say the strike is a crude, outmoded practice in modern times. What are your opinions about the right to strike?

3. What are the principal differences between the role of the mediator and arbitrator?

4. How does the collective bargaining process differ between public and private organizations?

5. Do you feel that public employees such as police officers and firefighters should have the right to join a union, bargain collectively, and strike? Why or why not?

6. As the president of a small nonunion baking company of 100 employees, you would like to introduce a grievance procedure for your employees. Develop a procedure which you feel would enable employees to resolve their formal complaints.

7. How important do you feel the supervisor is in avoiding strike situations? Discuss.

SUPPLEMENTARY READINGS

Baer, Walter. *Grievance Handling: 101 Guides for Supervisors*. New York: American Management Associations, Inc., 1970.

Elkouri, Frank, and Elkouri, Ena Asher. *How Arbitration Works*. 3d ed. Washington, DC: Bureau of National Affairs, Inc., 1973.

Huntley, G. "Diminishing Reality of Management Rights." *Public Personnel Management*, May 1976, pp. 731–37.

Hutchinson, John G. *Management Under Strike Conditions* New York: Holt, Rinehart, and Winston, Inc., 1966.

King, Geoffrey R. "Seniority, Technological Change, and Arbitration." *The Personnel Administrator,* September 1974, pp. 23–27.

Richardson, Reed C. *Collective Bargaining By Objectives.* Englewood Cliffs, NJ: Prentice-Hall Publishing Co., 1977.

Rime, Thomas Jr. "Arbitration: How to Avoid It." *Personnel,* May–June, 1970, pp. 29–34.

Smardon, Raymond A. "In Collective Bargaining, the Winner Can Be a Loser." *Harvard Business Review* 54 (July-August 1976): 6+.

Tagliaferri, Louis E. "Plant Operation During A Strike." *Personnel Administration,* March-April 1972, pp. 47–51 ff.

"The Unions Begin to Bend on Work Rules." *Business Week,* September 9, 1972, pp. 105–15.

Walton, Richard E., and McKersie, Robert B. *A Behavioral Theory of Labor Negotiations.* New York: McGraw Hill Book Company, 1965.

For Analysis: Making Coffee on Company Premises[1]

On February 10, 1961, the Sheridan Machine Company posted the following notice on all bulletin boards in the plant:

"Over the years the matter of making coffee, etc., has expanded to the point where the lost time involved has become very costly. We have installed brewed coffee machines for the convenience of office and engineering employees. Those employees who do not wish to bring their own beverages in thermos bottles will find the quality of the coffee in these machines quite good. Also, the proceeds from these machines will go into the employees' fund as do proceeds from the other vending machines.

In the interest of good management and the efficient operation of the plant, the making of coffee is to be discontinued. Effective Monday, February 13, 1961, all coffee pots, urns, and hot plates are to be removed from the

[1] Taken from S. H. Schoen and R. L. Hilgert, Cases in Collective Bargaining and Industrial Relations (Homewood, Ill.: Richard R. Irwin, Inc., 1969). All names have been disguised.

premises. No food preparations will be permitted after this date."

Sheridan Machine Company management enforced the provisions of the February 10 notice. The International Union of Electrical, Radio and Machine Workers filed a grievance to protest the company notice and its enforcement. Since the union and company were unable to agree about the employees' practice of brewing coffee and preparing other food on the premises of the company, the grievance was submitted for settlement to an arbitrator.

Both parties to the grievance agreed to the following facts: coffee making by the employees had been permitted for almost fourteen years as union representatives estimated. Representatives for the company estimated that this activity had continued during the negotiations of the three previous contracts. However, the question was not raised during negotiation of the last three contracts. Both parties agreed that the right of an employee to drink coffee was not at issue, this right being granted freely by the management.

The union contended that the issuing of the notice was illegal, since it was prohibited by the past-practice clause of the 1960 contract. Page 3 of the 1960 contract would indicate that the unilateral abolition of the right of employees to make their own coffee is a direct violation: "Practices and policies now in effect and not covered by this agreement shall continue in effect for the duration of this agreement unless changed by mutual consent between the Company and the Union."

To support its position, the union offered the following evidence: (1) Many employees were dissatisfied with the quality of coffee furnished by the machines installed by the company. (2) Expenditures for coffee by employees would be raised by as much as $3 per week. (3) The expense of bringing coffee from home would be increased because of periodic thermos bottle breakage. (4) The time involved in making coffee is minimal; the activity does not interfere with plant efficiency. (5) Plant efficiency is increased because of higher morale, with morale being boosted by the making of coffee to the individual taste. (6) Some supervisors in recent years had joined workers' coffee pools. (7) The issue was raised previously in a meeting attended by management in which a tool room foreman's order to his employees to cease making coffee was overruled by management, when the union offered the past-practices argument to support its protest. Management thus had acknowledged the validity of the union's position. (8) In negotiations of the 1957 and 1960 agreements, management had an opportunity to raise this issue, but it failed to do so.

Management contended that only the right to have coffee available constituted a past practice. The method of making coffee was not a past-practice but was within management discretion. Management contended that the question had not been raised seriously until recently for three reasons: (1) the participation by workers in making coffee had substantially increased and had been extended recently to include the preparation of shortorder dishes during working time before mealtime; (2) the introduction of a wide variety of utensils such as hot plates, sandwich grills, and frying and cooking pans constituted a fire hazard; (3) a wide enough variety of coffee to suit an adequate number of tastes was now available in the new machines installed by management.

Management further contended that these abuses interfered with plant efficiency, thus violating a management right stated in paragraphs 3 (a) and 3 (b) under Article II, Section 1 of the contract as follows: "It is the responsibility of the Management of the Company to maintain discipline and efficiency in its plant."

In this regard, management contended that the practice of coffee making took substantial time away from work, which detracted from plant efficiency and, therefore, must be curtailed. Management's notice was both reasonable and within its rights to manage the plant in an efficient, profitable fashion.

Questions

1. *Should this grievance be considered as a trivial dispute? Why is this the type of grievance which can be of serious consequence to both union and management interests?*

2. *Was management justified in posting its notice of February 10? Does management in this case have the right to prohibit the use of various utensils on its plant premises?*

3. *Which clause of the contract must be considered as being overriding in this case: the practices clause or the management rights clause? Are these clauses in basic conflict with each other?*

4. *What is the fundamental issue at stake for the management of the plant in this case?*

SELECTED PROFESSIONAL READING

Critical Issues and Problems in Collective Bargaining: A Management Perspective

JOHN H. JOHNSON, JR.

To cover all of the critical issues in collective bargaining facing management—or, for that matter, the unions, the employees, or the public—would be an impossible task because there are an increasing number of pressures on the collective bargaining process. Anticipating critical issues which will affect, alter, and shape the ultimate outcome of collective bargaining may best be done by examining the forces that determine what comes to the bargaining table for resolution.

Our form of collective bargaining is virtually unique. Most of our collective bargaining is done between two parties—management and union—with little or no involvement of a government representative. Even where a government mediator enters the bargaining, he is without power to compel the parties to settle or even to meet. Other than the 60-day "cooling off" period for situations which "threaten the national interest" or the occasional White House arm-twisting as was used in the 1967–68 copper strike, our negotiations are remarkably free of third-party interference.

I believe this to be desirable. In order to maintain this desirable condition, all parties in the bargaining process must continue to demonstrate to an ever-eager-to-intervene public and government that intervention is not required. By making settlements that demonstrate a recognition of all of the interests— management, employees, unions, and public—we can delay, and hopefully avert, intervention. To do this, all of us must be cognizant of the needs of the various groups involved in the collective bargaining process. Allow me to focus briefly on four areas of needs which, in the aggregate, may be properly termed critical issues and potential crisis points in collective bargaining: (1) the needs of the employee, (2) the needs of the union, (3) the needs of the employer, and (4) the needs of the public.

THE NEEDS OF THE EMPLOYEE

At the risk of stating the obvious, the paramount issue in any collective bargaining is to satisfy significantly the needs of the employees. If this is done, the collective bargaining agreement will be ratified. Hopefully, during the term of the agreement, labor relations can be conducted in a harmonious and productive climate.

Assessing the needs of the employee is not easy for the employee or his collective bargaining representative. Certainly if it is difficult for the persons most involved—the employee and someone who should be closely involved as his collective bargaining representative—it may be even more difficult for the management representative. The employee's perception of his needs is shaped by many internal and external factors, both economic and noneconomic. His economic needs receive the focus of his attention during the period immediately prior to negotiations and through the first few days after ratification of a new agreement. Of course, these economic needs may receive the most attention if he is out on strike. On the other hand, the employee's noneconomic needs from the collective bargaining process are continuing.

In framing his economic needs, the employee is, of course, governed by what he thinks he should be paid, based upon his perception of what his co-workers are paid, what he thinks his neighbors are paid, and what his wife thinks he should be paid. His economic needs increasingly tend to be shaped by economic settlements being made as a result of public-sector bargaining. The continued enlargement of public-sector bargaining inevitably leads to more opportunity for comparisons. Public-employee negotiations—whether actual negotiations, meet-and-confer, or the ever-present legislative lobbying—receive greater public attention and press coverage than do typical employer-employee private–sector negotiations.

The more the employee reads of what others are paid, the more he increases his evaluation of what he should be paid. For example, when he reads that the new collective bargaining agreement between the union representing city sanitation workers and his city government provides for an $18,000 a year minimum, it is difficult to overcome the employee's value judgment of "if a garbage collector is worth 18 grand, then I'm worth more than that."

In recent years we have been flooded with newspaper, radio, TV, and research accounts of worker discontent. A temporary peak may have been reached a couple of years ago with reports of the situation at the Lordstown, Ohio, GM Vega plant. Lordstown hopefully was an extreme example of a worker's alienation from his job. I think it may also be an extreme example of what results when an employee's needs for acceptable working conditions are not met by the collective bargaining process.

As I indicated earlier, the employee's non-economic needs continue throughout the term of the collective bargaining agreement. To the extent that he is dissatisfied with the contractual method of filling vacancies, assignment of overtime, absenteeism procedures, or even the job he is performing, he reflects his dissatisfaction with grievances, lower productivity, absenteeism, and, when carried to the extreme, sabotage. A sensitivity to the employee's needs to, if not actually enjoy, at least be able to tolerate the workplace will increasingly be a major issue to be resolved. This need will have an impact not only on the collective bargaining process, but also on the ongoing employee-employer relations.

The development and refinement of race-oriented equal employment opportunity during the last few years appears to be crystallizing into a few remaining issues for the collective bargaining process, most specifically in the retroactive seniority question. The courts—as in so many other areas—are developing several guidelines. Unfortunately, the courts are not addressing the problem that we will have to resolve in the collective bargaining process: how to meet the needs of the nonminority employee who can't use his seniority through no fault of his own. The developing female equal employment opportunity question will exacerbate this problem and exert further pressure on the collective bargaining process.

A final area of employee needs which will affect the collective bargaining process is the heightened interest in occupational health and safety. There seems to be little doubt that we will find more and more areas in the workplace where there are real or perceived health and safety hazards. The problem of adequately dealing with these hazards will significantly challenge the collective bargaining process.

THE NEEDS OF THE UNION

Having laid out a number of problems as to the needs of the employee—and you will note that I have and will continue to present problems and not solutions—allow me to forecast how the needs of the union may present critical issues in the collective bargaining process. In my view, most of our unions went through their infancy in the 1920s and 1930s, went through puberty in the 1930s and 1940s, and emerged into adolescence in the 1950s and 1960s. Most have now reached maturity. Just as each of us went through various stages of the life-cycle and encountered "growing pains," the growth of each individual union has presented collective bargaining with its share of "growing pains."

I believe that our labor relations system has seen the slaying of most of the old dragons: the sweat shop, subsurvival-level wages, favoritism, nepotism, and all other familiar old rallying cries of the trade unionists. I also happen to believe that unions did a worthwhile and commendable job in working to correct what were shortcomings of our economic system. I take comfort in the continuing reaffirmation by major responsible union leaders that they want to keep American unionism different from that common in other economic systems. Rather than working to overthrow the system, they believe they can best work within the system to gain a greater division of the rewards.

I hope they will keep reminding themselves of this; our system needs more supporters and fewer detractors. I do view with potential alarm the continuing strain placed on the collective bargaining process by those in union leadership roles who are unable to work within the process in a mature and professional manner. I hope they will not resort to methods more appropriate to an earlier age.

There is no doubt that unions are justified in seeking to improve the economic and noneconomic status of their members. There is also no doubt that management will continue to provide improved economic and noneconomic status for its employees. The formalization and attainment of these goals must be done with a maturity and responsibility which unions now have or must accept. To the extent the long-time mutually beneficial goals of economic growth and employment stability are sacrificed by immature union leadership, the collective bargaining process is jeopardized.

THE NEEDS OF THE EMPLOYER

At this point my union friends are probably quick to tell me, "Don't tell us how to run our business. Worry about yours." I don't find it that easy to separate the roles, rights, and responsibilities of the respective parties. The needs of management in the collective bargaining process will also lead to some crises. The continuing third-party involvement of government regulations, threatened legislation, increased taxation, foreign competition, and environmental and consumer advocates and the growing demands for shrinking new capital will focus more and more of the attention of management on the collective bargaining process. Increasing numbers of industries will feel an inability to meet the economic demands of employees and will more and more expect increased productivity and lower labor costs.

The result of an inability to resolve these conflicts is demonstrated by the railroad industry. Railroad employees, unions, and managements have been conducting their affairs without regard to economics, and the result has been a rail system almost totally dependent upon federal subsidies. A contrasting attempt to balance these interests can be seen in the steel industry where the experimental negotiating agreement and productivity bargaining have been serious efforts to solve the problems of prenegotiation inventory buying, postsettlement layoffs, and the market erosion of lower-cost imported steel.

THE NEEDS OF THE PUBLIC

The needs of the public may be the most illusory and difficult for the collective bargaining process to satisfy. Generally, the American public is a fickle lot. The steelworker who cries for protective tariffs for U.S.-produced steel listens to his Panasonic radio. The construction worker who proudly slaps a "Construction Feeds My Family" bumper sticker on his Toyota pickup is not concerned with losses of American automaking and steelmaking jobs through imports. The teamster on strike for higher wages grouses loudly as he reads of spreading "blue flu" among police seeking higher wages. The manufacturer concerned about shrinking profit margins insists that his contractor "settle at any price" to keep work going on the new factory. The list of contrasts goes on and on.

The point is that each of us tends to view every facet of our economic life with tunnel vision. Control the prices of those who sell to me, but don't control my wages, says the worker, be he laborer or corporate president. Control the wages of my employees, but don't control my prices, says the manager. Reduce pollution. Increase the water supply. Don't increase costs. Don't reduce jobs. All of these conflicting goals cannot be met. There must be a balancing of what the public can expect to receive. If not, the public will increasingly insert itself into the collective bargaining process to curb wage increases, to hold down prices, and to increase employee and management discontent.

The pressures on the collective bargaining process created by the attempts to meet the needs of the employees, the needs of the union, the needs of the employer, and the needs of the public will continue to be critical issues. The ability of the collective bargaining process to meet these challenges satisfactorily will determine the viability of the process. It will demonstrate the ability of our economic system to balance the counter-pressures created by the various needs. I am optimistic about the ability of both the collective bargaining process and the economic system to meet the challenge.

Research helps personnel specialists solve particular problems and evaluate proposed programs.

18

PERSONNEL RESEARCH AND PROBLEM SOLVING

Personnel Research Techniques

Personnel Information Decision System

Perceptions of Unfairness

Job Dissatisfaction

Absenteeism and Employee Turnover

The Problem: Absenteeism at Digitronics, Inc.

*Samuel Dominquez, personnel manager for Digitronics, Inc.,
quickly glanced over his quarterly personnel report. He was
due to go over the report with Plant Manager Jane Newberry
in about five minutes. The report contained information on a
wide range of personnel areas, including direct and indirect
labor costs; cost of employee benefits; new hires, transfers,
quits, and discharges; and data on the firm's absenteeism rate.*

*Digitronics is a medium-sized maker of computer
components located in Los Angeles, California. Digitronics sells
its parts to large computer manufacturers such as IBM and
Honeywell, Inc. The firm has enjoyed relatively peaceful labor
relations and is not unionized.*

*Sam walked a few doors down to Jane's office and took a
seat beside her desk. After exchanging a few pleasantries, they
turned their attention to the report.*

*Newberry: "Sam, all the data look pretty good. Our labor
costs are in pretty good shape, and our turnover is a little
below the industry average. But there seems to be one
problem, absenteeism. I see our overall absenteeism rate is
8.5 percent. That's pretty high, I believe. And the
quarterly trends are slightly increasing. How do our
absenteeism rates compare with industry averages?"*

*Dominquez: "Uh, Mary, I'm not sure. It's pretty hard to find
comparable absenteeism data. I guess most firms don't want
to air their dirty laundry. But I'll check around and see
what I can find."*

*Newberry: "O.K. Incidentally, just what does that 8.5 percent
absenteeism rate represent? How is it figured? Do you have*

*departmental breakdowns so we can see where the problem
is the greatest?"*

*Dominquez: "Well, the 8.5 percent figure is for the whole
company—all 1,200 employees. I'm pretty sure it
represents the total time lost to all kinds of absenteeism.
My assistant prepares the data, and I'm not positive just
how the statistic is computed. I'll check when I get back to
the office. I don't have any breakdown on that figure, but
it shouldn't be too hard to get."*

*Newberry: "I think we'll need some more details on that 8.5
percent figure. We need to compare departments, shifts, and
maybe even look at male and female rates. But Sam, the
real question is how can we get that rate down to about 3
or 4 percent?"*

*Dominquez: "Well Jane, I'm not sure. You know, absenteeism
is a real tough problem, and I don't think there's a whole
lot that can be done about it. Maybe we should hire a
consultant to look into the problem."*

For many managers and administrators today, people problems rank as the most frustrating and stressful work dilemmas. High levels of absenteeism and turnover, a steady stream of employee grievances, low morale, poor work attitudes, resistance to change, and large dosages of human conflict all curb employee productivity and push up operating costs. But the damage caused by extraordinary human problems often extends beyond the firm's current profit picture. An ineffectual and recalcitrant human resource group, coupled with the absence of sound personnel problem-solving techniques, may result in a gradual erosion of the organization's ability to remain competitive in today's complex and uncertain environment. In serious cases of personnel mismanagement, the survival of the organization may well be at stake.

The ability to conduct personnel research and effectively solve personnel problems is of critical importance to personnel administrators today. In contrast to years past, the personnel staff in many organizations is being called upon to play a more effective role in the diagnosis of human problems and the creation of policies and programs to solve them. The creation, implementation, and evaluation of many of the personnel programs discussed in this text—such as job enrichment, management development, the four-day workweek, flextime, and career development—usually involve some form of personnel research. Because human resource program management and personnel research are closely intertwined, the ability to perform research is rapidly becoming a basic requirement for middle and top level personnel administrators in organizations of all kinds today.

PERSONNEL RESEARCH

Personnel research is the investigation of facts related to human resource problems in order to eliminate or reduce the problems. Regardless of the discipline or subject area under study, the primary purpose of research is to seek the truth. Through personnel research, managers and administrators are able to substitute facts about human behavior for armchair theorizing, hunches, guesswork, and gut reactions. In the end, research helps the administrator manage more productively. Personnel research is not a luxury of the personnel department or something that should be done only "if the budget permits." A truly critical and necessary part of an ongoing human resource program, specific uses of personnel research include:[1]

● The measurement and evaluation of present conditions

● The prediction of conditions, events, and behavioral patterns

● The evaluation of current policies, programs, and activities

● The discovery of rational bases for revising current policies, programs, and activities

● The appraisal of proposed policies, programs, and activities.

Types of Research

Most research can be classified as basic or applied. *Basic research*, sometimes referred to as pure research, is undertaken simply to advance knowledge in a partcular field or about a given subject. It is knowledge for the sake of knowledge. The knowledge gained from pure research does not have an immediate application or particular use. While most basic research takes place within the confines of the scientist's laboratory, a great deal of basic research is also performed in human resource management. Most basic research in the personnel area is conducted by college and university faculty and private, nonprofit institutions.

Applied research is conducted to solve a particular problem; its results may be put to immediate use. The majority of personnel research in business firms and government agencies is of this type. Perhaps the earliest example of systematic, comprehensive applied research was the famous Hawthorne Studies which took place at the Western Electric Company's Hawthorne Works during the late 1920s.[2] Overall, the Hawthorne Studies involved thousands of employees and focused on the human behavioral areas of employee productivity, morale and job satisfaction,

---

1. Michael J. Jucius, *Personnel Mangement* (New York: Richard D. Irwin, Inc., 1971), pp. 534–35.

2. See F. J. Roethlisberger and W. J. Dickson, *Management and the Worker* (Cambridge, MA: Harvard University Press, 1939).

group dynamics, and leadership styles. Today, applied personnel research is still concerned with these areas, and expanded to include equal employment opportunity, job design, organization development, human resources planning, recruitment and selection, and labor–management relationships.

Personnel Researchers

Personnel research is conducted by individuals and a variety of public and private organizations. One study showed that $25 to $55 million were spent on personnel research annually, with 39 percent of the research conducted by private research organizations, 34 percent by academic institutions, 22 percent by agencies of the federal government, and 5 percent by business firms.[3]

FEDERAL GOVERNMENT
Many federal government agencies conduct both basic and applied research; perhaps, the most publicized government research has been done by the Government Accounting Office and Department of Defense concerning weapons systems and military readiness. In the personnel field, agencies within the Department of Labor, primarily the Bureau of Labor Statistics (BLS), conduct and report research. The Department of Labor's *Monthly Labor Review* contains the results of studies of a wide range of personnel and human resource topics.

PRIVATE RESEARCH ORGANIZATIONS
Many private organizations have been formed with the sole purpose of conduct-

ing pure and applied research in the personnel/industrial relations area. Some of these organizations include the National Industrial Conference Board (NICB), Bureau of National Affairs (BNA), and Brookings Institution.

PERSONNEL ASSOCIATIONS
Large national and international personnel associations periodically conduct research based on the practices and activities of their members' organizations. Some of these associations include the International Personnel Management Association (IPMA), American Society for Personnel Administration (ASPA), and the American Society for Training and Development (ASTD). The results of these studies are often reported in the association's journals, such as ASPA's *The Personnel Administrator* and ASTD's *Training and Development Journal*.

COLLEGES AND UNIVERSITIES
Institutions of higher learning not only disseminate knowledge but bear an important responsibility for creating knowledge as well. The collectivity of colleges and universities represents one of the greatest sources of basic and applied research in the personnel field. Many faculty members conduct research as a normal part of their employment responsibilities. In addition, many learning institutions also operate research centers to conduct both basic and applied research projects in conjunction with the business community. One of the best known university research centers is the University of Michigan's Survey Research Center where personnel have conducted pioneering studies in human behavior within an organization setting. Their long–standing work on employee job satisfac-

3. William C. Byham, *The Uses of Personnel Research*, Research Study 91 (New York: American Management Associations, Inc., 1968), p. 8.

tion trends remains one of the most sophisticated studies of workers' attitudes to date.

BUSINESS FIRMS

Many business firms conduct applied personnel research to solve a particular problem or evaluate a present or proposed program or project. Several larger firms, such as General Electric Company, IBM, and AT&T operate full-scale behavioral research departments. Most firms do not have a specialized personnel research function but require personnel administrators to perform research as a normal part of their jobs. Common examples of ongoing research responsibilities of personnel staff members may include:

Evaluating training and development programs

Conducting periodic wage and salary surveys

Predicting future human resource requirements

Conducting periodic employee attitude surveys

Conducting employee productivity studies

Validating selection and testing instruments

Finally, personnel administrators frequently receive requests from line managers to conduct special, ad hoc studies of some employee behavior problem. These studies are often requested because of some difficult personnel problem the manager is confronted with. Special studies of this type are an important part of the personnel department's service responsibility. Examples of research requests from other departments may include:

- Investigation of extraordinarily high employee grievances in a particular manufacturing department.

- A program to reduce absenteeism among clerical personnel.

- Evaluation of certain changes in a labor-management agreement which will impact on employee productivity.

- Development of a strategy to enable the employer to win a union certification election.

- Development of a special performance appraisal method for sales personnel.

Although line managers may occasionally conduct a personnel research project themselves, more normally they support the personnel staff throughout the project. For the research study to be successful, the personnel administrator generally needs the cooperation and assistance of the line manager. Assisting with the design of the study, providing performance data, allowing operative employees to be interviewed or to complete survey forms, and reviewing research results are some examples of the ways the line manager may support the personnel research effort. Personnel administrators can garner the support of line managers by explaining why research is necessary and showing how research results may help them perform their jobs more effectively.

Personnel Research Publications

The results of personnel research may be found in a wide variety of outlets. Reading all of the research literature in the field is, of course, unpractical—and also physically impossible—for a manager or administrator. However, the prudent manager and staff member will keep up to date on the major research results and use the findings to promote managerial effectiveness, employee productivity, and job satisfaction within the organization. An awareness of the important research is one way to keep abreast of the newly–developed policies, programs, and techniques that show promise for making organizations function more efficiently.

Scores of bulletins, research reports, working papers, and monographs containing personnel research are regularly published by numerous public and private organizations. But perhaps the most practical and expedient way for a personnel administrator to keep on top of the research is by regularly reading a selected group of personnel journals and magazines. The following list contains journals that frequently report research results in a variety of personnel areas.

Journals Written Primarily for the Academician
  Academy of Management Journal
  Administrative Science Quarterly
  Industrial and Labor Relations Review
  Journal of Applied Behavioral Science
  Journal of Applied Psychology
  Organization Behavior and Human Performance
  Personnel Psychology
Journals Written Primarily for the Practitioner
  Advanced Management Journal
  Business Horizons
  California Management Review
  Harvard Business Review
  Human Resource Management
  Management Review
  Monthly Labor Review
  Organizational Dynamics
  Personnel
  Personnel Administrator
  Personnel Journal
  Public Personnel Management
  Supervisory Management
  Training and Development Journal
Indices and Abstracts Containing Personnel Subjects
  Business Periodicals Index
  Employee Relations Index
  Management Abstracts
  Personnel Management Abstracts
  Psychological Abstracts

RESEARCH TECHNIQUES

Several different research techniques may be used to create and analyze knowledge; the choice of a particular method depends upon the purpose of the research and the type of problem under study. Familiarity with various research methodologies is important for two reasons. First, practitioners encounter a variety of human problems at work; the appropriate research technique must be applied to the particular study in question. The selection of an inappropriate research method may seriously affect the study's overall validity and usefulness. Second, a broad knowledge of research techniques is necessary in order to read and understand the studies that are reported by other employers and by researchers outside the organization. Practitioners must critically evaluate the research of others, differentiate between good and poor research, and train and develop research–oriented skills and abilities among subordinates. The primary research techniques used to conduct studies in personnel include:

Employee Surveys

The employee survey is the most widely used research technique among personnel administrators today. Two popular survey methods include the job satisfaction or *attitude survey* and the general purpose questionnaire.

JOB SATISFACTION SURVEY

Since the beginning of the human relations movement, managers have sought their employees' opinions and attitudes concerning a wide range of topics and issues. Because morale and job satisfaction have been important determinants of employee productivity, absenteeism, and turnover, for many years managers have systematically collected and analyzed data concerning employee attitudes to make jobs more satisfying and ultimately more productive.[4] For example, if survey results show that large numbers of employees are dissatisfied with supervision, rewards, decision making, or other conditions of work, management may make changes in the hope that employee discontent will disappear or be reduced. After changes in supervision, opportunities for advancement, or the pay system, another survey may measure whether or not attitudes have, in fact, changed. Thus, an attitude survey may be used to pinpoint areas of employee dissatisfaction and to appraise the effectiveness of the organizational changes that were introduced. Such "measure before, change, measure after" designs are commonly used to evaluate how effective change strategies have been in altering employees' attitudes.[5]

The nature and design of attitude surveys vary greatly, but most focus on employees' attitudes toward supervision, co-workers, the job, and the organization in general. Rather than creating an attitude survey, a personnel researcher should purchase commercially available instruments that have been tested for validity and reliability in actual organizational settings.[6] Homemade attitude surveys often contain confusing, ambiguous statements which may intentionally or unintentionally distort an employee's response. One of the most widely-used job satisfaction surveys is the *Job Descriptive Index* (JDI) which is available to researchers at a nominal cost. Sample questions on the JDI are shown in Figure 18–1.

For maximum effectiveness, employee surveys must be properly planned, administered, and analyzed. There are many different opinions about how employee surveys should be conducted, and Figure 11–5 highlights two broad, contrasting approaches: the traditional way and the organizational development way. As Figure 11–5 points out, the use of employee surveys via the organizational development approach involves greater employee participation in survey planning and analysis. The approach chosen for conducting the survey depends on several factors,

---

4. Although job dissatisfaction has been linked with absenteeism and turnover in many studies, the relationship between job satisfaction and productivity remains a controversy. See Arthur H. Brayfield and Walter H. Crockett, "Employee Attitudes and Employee Performance," *Psychological Bulletin* 52, no. 5 (September 1955): 396–424; and Charles N. Green, "The Satisfaction–Performance Controversy: New Developments and Their Implications," *Business Horizons* (October 1972): 31–41.

5. For a full treatment of experimental designs, see Donald T. Campbell and Julian C. Stanley, *Experimental and Quasi-Experimental Designs for Research* (Chicago: Rand McNally Publishing Co., 1963).

6. A description of various kinds of attitude surveys and how they may be obtained is included in Michael R. Carrell, "How to Measure Job Satisfaction," *Training* (November 1976): 25–27.

including the purpose of the survey, employees' needs, and management's attitudes about how surveys should be con-

FIGURE 18–1: *A Job Descriptive Index Sampler*

Think of the kind of supervision that you get on your job. How well does each of the following words describe this supervision? In the blank beside each word below, put:

y	if it describes the supervision you get on your job
n	if it does NOT describe it
?	if you cannot decide

Supervision on Present Job

Asks my advice _____
Hard to please _____
Influential _____
Quick tempered _____
Tells me where I stand _____
Stubborn _____

Think of the opportunities for promotion that you have now. How well does each of the following words describe these? In the blank beside each word, put:

y	for "Yes" if it describes your opportunities for promotion
n	for "No" if it does NOT describe them
?	if you cannot decide

Opportunities for Promotion

Good opportunities for promotion _____
Opportunity somewhat limited _____
Promotion on ability _____
Dead-end job _____
Regular promotions _____

Think of your present work. What is it like most of the time? In the blank beside each word given below, write:

y	for "Yes" if it describes your work
n	for "No" if it does NOT describe it
?	if you cannot decide

Work on Present Job

_____ Fascinating
_____ Boring
_____ Respected
_____ Challenging
_____ Frustrating

ducted. Personnel researchers should be aware of different strategies to implement and analyze surveys; the selection of a particular method will depend upon certain personal and organizational variables.

GENERAL PURPOSE QUESTIONNAIRE

Aside from collecting data about satisfying and dissatisfying work factors, personnel researchers often find it useful to gather workers' opinions about certain nonattitudinal areas related to their jobs. For example, employees may be asked to evaluate the organization's training and development function, orientation program, or a proposed flextime or job enrichment program. Because these questionnaires focus on an organization's particular problems or issues, they are generally custom designed by members of the personnel staff or an outside consultant. Items from a questionnaire concerning employee absenteeism are illustrated in Figure 18–2.

Interviews

Another research technique that receives widespread use is the face-to-face interview. Often held to evaluate proposed organizational changes, interviews are also used to evaluate changes that have taken place. To collect valid information using this technique, there must be trust and goodwill between the interviewer and respondent. An interviewer should stress that each individual's responses will be kept confidential and that only aggregate data will be reported.

The interview may take several forms. The *structured interview* asks the same questions of all respondents, much like a census taker who personally collects information from various households.

FIGURE 18–2: *Supervisory Absenteeism Questionnaire*

THE FOLLOWING QUESTIONS CONCERN THE *PRESENT* ABSENTEEISM CONTROL SYSTEM. PLEASE ANSWER ALL QUESTIONS.

1. At present, what is the absenteeism rate of your work unit?_____%

2. To what extent is employee absenteeism a productivity problem in your work unit?
   Not a problem at all   A very significant problem
       1   2   3   4   5

3. On the average, about how many hours per week do you feel you spend on problems related to absenteeism (talking with employees who call in to report an absence; calling absent employees; securing, training, and checking the work of replacement employees; counseling chronic absentees, etc.).
   0–1 hours_____   2–3 hours_____   4–5 hours_____   6–7 hours_____
   8 or more hours_____

4. Overall, I am satisfied with the present absenteeism control system.
   Strongly Agree Agree Neither Agree nor Disagree Disagree Strongly Disagree
       1   2   3   4   5

5. The present system allows employees to be absent and tardy too often.
   Strongly Agree Agree Neither Agree nor Disagree Disagree Strongly Disagree
       1   2   3   4   5

6. The present system has no rewards for employees who come to work regularly.
   Strongly Agree Agree Neither Agree nor Disagree Disagree Strongly Disagree
       1   2   3   4   5

7. The present system is difficult for employees to understand.
   Strongly Agree Agree Neither Agree nor Disagree Disagree Strongly Disagree
       1   2   3   4   5

SOURCE: Frank E. Kuzmits, *SUPERVISORY ABSENTEEISM QUESTIONNAIRE,* University of Louisville. Used by permission.

The *unstructured interview* is used to collect general opinions about work-related issues of interest to the interviewer and respondent. The interviewer usually begins the interview by asking a very broad question such as "tell me about the most satisfying parts of your job." The *open-ended interview* is a cross between structured and unstructured interviews and enables interviewees to freely respond to a structured question. For example, the interviewer may ask "What are your opinions about the new performance appraisal system?" Finally, many interviewers combine these approaches during an interview asking questions that are structured, unstructured, and open-ended.

Historical Studies

Personnel researchers often find tracking certain data for a time is beneficial in gaining a greater insight into human behavior. By isolating a small number of organizational and personal variables, a historical study analyzes patterns over weeks, months—or in some cases—years. For example, many organizations analyze absenteeism and turnover data to assess whether these problems are increasing, decreasing, or remaining unchanged. One example of a long-standing, historical study is a project mentioned earlier—the University of Michigan's Survey Research Center Job Satisfaction Survey.

Since 1958, the center has tracked a large sample of employee attitudes concerning overall satisfaction with work. Thus far, research indicates that most employees have been satisfied with their jobs and that workers' attitudes have changed little in over two decades. The results of the center's research and studies performed by the National Opinion Research Center are shown in Figure 18–3.

FIGURE 18–3: *Studies of Job Satisfaction*

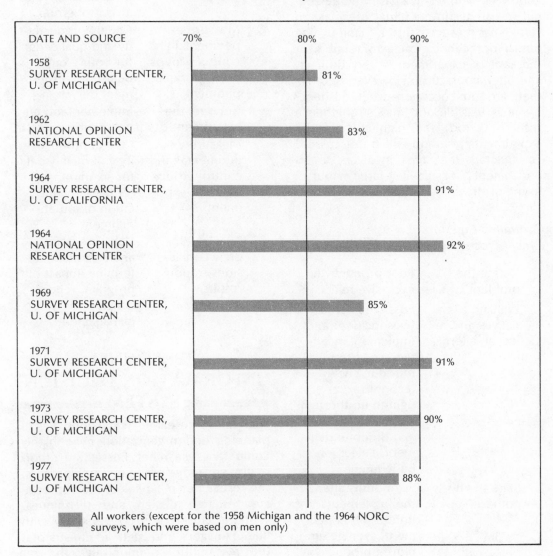

Adapted from Robert Quinn *et al, Job Satisfaction: Is There a Trend?* U.S. Department of Labor, Manpower Research Monograph no. 30, Manpower Administration, 1974, p. 4.

Controlled Experiment

Compared to the survey and interview, *controlled experiments* are rarely used in actual personnel practice. Unlike the scientist's laboratory or a professor's classroom where variables are created and controlled with relative ease, the personnel researcher in an actual organization setting has no such control. Manipulating human or technological factors simply for the sake of experiment is very difficult, and often impractical. However, because there are some occasions when this technique is feasible and may strengthen a research effort, the highlights of the experimental method will be discussed. To illustrate the steps involved, a job enrichment pilot study in a large manufacturing plant will be used.

Controlled Experiment Procedure	Example
1. Define the problem	Poor productivity, excessive rejects
2. Evaluate alternatives and select an alternative	Possible alternatives include: a) implement incentive pay system, b) introduce new technology, c) tighten up through closer supervision, and d) job enrichment. Select job enrichment.
3. State the hypothesis	Six months after the implementation of job enrichment, average employee productivity will have increased by 20 percent and the average rejects per employee will have decreased by 25 percent
4. Select experimental and control groups	Implement job enrichment in one area; select a similar area to serve as a control group
5. Measure experimental and control groups prior to the experiment	Collect productivity and quality data for both groups before the experiment begins
6. Conduct the experiment	Implement job enrichment
7. Measure experimental and control groups after the experiment	Collect productivity and quality data for six months after the implementation of job enrichment
8. Analyze data, draw conclusions, report results	Compare before and after data, determine impact of program, report conclusions to top management

PERSONNEL INFORMATION DECISION SYSTEM

High quality research takes a good deal of planning and organization by a highly competent researcher. Possessing a thorough knowledge of the research process, the researcher must select the appropriate research design and techniques. Working closely and cooperatively with line managers and staff administrators, the researcher communicates the research results, their implications, and desirable organizational changes or further research.

Extremely important in carrying out high quality personnel research is timely, accurate, and relevant personnel information. Without information, any form of decision making—including research—is impossible. Often times, personnel administrators are frustrated in their attempts to carry out meaningful research because they lack sound personnel data. A sophisticated absenteeism study, for example, would be impossible without relevant absenteeism data broken down by employee, supervisor, department and, perhaps, by other important categories such as age, sex, or job title. A comprehensive training needs survey cannot be undertaken unless the researcher can gather accurate information related to an employee's previous training and experience, current level of performance, and anticipated job changes. Not only is high quality information a key ingredient for a research undertaking, but it enables managers and administrators to make effective day-to-day decisions. Because of the importance of collecting meaningful information quickly and inexpensively today, more and more personnel managers are developing and implementing a formal *Personnel Information Decision System.* This information system is usually computer based, and designed to store and retrieve personnel data for applications in record keeping, personnel decision making, and personnel research.

Personnel managers and administrators have, of course, always had information systems to assist them in performing their jobs. Before the advent of electronic data processing, the personnel administrator's information system usually consisted of rows of filing cabinets packed with manila personnel folders. This rather inelegant technology was satisfactory for simply storing data, but totally inappropriate for meaningful personnel decision making and research, particularly in the larger organization. In a firm with several thousand employees, the cost of manually collecting data from employees' folders could conceivably outweigh the potential benefits of using the data to solve a personnel problem or conduct personnel research.

Computer technology has enabled significant advancements in the management of information in all areas. In the personnel area, computerized information systems enable administrators to store vast amounts of personnel data that may be easily and quickly retrieved. In addition to storage and retrieval, the computer may also be programmed to carry out practically any form of mathematical operation quickly with almost no chance for error. Reports and analyses that were too time consuming and laborious with manual systems may be processed in a fraction of the time with a computer system.

PIDS Model

A PIDS model is illustrated in Figure 18–4. The model contains five basic elements: inputs, transformation, outputs, feedback, and control. The input-transformation-output process turns raw personnel data into information that may be used to make personnel decisions and assist in the performance of personnel research. For example, sales forecasts and skills data inputs may be transformed into output data indicating that a 10 percent increase in assembly-line operators and 5 percent increase in sales personnel are required to produce and sell the firm's products for the coming year. Or, a transformation of skills inventory data and per-

FIGURE 18–4: *A Personnel Information Decision System (PIDS)*

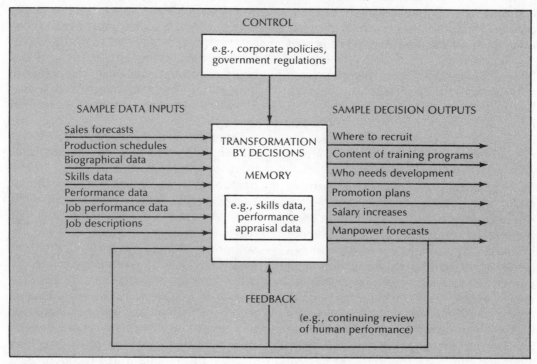

CONTROL

e.g., corporate policies, government regulations

SAMPLE DATA INPUTS

Sales forecasts
Production schedules
Biographical data
Skills data
Performance data
Job performance data
Job descriptions

TRANSFORMATION BY DECISIONS

MEMORY

e.g., skills data, performance appraisal data

SAMPLE DECISION OUTPUTS

Where to recruit
Content of training programs
Who needs development
Promotion plans
Salary increases
Manpower forecasts

FEEDBACK

(e.g., continuing review of human performance)

SOURCE: Paul S. Greenlaw and Robert D. Biggs, *Modern Personnel Management* (Philadelphia: W. B. Saunders Co., 1979), p. 15.

formance appraisal data may show that certain employees are in need of specialized training and development activities. The feedback element enables managers to continually review the effectiveness of their decisions so that decision processes may be changed as needed. For example, if equal employment goals are not being met, inputs may be altered to include more relevant information concerning the sources of qualified minority job candidates. Finally, the control mechanism acts as a guide in collecting and acting upon data generated by the system. The control element includes information about policies, standards, procedures, and government regulations. In effect, the control mechanism guides managers and admin-

istrators in using data effectively to accomplish organizational objectives. For example, the requirements outlined in the firm's affirmative action program may form an important part of the control element. In this case, the feedback element would inform decision makers of the extent to which the decisions are achieveing the firm's written equal opportunity goals.

RESEARCHING ▰ PERSONNEL PROBLEMS ▰

People problems represent some of the toughest and most burdensome dilemmas faced by managers today. One sometimes hears a manager claim, "if it weren't for people, my job would be a breeze." Of course, the mechanical side of organizational life can present burdens, too. But with proper preventive maintenance procedures, a machine or assembly line will generally hold up its end of the job. In addition, a machine is highly predictable; it never gets sick, is never late for work, never leaves early, and when switched on, will do the same thing time after time after time. Not only is a machine reliable, but it works without complaints, gripes, grumbles, or squawks—legitimate or otherwise. The machine fares well under verbal abuse and can even withstand physical abuse. An occasional kick, slam, scratch, poke, punch, or slap will probably roll off the machine—at least the sturdy ones—much like water off a duck's back. To top it off, a machine does all this for practically nothing. Wages or benefits are not necessary to keep the machine hard at work; it would never dream of asking for a raise, merit increase, or cost of living adjustment. Perhaps a little oil here and there, maybe some fuel of some sort, and periodic doses of tender loving care by its operator are about all it ever wants or needs. Yes, it is entertaining to envision how much easier organizational life would be if it weren't for people.

Entertaining perhaps, but the robot run organization is only a technocrat's dream that will never come true. With all their problems and promises, people will always be the key resource for any organization, regardless of how sophisticated and advanced our technologies become. Good managers waste little time wishing for impossible organizational utopias; instead they recognize the inevitability of human problems, create organization structures that minimize people problems, and deal with such problems when they occur.

One important responsibility of the personnel manager is to pinpoint and resolve human resource problems which claim a lion's share of management's time and effort. In many organizations—particularly large manufacturing firms—a small number of hardcore personnel problems require the special attention of the line management team and personnel staff. Solving these problems often requires a research study to learn more about the problem, followed by the implementation of one or more strategies to reduce or eliminate factors causing the problem. Included in the most pressing personnel problems are excessive employee absenteeism and turnover, job dissatisfaction, perceived unfairness, and excessive grievances.

Absenteeism

Employees' failure to show up for work creates problems of widely varying degrees for managers and administrators. The Monday morning absence of a personal secretary or administrative assistant may not present any real hardships for the boss, as the employees' work may often be put off until they return to work. But when 10 to 15 percent of the midnight–to–seven shift of a large manufacturer stays out on Friday night, havoc may result. Gaps on the assembly line force supervisors to transfer employees from noncritical areas to jobs where a worker must be present before the line can begin moving. Replacement employees must be quickly trained to perform unfamiliar jobs; even though the task is routine and easy to learn, their unfamiliarity with the job often creates quality and productivity problems. The supervisor must check replacement employees' work closely—this takes time that should be spent on other supervisory duties. In short, excessive employee *absenteeism* can significantly drain productivity and profits, creating innumerable problems for supervisors and the employees who work regularly. Nationwide, the total cost of absenteeism in 1978 including wage and benefit payments to absent employees and the estimated losses in profit, were a staggering $26.4 billion.[7]

The cost of absenteeism to individual organizations will generally parallel the size of the work force. In large manufacturing firms employing several thousand workers, the annual cost of employee absenteeism could easily amount to a six—and sometimes seven—digit figure. Decision makers should periodically compute the cost of absenteeism to their organizations; Figure 18–5 illustrates a procedure for making these computations. The resulting data will indicate the severity of the problem and the impact of absenteeism upon profits; a historical study indicates whether the total absence-related costs are increasing or decreasing.[8]

CAUSES OF ABSENTEEISM

Although absenteeism is one of the most complex employee problems faced by managers and administrators today, it is possible to isolate variables that influence employees' decisions to attend work. A model illustrating the interaction of these variables is shown in Figure 18–6. As the model suggests, personal characteristics affect the employee's motivation to attend and ability to attend. Put another way, absenteeism results when an employee cannot work (ill, missed the bus, sick child to care for), or does not want to attend work (job too boring, job too stressful, dislikes co-workers or supervisor, receives no rewards for attendance). These two variables often interact. For example, an employee may not feel up to par on a Monday morning following a long, boisterous weekend. Even though an employee may be tired but physically able to go to work, because the job is boring, the boss is hostile, the co-workers are unfriendly, or the union contract includes a liberal provision regarding sick leave, the employee may call in sick. Because each employee faces unique personal and work situations, no two employees will be absent for the exact same causes. Largely for this reason, employee absenteeism represents one of the organization's toughest personnel problems.

MEASURING ABSENTEEISM

Absenteeism represents one of many unique forms of employee behavior. Administrators will generally find it useful to compute and analyze these absenteeism measures:

TOTAL TIME LOST. Total time lost, one of the most popular measures, is used by the Bureau of National Affairs to study absenteeism in firms throughout the nation. The computation gives a percentage of total time lost to absenteeism. The formula for the measure is:

$$\frac{\text{Number of days lost through absenteeism for the period}}{\text{(avg. number of employees)} \times \text{(total days)}} \times 100$$

7. R. M. Steers and S. R. Rhodes, "Major Influences on Employee Attendance: A Process Model," *Journal of Applied Psychology* 63 (1978): 391–407.

8. Frank E. Kuzmits, "How Much Is Absenteeism Costing Your Organization?," *The Personnel Administrator* (June 1979): 29–33.

FIGURE 18–5: *Estimating the Cost of Employee Absenteeism*

Item	Acme International	Your Organization
1. Total man-hours lost to employee absenteeism for the period	78,336	
2. Weighted average wage/salary per hour per employee	$4.32	
3. Cost of employee benefits per hour per employee	$1.90	
4. Total compensation lost per hour per absent employee A. If absent workers are paid (wage/salary plus benefits) B. If absent workers are not paid (benefits only)	$6.22	
5. Total compensation lost to absent employees (total man-hours lost × 4.A or 4.B, whichever applicable)	$487,250	
6. Total supervisory hours lost on employee absenteeism	3,840	
7. Average hourly supervisory wage, including benefits	$9.15	
8. Total supervisory salaries lost to managing problems of absenteeism (hours lost x average hourly supervisory wage—item 6 x item 7)	$35,136	
9. All other costs incidental to absenteeism not included in the above items	$38,500	
10. Total estimated cost of absenteeism—summation of items 5, 8, and 9	$560,887	
11. Total estimated cost of absenteeism per employee (Total Estimated Costs) (Total Number of Employees)	$\dfrac{\$560,886}{1200} =$ $\$467.41$ per employee	=

SOURCE: Frank E. Kuzmits, "How Much Is Absenteeism Costing *Your* Organization?" p. 31. Reprinted with permission from the June 1979 issue of the *Personnel Administrator* copyright 1979, the American Society for Personnel Administration, 30 Park Drive, Berea, Ohio 44017.

The percentages may be used to determine the extent of an organization's absenteeism problem by comparing percentages among supervisors, departments, and plants to pinpoint problem areas. Administrators may also compare their total absenteeism rate to firms included in BNA's periodic reports on absenteeism and turnover. Figure 18–7 shows BNA absenteeism survey results for January through September, 1980.

ABSENCE OCCURRENCES. An absence occurrence is an absence of any length. For example, an employee absent on Monday collects one absence occurrence. An employee absent Monday, Tuesday, and Wednesday, also collects one absence occurrence. Why is it useful to gather this information? Perhaps this question can be answered by posing another: As a manager, which employee would create more problems at work: an employee who is absent twenty times a year for a total of twenty days, or an employee who is absent once for twenty days straight? Employees who collect numerous one-day absence occurrences present a much greater burden than the employee who may have one or two short-term illnesses. This statistic is valuable in pinpointing the chronic absentee who creates real headaches for the first-line supervisor.

FIGURE 18–6: *Factors Influencing Employee Attendance*

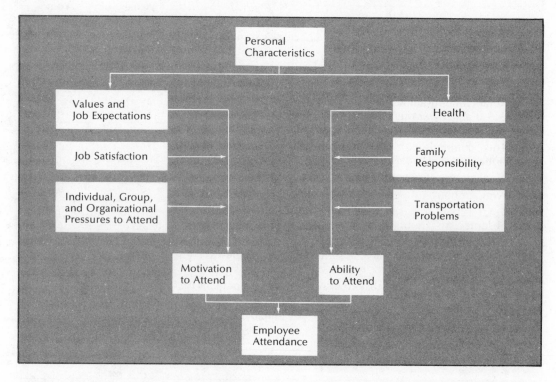

SOURCE: R. M. Steers and S. R. Rhodes, "Major Influences on Employee Attendance: A Process Model," *Journal of Applied Psychology*, 1978, 63, 393. Copyright 1978 by the American Psychological Association. Reprinted by permission.

TARDINESS. Tardiness is a form of absenteeism which can create work problems, particularly in manufacturing environments where machines and assembly lines are scheduled to start at a specific time. Excessive tardiness disrupts normal working operations, making it difficult for first level supervisors to synchronize the beginning of a shift operation.

PART ABSENCE. Employees will sometimes leave work for a portion of the day or request to leave work early. Because these part absences can also disrupt normal working operations and productivity, they should also be recorded separately.

RESEARCHING ABSENTEEISM

Historical studies are often useful in pinpointing absence problems. For example, a one year history of absence data may be studied by employee, work group, shift, department, and plant to determine which individuals and groups may be major contributors to the problem. In high absence areas, the results of attitude surveys and exit interviews should be analyzed to locate possible sources of dissatisfaction which may be partially responsible for the problem. Absenteeism costs should also be computed for high absenteeism areas, and interorganizational

FIGURE 18–7: *BNA Absenteeism Data*[1]

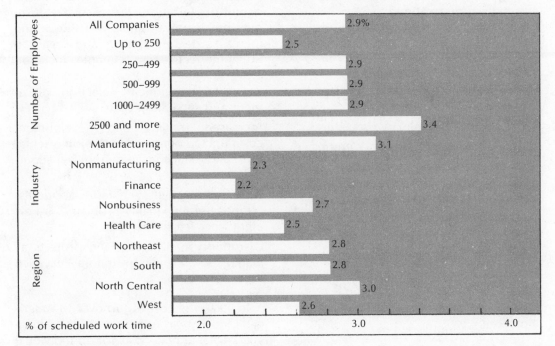

¹Includes 455 Employers with a total employment of 678,929

SOURCE: Reprinted by special permission from *Bulletin to Management: Personnel Policies Forum*, 1980, by the Bureau of National Affairs, Inc., Washington, DC

comparisons of absence data may be made by examining BNA survey data. An absenteeism audit may also be used to assess the overall effectiveness of a firm's absenteeism control system.[9] Audit procedures involve examining the variables which have an impact on employee decisions to attend work, including absenteeism policies and goals, discipline and rewards, alcoholism, employee selection practices, supervisory practices, and the absenteeism control information system.

9. Frank E. Kuzmits, "How Good Is Your Absenteeism Control System?," *Advanced Management Journal* (Winter 1980): 4–15.

REDUCING ABSENTEEISM

Because employee decisions to attend work result from a unique mix of personal and organizational factors, no single approach will solve the problem. The control of employee absenteeism in large, complex organizations will normally involve multiple strategies that include strengthening both the employee's motivation and ability to attend work. Specific strategies include:[10]

10. See *Employee Absenteeism and Turnover* (Washington, DC: Bureau of National Affairs, Inc., 1974): 4–7; and Kuzmits, "How Good is Your Absenteeism Control System?" pp. 4–15.

Strategies for strengthening the employee's motivation to attend

Match the employee with the job

Enrich the job

Reward good attendance

Provide human relations skills for supervisors

Use positive disciplinary procedures

Create small, cohesive work groups

Clarify attendance standards

Strategies for strengthening the employee's ability to attend

Create a safe, healthy work environment

Provide day-care facilities at the place of work

Create programs to assist troubled employees

Employee Turnover

As noted in Chapter 12, most personnel movement takes place through employee promotions, demotions, and transfers. Another form of employee movement involves *turnover:* the movement of employees into and out of the organization. Turnovers commonly result from resignations, discharges, and retirement. In relative terms, death is a very minor cause of turnover.

A certain amount of turnover is expected, unavoidable, and considered beneficial to the organization. New employees at the upper levels of the organization inject fresh blood into the firm by introducing new ideas, methods, and innovative, more effective ways of doing things. In addition, turnover may help rectify poor hiring and placement deci-

sions. Thus, some turnover renews a stagnating organization. But excessive turnover creates an unstable work force and increases personnel costs and organizational ineffectiveness. Examples include:

Increased recruitment, selection, placement and separation costs.

Increased training and development costs, including more on-the-job orientation and coaching required by supervision.

Lower productivity and more accidents, scrappage, and quality problems as new employees learn their jobs.

Disruption in programs and projects as managers and administrators leave in excessive numbers.

In 1980, the cost of turnover to American industry was estimated at $11 billion a year. Total annual costs for an individual firm will, of course, vary according to the size of the firm and the kinds of employees leaving. Because upper level managers and administrators require a great deal more training and development time and are much more difficult to replace, significant turnover among these employees will be quite costly to the firm. One mid–seventies estimate of the cost of recruiting, hiring, and training a nonexempt employee was $1,000 versus $14,000 or more for a manager.[11] Another mid–seventies estimate puts the cost of replacing a manager at $40,000.[12] Hiring an outside consulting firm to find a top level manager can add significantly to the cost of turnover. Headhunters—executive

11. Donald L. Hawk, "Absenteeism and Turnover," *Personnel Journal* (June 1976): 293.
12. Douglas T. Hall and Francine S. Hall, "What's New in Career Management," *Organizational Dynamics* (Summer 1976): 17.

search firms—may charge the company up to one-third of the annual salary of each new employee they deliver. Thus, a $75,000 per year vice-president will earn the search firm a fee of $25,000. Of course, this fee is only one of the many costs involved in replacing a top manager.

CAUSES OF TURNOVER

The causes of turnover are a complex mix of factors both internal and external to the organization. Figure 18–8 highlights the primary elements that have been determined to affect employee decisions to quit.[13]

General economic conditions have an important bearing on the overall availability of jobs. Thus, turnover closely follows economic swings; turnover is high during periods of growth or prosperity and low during recessions and low points in the business cycle. Local labor market conditions refer to not only the local economic conditions but also the supply-demand ratio for specific kinds of occupations and professions in a given geographical area. Thus, the outlook for a particular field could be good or poor regardless of general economic conditions. Personal mobility, or the extent to which one is bound to a particular area because of family or other social ties, is also a factor in deciding whether to leave a particular area. Employees who perceive a low degree of job security in their present jobs may be motivated to seek employment in organizations where they believe a greater degree of security exists. This perception is influenced to some extent by the involuntary transfers and terminations that occur. Finally, several demographic vari-

ables have been linked to the high turnover employee. Employees with a propensity to quit are low seniority employees dissatisfied with their jobs, or young employees. A large percentage of voluntary turnover occurs in the first few months of employment. Employees with relatively large families and important family responsibilities tend to remain on the job.[14]

MEASURING TURNOVER

Much like the absenteeism, turnover may be viewed as a multifaceted form of employee behavior. Thus, each form of turnover will be computed differently. Formulas for three popular turnover measures include:

Separation rate =
$$\frac{\text{Separations during the month}}{\text{Total employees at midmonth}} \times 100$$

Quit rate =
$$\frac{\text{Total quits}}{\text{Average working force}} \times 100$$

Avoidable turnover rate =
$$\frac{\text{Total separations} - \text{unavoidables}}{\text{Average work force}} \times 100$$

While all three formulas may provide important data for decision makers, most organizations use the total separation rate when computing their own turnover statistics. Recommended by the U.S. Department of Labor, the total separation rate is used by most companies that take part in BNA Surveys.[15] When making compari-

---

13. Hawk, "Absenteeism and Turnover," pp. 294–95.

14. L. W. Porter and R. M. Steers, "Organizational, Work, and Personal Factors in Employee Turnover and Absenteeism," *Psychological Bulletin* 80 (1973): 151–76.

15. BNA, *Employee Absenteeism and Turnover*, p. 2.

FIGURE 18–8: *Turnover*

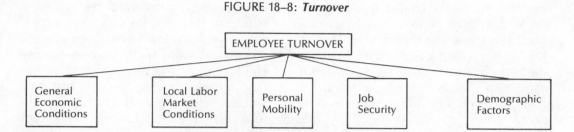

sons across firms, it is, of course, important that the same formula has been used throughout to avoid mixing apples and oranges. BNA turnover data for the first nine months of 1980 are shown in Figure 18–9.

RESEARCHING TURNOVER

Like employee absenteeism, permanent separation from the organization may stem from a variety of causes. Therefore, it is generally prudent to research the problem by using a variety of research methods. When researching turnover, management is usually concerned only with learning more about voluntary turnover—the reasons behind good employees quitting. Those who retire or are fired are generally not the focus of turnover research.

Most organizations analyze the problem using historical studies to spot high turnover work areas and to make interorganizational comparisons. Aside from quarterly BNA reports, turnover studies are published by the federal government and various personnel and management associations. Because job dissatisfaction is a significant cause of turnover, researchers often pinpoint specific areas of work that cause significant dissatisfaction. Attitude surveys can be most useful for this purpose, and general purpose questionnaires may also be used to collect opinions. Exit interviews are particularly valuable in discovering the causes of turnover. In fact, the prime reason for conducting the exit interview is to ask why the employee is quitting.

One interesting way to research turnover is to look at the opposite side of the coin and determine why people stay. In studying this question, researchers found that a variety of work and nonwork factors keep employees from leaving. Financial rewards were found to be an important factor, as were geographical location, social ties, and the local school system. Based on the likelihood of leaving, researchers developed four profiles to describe most employees:[16]

- Turnovers—highly dissatisfied at work, free of external pressures, and will quit at the first chance.

- Turnoffs—dislike job but stay because of pay, benefits, or some other extrinsic job reward.

- Turnons—highly satisfied and motivated at work but may leave if external pressures become significant.

- Turnons plus—highly motivated at work and satisfied with the local environment, likely to remain and continue to be productive.

16. Vincent S. Flowers and Charles L. Hughes, "Why Employees Stay," *Harvard Business Review* (July-August 1973): 49–60.

FIGURE 18–9: *BNA Turnover Data*

Average Monthly Rates: January–September 1980

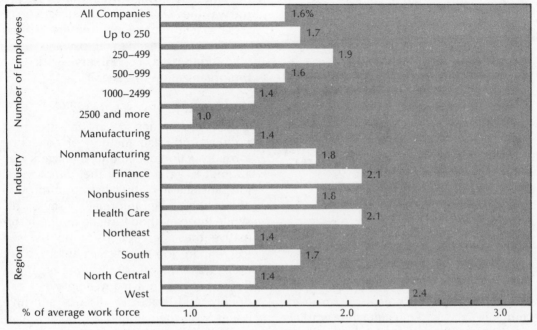

SOURCE: Reprinted by special permission from *Bulletin to Management: Personnel Policies Forum*, 1980, by the Bureau of National Affairs, Inc., Washington, D.C.

REDUCING TURNOVER

An organization's success in reducing turnover is closely tied to its success in pinpointing the real reasons why employees choose to leave or stay. Assuming that researchers have collected valid data on the causes of turnover, the next task is to implement policies, procedures, or programs to correct the deficiencies that exist. A turnover control program that works for one company may not work for another, as the underlying causes may vary significantly. Many companies have reported success in reducing turnover; their efforts began by researching the causes of the problem. Programs, policies, and other forms of organizational change that have reduced turnover include:[17]

- Programs designed to enhance job satisfaction may reduce turnover because of the link between job dissatisfaction and turnover. Such programs include fair and equitable wage and salary structures, competitive benefits packages, training and promotion possibilities, and employee grievance procedures.

- Valid selection procedures which place the right person in the right job.

17. BNA, *Employee Absenteeism and Turnover*, pp. 11–12.

- Proper orientation procedures.

- Close contact between the supervisor and new employee, so that the supervisor may iron out job problems and support the employee.

- Supervisory training and open lines of communication between the supervisor and employee.

- Explaining benefits to employees and how their total wage/benefits package compares to other firms in the area.

- Exit interviews and employee surveys to pinpoint areas of discontent.

Job Dissatisfaction

When some or even a few employees become dissatisfied, costly problems can result. Excessive absenteeism, turnover, and grievances often result when workers experience high levels of *job dissatisfaction*. While a price tag cannot be hung on job dissatisfaction, the economic cost of the outcomes of job dissatisfaction may be estimated. Aside from the obvious economic value of high job satisfaction, many managers also attach a social value to job satisfaction. As part of their social responsibility, many administrators strive to create rewarding and satisfying work environments for their employees. Therefore, managers have many reasons to recognize the significance of job satisfaction and understand the potential outcomes of both satisfying and dissatisfying work environments.

CAUSES

An employee's satisfaction is the "difference between the amount of some valued outcome a person receives and the amount of that outcome he feels he should receive."[18] Thus, an employee becomes dissatisfied when things are not the way they should be. Job satisfaction or dissatisfaction generally centers around certain issues dealing with pay and benefits, supervision, co-workers, work, and the organization in general.

MEASURING JOB SATISFACTION

Survey techniques are by far the most popular and valid method of collecting job satisfaction data. Some managers may attempt to get a feel for their employees' job satisfaction or dissatisfaction through observation or informal discussions. While these methods are, no doubt, informative, these perceptions cannot be used to compare job satisfaction among work units, departments, or different organizations. Further, not many employees can openly and honestly discuss sensitive issues with their immediate bosses, particularly if the employee feels the boss is a part of the problem!

Nonattitudinal organizational data are sometimes used as surrogate measures of job satisfaction's effect on absenteeism, turnover, and grievances. However, measuring job satisfaction through such indirect means has two pronounced shortcomings: First, job dissatisfaction may not be the sole cause of an absence, quit, or grievance. To illustrate, factors such as a child's illness, transportation problems, marital discord, drug addiction, or alcoholism may cause an employee's absence. Second, measuring job dissatisfaction by analyzing outcomes provides no information regarding the causes of the outcomes. One of the greatest benefits of a well-constructed job satisfaction survey is

---

18. Martin J. Gannon, *Organizational Behavior*, (Boston, MA: Little, Brown, and Company, 1979), p. 186.

that it will cover all significant job dimensions that affect job satisfaction. A valid and reliable paper-and-pencil survey is the least costly and most valid way to measure employees' satisfaction with their jobs and the conditions that surround their work.

RESEARCHING JOB DISSATISFACTION

Through proper survey techniques, management can learn a great deal about the attitudes of employees. This information is often researched through:

1. Average satisfaction indices (satisfaction with work, pay) for various employee groups (supervisory work groups, departments, plants, shifts, males, females) are compared with one another and against the organizational norm in order to spot areas of unusually high dissatisfaction.

2. The same data generated above are often analyzed by historical studies. This analysis will indicate the direction that various satisfaction indices are taking and, perhaps, evaluate any change programs the organization may have implemented to reduce job dissatisfaction.

3. Satisfaction indices are often correlated with absenteeism, turnover, grievances, or accidents to determine whether job dissatisfaction is linked to some other personnel problem. To illustrate, a survey of a work group with unusually high turnover may indicate that there is significant dissatisfaction with opportunities for advancement. This suggests that employees may be leaving for better opportunities in other companies and that management should study the problem further.

REDUCING JOB DISSATISFACTION

Survey results only pinpoint the type and extent of job dissatisfaction. The most difficult challenge for management and staff is to successfully implement the changes transforming dissatisfying experiences into satisfying ones. Because the sources and kinds of dissatisfaction vary from organization to organization and among departments and work groups within a single organization, management often makes organizationwide changes and other changes within smaller organizational subgroups. Based on the common dimensions of job satisfaction, a small sampling of policies and programs that may be implemented to improve satisfaction includes:

PAY AND BENEFITS: Strengthen pay and benefits to be more competitive. Pay incentive programs. Supplement the unemployment benefits program. Award bonuses for outstanding work.

WORK: Enrich the jobs through more decision making and control over the work, teamwork through small work groups, and greater variety of tasks. Train and develop employees to increase skills and abilities. Improve working conditions (temperature, lighting, safety).

SUPERVISION: Train and develop supervisors and/or hire new supervisors who clarify job responsibilities, let employees know where they stand, supervise fairly and justly, help people with work problems, solicit workers' opinions on decisions that affect their work, and go to bat for workers with upper management.

CO-WORKERS: Increase teamwork and cooperation by clarifying group goals, decreasing work group size to increase group cohesiveness, and involving groups in decision making for important decisions. Create group incentive pay and bonus systems. Enforce policies and standards for all group members fairly.

ORGANIZATION: Create greater opportunities for advancement. Base promotions on performance unless prohibited by union contract. Pursue affirmative action goals aggressively. Promote from within. Maintain open lines of communication throughout the organization.

Perceptions of Unfairness

Most employees expect to be treated fairly and justly in all aspects of their work; those who feel that the organization has treated them unfairly may react in one of many ways: Senior employees will often decide that they have invested too many years to risk creating a disturbance. Instead, they may do only as much as they have to do to get by until retirement. Or worse, senior employees may decide to get even with the supervisor or the company; they probably know how to cause the company trouble without getting caught. Young employees who feel the company has shortchanged them may feel less inclined to stay with the organization. Immediately following an incident of unfair treatment, an employee's short run response often will be low productivity, a lack of attention to quality, and the tendency to use excuses to be absent from the job. Sometimes employees will rationalize what occurred and after several months the incident may be forgotten.[19] If many of these incidents occur, or if an employee feels that other organizations will be more equitable, the long run consequence may well be that the employee leaves the organization.

The costs to an organization which has many employees perceiving unfair treatment are difficult to compute. Research has determined that employees' perceptions of inequitable treatment are very strong predictors of job absence and turnover, two costly employee behaviors.[20] The organizational costs which increase due to unfair treatment of employees include:

Direct Costs
  Lower production quantity
  Low production quality
  Greater absenteeism
  Greater turnover
Indirect Costs
  Less initiative
  Lower morale
  Lack of cooperation
  Spread of perceptions to co-workers
  Fewer suggestions
  Less self-confidence

MEASURING PERCEPTIONS OF FAIRNESS

Measuring employees' feelings about fair treatment is a difficult process. A manager's first impulse is to come right out and ask, but the probability of receiving an honest answer to a verbal question is low. The only practical alternative is to ask for written anonymous answers.[21] One advantage of using written questionnaires is that the possible sources of perceived inequity can often be identified. This can be accomplished by comparing the results between departments, over a length of time, and among the dimensions of fairness described in Figure 18–10.

19. Michael R. Carrell, "A Longitudinal Field Assessment of Employee Perceptions of Equitable Treatment," *Organizational Behavior and Human Performance* 21 (1978): 108–18.

20. John E. Dittrich and Michael R. Carrell, "Organizational Equity Perceptions, Employee Job Satisfaction, and Departmental Absence and Turnover Rates," *Organizational Behavior and Human Performance* 24 (1979): 29–40.

21. Michael R. Carrell, "How to Measure Job Satisfaction," p. 25.

FIGURE 18–10: *Organizational Fairness Questionnaire*

PAY RULES (nine questions). Perceptions of the fairness of one's pay relative to one's co-workers and the fairness of the rules for granting pay increases and promotions. Sample Statement: "The rules for giving pay raises are not fair to some employees."

PAY ADMINISTRATION (five questions). Perceptions of the fairness of the supervisor in administering the rules for pay raises and promotions. Sample Statement: "My supervisor rates people unfairly in considering people for promotion."

WORK PACE (eight questions). Perceptions of the fairness of the supervisor in maintaining a fair pace of work activity. Sample Statement: "My supervisor sees to it that all of us meet work standards."

PAY LEVEL (five questions). Perceptions of the fairness of one's pay relative to others' pay outside of the employing organization. Sample Statement: "Other companies in this area pay people doing my kind of job less than I am getting paid."

RULE ADMINISTRATION (four questions). Perceptions of the fairness of supervisors in maintaining acceptable forms of general behavior in the work place. Sample Statement: "My supervisor allows workers to tease other employees, be late to their work stations, and to act improperly in other ways."

DISTRIBUTION OF JOBS (six questions). Perceptions of the fairness of supervisors in distributing tasks to subordinates. Sample Statement: "My supervisor sees that everybody in my department does a share of the more unpleasant jobs."

LATITUDE (six questions). Perceptions of the fairness of supervisors in permitting subordinates latitude for planning and personal decision making on the job. Sample Statement: "In working with me, my supervisor is fair in letting me decide how to do my work."

SOURCE: Organization Fairness Questionnaire, © by John E. Dittrich, Ph.D., University of Colorado, 1977. Used by permission.

While equity and fairness are synonymous, the term *fairness* is found in labor law; for example, "a fair day's work for a fair day's pay." Fairness in disciplinary actions is required in many labor contracts; i.e., "no employee will be subject to disciplinary action except for just cause." Therefore, fairness should be incorporated into a questionnaire. Preferably, the personnel specialist will utilize an existing survey instrument which has been validated and is less likely to be biased. Sample questions from one such instrument, the Organization Fairness Questionnaire, appear in Figure 18–10.

RESEARCHING UNFAIRNESS

Organizations should measure employee perceptions as a routine matter. Employees surveyed on a regular basis become accustomed to filling out the forms and are more likely to give honest responses. If the organization waits until a crisis occurs, employees feel they are being patronized and suspect that the organization does not really care how they feel. Another advantage of conducting the fairness study on an annual basis is that organizations can analyze changes in employee perceptions and possibly pinpoint reactions to organizational changes.

REDUCING UNFAIRNESS

After reviewing the results of a survey of employee fairness/unfairness perceptions, management may find introducing one or more organizational changes necessary. Potential changes that may reduce perceptions of unfairness include:

- Reclassify jobs which appear inequitably paid.
- Change the method by which tasks are assigned to jobs.
- Alter the method of deciding promotions; i.e., base promotions solely on performance.
- Train supervisors to distribute the work load more fairly.
- Conduct wage surveys of the local labor market to determine compatability with local firms.
- Allow employees more latitude in planning and controlling their work.
- Ensure that policies, procedures, rules, and regulations are uniformly administered and enforced.

In summary, government agencies, private research organizations, personnel associations, colleges and universities, and individual business firms conduct personnel research. Within business firms, personnel research is usually conducted by the personnel or human resource staff. A sound personnel research function can significantly strengthen an organization's human resource program by evaluating present and proposed personnel policies, programs, and activities. Most research performed by personnel administrators is applied research to solve a particular problem or evaluate a proposed personnel program or activity. A key requirement for a sound personnel function is a valid and timely personnel information decision system (PIDS). Without relevant information, it will not only be difficult to carry out meaningful research, but the personnel administrator's day-to-day decision making effectiveness will be limited. In conducting personnel research, surveys, questionnaires, and interviews are used to gather employees' feelings and perceptions about job satisfaction and dissatisfaction. Although personnel administrators and line managers must confront a wide array of people problems, hardcore problems—absenteeism, turnover, job dissatisfaction, unfairness, and grievances—consume an inordinate amount of line and staff time.

The Solution

Samuel Dominquez, personnel manager for Digitronics, has displayed a considerable lack of knowledge about absenteeism control. Dominquez claims that comparable absenteeism data are hard to find, but he should know the BNA publishes quarterly absenteeism and turnover data for selected industries. Dominquez also needs to strengthen the firm's information system regarding absenteeism. The personnel information system should regularly compute absence data by department, work group, and job classification to determine where the problem is most severe. The information system should also regularly generate various kinds of abseenteeism statistics such as absences, tardiness, part-absences, and Monday/Friday absences. Finally, while Dominquez is correct in stating that "absenteeism is a real tough problem," there are policies and programs that have successfully combated the problem. If Dominquez regularly subscribed to a selection of personnel journals, he would be aware of contemporary techniques that organizations use to keep absenteeism at manageable levels.

KEY TERMS AND CONCEPTS

Basic Research	Controlled Experiment
Applied Research	Personnel Information Decision System (PIDS)
Attitude Survey	Absenteeism
Job Descriptive Index (JDI)	Turnover
Structured Interview	Job Dissatisfaction
Unstructured Interview	Unfairness
Open-ended Interview	Equity

FOR REVIEW

1. Describe the primary uses of personnel research.

2. Discuss the areas in which a business firm may find it beneficial to conduct applied research.

3. What are the steps involved in conducting a controlled experiment?

4. What causes employee absenteeism? How may absenteeism be reduced?

5. Is turnover good or bad for the organization? What problems may result from excessive turnover?

6. What is the most effective way to measure job dissatisfaction? In what different ways may job attitudinal data be analyzed?

7. What makes employees feel they are being treated unfairly? What personnel programs may be implemented to reduce feelings of employee unfairness?

FOR DISCUSSION

1. Assume you are a personnel manager in a large insurance company. At a luncheon meeting, a sales representative for MUSICO, a firm which sells piped in music in office buildings, claims "if you install MUSICO, your clerical employees will be happier and more productive." Could you set up a controlled experiment to determine the effects of MUSICO on employee morale and productivity? Should your company buy the MUSICO system?

2. In analyzing turnover records, you find that over one half of your MBA management trainees leave your large urban bank within one year of being hired. How would you conduct research on this problem? Speculate what some reasons for the turnover problem might be and offer some alternative solutions to eliminate or reduce these causes.

3. Whose responsibility is it to control employee absenteeism—the line manager's or the personnel manager's? Explain how the responsibility for controlling this problem might be divided.

4. Many companies employ outside consultants to research an organizational problem and recommend how to solve it. What are the advantages and disadvantages of using consultants rather than having internal personnel staff research a problem?

5. Research shows that the greatest percentage of absenteeism is accumulated by blue-collar and clerical workers and that managers and staff professionals are absent from their jobs very little.

What reasons account for this? Apply Figure 18–6 in formulating your answer.

6. The Schwartz Company implements an attitude survey once a year. The personnel manager found that job satisfaction increased overall among Schwartz employees from 1979 to 1980; the organization has done nothing specifically to improve job satisfaction. What could account for these results?

7. Why is relatively little basic research conducted within the organization by personnel researchers?

8. Assume your company has a significant turnover problem and you want to read upon the subject. At the library, (1) find out what organizations regularly publish turnover data, and (2) determine how these turnover figures are computed, and (3) gather some recent turnover data and report them to the class.

═══════ **SUPPLEMENTARY READING** ═══════

Byham, William C. *The Uses of Personnel Research. AMA Research Study 91.* New York: American Management Association, 1967.

Bernthal, Wilmer. "Research Foundations for Modern Personnel Administration: A Review and Appraisal." *The Personnel Administrator,* May-June 1965, pp. 25–27.

Goode, Robert. "How to Get Better Results From Attitude Surveys." *Personnel Journal,* March 1973, pp. 187–92.

Locke, E. A. "What is Job Satisfaction?" *Organization Behavior and Human Performance* 4 (1969): 309–36.

Miner, M. G. "Job Absence and Turnover: A New Source of Data." *Monthly Labor Review* 100 (1977): 24–31.

Morano, R. A. "Opinion Surveys: The How-To's of Design and Application." *Personnel* 51 (1974): 8–15.

Personnel Policies Forum. *Employee Absenteeism and Turnover.* Washington, DC: Bureau of National Affairs, Inc., 1974.

Price, J. L. *The Study of Turnover.* Ames: Iowa State University Press, 1977.

For Analysis: Better Bread Baking Company

The Better Bread Baking Company (BBBC) is a medium-sized manufacturer of bakery products located in New Albany, Indiana. BBBC employs approximately eight hundred blue—collar workers and ninety managers, staff, and administrative personnel. The company produces bread, rolls, donuts, and cakes for distribution through retail grocers. BBBC has been in existence for over fifty years, and has enjoyed good labor—management relations throughout most of its history. The company is not unionized.

Unfortunately, the past few years have seen a gradual erosion of the peace that traditionally characterized the relationship between labor and management. Turnover has become a real problem and supervisors report that grumbling along BBBC's long and winding production lines has become the rule rather than the exception. Employee absenteeism has become a particularly critical personnel problem. A gradual increase in employee absenteeism has led to production scheduling problems and a considerable overtime and weekend work—at time and one-half. To add to these problems, replacement employees' work is often of lower quality, resulting in supervisors having to spend inordinate time checking their work.

Jim Reeves, BBBC's plant manager, has decided that something must be done about the company's absenteeism problem. Reeves has been with the company for about twenty years, having started at BBBC in the shipping department as a clerk. Reeves has decided to start attacking the problem by calling his staff together for a conference, they were: Bob Davidson, Manager of Packing; Rodney Sipe, Manager of Baking; Dick Niemann, Manager of Sanitation; Charles Ferguson, Manager of Shipping; Donna Baker, Personnel

Manager; and Marsha Whitehall, Office Manager.

The meeting started promptly at 2 p.m. Whether engaged in a social tête-á-tête or a discussion about a problem at work, Reeves had a habit of getting to the point.

Reeves: "All right, you all know why we're here. I've spent a lot of time reviewing the plant's absenteeism and tardiness records for 1980, and I've come to two simple conclusions. One, our absenteeism rates are too high; two, we've got to do something about them. Our purpose for meeting today is to review all the pertinent records and decide what we are going to do. I want a clear cut plan for reducing our absenteeism problem. And I want it before we leave today, so let's get started.

O.K., now I'm going to throw the meeting open to anyone who wants to give us some ideas about how we can reduce our level of absenteeism to something we can live with. Any ideas?"

Not a word was spoken. Eyes were glued on the large, oval conference table. Fingers fidgeted. People shifted uncomfortably in their stiff chairs. Reeves, noticeably frustrated, glanced sternly about the room.

Donna Baker broke the ice: "Ah, Jim, maybe it would be a good idea to start off by reviewing some of the statistics I've been working on. As you'll notice on this chart, I've done an analysis for 1980 by department, showing the percent of leave taken for all reasons except vacations and holidays and the total tardiness for each department."

Reeves: "Good job, Donna. That gives us something to start with. Rodney, let's focus on your area for a moment. There seems to be no question that you have some real problems. Your absenteeism rates are the highest of all departments in the plant. What is the problem in Baking?"

Sipe: "Well, Jim, it's certainly true that my department suffers

Better Bread Baking Company

Absenteeism and Tardiness Data for 1980

Department	Hourly Employees	Total Absenteeism Paid	Total Absence Occurrences	Incidents of Tardiness Per Employee
Packing	137	6.8%	6.5	8.5
Baking	340	8.5%	7.2	9.3
Sanitation	198	5.9%	4.4	5.6
Shipping	111	4.5%	3.9	6.4
Administration	35	3.8%	3.3	3.9
Total	821	5.9%	5.1	8.7

a pretty high absenteeism rate. But we also have some of the toughest jobs in the plant. It gets awfully hot down there around those ovens, and I suspect a lot of employees just have to get away and take a day off every now and then. And you know another thing, I think we've got a higher percentage of younger employees than anyone else, and these young people don't give a damn about work. It seems like a lot of the young men and women are absent on Monday and Friday, particularly around holidays falling on Saturday or Sunday. And Derby weekend—Ha! Might as .well close down the Friday before Derby.''

Davidson: "I have to agree with Rod. The young people seem to be causing us real problems. And there's another big problem I have in my area. Several of my supervisors complain they're not sure what our policies are on absenteeism. Seems that many of the guys are interpreting the policy in different ways. And to add to that, we don't know how bad an employee's absence record has to be

*before we discipline or discharge. Maybe Donna could help
us out here a bit."*

*Baker: "The policy on absenteeism is spelled out in the
employees' handbook, which all employees should have.
[Baker picked up the handbook and turned to the section
on absenteeism.] The policy reads 'all employees are
expected to be at work on time as scheduled. Each employee
receives eight paid sick days per year, which are not
accumulative. BBBC will pay for one day per year personal
leave and two days per year to attend a funeral. In case of
jury duty or military leave, BBBC will pay the difference
between the pay for jury duty or military leave and regular
wages for the period. Absences beyond eight sick days per
year are not paid, and excessive unpaid absences are cause
for disciplinary action. Continued excessive absenteeism may
result in dismissal.'*

*"It seems that about two years ago we sent around a
memo stating that more than six days of unpaid absences
per year would be considered sufficient cause for dismissal."*

*Neimann: "Yes, but what about our loyal employees who have
put in a lot of years here, and who have special problems?
Like old Jim Cook. Hell, he's been on the line almost thirty
years, and his drinking problem affects his attendance every
now and then. But basically he's a good employee. We all
like him. And quite honestly, I think many of our
supervisors are lenient with the senior employees, and I
can't say as I really blame them. They're always there
when we really need them, like for overtime and holiday
work."*

*Ferguson: "And we all know we've got our share of Jim Cooks.
It would be interesting to know how much better our rates
would be if we didn't have the bottle to contend with."*

Whitehall: "I had an employee tell me something interesting the other day during a discussion on absenteeism. She said, 'There's no incentive to come to work regularly. Most supervisors don't seem to care about good attendance. I only missed two days' total last year—and I was really sick on those days—and no one showed a single iota of appreciation. Maybe I'll start taking my day a month like a lot of other people around here.' "

Reeves: "Well, hell, it seems a little strange to me that we should have to pat people on the back for simply doing what they were hired to do. But, then again, some of this behavioral science stuff I read every now and then says that people may be motivated by recognition. What do you think, Donna? You're our resident expert on the psychology of work."

Baker: "In our supervisory training programs, we tell supervisors of the importance of giving positive feedback— er—recognition to employees who do good work. I don't think we talk specifically about absenteeism, but it might not be a bad idea to include that in our program. I might add that some companies have found paying people for their unused sick leave beneficial."

Reeves: "Well, we're not going to even consider a plan like that. If you have a job, you come to work and do it. It's as simple as that. Besides, we can't afford to be giving money away."

Niemann: "I've got a couple of questions I'd like to throw out. First of all, how do our rates compare to other large baking companies? Maybe our record is not as bad as it looks. Second, it looks as though we've been hiring a lot of goldbricks lately. What is being done to minimize our problems at the hiring point?"

Reeves: "A couple of good questions. Maybe Donna can help us out here."

Baker: "Well, as far as the first question is concerned, I don't know how we compare to other baking firms, because the data aren't published. The national manufacturing rate was 2.9 percent for 1980, and our overall rate is somewhat above that. As for Bill's second question, we do all we can in personnel to hire the most qualified employee. We check each applicant's previous work record and ask former employers if they had any problems with the applicant. Every now and then when we get word that absenteeism was a problem with an applicant, we don't hire the person unless the skills are really needed. We also make sure new employees get copies of the employees' handbook and we ask them to read it carefully and contact us if they have any questions."

Sipe: "I don't think our supervisors know how to deal with problems the employees are having, and I think that it is affecting the absenteeism rate. I'm talking about both personal and work problems. I hear an awful lot of grumbling that our supervisors care only about one thing— production. I just can't help but think that a little more emphasis on good human relations would really have a positive effect on our attendance rate."

Whitehall: "I tend to agree with you, Rod. I've heard some of the same grumbling. But just what can we do specifically to get our supervisors to practice better human relations skills?"

Niemann: "Before we open that can of worms, I would just like to go on record as stating that the cause of the problem is not our supervision. I think our supervisors are doing just exactly what they are supposed to be doing— and that's getting the work out. I read enough management stuff to know that good human relations— whatever that is—is certainly not the answer to all *organizational problems. I think the cause of the problem is very simple. Some of our people would rather be somewhere else rather than at work. I think we should make it clearer to employees that excessive absenteeism must stop—or some people will be getting their walking papers. If you want to see people come to work regularly, that will do the trick—believe me.*

Sipe: *"Hold on a minute, Dick. Let me clarify what I mean about good human relations. What I'm saying is that we should provide some training on how supervisors should counsel employees who are having problems at home or work. And I'm really only talking about employees who are having trouble meeting productivity goals or trouble coming to work regularly. We may not realize it, but many times an employee who has no one to talk with looks to the supervisor to provide some help. And I think all this ties into knowing how and when to discipline an employee and being able to communicate why an employee is being disciplined."*

Reeves: *"Rodney, I think you've hit upon some good points here. Donna, what kind of supervisory training do we provide on counseling and discipline?"*

Baker: *"Well, of course we talk about the need to be good counselors during our supervisory training program. We have a pretty good film on counseling. But since we don't have a formal disciplinary program, training on disciplinary procedures is not an integral part of the program. Perhaps we need to think about developing a formal disciplinary system and to tie our absenteeism problem into the system."*

Reeves: *"Might be a good idea, Donna. Draft a proposal and let's go over it in a few weeks."*

Ferguson: *"I'd like to see some sort of plan dealing with alcoholism. I strongly feel this is a much bigger problem* than we're willing to admit, and I don't see anything being done to constructively deal with the problem. At a minimum, we should get the problem out in the open. I also think it's very important to have a company policy on alcoholism, stating our philosophy about the problem and how we intend to deal with it. For example, the policy could state that BBBC recognizes that alcoholism is a disease that is curable and that the company desires to assist alcoholic employees overcome their problems. At a minimum, I think we should strongly encourage problem drinkers to attend AA. Beyond that, maybe we could even consider some kind of employee assistance program."

Reeves: "I don't think we could afford a full-blown employee assistance program. Now you're talking about a bigger staff and more money."

Ferguson: "Well, maybe we can't afford a separate staff for handling employee problems, but something like AA would be very effective. And the price is right—Alcoholics Anonymous costs neither us nor the employee anything."

Reeves: "That sounds good. I'll get a memo out and tell supervisors about the need to get problem drinkers to attend AA meetings. I'll also state that no one will be fired—that is, unless they refuse to attend the meetings and their performance or absenteeism problems continue. [*Reeves glances at his watch.*] Okay, I see time is running out. Anybody else want to comment? All right. Good. We've got a lot accomplished this afternoon. I've been keeping a list of things we need to do, and I'm reasonably confident that we can reduce our absenteeism rate to reasonable levels if we all work hard and cooperate in this matter. First, our supervisors need to tighten up on excessive absenteeism. It's your responsibility to go back, spread the word around, and see that we closely monitor the problem and deal *appropriately with chronic offenders. Second, keep a close eye on your younger employees. When they start to get out of line, tell them about the need for punctuality and consistent attendance. Third, we need to modify our approach toward alcoholism. I want all our supervisors to be on the lookout for signs of alcoholism among our employees and counsel them on the problem rather than take a hard-nosed approach. I'll have my secretary get some materials from AA and see that they get distributed to all supervisory personnel. And fourth, we need to encourage our supervisors to be more considerate of employees' personal and work problems. Make sure they understand the importance of good communication and that they practice an 'open-door' policy.*

"If we all work hard at these things, we can lick this absenteeism problem and get our rates down to reasonable levels. So let's give it our best, and I want everyone to let me know how things are going in about six or eight weeks. That's all for today. Meeting adjourned."

Questions:

1. *How effective do you think Jim Reeves, BBBC Plant Manager, was in determining the causes of absenteeism and creating solutions to the problem? Why?*

2. *How effective do you think Donna Baker, Personnel Manager, is in controlling BBBC's absenteeism? Why?*

3. *How effective do you think the supervisors and middle managers of BBBC are in controlling the absenteeism problem? Why?*

4. *How effective do you think BBBC will be in reducing its absenteeism problem? Why?*

5. *Develop a strategy to reduce BBBC's absenteeism problems. Draw on material presented throughout the text.*

SELECTED PROFESSIONAL READING

Personnel Research for Problem Solving

FRED CRANDALL

Personnel research pervades all of the functional areas of personnel administration. In many respects, the future of the personnel administration field rests upon our ability to refine and develop techniques, practices and strategic approaches to the ongoing problems in personnel. Research has traditionally produced innovations in areas such as job analysis, staffing and performance measurements, job satisfaction and employee morale and personnel forecasting and planning. More recently research has provided answers to organizational problems in the areas of equal employment opportunity and equal pay administration.

Why then does there remain the doubt and skepticism about the practicality of PAIR research among practitioners and administrators? For years we have observed that there is a large gap between the subject matter and findings of personnel research efforts and the practical problems in the field. Concern over the sometimes "esoteric" nature of personnel research creates frustration on the parts of those who are involved in producing research as well as those who are involved in solving personnel problems. More importantly, however, much potential understanding and useful information is lost because of misunderstanding over the means and ends of personnel research. In the following paragraphs the relationship between personnel research and personnel problem-solving is outlined in an attempt to help bridge the gap between researchers and practitioners.

Problem-solving is a sequential and cyclical activity in an organization. The typical step-by-step process begins with the identification of a problem of importance and ultimately leads to the selection and implementation of a solution. Problem-solving is cyclical because of the dynamic nature of organizational problems—feedback from attempts at solution invariably leads to the identification of further problems in need of solution. Each stage of the problem-solving cycle for personnel is amenable to research. And the research strategy for each stage is aimed at obtaining the information required for that particular stage.

Problem identification: At the beginning of the problem-solving cycle, the identification of a problem can come from many sources. An active scan of personnel and employee relations programs is a means to highlight "problems" from time to time. However, in most cases problems arise for the personnel administrator when a program fails to operate according to plan, or when "something" unplanned happens. Thus, the first stage of problem-solving is often diagnostic, as we define the "something" that is wrong and translate it into terms that we can deal with.

Reprinted from the September 1978 issue of *Personnel Administrator*, 30 Park Drive, Berea, OH 44017, $26 per year.

Search for alternatives: Once the problem is defined, there is most often a variety of means to solve it. While in theory there are an infinite number of possible solutions, there is a much smaller number of alternatives that can be realistically considered. Criteria such as time available to solve the problem, monetary cost, expertise and practicality will quickly reduce the number of alternatives into a limited or "feasible" set.

At this second stage of problem-solving, research may be conducted to determine which alternatives should be considered for investigation. In the most limiting case, the time, cost and practicality criteria are so stringent that the search for alternatives is reduced to replicating previous problem-solving approaches and no active search for alternatives is attempted. Novel alternatives can prove costly and risky to the administrator, but should not be discounted without consideration if at all possible.

Investigation of alternatives: The investigation of alternatives involves the test of each in order to determine which should be chosen to solve the problem. If two or more alternatives are tested, employment of a structured research methodology is recommended including sampling procedures and appropriate statistical tests in order to test the potential effectiveness of the alternatives. Specific criteria for effectiveness of the tests may be determined in advance.

If only one alternative is investigated or little active search is attempted, obviously little investigation will be required. The administrator runs a risk in this case, however, that the alternative problem-solving approach chosen will fail and not be detected until the implementation or feedback stage.

Alternative selection: At this stage in the problem-solving cycle, one of the alternatives is chosen for implementation. For complex problems, many effectiveness criteria will be employed in order to reach a choice and the most feasible alternative may not be obvious until research is conducted.

Implementation and feedback: The imple-mentation of a solution and the practical experience that results from implementation takes place after the administrator has spent considerable energy and time exploring issues and making the choice of a course of action. By the time implementation begins, other problems in the organization have arisen and attention is focused elsewhere. Consequently, the feedback on implementation of problem-solving measures is often overlooked or not tested. Furthermore, since action is generally taken on only one alternative, there would generally be little opportunity to test solutions against each other or against a control group. If results are not monitored, though, another set of problems assuredly will develop.

Research can play many roles in the problem-solving process within your organization. The research output that appears in this publication and others can act as models for internal date gathering and analysis. Also, the results which are published can provide needed information for the understanding of similar problems/solutions for your organization.

Many practitioners perform research indirectly in the problem-solving process without realizing that they are engaging in a form of institutional research which may have wider application. The key to effective problem–solving, whether all of the formal steps are accomplished or less formal methods are employed, is developing timely and valid data at each step of the problem-solving process. Choice of appropriate research strategies can effectuate sound solutions.

Research methods appropriate to problem identification are basically survey and diagnostic instruments or review/audit techniques for analysis of records and programs. Ongoing review and analysis of organizational employment, compensation and training programs is a realistic means of identifying potential problems relative to governmental compliance programs. Alternatively, diagnostic surveys of employees and managers are a means of identifying problem areas which would not be apparent in personnel records.

Problem-Solving Research Methods and Results			
Stage of Problem Solving Cycle	Research Methods for Data Collection	Output of Research Results	Practicality of Results
Stage I: Problem Identification	Employee/manager surveys and diagnostic questionnaires; review & audit of personnel records and programs; forecasts of future scenarios	Analysis of problem scenario; trend predictions; control instruments	Helps to predict and avoid programatic crises. Continual audits help to focus on problem areas on a regular basis.
Stage II: Search for Alternatives	Retrospective organizational research to search for past ways of handling similar problems; library search for comparable problems in other organizations	Annotated bibliographies; library research reports; listings of feasible potential courses of action	Saving potentially repetitious analysis if problem has been addressed in-house or elsewhere previously.
Stage III: Investigation of Alternatives	Structured experimental or survey research methods; statistical analysis of personnel records; informal/judgmental assessment	Report on the expected impact of each alternative; results may be expressed in probabilities	The more thorough the investigation of each alternative, the more likely a more effective choice will be made.
Stage IV: Selection of "Best" Alternative	Choice based on statistical decision criteria or less formal individual/group decision methods.	Statement of a course of action, including specific details, costs and benefits	If more than one alternative is generated and specific criteria are applied, the choice is more clear cut and will help insure a more effective solution.
Stage V: Implementation of Solution	Measurements taken on implementation through formal sampling techniques, or informal observation	Reports generated on progress of problem solving; evaluation instruments with direct measurements are completed	Without research on the implementation stage, there may be no way of effectively measuring the impact of the solution.
Stage VI: Feedback	Analysis of impact of implementation through formal cost/ benefit or evaluation methodologies; informal/judgmental assessments	Analysis of evaluation reports; recommendations for future actions; listings of potential new problems	Feedback is an extremely important part of problem solving research. New problems are likely to develop and research on feedback can help avoid major crises.

For Stage II of problem-solving, research methods include both internal organizational analysis and external library search. The internal "search" is a means to discover, if at some previous time, similar problems had occurred and if so, how they were handled. The library search is a similar approach to ascertain if some other organization might have handled a similar problem. The research in this stage is most useful as a means of narrowing the list of alternatives to a feasible set.

In Stage III the feasible set of alternatives is

analyzed. The research methodology can be either a formal structured analysis or an informal assessment of alternatives. Formal research methods would include the pilot test of specific alternatives against control groups, or statistical tests of personnel records and other data which would provide precise and clear choice between alternatives based on the criteria per choice. Informal methods of assessing alternatives include general overall assessments using approximate or judgmental criteria. Obviously more formal research methods would be preferred if time and cost were not important, as the more precise the investigation of each alternative is, the clearer the choice between alternatives will be.

The fourth stage of the problem-solving process follows directly from the investigation of alternatives. No formal research methodology need be applied here; however, it is important to recognize that the actual course of action taken will depend upon the previous three steps, including criteria established, alternatives investigated and data collected. For the research purposes of Stages V and VI, it is very useful to outline the probable costs and benefits associated with the choice taken in order to estimate the effectiveness of implementation.

During implementation (Stage V), precise measurements on the impact of the choice taken will be the basis of feedback research (Stage VI). Research outputs for Stage V are mainly progress reports. The progress reports can then be contrasted with the choice criteria and expected costs and benefits as a basis for feedback to the next cycle of problem-solving. The important area of evaluation research, as a basis of feedback, is often overlooked. More often, approximate feelings and reactions are taken as measurements instead of focusing directly on the criteria that were used as the basis of choice and implementation. In effect, evaluation of problem-solving leads directly back to Stage I.

Personnel practitioners are constantly in need of innovative approaches to problem solving. Both external environmental pressures as well as the need to provide growth and development for individuals in organizations require novel answers to pressing problems. Provision for appropriate research methods to provide answers to our problems is a means to deal with such issues. In effect, the solution of PAIR issues in our organizations may be embedded within the context of our problems and all that may be needed is a means to address the problems. If a problem is large enough to be treated as such, it requires a problem-solving response. By addressing a PAIR problem as a research problem, we can both add to knowledge in the field and solve problems at home.

This accountant uses the same hot stove rule with her son that her employer uses with her.

19

DISCIPLINE AND COUNSELING

Causes of Poor Job Performance

Preventive Discipline

Supervisory Resistance to Discipline

Disciplinary Discharge

Hot Stove Rule

The Problem: Midwestern Chemicals

Bruce Helm slid from his seat in the forklift and sat on the edge of the loading dock. It was 10:00 o'clock in the morning—break time. He lit a cigarette, took a long pull, and blew about a half dozen smoke rings that quickly disappeared in the cool morning breeze. This was only his second day at Midwestern Chemicals—a small manufacturer of cleaning chemicals and solvents. The warehouse job seemed okay so far, Helm thought. The pay was not bad and benefits were pretty good. And he liked the fellow workers he had met so far.

All of a sudden, Helm's supervisor, John Huber, came running out of nowhere, shouting:

"Put that cigarette out! Put it out, you damn fool! Are you crazy? You want to blow us all to smithereens?" Huber grabbed the cigarette from Helm's hand and stomped it with his steel-tipped, thick-soled safety shoes.

Helm was startled. Silence befell nearby workers who had been enjoying their break.

"What's the problem?" Helm seriously asked. Huber replied, "This is a no smoking area. Look around you. There are fifty-gallon drums of flammable solvents practically within an arm's length of you. And you're puffing on a cigarette. How dumb can you get?"

Apologetically, Helm explained, "But I didn't know this was a no smoking area. Nobody told me. You didn't mention it yesterday when you showed me around the warehouse. Besides, I still don't see any no smoking signs."

Huber responded: "Well, the no smoking sign is covered up

by the stack of drums over there. But it should be obvious to everyone that you shouldn't smoke around these chemicals. Anyway, you've been warned. Any more problems and we'll have to let you go." Huber turned and strolled back to his office.

Helm cursed under his breath and went for a walk around the plant. He tried to get the incident out of his mind.

About a week later, Helm and three fellow employees were walking to their cars after work. Helm walked up to his van and said to his friends, "Come over here. I want to show you guys something." Opening the back of his van, Helm proudly displayed his new 12-gauge automatic shotgun. He said, "Those quail are in real serious trouble when the season opens next weekend. How do you like this beauty?" As Helm's pals were admiring the new shotgun, Huber drove by, saw the shotgun and brought his pickup to a screeching halt. Huber jumped out and howled, "Possessing firearms on company property is cause for immediate dismissal, Helm. It's in the union contract plain as day. You're fired. You other guys are witnesses." Huber jumped back in his pickup and sped away.

In even the most sophisticated organizations—with high quality, professionally-managed personnel programs and motivated, competent supervisors—a small percentage of employees will be unwilling or unable to achieve a satisfactory level of performance. Of course, the percentage of an organization's human resource group that may be considered unsatisfactory will vary considerably from firm to firm. Managers who view the employee as a resource rather than another factor of production will take positive steps to maintain high levels of employee satisfaction and productivity. Those who view the worker as a necessary evil will, more than likely, show little attention to employees' needs and, therefore, suffer an extraordinarily high level of "people problems" and performance shortfalls. Thus, in reality the administration may choose to minimize performance problems or to accept them. In the end, unsatisfactory performance is a management problem.

Unfortunately, some managers place the responsibility for performance problems on the shoulders of employees or the union. One occasionally hears a manager complain, "if it weren't for these #*@* employees of mine, I'd turn in a great performance!" But such an attitude reflects an inability or unwillingness on the part of the manager to assume a key managerial responsibility: the creation and maintenance of an effective, productive work group. While employees must shoulder the responsibility for meeting job standards, management must ensure that standards are defined, communicated, understood, and met. The buck stops at management's doorstep.

CAUSES OF POOR PERFORMANCE

Consider John Bradley, a press operator for a large printing company in Cincinnati, Ohio. His output is about 10 percent below standard and his quality level is often below standard. His absenteeism rate is about double the plant average. John is an unsatisfactory performer.

But why is John an unsatisfactory performer? Is he lazy and shiftless? Is his boss giving him a hard time for no reason? Is he an alcoholic? Was he assigned to a machine that frequently malfunctions? Is he really not sure what his standards are? Determining why an employee is performing at an unsatisfactory level is of critical importance, as a problem cannot be rectified unless its causes are known. Good managers not only pinpoint employee performance problems, but also recognize that productivity problems stem from a variety of causes. Rather than relying on a gut feeling or hunch, the prudent manager strives to uncover the true causes of employee performance prob-

lems and seeks solutions to eliminate or minimize those causes.

Organizational Shortcomings

Figure 19–1 illustrates the major sources of unsatisfactory performance.[1] Managers and supervisors often reluctantly agree that many employees perform unsatisfactorily because of managerial and organizational shortcomings. In this case, employee performance will improve only if the skills of managers and the quality of the organization's human resource programs are improved.

How may managerial and organizational shortcomings be spotted and reduced? Some organizations employ external consultants to study the organization's problems and uncover the specific causes of unsatisfactory employee performance. A small number of organizations maintain a group of internal consultants who perform basically the same task. More often, the personnel or human resource department researches performance problems and recommends solutions to minimize them. Finally, individual managers often spot problems that exist in their own work environments, and the correct these problems to enhance overall employee performance.

Throughout this text, we have focused on many policies and programs which will serve to minimize the managerial and organizational shortcomings illustrated in Figure 19–1. Examples of how some of the shortcomings shown in Figure 19–1 may be identified and reduced are shown in Figure 19–2.

---

1. This section is drawn from Lawrence L. Steinmetz, *Managing the Marginal and Unsatisfactory Performer* (Reading, MA: Addison–Wesley Publishing Co. 1969), Chapter 1.

FIGURE 19–1: *Sources of Unsatisfactory Performance*

	Unsatisfactory Performance	
Managerial and Organizational Shortcomings	**Individual Employee Shortcomings**	**External Influences**
• lack of proper motivational environment • personality conflicts with boss and/or co-workers • inappropriate job assignment • improper supervision • lack of training • failure to establish duties	• lack of motivation • laziness • poor personality • job dissatisfaction • fails to understand job duties • chronic absenteeism • alcoholism • mental illness • chronic physical illness • senility • sexual maladjustment	• family problems • mores and values that conflict with organizational expectations • labor market conditions • government action • union policies

Source: Lawrence L. Steinmetz, *Managing the Marginal and Unsatisfactory Performer*, © 1969, Addison-Wesley Publishing Company, Inc., Adaptation of Chapter 1, pages 1 through 17. Reprinted with permission.

FIGURE 19–2: *Potential Cures for Managerial and Organizational Shortcomings*

Shortcomings	*Potential Cures*
• Lack of proper motivational environment	• Through surveys and interviews, determine what environmental changes are necessary to increase employee motivation
• Personality conflicts	• Through face-to-face confrontations, conflicting employees must define the causes of conflicts and determine how they may be reduced. The physical removal of one employee (via transfer) may be necessary as a last resort remedy.
• Inappropriate job assignment	• Improve selection, testing and placement procedures; ease transfer procedures.
• Improper supervision	• Train or replace unqualified supervisors; employ assessment center techniques to improve selection decisions; clarify expectations for supervisors.
• Lack of training	• Implement a systems approach to training, strengthen overall training and development effort
• Failure to establish duties	• Improve job analysis procedures; strengthen job descriptions; improve orientation programs; clarify employee expectations through improved supervisory-subordinate communication; implement MBO for managers and administrators.

Employee Shortcomings

Often, the cause of unsatisfactory performance lies directly within the employee. Even properly trained employees who are aware of their job duties may not achieve the level of performance expected by management. While Figure 19–1 shows that this situation may stem from various causes, perhaps the most frequently-cited reason is that the employee simply lacks motivation. Social scientists claim that the work ethic is eroding and that young workers are placing less importance on work. While there is some evidence to support this belief, the extent to which attitudes toward work have changed over the past few decades or to what extent the changes have affected worker motivation are unknown. Even though the supervisory team is fully qualified and the organization maintains a strong human resource philosophy supported by a wide range of personnel policies and programs, a small percentage of workers will perform only marginally.

Several factors unrelated to the job may cause a worker to perform at substandard levels. Because very little research has been conducted about how external influences affect job performance, it is difficult to say which of these factors are the most problematic. For some individuals, however, these factors may have a very pronounced impact on job performance, particularly if employees have severe family problems. Given the divorce rate in the United States, a sizeable number of employees are experiencing serious conflicts with their spouses. Also, interaction between external factors and individual shortcomings is possible. For example, family problems may lead to alcoholism and peer pressure may negatively affect an employee's motivation to perform at the expected level.

Managers have only limited power to change an employee's basic motivational drives and the external factors that influence employees' behavior. For example, administration can do little to change an employee who holds a negative work ethic, or to remove a powerful, antagonistic union. Yet, management has a responsibility to correct performance shortfalls stemming from individual or external factors. One approach is to create and implement an employee assistance program to deal with extraordinary personal problems such as alcoholism, drug abuse, severe marital conflicts, or financial problems. Many such programs have corrected problems that have caused unsatisfactory performance. A second approach involves the application of employee discipline, the process designed to prevent unsatisfactory employee behavior.

OBJECTIVES OF DISCIPLINE

The primary objective of discipline is to motivate an employee to comply with the company's performance standards. An employee receives discipline after failing to meet some obligation of the job. The failure to perform as expected could be directly related to the tasks performed by the employee or to the rules and regulations that define proper conduct at work.

In effect, discipline is management's last resort measure to improve the performance of employees. Generally, discipline for poor task performance should not be applied while employees are being trained and learning the job. Nor should employees be disciplined for reasons beyond their control; for example, failure to meet output standards caused by a lack of raw materials. Discipline should only be applied when it has been determined that the employee is the cause of unsatisfactory performance.

A second objective of discipline is to create mutual respect and trust between the supervisor and employee. Improperly administered, discipline can create more problems: low morale, resentment, and ill will between the supervisor and employee. In this situation, any improvement in the employee's behavior will be relatively short-lived and the supervisor will need to discipline the employee again in the near future. The proper administration of discipline will not only immediately improve employee behavior but also minimize future disciplinary problems through a positive supervisor-subordinate relationship.

Approaches to Discipline

When someone breaks the rules, many approaches may be used to correct the problem. Most of us have observed the full range of alternatives to discipline in the supermarket as parents discipline their rambunctious children in different ways. Many children do not need to be disciplined; they understand "proper behavior" in the supermarket and behave accordingly. Sticking close to their parents, they don't crash the shopping carts into other patrons, or beg incessantly for candy bars or soda pop. Disciplined children gracefully take no for an answer. But other children are prone to treat the supermarket like a giant playground, running up and down the aisles, sampling fruit and candy, screaming and hollering, and just being general pains in the neck. Faced with such behavior, some parents immediately fly off the handle subjecting the child to public verbal and physical abuse. Shaking their fingers and fists, parents sternly warn the sobbing child that repeated rowdiness will result in further punishment. The child has been struck with the fear of God, at least for the time being. Other parents take a different approach to unsatisfactory child behavior. Calmly taking them aside, these parents clearly tell their errant children what is expected and why the misconduct creates problems for the store management and other customers. They speak to the child without charged emotions, threats, or abuse; treating the child with respect and maturity. Parents and their children walk away with a mutual understanding about what is right and what is wrong; there seems to be agreement on these matters.

These approaches to discipline are also common in all forms and sizes of organizations. Much like parents disciplining their children, supervisors administer discipline in different ways. Most of these techniques may be grouped into three categories: preventive discipline, punitive discipline, and positive discipline.

PREVENTIVE DISCIPLINE

Of all the approaches to discipline, the preventive approach is the most desirable. Through *preventive discipline*, people are managed in a way that prevents discipline from becoming necessary. Much like the individual who eats nutritious food and exercises regularly to avoid health problems, administrators who practice preventive discipline create an organization climate that is conducive to high levels of job satisfaction and employee productivity. In this case, the need to discipline will be minimal. To create a working environment that supports a preventive discipline approach, managers must:

- Match the employee with the job through effective selection, testing, and placement procedures.
- Properly orient the employee to the job.
- Clarify proper employee behavior.
- Provide frequent feedback to employees on their performance.
- Enable employees to address their problems to management through an open door policy and management–employee group meetings.

PUNITIVE DISCIPLINE

Punitive discipline, sometimes referred to as negative or autocratic discipline, is discipline through fear. Punitive discipline often involves threats, harassment, intimidation, and browbeating. Widespread in the early twentieth century, punitive discipline sees relatively little use in contemporary times, largely because of union protection and a greater acceptance of human relations methods and techniques. Punitive discipline still exists in some firms today, however, particularly among supervisors who prefer to do things the old way. Supervisory statements that indicate a punitive approach to discipline include:

Smith, if you're late one more time, you can pack up your tool bag and get the hell out of here. We don't need your kind.

Myers, you know there's no smoking in this area. If I see you smoking that pipe in this warehouse one more time, I'll see that you get transferred out of here so fast it'll make your head swim.

Borden, I see you're having some trouble making standard lately. I have one message for you: shape up or ship out. I've got enough problems around here without deadbeat employees like you.

Sussman, one more slipup like last night and you've had it. With your drinking problem, nobody will hire you—everybody in town knows you're a drunk. Maybe you'd like to see your wife and kids in the bread line.

The problem with punitive discipline is that it doesn't work—at least not over the long run. While this approach may immediately improve performance, any change is unlikely to be lasting. Other problems with punitive discipline include:

- Placing the emphasis of discipline on the employee, not the employee's act—where it belongs.
- Weakening, rather than strengthening the relationship between the employee and supervisor.
- Creating a desire to get even which the employee achieves by performing unsatisfactorily in other ways.

Punitive discipline should be avoided as an overall policy to correct unsatisfactory employee behavior. Today most employees will not respond positively to this approach; however, a small percentage of employees will change their behavior only if management adopts a get tough policy. Therefore, conflicts are resolved with these employees only through a supervisor's use of power and force. Such an approach should only be used sparingly and as a last resort.

POSITIVE DISCIPLINE

Positive discipline corrects unsatisfactory employee behavior through support, respect, and people-oriented leadership—helping rather than harassing the employee. Positive discipline is not an attempt to soft-pedal or side-step an employee problem. Rather, positive discipline is a management philosophy which assumes that improved employee behavior is most likely to be long-lived when discipline is administered without revenge, abuse, or vindictiveness. Positive discipline assumes that most employees are willing to accept personal responsibility for their work problems and to reverse their unsatisfactory performance with management's confidence and support. While positive discipline is not a panacea, this process offers a number of pluses over the punitive approach.

Positive discipline is much more than the simple act of a supervisor discussing performance problems with an employee. Rather, the positive discipline process includes a series of individual policies and procedures. The key elements in the positive disciplinary process are highlighted in Figure 19-3.

CLARIFY RESPONSIBILITY

The question of who should discipline is subject to some debate. In theory, the responsibility for discipline should fall upon the shoulders of an employee's immediate supervisor. Because the immediate supervisor is responsible for the employee's output, the supervisor should

FIGURE 19-3 *The Positive Disciplinary Process*

Clarify the Responsibility for Discipline

Define Expected Employee Behavior

Communicate Discipline Policy, Procedures and Rules

Collect Performance Data

Apply Progressive Discipline

Apply Corrective Counseling Techniques

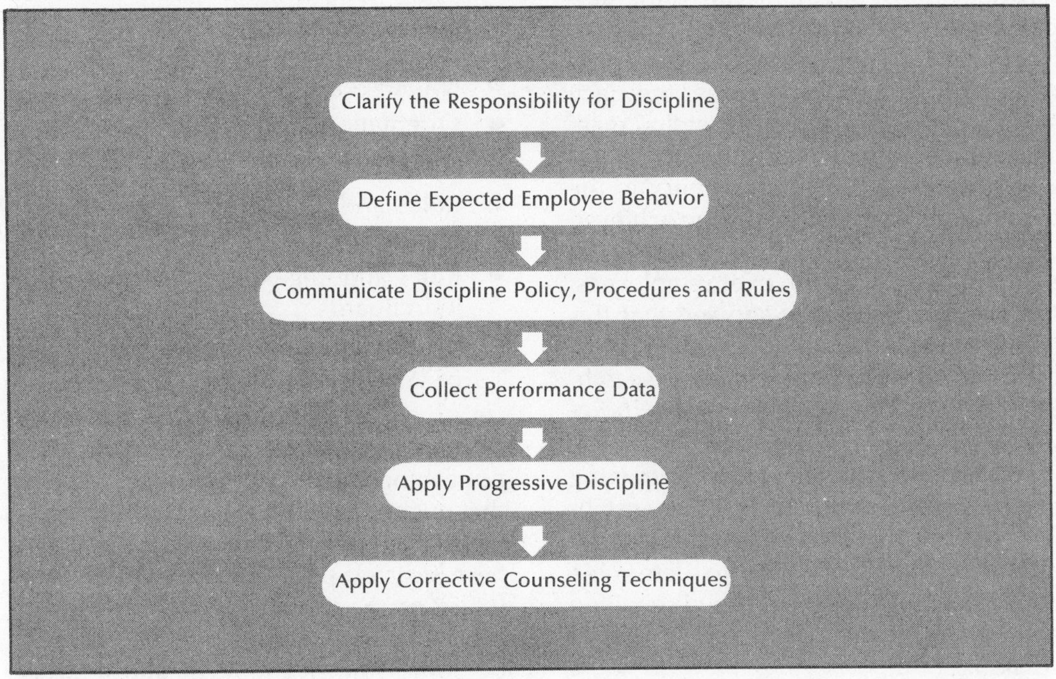

possess the authority to correct that employee's performance problems. Other managers and theorists, however, feel that decentralizing discipline responsibility will result in inconsistent application of discipline throughout the organization. An equitable and uniformly administered disciplinary system can take priority over other considerations; such uniformity may be achieved only by allowing the personnel or employee relations manager to apply the discipline. This approach also has its drawbacks: the personnel staff will be spending inordinate time on disciplinary matters, and the supervisor will lose control over subordinates.

To overcome the problem of where to place the responsibility for discipline, many organizations give the supervisor authority to issue lower level discipline, such as verbal warning or, perhaps, a written notice. For situations involving suspension or discharge, often the supevisor is required to consult with a personnel representative; in some cases, the decision is made by an upper level line manager or personnel executive. With this type of approach, fair consistency in the application of discipline can be achieved while the supervisor retains sufficient authority and control over employees' behavior. A BNA study showed that this method was generally followed by most companies that took part in the research. Results of the BNA study are shown in Figure 19–4.

Finally, the personnel staff's training and development division can help establish a uniform disciplinary system by teaching supervisors how to determine when an employee should be disciplined and how to actually conduct a disciplinary session.

DEFINE EXPECTATIONS

A central part of every disciplinary process is the definition of behavior management expects from its employees. Disciplining an employee for unsatisfactory performance is impossible unless management has clearly defined good performance. Management must ensure that written employee conduct standards are consistent with the organization's objectives and that standards are revised as new organizational goals are developed.

COMMUNICATE DISCIPLINARY POLICIES, PROCEDURES, AND RULES

Good communication is of utmost importance in maintaining satisfactory levels of employee performance. Management is responsible for telling employees precisely what is expected of them, and ensuring that all standards, rules, and regulations are clearly communicated.

These expectations are communicated by:

- Employees' Handbook
- Orientation Programs
- Union Contracts
- Rules and Regulations Distributed to Employees
- Rules and Regulations Posted on Bulletin Boards
- Supervisory-subordinate Discussions of Written Standards

Some companies' administrators avoid publishing rules and regulations, feeling that such a list is demeaning and condescending. As one executive put it, "We have resisted publishing the whole painful list on the theory that it is more insulting than useful, and that there is going to be some rule overlooked, and if every-

FIGURE 19–4: *Authority for Administration of Disciplinary Procedures*

| | % of Companies | | | | | |
| | Type of Industry | | | Size | | All |
	Mfg.	Nonmfg.	Nonbus.	Small	Large	Companies
Final authority for issuing disciplinary warnings—						
First-level supervisor	73%	79%	73%	68%	78%	74%
Supervisor & personnel rep	2	0	0	1	1	1
Department head	5	7	15	7	9	8
Dept. head & personnel rep	3	0	2	4	1	2
Plant manager (or other top line manager)	3	9	2	4	5	4
Top line mgr. & personnel rep	0	0	0	0	0	0
Personnel executive only	9	2	4	8	5	6
Final authority for ordering disciplinary suspensions—						
First-level supervisor	35	31	17	25	32	29
Supervisor & personnel rep	9	2	4	5	6	6
Department head	14	19	50	25	25	25
Dept. head & personnel rep	6	4	2	5	4	4
Plant manager (or other top line manager)	10	15	4	7	12	10
Top line mgr. & personnel rep	6	7	0	7	3	4
Personnel executive only	16	7	15	17	11	14
Final authority for disciplinary employee discharges—						
First-level supervisor	9	26	6	12	13	12
Supervisor & personnel rep	14	7	6	11	9	10
Department head	10	23	36	11	26	20
Dept. head & personnel rep	7	8	11	13	5	8
Plant manager (or other top line manager)	22	17	8	11	22	17
Top line manager & personnel rep	12	4	4	9	7	8
Personnel executive only	23	11	29	31	15	22

Note: Percentages may not add to 100 because of nonresponses.
Based on responses from 185 companies.

thing isn't spelled out, then you have no recourse and are in trouble. I speak particularly of the nonunion situation as evidently unionized companies feel that the contract must be all-inclusive in the matter of behavior."[2] Most firms formalize their rules for employee conduct. A BNA survey of 160 companies found that 85 percent put their rules and regulations in writing.[3] Figure 19–5 shows the percentages of companies with rules for various types of discipline problems.

COLLECT DATA

Before an employee is disciplined, there must be indisputable proof that some standard, rule, or regulation was violated. Discipline should not be a gut reaction by a supervisor. There must be no doubt that unsatisfactory performance has taken place; the collection of information clearly reflecting an employee's wrongdoing makes discipline more effective and easier to administer.

Some performance data are easy to collect; others are difficult. For example, an employee's absenteeism is routinely recorded and rarely subject to misinterpretation. Many companies with computerized absenteeism records furnish their supervisors with weekly or biweekly printouts so that employees requiring discipline for unsatisfactory attendance can be pinpointed. Production and quality statistics are routinely collected—often daily— in many manufacturing companies. Other areas of performance, however, are somewhat subjective and difficult to record. For example, as Figure 19–5 indicates, many firms have specific rules

against horseplay, carelessness, insubordination, and abusive or threatening language to supervisors. Inexperienced supervisors may ask what does "carelessness" mean? How do I know when an employee is "insubordinate?" When is an employee guilty of "horseplay"? While describing all possible occasions of unsatisfactory performance is impossible, upper line management should work closely with the training staff to ensure that supervisors are trained to recognize and record unsatisfactory performance in difficult areas.

Concrete, indisputable records of unsatisfactory performance are important for three reasons: First, the burden of proof lies with the employer. This practice stems from common law which suggests "an individual is innocent until proven guilty." Second, an employee is more likely to improve behavior if presented with facts about poor performance. Conflicting, disputable data will not motivate an employee to change. Third, if the unionized employee files a grievance indicating that discipline was unjustly applied, should the grievance reach arbitration, the arbitrator will look very closely at the proof that management has collected. If performance data are questionable or carelessly or sloppily recorded, the award will most likely go to the employee. The employer is required to document that there is "just cause" for suspending or discharging an employee.

APPLY PROGRESSIVE DISCIPLINE

Most companies follow a progressive disciplinary procedure. Two key characteristics of *progressive discipline* include a penalty commensurate with the offense, and a series of increasingly serious penalties for continued unsatisfactory perfor-

---

2. *Employee Conduct and Discipline* (Washington, DC: Bureau of National Affairs, Inc., 1973), p. 4.

3. Ibid., p. 1.

FIGURE 19–5: *Company Rules for Specific Disciplinary Problems*

Type of Offense	% of Companies Indicating Specific Rule*		
Attendance Problems	Small	Large	All
Unexcused absence	52%	62%	57%
Chronic absenteeism	51	55	53
Unexcused/excessive lateness	45	58	52
Leaving without permission	35	53	44
On-the-Job Behavior Problems			
Intoxication at work	39	56	48
Insubordination	35	55	45
Horseplay	35	53	44
Smoking in unauthorized places	33	52	43
Fighting	32	50	41
Gambling	28	51	40
Failure to use safety devices	36	46	40
Failure to report injuries	30	50	40
Carelessness	32	46	39
Sleeping on the job	26	51	39
Abusive or threatening language to supervision	26	48	37
Possession of narcotics	29	44	37
Possession of firearms or other weapons	26	40	33
Dishonesty and Related Problems			
Theft	38	60	49
Falsifying employment application	45	52	49
Willful damage to company property	36	56	46
Punching another employee's time card	32	52	42
Falsifying work records	35	45	40
Subversive activity	9	21	15
Other Problems—Outside Activities			
Unauthorized soliciting	29	46	38
Slowdown of production	22	35	29
Unauthorized strike activity	17	34	25
Wage garnishment	16	30	23
Outside criminal activities	10	30	20
Working for competing company	13	14	14

*Percentages are of all companies responding to checklist (N = 160).

Reprinted by special permission from *Bulletin to Management: Personnel Policies Forum*, 1973, by the Bureau of National Affairs, Inc., Washington, DC

mance. For nonunion firms, the progressive disciplinary system is often included in the employee handbook; unionized firms normally include the procedure in the labor-management agreement. The progressive disciplinary procedure in the contract between the Multi-Metals Division of the Vermont American Corporation and the International Association of Machinists and Aerospace Workers for 1977–1980 is shown in Figure 19–6.

APPLY CORRECTIVE COUNSELING

The final part of the positive discipline procedure is *corrective counseling*, which should solve the employee's problems

FIGURE 19–6: *Union-Management Progressive Disciplinary Procedure*

Unless otherwise noted, any proven infractions of the following rules will initiate the following disciplinary action, on an impartial and fair basis.

1st Offense = Action A:	Foreman will give verbal warning to employee, and written account to employee for record.
2nd Offense = Action B:	Oral reprimand form for file
3rd Offense = Action C:	Written reprimand form for file, union, company, employee, union hall
4th Offense = Action D:	Three days suspension without pay
5th Offense = Action E:	Discharge

General Plant Rules—Employees shall not:

a. Bring intoxicants or narcotics into, or consume intoxicants or narcotics in the plant or on the plant premises, excluding prescribed medicine.

> Disciplinary Actions D and E only
> E only if illegal narcotics

b. Report for duty under the influence of liquor or narcotics.

> Disciplinary Actions C, D and E

c. Smoke in prohibited areas.

> Disciplinary Actions B, C, D and E

d. Deliberately or through continued carelessness destroy, deface, or wrongfully remove the company's or another employee's property.

> Disciplinary Action E only

e. Alter time punched in or out on time card.

> Disciplinary Actions D and E only

f. Intentionally punch another employee's time card.

> Disciplinary Actions D and E only

g. Be guilty of unsanitary practices.

> Disciplinary Actions B, C, D and E

h. Be guilty of carelessness or recklessness, horseplay, or other disregard for the safety and comfort of fellow workers.

> Disciplinary Actions B, C, D and E

i. Roam about the plant, interfere with, or keep others from the performance of their duties.

> Disciplinary Actions A, B, C, D and E

j. Initiate an act of physical violence in the plant or on the plant premises, or directly threaten a supervisor, any salaried personnel, or any union employee with physical violence.

> Disciplinary Action E only

k. Participate in any gambling or other game of chance on company premises at any time.

> Disciplinary Actions A, B, C, D and E

FIGURE 19–6: *continued*

l. Bring firearms or other lethal weapons into the plant or on company premises at any time without permission.

Disciplinary Action E only

m. Refuse to obey the work orders of or refuse to perform work assigned by their supervisor.

Disciplinary Actions D and E only

n. Fail to wear safety glasses or other designated safety protection (clip-ons, goggles, coverall goggles, face shields, etc.).

Disciplinary Actions A, B, C, D and E

o. Receive more than two (2) sustained garnishments on separate indebtednesses during a contract year.

Disciplinary Action E only

p. Knowingly provide false information with regard to production, product control, equipment, equipment control, process, process control, doctors' excuses, or any phase of the company's operations.

Disciplinary Action E only

q. Leave the company premises without permission, for any reason, without clocking "in" and "out".

Disciplinary Actions A, B, C, D and E

SOURCE: Agreement between Multi-Metals and the International Association of Machinists and Aerospace Workers, AFL–CIO, 1977–1980, pp. 61–63. Used with permission.

rather than simply doling out penalty and punishment. For corrective counseling to be effective, the supervisor must be genuinely interested in helping an employee overcome problems and offer support, encouragement, and assistance.

While each counseling session will differ somewhat, there are a number of steps in each corrective counseling interview. Figure 19–7 illustrates each step and gives areas a supervisor may discuss with an employee being disciplined about excessive absenteeism.

One important way that the corrective counseling procedure differs from traditional autocratic techniques is that a supervisor avoids telling employees how to solve problems. Supervisors tend to tell employees the right thing to do. With therapeutic counseling, however, a su-

pervisor helps employees find solutions. Thus, employees are responsible for determining the most effective way to overcome the problem. With a greater problem–solving participation by the employee, the chances for a long lasting improvement in behavior are greatly increased.[4]

Supervisory Resistance to Discipline

Many managers and supervisors find disciplining an employee difficult and painful. Some supervisors will even put off discipline, preferring to trade off short range relief for possible future performance problems. Why is discipline some-

4. Steinmetz, *Managing The Marginal and Unsatisfactory Performer*, p. 83.

FIGURE 19–7: *Corrective Counseling: Absenteeism*

Get The Facts Before Counseling

- Make sure you understand the attendance policy
- Closely review the employee's attendance behavior
- Have a copy of absenteeism policies at hand, the employee's attendance record, and any other forms or documents that may be necessary

Discuss In Private

- Get away from the work area
- Keep phone calls and interruptions at a minimum
- Hold the discussion as soon as possible but at a time convenient to both of you

Put The Employee At Ease, But Get to The Point

- Offer the employee a comfortable seat
- Keep cool. Don't show anger or resentment

Describe The Problem, Using Facts

- Emphasize the act, not the employee
- State the problems caused by employee absence

  "Good attendance is really important for us to do a good job and produce a quality product. When people don't come to work, all kinds of problems can occur."

- Be specific—talk numbers and dates

  "About two weeks ago, we couldn't start the line in binding on the night shift because of absenteeism. It took us over an hour to get people shifted around and get the line going. A lot of employees really got upset because of all the moving around."

  "When I have to replace you, that employee just can't do the job as well as you can. Sometimes I have to spend a half hour or so making sure the replacement employee can do the job, and usually I have to check back every couple hours or so to make sure everything is going OK. I don't have to do that with you."

  "When everybody comes in, it makes my job and everybody else's so much easier."

  "Our absenteeism policies contain progressive disciplinary actions that relate to the number of absences an employee accumulates. The first step of the system requires that I discuss attendance with an employee who accumulates three occurrences within a twelve-month period."

- Go over attendance form(s) with the employee

  "Mary, you were absent on Friday, May 25; Monday, July 29; and Wednesday, August 22. Therefore, I must apply the first disciplinary step."

times a dreaded task? First, supervisors may find it distasteful to discipline an employee who is also a friend. Over the years, many supervisors build strong personal relationships with their employees. They may find disciplining employees they share lunch or evenings with extremely stressful and uncomfortable. The supervisor may not want to jeopardize this relationship because of a disciplinary

FIGURE 19–7: *continued*

- State the consequences of continued unsatisfactory performance.

    "If an employee accumulates five occurrences within a twelve-month period, he or she is placed on written probation—Step 2. Seven and nine occurrences within a consecutive twelve-month period will result in suspension and discharge, respectively."

Get Agreement On The Problem

- Make sure the employee understands policies and disciplinary system
- Make sure the employee agrees with the facts (even though he/she may not like the facts)

    "Do you have any questions concerning the new policies and disciplinary system?"

    "Do my records agree with attendance records that you may be keeping?" (If employees do not keep their own attendance records, suggest that they do.)

Involve the Employee In Problem Solving

- Get ready to listen
- Get the employee to talk about the problem—particularly work problems

    "What can we do to avoid another absence occurrence?"

    "Is there any aspect of your work situation that relates to your absenteeism?"

    "What can you do to make sure you are at work on time?"

- Avoid offering suggestions unless absolutely necessary
- Discuss the problem until you feel the employee reaches a satisfactory solution

Have Employee Sum Up Problem And Solution

    "OK, Marvin, now I would like for you to sum up the problem and tell me how you're going to make sure we don't have to go to the next disciplinary step."

State Goal, End In Positive Note

    "Mary, as you know, a calendar month of perfect attendance will remove one occurrence. Will you shoot for this?"

    "Barry, when you're here, you do a great job. You get along with the other employees, and we value and appreciate your efforts here. But as I mentioned earlier, good attendance is critical, and we need you here every workday. And please keep in mind I'm here to do whatever I can to make your job as satisfying as possible and one which you want to come to every day. If there's a work problem, let's talk about it."

    "OK, Pat, unless you have any questions, I'll let you get back to the press."

action. Second, some supervisors feel that the application of discipline forces them to play God. Uncomfortable in the role of judge and jury, they feel that the complexities of organizational life make it difficult, if not impossible, to define precisely what is right and what is wrong. Third, a supervisor lacking the skill and ability to discipline may rationalize, "If I try to discipline the employee, I'll probably make matters worse. So I'll just side-step the issue."

THE HOT STOVE RULE

One effective way to reduce supervisory resistance to discipline is to train supervisors to follow what is popularly known as the *hot-stove rule*. This rule suggests that applying discipline is much like touching a hot stove:[5]

- The burn is immediate; the cause is clear-cut.
- The person had warning; knowing the stove was hot the individual should have known what would happen if it was touched.
- The burn is consistent; all who touch the stove are burned.
- The burn is impersonal; the individual is burned for touching the stove, not because of who the individual is.

Like touching a hot stove, the application of discipline should also be immediate, with warning, consistent, and impersonal. These guidelines are totally consistent with the positive approach to discipline. Supervisors following these guidelines should experience less tension and anxiety when applying discipline and learn to view discipline as a supervisory responsibility rather than a personal dilemma. Briefly this is how the hot-stove rule applies to the discipline:

IMMEDIATE DISCIPLINE Some supervisors find it easy to procrastinate about discipline: "I'm busy today. I'll get to it tomorrow." But putting off discipline for a later date often reduces the impact. The greater the time between the offense and discipline, the less likely is the employee to

see a direct cause-and-effect relationship between unsatisfactory performance and the discipline.

How immediate should the discipline be? Discipline should be applied as soon as it has been determined that unsatisfactory behavior has taken place. Of course, the supervisor must fully investigate any issue which is not clear-cut. For example, a supervisor may issue an oral warning to an employee for a slow-down of production. A complete investigation of the problem, however, may have shown that a machine malfunction was, in fact, responsible for substandard output. In unionized firms misapplication of discipline may result in the filing of a formal employee grievance. At best, relations between the supervisor and employee will be cooled. Gathering the facts as soon as possible before disciplining is a good rule of thumb.

WARN EMPLOYEES An employee who receives unexpected discipline will more than likely raise cries of unfairness and favoritism. Discipline is more likely to be accepted without resentment if the employee had prior knowledge that certain behavior would necessitate disciplinary action. Thus, the personnel staff and supervisory team are responsible for ensuring that all employees realize unsatisfactory behavior will result in discipline.

Even though a disciplinary system is detailed in an employees' handbook or labor-management contract, good face-to-face communication between the supervisor and the work group is necessary if all employees are to understand the system and how it works. Too frequently written communications like an employee handbook are so quickly glossed over that the written word may not be fully comprehended or understood. Through frequent

---

5. See Douglas McGregor, *The Human Side of Enterprise* (New York: McGraw-Hill Book Co., 1960), p. 20.

oral communication, management can make sure that employees know what is expected of them and are aware of the consequences of unsatisfactory behavior.

CONSISTENT DISCIPLINE. Employees want to be treated fairly and impartially; feelings of unfairness result in low morale, absenteeism, turnover, and grievances. To minimize these problems, management must apply discipline consistently, without bias or favoritism. The consistent application of discipline means that:

- each employee who requires discipline, receives discipline,
- employees who commit the same offense receive the same discipline, and
- discipline is applied in the same way to all employees. That is, the tendency to apply positive discipline to one employee and negative discipline to another is avoided.

Consistent application of discipline is not an easy task; personality issues interfere. Because supervisors are human, they may occasionally overlook unsatisfactory behavior of likable employees and come down hard on those disliked. Consistency may also require that discipline be applied at an inconvenient time. Assume, for example, that a supervisor who commands a large assembly line with sixty employees has four employees requiring immediate discipline. If the supervisor reasons, "I'll discipline Joe and Harry this afternoon but I can't get to Mary and Frank until next week. If I spend all afternoon in disciplinary sessions, we won't meet our production quota this week," is making a mistake. Such inconsistency will generate more problems

than it avoids. A consistent, uniform disciplinary system may be difficult to achieve at times but it will help the supervisor avoid personnel problems and earn the respect and confidence of the entire work group.

IMPERSONAL DISCIPLINE. One significant drawback of punitive discipline is that the employee often takes personally the harsh, condescending methods that this technique involves. If a supervisor barks at an employee "This is your third warning, Richards. If you show up for work stinking like a distillery one more time, it's pink slip city. This isn't skid row, you know." With this approach, even though he may be guilty of the offense, Richards is likely to suffer a great personal indignity and harbor resentment and anger. Perhaps worse than that, the punitive approach does not find ways to overcome the employee's problems.

When discipline is applied impersonally, the supervisor focuses upon the act of unsatisfactory behavior, not the employee as a bad person. The most effective way to achieve this goal is to employ corrective counseling. Using the therapeutic method, the supervisor places less stress on why unsatisfactory performance took place than how the problem can be solved. With tact and maturity, the supervisor applies discipline in a supportive environment, emphasizing the improvement of performance rather than the infliction of punishment.

Disciplinary Discharge

An important part of the corrective discipline philosophy is salvaging the unsatisfactory employee. The primary emphasis is upon solving rather than getting rid of the problem. Consistent with good personnel management, this approach documents an organization's social responsibility to its human resource group. Nonetheless, administrators will occasionally find the ultimate disciplinary action necessary—discharge.

A great deal of colorful jargon describes the act of discharge. Employees talk about getting canned, sacked, booted, axed, a pink slip, or their walking papers. Perhaps the most common lament of the discharged employee is "I got fired."

An employee may be discharged because a company has severe financial problems, a plant closes, or the employee is continually ill and unable to perform the job. A disciplinary discharge occurs when an employee has committed a serious offense, repeatedly violated rules and regulations, or has shown a consistent inability to meet performance expectations. For example, in many disciplinary systems, the first offense of intoxication at work, insubordination, theft, willful damage to company property, or falsifying work records will result in discharge. One or two occasions of unexcused absenteeism, however, will generally result in a warning; several occasions will often bring a suspension followed by a discharge. Likewise, a salesperson's inability to meet a quarterly sales quota may result in a warning; failure to meet quotas for a full year may possibly result in discharge.

A discharge has consequences for both the employee and the employer. Loss of income is usually the most serious setback because an employee discharged for disciplinary reasons generally cannot collect company-provided supplemental unemployment benefits or unemployment insurance. For many employees, being dismissed becomes a personal failure which could possibly lead to serious family problems, alcoholism, or suicide. Upper level executives find job failure and dismissal is a particularly tragic event; many companies ease the financial and emotional trauma of dismissal through outplacement assistance programs.

Discharge is also costly to the company which loses many dollars invested in orientation, training, and development, not to mention the costs involved in hiring and training a replacement employee.

In relative terms, discharge is an infrequent personnel action. Most employees leave an employer voluntarily. The majority of employees perform their jobs satisfactorily; only a small percentage may be labeled unsatisfactory performers. Effective application of corrective discipline successfully prevents many employees from continually performing at unsatisfactory levels. Other factors also keep the disciplinary discharges at a relatively low level: Powerful unions are often instrumental in forcing the employer to not lay off a problem employee. A strong civil service program may also hold down discharges. Public officials sometimes state "It's impossible to fire an incompetent employee. There's nothing I can do." While a public manager, according to most personnel rules and regulations, can dismiss an unsatisfactory employee, the paperwork and case that must be built on an unproductive employee—in addition to the large number of hearings that are required—often make it extremely difficult and time consuming to discharge the unsatisfactory employee. Succumbing to the administrative burdens of discharge, a government official may say "it's easier to live with the problem employee than to get the employee discharged."

DISCHARGING THE MANAGER/PROFESSIONAL

Thus far, the discharge process has been described as the final step in the progressive disciplinary system which spells out what kinds and how many occasions of unsatisfactory performance must occur before an employee will be discharged. But such is not the case with managerial or professional employees. First, the upper–level employee is not a union employee subject to the work conditions and requirements that are included in the labor-management contract. Second, a detailed, written, progressive disciplinary system is rarely administered for managers and administrators. In fact, formal disciplinary systems almost exclusively refer to the operative and clerical level. This is not to suggest, however, that upper level employees are immune to discharge. Few companies will guarantee any employee a life-long job; in some firms, job security is much stronger for the production worker than the middle or top manager. Many managers testify "in my company, it's up or out. There's no deadwood here. But there are an awful lot of ulcers and short fingernails. And it's a smart practice to keep your resume current."

Because the executive or administrator's job is often difficult to evaluate, determining if and when an upper level employee should be discharged is difficult. Many poor managers are able to muddle along because their jobs and expectations have been poorly defined. Ill-defined jobs and performance standards also enable politics to significantly affect the promotion or discharge of an employee. This situation may be rectified by developing management by objectives work planning, evaluation, and control. With written, measurable objectives, there is less ambiguity about managerial performance. Many MBO programs have not only resulted in greater sales and profits but resulted in more effective personnel decisions about, for example, which employees to reward, to promote, or to discharge.

ALTERNATIVES TO DISCHARGING THE MANAGER/PROFESSIONAL EMPLOYEE

After deciding to remove a manager or administrator from the job, many superiors seek alternatives to firing. Some may kick the employee upstairs in a move which appears to be a promotion, complete with a prestigious title and greater salary. Other employees are strongly advised to take early retirement or demoted to less responsible jobs. The final alternative to firing is to dehire the employee. A dehired employee is encouraged to quit before being fired. At the end of a performance appraisal session, the employee may be told: "the job isn't right for you . . . have you considered other employment? I think it would be in your best interests to find employment more suited to your particular skills and abilities. . . . I like you, Fred, but the job isn't working out. You might want to use some of your lunch hours to check into other job opportunities around town."

Why dehire rather than fire an employee? Perhaps, the primary advantage of dehiring is that the employee may save face by leaving the company before being fired. Avoiding the disgrace and embarrassment of being discharged, the employee does not have to explain a firing to family members, friends, or prospective employers. The superior may even allow the dehired employee to seek other employment on company time.

The employer also benefits from the dehiring process. From a public relations point of view, dehiring indicates that the company has a moral obligation to its employees, and that it has a heart. Then too, most executives would much rather dehire a subordinate than face the stress and anguish that often accompanies the act of firing.

ADMINISTERING THE DISCHARGE DECISION

Companies may approach the problem of unsatisfactory performance in different ways. Many firms do everything they possibly can to avoid firing employees. Other employers have few or no qualms or regrets about firing employees who have toiled many long years with the company or who are upper or mid–level managers. Some administrators feel that the best interests of the company and the employee necessitate the rather direct approach of discharging an employee who has a minimal or nonexistent chance to perform satisfactorily.

The discharge decision should be taken seriously and carried out in a professional manner. While there are few real instances when an employee reporting to work has found the office door locked, the lock replaced, and personal belongings piled in the hallway, on many occasions firings have been badly bungled. Managers and professionals have received terse notes from their superiors, stating without any explanation whatsoever that "your services are no longer required as of two weeks from this date . . ." Other employees have been fired after being treated to drinks and lunch at the finest restaurant in town—presumably to soften up the employee for the blow.

Carrying out the discharge decision should involve tact, maturity, and careful planning. The discharge should be administered so that ill feelings between the employee and the company are minimized. As with the administration of any step in the disciplinary system, the discharge should be conducted unemotionally and without vindictiveness, revenge, or malice.

Considerations when discharging a managerial or professional employee include:[6]

NO SURPRISES. The discharge should not come as a surprise. The discharge should be preceded by documented warnings during the performance appraisals and meetings with the superior. On-the-spot dismissals are a sign of weak management.

PLANNING. The discharge interview should be carefully planned. The superior should be fully prepared.

PRIVACY. Absolute privacy is essential; interruptions must be avoided.

PROPER TIMING. Many executives prefer discharging an employee at the end of the day when the dismissed employee need not face fellow workers. Termination before important holidays should be avoided.

BE HONEST. Give honest, specific reasons why the dismissal is taking place. Don't pass the buck to others.

DON'T CRITICIZE OR INSULT THE INDIVIDUAL. Enumerate the person's strengths in addition to weaknesses. Give good advice wherever possible.

DETAIL THE FINANCIAL SETTLEMENT. Some companies use an indeterminate compensation cutoff date for executives or managers who remain on the payroll for a specified period until securing new employment. Usually, insurance benefits

---

6. Robert F. Westcott, "How to Fire An Executive," *Business Horizons* (April 1976): 34–36.

continue for the same period—usually a year. The financial settlement should be clear and put in writing.

COMMUNICATE THE PERSONNEL CHANGE. Tell the dismissed employee who will take over the job, if someone has been selected, and how the change will take place. Be sure that the successor knows the job expectations and try to maximize the new employee's chance for success.

In summary, many factors may cause an employee to perform unsatisfactorily; some reasons may be directly attributable to the management team or organizational shortcomings. Discipline should be applied only when the employee is the cause of unsatisfactory performance. The most effective approach to discipline involves the application of preventive discipline techniques. If it becomes necessary to apply discipline, however, it is important to use positive disciplinary methods. Positive discipline focuses upon solving the employee's problem rather than handing out punishment. Positive discipline is a process; each element in the process must be carried out for discipline to be maximally effective. Corrective counseling is a particularly important part of the positive discipline process. Corrective counseling helps build respect and trust between the supervisor and subordinate, because employees are encouraged to find solutions to problems. The more an employee participates in the problem–solving process, the greater the chances for a permanent improvement in an employee's behavior.

The Solution

The Midwestern Chemicals case presents serious problems that often take place in the application of discipline. First, it appears that Helm was not told about the no smoking rule. On the first day of work, the supervisor should have pointed out that smoking was not allowed in the warehouse. In fact, all rules and regulations should have been covered in detail on the first working day. Whether or not Helm was aware of the firearms rule is another matter. Was he given a copy of the union contract? Were the rules and regulations contained within the contract explained to him? Does the rule apply to firearms that are kept in the employees' cars?

Other problems are obvious in the way Huber administered

the discipline. He committed a serious error by disciplining Helm in the presence of his peers. Helm lost a great deal of face by being chewed out in front of the other workers; no doubt this resulted in bitterness and anger toward Huber. Discipline should always be applied in private. In addition, Huber applied punitive discipline, harassed, and intimidated Helm. Of course, he brought about an immediate change in Helm's behavior but he did so at a price: a good relationship with a subordinate. Huber should have used the positive disciplinary approach which focuses on solving the problem in a mature and respectful manner rather than a single application of punishment.

KEY TERMS AND CONCEPTS

Preventive Discipline	Progressive Discipline
Punitive Discipline	Corrective Counseling
Positive Discipline	Hot Stove Rule

FOR REVIEW

1. What are the three general causes of unsatisfactory employee performance?
2. Compare and contrast preventive, punitive, and positive discipline.
3. What steps are involved in the positive disciplinary process?
4. How may supervisory resistance to discipline be overcome?
5. What are some important considerations to keep in mind when discharging managerial or professional employees?

FOR DISCUSSION

1. In the past, punitive disciplinary measures were often used in disciplining employees. What reasons might account for this?

2. Briefly review the techniques for developing managers in Chapter 10. What would you include in a supervisors' training course in positive discipline and what developmental techniques would you use?

3. Under the therapeutic counseling method, the supervisor encourages employees to find solutions to problems. Why might this method be more effective than having the supervisor tell the employees how to solve their problems?

4. Assume you are responsible for training supervisors how to conduct employee discipline. What would you cover in the program?

5. Assume you were recently appointed the personnel director for a small bank. How would you communicate the company's rules and regulations to the employees?

6. If an employee shows up to work intoxicated, what action should the supervisor take? Should the supervisor counsel the employee about the evils of drinking? (Review the material on alcoholic employees in Chapter 18.)

7. In what ways does discharge of a lower-level operative employee differ from the discharge of a manager or professional? Do you feel these differences reflect an unfair and unjust system of making employee dismissals?

SUPPLEMENTARY READING

Fisher, Robert W. "When Workers are Discharged: An Overview." *Monthly Labor Review*, June 1973, pp. 4–17.

Mager, Robert, and Pepe, Peter. *Analyzing Performance Problems.* Palo Alto, CA: Fearon Publishers, 1970.

Miner, J. B., and Brewer, J. F. "The Management of Ineffective Performance." In Dunnette, M. D., ed. *Handbook of Industrial and Organizational Psychology.* Chicago: Rand McNally & Co., 1976.

Myers, Deborah, and Abrahamson, Lee. "Firing with Finesse: A Rationale for Outplacement." *Personnel Journal*, August 1975, pp. 432–34.

Shull, Fremont, and Cummings, L. L., "Enforcing the Rules: How Do Managers Differ?" *Personnel*, March/April 1966, pp. 33–39.

Stanton, Edwin. "The Discharged Employee and the EEO Laws." *Personnel Journal*, March 1976, pp. 128–33ff.

Wheeler, Hoyt. "Punishment Theory and Industrial Discipline." *Industrial Relations*, May 1976, pp. 235–43.

Wholburg, Wallace. "Effective Discipline in Employee Relations." *Personnel Journal*, September 1975, pp. 489–93ff.

For Analysis: Strand-O'Mally Publishing Company

The Strand-O'Mally Publishing Company is a large publisher of road maps, atlases, and books for both children and adults. Strand-O'Mally employs 9,800 employees in six states. There are many assembly-line type operations within its manufacturing facilities; good attendance is encouraged so that production bottlenecks, delays, and absenteeism-related problems are kept at a minimum. In order to control employee absenteeism, the company has instituted the following absenteeism policy and progressive disciplinary procedure:

STRAND-O'MALLY ATTENDANCE GUIDELINES

Absenteeism is defined as being absent from work on any scheduled workday, including scheduled overtime.

Each period of consecutive absence will be recorded as one occurrence, regardless of duration.

Employees who are not at work at the start of their shift, who leave more than two hours before the end of their shift, or who are away from work more than two hours, will be charged with an occurrence of absence.

Tardiness will constitute one-half of an absence occurrence.

Absences due to court ordered appearances, paid funeral attendance, lack of work, lunch punches, designated weather days, military obligation, jury duty, hospital confinement, work-incurred injury, or any company paid absence (sick days), will not be recorded as an occurrence of absence for purposes of disciplinary action or control. Absences other than those listed in this paragraph will be subject to the following procedure:

Step 1: Three occurrences within a consecutive twelve—
month period—verbal warning.

Step 2:   Five occurrences within a consecutive twelve—
          month period—written probation.

Step 3:   Seven occurrences within a consecutive twelve—
          month period—five-day layoff.

Step 4:   Nine occurrences within a consecutive twelve—
          month period—discharge.

Unfortunately, every firm, regardless of how well managed it is, will be faced with the need to discipline employees for unsatisfactory performance. Strand-O'Mally is no exception.

Described below are nine disciplinary actions which must be taken by Strand-O'Mally supervisors. Each disciplinary action should be role-played by students who play the roles of the supervisor and the employee. In carrying out the discipline, the supervisor is to use a corrective counseling technique. Before role playing begins, students playing supervisors should be familiar with the corrective counseling procedure and apply it to the positive disciplinary process.

ROLE PLAY 1: *Mary Marshall, a lithography press operator, has three absence occurrences. She's ready for step 1. She's been with you for about a year and does pretty good work. Her problem, however, is getting to work on time. While one occurrence was due to an all day absence, she has been anywhere from four to twenty-six minutes late four times. You're not sure what the problem is. You get along well with her, and she has given you no other problems.*

ROLE PLAY 2: *Bob Cohen has five occurrences and must receive disciplinary step 2. Bob is friendly, although a marginal employee. All of his absences have occurred on Monday and Friday. Cohen is a young, very bright, recent high school graduate, but he has a lackadaisical attitude about work and attendance.*

ROLE PLAY 3: *Allen Cahill just accumulated his seventh occurrence last week. He's in your office for step 3, a five-day layoff. He's a marginal employee, not particularly cooperative—actually difficult to get along with. Cahill's absences make him a particularly troublesome employee, and you really wish he'd quit.*

ROLE PLAY 4: *Ron Akers has three occurrences and he is in your office to receive disciplinary step 1. Ron was hired three months ago and is an excellent pressman—when he's around. But he has used all his personal leave days already, and has called three times during lunch hours to say he couldn't return to work. Ron's explanations were vague. A lot of people talk about Ron and his escapades; while rumors are rampant—ranging from alcoholism to migraine headaches to poker games—you have no facts.*

ROLE PLAY 5: *Mike Southern is due in your office to receive a step 2, written probation. He's twenty minutes late, but you see him coming down the hall. During the six months he has worked for you, Mike has been a true pain in the neck. He does just enough to get by. He's very argumentative and likes to give you and co-workers a hard time. In addition, Mike's language is abusive; he swore at you several times when he received his verbal warning at step 1.*

ROLE PLAY 6: *Val McCloud is in your office for disciplinary step 1. She's a long time, valued employee, having worked for Strand-O'Mally for over twelve years. She was almost a model employee, up to the past year or so.*

In recent months she's used all her personal days and has accumulated three occurrences. This is the first time she's had attendance problems, and she's very upset about it. Her work is good, although not quite up to the high productivity and quality she has demonstrated in the past.

You're not exactly sure what her trouble is; you know

only that she is raising four children: a nine year old, two teenagers, and a daughter who attends college. Her husband was killed in an auto accident a year and a half ago.

ROLE PLAY 7: *Kim Durango is in your office to receive step 3, a five-day layoff. An employee of yours for about a year, Kim's work is good, but she's been causing real problems because of her poor attendance. She's in the binding department, and her absences have caused several scheduling problems. You've talked about her with the department manager and personnel, and the decision is to transfer her upon her return to work.*

ROLE PLAY 8: *Scot Bledsoe is coming through your door now. Last week he accumulated his seventh occurrence, and is to receive a five-day layoff. The reason for his absence is no secret to anyone—he's an alcoholic getting progressively worse. Scot was your best employee when he first came to Strand-O'Mally six years ago, but a combination of marital and financial problems has destroyed his personal life—and now his job.*

You want to salvage Scot, but realize he's got to solve his own drinking problem. You have discussed the problem with the personnel manager who is sitting in with you during this meeting.

ROLE PLAY 9: *You knew Charley Basil wouldn't last long. Late for his first day of work, Charley barely made it through his probationary period. In the past few months, Steps 1, 2, and 3 have come mighty quickly for Charley. He accumulated his ninth occurrence last Friday when he left two and one half hours before quitting time. Today you've got to fire Charley.*

SELECTED PROFESSIONAL READING

Guidelines to Corrective Discipline

LEON D. BONCAROSKY

Employee discipline is a critical area of personnel administration and labor relations. In other areas of these fields, such as fringe benefits, performance evaluation or seniority, a decision favorable or unfavorable to an employee will not normally leave a permanent scar in the person's memory. However, an employee who has been suspended or fired has sustained a loss that may affect the rest of his or her work life. A suspension may result not only in loss of pay, but also in loss of future promotions. A dismissal not only severs an employee's income, but may also result in the inability to find suitable employment again. An employee's interest in having a disciplinary decision reversed or reduced is real and serious. On the other hand, a supervisor who has the responsibility for directing employees does not look on employee misconduct lightly, since it may appear a direct threat to his or her position and authority.

Some of the matters to be considered when discussing corrective discipline include the reasons why employee misconduct occurs and how discipline can be administered so that employees will have an opportunity to change their behavior. Another important topic is how discipline can be imposed in a corrective rather than a punitive manner. Finally, consideration should be given to the requirements for having a disciplinary decision sustained by an arbitrator. (A study conducted by the American Management Associations showed that 26.4% of arbitration cases dealt with discipline or discharge.)[1]

BASIC CAUSES: THE EMPLOYEE

First, let's consider some of the basic causes of employee misconduct. In essence, we will be dealing with the following question: Why do employees take action that will result in discipline? These causes can usually be attributed to the employee, the supervisor or the organization.

An employee can become an apparent disciplinary problem due to four basic reasons: lack of knowledge, personal desires, unsuitability to the job and emotional or external factors.

Lack of job knowledge can result in employees' failing to perform assigned tasks, failing to perform assignments correctly or causing damage to material or equipment. This type of situation, if diagnosed correctly by management, should not usually result in any disciplinary action and can be rectified by providing proper training for employees. An example of this situation is the recent collision of the Coast Guard cutter *Cuyahoga* with a freighter in the Chesapeake Bay. The cause of the accident appeared to be the lookout, who had not alerted the bridge of the collision course because he didn't understand his duties or the lights used in sailing. The lookout stated to a board of inquiry "that he was unaware of his duty to report whistle and horn signals to the bridge and that he did not know a red light is always posted on the left side of a ship."[2]

Some employees cause disciplinary problems due to their personal desires. They don't like their type of work, or they may be against authority figures and resent rules, regulations

---

1. P. Pigors and C. Myers, *Personnel Administration, A Point of View and a Method* (New York: McGraw-Hill, 1977), p. 301.

2. Harrisburg *Evening News*, October 26, 1978, p. 13.

or orders. The action they take is in the form of a protest. "In some [GM] plants worker discontent.has reached such a degree that there has been overt sabotage. Screws have been left in brake drums, tool handles welded into fender compartments."[3] For this type of situation, management should deal with the overall source of the problem. It must, however, remedy specific instances of misconduct by using disciplinary procedures.

Next, unsuitability to the job can lead to disciplinary problems. Employees may be fully aware of what is expected of them. They may even have the wholehearted desire to comply with all instructions and rules, but are unable to complete assignments. The responsibility for this type of problem is shared by management, since management is responsible for selection and placement of employees. Employees are also responsible, since they should inform supervisory personnel when they are unable to perform assignments. Means for remedying this type of situation include demotion to a less demanding position or termination.

Finally, employees can cause disciplinary problems due to emotional or external factors. Employees may carry their financial and family difficulties to work, responding inappropriately to work situations due to these external problems. This may account, as an example, for an act of insubordination to a supervisor. If employees create unusual problems, supervisors should look for external problems when investigating the misconduct. Privately talking to the employee and holding informal discussions with individuals close to the employee may help to determine the underlying problem and the alternatives for handling it.[4] "Employee-centered supervision," in which supervisors take an interest in employees both on and off the job, can prevent these problems from occurring.[5]

BASIC CAUSES: THE SUPERVISOR

The next cause of disciplinary problems is the supervisor. Some of the ways that supervisors can contribute to disciplinary problems include using an inappropriate method of supervision and giving improper assignments or orders.

Supervisors who consistently use an inappropriate method for supervising employees, such as the negative, authoritarian approach (the style typified by [Douglas] McGregor's Theory X), may be inviting disciplinary problems. These approaches basically ignore the human relations part of supervision and stress pressure, coercion and punishment. Employees may react to too much pressure and frustration with sabotage, slowdown and unnecessary waste and by resorting to psychological defense mechanisms such as aggressiveness and repression.[6]

Supervisors can also contribute to disciplinary problems by giving improper assignments or orders to employees. Assignments should be given to employees on the basis of what can reasonably be expected of them. This does not mean that employees should not be challenged. Instead, it means that supervisors should not give assignments to employees that they know are beyond their capabilities, since this can only result in improper job performance and frustration. Supervisors should also not direct subordinates to perform dangerous tasks that are not part of the employees' regular duties or to work with unsafe tools or equipment, since this may result in employees' refusing to perform orders. (This is one exception to the rule, "Do as directed and grieve later," since employees can rightfully

3. J. Gooding, "Blue Collar Blues on the Assembly Line," in *Management of Human Resources*, eds. P. Pigors, C. Myers and F. Malm (New York: McGraw-Hill, 1973), p. 223.

4. P. Wilkens and J. Haynes, "Understanding Frustration—Instigated Behavior," *Personnel Journal*, October 1974, p. 774.

5. R. Likert, "Motivation: The Core of Management," in *Management of Human Resources*, pp. 255–270.

6. G. Strauss and L. Sayles, *Personnel: The Human Problems of Management* (Englewood Cliffs, New Jersey: Prentice-Hall, 1967), pp. 127–131.

refuse to carry out assignments that may be deleterious to their health or safety.)

DON'T FORGET THE ORGANIZATION

The last cause of disciplinary problems is the organization. Some of the problems created by organizations include unsound and unnecessarily restrictive policies and regulations, and improper expectations. Unsound and unnecessarily restrictive policies only invite violations by employees. Policies and regulations should be clearly related to the overall performance of the job. Lastly, organizations may expect more from their employees than they can really produce or are paid to produce.

THE PROGRESSIVE DISCIPLINE PROCESS

When misconduct occurs, management must take action to redirect the employee. This is done through the use of disciplinary procedures. The procedure which has gained the acceptance of most arbitrators is progressive, or corrective, discipline. "Primarily as a result of arbitration awards, the doctrine of corrective or progressive discipline is now accepted industrial practice."[7] Corrective discipline, to offer clarification, does not apply to serious acts of misconduct, such as assault, accepting bribes or sabotage. It applies only to less serious offenses. The procedure involves increasingly severe penalties each time an employee is disciplined. Except for extremely serious acts, employees are not discharged for the first offense. Instead, the sequence of penalties is as follows: oral reprimand, written reprimand, suspension, and discharge.

An oral reprimand consists of clearly informing the employee that misconduct has occurred and that repetition could result in further disciplinary action. At this step, the supervisor should place great emphasis on determining why the misconduct occurred and helping the employee to determine how he or she can prevent a reoccurrence. The rep-

rimand should be given privately and immediately after misconduct has occurred, in order to add credibility and prevent a misunderstanding that the behavior has been condoned.[8]

The second step to progressive discipline is the written reprimand. This is the first formal step in the procedure. Psychologically, it has a greater effect on the employee, since the misconduct is now a matter of record. People in general appear to take matters more seriously when put in writing. Procedurally, the written warning can be clearly used as supportive evidence in possible arbitration should more severe disciplinary action be taken. It offers clear evidence to an arbitrator that management has attempted to use corrective disciplinary procedures.[9]

A letter of reprimand should contain the following information:

■ Facts surrounding the misconduct
■ The organizational policy or work rule that was violated
■ Previous counseling and oral reprimands
■ Reference to the fact that the written reprimand is disciplinary action for misconduct and that reoccurrence will result in further management action.[10]

Depending on the volatility of the situation, a supervisor may want to consider sending the letter by mail to avoid a confrontation at the work site.[11]

The third step in progressive discipline is suspension. An initial suspension, depending

---

7. M. Trotta, *Arbitration of Labor Management Disputes* (New York: AMACOM, 1974), p. 232.

8. R. Oberle, "Administering Disciplinary Actions," *Personnel Journal,* January 1978, p. 30.

9. To prevent possible misunderstanding, a written reprimand in itself can also be grieved; however, if the facts are clear to both parties since the employee has not suffered a real loss, it is highly improbable that such a reprimand will be grieved.

10. J. Justin, *How to Manage with a Union* (New York: IRWS, 1969), pp. 411–414.

11. Ibid., p. 414.

on the misconduct, should be for a period of "three, five, seven, but not exceeding ten working days."[12] Suspension should last at least three days in order to allow sufficient time for the discipline to sink in.[13] It also creates more of a socially embarrassing situation for the employee, since the latter is likely to be asked by neighbors and friends to explain his or her absence from work. Finally, suspension serves as a warning to the employee to modify his or her behavior or face the consequence of possible termination.

Depending on the circumstances of a disciplinary problem, an organization may want to consider two separate suspensions prior to discharge. This would seem appropriate for a minor problem, such as absenteeism.

The last step of progressive discipline is discharge. Many arbitrators refer to discharge as industrial capital punishment.[14] This is the most severe penalty that an organization or supervisor can give to an employee. It involves two aspects. For the employee, it means financial hardship, since income will stop. It also means that the employee may have difficulty in obtaining new work, since discharged people are closely scrutinized by prospective employers. For the organization, it means financial loss in terms of lost experience, and recruitment, placement and training expenses. For the supervisor, it means getting involved in an unpleasant experience which may have negative consequences, such as lost friends and ostracism by subordinate employees.

DISCIPLINE AND ARBITRATORS

Arbitrators are reluctant to sustain a discharge unless the reasons are morally and legally justified and the employee has been given a chance to correct the misconduct. The burden of proof in a disciplinary case falls on management. Unlike a court of law, management does not have to have an airtight case, but must prove to an arbitrator that the preponderance

of evidence shows that the discipline was a reasonable course of action.[15,16]

Arbitrator Carroll Daugherty has developed seven factors for determining whether management had "just cause" for a suspension or discharge. They are as follows:

1. Did the employee have prior warning that his or her conduct would result in discipline, including possible discharge?

2. Was the misconduct related to the safe, efficient and orderly operation of the company?

3. Was an investigation held?

4. Was the investigation fair and objective?

5. Did the investigation obtain circumstantial evidence that the employee was guilty?

6. Was the disciplinary decision nondiscriminatory?

7. Was the discipline reasonably related to the seriousness of the offense and the employee's record with the company?[17]

An alternative to progressive discipline (which would also be arbitrally sound when conducted properly) is the procedure developed by John Huberman. Initially used by a plywood mill in Canada, it consists of the following five steps:

1. A casual private reminder is given to the employee by the foreman when an incident of misconduct occurs.

2. Repetition of step 1 if misconduct reoccurs.

3. The shift foreman and department super-

---

12. Ibid., p. 422.
13. Ibid., p. 474.
14. Strauss and Sayles, *Personnel*, p. 311.

15. According to *Blacks Law Dictionary*, this term means that the "evidence . . . produces the strongest impression and has the greatest weight and is more convincing as to its truth."
16. R. Hilgert, "An Arbitrator Looks at Grievance Arbitration," *Personnel Journal*, October 1978, p. 558.
17. W. Baer, *Discipline and Discharge under the Labor Agreement* (New York: American Management Associations, 1972), p. 29.

visor discuss the next incident of misconduct with the employee. At this time, a great deal of effort is made to determine the cause of the misconduct and to help the employee prevent a reoccurrence. A written synopsis is made of the conversation.

4. If another incident of misconduct occurs, a final discussion with the employee is held by the foreman and the plant superintendent. The employee is asked to take the remainder of the shift off with pay and to reconsider his or her behavior. Also, the employee is warned that repetition will result in dismissal. The conversation is summarized in a letter.

5. Dismissal.[18]

A similar procedure has been used at a Goodyear plant in Wisconsin. Their experience with the program over a 2½-year period showed that 48% of their disciplinary cases proceeded to step 2, 35% to step 3 and 11% to step 4. Only 1% of the cases ended in dismissal.[19]

DISCIPLINE WITHOUT RESENTMENT
How can progressive discipline be administered so as to lessen resentment toward the supervisor or the organization and make the employee accept accountability for the consequences of misconduct? In approaching this dilemma, Douglas McGregor developed what is called the Hot Stove Rule. This rule or approach uses the analogy of touching a hot stove and undergoing discipline. When a person gets burned on a hot stove, that person doesn't blame the stove, but him or herself. Touching the hot stove involves four elements: The consequence is immediate; if an individual touches a hot stove, he or she will be burnt. Second, since a hot stove gives off radiant heat and the color of the metal may

change, individuals have been warned not to touch the stove. Next, the penalty for touching a hot stove is consistent; it always results in being burnt. Lastly, whoever touches the stove is burnt; the penalty is given in a nondiscriminatory manner.[20]

These four elements can be applied to the administration of discipline, and, if carried out, may result in the employee's blaming him or herself rather than the supervisor for the misconduct. Let's discuss this point in more detail.

Supervisors should begin the disciplinary process as soon as possible after misconduct has occurred and culpability has been determined. The more quickly the discipline follows the misconduct, the more likely it is that the employee will associate the discipline with misconduct, rather than with the person imposing the discipline. This does not mean that an employee should be disciplined without an investigation of the incident in order to expedite the connection. Instead, it means that after facts are gathered and the preponderance of the evidence indicates that a person is responsible for the misconduct, discipline should begin.[21] "How soon after an offense should discipline be applied? The general answer is that management may delay imposing a penalty for a reasonable time, but should have sufficient justification for the postponement. Arbitrators sometimes find that excessive delay resembles double jeopardy."[22]

When facts are not completely known to support disciplinary action, but the circumstances are such that immediate action must be taken, a person suspected of misconduct may be suspended, pending an investigation

---

18. J. Huberman, "Discipline without Punishment Lives," *Harvard Business Review*, July-August 1975, pp. 6–8.

19. Ibid., p. 8.

20. Strauss and Sayles, *Personnel*, pp. 311–321.

21. According to Trotta in *Arbitration of Labor Management Disputes*, p. 100, the degree of proof (i.e., preponderance of evidence, clear and convincing proof, and proof beyond a reasonable doubt) will vary with the seriousness of the misconduct. For misconduct involving moral turpitude, proof beyond a reasonable doubt would normally be required by arbitrators.

22. Baer, *Discipline and Discharge*, p. 60.

and a final disciplinary decision.[23] If disciplinary action is taken within a reasonable time after facts are gathered, this would normally preclude a defense of double jeopardy. If facts do not support a suspension, then the employee would be entitled to back pay.

The next part of the Hot Stove Rule is advance warning. Employees should receive warning that a particular act or misconduct will result in disciplinary action. Unexpected discipline is clearly unfair and will not usually be sustained in arbitration. One of the seven factors cited earlier dealt with advance warning: "Did the employee have foreknowledge that his conduct would be subject to discipline, including possible discharge?"[24] Employees can receive warning through such means as the orientation process, notices posted on bulletin boards, and work rules. "By giving advance notice of accepted standards of conduct, . . . [an employee] will equally enjoy the benefits and equally assume the responsibilities of his job."[25]

To offer clarification, merely because work rules are posted does not mean that management can take disciplinary action in a capricious manner for violations. To be meaningful and defensible in appeal proceedings, work rules or similar requirements must be consistently enforced by management. If management has at any time condoned violations of work rules, then management has in effect undermined their usefulness, since arbitrators will normally find a precedent of nonenforcement and thus sustain an employee's grievance.

If management has rules that have become nonenforceable, it must warn employees that enforcement will occur for future violations. This can be done by posting notices and meeting with employees.

Ideally, two employees who commit the same offense and have identical employment records should receive the same form and degree of discipline. Since these conditions do not usually exist, consistent discipline essentially means that a form of misconduct will result in discipline. Consistent discipline is accepted by most employees as fair and just. It also serves an educational purpose for all employees, since it sets behavioral limits, while inconsistent discipline leads to confusion and uncertainty.

To avoid any possible misunderstanding, consistent discipline does not mean that the form and degree of discipline should be determined by the offense. Each case must be determined on its own merits. Factors that should be included in making a decision include past-conduct record, seriousness of the offense, period of time that has lapsed since the last incident of misconduct, length of service, etc. There are two reasons why management should avoid imposing the same punishment on all employees. First, uniformity is inconsistent with the overall intent of the concept of "just cause." Second, any deviation will probably result in an allegation of discrimination.[26]

The last element of the Hot Stove Rule is nondiscrimination. It is admittedly difficult to impose discipline without causing the employee to feel resentment. However, resentment can be minimized if employees feel that their misconduct is the sole reason for disciplinary action. This can be accomplished by ensuring that the accused has every opportunity to confront his or her accuser at a predisciplinary investigation hearing. At the hearing, which should be confined to the act of misconduct, all supporting evidence should be presented by management, and the employee should be given an opportunity to respond and present a defense. By focusing on the act of misconduct, management is demonstrating this is the only reason for taking disciplinary action.

Nondiscrimination can also be furthered by

23. R. Schiffer, "Some Guideposts for Administering Discipline," *Personnel Journal*, February 1961, p. 36.

24. Baer, *Discipline and Discharge*, p. 29.

25. Justin, *How to Manage with a Union*, p. 372.

26. Schiffer, "Some Guideposts for Administering Discipline," pp. 37–38.

emphasizing to the employee in a counseling session subsequent to the disciplinary action that the primary concern of management is to prevent reoccurrence of misconduct, and that the only reason for the disciplinary action was the act of misconduct.

BASIC DISCIPLINARY PROCEDURE: A CHECK LIST

1. Secure the necessary facts related to the misconduct. Obtain verifiable information by interviewing witnesses and obtaining statements and all necessary supporting documentation.

2. Hold a meeting with the employee to discuss the allegation of misconduct. If requested, the employee is entitled to union representation.

3. Analyze all facts that have been obtained, including those presented by the employee. Determine if sufficient evidence exists to support disciplinary action.

4. If appropriate to the situation, determine corrective action. Consider the severity of discipline, and apply principles of progressive discipline.

5. Inform the employee of the disciplinary decision. Comply with all contractual requirements, such as notification.

6. Record all facts as soon as possible for a possible appeal. Do not rely on memory.

7. Upon return of the employee, hold a meeting to discuss the situation and counsel the employee on ways to prevent a reoccurrence.

NAME INDEX

Abrahamson, Lee, 677
Acheson, Dean, 469
Adams, J. S., 430
Alfred, T. M., 417
Alpander, Guvenc, 239
Ammerman, H. L., 95
Anderson, Harry B., 270, 271
Anderson, Howard J., 226
Anderson, J. W., 131
Anthony, Wilham P., 343
Apcar, Leonard M., 355
Applebaum, S., 376
Archer, W. B., 94
Argyris, Chris, 326
Arnold, M., 227
Ashford, Nicholas, 511, 532

Baer, Walter, 598
Barnard, Chester I., 41
Barnett, Nona, 241
Bass, B. M., 298, 305
Baumgartel, Howard, 376
Bayley, Susan, 160
Beach, Dale S., 577
Beer, Michael, 271, 376
Belcher, David W., 427, 435
Bell, C. H., 132
Bell, Cecil H., Jr., 354, 356
Benge, Eugene, 447
Benson, G. Philip, 218, 227
Berg, J. Gary, 460
Berg, Per O., 368, 369
Berliver, William M., 343
Bernard, Keith, 123, 125
Bernthal, Wilmer, 637
Bigelow, R. P. 227
Biggs, Robert D., 620
Biggs, William, 114, 172, 243, 252
Bingham, Eula, 518
Blake, R., 366, 376, 532
Blaustein, Saul J., 487, 488
Blood, Milton R., 254
Bogert, Jeremiah, 212
Bolt, John A., 219
Bowers, Charles P., Jr., 343
Brayfield, Arthur H., 614
Brewer, J. F., 677
Brookmire, David, 147
Bucalo, Jack, 255

Burack, E. A., 417
Burack, Elmer H., 58, 318
Burke, W., 376
Byars, Lloyd L., 36
Byham, William C., 192, 417, 611, 637

Calvin, Otto, 305
Campbell, Donald T., 368, 614
Campbell, John P., 331
Campbell, Thomas, 530
Carey, Alex, 82
Carrell, Michael R., 95, 131, 267, 430, 460, 499, 596, 614, 632
Carvey, Davis W., 533
Catalanello, Ralph, 333
Chamot, Dennis, 566
Cherns, A. B., 131
Chicci, David L., 192
Clague, Evan, 488
Claypool, Jeffrey, 496, 497
Colaser, Rollin, 305
Collette, Jerome A., 461
Conant, E. H., 131
Cone, Paul B., 343
Congemi, Joseph, 496, 497
Connellan, Thomas K., 343
Copperman, Lois, 129
Corn, Morton, 533
Crandall, Fred, 647
Crane, Donald P., 343
Cravens, Gwenyth, 333
Creitner, Robert, 268
Crockett, Walter H., 614
Cross, Frank, 192
Cullen, T., 292
Cummings, L. L., 131, 204, 267, 677

Dahl, D. R., 417
Dalton, Melville, 49, 400
Davis, L. E., 131
DeCotiis, Thomas A., 268
DeFee, Dallas, 255, 267
Dennis, Terry L., 192
Deric, Arthur J., 499
Dessler, Gary, 580
Detlefs, Dale, 481, 482
Dickson, W. J., 6, 610
Dimitroff, Nick, 267
Dittrich, John E., 95, 430, 460, 632, 633

Doeringer, Peter B., 192
Donnelly, James J., 112, 114, 115
Dorf, Paul, 456
Dowling, W., 376
Dressnack, Carl H., 23, 491
Drucker, Peter, 267
Duggan, Shirley, 157, 158
Dunnette, Marvin, 23, 95, 192, 223, 226, 331
Dwyer, James C., 267
Dyer, Frank J., 160
Dyer, L., 426

Ebel, Robert L., 160, 214
Eddy, William B., 372
Elbert, N. F., 267
Elkouri, Ena Asher, 598
Elkouri, Frank, 598
Endicott, Frank S., 182
English, Jack W., 23
Erdlen, John, 491
Esten, Marten, 541
Ewing, David W., 232, 592

Famularo, Joseph J., 160, 280
Farrell, Richard J., 492, 493
Farrell, W. T., 95
Feder, Barnaby J., 10
Fein, M., 131
Feldacker, Bruce, 552, 580
Field, Hubert, 160, 241
Filipowicz, Christine A., 525, 526
Fine, Sidney A., 78, 80, 81, 95
Fisher, Robert W., 677
Flanagan, J. C. 95
Fleishman, Edwin A., 268, 339, 594
Fleuter, Douglas L., 461
Flint, Jerry, 484
Flowers, Vincent S., 628
Foderaro, Diana, 501
Fogli, Lawrence, 254
Forbes, Ray, 219, 222
Ford, R. N., 131
Fossum, John A., 426, 586
Foulkes, Fred K., 46, 58, 533
Fox, Harland, 404
Fox, R. G., 131
Foy, N., 131
Frame, Robert M., 382
Franklin, Jerome L., 371
Frease, Michael, 125
Freeman, J., 335
French, Wendell L., 354, 356, 358, 549

Fulmer, William E., 506

Gadon, H., 131
Gannon, Martin J., 630
Gardner, James, 533
Gatewood, Robert, 149, 219
Gaylord, S. R., 226
Gellerman, Saul W., 268
Gibson, James L., 112, 114, 115
Gibson, Robert, 456
Glueck, William F., 370
Goldberg, Irving, 288
Goldstein, I. L., 210
Goldstein, R. C., 231
Golembiewski, R. T., 131
Gomersall, Earl R., 282
Goods, Robert, 637
Gordon, Francine E., 343
Green, Charles N., 614
Greenberg, Leon, 113
Greenlaw, Paul S., 114, 172, 243, 252, 501, 620
Grier, James, 15
Grimsley, Glen, 226
Guest, R. H., 110, 112
Guion, Robert M., 160, 192, 215
Gumbiner, Robert, 524
Gustafson, David, 192

Hackman, J. Richard, 132, 394
Hagburg, Eugene G., 566
Hagen, Elizabeth P., 216
Hall, Douglas T., 417, 626
Hall, Francine S., 417, 626
Hall, R., 174
Hammons, Henry E. II, 525
Harris, E. F., 594
Hass, Frederick C., 343
Hatfield, John, 222
Hawk, Donald, 626
Hawk, Roger, 176
Hedges, James N., 334
Heinen, J. Stephen, 335
Henderson, Richard I., 244, 437, 446, 448,
    449, 473, 482, 489, 500
Hendricks, John, 305
Heneman, H. G., Jr., 96, 417
Heneman, Herbert G. III, 268
Hennig, Margaret, 343
Hensler, W. J., 370, 417
Herzberg, Frederick, 394
Hess, Lee, 296
Higgens, James M., 195

Hodge, B. J., 343
Hodgetts, Richard M., 48
Holden, Peter B., 219
Holder, H. Birdie, 218
Hollingsworth, Thomas A., 58
Holly, William, 241, 264
House, Robert J., 331
Howe, R., 376
Hoyman, Michele, 160
Hubbartt, William S., 195
Hughes, Charles L., 628
Hulin, Charles L., 132, 254
Huntley, G., 598
Huse, Edgar F., 343
Hutchinson, John G.
Hyatt, James C., 456

Iacobellie, John, 195
Inman, James E., 492
Ivancevich, John, 107, 114, 115, 268, 365

Jackson, T. M., 232
Janger, Allen R., 54
Jaquish, Michael P., 192
Jarrett, Hilton F., 226
Jeanneret, Paul R., 78, 95
Johnson, John H., Jr., 602
Johnson, Lyndon B., 144
Jordon, Anne, 343
Jucius, Michael J., 610

Kahn, R., 376
Katz, Robert L., 319
Kearney, William J., 268
Kellogg, Marion S., 268
Kennedy, John F., 139
Kilbridge, M. D., 115, 131
Kilgour, John G., 562
Kimberly, John B., 331
King, Geoffrey R., 599
Kirkpatrick, Donald, 283, 294, 332–33, 343
Kisseloff, A., 227
Klingner, Donald E., 97
Knapp, C. L., 192
Koehn, Hank, 500
Koen, Clifford, 160
Koontz, Harold, 240, 540
Kotter, John P., 188
Kovach, K. A., 227
Kozlowski, Paul J., 487, 488
Kramer, Leo, 488
Kraut, Allen, 417
Kreis, S. Paul, 218

Krogman, Robert, 497
Kuzmits, Frank E., 367, 376, 525, 616, 622–23, 625

Laken, Martin, 331
Langsner, Adolph, 429, 461
Larson, K. Per, 489, 524–25
Lawler, E. E., 132
Ledvinka, James, 149, 160, 219
Legeros, C., 335
Levine, Edward L., 213
Levine, Marvin J., 566
Levinson, Harry, 325
Lewin, Kurt, 51
Likert, J. G., 361
Likert, R., 361
Lindsey, Fred, 473, 475
Lippett, Gordon L., 355
Littea, Michael P., 492
Locke, E. A., 433, 637
Loring, Rosalind, 333
Luthans, Fred, 268, 382

McCarthy, Maureen, 124
McClay, Robert, 524, 525
McConkie, Mark, 256
McCormick, Ernest J., 112, 160
McDonald, M. J., 132
McGehee, William, 290
McGlauchlen, D., 335
McGregor, Douglas M., 258–59, 674
McIssac, George S., 566
McKersie, Robert B., 404
McKinley, Richard N., 343
McLarney, William J., 343
Mager, Robert, 677
Maier, Norman R. F., 260, 263
Marquardt, L. D., 95
Marquiles, N., 358, 376
Marion, B. W., 281
Meader, Leland, 521
Mecham, Robert C., 78, 95
Meier, Grett S., 125, 126
Metcalf, Henry C., 5
Meyer, H. H., 258
Meyer, Herbert E., 4
Meyer, Mitchell, 404
Miller, E. L., 58
Miner, John, 376, 677
Miner, M. G., 637
Mitchell, H. H., 20
Mitchell, T. R., 132
Moore, B. E., 95

Moore, Russell F., 461
Morano, R. A., 637
Morgan, Henry M., 46, 58
Moses, J. L., 417
Mouton, J., 366, 376
Muczyk, Jan, 195
Munsberger, Gerald, 305
Murphy, John, 288
Mussberg, Walter S., 567
Myer, Herbert, 184
Myers, Charles, 58
Myers, Deborah, 677
Myers, M. Scott, 282

Newell, Gale, 305
Newstrom, John W., 118, 119, 120, 124
Nibler, Roger G., 533
Nielson, Warren R., 331
Nolan, R. L., 231
Norton, S. D., 399
Notkin, Herbert, 521
Novit, Mitchell S., 112, 116, 172, 205, 206

Oberg, Winston, 268
Odiorne, George S., 23, 268, 305
O'Donnel, Cyril, 540
Oldham, G. R., 132

Pati, Gopal, 318
Patten, Thomas H., 370, 500
Pauly, C. W., 229
Pearse, Robert F., 343
Peery, Newman, 323
Pete, Peter, 677
Peters, Lawrence, 174
Pettefer, G., 594
Pierce, Jon L., 118, 119, 120, 124
Pilenzo, R. C., 426
Pinto, P. R., 417
Porrau, Jerry I., 368–69
Porter, Lyman W., 394, 627
Preston, Paul, 58
Price, J. L., 637
Primoff, E. S., 95
Proehl, C. W., 131
Pursell, Elliott D., 226

Quinn, Robert, 617

Raia, A., 256, 268, 358, 376
Rasken, A. H., 567
Rhodes, S. R., 622, 624
Rich, Robert A., 271

Richardson, Reed C., 599
Rime, Thomas, Jr., 599
Robertson, David E., 152
Robinson, Ronda, 160
Roethlisberger, F. J., 610
Rose, Gerald, 220
Rosen, Hjalmar, 567
Rosen, M., 131
Ross, Alander, 530
Ross, Irvin, 567
Rue, Leslie W., 36
Rush, Harold M., 132, 370

Salinger, R. D., 306
Sassman, Thomas C., 482
Scheavoni, Michael J., 23
Schein, E. H., 364
Schick, Melvin E., 270
Schneider, Benjamin, 216
Schneier, Craig E., 296, 306
Schoenfeldt, Lyle, 160
Schrader, Jeff, 196
Schriesheim, Chester, 329
Schriesheim, Janet, 329
Schulhof, Robert J., 463
Schuster, Jay R., 461
Schwab, Donald P., 131, 204, 267–68, 426
Selfridge, R., 376
Sheehy, Gail, 417
Shetty, Y. K., 323
Sherwood, John, 117, 492
Shull, Fremont, 677
Shulz, Richard, 474, 475, 484, 490, 495
Simon, William A., 152, 153
Sish, Henry L., 38
Skjervhiem, Terry, 306
Sloan, Arthur, 542, 589
Smardon, Raymond A., 599
Smith, R. R., 227
Sokolik, S., 376
Sparks, C. Paul, 147
Sperry, Len, 296
Staats, Elmer B., 58
Stagner, Ross, 567
Stanley, Julian C., 368, 614
Stanton, Edwin, 677
Stanton, Erwin S., 183, 207, 208, 212
Stead, J. G., 533
Stead, W. E., 533
Steers, Richard, 255, 622, 624, 627
Steinmetz, Lawrence L., 656, 657
Stone, C. H., 95, 96
Stoner, A. F., 40

Stroeber, Myra H., 343
Stroh, Thomas F., 288
Stumm, D. A., 306
Sundberg, Norman D., 226
Suojanen, W. W., 132
Sutermeister, Robert, 113
Swallow, G. L., 132
Swanda, John, 353
Swindle, Orson, 343
Szilagyi, Andrew, 107, 108, 365

Tagliafern, Louis E., 599
Taylor, Frederick W., 5, 108
Taylor, J. W., 337
Tead, Ordway, 5
Thayer, Paul, 290
Thompson, David, 495, 496
Thorndike, E. L., 433
Thorndike, Robert L., 216
Tiffin, Joseph, 160
Toedtman, James C., 25
Towers, J. Maxwell, 329
Towle, Patrick M., 461
Tracey, William, 306
Traynor, W. J., 306
Trieb, S. E., 281
Trotta, Maurice S., 592
Turnbull, John, 58

Umstot, D. D., 132
Usery, W. J., Jr., 591

Vahaly, John, 499
Vaughn, J. A., 298, 305

Walker, C. R., 110, 112
Walker, James, 23
Wallace, Marc, Jr., 107, 108, 186, 365
Walton, Richard E., 599
Wangler, Lawrence A., 142
Wanous, John P., 187
Weihrich, Heinz, 540
Wells, Theodora, 333
Wendt, George, 139, 162
Westcott, Robert F., 675
Westin, Allan F., 213
Wheeler, Hoyt, 677
Whitney, Fred, 542, 589
Wholburg, Wallace, 677
Wickert, Fred, 286
Wikstrom, Walter S., 398
Wiley, W. W., 78, 95
Winpisinger, William W., 116
Within, Arthur, 204, 215
Woodman, Richard, 117, 492

Yoder, D., 95–6, 417
Yount, H. Hoover, 461

Zawacki, Robert, 125
Zerra, Yoram, 326
Zollitsch, Herbert G., 429, 461

Absenteeism, 621–26
Achievement Tests, 217
Adverse Impact, 149
Affirmative Action, 144–47
Age Discrimination in Employment Act of
  1967, 142, 157, 162, 208–09
Alcoholics Anonymous, 527, 528
  checklist for alcoholism, 527
Alcoholism, 525–30 defined, 528
Allis-Chalmers Manufacturing Company, 443,
  446
Alternate Work Schedules, 15
American Association of Industrial
  Management, 450
American Management Associations, 123
American Polygraph Association, 219
American Society for Personnel
  Administration, 11, 511, 518–20
Annual Review Record, 252
Application Blank, 208–12 defined, 208
  uses, 210–11
  weighted, defined, 211
Appraisal Process, 239–61
  evaluation 264
  interview 258–61
    format 259–61
    problems 258–59
  legal considerations, 241
  techniques 243–56
Appraisal Schedule, 256–57
Aptitude Tests, 216–17
Arbitration, 591–92
Assessment Center, 397–99
Authority, 40–43
  functional staff authority, 43
  line authority, 42
  staff authority, 42
Autonomous Work Groups, 116–17
  Sony Corporation, 117, 118

Background Checking, 211
Bakke v. *University of California*, 156
Behaviorally Anchored Rating Scales (BARS),
  253–54
Benchmark Jobs, 438
Benefit Formula, 478
Benefits, 473–79
  increases, major causes, 473–74
  types, 475

Bernreuter Personality Inventory, 217
Berol Corporation, 124–25
Blind Ads, 183–84
Blue Cross/Blue Shield, 489, 520
Bona Fide Occupational Qualification
  (BFOQ), 141
Boycott, 584
Brennan v. *Victoria Bank and Trust Company*,
  162

Cafeteria Approach, 492–95
  definition, 492
  steps in adaption, 495
California Psychological Inventory (CPI), 217
Call-in pay, 486
Campus Recruiting, 181–82
Career Management, 406–14
Career Opportunities in Personnel, 19
Career Patterns of Personnel Professionals,
  19–20
Castro v. *Beecher*, 209
Centralization and Decentralization, 41
Central Tendency, 242
Chain of Command, 41
Chemical and Atomic Workers Union, 518
Civil Rights Act of 1964, 10, 139, 142, 144, 154,
  156–57, 162, 209
Civil Service Retirement Program, 484
Classification Method, 440–42
  steps, 440–42
Coal Mine Safety Law, 511
Coates v. *National Cash Register Co.*, 157
Collective Bargaining and Grievance
  Handling, 575–605
  arbitration, 391–92
  bargaining structure, 577–78
  boycott, 584
  employer power tactics, 585–86
  fact-finding, 587
  good faith concept, 580
  grievance handling steps, 590–91
  interest arbitration, 588
  labor-management agreement, 581
  mediation, 586
  negotiations, 580
  picket, 584
  prenegotiation, 579
  reducing employee grievances, 592–96
  strike, 583–84

Compensatory Selection Model, 272
Completed Staff Work Concept, 52
Comprehensive Employment and Training Act (CETA), 197
Compressed Workweeks, 119–21
  defined, 119
Consumer Price Index (CPI), 484
Continental Can, 456
Corning Glass Works v. *Brennan*, 162, 163
Cost-Benefits Analysis, 52
Cost of Living Adjustment (COLA), 454, 456, 463, 467
Credit Unions, 490
Critical Incidents, 252
  checklist of, 252–53
Cross-Validation, 211

Davis-Bacon Act of 1931, 434–35
Decentralization and Centralization, 41
Degrees of Factors, 443
Demotion, 400–401
Departmentalization, 38
Dictionary of Occupational Titles (DOT), 77, 216, 440
  direct application, 180
Disciplinary Discharge, 671–75
Discipline and Counseling, 653–88
  approaches to discipline, 659–61
  causes of poor performance, 656
  disciplinary discharge, 671–75
  hot stove rule, 670–71
  objectives, 667–71
  supervisory resistance to discipline, 667–71
Discretionary Workweek, 121–25
  applications, 124–25
  flextime, 121–24
  staggered start, 124
  variable working hours, 124
  discrimination defined, 149
  dismissal pay, 485
Duke Power Company, 154

Economic Man Concept, 5
Eighty Percent Rule, 152
Employee Earnings and Benefits Letter, 497–98
Employee Job Satisfaction, 430
Employee Referrals, 180–81
Employee Retirement Income Security Act of 1974 (ERISA), 477–79, 497
Employee Services, 490–92
  defined, 490
Employee Surveys, 614–15

Employee Training, 275–313
  apprentice training, 286–87
  audiovisual techniques, 288
  conference/discussion, 288
  cost-benefit analysis, 292–93
  enlarged job responsibilities, 286
  evaluation, 290–96
  job instruction training (JIT), 286
  job rotation, 286
  lectures, 288
  objectives, 283–85
  off-the-job techniques, 287–90
  on-the-job techniques, 285–87
  off-the-job training:
    advantages and disadvantages, 289
  on-the-job training:
    advantages and disadvantages, 287
  program design, 285–90
  program implementation, 290–91
  programmed instruction, 288
  purposes for, 278–82
  training needs assessment, 283
  training process model, 282
  vestibule, 288
Employment Advertising, 183–84
Employment and Training Administration, 197
Equal Employment Opportunity, 10–11
EEO-1 Reports, 208
Equal Employment Opportunity Act of 1972, 142
EEOC v. *Local 638*, 161
EEOC v. *Multiline Cans, Inc.*, 157
Equal Pay Act of 1963, 139, 162–64, 196, 443, 453
Executive Order 11246, 144
Exempt Employees, 434
External Applicants, 177–78
  advantages, 177
External Influences Upon Personnel Management, 12–16
  labor market conditions, 13
  labor unions, 12
  legal, 11
  social, 13
  technological, 15
Extrinsic Rewards, 426

Factor Comparison Method, 447–50
Factor Evaluation System (FES), 450
Fair Labor Standards Act of 1938, 118, 162, 434
  child labor, 434
  minimum wages, 434

overtime compensation, 434
U.S. minimum wage changes, 434
False Negative, 174
False Positive, 174
Federal Insurance Contributions Act (FICA), 482, 484
Federal Wage Garnishment Act, 435
Female Managers, 333–36
Food Services, 490
Forced Choice, 245, 248
Forced Distribution, 250
Four-Fifths Rule, 152
Freedom of Information Act, 229
Fringe Benefits, 473

Garnishment, 435
Gate Hires, 180
General Aptitude Test Battery (GATB), 216
General Motors, 489, 530
Goal Setting, 433
Good Faith Bargaining, 580
Graphology Tests, 219
Grievance Handling, 589–96
Grievance Procedures in Nonunion Organizations, 592–93
Griggs v. *Duke Power Co.*, 153, 209
halo effect, 242

Hawthorne Studies, 6
Hay Guide Chart-Profile Method, 450
Health and Safety Programs, 524–25
Health Hazards, 511
Health Maintenance Organization (HMO), 520–24, 530
services, 522, 524
Health Maintenance Organization Act, 520, 530
Health Program Manager, 524
Hewlett Packard, 125
Hierarchy of Needs, 432–33
Hodgson v. *American Bank of Commerce*, 162
Hot Stove Rule, 670–71
Human Relations Philosophy 6–7
shortcomings, 7
Human Resources Outlook, 25
Human Resources Philosophy, 7–8
Hutchings v. *United States Industries, Inc.*, 158

IBM, 215
Individual Retirement Accounts (IRA), 490
Initial Applicant Screening, 208

Intelligence Tests, 215–16
Interest Tests, 217
Internal Applicants, 176–77
advantages, 177
Internal Revenue Code, 477
Internal Staffing and Career Management, 389–421
assessment centers, 397–99
benefits of career management, 413–14
career development, 411–13
career management, 406–14
career management success, 407
demotion, 400–01
individual career planning, 408–10
internal staffing policies, 403–06
layoff, 402–03
organizational career planning 407–08
promotion, 393–400
seniority, 395
transfer, 401–02
Internal Staffing Policies, 403–06
International Multi Foods Corporation, 456
Interview Employment, 219–22
steps, 220–21
Interviews, Research Technique, 615–16
intrinsic rewards, 426

Job, defined, 73
Job Analysis, 73–86
defined, 73
problems, 86–88
program implementation, 75–86
questionnaire compilation, 83
questionnaire samples, 84–85
steps, 75–86
Job Classification, defined, 73
Job Description,
defined, 73
elements, 89–91
sample job descriptions, 91, 92, 97
uses, 88–89
Job Design, 38
defined, 107
Job Dissatisfaction, 630–32
Job Enlargement, 114–15
Job Enrichment, 14, 115–16
union response, 116
Job Evaluation, 430, 435–50
committee, 436–37
defined, 73, 430, 435
methods, 438, 440–50
ranking method, 437
Job Family, defined, 73

Job Posting, 178–79
Job Rotation, 114
Job Service Improvement Program (JSIP), 198
Job Specialization, 108–11
    problems, 110
Job Specification, defined, 73

Kemper Insurance Companies, 529–30
    policies on employee alcoholism, 529
Kennedy, John F., School of Government, 519
Kentucky Department of Education, 250

Labor Force Participation Rate, 172
Labor Legislation, 552–54
Labor Market Statistics, 13, 171
Labor Organizing Drive, 558–62
Labor Unions, 537–72
    AFL-CIO merger, 545–46
    American Federation of Labor (AFL), 543–44
    Congress of Industrial Organizations (CIO), 544–45
    contemporary trends, 547
    controlling worker output, 549
    illegal organizing activities, 559–62
    impact on management, 540–41
    improved compensation, 550
    Industrial Workers of the World (IWW), 544
    job security, 548
    Knights of Labor, 542
    labor-management legislation, 552–54
    make-work activities, 549
    national labor union (NLU), 542
    organizing drive, 558–62
    preventative labor relations, 563
    union goals, 548–52
    union history, 541–47
    union security, 548
    union structure and management, 554–56
    white collar unionization, 547–48
Labor Reserve, 172
Law of Effect, 433
"Leisure Sharing" concept, 125
Leniency, 242
Line/Staff Conflict
    reducing conflict, 49–52
    sources of conflict, 47–49

McCormick, Ernest J., 78, 95
McDonnell-Douglas v. Green, 140

Management by Objectives (MBO), 99, 100, 253, 254, 255
Management Development, 315–46
    barriers to women, 333
    coaching, 325
    case study, 328
    committee assignments, 327
    defined, 317
    evaluation, 332–33
    female managers, 333–36
    in-basket exercise, 330
    job rotation and lateral promotion, 326
    management games, 329
    membership in professional organizations, 331
    needs assessment, 320–24
    off-the-job techniques, 327–31
    on-the-job techniques, 325–27
    problems, 336–37
    reasons for, 318
    role play, 329
    successful programs, 336–40
    understanding assignments, 327
Management Functions, 35–38
Management/Personnel Interaction, 47–52
Management Replacement Chart, 324
Manpower Information for Affirmative Action Plans, 197
Manpower Temporary Services, 186
Martin Marietta Corporation, 270
Maytag Company, 115, 118
    job enlargement program, 115
Mediation, 586
Medicaid, 476
Medicare, 476, 483
Military Leave, 486
Minimum Wages, 434
Monetary Responsibility Factor, 446
Monsanto Company, 120
Motivation, 431–32
Multiline Cans, Inc., 157
Multiple Hurdles Selection Model, 222

National Business Entrance Test, 218
National Council on Alcoholism (NCA), 525, 526, 528, 530
National Electrical Manufacturers Association, 450
National Institute for Occupational Safety and Health (NIOSH), 512
National Institute on Alcohol Abuse and Alcoholism (NIAAA), 525, 528, 530

National Metal Trade Association, 450
National Safety Council, 511
Neutrality Laws, 144
Nonexempt Employees, 434
Nonverbal Cue, 222

Occupational Illness, 512
Occupational Injuries
  defined, 511–12
Occupational Safety and Health Act (OSHA),
  231
Old Boy Network, 334
Olympia Machine Tool and Die Shop, 448,
  449
  Factor Comparison Method, 449
On-Call Pay, 486
Organization, 38–43
  authority, 40–43
  departmentalization, 38
  job design, 38
  span of control, 40
Organizational Development, 349–87
  change agent, 356
  data collection, 360
  definition, 355
  diagnosis, 360
  evaluation, 368–70
  forces leading to, 353
  Grid® OD, 365–67
  intergroup team building, 364
  internal change agent, 371
  intervention, 360
  job enrichment, 363
  MBO, 367
  objectives, 357–58
  organizational iceberg, 355
  personnel's role, 371, 382–87
  practices, 370
  prework, 359
  process and technologies, 359
  process consultation, 363
  sensitivity training, 362–63
  survey feedback, 364–65
  surveys, 360–61
  team building, 363
  technostructural activities, 367
  third party peacemaking, 364
  training and development, 362, 372–73
  values, 358–59
Organizational Iceberg, 356
Organizational Rewards, 432
Orientation Programs, 279–82

Orr v. MacNeill & Son, Inc., 162, 163, 164
Outplacement Programs, 491
Overtime Compensation, 434

Paired Comparison, 250–52
Part-time Work, 125–27
  job sharing, 125–26
  job splitting, 126–27
  permanent part-time, 127
Pay Equity, 451
Pay Increases 454–55
  across the board, 454–55
  merit, 455–56
Pension Benefit Guaranty Corporation
  (PBGC), 480
Pension Plan, 476
  supplemental, 477
  contributory, 477
  noncontributory, 477–78
  nonrefunded, 477
Pension Reform Act of 1974, 478, 480
Performance Appraisal
  definition, 237
  developmental objectives, 238–39
  evaluative objectives, 238
Performance Evaluation, 435–36
Performance Evaluation Monitoring System
  (PEMS), 270–72
Personal Absences, 486
Personality Tests, 217
Personal Leave, 486
Personal Staff, 42
Personnel Conflict. See Line/Staff Conflict
Personnel Department Functions, 43–47
Personnel Department Organization, 52–55
  jobs, 53
  structure, 53–55
Personnel Functions, 16–19
  acquiring human resources, 16
  compensation and health, 18
  designing and analyzing jobs, 16
  developing human resources, 17
  solving personnel problems, 18
Personnel Information Decision System, 618–
  20
Personnel Jobs, 53
Personnel Management
  associations, 11
  current problems and issues, 8–16
  past and present perspectives, 4–8
Personnel Planning Process, 188–90
  defined, 188

Personnel Recommendations, 212
Personnel Research and Problem Solving,
   607–50
   absenteeism, 621–26
   controlled experiment, 617–18
   employee surveys, 614–15
   historical studies, 616–17
   interviews, 615–16
   job dissatisfaction, 630–32
   personnel information decision system,
      618–20
   personnel researchers, 611–12
   personnel research publications, 612–13
   research techniques turnover, 626–30
   types of research, 610
   unfairness, 632–34
Personnel Roles, 43–47
   advice, 45
   control, 46
   policies, 44
   service, 45
Personnel Selection
   defined, 203
   elements of, 204–07
   objective, 204
   steps, 206
Peter Principle, 177, 178, 190
Pitney Bowes, Inc., 456
Point System 442–47
Polygraph Tests, 218–19
   polygraph, defined, 218
Poor Performance, Causes, 656
Position Analysis Questionnaire, 78
   sample page, 79
Positive Discipline, 661–67
Pregnancy Discrimination Act (PDA), 501–06
Prentice-Hall, 215
Preventive Discipline, 659
Preventive Labor Relations, 563
Privacy Act of 1974, 223, 227–29
Privacy Protection Study Commission, 229,
   230, 231
   recommendations, 230
Private Employment Agencies, 182–83
   source trust, 183
Problem Drinker, 526
Productivity, 112
Productivity Crisis, 8
Productivity Sharing, 463
Professionalism in Personnel, 11
Profit Center, 41
Profit Sharing, 491
Promotions, 393–400

Public Sector Collective Bargaining, 588–89
Punitive Discipline, 660

Quality of Working Life (QWL), 9, 119

Ranking, 248–49
Ranking Method, 438–40
Rating Scale, 244–45
   nongraphic form, 244, 246–47
   graphic form 244, 245
Recency, 243
Recreational Facilities, 491
Recruitment
   defined, 169
Red Circled Employees, 453
Reinforcement, 433
Relative Ability, 109
Reporting Pay, 486
Results-Oriented Job Description (ROD), 99–
   102
   samples, 101
Reverse Discrimination, 156–57
Robotics, 15
Rocky Mountain Data Systems (RMDS), 463
Rollins Environmental Services Corp., 518

Safety and Health, 9
Safety Hazards, 511
"Scanlon Plan," 463
   productivity sharing, 463
   positive effects, 465–66
   negative effects, 467–69
Scatter Diagram, 451–52
   samples, 451
Scientific Management, 5–6
Sears, Roebuck and Company, 142, 215
Sentry Insurance Survey, 214
Severance Pay, 485
Sick Leave, 486
Social Security, 455, 476, 477, 480–84, 497
   basic concept, 482
   schedule of taxes, 481
   benefits, 483
   problems, 484
Social Security (FICA), 126
Social Security Revision of 1975, 482
Span of Control, 40
Specialized Staff, 42
Sprogis v. United Air Lines, 209
Staffing Cost Analysis Techniques (SCAT), 186
Standard Metropolitan Statistical Area
   (SMSA), 144

State Employment Security Agencies (SESAS), 195, 196, 197
 various functions, 198
 strictness, 243
Strike (Labor), 583–84
Strong Vocational Interest Blank (SVIB), 217
Substantially Equal Concept, 139, 163
Supervisory Bias, 242
Supplementary Unemployment Benefits (SUB), 486, 488

Temporary Assignments in Personnel, 54
Texaco, Inc., 518
Thematic Apperception Test (TAT), 217
Thurstone Temperament Survey (TTS), 217
Title VII, 215
Turnover, 626–30
Typing Test for Business (TTB), 218
Typing Skills Tests, 218

Underemployed, 169
Underutilization, 144
Unemployment Insurance, 486
Unemployment Insurance Program, 1975, 487
Unfairness, 632–34
Uniform Guidelines on Employee Selection Procedures, 74, 77, 147
 section 1 (B) purposes of guidelines, 152
 section 2 (B) employment decisions, 148
 section 3 discrimination defined, 149
 section 4 (D) adverse impact and the "four-fifths rule," 152
 section 4 (C) the bottom line provision, 152–53
 section 4 information required, 153
 section 5 general standards for validity studies, 149
Union Goals, 548–52
Union History, 541–47
Union Structure and Management, 554–56
United Auto Workers, 530
United California Bank, 526
U.S. Administration of Veterans' Affairs, 143
U.S. Bureau of Labor Statistics, 13, 511
U.S. Civil Service Commission, 96, 143, 147, 440
U.S. Department of Health and Welfare, 143
U.S. Department of Justice, 147
U.S. Department of Labor, 76, 96, 143, 144, 147, 162, 164, 197, 231, 430
 standardized method for job analysis, 76
 Veterans Employment Service, 143, 197
 wage and hour division, 139, 142

U.S. Employment Services, 171, 172, 179–78, 216–17
 official aptitude test, 216
U.S. Equal Opportunity Commission (EEOC), 139–42, 147, 206–09, 214, 215
 description of categories, 145
U.S. Labor Force, 170
U.S. Minimum Wage Changes, 434
U.S. Occupational Safety and Health Administation (OSHA), 511, 512–20, 524, 530
 form 200, 516, 518
 form 101, 519
 penalties, 518
 problems, 518–20
 records, 515–16
 requirements, 514–15
 sample safety and health regulations, 520
U.S. Office of Personnel Management, 450
U.S. Postal Service, 526
U.S. Wage and Salary Administation, 426
U.S. Steel, 489
U.S. v. *Bethlehem Steel Corp.*, 209
United Steelworkers v. *Weber*, 156

Vacation, 485
Validity, 149
 criterion-related, 150
 predictive, 150
 concurrent, 151
 content, 151
 construct, 152
Vesting, 478, 480
 minimum vesting standards, 479
Vietnam Era Veterans Readjustment Act of 1974, 143, 195
Vocational Rehabilitation Act of 1973, 142

Wage Compression, 455–56
Wage Freeze, 433
Wage Levels, 426
Wage Surveys, 426–30
 data sheet, 428–29
Walker and Guest Study, 111, 112
Walsh-Healy Act, 435
 overtime example, 436
Weeks v. *Southern Bell Telephone and Telegraph Company*, 162
Weighted Application Blank defined, 211
Williams-Steiger Occupational Safety and Health Act, 512, 513, 514
Wirtz, Secretary of Labor v. *Basic, Inc.*, 158
Women Managers

  development activities, 334–36
  stereotypes, 333–34
Work Environment, 491
Work Incentive Program, 197
Work Sample, 217–18
Work Simplification, 117
  Cummins Engine Company, 117, 118
Work Standards, 243
Worker Instructions Scale, 81
Workers' Compensation, 492

Xerox, 215

Youngstown Sheet and Tube Company, 518